MAGILL'S CINEMA ANNUAL

MAGILL'S CINEMA ANNUAL

1991

A Survey of the Films of 1990

Edited by

FRANK N. MAGILL

SALEM PRESS

Pasadena, California   Englewood Cliffs, New Jersey

∞ The paper used in these volumes conforms to the American
National Standard for Permanence of Paper for Printed Library
Materials, Z39.48-1984.

LIBRARY OF CONGRESS CATALOG CARD NO. 83-644357
ISBN 0-89356-410-9
ISSN 0739-2141

First Printing

PRINTED IN THE UNITED STATES OF AMERICA

PUBLISHER'S NOTE

Magill's Cinema Annual, 1991, is the tenth annual volume in a series that developed from the twenty-one-volume core set, *Magill's Survey of Cinema*. Each annual covers the preceding year and follows a similar format in reviewing the films of the year. This format consists of four general sections: two essays of general interest, the films of 1990, lists of obituaries and awards, and the indexes.

In the first section, the first article reviews the career and accomplishments of the recipient of the Life Achievement Award, which is presented by the American Film Institute. In 1990, this award was given to the distinguished director David Lean. Following this initial essay, the reader will find an essay that lists selected film books published in 1990. Briefly annotated, the list provides a valuable guide to the current literature about the film industry and its leaders.

The largest section of the annual, "Selected Films of 1990," is devoted to essay-reviews of ninety-four significant films released in the United States in 1990. The reviews are arranged alphabetically by the title under which the film was released in the United States. Original and alternate titles are cross-referenced to the American-release title in the Title Index.

Each article begins with selected credits for the film. Credit categories include: Production, Direction, Screenplay, Cinematography, Editing, Art direction, and Music. Also included are the MPAA rating, the running time, and a list of the principal characters with the corresponding actors. This introductory information on a film not released originally in the United States also includes the country of origin and the year the film was released there. If the information for any of the standard categories was unavailable, the heading is followed by the phrase "no listing." Additional headings such as Special effects, Costume design, and Song have been included in an article's introductory top matter when appropriate. Also, the symbol (AA) in the top matter identifies those artists who have received an Academy Award for their contribution to the film from the Academy of Motion Picture Arts and Sciences.

The section of the annual labeled "More Films of 1990" supplies the reader with an alphabetical listing of an additional 193 feature films released in the United States during the year. Included are brief credits and short descriptions of the films. These films can be located, along with any cross-references, in the indexes.

Two further lists conclude the text of the volume. The first of these is the Obituaries, which provides useful information about the careers of motion-picture professionals who died in 1990. The second list is of the awards presented by ten different international associations, from the Academy of Motion Picture Arts and Sciences to the Cannes International Film Festival and the British Academy Awards.

The final section of this volume includes nine indexes that cover the films reviewed in *Magill's Cinema Annual*, 1991. Arranged in the order established in the introductory matter of the essay-reviews, the indexes are as follows: Title Index, Director Index, Screenwriter Index, Cinematographer Index, Editor Index, Art Director Index, Music Index, and Performer Index. A Subject Index is also provided. To assist the reader further, pseudonyms, foreign titles, and alternate titles are all cross-referenced. Titles of foreign films and retrospective films are followed by the year, in brackets, of their original release.

The Title Index includes all the titles of films covered in individual articles, in "More Films of 1990," and also those discussed at some length in the general essays. The next seven indexes are arranged according to artists, each of whose names is followed by a list of the films on which they worked and the titles of the essays (such as "Life Achievement Award" or "Obituaries") in which they are mentioned at length. The final listing is the Subject Index, in which any one film can be categorized under several headings. Thus, a reader can effectively use all these indexes to approach a film from any one of several directions, including not only its credits but also its subject matter.

CONTRIBUTING REVIEWERS

Amy Adelstein
Freelance Reviewer

Rebecca Bell-Metereau
Southwest Texas State University

Mary E. Belles
Freelance Reviewer

Jo-Ellen Lipman Boon
Freelance Reviewer

Beverley Bare Buehrer
Freelance Reviewer

Greg Changnon
Freelance Reviewer

Richard G. Cormack
Freelance Reviewer

Eugene H. Davis
Freelance Reviewer

Bill Delaney
Freelance Reviewer

Susan Doll
School of the Art Institute in Chicago

Gabrielle J. Forman
Freelance Reviewer

Dan Georgakas
Freelance Reviewer

Douglas Gomery
University of Maryland

Sidney Gottlieb
Sacred Heart University

Liane Hirabayashi
Freelance Reviewer

Eleah Horwitz
Freelance Reviewer

Andrew Jefchak
Aquinas College

Anahid Kassabian
Stanford University

Jim Kline
Freelance Reviewer

Patricia Kowal
Freelance Reviewer

Jo Lauria
Loyola Marymount University

Leon Lewis
Appalachian State University

Janet Lorenz
Freelance Reviewer

Blake Lucas
Freelance Reviewer

Marc Mancini
Loyola Marymount University

Cono Robert Marcazzo
Upsala College

Joss Lutz Marsh
Stanford University

John J. Michalczyk
Boston College

Robert Mitchell
University of Arizona

Marilyn Ann Moss
University of California, Riverside

Chon A. Noriega
Freelance Reviewer

Leslie A. Pearl
Freelance Reviewer

Carl Rollyson
*Baruch College of the
    City University of New York*

Robert Strauss
Freelance Reviewer

Gaylyn Studlar
Emory University

Terry Theodore
University of North Carolina at Wilmington

James M. Welsh
Salisbury State University

CONTENTS

CONTENTS

Life Achievement Award
David Lean

On April 16, 1991, David Lean died at the age of 83, a few short months after having been honored by the American Film Institute with its highest award for his contributions to filmmaking. The films for which Lean was honored form a paradoxical body of work. Lean's well-known films—*Summertime* (1955), *The Bridge on the River Kwai* (1957), *Lawrence of Arabia* (1962), and *Doctor Zhivago* (1965)—often feature Hollywood stars in leading roles and exotic international settings. As a result, they demonstrate the paradoxical mix of the familiar and the unfamiliar that American films so often embrace. While Lean's most famous productions share this aspect of American films and were often backed by American financiers, however, Lean never worked within the American film industry, nor did he ever become a "Hollywood" director. Instead, he was regarded as a distinctly British director, as his knighting in 1984 attests. Most important, his sensibility, reflected so often in his choice of subject matter, obviously was shaped by both his nationality and his beginnings in the modest British film industry.

Lean's career also was paradoxical because some of his films, now considered to be classics, were released originally to mixed or negative critical response, as was the case with both *Lawrence of Arabia* and *Doctor Zhivago*. Lean admitted that he became "very unfashionable" for a period of time. Like George Stevens, Lean often was regarded as a good director of honest human drama who succumbed to the temptations of advancing film technology (widescreen, color, stereo sound) and so lost his soul to cinematic spectacle. Lean claimed, however, that he became unfashionable because his kind of storytelling was no longer a priority within the film industry. The vitriolic critical response that greeted *Ryan's Daughter* (1970) was known to have contributed to the fourteen-year hiatus in Lean's film career. Not until 1984 was Lean enticed out of retirement to take up a project suitable for his talents. He began the monumental task of bringing E. M. Forster's novel, *A Passage to India* (1924), to the screen. In response to his efforts, and those of a number of notable collaborators, the film of *A Passage to India* (1984) received eleven Academy Award nominations, bringing the number of nominations that had been bestowed on Lean's films to a total of fifty-six, with Lean himself being the recipient of seven nominations (and two awards) for Best Direction, a phenomenal record, especially for someone whose films have been made outside of Hollywood.

Lean was born to a middle-class British family in 1908. His Quaker background distinguished him as different, and that particular religious difference would normally have cut off any possibility of an interest in film: Quakers simply did not go to see films. It is said that, after listening to a servant act out her favorite films, young Lean felt compelled to go to the "picture show." He saw his first film in 1922. Soon, he was fascinated by silent films, especially the epics of Rex Ingram, whose *The Four Horsemen of the Apocalypse* (1921), starring Rudolph Valentino, was the biggest box-office draw of the entire decade. That film's quest for a sense of authenticity in storytelling, as well as its combination of epic sweep, star charisma, and overwhelming visual power, would be qualities that would later characterize the films of Lean.

In spite of his family's initial shock at the suggestion that their son make films as a profession, Lean's father helped to arrange an interview at the Gaumont Studio. Lean was hired as a runner/messenger and was later entrusted with doing anything required, including serving as "wardrobe mistress" on a historical epic of the Crimean War, *Balaclava* (1930). He ended up in the editing rooms, literally cutting film with a pair of scissors as the editors of silent films did as standard procedure. He moved on to cutting sound newsreels and was hired by Movietone News in 1931.

As an editor, Lean's first big break came when he was hired to edit two theatrical films for director Paul Czinner including *As You Like It* (1936) starring Elisabeth Bergner and Laurence Olivier. A prestigious assignment on producer Gabriel Pascal's 1938 film version of George Bernard Shaw's play *Pygmalion* (1914) followed, as well as work on films of director Michael Powell, including *Forty-Ninth Parallel* (1941; known in the United States as *The Invaders*) and *One of Our Aircraft Is Missing* (1942). At the same time that Lean was hired to edit yet another adaptation of a Shaw play, *Major Barbara* (1905), in 1941, he was acting as an assistant director as well as an editor and was responsible for camera setups.

Offered an opportunity to direct, Lean evidenced the same demand for quality that would characterize his entire career. Instead of accepting any assignment, Lean waited until he had a script to his liking. Noël Coward provided that script, as well as himself as star, producer, and codirector for *In Which We Serve*, a 1942 naval saga based on a real-life episode of British wartime heroism. The film proved to be a tremendous success, so much so that the unlikely team of proper Quaker Lean and sophisticate Coward teamed again for *Blithe Spirit* (1946), a screen adaptation of a Coward stage play, and *This Happy Breed* (1947), the story of a lower-class family's trials and tribulations over the course of twenty years. *This Happy Breed* was particularly notable for starring Celia Johnson, who had offered a classic performance in a previous Lean film, the most famous of his early career, called *Brief Encounter* (1946).

Based on a Coward one-act play, *Brief Encounter* recounts, in flashback, the short-lived and unrequited romance between two unglamorous middle-aged people, a bourgeois housewife (Johnson) and a kindly doctor (Trevor Howard). They are married (but not to each other) when they meet by chance in a train station and proceed, almost against their will, to fall in love. For her work in the film, Johnson was named Best Actress by the New York Film Critics Circle, and Lean achieved an unprecedented honor: He was nominated for the Academy Award for Best Direction, marking the first time a British director was so named.

Lean followed the success of *Brief Encounter* with two adaptations of Charles Dickens' novels. *Great Expectations* (1947) was acclaimed on both sides of the Atlantic, but *Oliver Twist* (1951), with Alec Guinness as Fagin, was greeted with censorship problems rather than with critical praise. To his great surprise, Lean was accused of anti-Semitism in the depiction of Fagin, and the film was reported as being the impetus for a riot in Berlin. An edited version was shown to American audiences. Two undistinguished Ann Todd films—*The Passionate Friends* (1949; known in the United States as *One Woman's Story*) and *Madeleine* (1950)—followed, then *The Sound Barrier* (1952; known in the United States as *Breaking the Sound Barrier*), a film based on the British attempt to develop airplanes that would travel faster than the speed of sound. For his portrayal of a ruthless aircraft tycoon, Ralph Richardson was awarded with the New York Film Critics Award for Best Actor, and Lean once again demonstrated that not only did his tough attitude toward actors help elicit quality performances but that he possessed an unusual ability to make highly interesting films from unlikely dramatic material as well.

As his next directorial effort, Lean took on *Hobson's Choice* (1954), a comic vehicle tailored for the considerable talents of Charles Laughton. Also appearing in the film was John Mills, who had previously essayed the role of Pip in *Great Expectations*. Mills's screen debut as seaman Shorty Blake had been in yet another Lean film, *In Which We Serve*, and sixteen years later, Mills would win an Academy Award for Best Supporting Actor for his portrayal of Michael, the "village idiot," in Lean's *Ryan's Daughter*. This pattern of multiple collaborative efforts would mark Lean's professional relationship with other actors, such as Howard and Guinness, as well as his work with cinematographer Freddie A. Young, production designer John Box, and composer Maurice Jarre.

In 1955, Lean directed *Summertime*, the first of his large-scale, star-centered films. Set in Venice, *Summertime* tells the story of the magical experience of one lonely American tourist (Katharine Hepburn) with the city and with a seductive Italian merchant (Rossano Brazzi). Critics were divided as to whether the film's love story or the location shooting in Venice provided the most powerful appeal to viewers. In any case, all agreed that the film was a tremendous success, and Lean's "bankability" as a director was assured. Lean was drawn to another project involving the issue of Japanese prison camps during World War II, Pierre Boulle's book, *The Bridge on the River Kwai* (1952).

Producer Sam Spiegel owned the film rights to the Boulle novel, and from their uneasy collaboration would come both *The Bridge on the River Kwai* and *Lawrence of Arabia*. The former was a typical late-1950's blockbuster, filmed not only in Technicolor but also in Cinemascope. *The Bridge on the River Kwai* details life in a World War II prison camp in the jungles of Burma where British soldiers are forced by their Japanese captors to build a bridge. The leader of the prisoners, Colonel Nicholson (Guinness), becomes obsessed with completing the task, even though the wisdom of his actions is called into question by some of his own men. A British commando squadron is being dispatched to make sure that the bridge is destroyed before it can be used. The film won seven major Academy Awards including Best Picture, Best Direction, and Best Actor (Guinness). In spite of the ostensibly depressing subject matter, the film was also a box-office winner and its theme song was a tune whistled everywhere.

Toying with the notion of filming a biography of Mahatma Gandhi, Lean finally took up Spiegel's offer to do a film about T. E. Lawrence, "Lawrence of Arabia." After numerous disputes regarding casting, twenty months of filming began with newcomer Peter O'Toole as the enigmatic British leader of Arab forces during World War I. Working from a screenplay by Robert Bolt, Lean fashioned a film of astonishing visual grandeur that ambitiously attempted to capture the emotions of a self-doubting hero psychologically tortured by sexual and ideological conflicts. Again, Lean's effort was honored as the Best Direction and his film, Best Picture, by the Academy of Motion Picture Arts and Sciences in 1962. In spite of the acclaim, almost immediately after its Royal Invitational Premiere for Queen Elizabeth, the three-hour-and-forty-minute film began to be cut for distribution until a full thirty-five minutes were excised. Acknowledged as possibly the most beautiful film ever made, *Lawrence of Arabia* was finally restored in 1987 from an original negative and re-released in 1989.

After the tremendous success of *Bridge on the River Kwai* and *Lawrence of Arabia*, Lean chose a surprising project for his next film, Boris Pasternak's novel, *Doctor Zhivago* (1957). Lean defied Hollywood casting norms and assembled a cast made up largely of actors without star status, who were either newcomers such as Geraldine Chaplin or were those with whom he had worked previously, including Guinness, Richardson, and Omar Sharif in the title role. The $15-million film about a Russian doctor-poet who loves two women was dismissed by critics who generally echoed Judith Crist's commentary that Lean's film was "merely spectacular soap opera." Nevertheless, *Doctor Zhivago* was a huge box-office hit, grossing more than $200 million. The popularity of the film showed that, in spite of the critics' growing uneasiness with Lean's work, the public continued to respond to the romanticism and unrivaled pictorial values of Lean's filmic storytelling.

Those same qualities would infuse Lean's next project, *Ryan's Daughter*, a coming-of-age story set in Ireland in 1916. Bolt's screenplay centers on Rosy Ryan (Sarah Miles), an intelligent and sensitive young woman whose life in a small village takes a disastrous turn when she marries an older school teacher (Robert Mitchum) and then allows herself to be caught up in an affair with a troubled British officer (Christopher Jones). Rosy learns both the limits of passion and the unmatched virtues of love, even in a seemingly imperfect love such as the one that she shares with her husband, Charles. Compelling performances by Miles, Mitchum, Mills, and Howard were not enough to please the critics, who derided the film in terms that were unrivaled by the negative reviews of any previous Lean project.

Perhaps in response to the vicious critical attacks that were leveled at *Ryan's Daughter*, Lean retired soon after its release. An attempt to bring a new perspective to the story of the *H.M.S. Bounty* failed to make it to the screen in the late 1970's. Except for *Lost and Found*, a 1979 television documentary on Captain James Cook, Lean's career seemed over. The director's long-standing desire to make a film in India, however, was satisfied by the suggestion that he write the screenplay for and direct *A Passage to India*, a film project financed largely by Columbia Pictures and Home Box Office (HBO). Although it might be argued that some of the narrative changes that the film makes to Forster's novel clearly alter the intended political meaning of the book, the film was greeted as a masterpiece and hailed as marking the triumphant return of Lean to filmmaking. Yet Lean was not to make another film. At his death, he was still hoping to bring Joseph Conrad's novel *Nostromo* (1904) to the screen.

There is high irony in Lean's final return to creative triumph with *A Passage to India*, a film that reinforced rather than undermined the paradoxical tenor of his entire career. Making films that were both romantic but hardheaded, large-scale but intimate, boldly dramatic but also emotionally nuanced, Lean's sixty-year career as an international filmmaker suggests the powerful possibilities of visual storytelling and the paradoxical qualities of memorable filmmaking. While his bold personal vision might not have been the most subtle one ever to grace the screen, it remains a valuable, strikingly "cinematic" one that is increasingly rare in a technological age that is dominated by formulaic, derivative filmmaking, "high concept" marketing strategies, and the aesthetics of the small screen. Like Rosy Ryan's schoolmaster husband, Lean's obvious limitations seem to fade beside the great goodness of his virtues. All that it has taken for everyone else to see the magnitude of those virtues is a little time—and vision.

Gaylyn Studlar

SELECTED FILM BOOKS OF 1990

Adamson, Joe. *Bugs Bunny: Fifty Years and Only One Grey Hare*. New York: Henry Holt, 1990. An illustrated history of Warner Bros.' most popular cartoon character, this volume has chapters on Bugs's creators, his animated costars, and even a detailed filmography, complete with plot synopses.

Anderson, Christopher. *Citizen Jane: The Turbulent Life of Jane Fonda*. New York: Henry Holt, 1990. Of the two biographies of the controversial actress published in 1990, Anderson's is both the more detailed and the more critical.

Andrew, Geoff. *The Film Handbook*. Boston: G. K. Hall, 1990. This reference work contains brief critical and biographical essays on two hundred filmmakers.

Armstrong, Richard B., and Mary Willems Armstrong. *The Movie List Book: A Reference Guide to Film Themes, Settings, and Series*. Jefferson, N.C.: McFarland, 1990. Focusing on English-language films of the sound era, this useful reference work contains lists of films on more than 450 diverse topics—films about angels, films about zombies, films with dates in their titles, films with unusually long titles, and so on.

Bart, Peter. *Fade Out: The Calamitous Final Days of MGM*. New York: William Morrow, 1990. An insider's account of MGM/United Artists in the 1980's, blaming Kirk Kerkorian for the events that led to the studio's downfall.

Bergreen, Laurence. *As Thousands Cheer: The Life of Irving Berlin*. New York: Viking, 1990. Among his many other accomplishments, Berlin composed music for sixteen films. In this definitive biography, Bergreen depicts the prolific composer as a complex, driven man.

Billips, Connie J. *Maureen O'Sullivan: A Bio-Bibliography*. New York: Greenwood Press, 1990. A biographical, bibliographical, and critical study of the career of the actress, along with two short stories written by the O'Sullivans.

Boorstin, Jon. *The Hollywood Eye: What Makes Movies Work*. New York: Cornelia & Michael Bessie Books, 1990. Boorstin is a producer and screenwriter; his book is a useful study of the cinematic techniques that make a film work for its audience, using such films as *Citizen Kane* and *All the President's Men* by way of example.

Brouwer, Alexandra, and Thomas Lee Wright. *Working in Hollywood*. New York: Crown, 1990. A fascinating, nontechnical look at sixty-five different film occupations, from director to animal trainer, described through interviews with those in the business; this volume functions as an excellent description of how motion pictures are made.

Brown, David. *Let Me Entertain You*. New York: William Morrow, 1990. Subtitling his book *Quick Cuts and Slow Fades from a Life Among the Stars*, producer Brown offers this discursive review of his five decades of associations with show-business celebrities and characters.

Brownlow, Kevin. *Behind the Mask of Innocence*. New York: Alfred A. Knopf, 1990. This important study of the silent era examines many films, some long forgotten, which dealt with major social issues, such as crime, immigration, and women's suffrage. Thus Brownlow dispels the myth that early cinema was little more than pie-in-the-face slapstick.

Brunas, Michael, John Brunas, and Tom Weaver. *Universal Horrors: The Studio's Classic Films, 1931-1946.* Jefferson, N.C.: McFarland, 1990. Universal was the preeminent producer of horror films, including *Frankenstein, Dracula*, and many others. This volume provides cast and credits, plot summaries, and critical commentary for the eighty-five films the studio produced in this genre.

Bruskin, David N. *The White Brothers: Jack, Jules, and Sam White.* Metuchen, N.J.: Scarecrow Press, 1990. The White brothers specialized in comedy shorts from the silent era into the 1950's; Bruskin interviews them as a part of the Directors Guild of America's oral history series.

Bryson, John. *The Private World of Katharine Hepburn.* Boston: Little, Brown, 1990. Given unprecedented access to Hepburn, Bryson has produced this coffee-table book of photographs of the actress at home, with friends, and in a wide variety of intimate, unpretentious settings.

Buehrer, Beverley Bare. *Cary Grant: A Bio-Bibliography.* New York: Greenwood Press, 1990. A biographical, bibliographical, and critical study of the life and career of the late actor.

_____. *Japanese Films: A Filmography and Commentary, 1921-1989.* Jefferson, N.C.: McFarland, 1990. Buehrer examines eighty major films, the majority of which were released after 1945, providing plot summaries, information on cast and credits, and critical analysis in this survey of Japanese cinema.

Byrge, Duane, and Robert Milton Miller. *The Screwball Comedy Films: A History and Filmography, 1934-1942.* Jefferson, N.C.: McFarland, 1990. Byrge and Miller discuss fifty-three screwball comedies in chronological order, focusing on the writers, directors, and actors who made the genre popular.

Caine, Michael. *Acting in Film: An Actor's Take on Movie Making.* New York: Applause Theatre Book Publishers, 1990. The distinguished British actor offers useful tips on acting in cinema in this brief volume.

Carrier, Jeffrey L. *Jennifer Jones: A Bio-Bibliography.* New York: Greenwood Press, 1990. A biographical, bibliographical, and critical study of the life and career of the actress.

Cawley, John, and Jim Korkis. *The Encyclopedia of Cartoon Superstars.* Las Vegas, Nev.: Pioneer Books, 1990. Containing "biographies" of the featured characters in animated films and television, this volume is useful for its information on the more obscure cartoon characters.

Clagett, Thomas D. *William Friedkin: Films of Aberration, Obsession, and Reality.* Jefferson, N.C.: McFarland, 1990. This is a scholarly analysis of the films of the controversial American director.

Clark, Tom, with Dick Kleiner. *Rock Hudson: Friend of Mine.* New York: Pharos Books, 1990. Hudson's companion, a Hollywood publicist, offers this anecdotal account of the actor's career and of their relationship.

Coleman, Emily R. *The Complete Judy Garland: The Ultimate Guide to Her Career in Films, Records, Concerts, Radio, and Television, 1935-1969*. New York: Harper & Row, 1990. As its subtitle indicates, this volume is an exhaustive compilation of information on the actress/entertainer's career.

Combs, James. *American Political Movies: A Filmography*. New York: Garland, 1990. This work is a chronological filmography of American films with political themes.

Conquest, John. *Trouble Is Their Business: Private Eyes in Fiction, Film, and Television, 1927-1988*. New York: Garland, 1990. This reference work includes entries on 160 films of the private-eye genre; it is indexed by the name of the detective and by geographic locale.

Corman, Roger, with Jim Jerome. *How I Made a Hundred Movies in Hollywood and Never Lost a Dime*. New York: Random House, 1990. This is a volume of anecdotal memoirs from the prolific director of inexpensive and profitable exploitation films.

Darby, William, and Jack Du Bois. *American Film Music: Major Composers, Techniques, Trends, 1915-1990*. Jefferson, N.C.: McFarland, 1990. This volume analyzes the work of fourteen important or innovative composers, from the silent era to date, with regard to how their scores enhance the activity onscreen.

Davidson, Bill. *Jane Fonda: An Intimate Biography*. New York: Dutton, 1990. Davidson offers an admiring, if gossipy, account of the life of the controversial actress, activist, and fitness magnate.

De Cordova, Richard. *Picture Personalities: The Emergence of the Star System in America*. Urbana: University of Illinois Press, 1990. This scholarly work is a revisionist history of the evolution of the star system in American cinema between 1907 and 1925, using semiotics as an analytical tool.

Dika, Vera. *Games of Terror*. Rutherford, N.J.: Fairleigh Dickinson University Press, 1990. This scholarly analysis of nine "slasher" or "stalker" films, such as *Halloween* and *Friday the 13th*, concentrates on identifying the major elements of the genre.

Drew, Bernard A. *Motion Picture Series and Sequels: A Reference Guide*. New York: Garland, 1990. This reference work lists 936 English-language films in series or sequels, from the silent era to 1990; information provided includes studio, date, director, and stars.

Eberts, Jake, and Terry Ilott. *My Indecision Is Final: The Spectacular Rise and Fall of Goldcrest Films, the Independent Studio That Challenged Hollywood*. New York: Atlantic Monthly Press, 1990. Eberts founded the company that produced *Gandhi* and *Chariots of Fire*; in this volume, he details the business decisions that made and unmade the company.

Eyman, Scott. *Mary Pickford: America's Sweetheart*. New York: Donald I. Fine, 1990. This is a good biography of the silent-era star, with useful information on the founding of United Artists and Pickford's marriage to Douglas Fairbanks.

Flannery, Tom. *1939, the Year in Movies: A Comprehensive Filmography*. Jefferson, N.C.: McFarland, 1990. The year 1939 was one of the high water marks in American filmmaking; this reference work examines more than 125 films—major and minor—released that year, providing information on cast, credits, and plot.

Fowler, Karin J. *Ava Gardner: A Bio-Bibliography.* New York: Greenwood Press, 1990. A biographical, bibliographical, and critical study of the life and career of the late actress.

Gardner, Ava. *Ava: My Story.* New York: Bantam Books, 1990. Completed shortly before her death in 1990, this autobiography was written to tell Gardner's version of her story, particularly with regard to her tumultuous love life.

Gehring, Wes D. *Laurel & Hardy: A Bio-Bibliography.* New York: Greenwood Press, 1990. A biographical, bibliographical, and critical study of the life and career of the comic duo whose career spanned the silent and sound eras.

Giddings, Robert, Keith Selby, and Chris Wensley. *Screening the Novel: The Theory and Practice of Literary Dramatization.* London: Macmillan, 1990. This scholarly analysis of the transition of the novel to the screen features extended discussions of *Great Expectations* and *Vanity Fair.*

Gifford, Denis. *American Animated Films: The Silent Era, 1897-1929.* Jefferson, N.C.: McFarland, 1990. Most histories of film animation focus on post-Disney work; Gifford's book is a valuable annotated filmography of animation before the advent of sound.

Gottfried, Martin. *All His Jazz: The Life and Death of Bob Fosse.* New York: Bantam Books, 1990. The best biography so far of the complex choreographer and filmmaker.

Greene, Naomi. *Pier Paolo Pasolini: Cinema as Heresy.* Princeton, N.J.: Princeton University Press, 1990. A scholarly study of the career of the controversial Italian filmmaker.

Gronowicz, Antoni. *Garbo.* New York: Simon & Schuster, 1990. A Garbo intimate has prepared this biography, told mostly in Garbo's own words with instructions not to be published until after her death. A new perspective on the enigmatic legend.

Guynn, William. *A Cinema of Nonfiction.* Rutherford, N.J.: Fairleigh Dickinson University Press, 1990. A semiological analysis of documentary film, featuring an extended examination of the World War II classic *Listen to Britain.*

Hamilton, Ian. *Writers in Hollywood: 1915-1951.* London: Heinemann, 1990. This is a history of screenwriting in American film, from the silent era through the House Committee on Unamerican Activities' hearings and the notorious blacklist.

Hay, Peter. *Movie Anecdotes.* New York: Oxford University Press, 1990. An entertaining collection of anecdotes, culled from a variety of sources, on actors, producers, directors, and others involved in the film industry.

Heisner, Beverly. *Hollywood Art: Art Direction in the Days of the Great Studios.* Jefferson, N.C.: McFarland, 1990. This volume provides a studio-by-studio examination of the role of the art director in American films from the 1920's through the 1950's.

Helfer, Ralph. *The Beauty of the Beasts: Tales of Hollywood's Wild Animal Stars.*

Los Angeles: Jeremy P. Tarcher, 1990. Helfer is a prominent animal trainer; his book is a behind-the-scenes look at how filmmakers are able to incorporate exotic animals into their films.

Hilmes, Michele. *Hollywood and Broadcasting: From Radio to Cable.* Urbana: University of Illinois Press, 1990. A scholarly study of the relationship between the American film industry and the broadcast media of radio and television, which functioned as both rivals to and partners with the Hollywood studios.

Holston, Kim. *Richard Widmark: A Bio-Bibliography.* New York: Greenwood Press, 1990. This first book-length study of Widmark focuses on the actor's career rather than on his private life; it includes an extensive bibliography.

Jarlett, Franklin. *Robert Ryan: A Biography and Critical Filmography.* Jefferson, N.C.: McFarland, 1990. The most detailed look so far at the life and career of actor Robert Ryan; it features a detailed filmography.

Keith, Slim, and Annette Tapert. *Slim: Memories of a Rich and Imperfect Life.* New York: Simon & Schuster, 1990. Best known for her marriage to director Howard Hawks, Keith relentlessly pursued the good life among the rich and famous in the 1930's and 1940's; this autobiography was completed shortly before her death.

Kendall, Elizabeth. *The Runaway Bride: Hollywood and Romantic Comedy of the 1930's.* New York: Alfred A. Knopf, 1990. Kendall's book examines the role of women in Depression-era American comedies.

Lambert, Gavin. *Norma Shearer: A Biography.* New York: Alfred A. Knopf, 1990. Lambert offers an insightful biography on an important American actress of the 1930's.

Langman, Larry, and David Ebner. *Encyclopedia of American Spy Films.* New York: Garland, 1990. Focusing primarily on individual titles but also covering characters and organizations, Langman and Ebner provide casts and limited credits for approximately a thousand American films on the subject of espionage.

Lebo, Harlan. *Citizen Kane: The Fiftieth Anniversary Album.* New York: Doubleday, 1990. This profusely illustrated appreciation of Orson Welles's classic covers both the film's production and its reception.

Leff, Leonard J., and Jerold L. Simmons. *The Dame in the Kimono.* New York: Grove Weidenfeld, 1990. A lively account of Joseph Breen and the role of the Production Code in the censorship of Hollywood films between 1922 and 1966, focusing on the example of eleven key films to illustrate the issues faced by the studios and by the censors.

Lent, John A. *The Asian Film Industry.* Austin: University of Texas Press, 1990. This collection of essays provides a survey of the film industries of fifteen Asian countries, offering historical background as well as information on the current state of national cinema in East, South, and Southeast Asia.

Levy, Emanuel. *Small-Town America: The Decline and Fall of Community.* New York: Continuum, 1990. In this scholarly study, Levy demonstrates how the changing role of the small town in American cinema reflects similar changes in American culture.

Lourdeaux, Lee. *Italian and Irish Filmmakers in America*. Philadelphia: Temple University Press, 1990. This scholarly study places particular emphasis on the works of John Ford, Frank Capra, Francis Coppola, and Martin Scorsese.

McCann, Graham. *Woody Allen: New Yorker*. Cambridge, Mass.: Polity Press, 1990. Focusing on the theme of the contemporary urbanite's search for trust, McCann offers a scholarly analysis of Allen's films through his segment of 1989's *New York Stories*.

McGee, Mark Thomas. *The Rock and Roll Movie Encyclopedia of the 1950s*. Jefferson, N.C.: McFarland, 1990. This reference work provides information on the cast, credits, music, and public reception of thirty-five films that celebrated (or attempted to cash in on) rock and roll in its infancy.

McGhee, Richard. *John Wayne: Actor, Artist, Hero*. Jefferson, N.C.: McFarland, 1990. A comprehensive filmography highlights this study of John Wayne's screen persona.

Malone, Peter. *Movie Christs and Antichrists*. New York: Crossroad, 1990. Malone examines the "Christlike" qualities of characters in a variety of films, ranging from obviously biblically based epics to metaphoric interpretations of films such as *Star Wars* and *E.T.: The Extra-Terrestrial*.

Mank, Gregory William. *Karloff and Lugosi*. Jefferson, N.C.: McFarland, 1990. Mank provides a detailed filmography of the classic horror films in which Boris Karloff and Bela Lugosi costarred.

Mapp, Edward. *Directory of Blacks in the Performing Arts*. 2d ed. Metuchen, N.J.: Scarecrow Press, 1990. First published in 1978, this work has been updated and expanded to include eleven hundred entries on black performers, both living and dead. The volume includes both biographical information and film credits.

Miller, Mark Crispin, ed. *Seeing Through Movies*. New York: Pantheon Books, 1990. This valuable study of the state of American cinema at the beginning of the 1990's features six original essays on such topics as the blockbuster syndrome, the mall theater, and colorization.

Mordden, Ethan. *Medium Cool: The Movies of the 1960s*. New York: Alfred A. Knopf, 1990. This is a discursive and witty analysis of the films of the 1960's, a time in which the rules that had governed filmmaking for decades underwent a rapid transformation.

Murray, Bruce. *Film and the German Left in the Weimar Republic: From "Caligari" to "Kühle Wampe."* Austin: University of Texas Press, 1990. Murray offers a scholarly analysis of the film activity of the German Left between 1918 and 1933.

O'Brien, Tom. *The Screening of America: Movies and Values from Rocky to Rain Man*. New York: Continuum, 1990. A teacher and self-described populist looks at the social values reflected in contemporary American films.

Palmer, Christopher. *The Composer in Hollywood*. London: Marion Boyars, 1990. Focusing on the work of nine major composers who worked in Hollywood film from the 1930's to the 1950's, Palmer offers a detailed analysis of the composer's role in filmmaking. His avoidance of technical jargon makes the book accessible to the nonspecialist.

Parish, James Robert. *The Great Combat Pictures: Twentieth-Century Warfare on the Screen*. Metuchen, N.J.: Scarecrow Press, 1990. Along with a plot synopsis, this volume provides information on the cast, credits, and popular and critical reception of approximately three hundred English-language films on warfare from World War I to Vietnam.

_____. *The Great Cop Pictures*. Metuchen, N.J.: Scarecrow Press, 1990. Along with a plot synopsis, this volume provides information on the cast, credits, and popular and critical reception of hundreds of American police films, including many made for television.

Parish, James Robert, and Michael R. Pitts. *The Great Detective Pictures*. Metuchen, N.J.: Scarecrow Press, 1990. Along with a plot synopsis, this volume provides information on the cast, credits, and popular and critical reception of more than 350 American detective films, including many made for television.

_____. *Hollywood Songsters*. New York: Garland, 1990. This volume provides brief biographies of approximately one hundred actors who have had second careers as professional singers; it contains extensive indexes, with entries by song, album, film, and personal name.

Parks, Gordon. *Voices in the Mirror*. New York: Doubleday, 1990. The black photographer and filmmaker offers this autobiography.

Pflaum, Hans Gunther. *Germany on Film*. Detroit: Wayne State University Press, 1990. Pflaum, a major West German film critic, discusses the major feature films produced in the Federal Republic of Germany since 1962.

Phillips, Gene D. *Major Film Directors of the American and British Cinema*. Bethlehem, Penn.: Lehigh University Press, 1990. From Charles Chaplin to Ken Russell, Palmer analyzes the work of eight American and six British filmmakers.

Pierce, Arthur, and Douglas Swarthout. *Jean Arthur: A Bio-Bibliography*. New York: Greenwood Press, 1990. A biographical, bibliographical, and critical study of the life and career of the popular actress of the 1930's and 1940's.

Quirk, Lawrence J. *Fasten Your Seatbelts: The Passionate Life of Bette Davis*. New York: William Morrow, 1990. A solidly researched volume, this is the best biography so far of the late actress.

Rainey, Buck. *Those Fabulous Serial Heroines: Their Lives and Films*. Metuchen, N.J.: Scarecrow Press, 1990. This volume contains biographies of forty-six actresses who were featured in motion-picture serials between 1912 and 1956.

Rawlence, Christopher. *The Missing Reel*. New York: Atheneum, 1990. Subtitled *The Untold Story of the Lost Inventor of Moving Pictures*, this volume argues that Frenchman Augustin Le Prince, rather than Thomas Edison, was the true inventor of the motion-picture camera and projector.

Rebello, Stephen. *Alfred Hitchcock and the Making of Psycho*. New York: Dembner Books, 1990. Billed as the "complete inside story" of *Psycho*, Rebello's work is particularly strong on the marketing and subsequent reception of Hitchcock's most famous film.

Rentschler, Eric, ed. *The Films of G. W. Pabst: An Extraterritorial Cinema*. New

Brunswick, N.J.: Rutgers University Press, 1990. Austrian director Pabst's Weimar-era films have been highly regarded, while his later films have not. The essays in this volume evaluate the entire range of his career.

Rivadue, Barry. *Alice Faye: A Bio-Bibliography*. New York: Greenwood Press, 1990. A biographical, bibliographical, and critical study of the life and career of the actress/singer.

Rosen, David, with Peter Hamilton. *Off-Hollywood: The Making and Marketing of Independent Films*. New York: Grove Weidenfeld, 1990. This work contains case histories of thirteen independently made American films of the 1980's; it is useful both for information on individual films and for larger lessons on the business of contemporary filmmaking.

Rubin, Steven Jay. *The Complete James Bond Movie Encyclopedia*. Chicago: Contemporary Books, 1990. An extremely comprehensive reference work on the cinematic 007.

Schultz, Margie. *Ann Sothern: A Bio-Bibliography*. New York: Greenwood Press, 1990. This biographical, bibliographical, and critical study is the first book-length examination of the actress' life and career.

Segaloff, Nat. *Hurricane Billy: The Stormy Life and Films of William Friedkin*. New York: William Morrow, 1990. Segaloff had ready access to Friedkin in compiling this popular biography of the contentious American filmmaker.

Segrave, Kerry, and Linda Martin. *The Continental Actress: European Film Stars of the Postwar Era*. Jefferson, N.C.: McFarland, 1990. This reference work contains critical biographies, filmographies, and bibliographies for forty-one actresses from Italy, France, Germany, Greece, and Scandinavia.

_____. *The Post-Feminist Hollywood Actress*. Jefferson, N.C.: McFarland, 1990. This volume provides brief biographical sketches, filmographies, and bibliographies for fifty actresses born since 1940. The subjects range from established stars, such as Barbra Streisand, to newer stars, such as Glenn Close, Kelly McGillis, and Rebecca DeMornay.

Semsel, George S., Xia Hong, and Hou Jianping. *Chinese Film Theory: A Guide to the New Era*. Westport, Conn.: Greenwood Press, 1990. This work contains eighteen scholarly essays on Chinese film criticism between 1979 and 1989, a period when both Chinese cinema and film theory were rejuvenated by a relative freedom from state control.

Sennett, Ted. *Great Hollywood Westerns*. New York: Harry N. Abrams, 1990. Sennett offers a coffee-table history of the Western film genre, with chapters arranged by subject.

Siegal, Scott, and Barbara Siegal. *The Encyclopedia of Hollywood*. New York: Facts on File, 1990. Though this reference work on the American film industry contains entries on technical terms, the book's focus is on personalities, and it is most useful for its information on newly popular actors.

Skal, David J. *Hollywood Gothic: The Tangled Web of "Dracula" from Novel to Stage to Screen*. New York: W. W. Norton, 1990. Focusing on the efforts of Bram

Stoker's widow, Skal relates the complex story of how Stoker's vampire novel came to be immortalized on the screen by Tod Browning and Bela Lugosi.

Spoto, Donald. *Madcap: The Life of Preston Sturges*. Boston: Little, Brown, 1990. One of two books published in 1990 on the eccentric 1940's filmmaker, Spoto's volume is a solid contribution to the literature on the director's life.

Sragow, Michael. *Produced and Abandoned: The Best Films You've Never Seen*. San Francisco: Mercury House, 1990. This is an interesting compilation of reviews of films that are available on videotape and that were ignored by critics and audiences when they were originally released.

Stine, Whitney. *"I'd Love to Kiss You . . .": Conversations with Bette Davis*. New York: Pocket Books, 1990. Stine met Davis after publishing *Mother Goddam*, an account of her career. This book is based on conversations he had with the actress between 1972 and her death in 1989.

Strode, Woody, and Sam Young. *Goal Dust: An Autobiography*. Lanham, Md.: Madison Books, 1990. Strode was a black athlete who became an actor in the 1950's; this is his autobiography.

Sturges, Preston. *Preston Sturges*. New York: Simon & Schuster, 1990. Sturges' widow, Sandy Sturges, adapted and edited his unfinished memoirs and other personal papers for this "autobiography." Though not definitive, it is an entertaining supplement to Donald Spoto's biography, also published in 1990.

Thomas, Bob. *Clown Prince of Hollywood: The Antic Life and Times of Jack L. Warner*. New York: McGraw-Hill, 1990. Veteran Hollywood writer Thomas offers this anecdotal biography of one of the founders of Warner Bros.

Thomas, Tony. *Errol Flynn: The Spy Who Never Was*. New York: Citadel Press, 1990. This biography concludes that Flynn longed to be a serious person but continually succumbed to fleshly temptations. Thomas is skeptical of charges that the actor collaborated with the Nazis.

Truffaut, François. *François Truffaut: Correspondence, 1945-1984*. New York: Farrar, Straus & Giroux, 1990. Arranged in chronological order, this is a massive collection of letters from the French filmmaker and critic.

VanDerBeets, Richard. *George Sanders: An Exhausted Life*. Lanham, Md.: Madison Books, 1990. Written with the assistance of Sanders' sister, this is the most complete account so far of the life of the actor who specialized in playing villains and cads.

Van Gelder, Peter. *That's Hollywood: A Behind-the-Scenes Look at Sixty of the Greatest Films of All Time*. New York: Harper Perennial, 1990. Aimed at the lay audience and biased toward commercial successes, Van Gelder's work contains essays on the making of sixty American films.

Wayne, Jane Ellen. *Ava's Men: The Private Life of Ava Gardner*. New York: St. Martin's Press, 1990. Wayne is a veteran chronicler of the romantic affairs of Hollywood stars; Gardner's turbulent love life offers much grist for her mill.

Wick, Steve. *Bad Company*. New York: Harcourt Brace Jovanovich, 1990. Subtitled *Drugs, Hollywood, and the "Cotton Club" Murder*, Wick's book examines the murder of producer Roy Radin in a dispute involving the financing of Robert Evans' *The Cotton Club* in 1983.

Wood, Bret. *Orson Welles: A Bio-Bibliography.* New York: Greenwood Press, 1990. A biographical, bibliographical, and critical study of the actor/filmmaker, focusing on his lost, incomplete, and heavily edited works.

Wood, Richard, ed. *Film and Propaganda in America: A Documentary History.* Vol. 1, *World War I.* New York: Greenwood Press, 1990. This work reprints documents—primarily correspondence and memoranda, but also reviews—on American films, from 1913 to 1921, relating to the military activity that culminated in World War I, focusing on issues such as propaganda and censorship.

Wynn, Ned. *We Will Always Live in Beverly Hills: Growing Up Crazy in Hollywood.* New York: William Morrow, 1990. The son of Keenan Wynn, a sometime actor/screenwriter and full-time scenemaker, lived the wild life in Hollywood in the 1960's; he tells his story in this humorous memoir.

SELECTED
FILMS
OF
1990

AFTER DARK, MY SWEET

Production: Ric Kidney and Robert Redlin; released by Avenue Pictures
Direction: James Foley
Screenplay: Robert Redlin and James Foley; based on the novel by Jim Thompson
Cinematography: Mark Plummer
Editing: Howard Smith
Production design: David Brisbin
Art direction: Kenneth A. Hardy
Set decoration: Margaret Goldsmith
Sound: David Brownlow
Costume design: Hope Hanafin
Music: Maurice Jarre
MPAA rating: R
Running time: 114 minutes

Principal characters:
Collie . . . . Jason Patric
Fay . . . . Rachel Ward
Uncle Bud . . . . Bruce Dern
Bert . . . . Rocky Giordani
Doc Goldman . . . . George Dickerson
Charlie Vanderventer . . . . James Cotton
Jack . . . . Corey Carrier

Jim Thompson, author of *After Dark, My Sweet* and twenty-eight other novels, has experienced an enthusiastic reception for his work in the past few years both by the reading public and filmmakers eager to adapt his books to the screen. In addition to *After Dark, My Sweet*, two other films released in 1990 were based on novels by Thompson, *The Grifters* (reviewed in this volume) and *The Kill-Off*. Nevertheless, recognition for his work is something that Thompson barely realized during his lifetime; at the time of his death in 1977, all of his books were out of print in the United States. He did live to see two of his books adapted to the screen: *The Getaway* (1972), directed by Sam Peckinpah and starring Steve McQueen and Ali McGraw, and Thompson's most notorious novel, *The Killer Inside Me* (1976), directed by Burt Kennedy and starring Stacy Keach. Although both films were not totally faithful adaptations of Thompson's books, each film managed to capture a slice of Thompson's bleak, desperate worldview, one in which brutal, amoral, and sometimes psychopathic losers abound. Shortly after his death, two other film adaptations appeared, both from France: *Série Noire* (1979), directed by Alain Corneau and based on Thompson's 1954 novel *A Hell of a Woman*; and director Bertrand Travernier's *Coup de Torchon* (1982), based on *Pop. 1280*, written in 1964. Again, both films were only partially successful in translating Thompson's desolate vision of modern society to the screen. With *After Dark, My Sweet,* however—the most faithful film adaptation of one of his books—Thompson's world of drifters, con artists, and psychopaths has been fully realized in all of its sordid, mesmerizing splendor.

The film opens with Collie (Jason Patric) climbing out of a cave hideaway in the desert mountains of Southern California, then scuffling down a deserted road and wondering in a voice-over narration where he will end up next. His aimless wandering leads him to a roadhouse bar in a small desert town, where he orders a beer and attempts to make idle conversation, first with the gruff-looking bartender, Bert (Rocky Giordani), then with an attractive woman. The two begin to make fun of Collie's inane but harmless chatter until the bartender yells at Collie to leave his bar. When Collie protests, insisting that he has not done anything to deserve mistreatment, Bert grabs Collie by the shirt and Collie, in a sudden, shocking burst of violence, smashes Bert in the face with a lightning punch and leaves. The woman follows him in her car, apologizing for her rude behavior and offering to give him a ride. Collie finally agrees, and the woman takes Collie to her once-elegant but now run-down house on the outskirts of town. Introducing herself as Fay Anderson (Rachel Ward), a widow in need of a hired hand to help with the upkeep of her house and surrounding grounds, she offers him a place to stay in exchange for his help around her house, to which Collie agrees.

Later that evening, Uncle Bud (Bruce Dern), a former policeman turned cheap con artist, arrives, and Collie learns of their scheme to include him in a plot to kidnap the young son of a wealthy family in nearby Palm Springs. After Uncle Bud leaves, Fay has second thoughts about involving Collie in the kidnapping and persuades him to leave. Collie ends up in a truck-stop diner, where he slumps into a booth occupied by Doc Goldman (George Dickerson), the local general practitioner. Goldman immediately senses that Collie is in need of psychiatric help and asks him when he last received treatment. Collie admits that he has been in and out of several institutions over the past several years but insists that his illness is under control. Goldman suggests that Collie return to an institution as soon as possible, but then, seeing how seriously ill Collie is, decides to take Collie home with him.

Doc gives Collie a room of his own, and Collie helps Doc by doing small chores around Doc's combination house and office. Collie is haunted by the memory of Fay, however, recalling how helpless and desperate she seemed and how genuinely concerned she was for his well-being. Collie is also haunted by recurring images from his past: As a professional boxer under the name Kid Collins, he brutally and methodically beat an opponent to death. Collie finally decides to return to Fay and sneaks away one night to hitch a ride back to her house, where he is greeted with open affection by Fay. Soon after Collie's return, the two are joined by Uncle Bud, and they begin to plot the kidnapping.

Collie soon realizes that he was chosen as an accomplice primarily because of his fighting skills and because the others believe that he is mentally retarded and can be easily manipulated. Collie tells them that, despite his mannerisms, he is not stupid.

He also begins to suspect that the two are plotting to double-cross him in some way after the kidnapping has taken place. Despite his suspicions, Collie's affection for Fay increases, and she feels her affection growing for Collie. After she receives a call from Doc Goldman, however, who has learned of Collie's whereabouts and who tells her about Collie's history of mental illness, she runs away from Collie to seek refuge at Uncle Bud's. Collie, furious with Doc for telling Fay about his condition, threatens him over the phone but is appeased when Uncle Bud arrives and reassures Collie that the kidnapping will occur as planned.

The following day, Collie, dressed as a chauffeur, drives to an exclusive private boys' school, where he is supposed to impersonate the driver of the boy they plan to kidnap. Fearing that Uncle Bud and Fay are plotting to kill him and then make it look as if he acted alone in the kidnapping so that they can collect a reward from the boy's rich parents, Collie deliberately delivers the wrong boy to the rendezvous point. Collie then promises to return to the school and pick up the right boy, which he does with little difficulty. He delivers the passive, sickly boy, Charlie Vanderventer (James Cotton), to Fay and Uncle Bud, who are outraged at Collie's stupidity. Collie grabs Uncle Bud, yanks a gun out of his pocket, and accuses the two of plotting to kill him. It is obvious that Uncle Bud did intend to kill him, but Fay is incensed at the accusation and ultimately runs out of the house. Soon afterward, Charlie becomes deathly ill; Collie learns that the boy is diabetic and that Fay has been feeding him foods that aggravate his condition. Collie fears that Uncle Bud and Fay wish to kill the boy to ensure a safer getaway after collecting the ransom money. His suspicions are aroused further when, after stealing insulin from Doc Goldman and nursing Charlie back to health, Fay wakes him up one morning and tells him that Charlie has disappeared. Collie, determined to protect the boy, forces Fay to admit that she has hidden him. After Charlie is recovered from Fay's hiding place in a nearby forest, Doc Goldman makes a surprise appearance and overhears Collie and Fay arguing over her reasons for attempting to hide Charlie. When Doc threatens to expose them all to the police, Collie slugs Doc, killing him instantly. Collie and Fay escape with Charlie and drive to Uncle Bud's, where Collie confronts the old con man and demands that he collect the ransom money now before the situation is out of control. Uncle Bud confesses that his scheming and double-crossing have made for him many enemies, one of them being Bert the bartender, and that his status as a former policeman has not earned for him any inside information from his former police contacts; therefore, he has no idea if he can collect the money without walking into a police trap. Collie insists that Uncle Bud pick up the money anyway.

The three of them, along with a carefully concealed Charlie, drive to the local airport, where the money has allegedly been stored in a locker. Uncle Bud retrieves the bag containing the money but then is shot by Bert, who has been trailing Uncle Bud. Suddenly, dozens of law enforcement officers appear and Bert is gunned down. In the confusion, Collie, Fay, and Charlie drive away. Collie, realizing that Fay's affection and loyalty to him have always been genuine, decides to sacrifice himself to save her. He drives into the desert, then pretends that he means to kill the boy in order to make their escape easier. As he reaches for Charlie, he turns away from Fay, giving her easy access to the gun he has sticking out of his pocket. Fay grabs the gun and shoots Collie. As he collapses, mortally wounded, Collie tells her that she did the right thing, for now it will look as if he had forced her to participate in the kidnapping and she shot him to protect herself and the boy.

After Dark, My Sweet is not only the most faithful film adaptation of a Jim Thompson novel to date but also one of the most faithful film adaptations ever made. Director/coscreenwriter James Foley and producer/coscreenwriter Robert Redlin have managed to film every scene, every subtle nuance, suspicion, and grimace from the novel. On several occasions, huge chunks of dialogue and narrative are lifted straight from the novel and dramatized verbatim on the screen. Usually, such a literal approach to adapting a novel to the screen is avoided because dialogue from literature sounds stilted when dramatized word for word on film. This is especially true of noncontemporary novels such as *After Dark, My Sweet*, which was written in 1955—all of which makes the success of the film more remarkable.

What is even more impressive about the adaptation is that the film, like the novel, is told in first person from the point of view of a mentally unstable character. The usual objective, omnipotent camera point of view becomes completely subjective. The viewer sees, feels, senses everything from Collie's perspective. Thus, such questions of whether Fay and Uncle Bud are actually plotting to kill Collie after the kidnapping and of whether Fay really intended to kill Charlie by feeding him sugary food are filtered through Collie's beliefs, and because Collie has a history of mental illness and has been known to erupt in murderous violence when provoked, his perception of reality is highly unreliable. Thus, a fascinating and effective tension arises and bathes the action in a haze of psychotic delirium. The filmmakers add to this queasy view of reality with intense facial close-ups of the principal characters, long tracking shots with the camera following closely behind Collie as he paces and gazes at the world around him, and a series of abrupt, distorted flashbacks wherein Collie, in the boxing ring, is continually fouled by his opponent and then ultimately goes berserk, beating the man to death amid the screams of the crowd.

Two key characteristics of the film distinguish it from the novel. The novel explains the intricacies of the kidnapping plot in detail and de-emphasizes the emotional bond that develops between Collie and Fay. In the film, however, the kidnapping scheme is secondary to Fay and Collie's relationship. The result is that some of the film's plot developments are confusing, especially when Collie appears as the chauffeur. Nevertheless, by concentrating on the relationship between Collie and Fay, the filmmakers achieve what the novel lacks, namely a fully developed, always intriguing and finally emotionally moving portrait of two shifty, unstable, yet compassionate and noble human beings.

Much of the emotional effectiveness of the film comes from the principal actors, who endow their characters with sympathetic qualities even when they are acting despicable. Bruce Dern as Uncle Bud downplays the blatant seaminess of his character, speaking most of his dialogue in a quiet, bewildered tone of fake sympathy and savviness, resulting in a portrait of a small-time con artist completely overwhelmed by his own double-crossings and grandiose schemes. Rachel Ward as Fay softens Thompson's original character by playing her as less bitchy, less of an alcoholic loser, and more as a woman desperately in search of compassion and honesty. Jason Patric is nothing short of astounding as the childlike, dazed, and mentally unstable Collie. Patric gives Collie a wounded, innocent aura that makes him easy to like even after it is learned that he is a murderer and an escapee from a mental institution. Patric creates a fully alive and believable character, one with whom the audience can identify. Ultimately, Patric's Collie emerges as the strongest character of the three principals, the most intelligent, noblest, and most tragic.

Although Jim Thompson wrote most of his books in the 1950's and early 1960's, his vision of a world void of a moral code and peopled by rootless wanderers and psychopaths is hardly outdated. In fact, with the current economic instability in America and the continuous cutbacks in mental health care that have resulted in an upsurge in homeless individuals, most of whom suffer from mental illness or drug addiction, Thompson's bleak vision is sadly contemporary. The filmmakers must be commended for choosing to remain as faithful as possible to the vision of a man whose insights into the human condition are both timely and timeless.

Jim Kline

Reviews

American Film: Magazine of the Film and Television Arts. XV, July, 1990, p. 48.
Boxoffice. September, 1990, p. R69.
Chicago Tribune. August 24, 1990, VII, p. 40.
The Christian Science Monitor. August 23, 1990, p. 10.
Cosmopolitan. CCIX, August, 1990, p. 32.
The Hollywood Reporter. CCCXIII, June 26, 1990, p. 7.
Los Angeles. XXXV, July, 1990, p. 164.
Los Angeles Times. August 24, 1990, p. F8.
The New York Times. August 24, 1990, p. C11.
Newsweek. CXVI, September 3, 1990, p. 67.
Playboy. XXXVII, August, 1990, p. 24.
Rolling Stone. August, 1990, p. 46.
Variety. May 22, 1990, p. 19.
The Washington Post. August 24, 1990, p. C7.

AKIRA KUROSAWA'S DREAMS

Origin: Japan
Released: 1990
Released in U.S.: 1990
Production: Hisao Kurosawa and Mike Y. Inoue for Steven Spielberg and Akira
    Kurosawa USA; released by Warner Bros.
Direction: Akira Kurosawa
Screenplay: Akira Kurosawa
Cinematography: Takao Saito and Masaharu Ueda
Editing: Tome Minami
Production design: Yoshiro Muraki and Akira Sakuragi
Art direction: Yoshiro Muraki and Akira Sakuragi
Set decoration: Koichi Hamamura
Lighting: Takeji Sano
Visual effects: Industrial Light and Magic
Sound: Kenichi Benitani
Costume design: Emi Wada
Music: Shinichiro Ikebe
MPAA rating: PG
Running time: 120 minutes
Also known as: Dreams

> *Principal characters:*
> I . . . . Akira Terao
> Vincent van Gogh . . . . Martin Scorsese
> Old Man . . . . Chishu Ryu
> Snow Fairy . . . . Mieko Harada
> Mother . . . . Mitsuko Baisho
> Weeping Demon . . . . Chosuke Ikariya
> Power station worker . . . . Hisashi Igawa
> Private Noguchi . . . . Yoshitaka Zushi
> I (as a boy) . . . . Mitsunori Isaki
> I (as a young child) . . . . Toshihiko Nakano
> I's sister . . . . Mie Suzuki

Akira Kurosawa's Dreams consists of eight sequences that are connected only in
that the first two deal with youth, the final with advanced old age, and the middle five
with men at intermediate ages of maturity. At first consideration, this dream framework seems a great distance from Kurosawa's two preceding films, *Kagemusha: The
Shadow Warrior* (1980) and *Ran* (1985). Both of those films were epics in the formal
sense of depicting cataclysmic historical events with casts of thousands. The dreams
in this film usually highlight a small group, but they attain an epic resonance by
addressing the eternal questions of human existence.

Different dreams will surely appeal more strongly to some viewers than to others, and given their abstract style, individual dreams can yield different meanings to different viewers. As a group, however, they unambiguously assert a tragic vision of life. The pain of that vision is made bearable only by the beauty of Kurosawa's presentation. The director has written that dreams liberate "pure and earnest human desire." With a dazzling variety of styles and skills honed in fifty years of filmmaking, Kurosawa has captured his dreams on film.

The first dream, "Sunshine Through the Rain," features a five-year-old boy (Toshihiko Nakano) who has been told that on rainy days there are fox weddings in the forest which humans must not observe. On this particular rainy day, the boy slips into the forest where he soon comes upon such a wedding. Except for their fox faces, the creatures have human shapes, and they move with great precision, standing still from time to time as if they sense his presence. When the boy returns home, his mother (Mitsuko Baisho) responds to his tale by closing the door, shutting him outside, and telling him that he must go into the world and ask forgiveness from the foxes. The risk of being killed is high. The child arms himself and proceeds into a valley graced by a huge rainbow. He goes forward bravely yet humbly, fearful of death yet captivated by the rainbow.

In "The Peach Orchard" dream, the boy (Mitsunori Isaki) has entered his teen years. Chasing after a girl his own age, he comes upon a company of sixty life-size ceremonial dolls dressed in the traditional costumes of the Kyoho era. The group consists of emperors, empresses, ladies in waiting, musicians, courtiers, and servants. They are furious with him because his family has cut down a nearby peach orchard. The tearful boy is guiltless in the matter and asks if the orchard might be restored. After a solemn conference, the human dolls gracefully re-create the illusion of trees in full blossom with ballet movements in their Japanese robes. The enraptured boy's pleasure is completed when the dolls are magically transformed into actual peach trees. He reaches out to touch a branch, the dream dies, and he is left alone in a barren field.

The boy (Akira Terao) has grown to manhood in the third dream, "The Blizzard." He leads a four-man mountain-climbing party trapped in a blinding snowstorm. The climbers sink into waist-deep snow, desiring a sleep which means their death, when a snow fairy (Mieko Harada) appears to urge them on. The leader manages to awake his men, and they creep forward, counting their progress in inches. When the storm clears, they discover that they have been only a few feet from the safety of their tents. By struggling, they have survived.

An emotional turning point occurs in "The Tunnel." From this fourth dream onward, the more hopeful elements of the dreams fade. In this instance, a young man returning from war walks through a long tunnel. Upon emerging, his anticipated peace is disturbed by sounds of marchers behind him. He waits fearfully, and soon an entire platoon of soldiers emerges from the tunnel, men he has led to their death. The survivor, overcome with sorrow, asks their forgiveness and pleads for them to let him rest in peace.

In "Crows," an unseen man gazes at van Gogh paintings in a museum. The camera slowly enters the surface of a single canvas and the painted figures stir to life. The viewer-wanderer asks washerwomen where the artist may be found. Following their directions, he walks through various van Gogh landscapes. Sometimes the searcher is rendered realistically and the background is abstract, other times the conditions are reversed, and occasionally both are either realistic or abstract. Eventually the wanderer finds van Gogh (Martin Scorsese), but to all questions posed to him, van Gogh's only response is to work. The camera-wanderer's eyes turn aside for a moment and the painter is gone. Crows begin to gather and the camera retreats from the scene and the canvas, and the viewer is back in the museum. The viewer again stands before the famed van Gogh masterpieces and contemplates the menacing crows of his final work.

"Mount Fuji in Red" centers on a nuclear power plant where an accident has occurred. A terrified family is told by a learned man that each of the different gaseous clouds they see gets its distinctive color from a different lethal gas. The man explains that "they" had assured "us" the plant was safe, and then confesses that he was one of "them." The family turns to stare at an approaching cloud. When they look back to the man, he has committed suicide by leaping into the sea. The heat has become so intense that Mount Fuji has begun to melt. The family tries in vain to wave away the red fog which slowly masses about them.

"The Weeping Demon" is the most surreal of all the dreams. Following a global calamity, a man searches for other survivors and comes upon a demon with a horn growing in his forehead, who takes him to the rim of a valley. Below are a hundred horned men madly circling ponds such as those described in Dante's *Inferno*. All of them have been government officials or men of wealth, and their horns inflict upon them the same pain they inflicted on other living things and on the earth itself. The guide is forced to cut short his explanation, for his horn has also begun to throb.

The final dream, "Village of the Watermills," finds the wanderer discovering an idyllic village where the only power source is six elegant waterwheels. He encounters Old Man (Chishu Ryu) who informs him that, "People nowadays have forgotten that they are part of nature." To each observation that his ideas are outdated and inefficient, Old Man replies that so-called modern methods have led to the loss of Mother Nature, "and with that loss, the loss of the heart of mankind." When a cheerful band is heard playing, Old Man, who announces that he is 103, says it is a funeral procession. When the wanderer finds it odd that the music is so cheerful, Old Man declares that death is joyful when it comes in a natural way as part of the natural course of existence. Old Man takes up an instrument to join the festivities and the wanderer takes a farewell look at the serene village and its watermills.

The final dream is less a celebration of a natural way of life than a requiem for contemporary humanity. The child who could not restrain himself from intruding upon foxes has become a creature who commits terracide in an almost absent-minded fashion. Kurosawa mourns rather than mocks the fragility and pathos of human nature, but his judgment of the collective future is profoundly pessimistic.

The technical expertise required to realize any of the dreams was greater than that needed for a typical feature-length film. The fox sequence, for example, required the invention of a new method of implanting individual hairs upon each individual face. The dance sequences in various episodes required months of preparation by elite dance companies and specialized choreographers. The robes of the peach orchard are products of research in historical archives. The blizzard re-creation required three hundred bags of salt, four hundred bags of styrene foam, three giant jet engine fans, thirty bags of alum, and one million yen's worth of ice blocks. Experts on crows assisted on the van Gogh sequences and historical detail was authentic down to the very type of barleycorn seen being planted.

The actors in *Akira Kurosawa's Dreams*, mostly Japan's leading performers, succeed in the difficult task of sublimating their personas to the visual tableau. Seen most often is Akira Terao, who is the wanderer in six of the episodes. Old Man is played by Chishu Ryu, famous for his work with Yasujiro Ozu. For van Gogh, Kurosawa persuaded American director Martin Scorsese to step in front of the camera, and Scorsese's few moments on screen are riveting.

Akira Kurosawa has been recognized as a world-class director for decades, but few critics anticipated a work with the power of *Akira Kurosawa's Dreams* from a man who had just turned eighty. Ten years earlier, in 1980, the release of *Kagemusha* had set off a series of honors, including the Palme d'Or at the Cannes Film Festival followed shortly with a special life award. In September of 1982, the Venice Film Festival voted *Rashomon* (1950) the award of Lion Among Lions, the best film of all the films that had ever won the prestigious festival's highest award. When *Ran* was released, the film was heralded as Kurosawa's valedictorian and in 1989 the Academy of Motion Picture Arts and Science belatedly bestowed upon him a Life Achievement Award. But *Akira Kurosawa's Dreams* is no more a farewell effort than was *Ran*.

Dan Georgakas

Reviews
Boxoffice. October, 1990, p. R78.
Chicago Tribune. August 24, 1990, VII, p. 34.
Commonweal. CXVII, October 26, 1990, p. 612.
The Hollywood Reporter. May 11, 1990, p. 4.
Los Angeles Times. August 24, 1990, p. F1.
The New Republic. CCIII, October 8, 1990, p. 30.
The New York Times. August 24, 1990, p. B1.
The New Yorker. LXVI, September 10, 1990, p. 101.
Sight and Sound. LIX, Summer, 1990, p. 204.
Time. CXXXVI, September 10, 1990, p. 82.
Variety. May 11, 1990, p. 3.
The Washington Post. September 14, 1990, p. C1.

ALICE

Production: Robert Greenhut for Jack Rollins and Charles H. Joffe; released by
   Orion Pictures
Direction: Woody Allen
Screenplay: Woody Allen
Cinematography: Carlo Di Palma
Editing: Susan E. Morse
Production design: Santo Loquasto
Art direction: Speed Hopkins
Set decoration: Susan Bode
Sound: James Sabat
Costume design: Jeffrey Kurland
MPAA rating: PG-13
Running time: 106 minutes

> *Principal characters:*
> Alice .... Mia Farrow
> Joe .... Joe Mantegna
> Ed .... Alec Baldwin
> Dorothy .... Blythe Danner
> Vicki .... Judy Davis
> Doug .... William Hurt
> Dr. Yang .... Keye Luke
> Muse .... Bernadette Peters
> Nancy Brill .... Cybill Shepherd
> Alice's mother .... Gwen Verdon

Woody Allen was responsible for no less than eleven other productions starring
Mia Farrow prior to *Alice.* To her credit, Farrow met the challenge of those eleven
very diverse roles, and for each she created completely different characters. She
played the loving sister in *Hannah and Her Sisters* (1986); the simple but adorable
cigarette girl in *Radio Days* (1987); and the confused but kindhearted production
assistant in *Oedipus Wrecks* (one of the segments in the 1989 film *New York Stories*).
While each of these roles matured her as an actress, the limited partnership of Allen
and Farrow has created another motion-picture team which will have to rank with
those of Spencer Tracy and Katharine Hepburn, Fred Astaire and Ginger Rogers,
and even Stan Laurel and Oliver Hardy. By creating so many different characters for
the one actress, Allen stretches not only the actress but also the viewer.

Alice concerns itself with a simple Catholic girl who is sensitive but not very intelligent. She is a housewife and a somewhat detached mother who feels that there is
a void in her life. Alice (Farrow) is happily married to Doug (William Hurt), who is
an enormously successful businessman. While picking up the children from kinder-

garten one day, Alice catches the eye of Joe (Joe Mantegna). This momentary act of weakness creates feelings of guilt, in part because of her strict Catholic upbringing.

Three separate acquaintances suggest to her that a Dr. Yang (Keye Luke) might be able to help her recurring back problem. Dr. Yang is a Chinese herbalist, a first class psychologist, and a sage. Under hypnosis, Alice relives her first moment of falling in love with Doug. More interested in her personal life than her back complaint, Dr. Yang gives Alice a small bag of herbs with instructions that she take them at two-thirty that very day, also insisting that she take the children home from school. Alice complies with every detail. Sitting waiting for her children, she begins to talk to Joe—in fact, she does more than just talk. The once meek and shy Alice has become a romantic tigress out to make a kill. She arranges to meet Joe at the zoo. Her change of character has been entirely the result of the herbs, and when their effect wears off, she is unable to go through with her rendezvous.

What follows this incident is a series of meetings with Dr. Yang. At the end of each counseling session, he gives the unsuspecting Alice another small sachet of herbs, always accompanied by very explicit instructions. One batch of herbs allows Alice to speak with a deceased old flame, Ed (Alec Baldwin), who reappears as a ghost and is able to show Alice the New York skyline in a scene that is reminiscent of *Superman* (1978). Another type of herb invokes her own personal writing muse (Bernadette Peters). At one point, Dr. Yang prescribes an herb that makes her invisible, and another herb that will make any man she desires fall hopelessly in love with her. Instead, Alice chooses to divorce her husband, who she found was cheating on her. She leaves her rich life-style behind in order to go to Calcutta and be with Mother Theresa. On her return, she devotes herself to working with the less fortunate and lives in a rented apartment with hand-me-down furniture. Alice is now the happiest and most contented person in the world.

Throughout his motion-picture career, Allen has proven to be innovative, humorous, original, and, above all, consistent. As a director, his style is unique, and as a writer, his view of life only complements the finished article. With *Alice*, there is a definite departure from the usual, but his style is quite noticeable, despite the camouflage in employing a somewhat more supernatural approach. Outwardly, *Alice* deals with the thwarted ambitions of an upper-middle-class New York housewife, who confuses having an affair with trying to experience true love. Alice has completely lost her direction in life, and barely manages to remember her youthful dreams. Allen's setting is the perfect vehicle for exploring the deeper thoughts and feelings of an average well-meaning woman in her forties. While this may be a narrow band of experience, Alice represents those men and women who have allowed their true dreams to be buried under a mountain of material acquisitions.

Alice is a further attempt at understanding the human species. The groundwork for appreciating what Allen is trying to achieve has already been laid in his earlier works. This does not mean necessarily that each film builds on the one before, but when the screenwriter, director, and leading lady have collaborated in numerous previous productions, certain givens become apparent. An unfulfilled marriage is never the sole reason that men and women decide to divorce—usually, there is a deeper yearning for something that is more meaningful. Alice has found herself to be in a marriage that is quite stationary, with the possibility of going into reverse. For Alice, all that remains of her dreams as a young girl are the glowing embers. In a few more years, possibly, all hope of ever achieving something worthwhile may be long forgotten. The sands of time have slipped imperceptibly through her hands, and Alice stands looking into a future which has no meaning or direction. By chance or fate—the cause of such meetings is difficult to discern—Alice is given a chance to realize her longings by encountering Dr. Yang.

While Alice tries to explain that what seems to be bothering her is her back, the sage in Dr. Yang has already perceived that the trouble is much deeper. Alice is put under hypnosis. Instead of the conventional flashback, Dr. Yang's office is transformed into a fairground through the use of a simple red flashing light. There in front of Dr. Yang, Doug and Alice enact their first meeting together. This scene provides a window into the deeper world of Alice's past, and it is an attempt by Dr. Yang to discover what the root of her problem may be. The herbs which Dr. Yang prescribes are not medicinal but self-revelatory. Alice's malady is not in her back but in her life force, which is weak and almost exhausted. Dr. Yang represents wisdom that is cloaked in humility, while her husband Doug represents self-interest that is cloaked in the outward acknowledgement of his wife's dilemma. Doug's patronizing attitude and detachment contrast with Dr. Yang's deep interest in his patient. As a successful businessman, Doug does not want to step outside the bounds of convention, while Dr. Yang gives this virtual stranger every encouragement, and even the means for self-discovery.

By becoming romantically involved with Joe, who she knows is still in love with his former wife, Alice hopes that an affair will provide her with some of the answers that she seeks in her life. Even with Joe, she requires help from the ghost of her old flame, Ed, to encourage her to explore the extramarital relationship. Marriage is sacred ground upon which Alice is walking, as her Catholic upbringing strictly forbids such trysts. Like Lewis Carroll's Alice, who fell down the rabbit hole and came across the most amazing array of people and happenings, this modern Alice equally runs into the familiar and the unfamiliar. While her world is no Wonderland, so many incidents point toward Dr. Yang as someone who may have many of the answers to her questions that it is inconceivable that Alice could be as naïve as to miss all of his promptings. Even when she receives an herb that can make her disappear, in the style of *The Invisible Man* (1933), the anguished Alice is not prompted to probe deeper into the resources of the unconventional doctor of herbal medicine.

The one human-scale challenge that is presented to Alice is that of Nancy Brill (Cybill Shepherd). Apparently, Alice was instrumental in Nancy's success in becoming a television producer, and Alice believes that Nancy owes her a favor in return. Like nearly everyone else who knows Alice, Nancy treats her with quiet contempt and indifference, as Alice tries to break into writing for television. While it soon becomes obvious to Alice that she is not a writer, the attempt is at least praiseworthy. Allen hits on a universal subject which is experienced by everyone of every age. This ability to convey such everyday familiar needs is where *Alice* scores its many bull's-eyes.

Alice is carefully paced, which gives the subject matter time to unfold and tell its story without a sense of being rushed. By the time that Alice has finished her sessions with Dr. Yang and all her principal friends and acquaintances have been introduced, a certain sense of accomplishment has been achieved. What appears, in the final analysis, as a random series of meetings and happenings has the effect of telling all that could be told about Alice and her predicament. A simple conclusion is indeed fitting for a film that deals with the complexities of human suffering. Alice does what she always wanted to do with her life—help those less fortunate than herself. The film's satisfaction comes from Alice's own satisfaction in accepting herself and finding a purpose for her life.

Richard G. Cormack

Reviews

America. CLXIV, February 2, 1991, p. 93.
American Film: Magazine of the Film and Television Arts. XVI, January, 1991, p. 47.
Chicago Tribune. December 25, 1990, V, p. 10.
The Hollywood Reporter. CCCXV, December 3, 1990, p. 7.
Los Angeles Times. December 25, 1990, p. F1.
The New Republic. CCIV, January 28, 1991, p. 25.
The New York Times. December 25, 1990, p. A9.
Newsweek. December 31, 1990, p. 61.
Time. CCCXXXVII, January 7, 1991, p. 73.
Variety. December 3, 1990, p. 2.
The Washington Post. January 25, 1991, p. D1.

ANOTHER 48 HRS.

Production: Lawrence Gordon and Robert D. Wachs for Lawrence Gordon and
  Eddie Murphy Prods.; released by Paramount Pictures
Direction: Walter Hill
Screenplay: John Fasano, Jeb Stuart, and Larry Gross; based on a story by Fred
  Braughton
Cinematography: Matthew F. Leonetti
Editing: Freeman Davies, Carmel Davies, and Donn Aron
Production design: Joseph C. Nemec III
Art direction: Gary Wissner
Set decoration: George R. Nelson
Sound: Jerry Ross
Costume design: Dan Moore
Music: James Horner
MPAA rating: R
Running time: 98 minutes

> *Principal characters:*
> Reggie Hammond .... Eddie Murphy
> Jack Cates .... Nick Nolte
> Ben Kehoe .... Brion James
> Blake Wilson .... Kevin Tighe
> Frank Cruise .... Ed O'Ross
> Willy Hickok .... David Anthony Marshall
> Cherry Ganz .... Andrew Divoff
> Kirkland Smith .... Bernie Casey
> Tyrone Burroughs .... Brent Jennings
> Amy Smith .... Tisha Campbell

In 1982, Walter Hill, whose main talent is in making effectively violent action-adventure films such as *Red Heat* (1988), *Southern Comfort* (1981), *The Long Riders* (1980), and *The Warriors* (1979), made Eddie Murphy a film star in *48 HRS.* (1982). It begins with a spasm of violence (a Hill trademark, seen later in *Red Heat* as well as in *48 HRS.* and its sequel) by filming a prison break as one killer, a bad Indian named Billy Bear (played by stuntman Sonny Landham), escapes from a prison road gang, along with a psychopathic killer named Ganz (played by James Remar). Detective Jack Cates (Nick Nolte) and his partner trace Ganz and Billy Bear to the Walden Hotel, where, in a shoot-out, Cates's partner is murdered. Thwarted, Cates then turns to Reggie Hammond (Eddie Murphy), who is serving a three-year prison sentence with six months to go, and gets him released for forty-eight hours to assist him with the case, since Reggie had ties to the Ganz gang. The rest of the film is a quasi-comic action-adventure spectacle that proves to be a successful money-maker for Paramount Pictures. As Jack Kroll noted in his *Newsweek* review of the sequel

(June 18), however, the original was criticized for its racial stereotyping, misogyny, and mindless violence.

It is hardly a surprise, therefore, that a sequel called *Another 48 HRS.* would eventually follow, bringing back Nolte and Murphy, with Walter Hill again directing. Of the original scriptwriting team of four, only Larry Gross was involved in writing the screenplay for the sequel, which *Variety* criticized for its total creative bankruptcy, while *Newsweek* wondered what had happened to the wit and the irony of the original.

Clearly, Paramount Pictures counted on Eddie Murphy and Nick Nolte to carry the sequel. Apparently the studio knew that the story was weak, uninventive, and imitative, since the usual reviewers' screenings were not scheduled. As *Newsweek* critic Kroll pointed out, this often happens if a studio anticipates bad reviews. Fortunately for Paramount, the film was released into a summer market in which no single blockbuster seemed to dominate and overwhelm competing pictures.

The plot of *Another 48 HRS.* follows the same essential development of the original. This time, Detective Cates (Nick Nolte) has been suspended from the force for the unorthodox methods he has used in his efforts to identify and find a crime lord who is known only as the Iceman, and he is sure to be sentenced for manslaughter unless he can find the elusive and mysterious Iceman and clear himself within forty-eight hours. Meanwhile, Reggie Hammond (Eddie Murphy) is about to be released from prison again, several years after the first encounter, even though, back then, he only had a few months more to serve. Reggie was framed after his original encounter with Cates, who offered no assistance. Cates quickly forgot about Reggie after the original case was concluded. Now that Cates is himself being framed on a charge of manslaughter, he turns again to Reggie for help. Naturally Reggie is not inclined to cooperate.

Cates knows that the Iceman has put out a contract on Reggie's life. He visits Reggie in prison to suggest that they work together again on this case, but Reggie is not interested. He believes that he can take care of himself, and he does not want a "honky" partner in his life. The contract killers are two bad bikers, Willy Hickok (David Anthony Marshall) and Cherry Ganz (Andrew Divoff), the brother of the homicidal convict played by James Remar whom Cates and Hammond killed in the first film. Ganz's motive is revenge (the same motive Walter Hill gave to the Georgian drug dealer Victor in *Red Heat*, another trademark of the director-screenwriter).

The first half of the film pits Cates and Hammond against Hickok and Ganz. The last half is the story of detection, as the unlikely partners trace down the Iceman, with some help from kingpin convict Kirkland Smith (Bernie Casey). The tip is that the Iceman is an insider on the police force, and since Cates gradually becomes aware that his every move seems to be anticipated by his enemies, that makes sense. One possibility is Internal Affairs agent Blake Wilson (Kevin Tighe), who seems fanatical in his persecution of Cates, but this ultimately proves to be a false lead. Other possibilities are San Francisco police inspector Ben Kehoe (Brion James) and officer Frank Cruise (Ed O'Ross, who played the villain in *Red Heat*). The suspects are narrowed down in the final reel, and Cates has to deal with a problem of a betrayed friendship. He comes to the realization that he has been set up by one of his "friends" in the police department.

It is hard to believe that it has been eight years since Walter Hill directed the original *48 HRS.*, since the sequel resumes the action so smoothly. At that time, Nick Nolte got the lead billing and Eddie Murphy was merely a stand-up comedian trying to break into the motion-picture business. The film *48 HRS.* launched Murphy's film career, and he was excellent in such later films as *Trading Places* (1983) and *Beverly Hills Cop* (1984), the highest grossing comedy of all time. It is understandable that Murphy would return to the *48 HRS.* formula, since his film career could use a boost. Litigation concerning plagiarism in *Coming to America* (1988) had tarnished his image for many people, and films such as *The Golden Child* (1986) and *Harlem Nights* (1989) did not impress the critics, though *Harlem Nights* apparently made money, as did *Coming to America*, regardless of claims made by the studio's creative accounting system in court. In *Another 48 HRS.*, then, "the boys" are reunited and "back in town." Much of the action is replayed from the original. There is, for example, another bar fight, this time in a biker bar rather than a redneck bar, but the outcome is pretty much the same. There is the same kind of banter between Reggie and Cates. Murphy still loves his Porsche and still likes to sing "Roxanne." The desperadoes are cut from the same cloth, including Cherry Ganz, the biker-brother of the psychotic killer who was terminated eight years before. A female cop is killed by three bikers in the opening sequence, which parallels the initial violence of the original's prison work-gang escape. Walter Hill still directs violent action impressively, but there are fewer gasps this time around. Although Murphy gets top billing, and although he still plays the comedian, he is more laid-back and less effective than he once was. Nick Nolte seems to be working harder, but Hill's film does not represent his best work in 1990 (arguably Sidney Lumet's *Q&A*, reviewed in this volume, an internal-affairs vehicle released by Columbia pictures in April).

The biggest disappointment of *Another 48 HRS.*, however, is Murphy, who has forgotten how to subordinate his star persona to the role. Murphy's new, casual debonair image was created in *Harlem Nights*, where his character seemed to have been created by a tailor rather than a knowledgeable screenwriter. Murphy walked his way through that role as he does through this one. When he was younger (twenty-one years old at the time he made *48 HRS.*), he talked his way through his roles and created a distinctive style. One misses the energy and comic inventiveness and even the timing he employed so well in *Trading Places*. His approach began to change with *The Golden Child* and continued through *Coming to America* and *Harlem Nights*. Without the original Murphy, the sequel cannot succeed in measuring up to the original film, no matter how hard Nick Nolte may be working.

Consequently, the reviews were mixed. The *Variety* tally of critical reviews (June 13) did not bode well for this sequel. In Los Angeles, the only favorable review appeared in the *Los Angeles Times*. Of the other reviews in Los Angeles, one was ambivalent and six unfavorable. The film fared better in Chicago (six favorable, four unfavorable, and seven ambivalent), but it got bad press in New York (three favorable, nine unfavorable, and seven ambivalent). Jack Kroll of *Newsweek* considered *Another 48 HRS.* symbolic of cynical commercialism (June 18). Vincent Canby of *The New York Times* (June 8) blasted Murphy for a "lazy, unresponsive performance." In July, however, the film was still holding its place on the Associated Press listing of the ten top-grossing films, in the number-six position the weekend of July 6.

The picture cost close to $50 million to make, however, and both *Another 48 HRS.* and *Die Hard II: Die Harder* (1990; reviewed in this volume) were deemed safe risks, according to Aljean Harmetz, who reported in *The New York Times* (June 3) that National Research data put these two films "at the top, in a class by themselves." Certainly both sold tickets, but by mid-July *Another 48 HRS.* was losing ground and was pulled from some theaters. *Another 48 HRS.* might have done well competing against the likes of *Betsy's Wedding*, *Fire Birds*, and *Ghost Dad*, but it struggled to hold its own in a field of competition that included *Back to the Future Part III*, *Days of Thunder*, *Dick Tracy*, *Die Hard II*, *Gremlins II: The New Batch*, and *Total Recall* (all reviewed in this volume).

The first rule of making a sequel is to make it interesting and amusing and to keep it in the spirit and style of the original. The second rule is to find some way of advancing the formula so that it will be something more than the same old story recycled under a different title or number. *Another 48 HRS.* depended on the same formula and chemistry but shifted the importance from Nick Nolte, who got top billing in the original, to Eddie Murphy, who is no longer lean, mean, and hungry but merely slick, like the character he played in *Harlem Nights*. *Another 48 HRS.* offered the same predictable level of violence but failed to offer wit and irony. *Variety* pointed out accurately that it looked more like a remake than a sequel.

James M. Welsh

Reviews
Boxoffice. August, 1990, p. R61.
The Guardian. September 20, 1990, p. 24.
The Hollywood Reporter. CCCXII, June 6, 1990, p. 6.
Los Angeles Times. June 8, 1990, p. F1.
New York. June 25, 1990, p. 64.
The New York Times. June 8, 1990, p. C12.
Newsweek. June 18, 1990, p. 60.
Premiere. III, No. 10, June, 1990, p. 94.
Time. June 25, 1990, p. 77.
Variety. CCCXXXIX, June 13, 1990, p. 27.
Video. XIV, December, 1990, p. 76.
The Wall Street Journal. June 21, 1990, p. A12.
The Washington Post. June 8, 1990, p. B1.

ARACHNOPHOBIA

Production: Kathleen Kennedy and Richard Vane for Hollywood Pictures and Amblin Entertainment; released by Buena Vista Pictures
Direction: Frank Marshall
Screenplay: Don Jakoby and Wesley Strick; based on a story by Jakoby and Al Williams
Cinematography: Mikael Salomon
Editing: Michael Kahn
Production design: James Bissell
Art direction: Christopher Burian-Mohr
Set design: Carl J. Stensel
Set decoration: Jackie Carr
Special effects: Matt Sweeney
Visual effects: David Sosalla
Creature design: Chris Walas
Sound: Ronald Judkins, Terry Porter, David J. Hudson, and Mel Metcalfe
Costume design: Jennifer L. Parsons
Supervising entomologist: Steven Kutcher
Live spider coordination: Jim Kundig
Stunt coordination: Chuck Waters
Music: Trevor Jones
MPAA rating: PG-13
Running time: 109 minutes

> *Principal characters:*
> Dr. Ross Jennings .... Jeff Daniels
> Molly Jennings .... Harley Jane Kozak
> Delbert McClintock .... John Goodman
> Dr. James Atherton .... Julian Sands
> Sheriff Parsons .... Stuart Pankin
> Chris Collins .... Brian McNamara
> Jerry Manley .... Mark L. Taylor
> Dr. Sam Metcalf .... Henry Jones
> Henry Beechwood .... Peter Jason
> Milton Briggs .... James Handy
> Irv Kendall .... Roy Brocksmith
> Blaire Kendall .... Kathy Kinney
> Margaret Hollins .... Mary Carver

Dr. Atherton (Julian Sands), a noted specialist on insects and spiders (especially in identifying new ones), is on an expedition in Venezuela. He is joined by a photographer, Jerry Manley (Mark L. Taylor), on a trip to a sinkhole two thousand feet deep. Atherton hopes to find insects that have remained isolated and unchanged for millions of years. While there, he finds large spiders with no reproductive organs like worker bees or soldier ants. Later, Manley, not well from a bout with fever, retires to his cot, but he is not alone. One of Atherton's spiders has got out of the sinkhole and delivers a lethal bite to the photographer. Manley's body is shipped back to his small hometown of Canaima, California, for burial, but the deadly spider again hitches a ride.

From the funeral home, the spider makes its way out of a swinging door, is picked up by a crow (which it kills), and finally falls onto the new property of Ross (Jeff Daniels) and Molly (Harley Jane Kozak) Jennings and their two children (Garette Patrick Ratliff and Marlene Katz). The spider makes its home in the Jenningses' barn, mates with a domestic female spider, and begins to breed lethal offspring.

Ross, a doctor from San Francisco, has traded his life in the fast lane for country living and the practice of retiring Dr. Samuel Metcalf (Henry Jones). At the last minute, however, Dr. Metcalf, seeing retirement as the first step toward death, changes his mind, and Ross is left with no patients. Ross is befriended by Margaret Hollins (Mary Carver), who not only becomes his first patient but also throws a party to introduce him to more prospective patients. Margaret was diagnosed as having high blood pressure, but Ross finds otherwise and takes her off her medication. After the party, Margaret is bitten by one of the lethal spiders and dies. Dr. Metcalf blames her death on her high blood pressure and refuses to have an autopsy done. The gap left by the death of Ross's only patient is soon filled by the high school football team. When a spider gets into a player's helmet and kills him, Ross suddenly finds himself labeled Dr. Death.

After exercising one night, Dr. Metcalf suddenly has a seizure after being bitten by one of the spiders. He, too, dies, but now Ross knows the cause. Unfortunately, Ross (as the result of an incident in his childhood) is terrified of spiders and is still paralyzed by his fear of them.

Ross studies the dreaded topic and finds Dr. Atherton to be the most noted expert. Ross calls Atherton, who in turn sends a graduate student, Chris Collins (Brian McNamara), to investigate. When Collins realizes the magnitude of the situation, he calls Atherton. Soon the connection is made that the spiders came from Atherton's expedition via Manley's coffin. Ross and Collins assume the spider has established a nest in the mortuary, but it is not there. What is there are the dead mortician and his wife, bitten while eating popcorn during *Wheel of Fortune*. With the help of exterminator Delbert McClintock (John Goodman) of "Bugs-B-Gone," Ross and Collins plot the locations of all the victims on a map. In the very center of them all is Ross's house. While they find the first nest in Ross's barn, what they have not yet realized is that the primary spider has already made another nest in Ross's cellar.

It quickly becomes a man-versus-spider battle between the head spider and arachnophobe Ross. After a war in the basement, which practically destroys his wine cache, Ross burns the queen on the fuse box and then improbably propels her, flaming, into the pulsating nest with a shot from a nail gun. Having had enough of country life, the Jennings family moves back to San Francisco only to be subjected to an earthquake.

Arachnophobia's basic plot is very familiar. It is the story in which a "monster" comes to town, and one person tries to alert those who refuse to be alerted. Killings escalate until, finally, the hero prevails. A standard subplot is added to this scenario, in which the hero must overcome some personal fear to win against the evil force in a final battle. What helps to put this film a notch above the many B-films it seems to be imitating is its definite good humor about the whole topic and the performance of the actors.

First-time director Frank Marshall has a lengthy and distinguished list of films for which he has been producer, many of which were directed by Steven Spielberg; Marshall is a partner in Amblin Entertainment. His production of *Arachnophobia* attempts to produce maximum squeamishness in the audience while maintaining a high degree of humor; as a result, the film was advertised as a "thrillomedy."

As for the cast, Daniels is believable and sympathetic as Dr. Ross Jennings. The best part, however, belongs to John Goodman, the Rambo-like exterminator who has most of the film's best lines. Actually, the cast has a very familiar look: it is appropriately comfortable, just like the small town where the story is set. If audiences seem familiar with the town's population before they are introduced, there is good reason. Apart from their many film credits, the television credits of actors playing residents of the town of Canaima include the mother (who portrayed Margaret Hollins) from *Simon and Simon*, the lascivious librarian (the funeral director's wife) from the *Bob Newhart Show*, a reporter from cable television's *Not Necessarily the News*, Mary from *Santa Barbara* (Molly Jennings), and regulars from *House Calls* (Manley) and *Nutt House* (Collins), and, most obviously, Dan from *Roseanne* (Delbert McClintock).

Also among the cast were the innumerable spiders. Hollywood's best-known bug and insect expert, Steven Kutcher, researched dozens of spider candidates in his job of "casting" the starring role of the film. He even organized a "Spider Olympics" to test the skills of several different species. What was needed were spiders who could run, jump, walk upside-down, and spin webs. Finding one spider who could do all of this was important since director Marshall felt that substituting a mechanical spider would sacrifice the film's realism. Delena spiders from New Zealand were used to play the drone or soldier spiders, but to play the large and lethal star, an Amazonian bird-eating tarantula was chosen. (His several smaller relatives were played by smaller zebra-striped tarantulas.) Mechanical spiders were used, however, for some of the more difficult effects. These were supplied by Chris Walas who was also the creature effects supervisor on *Gremlins* (1984) and *The Fly* (1986) and who directed *The Fly II* (1989); it is virtually impossible to tell when they are used.

The film's opening sequence was filmed near Angel Falls in the heart of the Venezuelan rain forest. While there, the cast and crew stayed at a small enclave of huts near the base of the falls which was called Canaima. They enjoyed their stay there so much that the area's name was given to the fictitious California town in which the story takes place. (The town actually used for filming was Cambria, California.) The scenes in the giant sinkhole, however, were filmed on one of the largest sound stages in Hollywood, formerly Metro-Goldwyn-Mayer's famous Stage 30. There production designer James Bissell reconstructed a rain forest complete with waterfalls, massive trees, and gigantic spider webs. This care taken with realistic sets, the credible acting, the story's humor and creepy "monsters," which easily push an audience's psychological buttons, all help to make *Arachnophobia* more than simply another horror film.

Beverley Bare Buehrer

Reviews
Boxoffice. September, 1990, p. R66.
Chicago Tribune. July 20, 1990, p. C7.
The Hollywood Reporter. CCCXIII, July 16, 1990, p. 6.
Los Angeles Magazine. September, 1990, p. 167.
Los Angeles Times. July 18, 1990, Calendar, p. F1.
Magazine of Fantasy and Science Fiction. LXXX, January, 1991, p. 111.
New York Magazine. July 30, 1990, p. 51.
The New York Times. July 18, 1990, p. B1.
The New Yorker. July 30, 1990, p. 51.
Newsweek. CXVI, July 23, 1990, p. 64.
People Weekly. July 30, 1990, p. 11.
Premiere. IV, December, 1990, p. 37.
Rolling Stone. August 23, 1990, p. 45.
Sight and Sound. LIX, Autumn, 1990, p. 280.
Variety. CCCXL, July 18, 1990, p. 20.
The Wall Street Journal. July 19, 1990, p. A8.
The Washington Post. July 20, 1990, p. N33.

AVALON

Production: Mark Johnson and Barry Levinson for Baltimore Pictures; released by Tri-Star Pictures
Direction: Barry Levinson
Screenplay: Barry Levinson
Cinematography: Allen Daviau
Editing: Stu Linder
Production design: Norman Reynolds
Art direction: Fred Hole and Edward Richardson
Set decoration: Linda DeScenna
Sound: Gloria S. Borders
Costume design: Gloria Gresham
Music: Randy Newman
MPAA rating: PG
Running time: 126 minutes

> *Principal characters:*
> Hymie Krichinsky .... Leo Fuchs
> Dottie Kirk .... Eve Gordon
> Gabriel Krichinsky .... Lou Jacobi
> Sam Krichinsky .... Armin Mueller-Stahl
> Ann Kaye .... Elizabeth Perkins
> Eva Krichinsky .... Joan Plowright
> Izzy Kirk .... Kevin Pollak
> Jules Kaye .... Aidan Quinn
> Nathan Krichinsky .... Israel Rubinek
> Michael Kaye .... Elijah Wood
> Teddy Kirk .... Grant Gelt

Avalon, directed and scripted by Oscar-winning auteur Barry Levinson (*Rain Man*, 1988), is a glowing, humorous, bittersweet love letter—nostalgic, but in the best sense of wry observation—to a simpler time in this century, before progress destroyed family unity and tradition. Set in Levinson's hometown of Baltimore, it marks his return to the familiar and rewarding setting of his previous semiautobiographical successes—*Diner* (1982), a poignant tale of growing up in the 1950's; and *Tin Men* (1987), a sharp satire of aluminum siding salesmen.

Levinson, as in previous films, combines keen sociological insights with heartfelt storytelling, employing generous portions of laughter and tears. This time he focuses his unerring eye on the impact of expanding technology and suburbanization, spanning fifty years in the lives of the Krichinskys, a boisterous, affectionate, extended family of Russian immigrants, and their upwardly mobile, American-born offspring.

Avalon, however, is a departure in terms of Levinson's use of fable-like story elements. His tale is alternately narrated by a young boy, Michael Kaye (Elijah Wood), eyes full of naïveté, and an old man, Sam Krichinsky (Armin Mueller-Stahl), his nostalgic grandfather. Through their visions, Avalon, the Baltimore ghetto where the five Krichinsky brothers immigrated and raised families, is transformed, via the alchemy of memory and youthful bewilderment, into a land of perpetual wonder, much like the fabled paradise Avalon of Arthurian legend.

At the first of many Thanksgivings traditionally celebrated by the Krichinskys, Sam proposes to tell the story of his early experiences in America, while they await the arrival of his elder brother Gabriel. It would be disrespectful to carve the turkey without him. The generation born in America, including Michael's father, Jules (Aidan Quinn), and his Uncle Izzy (Kevin Pollak), look on bemusedly, having heard it all as children. On the Fourth of July, 1914, Sam landed in Baltimore. The sky was lit up with exploding rockets. It was the most beautiful place he had ever been. He fell in love, married, toiled in the family wallpaper hanging business, and reared a family. One Thanksgiving, however, Sam gives in to the children's impatience to eat and carves the turkey without Gabriel. Outraged, Gabriel storms away. At the next family circle meeting, they exchange violent words, sealing the rift between them and polarizing the others.

A number of Thanksgivings pass. In the meantime, Jules and Izzy open a store together, selling television sets, which have just arrived on the market. Jules moves his family to the suburbs, taking Sam and Eva (Joan Plowright) with him. The store, the first discount house ever, is a success, and Izzy, always the gambler, talks Jules into expanding the business. Jules and Izzy's enterprise now encompasses an entire warehouse of discount goods, a veritable "department store." Michael and cousin Teddy (Grant Gelt) almost start a blaze in the basement, and later the warehouse bursts into flames. Michael is relieved to learn that the fire was not his fault, but all of Jules's investment is lost. He parts company with Izzy, finding a job selling commercial time on television, and prospers.

Years pass. The split between Sam and Gabriel has become permanent. Sadly, when Eva dies of a heart attack, her funeral is attended only by the immediate family. Without her, Sam rapidly declines into senility. In the early 1960's, Sam is in a nursing home. On the television, coincidentally, is a Fourth of July celebration. At first, Sam fails to recognize Michael, who comes to introduce his own son "Sam." To the little boy, Sam is a geriatric stranger whose accent makes him "talk funny." He arrived a long time ago, explains Michael. "It was the Fourth of July, 1914. . . ." It remains to be seen if Michael will succeed in passing the old man's story, his family legacy, on to his son.

Avalon is drawn from research and stories that Levinson's grandfather told him as a child. Clearly, he is Michael, now matured, affectionately recoining his grandfather's stories. The result is a motion picture of considerable warmth, humor, and wisdom, and a testament to all immigrant forebears, regardless of their origins.

Avalon is not without shortcomings, notably a top-heavy development of the fable segments at the expense of character and overall story. There is also Levinson's ambiguity as to the point of view, which shifts uncomfortably from Sam to Michael to Jules, each personifying distinct ways of viewing the world. Sam's point of view is one of idealized memory (the past); Michael's, that of wonder (the future); and bridging the two is Jules, the salesman, his perspective one of pragmatic realism (the present).

While such a narrative design is not without merit, its expression tends to result in choppiness, as the story lurches from one character's focus to another's, telegraphing events, and mostly skimming the surface of experience but never quite diving beneath it. Not enough time is spent with any one character to facilitate identification. Instead of being one-dimensional, characters become symbolic, which makes them complex without being round and distances them from the audience.

On the rare occasions when symbolic identity merges with character, the result is a poignant moment of truth, as when Sam rues leaving Avalon. He is a father recalling his infant's first steps; he is the patriarch relinquishing his role, swept up in the winds of change. Similarly, Michael's anguished confession to Jules about setting the warehouse on fire is also such a moment of truth.

Levinson's portrait of Jules is by far the least successful. He remains a bland enigma poised between the two generations. Doubtless, it is difficult for Levinson the writer to perceive his own father, represented here. Jules symbolizes the generation of immigrant offspring first born in America. A generation of salesmen, they bridged the gap between their blue-collar parents (like Sam), and their children, who with the advantages of education, like Michael, entered the professions. Placed strategically in the center of the story, Jules seems to lack the backbone indicated by his pivotal role. Aidan Quinn's seamless, even-tempered portrayal betokens his confusion about what precisely motivates his character, instead of artful representation. For a salesman, he is sorely lacking in personality.

It is with the ancillary characters that Levinson shines, rendering them fully with a minimum of strokes. Cousin Izzy, played with admirable restraint by Kevin Pollak, is a succinct composite of the post-World War II gambler-businessman. Eva, though featured in only a few scenes, is a comic presence throughout. Her wrangling with her daughter-in-law and constant reproofs of Sam memorably depict her. Joan Plowright's understated characterization never falters. Similarly, Lou Jacobi's portrayal of the elder brother Gabriel is a work rich in comic understatement and brevity. His preposterous, indignant response to Sam's breach of respect—"You cut de turkey vid out me?"—is a masterpiece of acting.

Levinson's true art as a storyteller is the skill with which he weaves together all the elements of his subject—sociology, character, anecdote, history, and plot—into a whole fabric. He lays the foundation for story twists early and carefully nurtures them along, so that they appear inevitable and just but not predictable. The opening sequence, for example, depicting the first Thanksgiving, cleverly sets the stage for the critical scene in which Gabriel and Sam have their fateful falling out. As a result, Sam's hauntingly beautiful story of coming to America stands in vivid contrast to all that comes to pass, resonating eerily, as tradition and family disintegrate.

Levinson ingeniously incorporates the language and imagery of the times into the fabric of his tale. He has an infallible ear for the peculiar rhythms of speech and anecdotes of his characters, as well as an eye for absurdities. He fastens on just the right icons of an age: television in its infancy, trolley cars, Saturday film matinees, those inane model airplanes, sleeker and faster cars, and the newly launched discount store. Levinson works these icons into his narrative until they are inseparable from the destiny of his characters.

In documenting the dissolution of the family unit, Levinson accurately identifies television as one of the chief instruments of its demise. From its first inauspicious intrusion into the Krichinsky home, as a gift to Jules while convalescing, it alienates, usurping communication between family members—displacing, in fact, the storyteller's communal function. While it provides Jules with a prosperous, lifelong career, television takes him from his family. On Thanksgivings after the rift between Sam and Gabriel, it is this innocuous "storyteller" around which the family gathers, instead of around Sam, whose edifying stories humanized and linked family members. Finally, television is the baneful companion of Sam's old age, underscoring his abandonment by loved ones.

Nowhere is Levinson's insight into family more penetrating than in his account of the permanent rift between Gabriel and Sam. In Sam's cutting of the turkey, Gabriel rightly senses the first encroachment on the values which have sustained them through the years and during the roughest of times. Now that Sam has moved to the suburbs to enjoy his son's affluence, he need not have respect. The children may change their names, marry without ceremony, and move away, forgetting their roots, but surely the elders should set an example. This disintegration begins with the turkey, implies Gabriel, and proceeds from there.

Obviously, in secularizing his film, sanitizing it of all direct reference to the Krichinskys' Jewish identity, Levinson broadens his audience while avoiding the category of a so-called Jewish film. Whether this categorization would have been a pejorative and limiting assignation or merely an irrelevance, Levinson and his distributors were not willing to take a chance finding out; it is an issue that he skirts brilliantly. In this light, Thanksgiving is a shrewd compromise for a traditional holiday, as it is both ecumenical and American.

Some of the credit for *Avalon*'s success must be shared with other contributors, such as producer Mark Johnson, who has worked on all the films that Levinson has directed since *Diner* (1982), including *Rain Man*, which won the Academy Award for best picture in 1988. Director of photography Allen Daviau, who received three Oscar nominations for outstanding cinematography for *E.T.: The Extra-Terrestrial* (1982), *The Color Purple* (1985), and *Empire of the Sun* (1987), also brings his considerable skills to bear on *Avalon*. Grammy Award-winning singer-songwriter-composer Randy Newman wrote the music for *Avalon*, which was augmented by period classics from George Gershwin, Bing Crosby, and Al Jolson, to name a few. Oscar-winning editor Stu Linder and costume designer Gloria Gresham, veteran contributors to Levinson's films, also made valuable contributions.

Not surprisingly, *Avalon* garnered four 1990 Academy Award nominations—for best score, best costume design, best cinematography, and most original screenplay—but was passed over in the most coveted categories. Kevin Costner's *Dances with Wolves* (reviewed in this volume) was this year's Academy darling, sweeping the awards with twelve nominations, including best picture, best actor, and best director. Also nominated for best picture and best director were Martin Scorsese's *GoodFellas* and Francis Ford Coppola's *The Godfather, Part III* (both reviewed in this volume)—not at all a critical success. As always, it is impossible to understand the whimsy of the Academy, which nominated *Awakenings* and *Ghosts* (both reviewed in this volume) for best picture, but not *Avalon*, which was equally deserving.

Avalon will undoubtedly become a classic, *The Grapes of Wrath* for immigrants. Like all authentic, universal art, its faults are justified by the scope of genius they imply. Although the ending is rushed and the audience's sympathy is cut short, Levinson has presented a rare and wry fable of the human condition, one rich in ordinary miracles. Long after the credits have rolled, the laughter and delight linger.

Eugene H. Davis

Reviews
Chicago Tribune. October 19, 1990, VII, p. 38.
Commonweal. CXVIII, January 25, 1991, p. 54.
Films in Review. XLII, January, 1991, p. 55.
The Hollywood Reporter. CCCXIV, October 2, 1990, p. 10.
Los Angeles Times. October 5, 1990, p. F1.
The New York Times. October 3, 1990, p. B1.
The New Yorker. LXVI, October 22, 1990, p. 104.
Newsweek. CXVI, October 8, 1990, p. 66.
People Weekly. October 15, 1990, p. 12.
Time. CXXXVI, November 12, 1990, p. 104.
Variety. October 2, 1990, p. 2.

AWAKENINGS

Production: Walter F. Parkes and Lawrence Lasker; released by Columbia Pictures
Direction: Penny Marshall
Screenplay: Steven Zaillian; based on the book by Oliver Sacks
Cinematography: Miroslav Ondricek
Editing: Jerry Greenberg and Battle Davis
Production design: Anton Furst
Art direction: Bill Groom
Set decoration: George DeTitta, Jr.
Sound: Les Lazarowitz
Costume design: Cynthia Flynt
Music: Randy Newman
MPAA rating: PG-13
Running time: 121 minutes

Principal characters:

Dr. Malcolm Sayer	Robin Williams
Leonard Lowe	Robert De Niro
Eleanor Costello	Julie Kavner
Mrs. Lowe	Ruth Nelson
Dr. Kaufman	John Heard
Paula	Penelope Ann Miller
Dr. Peter Ingham	Max von Sydow
Anthony	Keith Diamond
Lucy	Alice Drummond
Rose	Judith Malina
Bert	Barton Heyman
Frank	George Martin
Miriam	Anne Meara
Sidney	Richard Libertini
Rolando	Dexter Gordon

Awakenings is the fictionalized account of Leonard Lowe, a man who spent decades in a sleeplike state and was briefly awakened with the help of neurologist Oliver Sacks. This heartbreaking and heartwarming story, which was adapted from Sacks's book and on which he served as technical director, was filmed on location at a functioning psychiatric hospital in Brooklyn, New York, not far from where the real story had taken place more than twenty years before.

The main titles appear over the warm tones of autumn in New York, where in the early 1930's, a young boy went to school and played with his friends until a neurological illness forced him to stay home, continuing his studies as best he could alone, and watching his friends from his bedroom window. The next scene takes place in 1969 at Bainbridge Hospital, where Dr. Malcolm Sayer (Robin Williams) nervously interviews for a staff position. Asked about his previous experience, Sayer passionately describes a five-year experiment involving earthworms. He has never worked with human subjects, and is terrified at the thought of doing so. Dr. Kaufman (John Heard) does not feel that Sayer has the necessary experience for the job; neither does Sayer, but he is hired nevertheless.

Despite his overwhelming shyness, Sayer dutifully endeavors to become acquainted with all the patients. In one of the film's thoughtfully placed comic moments, Sayer is scared out of his seat when he attempts to record notes on the chart of a woman who becomes hysterical at the sight of a pen. Although some of the patients are livelier than others, all of them are considered chronic and beyond help. An orderly named Anthony (Keith Diamond) tells Sayer that the employees refer to Bainbridge Hospital as "the garden" because all they do there is feed and water the patients. This disturbs Sayer, who cannot accept that there is nothing happening inside the minds of these mostly silent and immobile people. Sayer's curiosity is fueled by Lucy (Alice Drummond), a supposedly unresponsive patient, who responds when Sayer lovingly removes her eyeglasses, cleans them, and replaces them on her face.

Nurse Eleanor Costello (Julie Kavner) is touched by Sayer's concern and tenderness toward the patients. She defends and encourages him when he presents Dr. Kaufman with a theory that some of the patients who are considered unreachable can, in fact, be reached. Eleanor stays late to help Sayer search through dusty files for some clue that will connect these cases. They work well together, but when Eleanor suggests they go for a cup of coffee after work, Sayer becomes bashful and excuses himself to go home and spend another night alone with his plants.

That night, it occurs to Sayer that one thing the unresponsive patients have in common is that they were all survivors of the encephalitis epidemic that swept the world in the 1920's. Sayer visits Dr. Peter Ingham (Max von Sydow), who studied those encephalitic patients. Sayer wonders aloud what his patients must be thinking after all these years locked inside bodies that are unable to move, speak, or express themselves in any way. Ingham tells him that the patients are not thinking at all. When Sayer asks how Ingham knows this, Ingham replies merely that the alternative is unthinkable.

Sayer enlists much of Bainbridge's staff to help him experiment with ways in which to reach the catatonic patients. They find that, if they only look long enough and creatively enough, everyone will respond to something, such as a certain piece of music, geometric patterns, or the touch of another human being. In the case of Leonard Lowe (Robert De Niro), it is the sound of someone calling his name. Leonard, who is thirty-nine years old, is the boy that was seen in the film's first scenes. Sayer questions Leonard's mother (Ruth Nelson), who visits every day and helps care for Leonard. Sayer learns that, after contracting encephalitis as a boy, Leonard spent nine years living at home, during which time he gradually lost control over his body and suffered increasingly frequent bouts of catatonia, until finally Mrs. Lowe could no longer care for Leonard herself and brought him to Bainbridge. Although

Leonard cannot speak, Mrs. Lowe assures Sayer that Leonard can communicate with her in other ways. Sayer forms a special bond with Leonard when, with the aid of a Ouija board, Leonard "tells" Sayer to look up a poem that describes a caged panther which is alive but trapped beyond the ability to live.

Sayer makes a further connection between the condition of his patients and that of patients with Parkinson's disease. With the aid of Leonard's doting mother, Sayer convinces Kaufman to let him administer L-dopa, a drug that is used to treat Parkinson's disease, in the hope of bringing Leonard back to life. Over the course of days, Sayer experiments with the dosage and waits by Leonard's bedside for any sign of change. One night Sayer is shaken out of a nap to find that Leonard, previously unable to walk or even move, has disappeared. When Sayer finds Leonard in the hospital's day room, Leonard greets him by commenting on the quiet. Barely able to contain his excitement, Sayer explains that it is late and everyone is asleep. Leonard points out that not everyone is asleep. "No," replies Sayer, "you're awake."

Once Leonard is awake, his thirst for exploring the world around him is unquenchable. Sayer takes him for a drive through the neighborhood where Leonard used to live as a boy. Leonard rejoices in the simple pleasures of seeing his old school, eating an ice cream cone, and wading in the ocean. Later, at Sayer's home, they have a conversation in which Leonard reveals his awareness of the interest that Sayer has in Eleanor and she in him. Suddenly, Sayer is the inquisitive one, and Leonard the one who explains and encourages.

Eventually, the whole ward is given L-dopa, and as the staff rushes to witness the miracle of these long awaited awakenings, Leonard and Sayer smile at each other in private triumph. Suddenly the ward is bustling with elderly people who do not know that they are elderly—people who are only vaguely aware that they have been ill or "away" for some time and are anxious to feel the energy and freedom that they have lacked for so long. Sayer, Eleanor, and Anthony take the patients on a field trip that ends, to Sayer's distress and everyone else's delight, in a dance hall.

Notably absent from this journey is Leonard. He remains at Bainbridge in order to try to meet Paula (Penelope Ann Miller), the daughter of a resident stroke victim. Leonard follows Paula into the cafeteria where, with the encouragement of the hospital staff, he joins her for lunch. Paula is surprised to find that Leonard is one of the patients, and Leonard is glad not to be perceived as one. Paula shares with Leonard her concern that, although she visits and talks to her father often, she does not know if he hears her or is even aware that she is there. Leonard assures Paula, from his own experience, that her father knows.

Paula begins to visit Leonard whenever she is in the hospital, and the other patients continue to improve, until predictably and tragically, something goes wrong. Leonard, who has been on L-dopa longer than the others, begins to experience side effects. Small tics give way to a total loss of control over his body, and newfound energy gives way to aggravation and paranoia. The other patients see Leonard's deterioration and realize that their time of awakening is also to be brief. Although Sayer wants only to make Leonard comfortable, Leonard insists that Sayer record and learn from him, in the hope of helping others who are locked in the sort of prison to which Leonard must inevitably return. When all the patients have reverted to their vegetative states, Sayer views the films that he made of Leonard at his best and weeps, questioning his own part in bringing Leonard and the others back to life when they were only to have that life again stolen from them. Eleanor reminds him of Leonard's lesson: Take nothing for granted. As Sayer looks through photographs of Leonard, the message finally sinks in, and Sayer runs after Eleanor to ask her out for a cup of coffee.

The performances by Williams and De Niro are exquisite in their range of frustration to wonderment, agony to joy. Although *Awakenings* may suffer from accusations of too great a similarity to *Rain Man* (1988) or to *Charly* (1968), as well as too great a departure from Sacks's clinical account, screenwriter Steven Zaillian's script is fresh and deeply moving. In fact, his screenplay was selected to receive the Friends of the USC Libraries third annual Scriptor Award on January 26, 1991. The prestigious cast and crew of *Awakenings* were led by director and executive producer Penny Marshall, whose humor and attention to detail make her first drama a vehicle for spiritual awakening in her audience.

Eleah Horwitz

Reviews

Chicago Tribune. December 20, 1990, V, p. 1.
The Christian Science Monitor. December 28, 1990, p. 14.
The Hollywood Reporter. CCCXV, December 13, 1990, p. 9.
Los Angeles Times. December 20, 1990, p. F1.
The Nation. CCLII, January 7, 1991, p. 23.
The New Republic. January 7-14, 1991, p. 32.
New York. December 17, 1990, p. 68.
The New York Times. December 20, 1990, p. B1.
Newsweek. CXVI, December 24, 1990, p. 62.
People Weekly. XXXIV, December 24, 1990, p. 13.
Premiere. IV, October, 1990, p. 68.
Time. CXXXVI, December 24, 1990, p. 77.
Variety. CCXXX, December 12, 1990, p. 2.
The Village Voice. XXXV, December 25, 1990, p. 80.
Vogue. December, 1990, p. 94.

BACK TO THE FUTURE PART III

Production: Bob Gale and Neil Canton for Steven Spielberg; released by Universal
  Pictures
Direction: Robert Zemeckis
Screenplay: Bob Gale; based on a story by Robert Zemeckis and Gale
Cinematography: Dean Cundey
Editing: Arthur Schmidt and Harry Keramidas
Production design: Rick Carter
Art direction: Marjorie Stone McShirley and Jim Teegarden
Set decoration: Michael Taylor
Set design: Martha Johnston, Paul Sonski, Beverli Eagan, Nancy Nickelberry,
  Joseph G. Pacelli, and Lisa Newman
Visual effects: Ken Ralston and Scott Farrar
Sound: William B. Kaplan, Rick Alexander, Dennis Sands, and James Bolt
Costume design: Joanna Johnston
Stunt coordination: Walter Scott
Music: Alan Silvestri
MPAA rating: PG
Running time: 118 minutes

Principal characters:

Marty McFly/Seamus McFly	Michael J. Fox
Dr. Emmett Brown	Christopher Lloyd
Clara Clayton	Mary Steenburgen
Buford "Mad Dog" Tannen/ Biff Tannen	Thomas F. Wilson
Maggie McFly/Lorraine McFly	Lea Thompson
Jennifer	Elisabeth Shue
Bartender	Matt Clark
Barbed-wire salesman	Richard Dysart
Saloon old-timers	Pat Buttram
	Harry Carey, Jr.
	Dub Taylor
Marshal Strickland	James Tolkan
Gang members	Christopher Wynne
	Sean Gregory Sullivan
	Mike Watson

Back to the Future Part III is the third and last film in the series spawned by
director Robert Zemeckis' popular original, *Back to the Future* (1985). The film was
shot at the same time as *Back to the Future Part II* (1989), a calculated move that
ensured its release despite the dismal performance of the first sequel. In fact, the

lengthy trailer for *Back to the Future Part III* received better reviews than its pre-cursor.

Back to the Future Part III succeeds in large part because, like the first film, it explores the past, and not the future. In *Back to the Future*, Marty McFly (Michael J. Fox), a suburban teenager, travels back in time to 1955, where he must make sure that his parents fall in love, so that he will be born. In *Back to the Future Part III*, Marty returns to 1885, in order to rescue Dr. Emmett Brown (Christopher Lloyd), who is stranded there. Again, Marty must ensure the survival of his forebears, Sea-mus McFly (Michael J. Fox) and Maggie McFly (Lea Thompson), against a relative of Biff Tannen (Thomas F. Wilson), Buford "Mad Dog" Tannen (also played by Wilson).

Back to the Future Part III begins in Doc Brown's home in 1955, where Marty has returned in order to enlist Doc Brown's assistance in rescuing his future self from the distant past of the Old West. The premise of time travel requires both mental gymnastics and a willing suspension of disbelief. Doc Brown, it turns out, has bur-ied the customized De Lorean time machine in a nearby cave, along with instruc-tions on how to fix the broken circuit using 1950's technology. When Marty and Doc Brown excavate the vehicle in 1955, it affords one of the film's few historically in-sightful jokes. Given his 1950's perspective, Doc Brown is aghast that his future self would use an inferior circuit "made in Japan." Marty, a child of the 1980's, explains that Japan is where "all the best stuff is made," unaware of the change in the status of both American and Japanese products.

Once the De Lorean is fixed, Marty uses a drive-in theater as the runway, driving straight at the screen. Below the screen is a mural of Native Americans charging on horseback. When Marty leaps into the past, he confronts a real war party. The De Lorean is hit with an arrow in the gas tank and runs out of gas. On one level, the scene is one of several self-reflexive gags that allude to both classic and spaghetti Westerns. As Terrence Rafferty noted in *The New Yorker*, however, it also symbolizes how the film series itself has run out of gas after the frenetic one-upmanship of *Back to the Future Part II*. Indeed, the film then proceeds at a slower pace more suited to the Western, until the final attempt to return to the present.

Marty is taken in by Seamus and Maggie McFly, the parents of the first McFly born in the United States. The next day, he walks to Hill Valley in search of Doc Brown. Marty's knowledge of the Old West, however, is a product of Hollywood and television westerns. Dressed in a pink cowboy suit with atomic symbols, and wear-ing tennis shoes, he enters the local bar and proclaims himself Clint Eastwood. Buford Tannen and his gang proceed to rope Marty and drag him across town to the new courthouse and clock tower, which are under construction. Buford then hangs Marty, but Doc Brown arrives in time to shoot Buford.

Doc Brown's rescue creates further tension between the two men, and Buford leaves promising to shoot Doc Brown in the back. Marty pulls out a Polaroid photo-graph of Doc Brown's tombstone, which shows that Buford will carry out his threat within a week. As in the first film, the Polaroid becomes a reference point for the future. When Marty and Doc Brown resolve to fix the De Lorean and return to the present, the tombstone in the Polaroid begins to fade.

In order for the time machine to work, the De Lorean must reach eighty-eight miles per hour. Without gas, the car must be pulled or pushed up to speed. When a team of horses proves too slow, Marty and Doc Brown decide to commandeer a train engine and push the car down an unused track toward an unfinished bridge. If the De Lorean leaps into the future before it reaches the ravine, the car will land on the finished bridge that exists in 1985. Unfortunately, the next train does not arrive until the morning of the day that Buford is supposed to kill Doc Brown.

In the interim, Doc Brown saves schoolteacher Clara Clayton (Mary Steenburgen) from being hurled into a ravine when her horse spooks. The two fall in love at first sight, and a romance quickly develops, especially when Doc Brown discovers that Clara reads the works of futurist Jules Verne. Doc Brown's resolve to leave further weakens when he meets Clara at the town dance, even though Marty tells him that he has already altered history by saving her. The dance is interrupted when Buford thrusts a small gun into Doc Brown's back. Marty grabs a pie tin and hurls it at Buford, causing the gun to shoot astray. Before Marshal Strickland (James Tolkan) arrives on the scene, Marty challenges Buford to a shoot-out, but he schedules it to coincide with their escape. The telltale Polaroid, however, still shows a tombstone, although Doc Brown's name has disappeared. It is at this point that Doc Brown and Seamus McFly talk to Marty about his temper. Seamus' brother, Martin, never considered the future and died in a shoot-out; Marty's own temper will cause him to have an accident in the future.

Marty must face his temper problem when Doc Brown's lovesickness causes him to delay the escape. Doc Brown spends the night at the saloon, after he tells Clara that he must leave. When Marty arrives, Doc Brown has passed out after one drink, and before he can be revived, Buford appears outside the saloon taunting Marty. Marty manages to control his temper, but he must nevertheless confront Buford when Doc Brown is captured. Marty refuses to shoot and is gunned down by Buford. As Buford hovers over his victim, Marty kicks the gun out of his hand, and stands. Buford punches him, but Marty has hidden a stove door beneath his shirt. The illogic of the film's message is such that Marty learns to control his temper but gets to fight anyway. When Marshal Strickland arrests Buford, Marty notices that the tombstone has disappeared from the Polaroid picture.

Marty and Doc Brown rush to hijack the train. Meanwhile, Clara overhears a barbed-wire salesman (Richard Dysart) talk about Doc Brown's love confessions at the saloon the night before. She grabs a horse and races toward the tracks, where the two time travelers have begun to push the De Lorean up to speed. Clara jumps onto the train engine but is unable to reach Doc Brown, who is working his way to the De Lorean. Rather than sacrifice Clara in order to return to the present, Doc Brown uses Marty's hover board to rescue her. Marty returns to the future alone and barely ejects himself from the De Lorean before a train smashes into and destroys the time machine. Marty then runs to the home of his girlfriend, Jennifer (Elisabeth Shue), and awakens her. She believes that the events of *Back to the Future Part II* were an elaborate dream, although she has a computer printout that announces that the Marty of 2015 has been fired. The words later disappear when Marty refuses a challenge to drag race, a decision that also avoids the accident to which Doc Brown referred back in 1885. Marty and Jennifer drive to the train tracks to look over the wreckage and lament Doc Brown's isolation in the past. Suddenly, Doc Brown and Clara leap out of the past aboard a baroque train time machine. Doc Brown introduces his two children, Jules and Verne, and returns to the past. Despite Doc Brown's assurances that the future is not yet written, *Back to the Future Part III* leaves no doubt that everyone, except the Tannens, will live happily ever after.

Unlike the pointless futurism of *Back to the Future Part II*, the first and third films turn the series' present, 1985, into an uncertain future at the mercy of the past. Given the familiar terrain, these films parody the genre conventions and audience expectations for the 1950's and the Old West. In an era of diminished historical awareness, the future becomes a convenient mechanism for conceptualizing the link between the past and present; however, while other science fiction films, such as *The Terminator* (1984), have had more to say about that link, the *Back to the Future* series merely replicates the present across time.

Chon A. Noriega

Reviews
Boxoffice. July, 1990, p. R49.
Chicago Tribune. May 25, 1990, VII, p. 29.
The Hollywood Reporter. CCCXII, May 21, 1990, p. 4.
Los Angeles Times. May 25, 1990, p. F1.
New York. XXIII, June 11, 1990, p. 75.
The New York Times. May 15, 1990, p. B3.
The New Yorker. LXVI, June 18, 1990, p. 91.
Newsweek. CXV, June 4, 1990, p. 82.
Time. CXXXV, May 28, 1990, p. 88.
Variety. May 21, 1990, p. 2.
The Wall Street Journal. May 31, 1990, p. A12.
The Washington Post. May 25, 1990, p. D1.

BIRD ON A WIRE

Production: Rob Cohen for Cohen-Interscope Communications; released by
   Universal Pictures
Direction: John Badham
Screenplay: David Seltzer, Louis Venosta, and Eric Lerner
Cinematography: Robert Primes
Editing: Frank Morriss and Dallas Puett
Production design: Philip Harrison
Art direction: Richard Hudolin
Set decoration: Rose Marie McSherry
Special effects: John Thomas
Makeup: Sandy Cooper and Tom Case
Costume design: Wayne Finkelman and Eduardo Castro
Music: Hans Zimmer
MPAA rating: PG-13
Running time: 106 minutes

> *Principal characters:*
> Rick Jarmin . . . . Mel Gibson
> Marianne Graves . . . . Goldie Hawn
> Eugene Sorenson . . . . David Carradine
> Albert Diggs . . . . Bill Duke
> Joe Weyburn . . . . Stephen Tobolowsky
> Rachel Varney . . . . Joan Severance
> Marvin . . . . Harry Caesar
> Lou Baird . . . . Jeff Corey

The print media promotion for *Bird on a Wire* consisted of only two words: Mel
and Goldie. Sold first on the basis of Mel Gibson and Goldie Hawn's star appeal,
Bird on a Wire was then billed as a new genre hybrid, an action-romantic comedy,
that offered something for everyone. In a way it does, although the film as a whole
fails to offer a cohesive narrative upon which to hang these various audience hooks.
Instead, *Bird on a Wire* becomes an occasion to see the two stars bicker and fall
in love against the backdrop of Colombian drug deals, explosions, and car chases.
Thrown in for good measure is an ongoing argument over the corruption of 1960's
counterculture values.

In *Bird on a Wire*, Rick Jarmin (Gibson) has spent the past fifteen years assuming
various identities under the Federal Witness Protection Program, when his past catches
up with him. Jarmin, once a carefree college student, had flown to Mexico with a
friend to purchase marijuana, only to become blackmailed into working for two
corrupt Drug Enforcement Agency (DEA) officers. In order to protect himself, Jarmin turned state's witness. His fiancée, Marianne Graves (Hawn), however, was left

at the altar thinking that he had died in a plane crash.

The film begins with Eugene Sorenson (David Carradine), the DEA officer against whom Jarmin testified, getting out of prison, while the sound track plays the 1960's anthem "Age of Aquarius." Sorenson emerges from the prison like an aged hippie, with bare feet, long gray hair, and an exposed chest and stomach. Waiting for Sorenson is Albert Diggs (Bill Duke), the other DEA officer, who has eluded arrest all these years. Sorenson and Diggs arrive at the home of a Colombian drug lord in Atlantic City and are informed that their proposed deal will not be honored unless Jarmin is killed. Jarmin, after all, can still testify against Diggs, jeopardizing the entire operation. The scene acts as a mere plot device that establishes the premise for the remainder of the film, and it is the first and last time the audience sees the Colombian drug lords. The inclusion, however, of gratuitous shots of a children's birthday party, all in Spanish, serves to implicate the real culture beneath the otherwise blatant Latin stereotypes.

With help from an accomplice in the DEA, Joe Weyburn (Stephen Tobolowsky), Sorenson, and Diggs track Jarmin to a garage in Detroit, where he has worked for the past three months. At about the same time, Graves also stumbles onto Jarmin, when she pulls into the garage for gas on her way to an out-of-town business meeting. In the fifteen years since Jarmin's ostensible death, Graves has married, divorced, and become a successful corporate attorney. When she confronts Jarmin, he denies his true identity, and later he calls his protection officer in order to be relocated. Weyburn, however, has erased Jarmin's record from the computer, so that he is in effect on his own.

Later the next night, Graves returns to the garage to spy on Jarmin. As she looks on, Sorenson and Diggs arrive and manage to kill Jarmin's employer, blow up the garage, and shoot Jarmin in the rear end. Graves uses her car to distract the two killers, until Jarmin is able to reach her and escape. Back at Graves's hotel suite, the two former lovers argue over the path that each of their lives has taken. Jarmin criticizes Graves for having married a napalm heir four months after Jarmin's reported death and for having sold out her ideals to corporate America. Jarmin, for his part, recounts his ill-fated adventure in Mexico, which resulted in the death of their mutual friend. To his credit, the past fifteen years on the run have given him a down-to-earth experience and appreciation of blue-collar (and even gay) America.

Bird on a Wire, however, never does more than give lip service to the theme of money versus values. On an obvious level, the 1960's sound track and flashbacks reduce the conflict to a playing field of former hippies, in much the same way that everyone in *Lethal Weapon* (1987), another Mel Gibson film, is a Vietnam veteran. Beyond that, however, *Bird on a Wire* fails to evoke counterculture values in its flashbacks. Unlike *Lethal Weapon*, *Bird on a Wire* contains characters that never seem to possess a real history that motivates their present actions. For example, the flashback that is supposed to explain Graves's undying love for Jarmin consists of her yelling, "You're really freaking me out, man."

Without a strong, or even adequate, sense of history and character, *Bird on a Wire* becomes yet another special effects chase movie. In its attempt to maintain interest, the film continues the chase on land, air, and water. When Sorenson and Diggs force their way into Graves's hotel suite, Graves and Jarmin must crawl across a catwalk to the hotel restaurant. A standard car chase ensues, with Jarmin trying to get into the driver's seat and, having done so, almost getting run over by a train.

Jarmin then drives to a hair salon where he once worked, in order to retrieve the home address of his protection officer, Lou Baird (Jeff Corey), who has retired. Jarmin, it turns out, had once posed as a gay hairdresser highly respected as a genius with hair. These scenes are the high point of the film, both in terms of its rare homophobia-free humor and the sudden use of oblique camera angles. The tight quarters of the location, a renovated turn-of-the-century urban center, lend themselves to the unexpected whimsy of the camera.

Now on motorcycle, Jarmin and Graves stop at yet another of Jarmin's former places of employment, an animal hospital that he helped build. Sorenson and Diggs, however, arrive soon after in a helicopter. While Rachel Varney (Joan Severance), the veterinarian, fires her shotgun at the helicopter, Graves and Jarmin escape in a crop duster. After a crash landing, the two are forced to spend the night together in a cockroach-infested hotel before contacting Jarmin's protection officer. Graves and Jarmin have not yet been reconciled, and Jarmin continues to taunt Graves about her elitist attitude and new yuppie boyfriend. When Jarmin admits, however, that "Mr. Wiggly's been on bread and water for five years," Graves can no longer resist, and the two again become lovers.

The next morning, Graves and Jarmin visit Baird only to discover that the reason for his sudden retirement is that he is senile. Baird now works at a zoo where he had once placed Jarmin. Although senile, Baird is able to offer one coherent suggestion: that Jarmin use the zoo to trap his pursuers. Jarmin lures Sorenson and Diggs to an indoor rain forest exhibit that houses tigers, jaguars, alligators, and chimpanzees, among other wild animals. While Graves hides in the control room, Jarmin sets the animals loose and stalks the two men with a tranquilizer gun. The game of cat-and-mouse, however, goes on much longer than the relatively small size of the exhibit warrants. In the end, Jarmin and Sorenson slug it out on a rope bridge, which breaks, dropping Sorenson onto an electric fence. As Jarmin hangs precariously, he proposes to Graves and promises children, in order to inspire her to pull him to safety.

The film cuts to Graves and Jarmin's honeymoon aboard a yacht, which has "Mister Wiggly" emblazoned upon the sail. No longer does Jarmin chide Graves for her money and status in corporate America. In fact, the comic reference to Jarmin's penis suggests that the conflict was never really a case of money versus values, as Jarmin repeatedly claimed, but of sex versus values. In a film as thematically adrift as *Bird on a Wire*, Jarmin's class consciousness quite easily evaporates along with his celibacy.

Chon A. Noriega

Reviews

Boston Globe. May 18, 1990, p. 77.
Chicago Tribune. May 18, 1990, VII, p. 21.
Films in Review. XLI, August, 1990, p. 426.
The Hollywood Reporter. CCCXII, May 16, 1990, p. 4.
Los Angeles Times. May 18, 1990, p. F1.
The New Republic. CCII, June 11, 1990, p. 26.
The New York Times. May 18, 1990, p. B1.
Newsweek. CXV, May 28, 1990, p. 72.
Variety. CCCXXXIX, May 16, 1990, p. 2.
The Washington Post. May 18, 1990, p. B1.

BLACK RAIN
(KUROI AME)

Origin: Japan
Released: 1989
Released in U.S.: 1990
Production: Hisa Iino for Imamura Production, Hayashibara Group, and Tohoku-shinsha Film; released by Toei Company and Angelika Films
Direction: Shohei Imamura
Screenplay: Toshiro Ishido and Shohei Imamura; based on the novel by Masuji Ibuse
Cinematography: Takashi Kawamata
Editing: Hajime Okayasu
Art direction: Hisao Inagaki
Lighting: Yasuo Iwaki
Sound: Ken'ichi Benitani
Music: Toru Takemitsu
MPAA rating: no listing
Running time: 123 minutes

Principal characters:
Yasuko	Yoshiko Tanaka
Shigematsu	Kazuo Kitamura
Shigeko	Etsuko Ichihara
Shokichi	Shoichi Ozawa
Kotaro	Norihei Miki
Yuichi	Keisuke Ishida

On August 6, 1945, the world's first atomic bomb, a 12.5-kiloton uranium bomb nicknamed "Little Boy," was detonated over Hiroshima, Japan, killing and maiming thousands instantly. Thousands more were poisoned by the high level of radioactive fallout known as black rain. Shohei Imamura's compelling tale of three survivors of the blast who must later deal with the effects of radioactive poisoning is not an attempt to place blame and is not intended to be anti-American. It is instead a look at the reactions of the Japanese people to the *hibakusha*, the victims, and at the traditions that have shaped Japanese society. Certainly, the film is an intelligent, ironic reminder that it is humankind's obligation to control the power that they themselves have created.

Amid the charred bodies and devastation, Yasuko (Yoshiko Tanaka) and her aunt, Shigeko (Etsuko Ichihara), trudge through the debris, searching for Shigematsu (Kazuo Kitamura), Yasuko's uncle. They have all survived the blast of the bomb, but unaware of the consequences, they expose themselves to the radioactive fallout that permeates the moisture in the air and falls from the sky like oily, black rain.

Five years later, effects of the exposure surface, killing survivors of the "ground zero" as well as those who were exposed to the radiation in its aftermath. Back in the country village where Shigematsu is a respected landowner, the members of the family keep silent constant vigil over one another, as well as over their own bodies, looking for the slightest signs of betrayal. Tradition dictates that Yasuko must marry, but when details of her past are discovered, all potential marriage partners renege on their proposals. In a futile attempt to deny the truth, Shigematsu, who himself shows early signs of poisoning, obtains medical certificates declaring Yasuko's health, but that only raises suspicion and further ostracizes Yasuko.

Despite her family's objections, Yasuko falls in love with Yuichi (Keisuke Ishida), a young, traumatized veteran who cannot escape his wartime experiences. At first Shigematsu views Yuichi as an inappropriate suitor for his niece, too lower-class and too mentally unstable. Yet even this relationship is doomed, as Yasuko soon begins to exhibit symptoms of the radiation sickness. Each of the family members is forced to come to terms with a tragedy that they thought they had survived long ago. Each must face her or his prospective death, each in her or his own distinct way. For Yasuko, it is a resigned acceptance of fate. Her aunt reverts to superstition and mysticism. Shigematsu tries to maintain an aura of normality, laced with regret, as he watches the ambulance carry away his loved one.

Shohei Imamura is a rebel Japanese filmmaker, never falling into convention like the more tradition-bound family dramas of the celebrated director Yasujiro Ozu. Imamura worked for three years at Ozu's Shochiku Studios but rebelled against its more conservative, upper-class prevailing influence. Best known for his classic study of a serial killer, *Vengeance Is Mine* (1969), and the Cannes Film Festival's prestigious Palme d'Or winner, *The Ballad of Narayama* (1983), Imamura's inspired earlier work tended to be more highly stylized, sardonic portraits of societal outcasts driven by impure, almost primitive emotions. His protagonists were more often women rebelling against societal constraints. Imamura's other films include *The Pornographers* (1966), the mock *cinéma vérité A Man Vanishes* (1967), and his re-working of ancient myths, *The Profound Desire of the Gods* (1968).

If this film is uncharacteristic of Imamura's earlier work, it may be attributed in part to its origin. *Black Rain* is based on a classic of Japanese postwar fiction, the 1969 novel of the same name by Masuji Ibuse. The author used actual diaries and interviews with bomb survivors to chronicle the tragedy of the Hiroshima bombing. Many Japanese directors approached the author with the hope of translating the book to the screen, but Ibuse refused them all. It was not until the demand tapered off that Ibuse finally granted permission to the longtime pacifist Imamura, who years later chose to shoot the film in black and white with the hope of splicing in actual documentary footage of the Hiroshima devastation. The plan did not materialize, however, because Imamura discovered that archival coverage did not exist. The Japanese news media refrained from filming scenes of the aftermath until late in August and Imamura found that the edited, prettified versions that showed no trace of even a single human corpse were, obviously, useless. Re-creating the aftermath of the bombing on the film set, the director worked instead from his own recollections of a train ride he took through Tokyo following that city's firebombing in late August of 1945.

Imamura never sensationalizes the horror as one might expect from a Hollywood production; his controlled, understated, brief vignettes are far more chilling and unforgettable as a result of his restraint. The scenes help to contextualize postwar life for the *hibakusha* in general and the film's protagonists in particular. The film-maker never dwells on blame but explores instead the legacy that tragedy left behind and the rigid ancient Japanese traditions that have shaped Japanese society. Imamura examines the prejudices that arose against the very victims of the bomb, who were treated as lepers, constant reminders of failure by a society that wished to expunge that infamous day in 1945 from all memory. (The parallels to the late twentieth century's epidemic of acquired immune deficiency syndrome are obvious.) During his extensive interviewing prior to filming, Imamura found many of the survivors themselves were opposed to the *Black Rain* project. Perhaps they feared the director would glorify the tragedy. For Imamura, however, it was much more irresponsible, and unforgivable, to forget. The film received nearly unanimously favorable reviews, with most critics praising Imamura's restraint, his strong antiwar message that never turns into an anti-American tirade, and his formal control as the film smoothly shifts time periods and themes. The recurring device of Yasuko setting the family clock is somewhat laborious, and the character of Yuichi tends toward theatrics, but the compelling material and the impeccable acting of all three of the lead actors overshadow these minor flaws.

Patricia Kowal

Reviews

Chicago Tribune. September 21, 1990, VII, p. 41.
The Christian Science Monitor. February 15, 1990, p. 10.
ELLE. V, April, 1990, p. 169.
Film Comment. XXV, November, 1989, p. 68.
The Hollywood Reporter. CCCVII, May 25, 1989, p. 9.
Los Angeles Times. March 29, 1990, p. F7.
The Nation. CCL, March 5, 1990, p. 320.
National Review. XLI, October 27, 1989, p. 58.
The New Republic. CCII, February 12, 1990, p. 27.
New Statesman and Society. III, July 6, 1990, p. 36.
New York Magazine. XXIII, February 5, 1990, p. 58.
The New York Nichibei. January 18, 1990, XLVI, p. 3.
The New York Times. September 26, 1989, p. C13.
The New Yorker. LXVI, February 26, 1990, p. 106.
Variety. September 20, 1989, p. 29.
The Washington Post. April 27, 1990, p. D1.
Wigwag. I, April, 1990, p. 88.

THE BONFIRE OF THE VANITIES

Production: Brian DePalma; released by Warner Bros.
Direction: Brian DePalma
Screenplay: Michael Cristofer; based on the novel by Tom Wolfe
Cinematography: Vilmos Zsigmond
Editing: David Ray and Bill Pankow
Production design: Richard Sylbert
Art direction: Peter Lansdown Smith and Greg Bolton
Set decoration: Joe Mitchell and Justin Scoppa
Set design: Richard Berger, Robert Maddy, and Nick Navarro
Sound: Les Lazarowitz and James Tanenbaum
Costume design: Ann Roth
Music: Dave Grusin
MPAA rating: R
Running time: 125 minutes

Principal characters:
Sherman McCoy	Tom Hanks
Peter Fallow	Bruce Willis
Maria Ruskin	Melanie Griffith
Judy McCoy	Kim Cattrall
Jed Kramer	Saul Rubinek
Judge White	Morgan Freeman
Weiss	F. Murray Abraham
Reverend Bacon	John Hancock
Tom Killian	Kevin Dunn
Albert Fox	Clifton James
Ray Andruitti	Louis Giambalvo
Detective Martin	Barton Heyman
Detective Goldberg	Norman Parker
Arthur Ruskin	Alan King
Mr. McCoy	Donald Moffat
Caroline Heftshank	Beth Broderick
Pollard Browning	Kurt Fuller

The Bonfire of the Vanities, based on Tom Wolfe's 1987 satiric blockbuster novel about the Kafkaesque legal misadventures of a Wall Street bond broker, must have seemed an attractive opportunity for director Brian DePalma to return to satire, abandoned since his late 1960's and early 1970's debut films, such as *Hi Mom!* (1970) and *Get to Know Your Rabbit* (1972). Known for erotic horror, sexy thrillers, and stylish gangster films (*Carrie,* 1976; *Dressed to Kill,* 1980; *Scarface,* 1983; *Body Double,* 1984; *The Untouchables,* 1987), his best work is provocative, testing and stretching the limits of genre and medium. Touted as one of the new generation of filmmakers, DePalma, along with George Lucas, Steven Spielberg, Francis Ford Coppola, and Martin Scorsese, always leaves his personal stamp on his highly crafted films.

Unfortunately, his action-oriented sensibilities seem ill-suited to the rich ironies of Wolfe's arch Dickensian novel, which takes New York City to task, lampooning everything and everybody, from black power to the corrupt judicial system. The film is further flawed by a preachy, off-kilter script by Michael Cristofer (*Falling in Love*, 1984; *The Witches of Eastwick*, 1987) that substitutes shtick and vulgarity for humor. Mannered, stiff, or excessive performances by principals Tom Hanks, Kim Cattrall, and F. Murray Abraham detract as well. Under DePalma's belabored direction, Wolfe's devilish social commentary is reduced to low farce. Not even award-winning cinematographer Vilmos Zsigmond's ravishing camera work can compensate for the film's considerable failings. The film begins promisingly with a sensational time-elapsed exposure of Manhattan, from the point of view of a rooftop gargoyle surveying the shimmering, treasured kingdom below. Enter Peter Fallow (Bruce Willis), muckraking-journalist-turned-bestselling-author and heir to the keys to the kingdom for his exposé on corruption among the high and mighty. Drunk and stumbling swinishly from lackey to sycophant enroute to a lavish banquet given in his honor, he pontificates on his undeserved success, gained at the expense of his book's subject, one Sherman McCoy (Hanks), erstwhile Wall Street wizard and "Master of the Universe," whose philandering cost him everything: job, home, family, mistress, and most of all, his good name. Out of the ashes of McCoy's assassinated career rises the phoenix of Fallow, profligate, literary man, the toast of Manhattan. "What profits a man to gain the world if he loses his soul?" asks Fallow. In the course of recounting McCoy's fall from grace, he arrives at an answer.

It all begins the previous year when McCoy, returning from the airport with his mistress, Southern sexpot Maria Ruskin (Melanie Griffith), misses the turn back to Manhattan and becomes lost in the Bronx, which seems to Maria, with her Southern-born prejudices, like a black war zone. Sure enough, a pair of black youths, Henry Lamb (Patrick Malone) and Lockwood (Shiek Mahmud-Bey), waylay Sherman when he leaves the car to remove a tire blocking the expressway ramp. Maria slides behind the wheel of Sherman's Mercedes and rescues him, but not, apparently, without running over Lamb in her panic. Safely back at the couple's love nest, an East Side sublet, Maria convinces Sherman not to report the accident, citing the inevitable scandal that would result should their affair become public. Maria, the wife of aging, international industrialist Arthur Ruskin (Alan King), can ill afford to lose her meal ticket, and eminently reputable bond broker McCoy would also be ruined.

Meanwhile, Lamb, treated at a Bronx hospital for a broken wrist as a result of the accident, is readmitted after lapsing into a coma. He is not expected to recover consciousness. A flock of cynical crows quickly gather to feed off his comatose body. Black activist Reverend Bacon (John Hancock) threatens the district attorney's office with a Bronx uprising if they fail to find the driver of the Mercedes. His scam is to sue in behalf of Lamb's mother. Assistant District Attorney Jed Kramer (Saul

Rubinek), seizing upon the case for his own advancement, convinces his boss, district attorney and city mayoral candidate Weiss (Abraham), that apprehending and prosecuting the hit-and-run driver, doubtless a white man, will ensure Weiss's vote among the city's minorities. Has-been journalist Peter Fallow, about to be fired from his job for drunken incompetence, agrees to write a story that is sympathetic to Lamb, portraying him as an "honor student."

When the Mercedes is traced to McCoy, he arouses suspicion by refusing to let the police see it without the presence of his lawyer. Overnight, he becomes the subject of a relentless media character assassination, spearheaded by Fallow, who has thrown his lot in with Bacon. While Maria absconds to Italy with her new lover, artist Filippo Chirazzi (Emmanuel Xuereb), Sherman, who was not driving the car, is arrested and arraigned. The experience of being jailed completely demoralizes McCoy. He returns home to find the Reverend Bacon's followers picketing his apartment building. Upstairs, in his luxury condo, his wife, Judy (Cattrall), is conducting a dinner party, oblivious to his travails. Soon he learns that he is fired, Judy is leaving him, and the director of the building association wants him to move. Declaring himself dead, McCoy clears out everyone with his shotgun instead of killing himself.

Lockwood, arrested on new charges, makes a deal with the D.A.'s office to testify against Sherman in exchange for a reduced sentence. With Maria out of the country, Lockwood's perjured testimony will be sufficient to convict him. Meanwhile, the Reverend Bacon reveals to Fallow his hidden agenda, to sue the hospital for releasing Lamb with a concussion. Sherman was only a means to an end—a lucrative settlement from the hospital, to be split among Bacon, Mrs. Lamb, and her lawyer, Albert Fox (Clifton James). Selling himself out one more time, Fallow agrees to write the story of the hospital's negligence. By now, he realizes the possibilities of a book to be derived from this ludicrous play of human foibles.

Fallow learns from former girlfriend Caroline Heftshank (Beth Broderick), who was jilted by Chirazzi, that Maria was in the car with Sherman the night of the incident. Sherman and Maria's love nest, sublet from Caroline, was bugged by the building manager, who wanted to evict them. Fallow acquires the tape of a conversation between McCoy and Maria, in which Maria confesses to running over Lamb. Perhaps out of pity, he sends it to McCoy's attorney, who advises Sherman that, unfortunately, the tape cannot be used as evidence, as it was acquired illegally. If Sherman had taped it, it would have been admissible. Maria's husband dies suddenly, and she returns for his funeral. Sherman, inspired by the tape, goes to see her with his body wired in an attempt to tape her repeating her confession. His plan backfires when ever-lusty Maria attempts to seduce Sherman and discovers his wire. Kramer is handily nearby to benefit from her indignation. She agrees to let the "very handsome" assistant D.A. coach her testimony against Sherman. During Maria's perjured testimony against him, Sherman impishly triumphs, playing aloud the tape of Maria's confession, sprinkled with her customary lascivious expressions. Now it is he who boldly perjures himself, insisting to Judge White that he made the tape himself. The case against Sherman is dismissed, but not before Judge White delivers a thundering broadside against all the unscrupulous, greedy, self-promoting parties, black and white, involved in this travesty of justice. Back at the banquet in his honor, Fallow draws an ironic lesson from the events of the story, concluding that, while he may have lost his soul, he gained the world. He seems satisfied with the compromise.

Fans of Wolfe's titillating satire will find little in DePalma's self-conscious, lavishly lensed adaptation to remind them of the original. Though most characters are carried over from the book, with the exception of black Judge White, obtusely abstracted from Jewish Judge Kovitsky, their re-creation in the film borders on caricature. Kramer, for example, a fascinating study in Jewish insecurity, with his flexed muscles and worship of Irish stoicism epitomized by Detective Martin (Barton Heyman), is diminished to an ineffectual buffoon. His developing romance with an attractive Gentile juror, dropped from the film, is one of the novel's comic high points. Similarly, detectives Martin and Goldberg (Norman Parker), depicted waggishly by Wolfe as buddy cop clones, serve only pedestrian functions in Cristofer's script. Parker, a distinguished, talented actor (*Prince of the City*, 1981), is wasted on this abbreviated version of Goldberg. Judge White, substituted, according to DePalma, to lend "visual balance" and eliminate the prejudice suggested by a white judge freeing McCoy, appears sanctimonious and unreal. Earnestly spouting egalitarian homilies as alien to a New York City courtroom as palm trees, he is anything but amusing. To his credit, Morgan Freeman struggles bravely with the role. "Go home and be decent," he fulminates at the largely black courtroom spectators. Throughout, all the delicious ironies of character and ethnic identity, painted with genius and economy by Wolfe, are flattened in the film.

DePalma's broadly comic vision of the film apparently led him to seek out Hanks for the pivotal role of Sherman McCoy, which calls for an actor who is adept at drama as well as comedy. Hanks, although an immensely talented comic actor with dramatic credits in *Nothing in Common* (1986) and *Punchline* (1988), was clearly miscast. His portrait of blue-blooded McCoy, though well-intentioned, was a stretch reminiscent of Bill Murray's fiasco in *The Razor's Edge* (1984). Hanks's professed decision to play McCoy as a man vulnerable and posturing, insecure with his identity of "Master of the Universe," unfortunately reads as a compromise with the dramatic demands of the role. With his dandified speech and puckish eyes smarting, as when Goldberg coyly informs him of his right to an attorney, Hanks seemed to be resummoning his celebrated role from *Big* (1988)—that of a little boy in a man's body.

Willis, on the other hand, seems comfortable with his role as the reprobate Fallow, careening drunkenly from scene to scene until he sobers with the smell of McCoy's kill and temporarily resurrects himself. He is exquisitely smarmy when manipulating Lamb's teacher into calling McCoy's would-be robber an honor student. The scene that he shares with Geraldo Rivera playing a newsman ought to silence his critics once and for all. Willis' Cheshire-cat aplomb, next to Rivera's tense "frisking," demonstrates the difference between acting and pretending. Griffith, as the calculating Southern sexpot is superb. Given some horrendous malapropisms and puns, she triumphs admirably. Of all the characters taken from Wolfe's novel, hers is the most successful. In contrast, Cattrall's rendition of McCoy's supercilious wife Judy appears manic and askew—a caricature—as does Abraham's autocratic mayoral candidate Weiss. Rubinek plays Kramer gracelessly, in contrast with Hancock's artful portrayal of Bacon, obviously modelled after the Reverend Al Sharpton.

Midway through the film, Cristofer's script loses its edge. Apparently feeling the need to tell a more dramatic story than Wolfe's, he embarks on a course that becomes increasingly more absurd and melodramatic. He arranges an unlikely meeting between Fallow and McCoy, which is followed by McCoy's clearing his apartment of his wife's guests with a shotgun. Intended as an emotional turning point for McCoy, demonstrating newfound grit, it appears contrived and burlesque. Later, the scene between McCoy and his father, played skillfully by veteran actor Donald Moffat, in which their somewhat artificially inflated father-son conflict is resolved, renders a peculiar twist to McCoy's character arc and the film's message. McCoy Sr. may have changed by acquiescing to Sherman's perjury, but his son remains unaltered. Sherman begins unscrupulously, and he ends that way, even if he is justified. He has learned to play hardball with another set of sharks and he lost his material possessions, but how has he recovered his soul? By a singular act of deceit? The book condemns him to legal limbo, penniless and scrapping to stay out of jail. Here, Cristofer attempts closure with Judge White's unlikely diatribe, but it is spliced on and imposed, as is Kramer's melodramatic scramble after McCoy's tape—so much climactic piffle.

"Thank God it was a book first or it would never have gotten made," said De-Palma, in hindsight, of his film's outrageousness. On the contrary, it is DePalma's flawed interpretation that balks credibility.

Eugene H. Davis

Reviews

Chicago Tribune. December 21, 1990, VII, p. 23.
The Hollywood Reporter. CCCXV, December 17, 1990, p. 10.
Los Angeles Times. December 21, 1990, p. F1.
The New York Times. December 21, 1990, p. B1.
The New Yorker. LXVI, January 14, 1991, p. 76.
Newsweek. CXVI, December 24, 1990, p. 63.
Premiere. IV, October, 1990, p. 68.
Time. CXXXVI, December 24, 1990, p. 77.
Variety. December 17, 1990, p. 3.
The Wall Street Journal. December 20, 1990, p. A14.

C'EST LA VIE
(LA BAULE LES PINS)

Origin: France
Released: 1990
Released in U.S.: 1990
Production: Alexandre Arcady for Alexandre Films; released by the Samuel
   Goldwyn Company
Direction: Diane Kurys
Screenplay: Diane Kurys and Alain Le Henry
Cinematography: Giuseppe Lanci
Editing: Raymonde Guyot
Art direction: Tony Egry
Sound: François Groult
Costume design: Caroline De Vivaise
Music: Philippe Sarde
MPAA rating: no listing
Running time: 97 minutes

Principal characters:
Léna	Nathalie Baye
Michel	Richard Berry
Bella	Zabou
Léon	Jean-Pierre Bacri
Jean-Claude	Vincent London
Odette	Valeria Bruni-Tedeschi
Ruffier	Didier Benureau
Frédérique	Julie Bataille
Sophie	Candice LeFranc
Daniel	Alexis Derlon

The story of *C'est la vie* opens at the train depot at Lyon in 1958, where Léna Korski (Nathalie Baye) announces at the last moment that she is not coming with her two daughters but will join them later. Because their father is not coming with them either, thirteen-year-old Frédérique (Julie Bataille) and eight-year-old Sophie (Candice LeFranc) are panicked. As the train begins to move with the two tearful girls looking out the window, the theme of separation is announced for the first time.

Frédérique and Sophie arrive at the seaside resort of La Baule les Pins with the family maid, Odette (Valeria Bruni-Tedeschi), who is quite young herself and unused to such responsibility. The beach on the rugged Atlantic coast is a refreshing visual change from the all-too-familiar Riviera. The children are caught up in the universal seaside trance and experience their own small adventures in the shadow of the major adult tragedy gathering over their heads. Like the British film *The Fallen Idol* (1949), *C'est la vie* tells a story of tempestuous adult emotions as reflected through the eyes of a child. Viewers will also be reminded of the highly acclaimed Swedish film, *Mitt liv som hund* (1985; *My Life as a Dog*), in which twelve-year-old Ingemar is sent to stay with relatives in the country because his mother is dying of tuberculosis.

Léna is going to Paris to join her lover Jean-Claude (Vincent London), a penniless sculptor. Her husband, Michel (Richard Berry), has had to stay behind to mind his shop. When he finally arrives at the seashore and begins to suspect what is going on, the turmoil within the family begins. This is the main conflict of the story; however, it is told mainly through the points of view of Frédérique and her skinny little sister Sophie, a solemn, mischievous, adorable girl who dominates the film with her natural acting talent.

Like Jacques Tati's classic film *Les Vacances de Monsieur Hulot* (1953; *Mr. Hulot's Holiday*), the story begins and ends with a summer vacation at the seashore. It is further framed by shots of Frédérique writing in her diary to foster the illusion that the story is being told from her point of view. Yet, the filmmakers do not straitjacket themselves with this device; Léna and Jean-Claude are shown making love in a tent on the beach and spending an awkward evening at a nightclub with Léna's sister Bella (Zabou) and brother-in-law Léon Mandel (Jean-Pierre Bacri).

Léon and Bella have four children, and Bella is expecting their fifth in a few more months. As a result of being confined to the role of housekeeper, nursemaid, and mother, Bella has remained childlike herself. When she thinks the rules have been broken at a family bingo game, she pouts like a little girl and says that she will not play anymore. Léna, by explicit contrast, is being forced to grow up. She plans to move to Paris with her children and work as a secretary. Her spirit of independence is unusual for a Frenchwoman, especially at such an early date as 1958. She is the real protagonist of the story: Her decision to divorce her husband will bring much pain to her children, her husband, and herself. Nevertheless, the audience sympathizes with her and understands that not all women are meant to be complacent housewives and mothers like Bella.

Diane Kurys, who directed and coauthored *C'est la vie*, has a genius for creating visual symbols which tell the non-French-speaking viewer more than a thousand words of subtitles. When Michel arrives at the resort, Léna has just driven up in a brand-new Renault Dauphine. She is proud of her cheap little car, a symbol of her independence. On the pretense of testing its performance, the jealous Michel guns the engine and deliberately crashes into a tree. It is a scene reminiscent of *Shoot the Moon* (1982), in which the estranged husband (Albert Finney) uses his car to smash his wife's brand-new veranda.

C'est la vie, like *Shoot the Moon*, deals with the near impossibility of severing family bonds. A little later, Frédérique picks up a shard of the mirror that her parents have shattered and hysterically threatens to slit her own throat unless they stop fighting. Frédérique is being cut in two by their misguided efforts to cut their marital and parental ties. The parents suddenly stop fighting when they see it is not really anger they are feeling but their own heartbreak mirrored in their daughter's eyes.

The seaside itself is a visual metaphor. Childhood is like a long vacation which goes on and on and then is suddenly over. Kurys has done a marvelous job of directing the children in her film, both the principals and the extras that she recruited at La Baule-les-Pins. Her skill is comparable to that shown by the eminent French director François Truffaut in his classic *Les Quatre Cents Coups* (1959; *The 400 Blows*) and *L'argent de poche* (1976; *Small Change*). In *C'est la vie*, the children are all flirting with adulthood, impatient to grow up, even though they should be able to see from all the evidence around them that adulthood is not always so enviable. Frédérique is experimenting in the first steps of lovemaking with her cousin Daniel Mandel (Alexis Derlon), and even little Sophie is playing "doctor" with Daniel's younger brother. Throughout the film, the smallest child has been unable to tie his shoes and has to have someone else do it for him. Toward the end, he amazes himself by suddenly tying his own shoelaces. He jumps to his feet and runs after the older children, proudly proclaiming his achievement. He has made another step in the direction of adulthood; there is no turning back.

During the course of the story, a big stray dog has adopted the two families and has been able to insinuate himself so thoroughly into their affections that he is sleeping on their beds. In one of the final scenes, however, the maid Odette brings the dog to the edge of town and ties him to a road marker. She has to drag Frédérique and Sophie away, struggling, screaming, begging her to show pity, but it is impossible to keep the dog in a Paris flat. In fact, there is a hint that Frédérique and Sophie themselves may have to go to separate boarding schools when their mother begins to work, and so one separation follows another. The camera looks back at the dog sitting at the crossroads gazing after his friends, unable to understand that everyone must separate sooner or later.

Back at the beach, more and more people are leaving for home. An older couple says goodbye to the Mandels. It is clear that this couple has been coming here for many seasons, but now they are coming alone. The Mandels, who are smothering in children's sticky kisses, cannot see that they are looking at their own future in these older people, who have been sitting there all the summer envying the people who still have children and sharing vicariously in their family lives. The audience realizes that the Mandels' lonely future must have caught up with them long ago, however, because this was the summer of 1958.

The music throughout the film is unintrusive. A piano flirts with the main theme, a song entitled "La Bouche Pleine de Sable," and at the very end, as the camera pans across the empty beach, the delicate French song is finally put into words by a whole chorus of children. Their reedy, unsure voices give it more poignancy than could have been realized by the most polished professionals and remind the viewer of what can be done on a low budget if the filmmaker has something to say and says it with genuine feeling. Whatever the literal translation of the lyrics may be, the non-French-speaking viewer understands their meaning: Life goes on. There will always be children, although they will not be the same children. There will always be love and separation, happiness and grief. That is life, or, as the French say, "c'est la vie."

Bill Delaney

Reviews
Boston Globe. September 15, 1990, p. 14.
Chicago Tribune. November 16, 1990, VII, p. 44.
The Hollywood Reporter. CCCXIV, October 25, 1990, p. 5.
Los Angeles Times. November 9, 1990, p. F16.
The New Republic. CCIII, December 3, 1990, p. 26.
New Woman. XX, December, 1990, p. 32.
The New York Times. November 2, 1990, p. B6.
Rolling Stone. November 15, 1990, p. 163.
USA Today. November 7, 1990, p. D5.
The Washington Post. November 16, 1990, p. D7.

COME SEE THE PARADISE

Production: Robert F. Colesberry; released by Twentieth Century-Fox
Direction: Alan Parker
Screenplay: Alan Parker
Cinematography: Michael Seresin
Editing: Gerry Hambling
Production design: Geoffrey Kirkland
Art direction: John Willett
Set decoration: Jim Erickson
Sound: Bill Phillips
Makeup: David Craig Forrest
Costume design: Molly Maginnis
Music: Randy Edelman
MPAA rating: R
Running time: 138 minutes

Principal characters:
Jack McGurn	Dennis Quaid
Lily Kawamura	Tamlyn Tomita
Hiroshi Kawamura	Sab Shimono
Mrs. Kawamura	Shizuko Hoshi
Charlie Kawamura	Stan Egi
Harry Kawamura	Ronald Yamamoto
Dulcie Kawamura	Akemi Nishino
Joyce Kawamura	Naomi Nakano
Frankie Kawamura	Brady Tsurutani
Young Mini	Elizabeth Gilliam
Middle Mini	Shyree Mezick
Older Mini	Caroline Junko King

After the success of *Mississippi Burning* (1989), director Alan Parker tackles another controversial period in American history in *Come See the Paradise.* Parker employs a similar approach in both films, using a Caucasian to act as an interpreter between the audience and a minority experience. In both cases, the result is a flawed film, though more so with this film than his earlier effort. Though *Mississippi Burning* generated more controversy than this film, it was tighter and better made.

In 1948, Lily Kawamura McGurn (Tamlyn Tomita) and her daughter Mini (played at this point by Caroline Junko King) are walking to the train station to meet Jack McGurn (Dennis Quaid), who has just been released from prison. Mini asks her mother to describe Jack and how they met. As they walk, the film's plot unfolds. In 1936, Jack is an organizer for the Projectionists Union who leaves New York City after quarreling with his boss about scare tactics. Using a new name, Jack finds a job in Los Angeles as a film projectionist at a Japanese theater that is run by Hiroshi

Kawamura (Sab Shimono). Equally proud of his Japanese heritage and his success in the United States, Kawamura is disappointed by his children's lack of interest in their heritage. Charlie (Stan Egi) wants to become a baseball player, Harry (Ronald Yamamoto) has Hollywood ambitions, and Lily does not speak Japanese. The younger children—Dulcie (Akemi Nishino), Joyce (Naomi Nakano), and Frankie (Brady Tsurutani)—are no better.

Jack and Charlie quickly become friends. Through Charlie, Jack meets Lily, and they fall in love instantly. Despite Lily's and Jack's individual pleas, Kawamura is steadfastly opposed to the interracial marriage. The couple elope to Seattle, Washington, where, unlike in California, interracial marriage is permitted. Though brief, Jack and Lily's stay in Seattle is idyllic. Jack works at a cannery, and Lily takes care of their daughter Mini (played at this point by Elizabeth Gilliam). The conditions at the cannery are terrible, however, and Jack decides to renew his union activities. Lily and Jack quarrel, and the neglected Lily returns with Mini to Los Angeles. Upon her arrival, she learns that Japan has bombed Pearl Harbor and that her father has been arrested. Jack is also jailed because of his involvement in a protest; he learns that war has been declared after his arrest. Having been released from jail, Jack arrives in Los Angeles and is reconciled with Lily. Soon after, however, Jack is drafted into the army, and the Kawamura family, along with all persons of Japanese ancestry on the West Coast, receives orders to report to a racetrack that has been converted into an assembly center, where they will be processed and sent to "relocation camps."

Upon their arrival at the desert camp, each family is assigned to a hut. Gradually, an organized community forms in the camp, with baseball, dances, and other social events. Kawamura joins them after being released from prison. Although the family is supportive, he suffers further humiliations at the hands of young Japanese internees who believe that he gave information to the military. As he retreats increasingly from his surroundings, family unity begins to disintegrate. When filling out a loyalty registration, known as the "No-No" questionnaire, the family completely splinters. Charlie, who feels betrayed by his native country, refuses to say "yes" on two key questions. Harry takes this opportunity to enlist in the Japanese-American 442nd combat unit, which is recruiting from all the internment camps.

Jack is able to obtain some leave in order to visit the camp, but his stay is brief. On the night that he arrives, a protest by unhappy camp residents becomes a riot. Charlie takes part in the riot and is injured. Later, Jack goes AWOL and returns to the camp to see Lily and Mini (played by Shyree Mezick) and help the family. During his visit, he and Kawamura finally reconcile. When Jack asks him for advice, Kawamura replies "Just love Lily. That's enough," and persuades Jack to return to the army. Upon his return, Jack is met by the FBI, who confront him with his true identity and his unpleasant past. At the camp, the mentally and physically broken Kawamura walks into the desert to die. A quick succession of goodbyes follows: Dulcie finds work outside the camp at a sugar beet farm in Idaho but returns pregnant; Charlie is sent to the dissident camp, Tule Lake, pending repatriation to Japan; and Harry is killed in combat. When the internees are released in January, 1945, the

Kawamuras move in with relatives on a strawberry farm in California. The film ends with Jack's reunion with Lily and Mini.

In *Come See the Paradise*, Parker simply tries to do too much. The director explains in his production notes that he was inspired by a "haunting photograph by Dorothea Lange [of] a Japanese man sitting with his two grandchildren . . . awaiting deportation and internment." Combining this inspiration with a "folder full of scribbled notes on a story about a politically left-wing character in the States in the 1930's" and a desire to do a love story, Parker fashioned the plot for the film. Union organizing in the 1930's and 1940's, interracial marriage, and the Japanese-American internment are subjects that each deserve a separate film, however, and to combine all of them in one film is to shortchange all three.

Considering that Jack is one of the main characters, he shows little character development, particularly in relation to his union organizing activities. Used primarily to fill out his character, his involvement in union organizing results only in a series of rejections—by his first wife, his fellow workers, his brother, and Lily—and is not depicted as a source of strength for him or the people around him. After the internment and his separation from Lily, Jack's story is provided only in glimpses, and the sequence of events in his life becomes somewhat confusing. For example, it is never made clear that Jack went to jail because his true identity was discovered. Consequently, the reason that Lily and Mini are meeting him at the train station is equally unclear. Gaps such as these underscore the fact that Jack's character development is subordinated to his use as a plot device: He is the audience's window into the story, asking questions about Japanese-American culture and history that would not fit naturally in the script. In addition, the possible consequences of the interracial marriage are hardly addressed, except to explain why Jack and Lily left California. Only Kawamura objects to the marriage, but the couple never encounters racial prejudice from Americans. Such inferred open-mindedness during the 1930's and 1940's is optimistically unrealistic.

Of the three issues that are included in the film, the internment of Japanese Americans is handled with the most detail. Parker modeled the set for the camp on Manzanar, the largest of the internment camps. The camp scenes demonstrate Parker's sensitive direction and the extensive research to which he alludes in his production notes. The tragic irony of the internment is demonstrated by all-American activities such as a baseball game being played against the background of barbed-wire fences and gun towers or the incongruity of a sock hop followed by a protest. The constant dust, particularly during the scene at Kawamura's grave, is a grim reminder of the inhospitable environment in which they lived.

At least three key historical points, however, are handled less carefully. First, the most controversial question on the "No-No" questionnaire asked if the person rejected any allegiance to Japan. The script does show the dilemma faced by first-generation Japanese (Issei): If they answered "no," then they were branded disloyal to the United States; if they answered "yes," then they would have no citizenship, as they were not allowed to become American citizens. The film failed to point out the inherently damning implication for the second generation (Nisei)—that the person had an allegiance to Japan in the first place. The Nisei, who were American citizens by birth, had no national ties to Japan. If they answered "yes," then they were admitting an allegiance that they had never possessed; if they answered "no," then they, like the Issei, were considered disloyal. Second, the camp riot shows the soldiers facing pro-Japanese demonstrators. The actual protest, which took place in Manzanar on December 6, 1942, concerned the wrongful imprisonment of a Nisei. Portraying the riot as pro-Japanese justifies the soldiers' actions. Third, the film shows that the internees were released because the U.S. Supreme Court ruled that the camps were unconstitutional. In fact, the Supreme Court ruled that the government had no authority to intern citizens whose loyalty was proven. This distinction is important, for it was only in the 1980's that the U.S. government acknowledged that the internment was unconstitutional and unjustified.

It is important to remember that this film is first and foremost a Hollywood production, whose primary purpose is to entertain a large group of people. Based on these terms, *Come See the Paradise* is fairly successful. This emotionally draining film consists of a series of rejections, from Jack's rejection by his fellow workers and family to the Japanese-American community's rejection by the United States. Although there are reconciliations, the characters endure tragic losses, and the reunions are often bittersweet from the knowledge that they will be temporary and that they were achieved as a result of personal sacrifice. The love story is unabashedly romantic, which is refreshing in the light of the cynicism underlying many films of the 1980's.

The film benefits from visually stunning cinematography, a moving score, and excellent acting performances. The most memorable scenes are unspoken, allowing Michael Seresin's camera work and Randy Edelman's music to express themselves fully. The overhead shot showing hundreds of tagged people walking to the train station beautifully illustrates the extent of this national tragedy. Unfortunately, the film is hampered by a script that is filled with stilted dialogue and unrealistic monologues. Both Quaid's and Tomita's performances suffer as a result. On the other hand, Shimono and Shizuko Hoshi benefit from their characters' taciturn, proud natures. In particular, Shimono communicates Kawamura's heartbreaking deterioration using mostly gestures and facial expressions. An especially moving scene is Kawamura's arrival at the camp after being released from prison; in the looks exchanged between him and Mrs. Kawamura, the audience sees the tragic loss and shame that both of them feel. Egi, as Charlie, also gives a strong performance.

The love story swings in and out of the forefront of the film. After their first date, Jack and Lily spend a brief moment alone and their desire for each other almost overwhelms their prudence. In this scene, the chemistry between the two is palpable and is demonstrated by body language. Yet, when Jack declares his love to Lily after they are reconciled in Los Angeles, his speech is so unrealistic that it is embarrassing to hear. Despite being saddled with the most lines, Quaid and Tomita play their characters with depth and sensitivity. It is interesting that these two main characters have dual roles in the film: In addition to their characters in the story, both are interpreters. Jack is the character with whom audiences will identify; and Lily narrates the story to her daughter, who, like the audience, has only a marginal knowledge of the camp experience. Lily's narration frames the film. Such a framework can provide cohesion to a film that covers a great amount of time, or it can be interruptive. In this case, using Lily as a voice-over in some scenes is effective, as her narration is usually understated and unadorned. The breaks from the story to Lily and Mini's conversation, however, are disruptive.

Because it is the first major film about the camp experience, *Come See the Paradise* is historically and culturally important, and Parker bears a responsibility to depict the internment honestly. Unfortunately, Parker's status as an outsider makes it impossible for him to portray Japanese Americans as they really were. One could argue that the film was not made for a Japanese-American audience. On the other hand, given that Parker had a larger audience in mind, one wonders whether a mass audience would not have benefited more from a script that was written from the point of view of those who were there.

It is interesting that Parker demonstrates his inability to address directly the internment experience by using Jack and Lily's love story to frame the film. Although he has been criticized for his indirect approach to the subject matter in this film and in *Mississippi Burning*, one cannot fault him for demonstrating a degree of self-honesty; had he not provided a framework, his lack of firsthand knowledge would have been painfully obvious. *Come See the Paradise* is not a film about the internment of Japanese Americans during World War II; rather, it is Parker's interpretation of the internment.

Liane Hirabayashi

Reviews

American Film: Magazine of the Film and Television Arts. XVI, January, 1991, p. 48.
Boxoffice. December, 1990, p. R89.
Chicago Tribune. January 18, 1991, VII, p. 30.
The Christian Science Monitor. January 4, 1991, p. 12.
The Hollywood Reporter. CCCXII, May 14, 1990, p. 4.
The Hollywood Reporter. CCCXV, December 21, 1990, p. 6.
Los Angeles Times. May 15, 1990, p. F1.
Los Angeles Times. December 22, 1990, p. F1.
The New York Times. May 20, 1990, p. B17.
The New York Times. December 23, 1990, I, p. 42.
Newsweek. CXVII, January 14, 1991, p. 54.
Premiere. IV, October, 1990, p. 68.
Time. CXXXVII, January 14, 1991, p. 75.
Variety. May 14, 1990, p. 3.

THE COOK, THE THIEF, HIS WIFE, AND HER LOVER

Origin: France and Holland
Released: 1989
Released in U.S.: 1990
Production: Kees Kasander for Allarts Cook-Erato Films and Films Inc.; released
    by Recorded Releasing
Direction: Peter Greenaway
Screenplay: Peter Greenaway
Cinematography: Sacha Vierny
Editing: John Wilson
Production design: Ben Van Os and Jan Roelfs
Sound: Garth Marshall
Music: Michael Nyman
MPAA rating: no listing
Running time: 126 minutes

> *Principal characters:*
> Richard, the cook . . . . Richard Bohringer
> Albert Spica, the thief . . . . Michael Gambon
> Georgina Spica, his wife . . . . Helen Mirren
> Michael, her lover . . . . Alan Howard
> Mitchell . . . . Tim Roth
> Cory . . . . Ciaran Hinds
> Spangler . . . . Gary Olsen
> Harris . . . . Ewan Stewart
> Turpin . . . . Roger Ashton Griffiths
> Mews . . . . Ron Cook
> Grace . . . . Liz Smith
> Patricia . . . . Emer Gillespie

    Within the past few decades, critics and public alike have been shocked, scandalized, and infuriated by a host of nontraditional films. Gualtiero Jacopetti's *Mondo Cane* (1962), Alexandro Jodorowsky's *El Topo* (1971), Bernardo Bertolucci's *Last Tango in Paris* (1972), and Pier Paolo Pasolini's *Salo* (1975) attempt to make strong social and even political statements about society in striking and controversial ways. Although censorship and moral norms have been somewhat relaxed in film, especially in the 1970's and 1980's in the wake of these provocative works, Peter Greenaway's alluring film *The Cook, the Thief, His Wife, and Her Lover* still opens avenues for heated debate. It can evoke some of the same critical reaction as the earlier cinematic shockers in the light of its violent, scatological, necrophilic, and erotic elements. The film will above all raise the primordial issue of the fine line between art and pornography.

The Cook, the Thief, His Wife, and Her Lover could be a rousing tale right out of Giovanni Boccaccio's *The Decameron*, but with more of the taboo and erotic included. The narrative is straightforward. As the dark tale unfolds, one grotesque scene follows another to draw the viewer into a disturbing, ethereal world of love and horror. The gourmet restaurant Le Hollandais, a type of apocalyptic microcosm of a society breaking at the seams, provides the setting for the tale. It suggests a quasi-universal world, a cross between a futuristic European restaurant of haute cuisine and a decadent, urban American one where dogs grovel for delicacies in the bountiful garbage bins on the streets.

Georgina Spica (Helen Mirren), the beloved "possession" of the gangster Albert Spica (Michael Gambon), finds life oppressive in the presence of her brutish, boorish husband. For some odd reason, she tolerates his verbal and physical abuse. On one occasion, in the course of their nightly gastronomic adventures at Le Hollandais, however, she finds some respite from the incessant, degrading remarks of the insufferable animal Spica. She spies a quiet, sophisticated man all alone, poring over classic texts at his table. In a passion of pure, almost anonymous sex, a sizzling love affair commences and progresses nocturnally right under the ugly nose of Albert. Between courses, Georgina and Michael (Alan Howard) briefly meet in the bathroom or in the kitchen, protected by the sensitive, all-seeing cook, Richard (Richard Bohringer). When the affair is detected, Albert almost destroys the restaurant in pursuit of the daring adulterers. They manage to escape to the literary oasis of Michael's book depository, only to have Albert discover Michael and gorge him to death with his own texts, notably about the French Revolution. In a spirited act of vengeance, Georgina obliges the cook to prepare Michael's corpse as a gastronomic delight. She turns the table on Albert and forces him to eat the garnished cadaver. With no compunction, she guns him down and finally liberates herself from her oppressor.

On the surface, *The Cook, the Thief, His Wife, and Her Lover* is the story of an eternal triangle, an illicit affair, and a curious vendetta. Beneath this, however, is a black allegorical comedy about the nature of oppression. In essence, the powerful, manipulative, and abusive creatures themselves fall victim to the violence by which they live. In a cathartic way, the audience can cheer on Georgina as she extracts retribution from Albert for her life of sheer misery and, more significantly, for the death of her only source of love.

The unique quartet of characters is carefully crafted to populate the bizarre universe of this posh, gourmet restaurant frequented by Albert Spica. The gangster, affecting the traits of a cultured gentleman, is anything but that. His controlling force obliges each person from cook to wife to become a marionette in a tragicomic puppet show that is announced with the obvious ascent and descent of the theater curtain. Michael Gambon plays his role with a viciousness and vileness that allows the audience not a drop of sympathy for him at the conclusion. He indeed gets his just "desserts." Georgina, on the other hand, tears at the audience's heartstrings, for she is shown victimized at every turn. Her only outlet in this oppressive milieu is the unbridled passion she shares with Michael. Rivaling and even surpassing her roles in *White Nights* (1985) and *The Mosquito Coast* (1986), Helen Mirren creates a power-ful character who cries out for emancipation. The taciturn Michael, played coyly by the British stage actor Alan Howard, is the catalyst in the whole affair. He falls prey to Georgina's charm and burst of passionate love, and finds utter joy in a life nor-mally marked by silent texts and gourmet dishes. As protector and confidant, the French chef Richard, subtly played by Richard Bohringer from *Diva* (1982), helps orchestrate the affair between his exotic courses. He is truly an artist in his profes-sion, but his creative genius is equally abused by Spica, his most flamboyant client.

The tense film is richly multilayered. On one hand, the image of "woman as ob-ject" dominates the narrative in a way that is reminiscent of the Zampano-Gelsomina relationship in Federico Fellini's *La Strada* (1954). It creates a superb tension within the viewer's mind insofar as Spica acts impulsively toward Georgina and those around him. At one instant, he can lash out at her and almost destroy her; at the next in-stant, he can passionately devour her.

Peter Greenaway's original script also delves into the cultural level of society. The restaurant itself is at the frontier of civilization, as the roving, snarling dogs fight over remnants at the restaurant's doors. On the personal level, it is not money, power, or fine food that makes one cultured, as is evident in Spica's case. It is the apprecia-tion of beauty and good taste and the sensitivity to carry this out in one's personal philosophy of life. Georgina's gentleness and openness, as well as Michael's scholar-liness and understanding, draw them together and reveal them at one moment as idyllic dwellers in the Garden of Eden.

One of the most controversial and disturbing aspects of *The Cook, the Thief, His Wife, and Her Lover* is the critical level of violence. This has created a major di-lemma whether the film should receive an "A" rating for special artistic adult works or the more traditional "X." Spica's harsh physical and verbal treatment of Geor-gina, his grotesque covering of one of his enemies with excrement, his ramming of a fork into the cheek of one of his crony's companions, and the eviscerating of the boy soprano are most unsettling. Greenaway purports to avoid sensationalism with this serious tone of violence, yet he cannot avoid it. Spica's horrifying treatment of the members of his entourage reflects both the vulnerability of the human being and the bestiality of a man without morals.

In every frame, the lavish sets delight and stimulate the eye. Metaphorical color and aesthetic composition work together to create one of the most unusual artis-tically designed films in recent cinema history. At one moment, the stylized set of the kitchen exudes a futuristic tone, as in *Blade Runner* (1982), while at the next, it has a medieval or baroque quality to it. In an early sequence of the film, Spica's retinue dresses in clever imitation of the restaurant's large canvas of the Dutch Ba-roque painter Frans Hals, in his *Banquet of the Officers of the St. George Militia of Haarlem*, while the camera pans over the rich still-life decor that leaps out of a traditional Baroque painting. The rose-tinted white bathroom with central urinals evokes a twenty-first century decor. Greenaway's past experiences with art and his sensitivity to it have helped create these highly stylized sets, but not without the significant collaboration of his director of photography, Sacha Vierny. Established in the industry with Alain Resnais (*Hiroshima mon amour*, 1959; *Last Year at Marienbad*, 1961; *La Guerre est finie*, 1966), Vierny now continues to find artistic license working with Greenaway (*A Zed and Two Noughts*, 1986; *Belly of an Architect*, 1987; *Drowning by Numbers*, 1988). Vierny's tracking camera uncovers one finely designed composition after another. In the realm of sound, Michael Nyman's musical compositions are as stylized as the sets. Sung by the boy soprano, the haunting and melodious chant "Wash Me of My Iniquity" adds profound, metaphorical depth.

Peter Greenaway's *The Cook, the Thief, His Wife, and Her Lover* has the power to shock and to provoke, or to stimulate and to educate. Its allegorical statement about oppression—be it personal or political—and its aural and visual aesthetics make the difference between pornography and art.

John J. Michalczyk

Reviews
Boxoffice. May, 1990, p. R40.
Chicago Tribune. April 6, 1990, VII, p. 41.
Film Comment. XXV, November, 1989, p. 72.
Films in Review. XLI, October, 1990, p. 488.
Los Angeles Times. April 13, 1990, p. F12.
The Nation. CCL, May 7, 1990, p. 644.
The New Republic. CCII, April 23, 1990, p. 26.
New Statesman and Society. II, October 20, 1989, p. 48.
The New York Times. April 6, 1990, p. B1.
The New Yorker. LXVI, May 7, 1990, p. 88.
Newsweek. CXV, April 23, 1990, p. 73.
Time. CXXXV, April 9, 1990, p. 95.
Variety. CCCXXXVI, September 13, 1989, p. 39.

CYRANO DE BERGERAC

Origin: France
Released: 1990
Released in U.S.: 1990
Production: René Cleitman and Michel Seydoux for Hachette Première, Camera One, Films A2, D. D. Prods., and UGC; released by Orion Pictures
Direction: Jean-Paul Rappeneau
Screenplay: Jean-Paul Rappeneau and Jean-Claude Carrière; based on the play by Edmond Rostand
Cinematography: Pierre Lhomme
Editing: Noelle Boisson
Set design: Ezio Frigerio
Sound: Pierre Gamet and Dominique Hennequin
Makeup: Jean-Pierre Eychenne
Nose creation: Michele Burke
Costume design: Franca Squarciapino (AA)
Music: Jean-Claude Petit
MPAA rating: PG
Running time: 138 minutes

> *Principal characters:*
> Cyrano de Bergerac . . . . Gérard Depardieu
> Roxane . . . . Anne Brochet
> Christian de Neuvillette . . . . Vincent Perez
> Comte de Guiche . . . . Jacques Weber
> Ragueneau . . . . Roland Bertin
> Le Bret . . . . Philippe Morier-Genoud
> Vicomte de Valvert . . . . Philippe Volter
> Carbon de Castel-Jaloux . . . . Pierre Maguelon
> Roxane's handmaid . . . . Josiane Stoleru
> Montfleury . . . . Gabriel Monnet

In any production of *Cyrano de Bergerac*, the length of the protagonist's nose is a good indication of the spirit in which the piece will be interpreted. In the 1950 American film version of the play, José Ferrer wore an impossibly long nose, like the end of a broom handle stuck in the middle of his face. Anyone with such a nose would not be merely eccentric but cross-eyed and completely insane. Ferrer seemed continually upstaged by his own nose: He was forced into histrionics above and beyond the call of the title role simply in order to live up to the grotesque proboscis with which Stanley Kramer and his makeup department had provided him. By contrast, the tasteful French film adaptation of one of their own literary treasures makes the Ferrer version look like a burlesque.

Gérard Depardieu is highly regarded in his own country but did not receive international acclaim until he starred in *Jean de Florette* (1986), which evoked the unusual spectacle of around-the-block lines of American moviegoers waiting to see a film with subtitles. The public did not flock to the new production of *Cyrano de Bergerac* in order to see another version of a familiar play—they went to see how Depardieu would play Cyrano. His nose, as the Vicomte de Valvert (Philippe Volter) tells him, is "rather large"; however, it is not large beyond the realm of possibility, and Depardieu's reading is correspondingly restrained.

It is very difficult for an actor to play the title role in this play without making Cyrano appear to be a bully, a braggart, and a lunatic. Depardieu somehow is able to make the swashbuckling, loquacious hero not only believable but also modest. Beginning with the famous opening scene in which Cyrano prevents a whole theater audience from witnessing a play because he dislikes the star, Depardieu is credible and sympathetic. In the even more famous duel between Cyrano and Valvert which immediately follows, Depardieu seems to find exactly the right note of malice and good humor. He achieves this in part through a slight alteration of Edmond Rostand's original play: Instead of Cyrano concluding his impromptu ballade with a vicious swordthrust, he disarms the Vicomte and merely presses him on the nose with his finger as he ends with the words "je touche!" (Unfortunately, Valvert is unwilling to leave it at that and ends up badly wounded, as in the original.)

Rostand's play was written in rhyming alexandrine couplets, a form similar to that perfected by France's two greatest dramatists, Pierre Corneille and Jean Racine. The rhyme and meter were disregarded in Ferrer's 1950 version of the play, as they are in most English-language stage productions. After seeing Depardieu's French version, the American viewer, even if his or her knowledge of French is minimal, can see that the play must lose much of its charm when translated into a foreign language. English subtitles to foreign films are typically insensitive and fragmentary; often they evoke laughter because they were so obviously written by someone familiar with his own language but not with English. In this French production of *Cyrano de Bergerac*, however, the subtitles were tastefully created by the multitalented novelist and linguist Anthony Burgess, who published a complete translation of *Cyrano de Bergerac* in 1971. His subtitles are cleverly rhymed and convey at least the spirit of Rostand's romantic poetry. The poetic aspect of the film is nowhere more important than in the balcony scene, in which the handsome but inarticulate Christian de Neuvillette is wooing the beautiful Roxane while Cyrano hides in the shadows telling him what to say. Depardieu and his two talented costars, Anne Brochet and Vincent Perez, make this scene entirely credible, even though there is danger that Cyrano will look like a panderer and Roxane will look like a giddy schoolgirl for allowing herself to be deceived in such a blatant manner. The audience needs to be reminded that this is not literal truth but poetic truth. The impression of rhyme and meter that is preserved in the subtitles lends the scene a certain poetic license which is lost when Rostand's masterpiece is presented in plain English prose.

Like other great actors, such as Charles Laughton, Marlon Brando, Laurence Olivier, and Alec Guinness, Depardieu's secret is simple: He does not "act" at all but actually "becomes" the character he is playing. This requires nothing more or less than genius and cannot be taught by any method in any acting school. By 1990, Depardieu was on his way to becoming an international superstar. He appeared in his first English-language film, *Green Card* (1990; reviewed in this volume), which received widespread critical approval and gratifying receipts at the box office. He is not a handsome man, nor is he blessed with a naturally graceful physique—he has a bearlike build and a nose that needed little augmentation for the role of Cyrano. His rare ability to crawl into the skin of the character he is playing, however, gives him a commanding presence that makes up for any of his deficiencies. Such an actor not only gives memorable performances himself but also is capable of drawing superior performances from the other members of a cast.

The director, Jean-Paul Rappeneau, had an opportunity to "open up" the play for motion-picture audiences in the same way that Olivier opened up *Henry V* (1944) in his film version of Shakespeare's historical drama. Just as Olivier made a grand spectacle of the Battle of Agincourt, Rappeneau has done the same thing with the battle between the French and Spanish armies at the bloody Siege of Arras, which occurred during the Thirty Years War. The production required two thousand actors and extras, three hundred swords, five hundred pikes, one hundred and fifty muskets, one hundred pistols, two howitzers, and a dozen cannons. Franca Squarciapino received an Academy Award for costume design. As with the marvelous *Jean de Florette* and its sequel *Manon des sources* (1986; *Manon of the Spring*), a French company has invested an unusually large sum of money in a brilliant production. *Cyrano de Bergerac* will undoubtedly remain the definitive film version of the famous play for many years to come.

The battle scene forms the climax of the film. At Arras, amid the smoke and confusion, the three principals are brought together for the last time. Christian is fatally wounded and the grief-stricken Roxane decides to retire to a convent, where Cyrano comes to visit her faithfully and bring her news of the court. In Cyrano's long death scene, Depardieu again finds exactly the right note. The audience feels genuine pity for him and is not, as in the Ferrer version, secretly relieved that the assault on their eardrums is finally about to end. In every famous scene of this famous play, Depardieu is dignified and convincing. The audience is made to understand that Cyrano is essentially a gentle, sensitive person who feels compelled to act outrageously, just as people tend to behave differently from their true characters if they wear an outlandish costume at a masquerade party. Cyrano is so mortified by what he considers to be his horrible deformity that he is driven to deeds of desperation. When he goes to fight a hundred armed men single-handed, it is not the action of an exhibitionist or a maniac but that of a man who does not care whether he prolongs his painful existence. Even in the outrageous scene in which Cyrano pretends to have fallen out of the moon in order to prevent Roxane's ardent lover the Comte de Guiche (Jacques Weber) from interrupting her hastily arranged marriage to Christian, Depardieu makes his character completely credible. In fact, he demonstrates that Cyrano's behavior from beginning to end has a common denominator: It is intended to provoke just such a violent death as eventually occurs. When he dies in the arms of his beloved Roxane at the Convent of the Ladies of the Cross, it is the perfect consummation of his dreams.

Bill Delaney

Reviews

Chicago Tribune. December 25, 1990, V, p. 11.
The Christian Science Monitor. November 16, 1990, p. 12.
The Hollywood Reporter. CCCXV, May 22, 1990, p. 4.
The Hollywood Reporter. CCCXV, December 18, 1990, p. 10.
Los Angeles Times. December 18, 1990, p. F1.
The New Republic. CC, December 10, 1990, p. 28.
The New York Times. November 16, 1990, p. B7.
Time. CXXXVI, November 19, 1990, p. 112.
The Times Literary Supplement. January 18, 1991, p. 15.
Variety. April 5, 1990, p. 10.
The Washington Post. December 20, 1990, p. D1.

DANCES WITH WOLVES

Production: Jim Wilson (AA) and Kevin Costner (AA) for Tig Productions;
  released by Orion Pictures
Direction: Kevin Costner (AA)
Screenplay: Michael Blake (AA); based on his novel
Cinematography: Dean Semler (AA)
Editing: Neil Travis (AA)
Production design: Jeffrey Beecroft
Art direction: Wm Ladd Skinner
Set decoration: Lisa Dean
Sound: Russell Williams II (AA), Jeffrey Perkins (AA), Bill W. Benton (AA), and
  Greg Watkins (AA)
Costume design: Elsa Zamparelli
Music: John Barry (AA)
MPAA rating: PG-13
Running time: 181 minutes

Principal characters:
Lieutenant Dunbar	Kevin Costner
Stands with a Fist	Mary McDonnell
Kicking Bird	Graham Greene
Wind in His Hair	Rodney A. Grant
Ten Bears	Floyd Red Crow Westerman
Black Shawl	Tantoo Cardinal
Timmons	Robert Pastorelli
Lieutenant Elgin	Charles Rocket
Major Flambrough	Maury Chaykin
Stone Calf	Jimmy Herman

Dances with Wolves dominated the Academy Awards by receiving twelve nominations and winning seven for Best Picture, Best Director (Kevin Costner), Best Adapted
Screenplay (Michael Blake), Best Cinematography (Dean Semler), Best Film Editing (Neil Travis), Best Original Score (John Barry), and Best Sound (Russell Williams II, Jeffrey Perkins, Bill W. Benton, and Greg Watkins). In a year in which the
United States became engulfed in a major overseas conflict with the Iraqi nation,
Dances with Wolves arrived at a time when the country was in desperate need of a
spiritually uplifting jolt. The film was duly rewarded for supplying this much-needed
affirmation of the positive forces inherent in nature and people's ability to recognize
these forces and align themselves accordingly despite overwhelming opposition from
without and from within. This is a film rich in mythic themes, boldly dramatizing
the death, rebirth, and spiritual transformation of a man who dares to stray from the

traditional path of accepted behavior into the unknown wilderness in order to find his true self. A wide assortment of films have embraced the mythic theme of the hero's journey to spiritual transformation; such films as *The Wizard of Oz* (1939), *The Searchers* (1956), *Star Wars* (1977), and *Rain Man* (1988) all deal with characters who stray into uncommon territory and gain life-affirming enlightenment from the experience. *Dances with Wolves*, however, is able to develop and sustain the theme of spiritual transformation more successfully than any other film in recent memory.

The film begins with the hero's symbolic death and rebirth. John J. Dunbar (Kevin Costner), a Civil War soldier fighting for the Union, is wounded in battle and wakes up on a crude operating table, slated to have his foot amputated. Choosing to die rather than to be mutilated, he drags himself off the table and mounts a horse. After whispering "Forgive me, Father," he rides between the opposing armies, flinging his arms out in a crucifixion pose, expecting to be killed by the Confederate troops. Instead, his action serves to distract the Confederate troops long enough for the Union soldiers to attack and defeat the opposing army. Dunbar becomes a hero, is promoted to lieutenant, and is given a choice of posts to serve out the remainder of his military term. Sickened by the slaughter and insanity of war, Dunbar chooses the most remote of all posts, Fort Sedgewick, located deep in the uncharted Western wilderness.

Dunbar travels into the wilderness with Timmons (Robert Pastorelli), an extremely uncouth wagon driver. When the two finally reach Fort Sedgewick, they find it deserted and in shabby disrepair. Nevertheless, Dunbar is determined to stay and wait for replacement troops, and he struggles to adapt to the wide expanse of wilderness. One day, he spots a lone wolf approaching the fort. At first, he draws his rifle, ready to shoot the wild animal. At the last moment, however, he decides against killing it. He befriends the animal which, along with his horse, serves as a symbol of the primitive forces of nature that connect humanity with other forms of life. By daring to acknowledge that primitive connection between himself and his savage, natural environment, Dunbar takes another step in the direction of his spiritual transformation.

Dunbar's biggest step toward spiritual enlightenment occurs during his encounters with a tribe of Sioux that is camped within a day's ride from the fort. After various tribe members attempt to steal his horse on three separate occasions, each encounter becoming more aggressively hostile, Dunbar decides to confront the tribe on their own land. Before reaching their camp, he first encounters a woman from the tribe, who is attempting to commit suicide. Dunbar stops her and rides into the Sioux camp with the bleeding woman in his arms. When Dunbar tries to explain that the woman is hurt, the Sioux yell at him to get off their land, which he finally does, frustrated by his inability to communicate his intentions to the tribal leaders.

The leaders of the tribe later meet and decide that the best way to deal with Dunbar is to learn if he knows whether other white settlers will follow after him and, if so, in what numbers. Gradually, after several encounters, Dunbar and the Sioux leaders begin to develop a mutual trust and tolerance for one another. In order to gain information about Dunbar's intentions, the holy man of the tribe, Kicking Bird (Graham Greene), enlists the help of his adopted daughter, Stands with a Fist (Mary McDonnell), a white woman who has lived with the Sioux since childhood and who has a vague remembrance of rudimentary English. She is the woman whom Dunbar saved from committing suicide, which he learns was because of her grief over the death of her Sioux husband. When Dunbar is invited to the camp, he talks with Kicking Bird using Stands with a Fist as an interpreter, although he is purposefully vague in giving information about the intentions of other white settlers migrating into the area. One of the things he learns from Kicking Bird is that the tribe is in desperate need of finding buffalo to supply them with food, clothing, and shelter.

Soon after Dunbar's visit with the tribe, he awakens one night in his fort to the sound of thunder and the violent shaking of the earth. When he investigates, he finds a huge herd of buffalo galloping near the post. He immediately rides to the Sioux camp to alert them and inadvertently interrupts one of their sacred dances, for which he is soundly beaten. When he is finally able to communicate his news of the buf-falo, he is hailed as a hero. He is invited to accompany the tribe as they follow the buffalos' trail. What follows is a breathtaking action sequence involving Dunbar and the Sioux hunters, who ride into the thunderous buffalo herd and kill many of the fiercely powerful animals. Afterward, Dunbar celebrates with the Sioux as they laugh, eat, and swap tales of the hunt. When Dunbar again returns to his post, he feels lonely for the first time.

Dunbar decides to return to the Sioux camp for a visit and is followed by the wolf he has befriended, Two Socks. When he dismounts and tries to prevent Two Socks from following him, the two playfully chase each other. This act is watched by Kicking Bird and the other approaching Sioux visitors, which earns Dunbar his Sioux name, Dances with Wolves. Dunbar learns that the Sioux are planning to do battle with the Pawnee, and he asks to accompany them. Instead, Kicking Bird re-quests that Dunbar stay behind and watch over the remaining tribe members, to which Dunbar agrees. During his stay, he and Stands with a Fist trade information about each other's pasts and eventually become lovers.

Scouts from the camp return with the news of an approaching band of Pawnee. Dunbar rides back to his post and retrieves a stockpile of rifles, which he then di-vides among the Sioux women and the older men of the tribe. When the Pawnee at-tack, they are severely and savagely slaughtered by the Sioux, who afterward wildly celebrate their victory. When the other Sioux warriors return from their own vic-torious battle, Kicking Bird learns of the romance that has developed between Dun-bar and Stands with a Fist and presides over their marriage. Dunbar attends the marriage ceremony dressed in his best army uniform. The next time Dunbar ap-pears, however, he is dressed in Sioux buckskins, lives in his own Sioux lodgings, and fluently speaks the language of the Sioux. Dunbar's spiritual transformation is now complete. Yet, one final test of his new spiritual self remains.

When winter approaches, the Sioux prepare to migrate to their winter quarters. As the tribe begins its journey, Dunbar returns for the last time to the fort in order to retrieve his journal, which he fears might be used to track down the tribe if it falls into the hands of returning troops. Dunbar's worst fear is realized when he reaches the fort and sees that troops have arrived. Before he can escape and return to the Sioux, he is spotted and his horse is shot from under him. He is captured, tortured, jailed, and branded a traitor when his true identity becomes known. The commanding officer tells Dunbar that, if he agrees to help track down the Sioux, the commander will ensure that Dunbar's punishment for aiding the tribe will be less severe. In an act that affirms his total spiritual transformation, Dunbar gives his reply in the Sioux language, repeating over and over again his new Sioux name.

Dunbar is shackled, and a small troop of soldiers begins to transport him back to headquarters for court-martial. Along the way, Two Socks appears and the soldiers gleefully open fire on the wolf, eventually killing it. This act stands in marked contrast to Dunbar's own initial reaction to the wolf and is symbolic of the spiritual gap that now separates him from the morally bankrupt soldiers. Soon afterward, the troop is attacked by Sioux warriors, who have returned to investigate Dunbar's disappearance. After a fierce battle, the Sioux kill the troop and rescue Dunbar. A joyful reunion takes place when Dunbar is united again with Stands with a Fist and the rest of the tribe. Dunbar later meets with the chief, Ten Bears (Floyd Red Crow Westerman) and the other tribe leaders to tell them that he must leave the tribe in order to prevent soldiers from tracking him down and using him as an excuse to wage war with the Sioux. After a tearful farewell, during which the tribe's most fierce warrior, Wind in His Hair (Rodney A. Grant) shouts from the surrounding cliffs his pledge of eternal friendship with Dances with Wolves, Dunbar and Stands with a Fist separate from the tribe and ride away together.

What makes Dunbar's spiritual transformation so moving and effective is that the progression of events leading to the transformation is completely believable. Discounting the overt symbolism that permeates the film, the basic story is told with honesty and compassion and is filled with adventure, humor, and stunning visual beauty. For a film that is more than three hours long, the story is compelling enough and told with such emotional diversity that time seems suspended as the action unfolds and envelops the audience.

The film is epic in its scope and grandeur, yet it still has the feel of an intimate, personal drama. This effect is attributable to the story itself, which, although set during one of the most dramatic periods of U.S. history and dealing with such grand themes as the settling of the West and the final years of Native American freedom, still remains a very intimate tale, that of one man's search for personal fulfillment. Director Costner and screenwriter Michael Blake emphasize this intimacy by having Dunbar read passages from his journal in a voice-over narration and by telling the action almost exclusively from Dunbar's point of view. They also dramatize the story by punctuating the film with a diverse emotional texture, following intense dramatic scenes with quiet or humorous ones that again stress the personal drama of the story. This intimate emotional diversity is well illustrated during the three scenes in which the Sioux try to steal Dunbar's horse. In the first attempt, Dunbar is bathing in a nearby stream and must chase Kicking Bird away from the horse by running after him while stark naked. In the second attempt, three young Sioux boys try to steal the horse while Dunbar is asleep. When he hears them approaching, he finds his gun and rushes out of his tiny sleeping quarters, hitting his head on the top of the door and knocking himself unconscious while the boys ride away with his horse. The horse escapes by itself, however, and returns to the now snoring Dunbar. In the third attempt, a troop of the most fierce Sioux braves rides into Dunbar's camp, with Wind in His Hair screaming his defiance at Dunbar as Dunbar holds a pistol inches away from the warrior's face. After the braves have galloped away, Dunbar turns back toward his fort, staggers, and faints from the shock of the confrontation. Meanwhile, his horse has once again escaped from the Sioux and returns to find Dunbar passed out in the dirt. Each of these scenes is filled with intense drama which is later defused by comic humor, a dramatic pattern that is used effectively throughout the film and which gives the story a satisfying emotional diversity that maintains a level of action that is intimate and involving.

Another factor that allows the audience to willingly accept the action of the story is the low-key acting of the principals, most notably Costner's performance as Dunbar. Costner is surrounded by grandeur and spectacle, yet his reactions to his surroundings are almost deadpan. Costner's calmness, his subtle delivery, and his nearly deadpan expression are matched by Graham Greene's portrayal of Kicking Bird. Both actors emphasize a quiet curiosity that links their characters, making Greene's Kicking Bird a sympathetic and believable role model for Costner's Dunbar to emulate. Mary McDonnell's portrayal of Stands with a Fist also emphasizes the calmness and gentleness of her character, which makes it easy for the audience to accept Dunbar's attraction to her.

Costner and Blake are trying to present Native Americans in a much more favorable light than other Westerns of the past, which have usually concentrated on the plight of the noble white settlers and their battles against the savage, hostile natives. Yet the filmmakers come close to overly glamorizing the life of the Sioux. Overall, the portrayal seems accurate and is convincing from a dramatic point of view. What seems inaccurate is the portrayal of the white settlers and soldiers, who are all depicted as insane, stupid, or sadistic. Also, Costner's attempts to gain sympathy for his character—in the scenes in which he is repeatedly beaten by the soldiers and especially when the soldiers shoot the wolf—are maddeningly melodramatic and ring false when compared to the compelling believability of the rest of the film. Nevertheless, considering the dramatic scope and overall integrity of the rest of the film, Costner, his crew, and his cast must be commended for creating one of the most visually beautiful and dramatically powerful retellings of one of the oldest, archetypal mythic tales, that of a hero's journey to spiritual enlightenment. Costner, who believed so strongly in the film that he financed part of it with his own money, must also be praised for almost single-handedly reviving what many felt was a dead genre—the Western. Along with the horribly dated 1931 epic *Cimarron*, *Dances with Wolves* is only the second Western to win the Academy Award for Best Picture, an achievement that almost guarantees the resurrection of this most highly underrated and most purely American film genre.

Jim Kline

Reviews

Chicago Tribune. November 9, 1990, VII, p. 31.
The Hollywood Reporter. CCCXIV, November 5, 1990, p. 5.
Los Angeles Times. November 9, 1990, p. F1.
The New York Times. November 9, 1990, p. B1.
The New Yorker. LXVI, December 17, 1990, p. 115.
Newsweek. CXVI, November 19, 1990, p. 67.
Premiere. October, 1990, p. 84.
Smithsonian. XXI, November, 1990, p. 25.
Time. CXXXVI, November 12, 1990, p. 102.
Variety. November 5, 1990, p. 2.
The Washington Post. November 9, 1990, p. C1.

DAYS OF THUNDER

Production: Don Simpson and Jerry Bruckheimer; released by Paramount Pictures
Direction: Tony Scott
Screenplay: Robert Towne; based on a story by Towne and Tom Cruise
Cinematography: Ward Russell
Editing: Billy Weber and Chris Lebenzon
Art direction: Benjamin Fernandez and Thomas E. Sanders
Set decoration: Thomas L. Roysden
Sound: Charles M. Wilborn
Costume design: Susan Becker
Stunt coordination: Gary McCarty
Music: Hans Zimmer
MPAA rating: PG-13
Running time: 107 minutes

Principal characters:
Cole Trickle . . . . Tom Cruise
Harry Hogge . . . . Robert Duvall
Dr. Claire Lewicki . . . . Nicole Kidman
Tim Daland . . . . Randy Quaid
Rowdy Burns . . . . Michael Rooker
Russ Wheeler . . . . Cary Elwes
Big John . . . . Fred Dalton Thompson
Buck Bretherton . . . . John C. Reilly
Aldo Bennedetti . . . . Don Simpson

A major release in the summer of 1990, *Days of Thunder* featured Tom Cruise in an action film specially tailored to his image. The production reunited Cruise with director Tony Scott and producers Don Simpson and Jerry Bruckheimer—the team responsible for Cruise's blockbuster hit *Top Gun* (1986). The close resemblance between *Days of Thunder* and *Top Gun* escaped few reviewers or audience members. The film was heavily criticized and proved to be a box-office disappointment. Actually, the narrative structure of *Days of Thunder* is typical of many of Cruise's films, which over recent years have formulated a specific image for the popular young actor. An examination of these films reveals not only how certain images are constructed for high-profile, money-making actors but also how material is adapted to suit that image.

Cruise has appeared in a number of melodramas in which his character is a cocky young man who enters a male-dominated profession through the tutelage of an older father figure. The Cruise character turns out to be a natural at his craft, which forms a tight bond between the young man and his mentor. He then becomes romantically involved with a strong, older woman, and their relationship helps him to mature. Other characters in the narrative often include an archrival, who exists to challenge the Cruise character's skill and test his maturity. A disagreement or break with his mentor results in much soul-searching on the part of Cruise until the pair reunite to overcome the central challenge created or represented by the archrival.

A short survey of Cruise's films to date indicates that *Top Gun, The Color of Money* (1986), and *Cocktail* (1988) have followed this formula. In *Top Gun*, the archetype of the Tom Cruise film, the actor stars as Maverick, a brash fighter pilot whose flying skills land him in Top Gun, the navy's elite aviation training school. A beautiful but older instructor begins a romantic relationship with Maverick, which helps him to mature emotionally. A rival pilot competes with Maverick for honors at Top Gun until a personal tragedy results in Maverick's decision to drop out. With the support of an experienced officer who acts as his mentor, Maverick is later reunited with his group to help thwart an attack on a U.S. military vessel by an ambiguous enemy. *Top Gun* became the number-one film of 1986 (with $79.4 million in theatrical rentals) and established Cruise as a major adult actor. Prior to that, he was known primarily for roles that emphasized his status as a teen idol.

The Color of Money teamed Cruise with veteran star Paul Newman, who reprised the character of Fast Eddie Felson from *The Hustler* (1961). Cruise stars as Vincent, an unrestrained but naïve pool player whose natural talent attracts the attention of Fast Eddie. Newman's character becomes the young man's coach in the hopes of regaining the prestige and financial rewards he had enjoyed as a pool hustler in his youth. A streetwise woman serves as Cruise's manager and girlfriend, while an established top-money player represents his archrival. A major confrontation occurs when Fast Eddie ends his association with Vincent and returns to honest pool playing. The test of merit and skill is represented by a pool competition in Atlantic City in which Vincent purposefully throws his game with Fast Eddie in order to raise the odds against himself. In the final scene, Vincent is reunited with Fast Eddie but not as members of the same team; instead they are competitors in a solitary game to reveal who is the better player.

Cocktail is undoubtedly the weakest of the series, with Cruise wasted in a film that merely exploits his physical appearance. Here, Cruise plays a bartender who acquires his barroom skills from a master bartender, played by Bryan Brown. Both an older woman and a mature girl teach him about the responsibilities of relationships, while a clash with the other bartender over another woman leads Cruise's character down the path of self-discovery. Cruise's role in this film cemented his image as an eager young man who learns a craft from a seasoned father figure. Later performances in the Oscar-winning films *Rain Man* (1988) and *Born on the Fourth of July* (1989)—in which Cruise does not play this type of role—did little to alter this image.

Days of Thunder offers a well-crafted example of the Tom Cruise film in which all the characteristics fall neatly into place. Cruise stars as rookie stock-car driver, Cole Trickle, who is hired by a wealthy car salesman, Tim Daland (Randy Quaid), to race the NASCAR circuit in the South. This time around, the mentor figure is a veteran racing-team leader named Harry Hogge (Robert Duvall), who serves as a surrogate father as he teaches Cole the finer points of stock cars. Despite her assertion that race-car drivers are "infantile egomaniacs," Dr. Claire Lewicki (Nicole Kidman) reluctantly becomes involved with Cole after she meets him in the emergency room following an accident on the track. As with Kelly McGillis in *Top Gun*, Kidman's height and stature physically represent her superiority and maturity over the Cruise character. Cole battles two rivals in the film, veteran driver Rowdy Burns (Michael Rooker) and ruthless newcomer Russ Wheeler (Cary Elwes). Eventually Rowdy and Cole settle their differences, while Wheeler proves to be his true adversary.

Following the established formula, Cruise's character breaks with his mentor before realizing his true talent and worth. In *Days of Thunder*, this moment of self-discovery occurs after Cole's accident has made him afraid to race, causing the disbanding of his racing team. Recognizing that he "is more afraid of being nothing than (he) is of being hurt," the determined young driver enlists the aid of Harry and enters the Daytona 500. To the surprise of no one, Cole wins. The freeze frame that concludes the film is not of Cole and Claire but of Cole and Harry, emphasizing the importance of male bonding to the story line.

Aside from the narrative structure and central character, these films share a certain approach to setting. Each film uses a specific subculture as a backdrop—the military in *Top Gun*, the seedy world of pool halls and back alleys in *The Color of Money*, and the glamorous singles-bar scene in *Cocktail*. Each subculture features an established vocabulary, a special knowledge, and an arena, where Cruise's character must test his inner strength and prove his skills. In *Days of Thunder*, that subculture is the world of stock-car racing, a sport associated with but not exclusive to the South. Like the milieus of the other Cruise films (with the possible exception of *The Color of Money*), the unique characteristics of the racing environment have been obliterated in *Days of Thunder*. The subculture has been made to conform to the conventions of a Hollywood melodrama. Consequently, the sport has been homogenized for mainstream audiences.

Despite the sport's long-standing association with the South (most of the major tracks are located there), little exists in *Days of Thunder* to indicate this link. The South is merely a backdrop, not a force that propels the action or defines the characters. Few speak with Southern accents in the film. In terms of the major characters, only Michael Rooker and Robert Duvall portray Southerners, though their characters' heritage is never an issue. Actual participants in the sport, including champions Richard Petty, Junior Johnson, and Cale Yarborough, have maintained, even emphasized, their Southern identity to build a closeness with their fans. Aside from Harry Hogge's obvious disgust upon learning that Cole Trickle is a Yankee, the peculiarities of the region and the unique culture of its inhabitants have been omitted from the film to appeal to the broadest audience possible. Cruise's handsome Hollywood features and clean-cut image are at odds with the rough nature of the rural white Southern males who have traditionally dominated the sport, so the producers have eliminated that element.

A few of the early stock-car racers had been bootleggers, who honed their driving skills while hauling illegal alcohol in souped-up cars of their own making. Though a minority, these drivers were among the most proficient drivers and organizers, propagating their own legends with tall tales to the press and amazing feats of driving on the track. Little is made of this colorful history in *Days of Thunder* except for a scene in which Cole's racing team relaxes with a few quart jars of moonshine, courtesy of Harry, whose accent, personality, and skill recall the drivers of that earlier era of racing. The scene concludes with a practical joke in which some phony state troopers "arrest" the team for transporting moonshine across the state line. Though an indirect reference to the sport's heritage, only fans of the sport will understand its significance and the difference between Harry's generation and Cole's.

The noisy, gritty aspects of the sport are replaced by director Tony Scott's glamorous sunrise/sunset shots of the racetracks, which have been romanticized into arenas of personal honor by Scott's luxurious cinematography. In addition, the production team made extensive use of a number of cameras placed inside cars engaged in actual races, emphasizing the speed and danger of the sport over its dependency on finely tuned machinery and mechanical skills.

Though diehard stock-car fans may lament how *Days of Thunder* eliminated certain aspects of the sport to suit the image of its star, the film seems an idea whose time has come. The recent rise in box-office revenues for racing indicates the increased popularity of all forms of the sport across the country, a result, in part, of the use of in-car cameras at important races. As prominent celebrities have become interested in various forms of auto racing, including Cruise and Lorenzo Lamas, who joined such stars as Paul Newman and James Garner on the track, women spectators have increased to 43 percent of the overall racing audience. Racing has become big business as nationally based sponsors compete with one another to support popular drivers. As racing, including stock-car racing, pushes further into the mainstream culture, it is only natural that Hollywood would provide a big-budget, star-studded venue to open the doors wider.

Susan Doll

Reviews
Boxoffice. August, 1990, p. R59.
Chicago Tribune. June 27, 1990, V, p. 1.
Chicago Tribune. June 29, 1990, VII, p. C.
Films in Review. XLI, October, 1990, p. 481.
The Hollywood Reporter. CCCXIII, June 27, 1990, p. 10.
Los Angeles Times. June 27, 1990, p. F1.
The New York Times. June 27, 1990, p. B1.
The New Yorker. LXVI, July 16, 1990, p. 73.
Newsweek. CXVI, July 9, 1990, p. 65.
Time. CXXXVI, July 16, 1990, p. 87.
Variety. CCCXXXIX, June 27, 1990, p. 2.

DICK TRACY

Production: Warren Beatty for Touchstone Pictures, in association with Silver
Screen Partners IV; released by Buena Vista
Direction: Warren Beatty
Screenplay: Jim Cash and Jack Epps, Jr., with special consultant Bo Goldman;
based on characters created by Chester Gould
Cinematography: Vittorio Storaro
Editing: Richard Marks
Production design: Richard Sylbert (AA)
Art direction: Harold Michelson
Set decoration: Rick Simpson (AA)
Visual effects: Michael Lloyd and Harrison Ellenshaw
Special makeup effects: John Caglione, Jr. (AA) and Doug Drexler (AA)
Costume design: Milena Canonero
Music: Danny Elfman
Song score: Stephen Sondheim
Song: Stephen Sondheim, "Sooner or Later (I Always Get My Man)" (AA)
MPAA rating: PG
Running time: 110 minutes

Principal characters:

Dick Tracy	Warren Beatty
Big Boy Caprice	Al Pacino
Breathless Mahoney	Madonna
Tess Trueheart	Glenne Headley
Kid	Charlie Korsmo
Flattop	William Forsythe
Itchy	Ed O'Ross
Chief Brandon	Charles Durning
88 Keys	Mandy Patinkin
Lips Manlis	Paul Sorvino
Pruneface	R. G. Armstrong
Mumbles	Dustin Hoffman
D.A. Fletcher	Dick Van Dyke
Bug Bailey	Michael J. Pollard

One may disapprove of his purportedly womanizing offscreen ways, but it should
be evident that Warren Beatty's creative genius and crystal-clear vision have earned
for him a place among an elite group of master filmmakers. Despite Beatty's penchant for multiple takes and his predilection for agonizing over every decision, the
end result is nothing short of brilliant. Beatty has created in *Dick Tracy* a film that
looks unlike any other and has succeeded in bringing real-life dimensionality to
Chester Gould's long-running comic strip. With its unique primary Sunday comics

colors, impressive matte paintings, and backlot sets, *Dick Tracy* displays a visual depth reminiscent of an earlier time, when such film artistry was applauded. In fact, Beatty has achieved over the years a level of craftsmanship that is comparable in cinematic importance to that of the late director Orson Welles.

Dick Tracy is a sweetly simplistic tale of good versus evil, with a convoluted plot that keeps the viewer involved. The story revolves around the straitlaced police detective Dick Tracy (Beatty) and his attempts to put an end to the underworld dealings of criminal kingpin Big Boy Caprice (Al Pacino), a walnut-cracking crime lord with a penchant for bogus quotations, and his gang of grotesque accomplices, who include the demented deadly duo of Flattop (William Forsythe) and Itchy (Ed O'Ross). Big Boy has usurped the territory of Lips Manlis (Paul Sorvino), including the sexy chanteuse Breathless Mahoney (Madonna), and has rallied the City's crime bosses into one organized syndication. Aided by a mysterious, faceless villain known only as The Blank, the Mob maneuvers to frame Tracy and take control of the City.

As Tracy fends off evil at every turn, his personal life becomes increasingly complicated as well. His longtime sweetheart, Tess Trueheart (Glenne Headley), and the street urchin they unofficially adopt, the Kid (Charlie Korsmo), conspire to persuade Tracy to retire from the streets and take a safe desk job. Breathless, however, has other plans. Pop icon Madonna uses her own persona to play the character with such searing pain that even at her most camp, Breathless is never cartoonish. When she makes one final play for Tracy, she pleads: "You don't have to sleep with me. Just tell me you want to."

From impeccable matte paintings and set designs that combine to create a hauntingly beautiful yet generic world, to the use of shot foregrounding and backgrounding inspired by Welles's *Citizen Kane* (1941), the filmmakers produced a flawless film that not only looks but also feels like a comic strip. Even the violence is done in cartoon fashion, without a single drop of blood ever appearing on screen. Yet the characters are three-dimensional with very real and (particularly for the women) very adult emotions.

Unfortunately, *Dick Tracy* did not enjoy the same kind of box-office excitement as *Batman* (1989) did the previous summer. Technically, *Dick Tracy* is a more inspired film, yet its drawing power seemed to be hindered by several factors. First, Chester Gould's comic strip, which first appeared in 1931, lacks the emotional complexity and dark side that *Batman* offered (but was only vaguely hinted at in Tim Burton's highly flawed film). Further, *Batman* is a character more deeply ingrained in American culture, resulting from both comic books and the television show of the 1960's. In addition, *Batman* was able to capitalize on the star appeal of cult hero Jack Nicholson. Although a contemporary of Beatty, Nicholson has managed to maintain, and in fact strengthen, his popularity, while Beatty has appeared in relatively few films in the past ten years to which younger audiences can relate, has shunned the press, and has grown increasingly reclusive. His refusal to publicize his masterpiece, *Reds* (1981), is often cited for the film's weak reception by American audiences.

Few filmmakers have had to endure the scrutiny and relentless criticism that Warren Beatty has. Perhaps his sensuous good looks have stood in the way of public acclaim, but Beatty has been nominated for a total of eleven Academy Awards and has twice been nominated in all four of the acting, producing, directing, and writing categories—a feat shared only with Orson Welles. *Heaven Can Wait* (1978) is a charming update of *Here Comes Mr. Jordan* (1941), and the film for which Beatty won an Academy Award for Best Director, *Reds*, is a courageous biography of American leftist journalist and Communist sympathizer Jack Reed. Beatty burst onto the producing scene with *Bonnie and Clyde* (1967), an American film masterpiece that broke cinematic ground and shocked viewers by combining humor with graphically depicted violence.

The cast list of *Dick Tracy* is a tribute to Beatty's high regard as a director. Such respected actors as Dustin Hoffman, Charles Durning, and Paul Sorvino appear in cameo roles, as well as two of Beatty's *Bonnie and Clyde* costars, Estelle Parsons and Michael J. Pollard. Perhaps the most enjoyable surprise performance is that of Al Pacino, the intense actor whose previous work includes *The Godfather* (1972). As the hunchback Big Boy Caprice, Pacino unleashes a comic performance of immense proportions that seems to satirize his own past roles, particularly the crime lord in *Scarface* (1983). His role in *Dick Tracy* could easily have overshadowed the entire film, like Jack Nicholson's Joker in *Batman*, but to Beatty's credit, no one element overtakes the others.

Early in the film, the Kid tells Tess, "I don't like dames," to which she responds, "Good. Neither do I." Neither, apparently, does Warren Beatty, for the women in *Dick Tracy* are far from the helpless, mindless kind that populate the majority of today's films. Even Breathless, with her abundant cleavage and wanton ways, is anything but a "dumb broad," and Tess proves herself to be a self-sufficient, independent woman who remarks, "When you play in the street, it's part of the game. Just don't ask me to like it." Women in Beatty's films have always been intelligent and very adult.

The screenplay is credited to Jim Cash and Jack Epps, Jr., the duo noted for the insipid dialogue of such films as *Top Gun* (1986) and *Legal Eagles* (1986). The clever, incisive writing of *Dick Tracy* is undoubtedly more the work of Beatty and Bo Goldman, the renowned script doctor and writer of *Melvin and Howard* (1980) and *Shoot the Moon* (1982). It is difficult to believe that Cash and Epps could have conceived that when things begin to unravel for Big Boy, he would testily remind himself, "A man without a plan is no man. Nietzsche," or when Tracy threatens to sweat a confession out of Breathless under hot lights, that she would respond with this classic screenplay line: "I sweat a lot better in the dark."

Beatty's homage to the crime films of the 1930's is achieved with the use of montages that occur at crucial plot points. Beatty takes an inspired turn by juxtaposing sentimental, slow Stephen Sondheim songs against quicker-paced, action-packed cutting patterns, giving the montage sequences a slightly offbeat cadence.

Some critics chastised Beatty for his low-key portrayal of the square-jawed detective. His Tracy is a man of surprising vulnerability, combined with a smoldering sensuality, a quintessential man of the 1990's, facing the continuing dilemma of balancing work with love and family. Beatty knew that he could not merely re-create the sweetness and simplicity of the 1930's without a fresher perspective. It is unfortunate that the film had to be encumbered by excessive, gross merchandizing at the hands of Disney, but with its cohesive diagenetic world, *Dick Tracy* is an inspired piece of filmmaking that will no doubt leave an indelible mark on film history. The Academy of Motion Picture Arts and Sciences snubbed *Dick Tracy*, ignoring its director and failing to nominate the film for the Best Picture category. Despite the film's technical accomplishments, the simplicity of the story, while keeping with its comic strip origins, could not compete with the more "politically correct" message of first-time director Kevin Costner's revisionist Western, *Dances with Wolves* (1990; reviewed in this volume). The originality of *Dick Tracy* deserved to be publicly acknowledged by Beatty's fellow filmmakers; yet nobility of subject matter—specifically in the case of the inaccurate *Awakenings* (1990; reviewed in this volume)—and big box-office receipts—*Ghost* (1990; reviewed in this volume)—clearly clouded the voters' recognition of true artistic vision. One cannot help but question the criteria employed during the Academy's selection process; are good intentions more important than artistic endeavors?

Dick Tracy was preceded by the animated short *Roller Coaster Rabbit*, which marked the return of the characters from *Who Framed Roger Rabbit* (1988). While Steven Spielberg should be applauded for his attempt to return animation to a more sophisticated level than is prevalent on Saturday morning cartoons (with their lazy cutting patterns and simple "talking heads" approach), praise for this short should be kept in perspective. While the point-of-view shots from the roller coaster are imaginative and its self-reflexiveness addresses the film medium and animation techniques themselves, *Roller Coaster Rabbit* is far from original: Warner Bros.' *Duck a Muck* (1953) was the first animated film to display cartoon characters having conversations with their animators.

Patricia Kowal

Reviews
Boxoffice. August, 1990, p. R58.
Chicago Tribune. June 15, 1990, VII, p. 39.
Films in Review. XLI, October, 1990, p. 478.
The Hollywood Reporter. CCCXII, June 1, 1990, p. 4.
Los Angeles Times. June 15, 1990, p. F6.
The New Republic. CCIII, July 9 & 16, 1990, p. 32.
The New York Times. June 15, 1990, CXXXIX, p. B1.
The New Yorker. LXVI, July 2, 1990, p. 56.
Newsweek. CXV, June 25, 1990, p. 44.
Time. CXXXV, June 18, 1990, p. 74.
Variety. June 1, 1990, p. 3.

DIE HARD II
Die Harder

Production: Lawrence Gordon, Joel Silver, and Charles Gordon for Gordon
  Company and Silver Pictures; released by Twentieth Century-Fox
Direction: Renny Harlin
Screenplay: Steven E. de Souza and Doug Richardson; based on the novel
  58 Minutes, by Walter Wager
Cinematography: Oliver Wood
Editing: Stuart Baird and Robert A. Ferretti
Production design: John Vallone
Art direction: Christiaan Wagener
Set decoration: Robert Gould
Special effects: Al DiSarro
Visual effects: Industrial Light and Magic
Costume design: Marilyn Vance-Straker
Stunt coordination: Charles Picerni
Music: Michael Kamen
MPAA rating: R
Running time: 125 minutes

> *Principal characters:*
> John McClane .... Bruce Willis
> Holly McClane .... Bonnie Bedelia
> Dick Thornberg .... William Atherton
> Al Powell .... Reginald VelJohnson
> Colonel Stuart .... William Sadler
> Trudeau .... Fred Dalton Thompson
> Barnes .... Art Evans
> Lorenzo .... Denis Franz
> Captain Grant .... John Amos
> Ramon Esperanza .... Franco Nero
> Samantha Coleman .... Sheila McCarthy

In the summer of 1990, a period notable for its numerous sequels and ubiquitous violence, there was but one aesthetic virtue: to be unabashed. Films such as *Die Hard II: Die Harder* and *Robocop II* (1990; reviewed in this volume) at least made no pretense of a social message; the entertainment was admittedly exploitative, based on a game of special effects one-upmanship. Nevertheless, the National Coalition on Television Violence condemned the action films, which collectively cost at least $250 million to produce, for the high number of violent acts per hour. While not included in the tally, *Die Hard II: Die Harder* easily tops the list.

The sequel to *Die Hard* (1988) uses the exact same premise as the original film.

Detective John McClane (Bruce Willis) is about to be reunited with his wife, Holly McClane (Bonnie Bedelia), for Christmas, when he stumbles upon a terrorist operation that endangers them both. Given the incompetence of the local police, it is up to McClane to outfox the well-armed terrorists and save his wife. Meanwhile, an unscrupulous reporter, Dick Thornberg (William Atherton), jeopardizes the situation when he broadcasts sensitive information. Even Al Powell (Reginald VelJohnson), the chair-bound, Twinky-eating black police officer who aided McClane in *Die Hard*, appears in a brief cameo.

Die Hard II which opened on the Fourth of July, was pegged at once as an all-American version of the perennial James Bond series. The qualities upon which the comparison was based included the high production values, state-of-the-art special effects, and preposterous action sequences. The crucial difference, however, is that McClane is blue-collar. Also—so far, at least—McClane's *raison d'être* has been the protection of his career-oriented wife. In fact, the violence in both *Die Hard* films appears to be a displacement of McClane's repressed emotions about his wife's increasing independence and social status. In *Die Hard*, after all, Holly McClane relocates to Los Angeles without her recalcitrant husband to pursue a lucrative job. By the film's end, the entire corporation and its new headquarters are in ruins.

Die Hard II begins with flat-footed exposition in which McClane, now famous, explains that he has moved to Los Angeles and is now in Washington, D.C., awaiting the arrival of his wife, in order to spend Christmas vacation with his in-laws. These details are delivered rapid-fire to an airport police officer issuing him a parking ticket. Much of the setup is presented in such an obvious manner, which is unfortunate, since the film devotes much time to putting the different plot elements into place.

In *Die Hard II*, Ramon Esperanza (Franco Nero), a Central American dictator and "the biggest drug dealer in the world," is being flown into Washington, D.C., to stand trial. Meanwhile, Colonel Stuart (William Sadler) and other former Army Special Forces commandos prepare to seize the airport and rescue Esperanza. Like Stuart, Esperanza is a rabid anti-Communist. When the U.S. Congress cut military aid in response to human rights violations, Esperanza resorted to drug trade for additional income, presumably with Stuart's help. *Die Hard II* provides a post-Cold War interpretation of recent U.S. foreign policy in Central America and the Caribbean. As a result, the right-wing zealots who shaped that policy are placed on a par with the usual Latin American villains. As a character, Esperanza is clearly based upon dictator Manuel Noriega, who was brought to the United States to stand trial after the U.S. invasion of Panama. Like Noriega, Esperanza is depicted as a long-time U.S. ally in the ostensible struggle against communism. In appearance, however, Esperanza looks more like Fidel Castro, with military fatigues, a long, gray beard, and a trademark cigar, while the diversion of funds that brings Esperanza to trial refers more to the Contragate scandal than to Panama.

Colonel Stuart's crack unit commandeers a nearby church as its base of operations, since the main electrical cable runs through the church grounds. In contrast to the high-tech terrorists, McClane is presented as someone uncomfortable with even basic technologies. Instead, he relies upon his instinct when he spots two of the terrorists in the airport, and follows them. McClane confronts the two men and shoots one, who carries a Glock 17, a porcelain gun used by terrorists to elude metal detectors. Despite the evidence that something is about to happen, the airport police captain, Lorenzo (Denis Franz), refuses to investigate.

Undaunted, McClane follows Lorenzo to the control tower and confronts Trudeau (Fred Dalton Thompson), the chief air traffic controller. Just then, the runway lights shut down, and Colonel Stuart cuts into the Federal Aviation Administration's (FAA) hot line and delivers his demands. McClane and Samantha Coleman (Sheila McCarthy), a television reporter, are evicted from the now-disabled control tower, while Trudeau makes plans to divert the incoming planes with enough fuel to reach another airport. Meanwhile, Barnes (Art Evans), the airport's chief engineer, sets out with an airport police escort to borrow new hardware that can be used to build an alternative control tower.

McClane refuses to be excluded from the action and arrives in time to save Barnes from an ambush that nevertheless leaves the police officers dead and the vital hardware in flames. To make matters worse, Colonel Stuart decides to punish the airport for Barnes's attempt to restore power. Posing as an air controller, Stuart signals an airplane from London to land and then resets ground level at minus two hundred feet on the control panel. The disabled tower is unable to warn the plane, which prompts McClane to grab two makeshift torches and head for the runway. McClane's efforts fail to stop the plane from crashing; and the plane is quickly consumed in a fireball, although it is supposed to have been low on fuel. The film, however, works against the illogic of its special effects on an emotional level. Before the crash, several interior shots of the plane linger on the passengers as they prepare to land, so that the viewer identifies with them. The crash, then, becomes perhaps the most extreme example of a film's manipulation of audience expectations, involving as it does several hundred lives. While McClane lies on the runway sobbing, Captain Grant (John Amos) arrives with a Special Forces platoon. Since Grant taught Stuart everything he knows, he—and not McClane—will be the one who can outfox Stuart.

Meanwhile, the ever-resourceful Barnes manages to convert the outer marker beacon into a one-way voice transmitter and warns the other planes not to land. Reporter Dick Thornberg, who happens to be on the same plane as Holly McClane, overhears and tapes the transmission. In his constant bid to break into the network news, he phones in the story live, wreaking havoc at the airport. Holly, who knocked out Dick's front teeth in *Die Hard* after he interviewed her children, grabs a stun gun and zaps Dick in mid-sentence.

With Captain Grant on the scene, McClane's talents remain unrecognized. Still, he manages to reach Esperanza—who has taken control of the plane—after he lands, but before Colonel Stuart's men arrive. McClane shoots Esperanza in the shoulder but is soon outgunned and forced to retreat to the cockpit. When Stuart orders the men to toss their hand grenades into the cockpit, McClane quickly straps himself into the pilot's seat and ejects himself. The scene is one of the more innovative uses of special effects. Shot from overhead, the viewers see McClane hurled from the explosion and toward the camera until he is in close-up, and then begin to fall back to earth.

McClane is now allowed to join Grant's unit in an assault on the church. Stuart's men manage to escape on snowmobiles, even after McClane gives pursuit and shoots at them point-blank. It is at this point that he realizes that Grant and his men are part of Stuart's operation and had used blanks to fool the police. McClane, however, is unable to reach the hangar where Stuart and Grant have reconnoitered. Coleman, a reporter as persistent as Thornberg but not as unscrupulous, offers her helicopter. In the most improbable scene in the film, the helicopter deposits McClane on the wing of the plane as it attempts to take off. McClane jams the flaps with his coat, so that Grant and then Stuart are forced onto the wing for some one-on-one combat. Grant is thrown into the engine, which curiously fails to shut it down. At last, McClane himself is thrown from the wing, but he manages to pull the fuel dump lever. The plane speeds down the runway, leaving a trail of fuel behind it, which McClane then lights.

In a replay of the first plane explosion, the audience now sees McClane sprawled in the snow laughing. The explosion and fire trail will provide a guide for his wife's plane to land. When at last the couple is reunited, Holly's first expression proves unintentionally funny: "Oh John, why does this keep happening to us?" The answer: box office. In any case, these violent interludes appear to be the real and metaphoric basis of their marriage.

Chon A. Noriega

Reviews

Baltimore Sun. July 3, 1990, sec. E, p. 1.
Baltimore Sun. July 4, 1990, sec. G, p. 1.
Boxoffice. August, 1990, p. R57.
Chicago Tribune. July 4, 1990, V, p. 1.
The Christian Science Monitor. July 6, 1990, p. 12.
The Hollywood Reporter. CCCXIII, June 28, 1990, p. 6.
Los Angeles Times. July 3, 1990, p. F1.
The New York Times. July 3, 1990, p. B1.
Newsweek. CXVI, July 9, 1990, p. 66.
Premiere. IV, December, 1990, p. 36.
Variety. June 28, 1990, p. 2.
Video. XIV, February, 1991, p. 53.
The Wall Street Journal. July 5, 1990, p. A9.

EDWARD SCISSORHANDS

Production: Denise Di Novi and Tim Burton; released by Twentieth Century-Fox
Direction: Tim Burton
Screenplay: Caroline Thompson; based on a story by Tim Burton and Thompson
Cinematography: Stefan Czapsky
Editing: Richard Halsey
Production design: Bo Welch
Art direction: Tom Duffield
Set design: Rick Heinrichs, Paul Sonski, and Ann Harris
Set decoration: Cheryl Carasik
Sound: Petur Hliddal
Special makeup effects: Stan Winston
Costume design: Colleen Atwood
Music: Danny Elfman
MPAA rating: PG-13
Running time: 98 minutes

Principal characters:

Edward Scissorhands	Johnny Depp
Kim	Winona Ryder
Peg	Dianne Wiest
Jim	Anthony Michael Hall
Bill	Alan Arkin
Joyce	Kathy Baker
Kevin	Robert Oliveri
Helen	Conchata Ferrell
The inventor	Vincent Price

Edward Scissorhands is a modern fairy tale complete with princess, an evil ogre, and an enchanted, artificial boy who is fashioned out of machinery parts by an eccentric inventor. Mixing themes from such films as *The Bride of Frankenstein* (1935), *The Wizard of Oz* (1939), *Pinocchio* (1940), and *Willy Wonka and the Chocolate Factory* (1971), along with large doses of satire aimed at modern suburban society, *Edward Scissorhands* tells a simple moral tale that is both charming and profoundly moving.

The film begins with a prologue. An old woman stares out the window of her comfortable suburban home, watching a light snowfall. The woman's young granddaughter lies in a large bed and, glancing out the window, asks her grandmother to explain why it snows. The woman then begins to relate the story about the boy who had scissors for hands. The scene shifts to a small suburban community with identical-looking houses, except that each house is painted a different bright, basic color. Peg Boggs (Dianne Wiest) is seen making her rounds as the local Avon Lady representative and decides to pay a visit to the mysterious, unique, gothic-style mansion on the hill at the end of the block. When Peg breaks through the mansion's tangled outer brush, she is shocked and pleased to see that the inner area around the building contains a beautifully manicured garden featuring fabulous statues clipped out of bushes and hedges.

Peg receives no answer to her knocks, but she enters anyway and wonders at the sight of massive, fanciful machinery. She walks up the ancient stone steps to a loft, where she spots a figure cowering in the shadows. When the figure approaches her, Peg nearly flees in terror. The figure is a young man dressed in black leather, his pale white face covered with scars, his long, stringy black hair sticking nearly straight up, and his hands a mass of sharp, daggerlike scissors. Despite his nightmarish appearance, the young man's face beams a look of total innocence and helplessness. When Peg asks him his name, he replies Edward (Johnny Depp) in a timid voice. Peg recognizes the look of helplessness in his face and decides to take him home with her. Peg shows the dazed and curious Edward around her house and tries to treat his facial scars with some of her Avon products. Later, around the dinner table as he struggles to skewer his food with his awkward scissor hands, Edward meets Peg's husband Bill (Alan Arkin) and their young son Kevin (Robert Oliveri), both of whom try to remain casual about Edward's strange appearance and habits.

Soon the gossipy neighbors are buzzing with curiosity about the strange newcomer living with the Boggses. Finally, they congregate on the Boggses' front steps and persuade Peg to arrange a barbecue so they can meet Edward. During the barbecue, Edward opens beer cans with his sharp scissor hands, roasts his food shish kebab-style on his blades over the barbecue, and samples various dishes supplied by the curious women neighbors. He also shows off some of the hedge sculptures that he has cut in the Boggses' backyard, one of them in the shape of a dinosaur, another in the shape of the Boggs family members. Soon Edward is fashioning other unique hedge sculptures for the neighbors, which gives the bland suburban tract a touch of whimsy. Later, he graduates to pet grooming and finally to hairstyling, creating fabulously unique haircuts for the women. He also accompanies Kevin to school as a show-and-tell subject and creates an impressive series of cutout dolls. Edward has become a celebrity, a delightful, curious addition to the otherwise nondescript neighborhood.

When the Boggses' daughter Kim returns from a camping trip, she is shocked to find Edward in her bedroom. Gradually, she realizes that he is harmless and endowed with a sweet innocence that contrasts sharply with the brutish character of her boyfriend, Jim (Anthony Michael Hall). Edward is smitten by Kim's beauty and stares at her with a worshipful longing. Jim laughs off Edward's presence, treating him as a freak. With the coaxing of Peg and sexy neighbor Joyce (Kathy Baker), Edward looks into the prospect of opening up his own beauty salon. He accompanies Joyce to the site of the shop, and Joyce tries to seduce him in the back room. Edward, not understanding Joyce's actions, runs out of the shop. Later, he accompanies Peg to the local bank and applies for a loan. His loan is quickly turned down due to his nonexistent job and credit history.

Soon after the fiasco at the bank, Jim persuades Kim to elicit Edward's help in breaking into Jim's own house and stealing his stingy father's elaborate electronics equipment, which Jim hopes to sell so that he can buy a van. Eager to please Kim, Edward agrees to help by using his blades to pick the locks on the room that contains the electronics equipment. After successfully opening the locked room, however, Edward sets off the burglar alarm and is trapped inside the room while the others flee. Edward is arrested for breaking and entering and, after spending a night in jail, is eventually released into the Boggses' custody. Thinking that he attempted the robbery in order to raise money for his beauty salon, Bill Boggs tries to give Edward a crash course in morality. Edward, however, is more interested in knowing about how Kim feels for him. Kim realizes that Edward is in love with her, and she too begins to feel strong emotions for him, especially after the robbery when he took full blame for the incident in order to protect her.

Christmas approaches, and the Boggses prepare for their annual Christmas party to which the entire neighborhood is invited. The neighbors have begun to turn on Edward, however, after the robbery attempt and Joyce's claim that Edward tried to rape her in the beauty shop. While the Boggs family adorns their household with Christmas decorations, Edward fashions a huge ice sculpting of an angel in the front yard. After Jim arrives and provokes him, however, Edward runs away in a fit of rage. Kim criticizes Jim, who skulks away to get drunk. Meanwhile, Edward roams the neighborhood, randomly chopping down his own hedge sculptures. Finally, after the neighbors call the police, he sneaks back to the Boggses' house and finds Kim alone. Kim admits that she is in love with him and asks Edward to hold her. His reply is heartbreaking: "I can't," he says in his childlike voice. Kim snuggles next to him as he stares at her in bewilderment, thinking back to the days when his lonely, eccentric creator (Vincent Price) built him out of machinery parts, instructed him in the ways of the world, and then died before he could fashion Edward with hands.

When Edward awakes from his reverie, he notices Kevin walking down the street, while Jim and a drunken friend drive recklessly down the street in a van. Edward rushes out of the house just in time to push Kevin out of the way of the van. His action is misunderstood, however, when he accidentally cuts Kevin. A crowd of angry neighbors forms and hurls insults at Edward. Then Jim shows up and attacks him. Edward injures Jim, then runs back to his old mansion on the hill, followed by the police and later by the neighbors. Kim follows too and sneaks into the mansion, where she finds Edward cowering in the shadows of the attic. When she tells Edward that she loves him, Jim suddenly appears with a gun and begins to shoot at Edward. A fight erupts, and Jim falls out of a window to his death. Realizing the hopelessness of his situation, Edward turns to Kim and says goodbye. A tearful Kim leaves Edward and returns to the crowd of neighbors, telling them that both Jim and Edward were killed in the fight.

The scene then returns to the old woman and her granddaughter. It becomes apparent that the little girl's grandmother is, in fact, Kim. The girl asks her if Edward is still living in the mansion, and she replies that he is. When the girl asks how she can be so sure, the old woman replies that long ago before Edward made his visit, it never snowed in the neighborhood, but since he returned to his mansion it has snowed ever since. The scene then shifts to the mansion on the hill where the ageless Edward furiously cuts at a huge slab of ice, the snowlike cuttings flying out of the window and falling across the community below.

Edward Scissorhands, with its fanciful sets—cartoonish sculptures, a gloomy and enchanted castle filled with strange machines shaped like human legs and torsos, its quirky suburban housing tract with each house the same except for its color—and the lighthearted attitude of the neighbors when confronted with the bizarre, has the feel and flavor of a whimsical fairy tale. Along with the whimsy, however, is wickedly funny satire aimed at modern society's inability to deal with anything unique or innovative. When Edward first appears, he is treated as something of a curiosity, a diversion from the community's normal, boring routine. His celebrity status depends on his blatantly obvious physical deformity, which is unique enough to earn him an appearance on the local television talk show modeled after other contemporary television interview programs, which usually feature people with sensationalistic habits or beliefs (transvestites, neo-Nazis, or Satan worshippers). When Edward's uniqueness becomes commonplace, when his extraordinary talents have become trivialized to the point of blandness and then later exploited and corrupted by the selfish purposes of others, the society that first labeled him a harmless diversion now treats him as an untrustworthy freak to be shunned and ultimately banished. Ironically, Edward himself longs to be part of this creatively bankrupt community. Like Pinocchio and, most especially, the monster from *The Bride of Frankenstein*, he longs to be normal but ultimately realizes he can never fit into a society that rewards conformity and distrusts the unique and unusual.

The impact of the film's serious underlying theme is made more effective because it is wrapped and delivered in such an offbeat, colorfully enchanting veneer. The film's effectiveness is also enhanced by the fact that its message is presented more visually than verbally. For example, to illustrate the almost robotlike routine of the community, there is an amusing scene of the women neighbors gathered on a street corner gossiping about Edward, then scattering as their husbands drive up one by one in a long parade of cars, creating a mini traffic jam as they arrive home from work. Edward's character is established almost completely without dialogue, his thoughts and feelings communicated by his expressions and actions. Johnny Depp, who is brilliant as the innocent, compassionate Edward, studied Charlie Chaplin's movements in his classic silent films while preparing for the role.

Director and writer Tim Burton, known for his colorfully cartoonish flourishes and eccentric characters in such films as *Pee-wee's Big Adventure* (1985), *Beetlejuice* (1988), and *Batman* (1989), has finally populated a film with actors that do justice to his distinctive visual style. Burton's previous films have all contained an exciting, toylike artificiality, yet his ability to generate exciting performances from his actors has been sporadic at best. In *Edward Scissorhands*, however, the entire cast is uniformly excellent, especially Dianne Wiest as the eternally optimistic Peg, Kathy Baker as the exaggeratedly sexy Joyce, Alan Arkin as the bland, unfazed Bill, and Winona Ryder as beautiful, ethereal Kim who, along with Depp as Edward, gives the most emotional depth to her character. Danny Elfman, who has written the musical scores for all of Burton's films, surpasses his previous successes with his music for *Edward Scissorhands*. Mixing musical themes that conjure up such works as the music from Walt Disney's *Pinocchio*, Peter Ilich Tchaikovsky's *The Nutcracker* (especially "The Dance of the Sugar Plum Fairy"), and the song, "Sunrise, Sunset," from *Fiddler on the Roof* (1971), Elfman's use of full orchestra and boys' choir perfectly complements the fairy-tale wonder of the story.

The overall effect of the film is one of a lighthearted, yet profoundly touching, fable. Edward, horribly disfigured, his ominous, knife-like blades a threat to himself and society, is actually more human, compassionate, and loving than the people around him, who have sacrificed their humanity for conformity. Although he is unable to touch anyone physically, Edward does touch one other person deeply and profoundly and, in doing so, moves the viewing audience with his childlike simplicity and sincerity.

Jim Kline

Reviews
Chicago Tribune. December 14, 1990, VII, p. 41.
Commonweal. CXVIII, February 8, 1991, p. 100.
The Hollywood Reporter. CCCXV, December 3, 1990, p. 7.
Los Angeles Times. December 7, 1990, p. F1.
The New York Times. December 7, 1990, p. B1.
The New Yorker. LXVI, December 17, 1990, p. 116.
Newsweek. December 10, 1990, p. 87.
Premiere. October, 1990, p. 73.
Time. CXXXVI, December 10, 1990, p. 87.
Variety. December 3, 1990, p. 2.
The Washington Post. December 14, 1990, p. B1.

THE FIELD

Origin: Great Britain
Released: 1990
Released in U.S.: 1990
Production: Noel Pearson for Granada Film; released by Avenue Pictures
Direction: Jim Sheridan
Screenplay: Jim Sheridan; based on the play by John B. Keane
Cinematography: Jack Conroy
Editing: J. Patrick Duffner
Production design: Frank Conway
Art direction: Frank Hallinan Flood
Set decoration: Josie MacAvin
Sound: Kieran Horgan
Makeup: Tommie Manderson
Costume design: Joan Bergin
Music: Elmer Bernstein
MPAA rating: PG-13
Running time: 107 minutes

Principal characters:
Bull McCabe	Richard Harris
Bird O'Donnell	John Hurt
The American	Tom Berenger
Tadgh McCabe	Sean Bean
Widow	Frances Tomelty
Maggie	Brenda Fricker
Tinker girl	Jenny Conroy
Father Doran	Sean McGinley
Flanagan	John Cowley

Ireland has been immortalized in the literature of William Butler Yeats, John Millington Synge, and James Joyce, yet it is against the background of the hardship and turmoil of the potato famine that Ireland is most remembered. *The Field* deals with the generation that remained in Ireland, rather than emigrate to the New World. These were mostly simple country folk who lived by their wits and hard work. Writer-director Jim Sheridan, who portrayed Christy Brown in *My Left Foot* (1989) extremely successfully, delves into yet another aspect of Irish life, this time through the character of Bull McCabe (Richard Harris).

Scraping a meager existence by milking cows and growing vegetables, the McCabe family barely manages to make a living. Maggie (Brenda Fricker) and Bull have not spoken a single word in more than eighteen years. Their son, Tadgh (Sean Bean), shows no interest in making anything of a life for himself. Bull is very proud of his field, cultivated over the years with baskets of seaweed carried up from the shores. Bull's livelihood is threatened when the field is put up for auction by the owner. Thinking that he has the right to buy the field outright, even before the field goes to auction, Bull gathers together his life savings, which he has kept in small cups and pots dotted around the house. These entire life savings amount to fifty pounds, which he offers the auctioneer. The offer is refused. When Bull tries to buy the field at the auction, an Irish-American developer (Tom Berenger) easily outbids Bull. In his rage, Bull warns the American that he does not know what he is doing in trying to take this field from him and his family. One evening, while the men of the village are socializing over their pints of beer, Bull is informed that the American has gone down to the river. Seizing his opportunity, Bull confronts the American and has his son fight him in order to drive home the point that the field belongs to the McCabe family. Overtaken by fury, Bull crashes the American's head against a rock—killing him. All police investigations fail to find the culprit and Bull is never charged with the murder.

Outwardly, *The Field* deals with the intrusion of an outsider who believes that money will buy both the rights to a piece of Ireland and its tradition. Bull has nurtured his field to the point that there is nothing more in life to live for. When that reason for living is threatened, he becomes a man obsessed. Tradition plays a very important part in the lives and culture of the Irish, and since the setting is in the 1930's, memories of the great potato famine (1845-1849) still play an important part in how people view life. Bull's own parents had rented this field, and he had dutifully taken on the same task. In a sense, the American entered a world that was still firmly rooted in the past, and money cannot buy a piece of tradition. Bull's own traditional ways are equally being challenged, and his belief is that what was done in the past should carry on into the future. With so much invested in the field, he believes that he has a right to it that is above the law.

From the very first words that are uttered by Bull McCabe, it is clear that his field holds some dark and mysterious secret. Yet, the focus of the film moves away from developing this theme and takes up with the story of his son, Tadgh. This has the effect of throwing the first section of the story into two separate parts without there being any obvious connection between them. By taking up the story of Tadgh McCabe, the real story concerning the field is eventually discovered, but this method has the effect of creating a lull in the film. When the father and son both attend the same Saturday night dance, Bull encourages Tadgh to dance with a nice lass from the village. Tadgh has his eye on a pretty but rough redheaded gypsy girl (Jenny Conroy). In his usual brassy way, Bull stops his son from dancing with the gypsy and starts dancing an Irish jig. The company enjoys the revelry. Tadgh is embarrassed into dancing as fast with his partner as Bull is dancing with the gypsy girl. Tadgh's partner falls to the ground and Tadgh rushes from the dance hall. This is the first of many incidents in which Bull tries to make a man of Tadgh, in Bull's view, and utterly fails. To Bull, the gypsy girl and her culture represent everything that is abhorrent to him. They are a displaced people without any land, and he will not have his son associate with those who have no respect or love for the land. In Bull's opinion, traveling people—like the gypsies—do not care about the land and its intrinsic value. While this piece of pastureland may appear to the casual observer as insignificant, to the proud and intransigent Bull the field represents stability, ownership, and family tradition.

Little by little, Bull is almost forced into revealing his innermost secrets. One afternoon, without any regard for another man's privacy, he storms into the house of Father Doran (Sean McGinley). Without explanation, Bull demands the reason that his piece of property should be so interesting to the American. Neither the priest nor the American appear particularly interested in his plight. Realizing the possibility of defeat, Bull softens and begins to bare his soul before the two men. This is one of Harris' finest moments in the film. He brings to the part a realism that makes his revelations all the more heart wrenching. He plays the part of Bull McCabe in a way that embodies the man's pain and helplessness, while at the same time showing his steadfast resolve to hold onto his tiny parcel of land. During the Great Famine, Bull's brother had been sent away to America because the field could not support all his family. Indeed, his mother had died bringing in the harvest, and she lay unattended until evening when the other men had finished their grueling day's work. Bull explains that the field means more to him than they will ever know, and he leaves with the vow that neither the church nor the legal profession will stand in the way of him keeping the field. One dark secret that Bull does not reveal that eventful afternoon is that he believes that he was the cause of his eldest son's suicide.

Faced with an American with a seemingly unlimited supply of money, an indifferent priest, a son who has little interest in the family field, and the threat of eviction from the only tangible property belonging to him, Bull McCabe is finally driven to despair. While the similarity between William Shakespeare's King Lear and Bull may be only coincidental, one does exist. Perhaps both men mistakenly put great stock in children who did not share the same values, and neither of them would listen to reason when it was offered. Sorrow upon sorrow is now heaped on the head of Bull, whose only wish in life was to see his field passed on to his son. Like Lear, Bull also has his fool who is constantly at his side. Affectionately known by the name of Bird O'Donnell (John Hurt), Bull relies on him more than he will ever admit. Just as the simple relationship between King Lear and the fool is touching, equally there is a realization that Bull depends on this half-wit for comfort and advice, even if Bull does treat him harshly at times. Hurt's portrayal of the fool-like character is masterful in its execution. Unlike other cultures, early twentieth century Ireland permitted the simple-minded person to remain a part of village life, rather than to be institutionalized. Bird is a constant companion to Bull, a sort of unpaid village adviser, as there is nothing that Bull does not know concerning the happenings in and around the village. Bird, like his counterpart in *King Lear*, warns Bull of the consequences of his actions, but Bull pays little heed to his words.

The message of *The Field* is clear and strong—the famine of the mid-1800's is still causing considerable pain and torment. By devoting every ounce of his energy to the preservation of his field, Bull has lost his sense of proportion. When the body of the American is pulled from the lake, Bull realizes that his time has run out. There is nothing left for Bull to live for, and in a last mad act of despair, he drives his herd of cattle over the edge of the cliff to their deaths. Tragedy plays one final scene. Tadgh, trying to avert his father's madness, is thrown over the cliff by the advancing animals. As Bull's son lies before him, lifeless on the rugged Irish coast, and with murder on his hands, Bull slashes violently at the waves of the advancing sea in an effort to stop the ocean from taking away his son. Like the old mythical Irish character Cuchulainn, Bull walks further into the white surf, leaving nothing for any future McCabe generation.

Richard G. Cormack

Reviews

Boxoffice. December, 1990, p. R90.
The Christian Science Monitor. January 4, 1991, p. 12.
The Hollywood Reporter. CCCXV, December 13, 1990, p. 9.
Los Angeles. XXXV, December, 1990, p. 218.
Los Angeles Press Telegraph. February 9, 1991, p. C5.
Los Angeles Times. December 20, 1990, p. F11.
Los Angeles Times. December 31, 1990, p. F7.
National Catholic Reporter. XXVII, January 11, 1991, p. 22.
The New York Times. December 21, 1990, p. B6.
Premiere. February, 1991, p. 112.
San Francisco Chronicle. January 11, 1991, p. E4.
Variety. September 17, 1990, p. 2.
The Village Voice. January 1, 1991, p. 62.
The Washington Post. January 25, 1991, p. D7.

FLATLINERS

Production: Michael Douglas and Rick Bieber for Stonebridge Entertainment;
 released by Columbia Pictures
Direction: Joel Schumacher
Screenplay: Peter Filardi
Cinematography: Jan De Bont
Editing: Robert Brown
Production design: Eugenio Zanetti
Art direction: Jim Dultz
Set decoration: Anne L. Kuljian
Special effects: Philip Cory and Hans Metz
Sound: David MacMillan
Costume design: Susan Becker
Stunt coordination: Bill Erickson
Music: James Newton Howard
MPAA rating: R
Running time: 111 minutes

Principal characters:

Nelson Wright	Kiefer Sutherland
Rachel Mannus	Julia Roberts
David Labraccio	Kevin Bacon
Joe Hurley	William Baldwin
Randy Steckle	Oliver Platt
Winnie Hicks	Kimberly Scott
Billy Mahoney	Joshua Rudoy
Rachel's father	Benjamin Mouton
Nelson (as a child)	Aeryk Egan
Winnie (as a child)	Kesha Reed
Anne	Hope Davis
Uncle Dave	Jim Ortlieb
Labraccio (as a child)	John Joseph Duda

The premise for *Flatliners* is a good one. For modern pioneers, the most logical "place" to explore next is life after death. Accounts from those who have died and been brought back to life by the advances of modern medicine have been tantalizing. What if instead of accidentally dying and accidentally being brought back to life, *Flatliners* asks, explorers went into a controlled experiment in which they experienced death with the sure knowledge that they would be revived. This voyage is the vision of medical student Nelson Wright (Kiefer Sutherland). To aid him in his illicit experiment, he enlists four of the brightest of his fellow students: Rachel Mannus (Julia Roberts), Dave Labraccio (Kevin Bacon), Joe Hurley (William Baldwin), and

Randy Steckle (Oliver Platt). At first, the four are reluctant to participate, but each finds his or her own reason for finally helping Nelson become the first death scout.

Nelson is purposely frozen until he flatlines—a condition in which he has neither a heartbeat nor brainwaves. He is given one minute to explore and then the team quickly moves into emergency revival routines. Recovered, Nelson marvels at his sharpened senses, but later, in an alley in Chinatown, a far away dragging sound he hears is soon discovered to be his long-dead dog, Champ. Nelson does not tell his coconspirators about this discovery, and soon a bidding war evolves to see who will go next. Although Rachel wants to go, Hurley wins when he bids to stay dead one minute and thirty seconds. While dead, ladies' man Hurley relives his life with an emphasis on the women he has known. The next explorer is Labraccio who outbids Rachel with a time of two minutes and twenty seconds. Appropriately, Labraccio "dies" on Halloween, but while on the table, Nelson starts fooling around, counting incorrectly on purpose and miscalculating time. Frantically, the others are finally able to revive Labraccio.

During all this experimenting, however, strange things have begun to happen. Nelson has again seen Champ and has followed him through subway corridors. There he runs into a little boy (Joshua Rudoy) he saw during his death experience. This little boy, however, assaults Nelson. Later he appears in Nelson's apartment and again attacks him. Hurley, who has made a habit of videotaping the women he has sex with without their permission, suddenly believes that he is seeing one of his private tapes playing on a school television. Later, they seem to be on televisions in a store window. For Labraccio, trouble comes in the form of a little black girl (Kesha Reed), who starts hurling epithets at him while riding on the subway. No one else sees Champ, the little boy, the videotapes, or the little black girl, only those who saw them in their death experiences. Furthermore, none tells the others about what he has seen.

Finally, it is Rachel's turn. Rachel, who has been collecting the death fears and experiences of patients in the hospital, flatlines and begins to relive her father's suicide: It happened when she was a little girl, and her mother says that it was Rachel's fault. It is a terrible and unfounded guilt with which she has been living for years. While Rachel is "dead," water short circuits the electrical system, and she is out for five minutes. She is revived and later sees her father (Benjamin Mouton) in a washroom mirror. He again appears as the cadaver she is dissecting in anatomy class.

The group now discovers that each has brought back something from the death experience. Labraccio has brought back Winnie Hicks, a black girl he teased as a child. He finds her (Kimberly Scott) living nearby and apologizes to her to atone for his behavior. Similarly, Rachel relives her father's suicide, seeing it for what it was: the desperate act of a drug addict. He asks for her forgiveness and her guilt is lifted. Nelson, however, cannot rid himself of the boy who is tormenting him. It is Billy Mahoney, a boy Nelson tormented and accidentally killed when they were both children. Nelson suffers a nervous breakdown and flatlines himself to "get" Billy. He is dead for more than nine minutes before the others arrive. During that time, however, he finds Billy, who simply smiles at him and walks off with Champ. Nelson runs back to his life and is revived.

There are several solid performances in *Flatliners*. Sutherland—who worked with director Joel Schumacher previously in *The Lost Boys* (1987)—brings a brooding egoism to the character of Nelson who is always claiming proprietary ownership of the experiment and is pushed over the edge by it. Roberts adeptly walks the line between the hard scientist and the emotional little girl, who desperately needs to be reassured that the father she loved as a child has gone to a good place and has found happiness. Bacon's Labraccio is the skeptic who tries to provide a voice of reason for the group. William Baldwin, brother of Alec Baldwin of *The Hunt for Red October* (1990; reviewed in this volume), provides Hurley with a sleaziness that gives new meaning to sex, lies, and videotapes. (Viewers can only imagine what he must go through to find atonement since his burden is left unresolved.) The least developed character of the five is Oliver Platt's Steckle, the self-styled chronicler of the experiments who plans on writing a book about his life pompously titled *Genesis of a Doctor*.

Although the cast is young, the film does not rely on top rock-and-roll songs to provide the music. There is one up-tempo song, "Party Town," written by Dave Stewart of the Eurythmics, but the bulk of the score, which was written by James Newton Howard, has a classical, even spiritual, sound to it. This spirituality also is echoed in the film's sensational sets. Joel Schumacher, the acclaimed director of *St. Elmo's Fire* (1985), *The Lost Boys*, and *Cousins* (1989), told director of photography Jan De Bont—*The Jewel of the Nile* (1985), *Die Hard* (1988), and *Black Rain* (1989)—and production designer Eugenio Zanetti—*Slam Dance* (1987)—to take risks and create their own world. As a result, the film is very visually interesting. Life-after-death scenes are filmed in grainy black and white, occasionally focusing in with color. Humanity's eternal struggle with death and attempts at interpreting it are reflected in the Gothically stylized and symbolic sets. In the lab where the experiments take place, ominous lighting streams through the iron gratings in the floor, evoking the underworld, while angels populate the columns on the surrounding walls and seem to provide a degree of divine protection.

Besides these soundstage sets, use was well made of several locations in Chicago. Loyola University's Lake Shore Campus was used for exterior medical school shots, while the Museum of Science and Industry became the exterior of the lab building. Fog and steam permeate the air, the streets, and the buildings in Schumacher's film, while innovative and sensational lighting lends greatly to the film's atmospherics.

These surroundings set off well the promising premise offered by writer Peter Filardi. Initially inspired when a friend of Filardi had a near-death experience on the operating table, the story relies on research into published accounts of near-death experiences. In them, almost all those who died accidentally reported positive experiences of a tunnel leading to a beautiful white light and friendly voices, while those who had attempted suicide had troubled and emotionally painful near-death experiences. Filardi, therefore, assumes those who choose near-death will find yet another option: facing their own guilt. *Flatliners* is a film about atonement and forgiveness. It is filled with wonderfully atmospheric sets, good performances, and a great premise. Unfortunately, they are eventually subverted by a simplistic resolution.

Beverley Bare Buehrer

Reviews

Chicago Tribune. August 10, 1990, p. C7.
Cosmopolitan. September, 1990, p. 48.
Films in Review. XLI, November, 1990, p. 559.
The Hollywood Reporter. CCCXIII, August 1, 1990, p. 5.
Los Angeles Times. August 10, 1990, p. F4.
Maclean's. August 13, 1990, p. 58.
The New York Times. August 10, 1990, p. B6.
People Weekly. August 20, 1990, p. 12.
Playboy. October, 1990, p. 18.
Premiere. IV, December 1990, p. 37.
Rolling Stone. August 9, 1990, p. 37.
Variety. CCCXL, August 1, 1990, p. 2.
Video. XIV, March, 1991, p. 48.
Vogue. CLXXX, November, 1990, p. 266.
The Wall Street Journal. August 16, 1990, p. 12.
The Washington Post. August 10, 1990, p. N49.

THE FRESHMAN

Production: Mike Lobell for Lobell/Bergman Productions; released by Tri-Star
  Pictures
Direction: Andrew Bergman
Screenplay: Andrew Bergman
Cinematography: William A. Fraker
Editing: Barry Malkin
Production design: Ken Adam
Art direction: Alicia Keywan and Dan Davis
Set decoration: Gordon Sim and Gary J. Brink
Costume design: Julie Weiss
Music: David Newman
MPAA rating: PG
Running time: 102 minutes

Principal characters:
Carmine Sabatini	Marlon Brando
Clark Kellogg	Matthew Broderick
Victor Ray	Bruno Kirby
Tina Sabatini	Penelope Ann Miller
Steve Bushak	Frank Whaley
Arthur Fleeber	Paul Benedict
Larry London	Maximilian Schell
Dwight Armstrong	Kenneth Welsh
Chuck Greenwald	Jon Polito
Lloyd Simpson	Richard Gant

Matthew Broderick and Marlon Brandon star in this offbeat comedy about a young
film student who finds himself caught in a series of insane, uncontrollable circumstances that ensnare him in illegal activities. Clark Kellogg (Broderick) leaves behind Vermont and an enthusiastic animal rights activist stepfather (Kenneth Welsh)
in search of a new life as a freshman in the film department at New York University.
In less than an hour's time, Clark meets the streetwise con artist Victor Ray (Bruno
Kirby), who cleverly swindles Clark out of his textbook funds. Pressured by his arrogant and unsympathetic professor, Arthur Fleeber (Paul Benedict), Clark becomes
desperate for part-time work. His prayers for salvation seem to be answered when
he spies Victor passing by, but Clark quickly discovers that Victor has a gambling
problem and has lost the money wagering at the race track. Victor has a plan, however, and proposes that Clark meet his uncle, Carmine Sabatini (Marlon Brando), a
respected importer who bears an uncanny resemblance to Don Vito Corleone, the
title character from director Francis Ford Coppola's epic masterpiece *The Godfather*
(1972). This intertextuality permeates *The Freshman*, as typified by the scenes in

which Fleeber, the pompous film professor, pretentiously analyzes *The Godfather, Part II* (1974) in class.

Carmine takes an instant liking to Clark and offers him a job retrieving cargo from the airport for a hefty salary. Clark hesitates, but Carmine applauds his suspicious and cautious nature and gives Clark his solemn promise that nothing illegal is transpiring. Driven by the prospect of impoverishment and lured by Carmine's comforting paternalistic nature, Clark finds himself transporting an endangered Komodo dragon across state lines and delivering the Indonesian lizard into the hands of a peculiar Teutonic chef, Larry London (Maximilian Schell). As Clark soon discovers from the pair of federal agents (Jon Polito and Richard Gant) who pressure him into entrapping Carmine, the Komodo dragon is destined to be the main course at the next meeting of The Gourmet Club, a pricey exotic culinary experience to be hosted by Sabatini and London. Feeling as though he has lost all control over his life, Clark soon finds the situation growing even more complicated when Carmine announces that he will marry his feisty daughter, Tina (Penelope Ann Miller). Even though he is strongly attracted to her, Clark has no desire to wed yet. Longing for a return to normality, Clark must choose between self-preservation and his increasing sense of loyalty to the beneficent Carmine.

While *The Freshman* is not offensive, neither is it inspired filmmaking; it is for the most part merely disposable entertainment. The plot defies logic at points, and the film suffers from expositional overload at the end as it attempts to pull together all the illogical loose ends. Furthermore, one never gets the sense that Clark is really a person passionate enough to pursue the study of film. He never talks about films or filmmaking, and the only indication that he is even in film school are several extraneous scenes with Fleeber in class, a whacky roommate (Frank Whaley), and a poster of Buster Keaton on the wall of his dormitory room (which in itself is problematic since "The Freshman" was the title of the 1925 film by Keaton's silent rival, Harold Lloyd). In fact, Clark's being a film student is incidental to the story line, since it serves only to set up an amusing parody of Marlon Brando's roles in *The Godfather* and *The Godfather, Part II*.

While it is refreshing to witness Brando's commanding presence once again, one cannot help but wonder whether the character of Carmine Sabatini or the plot itself is actually that humorous or if it is simply entertaining to watch the king of Method Acting reprise one of his most famous roles. Brando is certainly not to blame, for he does succeed in imbuing his character with an inner warmth and a longing for the straight life that he never had and never will know; and the sight of Marlon Brando on ice skates, gracefully gliding along, is well worth the viewing. The actor won his first Oscar as Best Actor for his performance in *On the Waterfront* (1954), and another for *The Godfather*. In addition, Brando was nominated for Academy Awards for *Viva Zapata!* (1952), *Julius Caesar* (1953), *Sayonara* (1957), *Last Tango in Paris* (1972), and *A Dry White Season* (1989).

In an interview with David Letterman, Matthew Broderick confessed that Brando had his lines read to him through an earpiece on the set. The young actor seemed somewhat disillusioned by this realization; in *The Freshman*, there are several scenes in which Broderick appears to be rather annoyed with Brando's technique, as well as others in which he is appropriately in awe of the veteran actor. As the star of such films as Neil Simon's *Brighton Beach Memoirs* (1986) and *Biloxi Blues* (1988), Matthew Broderick is adept at portraying the slightly overwhelmed, affable, "nice guy" who is swept along by life. It remains to be seen, however, if the actor will be able to make the transition to a more mature leading man. There are moments in *The Freshman* in which Broderick, who at twenty-eight is beginning to show his age, is less than convincing as a naïve, innocent teenager.

Perhaps it was Marlon Brando's presence that inspired the other actors, for performances are consistently good. Award-winning actor Maximilian Schell, a man who along with Brando and an elite group of others will be remembered as most having influenced acting styles in the cinema, contributes a rare comedic role in an American film. Bruno Kirby is a talented character actor whom audiences will recognize as Billy Crystal's best friend in *When Harry Met Sally* (1989) and as Robin Williams' commanding officer in *Good Morning, Vietnam* (1987). The actor also appeared opposite Robert De Niro and Sean Penn in *We're No Angels* (1989), as well as in *Tin Men* (1987) and *The Godfather, Part II*. Penelope Ann Miller made her film debut in *Adventures in Babysitting* (1987), then went on to star opposite Don Johnson in *Dead Bang* (1989). Other notable performances include Frank Whaley from Oliver Stone's *Born on the Fourth of July* (1989) and *Field of Dreams* (1989) and veteran stage actor Paul Benedict, who may be recognized as the Off-Broadway director in *The Goodbye Girl* (1977) and the butler in *Arthur II: On the Rocks* (1988).

Wildlife enthusiasts expressed concern over the stunts required of the endangered Komodo dragon lizard, but seven lizards from Southeast Asia of a more expendable nature, called water monitors, were used in its place, with each having its own purpose. Exotic animal trainers Jules Sylvester and Jim Brockett trained and tamed the water monitors for months prior to filming.

Before the film was released, Marlon Brando told the Toronto press that *The Freshman* was one of the worst films with which he had ever been involved. A few days later Brando recanted, saying that he was wrong about the quality of the film, that it contains memorable moments of high comedy. Actually, Brando is right in both remarks. At times the film is amusing; at others, trite and predictable. *The Freshman* could very easily have been entitled "The Sophomore" in respect of its sophomoric sense of humor.

Patricia Kowal

Reviews

Boxoffice. CXXVI, September, 1990, p. R66.
Chicago Tribune. July 27, 1990, VII, p. 27.
The Christian Science Monitor. LXXXII, July 20, 1990, p. 14.

Drama-Logue. XXI, July 26-August 1, 1990, p. 23.

Films in Review. XLI, November, 1990, p. 555.

The Hollywood Reporter. CCCXIII, July 17, 1990, p. 6.

Los Angeles. XXXV, September, 1990, p. 167.

Los Angeles Times. July 20, 1990, CIX, p. F1.

New Woman. September, 1990, p. 52.

The New York Times. July 20, 1990, CXL, p. B1.

The New Yorker. LXVI, July 30, 1990, p. 78.

Newsweek. CXVI, July 23, 1990, p. 64.

Time. CXXXVI, July 23, 1990, p. 79.

Variety. July 16, 1990, p. 2.

Video. XIV, March, 1991, p. 47.

The Wall Street Journal. August 2, 1990, p. A9.

GHOST

Production: Lisa Weinstein for Howard W. Koch; released by Paramount Pictures
Direction: Jerry Zucker
Screenplay: Bruce Joel Rubin (AA)
Cinematography: Adam Greenberg
Editing: Walter Murch
Production design: Jane Musky
Art direction: Mark Mansbridge
Set decoration: Joe D. Mitchell
Visual effects: Ned Gorman, Bruce Nicholson, John Van Vliet, Katherine Kean, and Richard Edlund
Sound: Jeff Wexler
Costume design: Ruth Morley
Music: Maurice Jarre
MPAA rating: PG-13
Running time: 122 minutes

> *Principal characters:*
> Sam Wheat . . . . Patrick Swayze
> Molly Jensen . . . . Demi Moore
> Oda Mae Brown . . . . Whoopi Goldberg (AA)
> Carl Bruner . . . . Tony Goldwyn
> Willie Lopez . . . . Rick Aviles
> Louise . . . . Gail Boggs
> Clara . . . . Armelia McQueen
> Subway Ghost . . . . Vincent Schiavelli
> Emergency room ghost . . . . Phil Leeds

Rarely does a film so successfully combine the elements of comedy, suspense, science fiction, and romance. *Ghost* is a modern parable of good and evil that sacrifices common knowledge and documented fact for a vision of how things might be in the world beyond this one, and what might happen when a soul is caught in between.

Sam Wheat (Patrick Swayze), a corporate banker, and Molly Jensen (Demi Moore), a sculptress, are in love. As they prepare to move into their new loft apartment in New York, they celebrate their luck in finding each other, symbolized by a penny that Sam finds among the redecoration rubble. Their relationship would be perfect except for one thing: Sam cannot bring himself to say the words, "I love you." Molly knows that Sam loves her, but she would like to hear those words. The best response Sam can muster is, "Ditto!"

On their way home from an evening out, Molly brings up the subject of marriage. Just when it seems that Sam is about to overcome his inability to express his feelings, their conversation is interrupted. Willie Lopez (Rick Aviles) steps out of the shadows and demands Sam's wallet. Despite Sam's compliance, Lopez shoots him. Molly screams for help, but this is New York, and Sam dies waiting for the ambulance.

Sam does not feel dead, though. He sees a beam of sparkling white light descend toward him, but he is more concerned with the sight of Molly weeping over a body. Only after checking Molly for injury and trying to stop her tears does Sam realize that it is his body she is holding. Unable to make Molly hear him, Sam follows the ambulance to the hospital. There, an elderly man (Phil Leeds) appears to recognize Sam. As the man tells Sam that he is there to meet his wife, the beam of sparkling white light descends over a female heart attack victim whom the doctors have just pronounced dead. The man disappears before Sam can discover why they were able to communicate but he and Molly cannot.

Sam attends his own funeral, where his friend and coworker Carl Bruner (Tony Goldwyn) attempts to comfort Molly. Carl further offers to help Molly go through Sam's things. At the loft, Sam sits in the window, watching Molly and Carl sort through his belongings and mourn his senseless death. Sam is so pained at his inability to comfort Molly that he fails to notice that Carl is looking for something specific.

Later, Carl persuades Molly to take a walk with him. Shortly after they leave, Willie Lopez breaks in and begins searching the loft. Sam futilely tries to attack Lopez, demanding to know who he is and why he is in Sam and Molly's home. When Molly returns from her walk before Lopez has left, Sam's anger turns to fear. If he cannot touch her or make himself heard, he will be unable to protect Molly from this murderer, who is now hiding behind a door and peering lasciviously at her. In his frenzy, Sam discovers that although the humans are not aware of him, Molly's cat is. Sam hisses at the cat, who reacts, attracting Molly's attention. Lopez runs, leaving Molly safe for the moment but unaware of the danger from which Sam saved her.

Determined to find a way to protect Molly, Sam follows Lopez in search of more information. What he finds is that Lopez was hired by his trusted associate, Carl. Carl is several million dollars in debt and was planning to obtain account numbers from Sam's files for an elaborate scheme of computerized embezzlement. Carl had only intended for Lopez to steal Sam's wallet, which contained his computer access code, but Lopez tells Carl to consider Sam's murder a bonus. The wallet did not contain the information Carl needed, and with Lopez now expecting a generous fee, Carl's need is even greater. He tells Lopez to do whatever it takes to find the access code.

Devastated, Sam leaves for the loft. On the ride home, Sam is attacked by another ghost, the Subway Ghost (Vincent Schiavelli), who claims the subway as his territory and throws Sam off the car, breaking a glass window in the process. Sam sees the passengers react to the broken window and realizes that, unlike Sam, this ghost is able to manipulate his surroundings. Before Sam can discover how, the Subway Ghost is gone.

Sam exits the subway station in fear and confusion, and begins to wander the streets in search of help. He happens, perhaps too coincidentally, upon the establishment of a psychic. Oda Mae Brown (Whoopi Goldberg) is a charlatan who, assisted by her sisters Clara (Armelia McQueen) and Louise (Gail Boggs), is skilled at making paying customers believe that she is in contact with their dearly departed. It seems logical to Sam that, since he is the dearly departed, Oda Mae would be just the person to help him. He finds that, although Oda Mae cannot see or feel him, she can hear him clearly. Sam asks Oda Mae to help him communicate with Molly, but Oda Mae, convinced that she is not actually psychic (as supposedly were her mother and grandmother) but merely going insane, wants nothing to do with Sam. In order to persuade her, Sam spends hours serenading Oda Mae with a charmingly off-key rendition of "I'm Henry the Eighth, I Am" until she finally agrees.

Persuading Oda Mae is only the first step; it proves much more difficult for Oda Mae to persuade Molly that she really is speaking for Sam. When Oda Mae tells Molly that Sam loves her, Molly counters that Sam would never say that. It is only when Sam instructs Oda Mae to say "Ditto!" that Molly begins to believe.

In addition to the looming threat of Lopez and Molly's valid skepticism of Oda Mae, Sam is faced with the threat of Carl trying to seduce Molly. Sam watches in anguish while the man who is ultimately responsible for his murder works to gain the trust and affection of his beloved Molly. Carl discourages Molly from believing that Oda Mae is what she says she is. On Carl's advice, Molly goes to the police and discovers that Oda Mae has a long and colorful police record. In one of the film's funniest scenes, an officer shows Molly one report after another revealing Oda Mae's various personas adopted over the years to carry out the numerous scams from which she has made her living. Molly leaves the police station convinced that she has been the victim of a cruel hoax.

Desperate to find a way to convince Molly that he is still on earth and trying to help her, Sam returns to the subway and runs through car after car in search of the Subway Ghost. Furious that Sam has again invaded his domain, the spirit threatens Sam, but Sam vows not to leave the subway until the other ghost reveals his secret. Anger is what keeps this ghost so painfully connected to the living world. The Subway Ghost teaches Sam how to focus his anger onto the objects he wishes to control. With this new knowledge, Sam returns to Oda Mae, who is now besieged by ghosts waiting to converse through her with their still-living loved ones. Sam convinces Oda Mae to try again with Molly, and this time, while Oda Mae pleads with Molly through a closed door, Sam passes through the door and hands Molly a penny, instructing Oda Mae to tell her that it is for luck. Molly opens the door.

Finally having brought Molly and Oda Mae together, Sam begins his mission of justice. He must expose Carl before any further harm can come to Molly. With Sam, Molly, and Oda Mae working as a team, justice is quickly served. Oda Mae and Sam retrieve the embezzled funds from Carl's account and turn them over to a charity, much to Oda Mae's chagrin. Both Carl and Willie Lopez meet with death and, in doing so, show Sam the dark and eerie counterparts to the sparkling white light that claimed the woman in the hospital and tried to claim him. Molly and Sam are able to say a touching final farewell before Sam exits into an image of light and love.

The stunning and diverse visual effects in *Ghost* were created by some of cinema's most prestigious effects makers. Bruce Nicholson served as supervisor and Ned Gorman as producer for Industrial Light and Magic, John Van Vliet and Katherine Kean design for and co-own Available Light Limited, and four-time Academy Award winner Richard Edlund represented his own Boss Film Corporation.

Ghost is the first film directed solely by Jerry Zucker, who is known for his collaborations with David Zucker and Jim Abrams on such films as *Airplane* (1980), *Ruthless People* (1986), and *The Naked Gun: From the Files of Police Squad* (1988). *Ghost* was named Favorite Dramatic Motion Picture at the seventeenth annual People's Choice Awards (1991). The film has also become the highest grossing foreign film in many countries, with a world-wide box office surpassing $400 million.

Eleah Horwitz

Reviews

Afro-American. September 8, 1990, p. B7.
Chicago Tribune. July 13, 1990, VII, p. 33.
Films in Review. XLI, October, 1990, p. 477.
The Hollywood Reporter. CCCXIII, July 9, 1990, p. 10.
Jet. LXXVII, July 23, 1990, p. 64.
L.A. Weekly. July 27, 1990, p. 33.
Los Angeles Times. July 13, 1990, p. F1.
The New York Times. July 13, 1990, p. B1.
Newsweek. CXVI, July 16, 1990, p. 61.
Time. CXXXVI, July 16, 1990, p. 86.
Variety. CCXXVIII, July 9, 1990, p. 2.
Village View. July 13, 1990, p. 8.
The Wall Street Journal. July 12, 1990, p. A9.

THE GODFATHER, PART III

Production: Francis Ford Coppola for Zoetrope Studios; released by Paramount
  Pictures
Direction: Francis Ford Coppola
Screenplay: Mario Puzo and Francis Ford Coppola
Cinematography: Gordon Willis
Editing: Barry Malkin, Lisa Fruchtman, and Walter Murch
Production design: Dean Tavoularis
Art direction: Alex Tavoularis
Set design: Maria Teresa Barbasso and Nazzareno Piana
Set decoration supervision: Gary Fettis
Set decoration: Franco Fumagalli
Sound: Clive Winter
Costume design: Milena Canonero
Music: Carmine Coppola and Nino Rota
MPAA rating: R
Running time: 161 minutes

> *Principal characters:*
> Michael Corleone . . . . Al Pacino
> Kay Adams . . . . Diane Keaton
> Connie Corleone Rizzi . . . . Talia Shire
> Vincent Mancini . . . . Andy Garcia
> Don Altobello . . . . Eli Wallach
> Joey Zasa . . . . Joe Mantegna
> B. J. Harrison . . . . George Hamilton
> Grace Hamilton . . . . Bridget Fonda
> Mary Corleone . . . . Sofia Coppola
> Cardinal Lamberto . . . . Raf Vallone
> Anthony Corleone . . . . Franc D'Ambrosio
> Archbishop Gilday . . . . Donal Donnelly
> Dominic Abbandando . . . . Don Novello

In retrospect, the first two *Godfather* films by Francis Ford Coppola seem both
remarkably patient and effortless. There is very little noticeable straining after pro-
fundity or nervous concern for relevance, dramatic intensity, or resonance. Yet, by
almost universal agreement, both of these films are compelling, richly textured, and
deeply insightful about the psychology and the culture of crime. The actors and,
more importantly, the director radiate confidence, evident in the unhurried pace as
well as the skillfully constructed rhythm that are arguably the most commonly overlooked and undervalued features of *The Godfather* (1972) and *The Godfather, Part II*
(1974). A superficial look at these films may be very misleading. Most viewers recall

first and foremost the eruptions of violence, and perhaps because they are often so shocking and vivid, these moments tend to obscure the much more characteristic languor of the films. Put most simply, Coppola typically takes his time letting the action unfold and the characters develop or reveal themselves. The opening scene of *The Godfather*, for example, the almost agonizingly protracted and static dialogue between Vito Corleone (Marlon Brando) and a suitor asking for a favor, uses visual style—long takes, slow, almost timid camera movements, scrupulously chosen camera angles—slowly to establish the old don not only as a man of imposing physical power but also as a custodian of unexpected virtues: patience, restraint, and a penchant for the careful consideration of everything before him. This simple scene is tense and evocative, illustrating that it is a great artist who knows how to reach the depths through the surfaces, the profound through the trivial, the dramatic through the immobile.

Yet, there is little of this patient and confident artistry to be found in *The Godfather, Part III*. It is a long film not because it is artfully slow but because it nervously piles up dramatic and spectacular incidents in an attempt to achieve some kind of accumulated power or meaning. While the frantic style of *The Godfather, Part III* may betray Coppola's loss of directorial self-confidence or his unwillingness to gamble that a new generation of film-goers will be captivated by cinematic subtleties, it may also be that he conceived of this style as the suitable vehicle for telling the story of the last days of Michael Corleone (Al Pacino), a gangster on the verge of a nervous breakdown, set in a world so corrupt that the crimes of the Corleones seem almost inconsequential.

The film begins in a grand manner with a deeply evocative shot that subtly but purposefully recalls the opening shot of Orson Welles's *Citizen Kane* (1941): Coppola's camera moves slowly through the ruins of the Corleone family compound in much the same way as Welles's camera surveyed Charles Foster Kane's Xanadu, and each of these settings serves as an embodiment of the owner's vulnerability and precariously maintained, but ultimately self-destructive, power. This opening visual analogue also helps set a mood and introduce a key theme: Like *Citizen Kane, The Godfather, Part III* is relentlessly nostalgic, and the plot revolves around Michael's attempt to return to a state of innocence by making all his business assets and interests legitimate. His father had this in mind as well, and in a memorable scene from *The Godfather*, Vito fantasized longingly about a future Senator Corleone or President Corleone even as he realized that Michael had inescapably been drawn from his carefully protected life into becoming the heir apparent of the crime family. Now for Michael, several decades after his initiation as the don, this desire for legitimacy is a psychological necessity as well as a dream: At stake, Coppola would have the viewer believe, is Michael's mental and spiritual health.

Michael's plan to become respectable is carefully orchestrated. He donates a tremendous amount of money to the Catholic Church and is rewarded by an elaborate ceremony that makes him a member of the Order of St. Sebastian, followed by a large reception and dance. The earlier *Godfather* films established that ceremonies and dances are ironic occasions, used to dramatize the continuation rather than the eradication of tensions and problems, and this pattern holds true in this film as well. The gift to the Church is part of Michael's attempt to maneuver himself into a position where, with the support of the Vatican, he can shift all of his family's remaining resources into an international corporation, thereby reconciling his two most cherished desires: for power and for legitimacy. The dinner-dance that celebrates the completion of the first phase of his plan, however, introduces characters who represent the many serious difficulties that are yet to be overcome. Michael's retreat from criminal activities leaves a void that is filled by thoroughly disreputable mobsters such as Joey Zasa (Joe Mantegna), whose mannered respect for Michael at the party marks him as an inveterate and dangerous enemy. The one uninvited guest, Vincent Mancini (Andy Garcia), an illegitimate son of Michael's oldest brother Sonny, may turn out to be a powerful ally and ease Michael's transition to respectability, but at the party he only causes trouble, assaulting Zasa. Finally, enemies come in all shapes and forms: The canny Archbishop (Donal Donnelly) is an unctuous, shady character who prefigures the most dangerous criminals that Michael has yet to face— the international capitalists and financiers who are intimately connected with the Vatican.

Because of the great number of characters that Coppola weaves into the plot and the emphasis on episodic melodramatic incidents, the film sometimes seems fragmentary, but beneath all the action is an intricately (though not completely successfully) choreographed deep structure. Like William Shakespeare, his often-acknowledged model, Coppola charts his themes on several different but interrelated levels. *The Godfather, Part III* is, most obviously, a crime story, and much of the action revolves around the conflict between rival gangs and Vincent's struggle to become the new don. For Coppola, however, crime is too important to be left solely in the hands of the criminals, and the film veers toward a broader social and political analysis. Like Bertolt Brecht, who concluded one of his studies of crime, *Die Dreigroschenoper* (1928; *The Threepenny Opera*, 1949), with the rhetorical question "What is the robbing of a bank to the founding of a bank?", Coppola suggests that gangsterism is not an aberration but the norm, the way of the world, and that the meanest streets are not in Brooklyn or Sicily but in the banking centers of Europe and the Vatican, fronts for the truly vicious and powerful criminals. This is the legitimacy which Michael aspires to—an irony that Coppola never satisfactorily controls and which thus tends to make Michael's quest seem misguided and uncharacteristically blind, rather than admirable.

The film not only turns outward to broad levels of action and political meaning but inward as well. Like the earlier films, *The Godfather, Part III* is an examination of a domestic family as well as a crime family. Kay (Diane Keaton) is particularly important in *The Godfather, Part II* as a guide for the audience's judgment of her husband, Michael: Her growing horror at his actions and her final repudiation of him place Michael beyond sympathy. In the third installment, however, she is used for a much different purpose, and her new (although in some respects inexplicable) warmth toward Michael is an integral part of Coppola's attempt to make him an object of sympathetic concern, rather than judgment. In a film so haunted by the fear that the sins of the father will continue to be visited upon the children, it is not surprising that Coppola intertwines Michael's fate with that of his daughter and son. Mary (Sofia Coppola) falls in love with Vincent and predictably pays the price for becoming attracted to his dangerous vitality. (Critics who rightly chastise Coppola for casting such an inept actress as his daughter in this part should also chastise him for his inept direction of her and his strikingly weak scripting of the part of Mary—for setting her up as only an icon of innocence rather than a fully realized dramatic character.) The fate of Anthony (Franc D'Ambrosio) is equally melodramatic but in a sublimated, rather than literal, way. He chooses opera rather than law as a career, and in a curious way, perhaps his father's objections to this choice are well grounded. In the stunning conclusion to the film, the opera that Anthony sings parallels and introduces the deadly violence from which the Corleone family is finally never able to escape.

The last level on which *The Godfather, Part III* operates is in some ways the weakest. Coppola is rightly fascinated by Michael, and the film is, in part, a psychological character study of an aging man who is struggling to set his house and mind in order. Tragic grandeur does not sit well on Michael Corleone, however, and it is somewhat strained, even fraudulent, to portray the last years of his life as an emotionally moving attempt to gain spiritual tranquility, forgiveness, redemption, and financial security. Pacino's acting is remarkable, but he has been set on the wrong path. Coppola gives Michael the fits of madness, exhaustion, and final despair of Shakespeare's King Lear over the sacrifice of innocence—his own and his daughter's. It might have been more fitting, instead, to give him the cynical but penetrating lucidity of *Hamlet*'s Claudius and *Richard the Second*'s Henry Bolingbroke, each profoundly aware of how his life has placed him in need of but also beyond redemption, forgiveness, and tranquility.

There are many weaknesses in *The Godfather, Part III*—for example, the inclusion of many unnecessary characters—but there are also many disturbing inconsistencies and problems that are posed by the film that are not necessarily weaknesses. For example, it is Coppola's choice to rely on melodrama and nostalgia as his primary vehicles for portraying and analyzing the passions of his key figures. As a result, the film contains tremendous hysterical energy and fosters a kind of dramatic engagement with various characters that substitutes for a more clearheaded assessment of them. This makes for an exciting, but in some ways irresponsible, film. Vincent, the callous and casual murderer of the two men who come to kill him early in the film, is nevertheless the film's romantic hero. Michael—the emotionless murderer of his own brother in *The Godfather, Part II*—is "humanized" by being placed in the company of ostensibly far more reprehensible villains, who do not have families like his and are not connected to a noble heritage as he is. Nostalgia is often invoked, but rarely displayed, and each time the past is closely examined (in any of the *Godfather* films) it is revealed to be corrupt.

Thus, this film is filled with many ironies, not the least of which is that, despite its superficial concern for legitimacy and respectability, it is, like the world it represents, patently amoral, beyond good and evil as standards of judgment or relevant models of conduct. Yet, it poses a great challenge: To an observant and thoughtful audience, one of the most provocative aspects of *The Godfather, Part III*, a flawed but complicated and powerful film, is that—sometimes intentionally, sometimes unintentionally—it calls into question as well as celebrates the perennial fascination with power, violence, and ambition. All the densely interrelated *Godfather* films confirm that this fascination is ultimately an offer that one can neither refuse nor accept.

Sidney Gottlieb

Reviews

Chicago Tribune. December 25, 1990, V, p. 1.
The Hollywood Reporter. CCCXV, December 17, 1990, p. 10.
Los Angeles Times. December 23, 1990, Calendar, p. 9.
The New Republic. CCIV, January 21, 1991, p. 26.
The New York Times. December 25, 1990, p. A9.
The New Yorker. LXVI, January 14, 1991, p. 76.
Newsweek. CXVI, December 24, 1990, p. 58.
Premiere. IV, October, 1990, p. 73.
Time. CXXXVI, December 24, 1990, p. 76.
Variety. CCCXLI, December 17, 1990, p. 3.
The Wall Street Journal. December 27, 1990, p. A7.

GOODFELLAS

Production: Irwin Winkler; released by Warner Bros.
Direction: Martin Scorsese
Screenplay: Nicholas Pileggi and Martin Scorsese; based on the book *Wiseguy*, by Pileggi
Cinematography: Michael Ballhaus
Editing: Thelma Schoonmaker
Production design: Kristi Zea
Art direction: Maher Ahmad
Set decoration: Les Bloom
Sound: James Sabat and Tom Fleischman
Costume design: Richard Bruno
Stunt coordination: Michael Russo
MPAA rating: R
Running time: 146 minutes

Principal characters:
Jimmy Conway	Robert De Niro
Henry Hill	Ray Liotta
Tommy DeVito	Joe Pesci (AA)
Paulie Cicero	Paul Sorvino
Karen Hill	Lorraine Bracco
Billy Batts	Frank Vincent
Young Henry	Christopher Serrone

One of an elite group of filmmakers with a clear-cut vision and compelling directorial style, Martin Scorsese personifies a definite argument for the auteur theory of filmmaking; his body of films stands as a definitive text, exhibiting recurring themes over which he obsesses. His work is the epitome of form mirroring content. In his latest work, *GoodFellas*, Scorsese's ironic treatment of a factual account offers a viscerally accessible look at organized crime without the burden of blatant moralizing.

Ever since he was a child, Henry Hill (Ray Liotta) wanted to be a gangster. Everything about life in the Mafia appealed to him. These were men who saw what they wanted and took it. They never wasted their time pursuing the American Dream; they lived it. The young half-Irish, half-Sicilian Hill (Christopher Serrone) worked his way up through the ranks of the neighborhood Brooklyn gang run by Paulie Cicero (Paul Sorvino). Even at an early age, the smart and resourceful Henry basked in the power and the illusion of influence that came from his association with these gangsters. When Henry takes his first "fall like a man," the respected Jimmy Conway (Robert De Niro), a "goodfella" who loved to steal, conveys to his young protégé the following ethics: "Never rat on your friends and always keep your mouth shut."

By the time he was twenty-one, Henry was ensconced in mob life, seduced by its adolescent glamour. He belonged to a family that seemed to care about him and encouraged his indulgences: the socializing, the money, and the thrill of living life on the edge. It was an intoxicating journey into another world, and Henry reveled in the power and the celebrity status that came with being a "wiseguy." His wife, Karen (Lorraine Bracco), is naïvely seduced by material excess and later defends the actions of the brotherhood as merely "blue-collar guys who could only make a few extra bucks by cutting a few corners." Before long the Jewish Karen is describing amounts of money in inches with her fingers and rewarding her husband with oral sex. It was, as Henry tells us, "a glorious time."

When the psychotic and volatile Tommy (Joe Pesci) senselessly kills a mob member (Frank Vincent), whom he should have obtained special permission to murder, or "whack," Henry begins to realize that the "rules" of the game may not carry the same weight for the others. The self-deluding Henry's faith is further eroded when a twist of fate lands him in prison. He realizes that only the "wiseguys" themselves are looked after properly and, in an attempt to sustain Karen's accustomed life-style, the resourceful Henry begins supplying drugs to the other convicts.

Once out of prison, Henry becomes involved in cocaine trafficking, despite stern warnings from Paulie. All seems well when the goodfellas mastermind the heist of the century by stealing six million dollars in cash from Lufthansa Airlines, but things unravel when the others begin spending money ostentatiously without Jimmy's approval and it is discovered that the police have found the getaway truck that was not disposed of properly. Jimmy's paranoia grows and he begins to cut every link between him and the robbery, ordering the death of several of his partners. When Tommy receives the highest honor that can be given, to be made a part of a mob, Henry further realizes that he will always be an outsider, that by virtue of his Irish heritage he can never truly be accepted into the Mafia, no matter how loyal he remains or how deeply he believes in the rules. As he watches his companions become increasingly unstable and his own life unravel in the midst of drug abuse, Henry suspects that the honor and sense of belonging to a family is really a sham. He was too loyal to his undeserving friends and naïvely believed too deeply in the rules, which means little in the face of paranoia and greed. Yet for Henry, life in the mob is an even stronger addiction than drug abuse. Henry never does change; he merely regrets the unfortunate turn of circumstances that could forever leave him "just an ordinary schnook."

Some critics have argued that the film is disappointing in its narrative structure: It does not have a neat, convenient arc to its story line or adhere to a three-act screenplay structure. The problem lies in the fact that this film was based on a true life story and, unfortunately, real life does not always present itself in a neatly constructed package and few people have the pleasure of experiencing a resolution or a third act to their stories. In Scorsese's defense, he was given a text, a story that consisted of well-defined events and definite plot points to which he had to adhere. The film's lack of resolution is underscored most graphically in the film's postscript, in which it is revealed that Henry Hill used his new identity to set up further criminal activities and that he was consequently arrested. It is unfortunate that many reviewers seemed to expect the director to somehow alter the course of events. If Scorsese had wanted to tell that kind of a story, however, he undoubtedly would have worked from an original fictional screenplay and not from someone's real-life escapades.

Scorsese's past work has, for the most part, conveyed the main character's potential for change. He may want to change and know that he must change, but the main character in Scorsese's films very often is not able to initiate a deep or long-lasting transformation. This often results in the presence of intense conflict within the character. For example, Scorsese's protagonist, Charlie, in *Mean Streets* (1973), is deeply conflicted and troubled by religious and sexual guilt, tortured to the point of paralysis. It is interesting to note that the film that garnered the most critical acclaim as the best film of the 1980's, Scorsese's *Raging Bull* (1980), a highly stylized work based on the life of boxer Jake La Motta, revolved around a character who also changed little throughout the course of the story. In an interview in *Film Comment*, Scorsese defended his storytelling technique in *GoodFellas* as closely mirroring the free-flowing style of both Nicholas Pileggi's book and Henry Hill's own arrogant way of telling his story. Scorsese explained: "[I]t would make a fascinating film if you just make it what it is—literally as close to the truth as a fiction film, a dramatization, could get. No sense to try to whitewash."

Further criticism centered on the film's violent nature. Again, it is difficult to interpret visually a story about men for whom violence is an integral part of their lives without displaying that violence. Scorsese's depiction of brutality is restrained, limited to a few isolated moments that are done in an almost comical fashion, thus accentuating the commonplace acceptance of the role of violence. Scorsese cannot compare to the gratuitous violence employed by director Brian DePalma, whose misogyny reached a career high in *Body Double* (1984).

Henry's narration (often foregrounded with a freeze-frame device) offers the viewer essential keys to understanding motivations that otherwise might be difficult to convey amid this duplicitous world. Scorsese furthers the gangster genre by providing a unique and previously untapped perspective: the inclusion of a distinct female viewpoint provided by Karen's voice-over, which offers an insight lacking in Francis Ford Coppola's epic, *The Godfather* (1972). More accessible than *The Godfather* saga, *GoodFellas* facilitates the viewer's understanding of the allure of mob life. By providing an outsider's viewpoint (having the main protagonist be of mixed ethnic background rather than purely Sicilian), it enhances the audience's identification with Hill's aspirations, more so than had he been born into "the Family," as was Coppola's Michael Corleone. The film, therefore, does not read as a complete, all-encompassing indictment of Italian culture, but rather as an isolated moment in time and space.

Following previous critical acclaim, particularly for his portrayal as the crazed boyfriend in *Something Wild* (1986), Ray Liotta gives an impressive performance in his first starring role. The actor imbues Henry with a childlike innocence and eagerness to please, combined with a very adult desire to maintain order and to diffuse tension among the wiseguys.

Despite winning nearly every major film critics award, Scorsese's *GoodFellas* failed to capture the Academy Award for both Best Picture and Best Director, with votes going instead to first-time director Kevin Costner's revisionist Western *Dances with Wolves* (1990; reviewed in this volume). Perhaps even more surprising was the Directors Guild of America's snub of Scorsese. Critics have speculated that even superlative filmmaking could prove to be no match for the more sentimentally humanistic, "politically correct" tale of the tragic exploitation of the American Indian. While Costner's effort was admirable, the large part of the film's appeal rested in the seductive, romantic treatment of the frontier, in definite contrast to Scorsese's more brutally honest exposé of life in the Mafia. It is interesting to note that Scorsese has never been awarded an Oscar for any of his films, despite the fact that *Raging Bull* is considered by most critics to be the best film of the decade.

What Scorsese offers in *GoodFellas* is fast-paced, stylistically driven filmmaking that succeeds in seducing its audience with its glamour, in much the same way as Henry Hill is attracted to life in the Mafia.

Patricia Kowal

Reviews
Boxoffice. CXXVI, November, 1990, p. R82.
Chicago Tribune. September 21, 1990, VII, p. 31.
Commonweal. CXVII, December 7, 1990, p. 720.
Daily Variety. LVII, 1990 Anniversary Issue, p. 304.
Drama-Logue. XXI, September 27-October 3, 1990, p. 6.
Film Comment. XXVI, September/October, 1990, p. 25.
Film Journal. XCIII, October 9, 1990, p. 55.
The Hollywood Reporter. CCCXIV, September 7, 1990, p. 7.
L.A. Weekly. September 28, 1990, XII, p. 27.
Los Angeles Times. September 19, 1990, p. F1.
New York Magazine. XXIII, September 10, 1990, p. 32.
The New York Times. September 19, 1990, p. B1.
The New Yorker. LXVI, September 24, 1990, p. 98.
Newsweek. September 17, 1990, p. 54.
Outlook. September 18, 1990, CXV, p. C1.
Rolling Stone. RS 588, October 4, 1990, p. 48.
Time. CXXXVI, September 24, 1990, p. 83.
Variety. September 7, 1990, p. 2.

GREEN CARD

Origin: Australia and France
Released: 1990
Released in U.S.: 1990
Production: Peter Weir for Touchstone Pictures; released by Buena Vista
Direction: Peter Weir
Screenplay: Peter Weir
Cinematography: Geoffrey Simpson
Editing: William Anderson
Production design: Wendy Stites
Art direction: Christopher Nowak
Set decoration: John Anderson and Ted Glass
Sound: Pierre Gamet
Music: Hans Zimmer
MPAA rating: PG-13
Running time: 108 minutes

Principal characters:
George Faure	Gérard Depardieu
Brontë Parrish	Andie MacDowell
Lauren	Bebe Neuwirth
Phil	Gregg Edelman
Brontë's lawyer	Robert Prosky
Mrs. Bird	Jessie Keosian
Gorsky	Ethan Phillips
Mrs. Sheehan	Mary Louise Wilson
Brontë's mother	Lois Smith
Brontë's father	Conrad McLaren
Anton	Ronald Guttman
Oscar	Danny Dennis
Mr. Adler	Stephen Pearlman
Mrs. Adler	Victoria Boothby

Australian filmmaker Peter Weir handles his typical subject of culture clash with a light touch in *Green Card*. The script, authored by producer/director Weir, is rooted in the fairy tale of the frog prince. In the tale, the amphibious title character intrudes on the pampered life of a princess, as a result of a bargain struck between them; after the princess reluctantly fulfills her side of the agreement, allowing the frog to eat from her plate, drink from her cup, and sleep in her bed, the animal is transformed into a handsome (human) prince. In *Green Card*, an agreement between the two central characters similarly involves thwarted potential: in the modern guise of a green card, permitting the Frenchman George Faure (Gérard Depardieu, in his first major English-language role) to fulfill his commercial promise as a musician in the United States, and an exclusive Upper Westside apartment, boasting a greenhouse to provide Brontë Parrish (Andie MacDowell) the opportunity to exercise her horticultural skills. Furthermore, the raffish George and the evasive Brontë also appear to be lacking as fully emotional, spiritual, and sexual beings.

The two enter into a marriage of convenience in order to raise George's status in the eyes of the U.S. Immigration and Naturalization Service (INS) and Brontë's status in the view of the apartment's priggish tenants' association. George's marriage to an American citizen legitimizes him for the government; Brontë's show of stability as a married woman establishes her acceptability to the association.

Following a perfunctory wedding, George and Brontë part, expecting never to see each other again. Cupid, however, has other plans, employing such unlikely agents as INS officials involved in a crackdown of green-card motivated marriage scams. In one of the film's most amusing sequences, Brontë has arranged for George to be present in the apartment for an initial interview with investigators from the INS, who have been quizzing her equally prying neighbors, especially the tiny but formidable Mrs. Bird (Jessie Keosian). George and Brontë's slapdash attempt to impersonate newlyweds is punctuated by a broadly improvised story about their first meeting and interrupted by an unpropitious phone call from Brontë's fastidious boyfriend, Phil (Gregg Edelman). This dubious show of married life is capped by George's muddled direction of one of the investigators to the bathroom, the location of which George, arriving mere minutes before the agents themselves, has no clue. Throughout the scene, Depardieu, for whom Weir conceived the film, masterfully wields his freewheeling charm to sweeten George's alarmingly anarchic imagination.

Brontë unhappily concludes that George must stay at the apartment with her for a crash course in intimacy, so that they can pass individual, in-depth interviews with the INS. This plot device of forced cohabitation enables Weir to set in relief the culture clash that the two represent: his intoxicatingly strong coffee versus her decaf, his red meat versus her "trail mix," his street-smart cynicism versus her university-bred "political correctness." He is waiting for his life to begin; she expects hers to continue as it is. He has survived the urban jungle through juvenile delinquency and petty thievery; she, a member of the Green Guerillas (an actual, all-volunteer ecological movement to which MacDowell herself belongs), blankets the city's concrete and rubble with gardens. In one of their numerous confrontations over the course of their weekend together, George, the pragmatist, declares to Brontë, the idealist, that inner-city children would benefit more from a good meal than from potted plants.

This statement epitomizes the fundamental difference that separates them: George embodies restless, sensual animalism; Brontë, self-contained, bloodless vegetable life. George's contribution to Brontë's greenhouse, a goldfish, adds to it a spark of animal life. He also starts a vegetable garden, in the process, uprooting the weeds that constitute Brontë's research. In the same way, he disrupts her controlled, antiseptic life in order to plant there something vital and nourishing. She, on her part, provokes this nurturing, sustaining, and ultimately sacrificial side of George's na-

ture. By the film's end, in classic "odd couple" style, each has adopted the characteristics of the other: Forced to part for "failing" the INS test, Brontë clings fero-
ciously to George, while he, holding fast to principle, surrenders to deportation after
first protesting Brontë's innocence in the deception.

The turning point in the relationship is also the film's most wildly comic scene.
Brontë's bohemian friend, Lauren (Bebe Neuwirth), startles Brontë by appearing with
George at a dinner party that is hosted by Lauren's parents, the Adlers. Brontë hopes
to overcome Mrs. Adler's (Victoria Boothby) resistance to donating her magnificent
trees to the Green Guerillas, as the couple intends to move from their penthouse.
The gathering's brittle, upper-crust atmosphere is shattered by a piano performance
that is requested of the sometime composer George, as he pounds out dissonances
on the keys. "It's not Mozart," he cheerfully announces (Wolfgang Mozart—that
perfect of classical composers—is invariably heard whenever Brontë turns her cassette player on). Yet, George also improvises a wistful, lyrical plea for destitute
children to enjoy the beauty of gardens and parks. Depardieu here suggests the range
that has marked his career, which spans more than seventy films: He is alternately
clumsy, savage, endearing, tender, and sly. The scene closes with a wink by George
to Brontë, whose radiantly conspiratorial expression fills the screen.

Back in Brontë's apartment, the two huddle over Brontë's family photo album and
share incidents that are still vivid in their lives. They finally part to their respective
beds, and as the scene shifts from one to the other undressing for the night, the
camera reveals each's vulnerability to a yearning for the other. The next day, the two
produce a series of snapshots that chronicles their fictional courtship and honeymoon. In their play, George and Brontë develop a joyously spontaneous language.
Blissfully fluid in their identities, they are relaxed with one another, as trusting and
eagerly inventive as children.

Significantly, it is the emotional directness of music that hints all along at the
rightness of these two seeming opposites. The film opens with the raw, exuberant
drumming of a young street musician, whom Brontë tips; Brontë's first love affair
was with a musician; and when Brontë asks George, for the purposes of the INS interview, why he fell in love with her, he responds, "Because I began to hear music
again." George shares a last name with the composer Gabriel Faure; known for his
highly personal style, Faure bridged the gap between the Romantic composers of the
nineteenth century and the moderns of the twentieth. George himself reveals a singular, complex personality, compellingly old-fashioned and contemporary at the same
time.

Brontë's name is also illustrative of her character. The Brontë sisters were Vic-
torians who wrote novels in which passion seethed just below the surface. This symbolic use of names reinforces the fairy tale feel of *Green Card*, which was criticized
by some as fluff. Strains of believability do weaken the plot: Is it necessary for a
husband to know such minutiae about his wife as the brand of her cold cream? Why
does Brontë resist telling her parents and boyfriend about the ruse? Would an idealistic woman really enter into a sham marriage for an apartment? Such plot points

are manipulated for their comic possibilities rather than unfolding as the plausible actions of realistic characters.

Weir, however, has a history of making genre films with a difference: *Gallipoli* (1980), a war picture; *The Year of Living Dangerously* (1982), a romantic thriller; and *Witness* (1986), a crime story, all are enriched by social and political overtones. *Green Card* may resemble a stock screwball comedy with its antic, impertinent humor and slapstick, its eccentric characters and its exploitation of the war between the sexes, but its scope consciously includes a dimension of social comment. The 1930's, when the genre flourished, witnessed economic and social uncertainty, which sent values into turmoil. In reviving the genre, Weir may intend to reflect that era's confusion and perversity in the troubled years ending the twentieth century. Housing and employment, the relevance and seriousness of marriage are no longer givens in contemporary society. *Green Card* intimates these issues, and consequently chafes against the constraints of its form. Yet, these issues also cause the film to generate a poignance that lingers in the conscience. *Green Card* ends with the exhortation of a gospel choir to "Keep Your Eyes on the Prize," an anthem of the Civil Rights movement.

In the tradition of romantic comedies, *Green Card*'s credibility depends on the chemistry of its leads, and Depardieu and MacDowell do convey archetypal charm and attraction as the tough-but-tender, diamond-in-the-rough hero and the repressed, skittish heroine. The production design by Wendy Stites, the art direction by Christopher Nowak, and the set decoration by John Anderson and Ted Glass attentively detail Brontë's tremulous femininity: the Matisse prints on her walls and the straw hats, shawls, and loosely draped jumpers that she wears. The rounded angles and circular tracking of Weir's camerawork embrace what is on the screen the way a wedding ring—a central image in the film—embraces the finger, and as George and Brontë finally embrace life and each other.

Amy Adelstein

Reviews
Chicago Tribune. January 11, 1991, Section 2, p. 4.
The Christian Science Monitor. December 21, 1990, p. 12.
The Hollywood Reporter. CCCXV, December 2, 1990, p. 6.
Los Angeles Times. December 22, 1990, p. F1.
The New York Times. December 25, 1990, Living Arts, p. 11.
Newsweek. CXVII, January 7, 1991, p. 55.
Premiere. IV, January, 1991, p. 12.
Variety. December 21, 1990, p. 2.
The Wall Street Journal. January 10, 1991, p. A12.
The Washington Post. January 11, 1991, p. D1.

GREMLINS II
The New Batch

Production: Michael Finnell for Amblin Entertainment; released by Warner Bros.
Direction: Joe Dante
Screenplay: Charlie Haas; based on characters created by Chris Columbus
Cinematography: John Hora
Editing: Kent Beyda
Production design: James Spencer
Art direction: Joe Lucky and Rick Butler
Set decoration: John Anderson
Special effects: Rick Baker and Ken Pepiot
Visual effects: Dennis Michelson
Sound: Ken King and Douglas Vaughan
Sound effects: Mark Mangini and David Stone
Costume design: Rosanna Norton
Stunt coordination: Mike McGaughy
Music: Jerry Goldsmith
MPAA rating: PG-13
Running time: 106 minutes

> *Principal characters:*
> Billy Peltzer . . . . Zach Galligan
> Kate Beringer . . . . Phoebe Cates
> Daniel Clamp . . . . John Glover
> Grandpa Fred . . . . Robert Prosky
> Forster . . . . Robert Picardo
> Dr. Catheter . . . . Christopher Lee
> Marla Bloodstone . . . . Haviland Morris
> Murray Futterman . . . . Dick Miller
> Sheila Futterman . . . . Jackie Joseph
> Katsuji . . . . Gedde Watanabe
> Mr. Wing . . . . Keye Luke
> Microwave Marge . . . . Kathleen Freeman

There is an art to making sequels, as was demonstrated by the summer season of 1990. The original idea has to be imitated in such a way that the sequel will seem to be something other than a remake, as *Another 48 HRS.* (1990; reviewed in this volume) failed to do, even though the original's director, Walter Hill, was brought back to work with Nick Nolte and Eddie Murphy. *Robocop II* (1990; reviewed in this volume) experimented with a new director and forgot the human side of its robot peacemaker. The more successful sequels stayed with the talents who understood why what they had done had worked, but who also had the ingenuity to experiment so that the sequel would have something fresh to offer. The two best sequels of the summer of 1990 were inventive enough, and daring enough, to try something new, and both of them attempted to capitalize on motion-picture nostalgia in amusing ways. The first sequel to take this approach was *Back to the Future Part III* (reviewed in this volume), which offered a Hollywood conception of the Old West populated by some Hollywood old-timers and recognizable props and settings from the classic Westerns. The second sequel to follow this trend was *Gremlins II: The New Batch.*

Gremlins II is indescribably silly, but it is also amusing and entertaining. Director Joe Dante was brought back to create another high-tech inferno, this time with Charlie Haas rather than Chris Columbus as screenplay writer, and without Chris Walas, who created the original creatures. Zach Galligan and Phoebe Cates were both back, however, along with everyone's favorite Mogwai, Gizmo, the star of the original creature-feature, but what made this sequel distinctive and compelling was its shift in tone. It was a horror picture with a distinctive sense of humor.

The sequel is set in New York City, mainly at the so-called Clamp Centre, the corporate headquarters of high-roller Daniel Clamp (John Glover), who seems to be a parody of both Donald Trump and Ted Turner. Mr. Clamp, who has written a book entitled *I'll Take Manhattan*, develops real estate and also runs a media empire. His logo is a globe squeezed into a bagel shape within the clutches of a giant clamp. The person behind this caricature is not such an ogre, however, but an overgrown kid who is quite pleased with himself and exudes a childlike sense of self-centered wonder and awe over what he has created.

Billy Peltzer (Zach Galligan) and Kate Beringer (Phoebe Cates) have moved from Kingston Falls to New York City, and both of them work at the Clamp Centre. Billy works on the corporate side, where he is watched over by his supervisor Marla Bloodstone (Haviland Morris) and an efficiency expert named Forster (Robert Picardo). Kate is a tour guide at the Clamp Centre, which includes a genetics laboratory headed by Dr. Catheter (Christopher Lee) and a television studio with its own star, Grandpa Fred (Robert Prosky), who introduces late-night horror films for insomniacs. The genetics laboratory sets the stage for later mischief and the possibility of several grotesque Gremlin mutants: a bat Gremlin (who eventually becomes a gargoyle), a spider Gremlin, and even a talking Gremlin, for example. This bit of invention is a stroke of comic genius.

The plot is quite skimpy. Clamp wants to build a huge office complex in Chinatown and has to deal with the ancient Mr. Wing (Keye Luke), who looks after Gizmo. Mr. Wing dies before long, the demolition crews come in, and Gizmo escapes. He is captured and taken to Dr. Catheter's genetics laboratory at the Clamp Centre. Billy rescues him, but Gizmo then escapes from Billy's filing cabinet and gets wet, thanks to a bumbling maintenance man trying to fix a water fountain. As a result, a new batch of Gremlins is spawned, and they infiltrate the Clamp Centre. (Part of the original formula was that Gizmo would reproduce only under special circumstances, if doused with water or if fed after midnight.) One of the new batch takes a brain stimulant in the genetics laboratory and becomes the mischievous mastermind of the Gremlin takeover. He talks with Tony Randall's voice (imitating the accent and manner of William F. Buckley, Jr.), and eventually he sings and performs. Taking care of this Gremlin crisis is more of a challenge than the first round, though Billy, who knows their habits, is up to the challenge. Several critics found the sequel superior to the original.

The original Gremlins were awful creatures, but *Gremlins II* is not so hellish as the original. Instead, it is amusing and constantly satiric. It is packed with media celebrities and character actors and pokes fun at filmgoers, television viewers, and popular culture in general. At one point, for example, the Gremlins seem to invade the film theater and cause the film to catch fire and break, leaving the screen momentarily empty. Then the Gremlins, who have taken over, start to make shadow puppets with the projection beam and then begin to show another film, which seems to be a black-and-white pornographic film, until someone goes to the management to complain. Fortunately, Hulk Hogan happens to be in the audience of this film-within-a-film and intimidates the Gremlins into reinstating the right film.

Amusing cameos continue as Leonard Maltin appears to do a review of the video of the original *Gremlins* (1984), until the new batch attacks him and pulls him out of the picture. Top Warner Bros. animator Chuck Jones directed the opening credits, which tells the audience that the film is really a sort of cartoon. The Warner Bros. logo first appears with Bugs Bunny and Looney Tune music, but Bugs is soon usurped by Daffy Duck, who tells the audience that Bugs has had the limelight for fifty years, which is long enough. As the end credits roll, Daffy is back to comment about how long and boring the credits are and to make fun of those who stay around to read them. Daffy sets the tone of the entire picture.

Robert Prosky plays the late-night master of ceremonies Grandpa Fred, who introduces trashy horror films on cable television, outrageously made up as a fat Count Dracula and a spoof, as *Variety* noted, of the Grandpa character on the old television series *The Munsters*. British horror star Christopher Lee appears as Dr. Catheter, a mad scientist who experiments in genetic engineering and regrets his experiment after the Gremlins take over. Keye Luke, who plays Mr. Wing, is the most famous Oriental character actor to have worked in Hollywood. He has appeared in more than 150 films and was the star of thirteen Charlie Chan pictures. The wall-to-wall homage of *Gremlins II* is wonderfully orchestrated. The real star of this picture, though, is John Glover, who provides a brilliant caricature playing multimillionaire Daniel Clamp, who will surely remind most viewers of Donald Trump, despite the disclaimer at the end of the picture. The bombshell for whom Clamp seems to fall in the final reel is named Marla, also the name of one of Trump's celebrity playmates.

Ultimately, *Gremlins II* succeeds thanks to the playful nature of the screenplay written by Charlie Haas, a journalist and humorist who obviously enjoys satirizing popular culture and the Ted Turner approach to classic films. Haas makes fun of colorization, for example, with an announcer on Clamp's cable television network, hyping a new version of *Casablanca* (1942), "now in full color, with a happier ending." The screenplay makes fun of Muppet Miss Piggy, celebrity film reviewers (with Leonard Maltin genially going along with the satirical attack on what he represents),

Broadway blockbusters, and cable television itself. Also subject to this ribbing are media logos—that of *Batman* (1989), in particular—corporate egos and commercial glut, corporate ambition and power lunches. The satire is perfectly captured in the salutation "Have a powerful day." Critic John Simon, a guardian of High Culture, grumbled that *Gremlins II* is "too timid to be significant," but most viewers will find ample significance here.

Finally, *Gremlins II* succeeds because of the special-effects designs of coproducer Rick Baker, who won Academy Awards for his work on *An American Werewolf in London* (1981) and *Harry and the Hendersons* (1987). The sequel has more to offer than sheer spectacle, but it needs the spectacular effects in order to reach its finale, and Baker's work is nothing short of impressive.

Discussing *Gremlins II* with James Greenberg of *The New York Times*, director Joe Dante noted that the film had "the esthetics of a cartoon" and was intended as a "parody of the first film and movies like it." Dante and his collaborator Mike Finnell did not want merely to repeat themselves and demanded artistic freedom as a condition for making the sequel. They got what they wanted and were able to do in the sequel what they could not have done in the original, and with a budget of $32 million. Most important, they seemed to enjoy what they were doing. The film appears to be witty, inventive, and spontaneous, an outstanding self-parody, and a pleasure to watch.

James M. Welsh

Reviews
Baltimore Sun. June 15, 1990, p. 16.
Boxoffice. August, 1990, p. R59.
Chicago Tribune. June 15, 1990, VII, p. 38.
Films in Review. XLI, October, 1990, p. 485.
The Hollywood Reporter. CCCXII, June 4, 1990, p. 6.
Los Angeles Times. June 15, 1990, p. F1.
National Review. August 6, 1990, p. 48.
New York Magazine. June 25, 1990, p. 61.
The New York Times. June 10, 1990, sec. 2, p. 15.
The New York Times. June 15, 1990, p. B9.
The New York Times. August 12, 1990, Sec. 2, p. 11.
The New Yorker. LXVI, July 2, 1990, p. 54.
Newsweek. CXV, June 18, 1990, p. 59.
Time. CXXXVI, July 2, 1990, p. 64.
Variety. CCCXXXIX, June 4, 1990, p. 2.
Variety. CCCXXXIX, June 6, 1990, p. 23.
The Washington Post. June 15, 1990, p. C1.

THE GRIFTERS

Production: Martin Scorsese, Robert Harris, and James Painten for Cineplex Odeon
   Films; released by Miramax Films
Direction: Stephen Frears
Screenplay: Donald E. Westlake; based on the novel by Jim Thompson
Cinematography: Oliver Stapleton
Editing: Mick Audsley
Production design: Dennis Gassner
Art direction: Leslie McDonald
Set design: Nancy Haigh
Sound: John Sutton
Costume design: Richard Hornung
Music: Elmer Bernstein
MPAA rating: R
Running time: 119 minutes

> *Principal characters:*
> Roy Dillon .... John Cusack
> Lily Dillon .... Anjelica Huston
> Myra Langtry .... Annette Bening
> Bobo Justus .... Pat Hingle
> Simms .... Henry Jones
> Irv .... Michael Laskin
> Mints .... Eddie Jones
> Cole .... J. T. Walsh
> Hebbing .... Charles Napier

From the first divided images of *The Grifters*, it is clear that the focus will be
split. The shortcomings here lie less with the tale itself than with its handling. The
precise brand of dark and treacherous filmmaking that this release asks to be placed
alongsid seldom lends its storytelling to such multiple perspectives.

The opening sequence alternately trails the three "grifters" on their day's individual shady undertakings. Lily Dillon (Angelica Huston) coolly manipulates racetrack
stakes for unseen bookies while skimming a nice nest egg in the process. Mrs. Myra
Langtry (Annette Bening) attempts to cash in both her last fake jewels and her body.
Roy Dillon's (John Cusack) game is the slight-of-hand trick of slipping tens on the
bar in the place of twenty dollar bills and then leaving with the change. This is just
the sort of small-time con that Roy assumes will never land him in prison. It does,
on this occasion, land him a powerful blow to the stomach. Roy dismisses the seriousness of the injury that evening to Myra, who is his lover but far from his confi-
dante. Soon after, with her work bringing her near the Los Angeles area, Lily de-

cides to pay the first visit to her twenty-five-year-old son since he set out on his own eight years ago.

Roy tries to cover his hostility with detached civility toward his very young mother, but he almost immediately collapses from internal bleeding. This unexpected vulnerability allows Lily the opportunity to act with the ferocity of a mother tigress. She calls on her connections and whisks Roy to the hospital, saving his life. After recovering, however, Roy regards Lily with more spite than ever. Resentful of his unhappy childhood, he scoffs at her advice to get out of the life of graft. Lily also takes an instant, suspicious dislike toward Myra and urges Roy to get rid of her. Defying his mother, Roy leaves on an apparent holiday with Myra, while Lily is left to suffer the consequences of the spontaneous maternal instincts that have sidelined her racetrack obligations. Ironically, she too is hit in the stomach. Roy's excursion is actually to garner the hospital fees in order to pay Lily back and avoid her reentry as a controlling force in his life.

After finally glimpsing him in fleecing action, Myra reveals big plans to use Roy as her new partner in big-time con games. But the very same deep-rooted fears of being controlled by a manipulative woman are quickly triggered in Roy, and he casts Myra away. Furious, she accuses him of incestuous motivations of which he seems unaware. Myra's elaborate revenge scheme succeeds in putting Lily on the run, but it is Myra's body that is found alongside Lily's suicide note. Unemotionally, Roy goes along and incorrectly identifies the body. The only means of controlling power to which the bitter young man has left to cling is the denial of his petty stash of money when Lily arrives. He of all people should have realized, however, the lengths to which Lily would go in her desperation for survival.

Following all three petty grafters with equal diligence may have proven successful in the hard-boiled prose of Jim Thompson, on which the screenplay was based. The filmmakers chose to transplant his novel's 1950's characters point-blank into the 1990's. They also hold with a novelistic disinclination toward selecting a main character—one character through which the story could be filtered to the viewer. The resulting cinematic adaptation details the convoluted machinations of the principals in such a way as to deaden, rather than enliven, the story. Because films generally cannot be sustained over the broader scope that fiction can, the convention of focusing on a main character often streamlines the narrative into a more workable form. Such characters hold the viewer's interest largely with their potential for development. In the case of *The Grifters*, maintaining the triad of distinctly unredeemable individuals puts a burden on the story to be driven by other means.

The overreaching quality of director Stephen Frears's stylized omniscience works best in his earlier, more political films, such as *My Beautiful Laundrette* (1985) and *Sammy and Rosie Get Laid* (1987). The approach seems particularly ill at ease with the tone and subject matter of the pulp fiction that is brought to the screen. Unfortunately, much of *The Grifters* is devoid of those interesting tensions which might have existed. The characters are presented, but at a calculated distance that does not foster identification or evoke suspense. High angles often make the experience resemble an examination of flies under a microscope—academic and dimensionless. Films that purposely flatten drama must have a larger purpose, but there seems to be a lack of authority controlling the images; much of the meaning of these images hovers out of reach. To be made more compelling, the plot might have been structured to withhold some bits of information over others. Instead, it plods through everything so thoroughly that there are few surprises and little sense of building, no matter how awful the final deed may be. By denying both character and dramatic possibilities, the film leaves only the playing out of who shall emerge the grim victor. Because there is so little doubt on that score, the last scene delivers a hollow climax, even while it screams.

Critics admired the film mainly for its uncompromising depiction of nonchanging characters. Pauline Kael went as far as likening Bening's Myra to a legitimate femme fatale in the *film noir* tradition. Alongside the established works of this genre (many drawn from similar fiction sources), however, a noticeable difference in character treatment becomes apparent. What epitomizes the femme fatale icon above all is her "unknowability." Myra, like her endlessly paraded unclothed physique, is an open book. Memorable examples of the *film noir* canon—such as Huston's own father's classic *The Maltese Falcon* (1941)—achieve intrigue by keeping the depth of the female's duplicitous nature from the audience as well as the film's male protagonist. With *The Grifters*, that kind of simple mystery story allure is not possible. In fact, the moment at which surprise is played (with an abrupt cut out of the murder scene) is laughable. The flashbacks in which Myra retells her glorious past also work rather awkwardly against the tone. Their excessive humor grinds down the pace and diffuses valuable tension. The film could have been sharper had its focus stayed on Roy and not clouded a pivotal moment. This sequence is further taxing because the audience must struggle with the extent to which they are expected to believe that the two unsavory characters are unfathomable to each other.

While a *film noir* need not always be a detective story or even a mystery, it is little else if not subjective. Characterized by a paranoia and claustrophobia, these dark films draw in the viewers despite themselves. There are hints of this paranoia in Roy's extreme hostility toward Myra and her plan, and the most palatable crackle of electricity certainly exists in the screen moments between Lily and Roy. Such scenes, however, are few and far between. One longs for more exploration of the mother/son conflict and less of Myra's disrobing.

Perhaps its aim is along more modernist lines, such as producer Martin Scorsese's own *Taxi Driver* (1976). Unlike that film, however, *The Grifters* does not master that which it proposes to deal with and transcend history and audience expectations. A sense of urgency cannot be made up for merely with stylishly dark compositions or baroque flashback offerings. There is little evidenced of the illusive narrative quality that sustains the twenty-four characters through the converging events in the world of Robert Altman's *Nashville* (1975). Frears's film does not make enough use of the elements at its disposal. With their grime-coated artiness, the film's creators were attempting to make a great film over a good, watchable film, but they do not exactly hit their mark—they merely smudge it. Understandably mesmerized by the sheer reined-in power of an actress such as Huston, many critics were distracted from this point.

The film's integrity is based largely on the diligence of its cynical view of its characters and their inability to change even given their one brief moment of opportunity. The performances are certainly fine, especially with Cusack's newly tapped dark side, and there are undeniably those glimpses of rage and regret that ring true to anyone who has ever feared, loved, and hurt someone. Yet, the enthusiastic praise that the film received can seem distinctly amiss during its long, fidgety moments. In fact, *The Grifters* received four Academy Award nominations, for Best Actress, Best Supporting Actress, Best Director, and Best Adapted Screenplay. The Los Angeles Film Critics Association named Anjelica Huston Best Actress, and the National Society of Film Critics voted Huston Best Actress and Annette Bening Best Supporting Actress.

Mary E. Belles

Reviews

Boxoffice. CXXVI, November, 1990, p. R81.
California Magazine. XV, November, 1990, p. 164.
Chicago Tribune. January 25, 1991, VII, p. 29.
Film Comment. XXVI, November, 1990, p. 30.
The Hollywood Reporter. CCCXV, December 5, 1990, p. 5.
The L.A. Weekly. February 1-7, 1991, XIII, p. 33.
Los Angeles Times. December 5, 1990, p. F1.
The New Republic. CCIII, December 17, 1990, p. 26.
New York Magazine. XXIII, December 10, 1990, p. 84.
The New York Times. December 5, 1990, CXL, p. B1.
The New Yorker. LXVI, November 19, 1990, p. 127.
Newsweek. CXVII, February 4, 1991, p. 71.
Rolling Stone. November 29, 1990, p. 117.
Screen International. December 1, 1990, p. 22.
Time. CXXXVII, February 11, 1991, p. 79.
Variety. September 14, 1990, p. 2.
Variety. CCCXL, September 24, 1990, p. 84.
Vogue. CLXXX, November, 1990, p. 272.
The Washington Post. January 25, 1991, p. D1.

HAMLET

Production: Dyson Lovell for Warner Bros., Nelson Entertainment, and Icon; released by Warner Bros.
Direction: Franco Zeffirelli
Screenplay: Christopher De Vore and Franco Zeffirelli; based on the play by William Shakespeare
Cinematography: David Watkin
Editing: Richard Marden
Production design: Dante Ferretti
Art direction: Michael Lamont
Set decoration: Francesca Lo Schiavo
Sound: David Stephenson
Costume design: Maurizio Millenotti
Music: Ennio Morricone
MPAA rating: PG
Running time: 135 minutes

Principal characters:

Hamlet	Mel Gibson
Gertrude	Glenn Close
Claudius	Alan Bates
Laertes	Nathaniel Parker
The Ghost	Paul Scofield
Polonius	Ian Holm
Ophelia	Helena Bonham-Carter
Horatio	Stephen Dillane
Guildenstern	Sean Murray
Rosencrantz	Michael Maloney
The Gravedigger	Trevor Peacock
Osric	John McEnery
Bernardo	Richard Warwick
Marcellus	Christien Anholt
Francisco	Dave Duffy
Reynaldo	Vernon Dobtcheff
Player King	Pete Postlethwaite
Player Queen	Christopher Fairbank

The plot of *Hamlet* is pure Jacobean revenge drama: A troubled son must kill the uncle who has murdered his king-father, usurped the throne, and bedded and married the widowed queen, Gertrude. Yet, is the ghost of King Hamlet truly the spirit of his beloved father, or a demon sent to betray him? How can he avoid torturing his infatuated mother if he is to be the instrument of vengeance on her new husband, his uncle Claudius? Can his own affection for gentle Ophelia survive these revelations of sexual criminality? Is action worthwhile in a world that seems rotten to the core? In the end, Prince Hamlet takes action with a vengeance: He stabs counsellor Polonius through a tapestry; he casually orders the deaths of the two schoolfriends whom Claudius sets upon him; he abruptly abandons Ophelia, which leads to her madness and suicide; and when the curtain falls, his own corpse lies surrounded by those of Ophelia's brother Laertes, his uncle, and his mother.

Although William Shakespeare's *Hamlet* is a revenge play as surely as *Once Upon a Time in the West* (1969) is a Western, like Sergio Leone's baroque frontier epic, the play thwarts our expectations of the genre as much as it fulfills them. The play as Shakespeare wrote it is, for one thing, enormously overlong: It winds through nearly four hours of self-questioning indecision, "unnecessary" scenes, and fascinating superfluities to the final bloodbath. Every production of *Hamlet* is thus necessarily a rewriting of the play because no company—including Shakespeare's own Globe Theatre (with the Bard probably playing the ghost)—has ever staged the play at full length. To do so would be to purchase textual purity at the price of drama. Laurence Olivier's famous 1948 version runs only seven minutes longer than Franco Zeffirelli's production.

Every cut in this new *Hamlet* reinflects what remains. When he cuts the opening scene, in which semi-anonymous soldiers encounter the ghost, Zeffirelli cuts a certain feeling for the common man from his film, and must supply by other means the atmosphere and suspense that he loses—hence, the chase by Hamlet (Mel Gibson) through the moonlit castle to find and face the spirit of his father. He also creates, however, room for an opening that underscores the play's family plot. Zeffirelli delves into the prehistory of the play to bring back Gertrude (Glenn Close) weeping inconsolably over the tomb of her newly dead husband, and he grants to Claudius (Alan Bates) the privilege of the first line—his pregnant apostrophe to Hamlet, "Think of us as a father." In erasing all reference to Prince Fortinbras, who arrives from the North to take over Denmark at the end of the play, he acknowledges that the modern audience (unlike the audience of 1600) makes no intimate connections between the body of the state and the body of the ruler. In so doing, however, he also reduces Hamlet's stature—he becomes more a tortured man, less the "sweet Prince," who was "like to have proved most royal." Again, Hamlet's long exchanges with the traveling players are swept from Zeffirelli's version: Gone is the player-king's recitation of a stagy set-piece on the death of Hecuba, Queen of Troy—but with it, the meditations of Hamlet, himself the quintessential actor (faking lunacy to sniff out the truth of his uncle's guilt), on the player's self-induced tears and "truthfulness" in acting. Most successfully, Zeffirelli merges the half-crazy "Mousetrap" scene (wherein Hamlet stages for Claudius a play that re-enacts his crime) with the disturbing scene in which Hamlet taunts Ophelia (Helena Bonham-Carter) and denounces her sexual corruptibility. Shakespeare's point, that his mother's incest has destroyed the Prince's faith in women, emerges powerfully—all the more so because Gertrude now watches the exchange.

There will be much debate about Zeffirelli's *Hamlet*: many a professor will brush off a dog-eared copy and declare the film to be a travesty of the text. Yet that is not really the point. There is no definitive *Hamlet*—Shakespeare himself did not leave one. The questions that must be asked are these: Is this *Hamlet* an aesthetically fulfilling work in its own right? Does it function on its own terms, as an interpretation for a modern mass audience of a compelling story that gives shape to some of the deepest-rooted human fears and aspirations? Does it, in short, satisfy (as Zeffirelli set out to do, and as perhaps only Shakespeare has ever truly succeeded in doing) both the critics and the "groundlings," the intellectuals and the fans who flocked to see Zeffirelli's chosen Hamlet, Mel Gibson, in *Mad Max* (1979)?

The short answer is that Zeffirelli nearly succeeds. He and Gibson restore to the audience the Prince who can be coarse, cruel, and violent, banishing the romanticized wimp of a thousand schoolboy productions. Gibson's screen persona generates a sense of cliff-edge tension and manic physicality. Unfortunately, Zeffirelli also throws too much weight on Gibson's shoulders by consistently cutting the text around the figure of the prince: Claudius's great abortive confession vanishes, for example, in favor of more of the same from his nephew, whose lighthearted exchanges with Horatio (Stephen Dillane) or the players are also dropped to leave room for more serious stuff. The variety of the play and of the central role suffers as a result. Further, Gibson is not well served by his director in his soliloquies: He starts every one by sloping round a corner and putting on his Shakespeare face for the inevitable close-up, and he delivers them all in a monotonous half-whisper (presumably respectful). Only the "Yorick" speech in the graveyard, perhaps because he is here released into the open air and allowed to act with his body as well as his voice (a good voice, but short on the range that the role demands of an actor), flashes into life.

Other performances in this new *Hamlet* include Alan Bates as a devious, almost schizophrenic, Claudius and Paul Scofield as a haunting Ghost, both of whom have previously played the central role of the Prince. Ian Holm, another Royal Shakespeare Company veteran, appears to enjoy playing the pompous Polonius; he also brings an edge of conviction to his relationship as father to his daughter Ophelia, making more credible her lapse into madness after his death at Hamlet's hands.

As Gertrude, Glenn Close is magnificent. The Queen is a notoriously difficult role to play—her relationship with Hamlet is perhaps the emotional core of the play, yet she has comparatively few lines to speak. Here, the medium of film—above all, the peculiar physicality of acting style that the screen demands—serves the text superbly well. Close as Gertrude combines stature and presence with a yearning sensuality that makes credible both her dignity as dead King Hamlet's queen and her need for his replacement's baser charms. Her crucial confrontation with her son Hamlet is electrifying. Olivier's Hamlet pinned his Gertrude upon her own incestuous bed to hammer home to her the truth of her sexual guilt. Gibson and Zeffirelli, however, playing to perfection off the earlier film version and scholars' theories, up the stakes: The hammering is done with manic and agonizing relish. The sexual supercharge of the mother-son relationship, however, does have the side effect of making Bonham-Carter's sexualized mad scene as Ophelia strangely redundant.

Issues of sexual-familial betrayal underscore the whole of Zeffirelli's wonderful last act. Here, when his Hamlet is at last granted action—duelling Laertes (Nathaniel Parker), outwitting the king, playing to the crowd—Gibson comes into his own. So does Close's Gertrude: The very camera acknowledges her presence at the center of the play. As she sweats and retches, holding her bursting temples, dying by agonizing degrees, the camera's eye becomes her eyes fixed on the poisoned cup that Claudius had set for Hamlet and that she has drunk, then on her guilty bedmate, then on the beloved son whom she must use her last breath to warn.

Zeffirelli's background in architecture and set design is abundantly evident in his *Hamlet*, and he is ably abetted by Dante Ferretti, a designer who shares his operatic imagination and who was justly nominated for an Academy Award for his work on Terry Gilliam's fantasy *The Adventures of Baron Munchhausen* (1989). Zeffirelli's own film of Giuseppe Verdi's opera *Otello* (1986) was less grandly stylized than his *Hamlet*. Somber and massive castle interiors fit for Wagnerian extravaganza mix with solid detail of grey walls and harsh landscape (making the most of locations in Scotland and Kent), slashed by color every time a character spins across a courtyard. Sound, too, is finely used. It brings a sense of echoing, cold reality to the stone spaces of Elsinore castle; while a score that combines classic orchestral sounds with nontraditional instrumentation builds the edgy emotional atmosphere of the film.

Zeffirelli's 1968 *Romeo and Juliet* caught the mood of a generation, providing, for the first time, Shakespeare's teenaged lovers played by real teenagers. It started a new wave of filmic reinterpretations of the classics, which remain classics only if they continue to be rich in meanings for new times. If his *Hamlet* does not represent quite such a cinematic watershed, it is a superbly crafted film that will fuel arguments and emotions about the play for a generation. One is tempted to think this is what Zeffirelli (who first came to the play in 1964) signalled in the opening credits: first Elsinore, and then Shakespeare's title, *Hamlet*, take the eye, growing larger and larger until it encompasses and breaks the boundaries of the screen.

Joss Lutz Marsh

Reviews
Chicago Tribune. January 18, 1991, VII, p. 31.
The Christian Science Monitor. January 4, 1991, p. 12.
The Hollywood Reporter. CCCXV, December 19, 1990, p. 6.
Los Angeles Times. December 19, 1990, p. F1.
The New York Times. December 19, 1990, p. B1.
Newsweek. CXVI, December 31, 1990, p. 61.
Premiere. IV, January, 1991, p. 12.
Time. CXXXVII, January 7, 1991, p. 73.
Variety. December 19, 1990, p. 2.
The Washington Post. January 18, 1991, p. C1.

THE HANDMAID'S TALE

Production: Daniel Wilson; released by Cinecom Entertainment Group
Direction: Volker Schlondorff
Screenplay: Harold Pinter; based on the novel by Margaret Atwood
Cinematography: Igor Luther
Editing: David Ray
Production design: Tom Walsh
Art direction: Gregory Melton
Set decoration: Jan Pascale
Special effects: Tom Ward
Sound: Danny Michael
Makeup: Jeff Goodwin
Costume design: Colleen Atwood
Music: Ryuichi Sakamoto
MPAA rating: R
Running time: 109 minutes

Principal characters:
Kate	Natasha Richardson
Commander	Robert Duvall
Serena Joy	Faye Dunaway
Nick	Aidan Quinn
Moira	Elizabeth McGovern
Aunt Lydia	Victoria Tennant
Ofglen	Blanche Baker
Ofwarren/Janine	Traci Lind

A tony cast and creative team bring good ideas to this adaptation of Margaret Atwood's bestselling dystopian novel. Playwright Harold Pinter's script once again makes a tough-to-film, highly internalized story accessible and gripping, although *The Handmaid's Tale* did not require the audacious invention that, say, *The French Lieutenant's Woman* (1981) demanded. Tom Walsh's production design wittily conveys the color-coded coldness of the story's future Fascist theocracy, incorporating at the same time chillingly convincing aspects of contemporary American life. Director Volker Schlondorff exerts the same pleasing balance of fidelity to source material and cinematic boldness that has marked his better film adaptations—*The Lost Honor of Katharina Blum* (1975), *The Tin Drum* (1979), *Death of a Salesman* (1985), and, to a lesser extent, *Young Törless* (1966) and *Swann in Love* (1984).

Yet for all the clarity, humanism, and offbeat humor they have added to Atwood's mix, Schlondorff and company have failed to relieve *The Handmaid's Tale* of its fundamental, hysterical preposterousness. The film, like the book, is rich with insights into both the Fascist mind and feminist paranoia, and, considering the human rights abuses that some Middle Eastern theocracies indulge, Atwood's speculative nightmare vision should not seem too impossible to believe. Yet it does.

In a near-future United States that has undergone widespread ecological catastrophe and a Christian fundamentalist coup, the new republic of Gilead is implementing some severe social engineering techniques. The programs are based partly on the need to preserve the race and partly on grossly misinterpreted Biblical principles, but the main thrust to all of it is a deeply reactionary, white patriarchal pathology bent on doing away with all minorities and sexual deviations, and all women's rights.

Like many families, that of Kate (Natasha Richardson) tries to escape from the institutionalized madness, but they are caught at the Canadian border. Kate's husband is killed and her young daughter given to a powerful family. Kate is tested and discovered to be fertile; since pollution has rendered most women incapable of childbearing, this saves Kate from the usual punishment for trying to escape: cleanup duty in one of the many toxically contaminated zones. Instead, Kate is sent to the handmaid's training center, where fertile women are indoctrinated by hate-filled, cattleprod-wielding matrons (called Aunts) to appreciate their new calling in life: bearing children through loveless couplings for the power elite. The concept is based on the Genesis story of Rachel and her handmaid. At the center, intelligent Kate forms an encouraging alliance with Moira (Elizabeth McGovern), a no-nonsense lesbian whose fertility is the only thing standing between her and the hangman's noose. Kate eventually helps Moira mug an Aunt (Victoria Tennant) and escape. Yet Kate balks at running away and joining the underground resistance herself.

Her training complete, Kate is assigned to the heavily guarded home of Fred (Robert Duvall) and Serena Joy (Faye Dunaway). Also known as the commander, Fred is in charge of combatting insurrection for the Gilead government. Serena Joy, a former television evangelist who, like all women in the new republic, is now proscribed from reading, hopes that this latest Offred (handmaids are addressed by the word "Of" followed by their commander's name to signify his ownership and their own marginalized state of existence) will hurry and get pregnant before she causes the problems that previous handmaids did.

During the times of the month when Kate/Offred is at her fecund peak, a bizarre ceremony is performed in which Fred copulates with her while she lays at the edge of a bed with Serena Joy's legs wrapped around. If Fred makes the least caress or bit of eye contact, it is with his wife, not Offred. No words are uttered. Yet Fred does want to communicate with Kate. Breaking all rules, he invites her repeatedly into his private study, where he attempts to get to know her. They drink and play Scrabble; he gives her prerevolutionary fashion magazines to read and nice clothes to replace momentarily the red habit handmaids are always required to wear. Instinctually aware that something is amiss and worried that Offred is taking too long to get pregnant, Serena Joy encourages her into yet another forbidden diversion. She enables Kate to visit the garage apartment of her husband's chauffeur, Nick (Aidan Quinn), at night. Nick is secretly involved with the underground, and he and Kate quickly fall in love.

One night, Fred takes the biggest risk of all. He dresses Kate in a sexy evening

gown and then has Nick drive them to a secret brothel, where Gilead's most powerful men indulge all of their now-outlawed vices. Kate is astonished at the hypocriti-
cal setup, where once again the women who staff the place are totally enslaved to
their male masters. Kate finds her old friend Moira working there; her rebel group
was captured, but she was considered too attractive to be executed. Serena Joy discovers her husband and Kate's excursion and flies into a rage. This has happened before, and for once the law is on her side—fraternizing with a commander is enough
to have a handmaid shipped to the toxic wastelands. Kate goes to Fred's den, begging for help. Apologetically, he explains that there is nothing he can do for her. Yet
Kate and Nick have already planned Fred's murder. She stabs the commander and,
with Nick and other rebels' assistance, escapes to a mountain hideaway where, alone
(Nick having gone to fight), she awaits the birth of her baby.

Atwood's novel is told in subjective flashbacks, with little direct action. Pinter
does an admirable job of taking the story out of Kate's head and presenting it in
chronological, dramatically building order. This process, along with the carefully
controlled performances of Duvall and Dunaway, helps humanize the commander
couple beyond the villainous monsters they appeared to be in the book. It also helps
widen the film's scope from schematic feminist parable to an incisive look at the
impossibility of dictating human nature. Duvall's commander is not so much an
abject hypocrite as a man who, despite his rigid religious/political dogmatism, cannot suppress his desire for fully dimensional love.

These are admirable additions to Atwood's story, but they are achieved at the
expense of the novel's greatest strength: the complex and fascinating revelation of
Kate's character. A former librarian, her narration in the book was an intriguing
combination of intelligent insight, natural longing, and demoralizing fear. She had a
perfect take on the terrifying absurdity of the new regime, yet she constantly had to
modify her behavior because, no matter how much smarter she was than her captors,
she clearly understood that she was totally at their mercy.

Natasha Richardson is a fine, subtle actress, who proved in the title role of *Patty
Hearst* (1988) that she can project much feeling as a captive, mentally gagged woman.
Yet Kate, as Atwood imagined her, was anything but intellectually silent. Transferred to the more literal medium of film, it is hard to create a character of such rich
mental and emotional depth while essentially keeping your mouth shut. Richardson
is careful, quiet, and given to ironic smiles; she appears bemused and defensively
disengaged, and, although it is not a bad performance, it is probably the film's biggest liability. Audiences do not go with the fantasy because the identification figure
seems to be too spiritually passive.

Yet the overall focus of the film, as is the novel's, is the indominability of the
female spirit. It is apparent in Moira's spunky refusal, even upon her recapture, to
capitulate to overwhelming brainwashing (even working at the brothel is not so bad,
the lesbian tells Kate; the place is full of attractive, affection-starved women). It is
apparent in the very human responses to an otherwise dehumanized birthing ritual,
in which the handmaid mother Ofwarren (Traci Lind) is made an object of hysterical

worship by dozens of other attendant handmaids, of jealous scorn by the barren commanders' wives, and ultimately of little value by the system that immediately takes her newborn baby away from her. It is also apparent in the controlled explosions of savage frustration that the regime calls salvaging, stadium-sized events in which offenders are hanged or—if accused of any one of myriad unsanctioned sexual crimes—beaten to death by hordes of furious handmaids.

The connection between sexism and brutality informs every frame of *The Handmaid's Tale*. The dialectic is explored completely and intelligently, while the plot unfolds with unlikely swiftness. Yet Atwood's book remains the kind of novel that is too internalized to be transferred to the screen with complete success. The result is neither cautionary nor fancifully inventive enough; realism and fantasy elements cancel one another, leaving the viewer colder than the emotionally richer novel did.

Robert Strauss

Reviews
Boxoffice. April, 1990, p. R27.
Chicago Tribune. March 16, 1990, VII, p. 36.
Commonweal. CXVII, April 20, 1990, p. 257.
Films in Review. XLI, June, 1990, p. 368.
The Hollywood Reporter. CCCXI, March 7, 1990, p. 4.
The Humanist. L, May, 1990, p. 25.
Los Angeles Times. March 7, 1990, p. F1.
The New York Times. March 7, 1990, p. C17.
Newsweek. CXV, March 26, 1990, p. 54.
The Times Literary Supplement. November 2, 1990, p. 1181.
Variety. February 12, 1990, p. 2.

HAVANA

Production: Sydney Pollack and Richard Roth for Mirage; released by Universal Pictures
Direction: Sydney Pollack
Screenplay: Judith Rascoe and David Rayfiel; based on an original story by Rascoe
Cinematography: Owen Roizman
Editing: Fredric Steinkamp and William Steinkamp
Production design: Terence Marsh
Art direction: George Richardson
Set decoration: Michael Seirton
Sound: Peter Handford
Costume design: Bernie Pollack
Music: Dave Grusin
MPAA rating: R
Running time: 145 minutes

Principal characters:
Jack Weil	Robert Redford
Bobby Durán	Lena Olin
Joe Volpi	Alan Arkin
Arturo Durán	Raul Julia
Menocal	Tomás Milián
Marion Chigwell	Daniel Davis
Julio Ramos	Tony Plana
Diane	Betsy Brantley
Patty	Lise Cutter
Professor	Richard Farnsworth
Meyer Lansky	Mark Rydell
Willy	Vasek Simek
Baby Hernandez	Fred Asparagus
Mike MacClaney	Richard Portnow
Roy Forbes	Dion Anderson
Captain Potts	Carmine Caridi
Corporal	James Medina

On the very eve of revolution (just the time, he says, to make a killing), professional poker-player Jack Weil (Robert Redford), on the wrong side of forty and getting a little desperate, travels to Havana for the game of a lifetime, only to find a bigger game that may force him to show his hand—and his heart.

On the ferry from Florida and on the lookout for spare cash, he spots Bobby Durán (Lena Olin), a beautiful woman with a carload of stolen radios that she must get past dictator Batista's police to Fidel Castro's revolutionaries. Weil has morals that are as seamy as his face: He smuggles for her, but for a price. Though his youth has faded, however, his idealism has not. The one thousand dollars that he demands for running the customs mysteriously finds its way back into Bobby's purse. Maybe, as her revolutionary-aristocrat husband Arturo (Raul Julia) suspects, it is her beauty, not her cause or her commitment, that Weil believes in.

In order to challenge the big players, Weil must first convince his old friend Joe Volpi (Alan Arkin), the owner-manager of the glittering Lido Casino (modeled on the Havana Hilton), to host the high-stakes game. "The players I'm talking about, they don't walk up three floors," Weil says—not to apartments like his own, with its seedy furniture and bullfighting poster peeling from the wall. There is a touch of pathos in his macho claim: "I can make it happen." In the end, only a poker-faced virtuoso display of his card skills at a sleazy rival casino persuades Volpi. While Weil pushes Volpi to play host, however, he cannot shake his attraction to Bobby, and their meetings become less the product of chance as the eight days to revolution tick by.

The Duráns' political cadre has been infiltrated, and a few days later, while Weil sleeps with two bimbo tourists who want to see the "real" Havana, Cuban terror squads raid the Duráns' house, seize Bobby, and (the newspapers say) slaughter her husband. Staked by Volpi for his big game at last, Weil finds his opponents include the head of the secret police, Menocal (Tomás Milián), who is fresh from torturing Bobby. From here on, outfoxing Menocal in a bigger game takes over from outsmarting him at cards, but gambling remains the film's central metaphor.

Weil has Bobby released from custody. Back in his apartment, battered and shocked, she tries to take in Arturo's death, her own survival, and the answering tenderness that she feels for Weil, who is offering her rest. The cause comes first, however, and while Weil sleeps, she runs. He travels across the country and under fire, without knowing a word of Spanish, in order to take her from Arturo's family home and from the guerrillas, her "family." For a single day, she is his, until he reveals what he has learnt from Menocal—that Arturo is alive because the police chief has kept him as an insurance policy. Weil pays for Arturo's release with his final stake—a diamond sewn under the skin of his arm, the gambler's last chance. He lingers on the causeway that leads down to the ferry until she comes to bid him goodbye. "Were you waiting for me?" she asks. "All my life," he smiles.

Havana is the story of how an apolitical outsider gives his last shot in the cause of someone else's revolution and for love of a woman he will win only to lose, and of how a woman who wants to change the world changes one man. It is the story, of course, of *Casablanca* (1942), the American myth of romance, and of the romance of politics, and *Havana* acknowledges its parentage every time Redford lights Olin's cigarette.

It is hard to say how far Sydney Pollack and writer Judith Rascoe believe that opposites attract. To Redford's sardonic loner, the quintessential American hero and the latest in the long line of free agents that he has personified since the 1960's, they oppose, it seems at first sight, Olin's passionately committed insider who feels herself "part of something bigger than myself." Yet, there is no simple contrast here. Weil's "innocence" was always partly a front; he proves capable of a romantic attachment that effaces his very sense of self, even of survival, and in a quiet epilogue, he is left reading the papers for news of the world. Bobby is, in a sense, no less of an equivocal American type. The revolution and the people are not her own: An immigrant and bit-actress, perhaps she has simply found the mask or role that makes her believe that she is a player in history.

The first hour of *Havana* is an example of good updated old-style filmmaking—a Hollywood epic that does not duck the realpolitik, with tension and tempo riding on the atmosphere of the recreated Cuban city of corruption. Fine camerawork puts a neon-glossed spin on production designer Terence Marsh's giant set, one of the biggest in motion-picture history: While the film stays in the streets, strip joints, and casinos, it positively steams off the screen. The scene in which Weil entertains the female tourists while the Duráns' home and bodies are torn apart is one of the sleaziest and sharpest stretches of cross-cutting in years.

Then the problems start, however, and they are big problems: Olin's Bobby never melts, though the audience is meant to believe that she sleeps with Weil days after burying her husband—a veritable black hole at the center of the plot. In addition, Pollack lets his political sympathies dictate the script not once but several scenes too often. *Havana* provides too much of a not-so-good thing, and is simply a half-hour too long.

Although the film gets caught in its own web of words, its literacy is also a pleasure: A raft of talkative minor characters sparkle, from Arkin's club owner surveying the destruction from his balcony as if revolution were one final wild party, to Daniel Davis' CIA operator posing as an effete writer for "Gourmet" magazine (his kind of game, he tells Weil as they board the last ferry out of Havana, is "never over, so we never lose"). Redford, meanwhile, delivers lines that mingle macho straightforwardness with dry wit. "You want to tell me which car?" he asks naïve revolutionary Bobby as she turns to leave without describing the wagon that he is to drive off the ferry for her, "Or shall I just try them all?" His performance is hard to fault, and his honesty in opting to act his age is commendable. This is an all-star, no-star performance, and the edge of improvisation and body language (flicking cards like darts, for example) that he brings to the overblown script work wonderfully against the film's wordiness and glossy surface sheen. Everyone who has him pigeonholed should hear him deliver a come-on line to Olin that would have made Humphrey Bogart swallow his cigarette: "If you want suave, I can be suave. . . . But how many crude guys do you know?"

Joss Lutz Marsh

Reviews
Chicago Tribune. December 12, 1990, V, p. 1.

The Hollywood Reporter. CCCXV, December 10, 1990, p. 10.
Los Angeles Times. December 12, 1990, p. F1.
The Nation. CCLII, January 7, 1991, p. 22.
The New York Times. December 12, 1990, p. B3.
Newsweek. CXVI, December 17, 1990, p. 68.
Premiere. IV, December, 1990, p. 22.
Time. CXXXVI, December 17, 1990, p. 91.
Variety. CCCXLI, December 10, 1990, p. 2.
The Washington Post. December 12, 1990, p. G1.

HENRY AND JUNE

Production: Peter Kaufman for Walrus and Associates; released by Universal Pictures
Direction: Philip Kaufman
Screenplay: Philip Kaufman and Rose Kaufman; based on the diary of Anaïs Nin
Cinematography: Philippe Rousselot
Editing: Vivien Hillgrove, William S. Scharf, and Dede Allen
Production design: Guy-Claude François
Art direction: Georges Glon
Set decoration: Thierry François
Sound: Jean-Pierre Ruh
Costume design: Yvonne Sassinot de Nesle
Original source music: Mark Adler
MPAA rating: NC-17
Running time: 136 minutes

> *Principal characters:*
> Henry Miller .... Fred Ward
> June Miller .... Uma Thurman
> Anaïs Nin .... Maria de Medeiros
> Hugo .... Richard E. Grant
> Osborn .... Kevin Spacey
> Eduardo .... Jean-Philippe Ecoffey
> Jack .... Bruce Myers
> Publisher/editor .... Jean-Louis Buñuel
> Spanish dance instructor .... Feodor Atkine
> Emilia .... Sylvie Huguel
> Brassai .... Artus de Penguern

Henry and June, based on Anaïs Nin's diary chronicling her love triangle with the writer Henry Miller and his wife June, is clearly a labor of love for director Philip Kaufman—whose credits include *The Right Stuff* (1983) and *The Unbearable Lightness of Being* (1988)—and wife Rose Kaufman, with whom he wrote both *The Wanderers* (1979) and this screenplay. The Kaufmans have been fans of Miller and Nin since their college days. Miller's *joie de vivre*, captured in his series of ribald, picaresque, autobiographical novels, inspired generations of young would-be writers. For Kaufman, meeting Miller in the 1960's was such a turning point. He dropped out of Harvard Law School and wrote a novel. With the encouragement of Nin, whom he had met in Chicago in 1962, that novel became his first film, the award-winning *Goldstein* (1963). Such personal artistic wellsprings, however, do not always lend themselves to objective validation. *Henry and June* remains at best a rather private homage, one that, remarkably, misses the true spirit of these historical characters.

As the story begins, Nin (Maria de Medeiros), a not-so-recent French bride, feels stifled by her unimaginative husband, American-born banker Hugo (Richard E. Grant). Life in their cozy country home, miles from Paris, is unstimulating. As revealed in her diaries, she yearns for deeper creative and sexual expression—and for people who are alive. Enter Miller (Fred Ward): uncouth, bohemian, burning with raw genius. One day Hugo brings him home for dinner along with Osborn (Kevin Spacey), a banker and frustrated writer, who introduces Miller to Nin. Anaïs is immediately drawn to Miller. Awed by his genius and vitality, she writes in her journal, "I have met Henry Miller. He is a man whom life makes drunk. He is like me."

Soon Henry is telling her of his tortured love for his wife June (Uma Thurman), who, according to Miller, abandoned him in Paris to be with her lesbian lover in New York. Miller enlists Anaïs to help him understand June, unravel her mystery, and release him from her hold on him. When June visits Paris, however, she reclaims Henry and, amazingly, puts Anaïs under her spell as well. After her return to New York, Henry seduces Anaïs, practically under her husband Hugo's nose. Thus begins their impassioned relationship, fueled by an avalanche of love letters. They revel in their lusty trysts, eating, drinking, writing, and experiencing Paris as only lovers can. That the affair is illicit is not a small part of its allure. Yet, one night Henry is impotent, and, though Anaïs reassures him, both understand that their love is doomed.

When June returns to Paris, bemoaning Henry's depiction of her in his yet-to-be-published manuscript (*Tropic of Capricorn*, 1939), Anaïs is caught in the crossfire. She admits that she has been sleeping with Henry. Enraged, June flees, hurling their precious manuscripts down upon them as she exits. The next day finds Anaïs taking back her belongings from Henry. He begs her to stay, to marry him, but it is too late. Happily, Hugo pulls up at Osborn's as if on cue, offering her a ride home. Anaïs is changed. Having suffered and loved, she is a woman now. They pass Henry pedaling his bike, and he waves as if nothing has happened. His smile seems to betoken his habitual motto in the face of life's adversity: "always merry and bright."

For a work that may be presumed to be a homage to Miller and Nin, Kaufman's portrait is one-sided and sensational, glossing over the intellectual aspects of their relationship and glorifying the physical. Art in general, and their own writing in particular, seems only a pretext for their steamy trysts. In one telling scene, Henry is shown editing Nin's manuscript on D. H. Lawrence, red-penciling glibly, only to provoke her defensiveness. It is a caricature of competing artists, intended to show Nin's grit. In point of fact, Miller was very supportive of her work, while she in turn dedicated herself to launching his career. Lip service to their world of ideas comes full turn in the climax, when June, in a gesture that could only be called excessively symbolic, showers their manuscripts down upon their heads.

Ironically, Kaufman has overlooked the poetry in his subjects' lives, settling for an image of Henry that is strictly "Neanderthal," as Osborn jealously sums him up; and a portrait of June, the smoldering goddess of Henry's million-word-long fictive panegyric, *The Rosy Crucifixion* (1965), that is disappointingly drab and coarse. As played by Uma Thurman, whose credits include *Dangerous Liaisons* (1988) and *The Adventures of Baron Munchausen* (1989), June is a sulky vamp, more waif than seductress, with all the clumsy allure of an aspiring B-film star. Her Brooklyn accent is thick enough to cut. She is, by all accounts, a woman of magnificent conceits, lies, and self-creations, centerless and incandescent. Thurman reduces her to a shrill and false note.

Similarly, Fred Ward's rendition of Henry is monochromatic and crass. It appears to be a masterstroke of bad cross-casting, unless the objective is the superficial notion of Miller. Ward, lauded for his role as the earthy police officer in *Miami Blues* (1990; reviewed in this volume), relies on Miller's alleged conversational tick of humming, reducing it to a constant growl. He grunts his lines, explodes like a madman when June pushes him too far, and turns seductive with all the charm of a rattlesnake. In short, he behaves like a Neanderthal. In Ward's mouth, all of Henry's brilliant observations—his diatribe on money, for example (excerpted from Miller's essay "Money and How It Gets That Way")—seem thick-tongued and incongruous. Miller was a brilliant conversationalist, turning his handicaps, his Brooklynese and ticks, his "you know"'s, to advantage in a vibrant song. Unhappily, Ward has mistakenly built his character on the narrator of Miller's novels, "Val," a relentless toiler in the trenches of fornication, a poet-gangster, a barbarian-genius—in short, an amplified fiction, a legend created by the writer Miller.

As for Nin, her desperate quest for a middle road between her duty as a wife and her need to go beyond the contemporary limitations placed on European women of the 1930's, and not incidentally to satisfy her creative and sensual side, is reduced to a series of erotic interludes with Henry and June. Maria de Medeiros' magnificent portrayal of Nin is the film's one saving grace. Despite a minimum of credits, appearing in *Silvestre* (1980) and *La Lectrice* (1988), she is accomplished and promising. Not only does she resemble Nin uncannily, but she brings her to life on all levels as well: spiritual, psychological, and, not least of all, sensual. To the degree that Ward's Miller is one-dimensional, her re-creation of Nin is multifaceted, sparkling with nuance and organic subtlety. Her Nin is a woman deliciously ambivalent about her sexual proclivities, open, vulnerable, and courageous.

Other characters, notably Hugo, played with appropriate forebearance by Richard E. Grant, never rise above caricature. Hugo closes his eyes to Anaïs' affairs, dutifully avoiding perusal of her diaries, the very diaries Nin respectfully refrained from publishing until Hugo's death in 1977. In real life, he was violently jealous of Henry and was not quite the fool that Kaufman depicts. His convenient disappearance from the story during Anaïs' affairs, without a word of explanation in the script, is made all the more ludicrous by his reappearance to pick up the pieces at the end.

Kaufman takes liberties with Nin's text, distorting the events of the diary, borrowing from Miller's *roman à clef Tropic of Cancer* (1934), and creating his own meta-fictions and extensions of the facts to heighten the drama. At times this works to advantage, as when Kaufman has Miller recount to Nin how, before embarking on his boat to Europe, he doubled back to their apartment to find June, along with her lesbian lover, entertaining June's benefactor Pop. While Henry was spying on them from the window ledge, June shut the window on his tie, and he dangled precariously by the neck, high above the streets of Brooklyn. It never happened—Miller left for Europe, as much in the dark about June's liaisons as ever. Kaufman's invention shows Miller's need and habit, as a writer, to dramatize and turn his own life into legend. At times, Kaufman's creations seem contrived and excessive, as when, following the wonderful scene when Henry proves impotent, Anaïs wanders the Carnivale and is attacked and raped by a man in a mask who conveniently proves to be her Hugo. Thus, immediately on the heels of Henry's emasculation, Anaïs is shown unsympathetically seeking new thrills. Is Kaufman aware of the implications of this juxtaposition? Did Nin know it was Hugo all along? Such ambiguities are evident throughout the film, blurring the characters and their motives.

One brilliant fabrication of Kaufman worthy of mention is the deliciously ironic scene when Henry is nearly caught in bed with Anaïs. As Hugo blithely lingers in the kitchen over a hot bun from the oven, prepared by the maid (who is in on the joke), Anaïs and Henry cavort upstairs in Hugo's bed. Later, the cuckolded Hugo innocently invites Henry to join him and Anaïs in bed. It is a scene reminiscent of Kaufman's best absurdities in *The Unbearable Lightness of Being*, for which he won an Academy Award nomination.

Comparisons with this widely applauded film are inevitable, as the subject matter—the erotic—is a common denominator. Based on Milan Kundera's brilliant novel of love amid the deployment of Russian tanks in Prague in 1968, *The Unbearable Lightness of Being* also features a man of sexual largesse, an affable, philandering Czech doctor. Unlike Kaufman's Miller, however, the hero of Kundera's novel is painted with a full palette of colors and enlists the audience's sympathy. In *The Unbearable Lightness of Being* Kaufman celebrates the sensual; in *Henry and June*, only the sexual. Yet it is difficult to imagine why *Henry and June* became the precedent case for establishing a new Motion Picture Association of America code, NC-17: no children under seventeen admitted. Little flesh is actually shown. Undoubtedly it is the film's incessant concern with the subject of sex which justifies this rating. Surely Miller is chuckling in his grave, delighted to revive his old nemesis, the hellhounds of censorship.

Even for devotees of Miller and Nin, *Henry and June* is disappointing, titillating rather than satisfying the appetite for insight into the lives and loves of these two pioneering writers and their shared central enigma of June, who drove both Miller and Nin to plumb her mystery in their voluminous writings. All the more frustrating, as Kaufman's vibrant re-creation of Parisian bohemia of the 1930's—replete with seedy Montmartre pickpockets, lush bordellos, nude contortionists, and bawdy Carnivale nights—provides an alluring setting. Credit for cinematic vérité must be shared with cinematographer Philippe Rousselot, who won an Academy Award nomination for *Hope and Glory* (1987) and *The Bear* (1988); and production designer Guy-Claude François. In the final analysis, Kaufman's *Henry and June* is an uneven pastiche of inspirations and misdirections, with a brilliant but unconnected portrait of Nin at the center.

Eugene H. Davis

Reviews
Chicago Tribune. October 5, 1990, VII, p. 28.
The Christian Science Monitor. October 10, 1990, p. 10.
The Hollywood Reporter. CCCXIV, October 5, 1990, p. 6.
Los Angeles Times. October 4, 1990, p. F1.
The New Republic. CCIII, November 5, 1990, p. 26.
The New York Times. October 5, 1990, p. B3.
Newsweek. CXVI, October 22, 1990, p. 73.
Premiere. November, 1990, p. 92.
Vanity Fair. LIII, November, 1990, p. 72.
Variety. CCCXL, September 17, 1990, p. 2.
The Washington Post. October 5, 1990, p. D1.

HOME ALONE

Production: John Hughes; released by Twentieth Century-Fox
Direction: Chris Columbus
Screenplay: John Hughes
Cinematography: Julio Macat
Editing: Raja Gosnell
Production design: John Muto
Art direction: Dan Webster
Set design: Bill Fosser and Karen Fletcher-Trujillo
Set decoration: Eve Cauley and Dan Clancy
Sound: Jim Alexander
Costume design: Jay Hurley
Music: John Williams
MPAA rating: PG-13
Running time: 102 minutes

Principal characters:
Kevin . . . . Macaulay Culkin
Harry . . . . Joe Pesci
Marv . . . . Daniel Stern
Kate . . . . Catherine O'Hara
Peter . . . . John Heard
Marley . . . . Roberts Blossom
Gus Polinski . . . . John Candy
Linnie . . . . Angela Goethals
Buzz . . . . Devin Ratray
Uncle Frank . . . . Gerry Bamman
Megan . . . . Hillary Wolf
Santa . . . . Kenneth Hudson Campbell

Home Alone surprised everyone when it emerged as the third most successful film of 1990. At a cost of $18 million to produce, *Home Alone* earned more than ten times that amount domestically in its first three months of release.

Home Alone tells the story of every child's worst nightmare and best fantasy rolled into one. Eight-year-old Kevin McAllister (Macaulay Culkin), the youngest of a seemingly endless family, is accidentally left behind when the rest of his clan flies to Paris for Christmas. Kevin, used to being under the often insensitive thumbs of his parents and siblings, has the freedom to do anything he wants for the first time in his life—until circumstances force him to defend his home against two burglars.

The story begins with a look at the chaotic McAllister household, which is brimming over with people—some who actually live there and others who are out-of-town relatives sleeping over the night before their joint trip to Paris. Considering the circumstances, there certainly is not anything out of the ordinary here in this upper-middle-class suburban home. Children are running everywhere and parents are packing suitcases. A police officer (Joe Pesci), presumably making rounds through the neighborhood, is trying, in vain, to catch the attention of anyone who will listen.

In the middle of this pre-vacation family chaos, the audience is given its first glimpse into the helpless side of young Kevin's character. When he is faced with an order to pack his own suitcase, something he has never done before, he panics. His older siblings reinforce Kevin's ineptitude with their nasty comments, increasing the audience's sympathy for him. Kevin, who seems somewhat accustomed to being picked on, wanders downstairs to where the police officer is waiting patiently and senses something sinister when he spots a gleaming gold tooth in the man's smile. After all, as every young boy knows, only villains, from pirates to James Bond's resilient enemy Jaws, wear such noticeable oral imperfections. Kevin's keen observation alerts the viewer that there is more to the eight-year-old than merely serving as a punching bag for his bullying brothers and sisters.

Kevin can take a lot of verbal abuse from his family, but he does draw the line when it comes to something very important to him—food. Buzz McAllister (Devin Ratray), the crudest and largest sibling, devours the last of the cheese pizza, the only kind that Kevin likes. Kevin reacts by head-butting Buzz in the stomach, which sets off a chain reaction of kitchen mishaps, ending with a sharp rebuke from insensitive Uncle Frank (Gerry Bamman) and the confirmation that Kevin is, indeed, the unappreciated member of the family. Only the audience understands what drove small Kevin to challenge his oversized brother as he is sent to bed in the scary converted attic without dinner.

With the conviction of a child who knows that he has been wronged but realizes that no one understands, Kevin wishes out loud that his family would disappear. This outburst shocks his mother (Catherine O'Hara), though more than likely does not surprise the children in the audience. The finality of the attic door closing Kevin in for the night sets the stage for that wish to come true.

The transformation from a story about a family to a story about a young boy is deftly handled. In a plane somewhere over the Atlantic Ocean, Kevin's mother has a nagging feeling that she has forgotten something. Simultaneously, Kevin, having woken up and wandered down out of the attic into the now strangely peaceful house, becomes convinced that he, miraculously, has wished away his family. Out of a combination of fear and glee, he screams "Mom!" The camera flashes back to the transatlantic jet as she instantly remembers what, or rather who, she has left behind.

Though his mother is distressed, Kevin adjusts quickly to his newfound freedom. After all, he is really a young boy who is old enough to think about rebellion but who is too young to do anything effective about it. Hughes's long-winded indulgence of Kevin will not disappoint anyone who expects this new freedom to include rifling through Buzz's secret box (including the obligatory copy of *Playboy*), eating enormous ice cream sundaes, and bouncing on his parents' bed while eating popcorn. The predictable explorations of shaving and using after-shave and antiperspirant, however, are somehow transparent. They appear to be acted by a child who is told to act like an adult, rather than by a child who is pretending to be an adult. When comparing this performance to that of Tom Hanks in *Big* (1988), Culkin's mannerisms seem contrived.

On his own, Kevin does have to face his two childhood fears. First, he overcomes his fear of the furnace in the basement, which in Kevin's childish imagination comes alive, reminiscent of a Stephen King creation. Later, he will meet Marley (Roberts Blossom), the old man who lives next door and who is rumored by Buzz to be an ice-shovel murderer. *Home Alone* is a children's film, but in exploiting childhood fears as well as delights, it has earned its PG-13 rating.

Perhaps the most pervasive theme in *Home Alone* is that of fantasy. The film excels in this aspect as it displays a wonderful winter spectacle of Christmas lights, sparkling snow, carolers, and a local Santa's village. When the reality of being alone begins to hit Kevin, it is to Santa (Kenneth Hudson Campbell) that he goes to plead for the return of his family for Christmas. In this scene, Hughes shows his skill in revealing the child within. As the young boy tells Santa that he knows that he is a fraud, the audience is set up for the confirmation that, sadly, the insecure and innocent boy that had existed before has been replaced by a grown-up. The audience assumes that, just as Kevin overcame his childish fear of the furnace, he also lost his fantasies of Christmas. This is a glorious setup, however, as Kevin matter-of-factly reveals that he knows that this phony Santa works for the real one, who is too busy to be everywhere at once.

The fun finally begins when Kevin discovers that his house is next on the list of burglars Harry (Joe Pesci)—the suspicious police officer—and Marv (Daniel Stern). The suddenly resourceful boy sheds his insecurities and devises a multitude of ruses and booby traps in order to defend his territory. His preliminary diversion tactics provide some of the film's best moments, including the clever use of a video cassette recorder and a gangster video. These tactics only work temporarily, however, and Kevin prepares a multiphase battle plan.

This Christmas comedy creates its best laughs from its slapstick, which is performed with perfect timing by the scheming criminals Harry and Marv. With Kevin's house as their prime target, they sneak around the neighborhood trying to determine if Kevin's house is really vacant, while ransacking more minor pickings. It is difficult to tell whether Hughes intended to reincarnate Laurel and Hardy in this pair, or to re-create the incompetence of Chevy Chase in his most recent production success, *National Lampoon's Christmas Vacation* (1989). In any case, the comedy is in the action, not the dialogue. To the audience, it is a classic circus setup—the audience guesses what is going to happen to the poor clowns next. Marv is left with the imprint of an iron on his face, Harry is tarred and feathered, and Kevin is both hero and role model to the children in the audience, staying one step ahead of the thieves while managing to maintain an innocent expression throughout. There is an amusing line, however, when the dimmer of the dim-witted burglars, Marv, reveals that his reason for flooding burgled homes is to develop their underworld reputation as "the wet bandits."

The musical score by John Williams works best when it enhances the timing and tension of the slapstick comedy. Predictable old favorites such as *White Christmas* and *Santa Claus Is Comin' to Town* are also effectively scattered throughout the score, setting the pace and emotional tone of the film. The two original numbers by Williams, however, leave the audience with no strong musical identification, as the themes of *Jaws* (1975), *Star Wars* (1977), and *E.T.: The Extra-Terrestrial* (1982) did.

On Christmas day, loneliness sets in, and Kevin begins to wish that his family would reappear. Because this is a Christmas film, it is no surprise that his mother, who has been justly punished for her insensitivity by having a terribly difficult journey back, arrives home to make his most recent wish come true. Her guilt is severe enough that the audience is convinced that Kevin will not be looked over again. The rest of the family soon files in and the McAllisters are together for Christmas. None of this should surprise the audience, who presumably come to see Christmas films for their delightful emotional appeal rather than for an intricate story line.

Except for the brief and surprisingly lackluster cameo appearance by John Candy, which seemed to be more of an excuse to reunite the cast from *Uncle Buck* (1989) than a necessary plot element, this is a delightful look at Christmas, families, and happy endings. No one, except for the bad guys, is left unhappy in *Home Alone*.

Leslie A. Pearl

Reviews
Chicago Tribune. November 16, 1990, VII, p. 43.
The Christian Science Monitor. December 7, 1990, p. 12.
The Hollywood Reporter. November 12, 1990, p. 8.
Los Angeles Times. November 16, 1990, p. F6.
New Statesman and Society. III, December 14, 1990, p. 30.
The New York Times. November 16, 1990, p. B7.
Newsweek. CXVI, December 3, 1990, p. 67.
Premiere. IV, October, 1990, p. 74.
Time. CXXXVI, December 10, 1990, p. 94.
Variety. November 12, 1990, p. 2.
The Washington Post. November 16, 1990, p. D7.

HOUSE PARTY

Production: Warrington Hudlin; released by New Line Cinema
Direction: Reginald Hudlin
Screenplay: Reginald Hudlin
Cinematography: Peter Deming
Editing: Earl Watson
Production design: Bryan Jones
Art direction: Susan Richardson
Set decoration: Molly Flanegin
Special effects: Michael Sullivan
Sound: Oliver Moss
Makeup: Laini Thompson
Costume design: Harold Evans
Music: Marcus Miller
Songs: Kid 'n Play, "Fun House"; and Today, "Why You Gettin' Funky on Me"
MPAA rating: R
Running time: 100 minutes

Principal characters:
Kid	Christopher Reid
Pop	Robin Harris
Play	Christopher Martin
Bilal	Martin Lawrence
Sidney	Tisha Campbell
Sharane	A. J. Johnson
Stab	Paul Anthony
Pee-Wee	Bowlegged Lou
Zilla	B. Fine

  House Party is a black independent feature that translates the white teen film genre to the black middle-class experience. Director Reginald Hudlin and his brother Warrington, who produced the film, set out to depict the "hip-hop sub-culture of today's Black teenagers." Like *Risky Business* (1983) and *Ferris Bueller's Day Off* (1986), *House Party* takes place in a suburban milieu that alternates between high school and parties, and is notable for the absence of parents.
  House Party, however, deviates from the white teen film in its awareness of race and class, as well as of the film stereotypes and conventions for blacks. The first sign is implicit in the use of a previously all-white genre. The Hudlin brothers go one step further, in depicting an unnamed urban area in black middle America. There, removed from the film stereotypes of Harlem, Watts, and other urban ghettos, *House Party* can explore a metaphoric black space in which the projects and suburbs are worlds apart, yet somehow within a short walk of one another.

While the geographic boundaries are vague, the implications of crossing them are not. In *House Party*, the lush suburban living rooms, furnished with antiques and empty of parents, offer a space for the teenagers to test their boundaries, while a glimpse into a project living room reveals the silent weight of an impoverished extended family. The elements that unite these two spaces are the teenagers themselves and a ubiquitous television consumer show. While class issues are central to most of John Hughes's teen films, such as *The Breakfast Club* (1985), *Pretty in Pink* (1986), and *Some Kind of Wonderful* (1987), the images of the projects in *House Party* prohibit the usual resolution of class conflict.

Given the genre within which it operates, *House Party* walks a fine line between a celebration of black youth culture and social message. The filmmakers themselves are self-conscious in raising three issues common to American youth of all races: alcohol abuse, birth control, and father-son relationships. Beyond this, the film uses humor to explore the misperceptions of those white authority figures whose mistakes have a significant impact on black youth: high school administrators and the police.

House Party begins with Kid (Christopher Reid) in bed, having a dream about a party that blows the roof off the house. As the end credits roll, that same roof will land on the two white police officers who antagonize the entire black community. As a framing device, the dream sequence establishes the film narrative as a middle-class, teenage wish fulfillment, a device perhaps inspired by *Risky Business*. The film itself chronicles the next twenty-four hours, as Kid and his friends prepare for a party at the house of their friend Play (Christopher Martin).

Kid and Play, members of the rap group Kid 'n Play, plan to use the party as a chance to demonstrate their rap skills and thereby impress Sidney (Tisha Campbell) and Sharane (A. J. Johnson). Kid, however, displaying all the awkwardness of a teenager, bumps into three bullies in the high school cafeteria: Stab (Paul Anthony), Pee-Wee (Bowlegged Lou), and Zilla (B. Fine), all members of Full Force, a highly successful rap group and production team. Stab calls Kid's dead mother a whore and then punches him repeatedly after an upset Kid flings Jell-O at him. The Jell-O hits a portrait of former president Ronald Reagan, and the two end up in the principal's office, where the white principal misreads the situation, believing that Stab called Kid's mother a garden tool, or hoe.

Once outside school, Stab, Zilla, and Pee-Wee pursue Kid, especially since Kid variously taunts the three as hoods and homosexuals. Another impediment to Kid's debut as a rapper comes when Kid's father, Pop (the late Robin Harris), receives a note from the principal and grounds Kid for the night. Kid must sneak out of his house while his father naps in the living room. On the street, not watching where he walks, Kid steps in front of Stab's Jeep. He is then chased to a black fraternity alumni party, where the police arrive. The adults refuse to press charges, explaining that the teenagers need "discipline, not solitary confinement." The police, however, miss the point and conclude that the adults are too afraid to talk.

While Kid struggles to reach Play's house, Play prepares for the party, taking advantage of his friend Bilal (Martin Lawrence), who provides the stereo equipment. When Play's car, loaded with equipment, proves unable to accommodate Bilal and a female passenger, Play leaves a furious Bilal behind.

Once everyone has arrived at Play's house, Kid and Play are able to demonstrate their new dance moves and engage in a rap duel. Sidney and Sharane both make advances to Kid, who cannot make up his mind, although he seems to prefer Sharane. Play, however, explains why he has a better claim on Sharane: She is a project girl with no privacy and therefore requires a boyfriend with a car. Sidney, on the other hand, comes from a well-to-do family and has her own bedroom. In the end, Kid walks Sharane and Sidney to their respective homes and discovers that he has much more in common with Sidney. When the two end up in Sidney's bed, Kid asks her if she is on the pill; when she answers that she is not, Kid retrieves a condom from his wallet. The condom, however, has melted, and a disappointed Kid must wait.

Although *House Party* addresses the issue of birth control head-on, the class dimensions of its message are troublesome. Kid admits that he might not have asked about birth control with another woman. Play later makes the implication explicit, when he explains that it is the woman's problem if she becomes pregnant. Since Play and Sharane have become involved by this point, his intentions are both clear and unchallenged. In fact, a certain ambivalence about the projects runs throughout *House Party*. While white teen films often use ghetto culture as a liberating force for uptight white teenagers, as in *Adventures in Babysitting* (1987), here it is an unsettling presence that the film cannot and, to its credit, does not incorporate into its humor.

After Kid has left Sidney's house, he is again pursued by the three bullies. Once again, the police catch up with them and this time arrest all four. In jail, Kid finds himself the object of the other prisoners' sexual desires and must hold them at bay with an improvised rap song about safe sex. The so-called message, however, turns out to be a prolonged setup for an antihomosexual remark, delivered once Kid is bailed out by his friends.

House Party has trouble with its self-conscious messages. The treatment of the issue of teenage alcohol abuse consists of a series of shots of a male who drinks too much and passes out. The father-son relationship remains unexplored: Instead, Pop is seen roaming the neighborhood in search of Kid, so that he can punish him. In the last scene, he appears at Kid's bedroom door with a belt and announces, "Your ass is mine." Rather than comment on family life, the line puts an ironic twist on Kid's antihomosexual taunts and near-rape in jail.

For ethnic filmmakers, the desire to "do the right thing," often gets twisted into an imperative to do all things in one film, since there might not be another chance. *House Party* does fall short in its use of homosexual stereotypes and its class-skewed message about birth control; when judged against the white teen films, however, *House Party* does at least introduce some serious and open-ended issues into an otherwise escapist genre. Perhaps the most important impact of the crossover success of *House Party*, however, will be to put another foot in the door that black filmmaker Spike Lee continues to push open. There are, after all, too many stories in the black experience for one or two filmmakers to tell. In an era of increasing racial conflict and violence, these stories are needed more than ever.

Chon A. Noriega

Reviews

American Film: Magazine of the Film and Television Arts. XV, April, 1990, p. 50.
Boston Globe. March 22, 1990, p. 85.
Chicago Tribune. March 9, 1990, VII, p. 36.
The Guardian. March 21, 1990, p. 20.
The Hollywood Reporter. CCCXI, January 25, 1990, p. 4.
Los Angeles Sentinel. March 22, 1990, p. B8.
Los Angeles Times. March 9, 1990, p. F4.
The Nation. CCL, April 2, 1990, p. 467.
The New Republic. CCII, April 9, 1990, p. 26.
The New York Times. March 9, 1990, p. C14.
Newsweek. CXV, March 26, 1990, p. 55.
Time. CXXXV, March 26, 1990, p. 71.
Variety. CCCXXXVIII, February 7, 1990, p. 32.
The Village Voice. March 13, 1990, p. 67.

THE HUNT FOR RED OCTOBER

Production: Mace Neufeld; released by Paramount Pictures
Direction: John McTiernan
Screenplay: Larry Ferguson and Donald Stewart; based on the novel by Tom Clancy
Cinematography: Jan De Bont
Editing: Dennis Virkler and John Wright
Production design: Terence Marsh
Art direction: Dianne Wager, Donald Woodruff, and William Cruse
Set decoration: Mickey S. Michaels
Sound: Richard Bryce Goodman
Sound Editing: Cecelia Hall (AA) and George Watters II (AA)
Makeup: Wes Dawn and James R. Kail
Costume design: Darryl M. Athons and Gary R. Sampson
Music: Basil Poledouris
MPAA rating: PG
Running time: 135 minutes

Principal characters:
Captain Marko Ramius .... Sean Connery
Jack Ryan .... Alec Baldwin
Captain Bart Mancuso .... Scott Glenn
Captain Second Rank Vasily Borodin .... Sam Neill
Admiral James Greer .... James Earl Jones
Ambassador Andrei Lysenko .... Joss Ackland
Jeffrey Pelt .... Richard Jordan
Ivan Putin .... Peter Firth

Submarines have long been the setting for action films. Such adventures as *Destination Tokyo* (1943), *Run Silent, Run Deep* (1958), and *Ice Station Zebra* (1968) make full use of the conflicting dramatic potentials of a submarine setting: freedom of movement versus claustrophobia, stealth versus vulnerability, graceful movement through water versus murkiness of environment, human bravery and steely technology against underwater fragility.

With time, however, the submarine film drifted away from its more earnest conventions. Many of its most memorable examples portrayed submarine life in a farcical (*Operation Petticoat*, 1959), whimsical (*Twenty Thousand Leagues Under the Sea*, 1954), or fantastic manner (*Thunderball*, 1965). With the success of *Das Boot* (1982), the genre tacked back into seriousness and even into sober speculation. The huge success of author Tom Clancy's taut, intricate, and erudite novel, *The Hunt for Red October*, therefore begged for a Hollywood adaptation. Veteran producer Mace Neufeld and director John McTiernan teamed to create a motion picture that improves upon much of the sourcebook's character development, though at the expense of what may have been the novel's greatest strength: its deep, espionagelike revelations of military technology.

The film's opening immediately introduces Soviet submarine captain Marko Ramius (Sean Connery), a ramrod-straight officer who seems utterly unaffected by the gray, cold Murmansk environment that envelops him. Quickly the film crosscuts to its second lead character, Central Intelligence Agency (CIA) analyst Jack Ryan (Alec Baldwin), who has been assigned to examine a photograph of a new Soviet submarine, which appears to have two unexplained openings in its hull. Ryan indicates to his superior, Admiral James Greer (James Earl Jones), that he suspects these doorlike openings to be part of a nearly silent propulsion system that will render the submarine virtually invisible to sonar and will give the Soviets a dangerous first-strike capability.

Ramius has concluded the same. Though he is to captain the revolutionary new ship, the *Red October*, Ramius begins swiftly to alter the submarine's intended trial mission. He is especially disturbed to find a Komitet Gosudarstvennoi Bezopasnosti (KGB) officer in his cabin. These two are clearly at opposite ends of the pre-*glasnost* spectrum; cinematographer Jan De Bont conveys this by placing each actor at extreme opposites of the screen. Indeed, Ramius is often positioned to the side or on the edge of the frame. The technique is a clever visual shortcut to Ramius' personality: This is a near-outsider who has been forced to the boundaries of conventional Soviet military thinking. What kind of thinking—warlike or not—is not clear at first; this uncertainty is what lends suspense to much of Ramius' initial actions: He strangles the KGB operative in his cabin, burns his military orders, confiscates the second key necessary to fire the submarine's thick array of nuclear-tipped missiles, and sends the hulking *Red October* off to an unplanned mission—one about which only a few of his fellow trusted officers know.

Ramius' rogue plans are a pivotal plot point: They unleash a flood of narrative complications. Fifty-eight Soviet ships head out in pursuit of the *Red October*. The Americans question whether this is not a major Soviet military offensive. Soviet officials, in turn, hide the truth from their U.S. counterparts. American spies uncover what is really happening. A second KGB operative seems to be trying to sabotage the *Red October* from within. Ultimately, the Soviets themselves ask for the United States' help in hunting down the dangerous submarine, claiming that Ramius' mission is to singlehandedly start World War III.

In a darkly lit, foreboding conference room, Jack Ryan—a relatively ordinary man thrust into extraordinary circumstances—boldly gives his interpretation to an assembly of high-ranking government leaders: that Ramius, a Lithuanian, is defecting to the West and is bringing *Red October* as his prize. Indeed, the filmmakers have planted clues to Ramius' real motives all along: When he happens upon the KGB operative in his room, for example, he is reading a book belonging to Ramius on Armageddon.

Several other factors are introduced to complicate this adventure: A U.S. submarine captained by Bart Mancuso (Scott Glenn) has discovered a way to pursue the not-quite-silent *Red October.* Ryan soon joins Mancuso on his submarine—a plot device meant to tighten an increasingly complicated story line and to give the audience a heightened sense of involvement and jeopardy. (By this point Ryan has become the point of view with which the audience identifies.) Also, another Soviet submarine captain becomes adept at second-guessing Ramius' movements.

Up to this point, *The Hunt for Red October* is top-heavy in narrative exposition. In the last third of the film this changes. Action comes swiftly. The second Soviet submarine fires torpedoes at *Red October.* Ramius uses wily tactics to avoid them. The remaining, still unidentified KGB crew member sabotages one system after another and is hunted down in a tense shooting duel amid the forest of nuclear missiles. The resolution, which comes after a false climax, occurs when the second Soviet submarine is blown up by one of its own torpedoes. (By this point, in a bit of credibility-straining plot mechanics, Ryan and Mancuso have come aboard *Red October* via a small transfer submarine.) On the surface, Soviet sailors applaud what they believe to be the destruction of their renegade *Red October.* The *Red October,* however, is intact. It sails into a cold, gray Maine harbor (in imagery that echoes the film's opening), where Ryan and Ramius find one more common interest: fishing.

The Hunt for Red October succeeds in large part through its use of special effects. Underwater films have always suffered because of the images' inherent murkiness and constraint. Industrial Light and Magic, a division of Lucasfilm, overcame many of the genre's visual limitations by re-creating the film's environment through detailed miniature models, computer-generated propeller swirls, and, ironically, not a drop of water. The film's more conventional images abet the overall look: Shallow depth of field shots, extreme close-ups, Dutch angles, and monochromatic lighting all serve as visual correlatives to the characters' moods and feelings. Color, lighting, and graphics, especially, help organize the intricate, crosscut plotting, for one of the film's greatest challenges is to keep the location, characters, and action clear and well-situated to the viewer.

There are narrative elements that strain credibility, though. Ryan's predictions of Ramius' action's are preternatural. In the midst of heated action, Bart Mancuso is somehow able to pilot the Soviet *Red October* itself, unfamiliar controls and language notwithstanding. Also, the English-Russian language translation problems are handled somewhat awkwardly. Some of these problems were inherited from the novel. The filmmakers did try to compensate by fleshing out the characters. Ryan is introduced far earlier in the film, for example, and is given one more complicating trait: his fear of flying. Aspects of personality, too, are often cleverly translated through a single shot: Ramius' calm dining while his ship is under siege conveys an unusual sangfroid. Yet the limitations of time (despite the film's 135-minute-long running time) shortchange other points of characterization: The book's Ramius has more complex reasons for defecting. As the story stands, the viewer is left to wonder why the Soviet captain seems to welcome the chase and even encourages it by informing the Soviets of his defection so early. Is it an act of defiant revenge for his wife's death? It is hard to tell. Finally, the novel's greatest strength—its detailed, technological intelligence—is virtually lost in the film. *The Hunt for Red October,* as a result, succeeds as a one-dimensional but satisfying thriller.

Marc Mancini

Reviews
Boxoffice. April, 1990, p. R26.
Chicago Tribune. March 2, 1990, VII, p. 37.
The Christian Science Monitor. March 9, 1990, p. 10.
Entertainment Weekly. March 9, 1990, p. 4.
Films in Review. XLI, June, 1990, p. 361.
The Hollywood Reporter. CCCXI, February 26, 1990, p. 4.
Los Angeles Times. February 2, 1990, p. F1.
The New York Times. March 2, 1990, p. B1.
Newsweek. CXV, March 5, 1990, p. 63.
Time. CXXXV, March 5, 1990, p. 70.
Variety. February 26, 1990, p. 2.
Video. XIV, October, 1990, p. 61.

THE ICICLE THIEF
(LADRI DI SAPONETTE)

Origin: Italy
Released: 1989
Released in U.S.: 1990
Production: Ernesto di Sarro; released by Aries Film Releasing
Direction: Maurizio Nichetti
Screenplay: Maurizio Nichetti and Mauro Monti
Cinematography: Mario Battistoni
Editing: Rita Olivati
Production design: Marco Mandelli
Set decoration: Ada Legori
Sound: Amedeo Casati
Costume design: Maria Pia Angelini
Music: Manuel de Sica
MPAA rating: no listing
Running time: 90 minutes

Principal characters:

Antonio	Maurizio Nichetti
Maria	Caterina Sylos Labini
Model	Heidi Komarek
Bruno	Federico Rizzo
Paolo	Mattio Auguardi
Don Italo	Renato Scarpa
Television producer	Lella Costa
Film critic	Claudio G. Fava
Maurizio Nichetti	Himself
Mother	Carlina Torta
Father	Massimo Sacilotto

Maurizio Nichetti's *The Icicle Thief* is a clever and charming satire on the power of television: how it can affect the content of serious drama with its countless commercial interruptions and how it manipulates the attention span of its audience. By telling his story from four different points of view, blending neorealism with flashy television advertisements for soap, floor wax, and candy, Nichetti creates a surrealistic world where a sexy, contemporary model moves in with a poor, starving post-World War II family, a film director watches in horror as his cinematic masterpiece is distorted to fit the confines of commercial television, and members of a typical modern family watch the televised madness from their living room without any idea that something is peculiar about the evening's entertainment.

The film begins at a television studio where acclaimed film director Maurizio Nichetti (played by Nichetti himself) is to be interviewed by a snobbish film critic

(Claudio G. Fava) prior to the showing of Nichetti's neorealistic masterpiece, *The Icicle Thief.* Nichetti is nervous about his film being shown on television, fearful of the inevitable commercial interruptions and how they will affect the dramatic flow of his film. As the critic babbles on about the metaphorical symbolism of the film (actually, the critic has never even seen the film), the scene shifts to the living room of a suburban family preparing for an evening around the television set: Father (Massimo Sacilotto) reads his paper, Mother (Carlina Torta) talks on the telephone, their son plays with his building blocks, and their daughter plays with the TV's remote control. Throughout the showing of Nichetti's "masterpiece," this family pays little or no attention to the film.

As Nichetti's film is presented, it becomes obvious that the film is a parody of Vittorio de Sica's neorealistic classic, *The Bicycle Thief* (1948). Like de Sica's film, Nichetti's version is filmed in gritty black and white and concerns itself with a poor family struggling to survive in post-World War II Italy. Even the characters' names are taken from de Sica's original: Antonio (also played by Nichetti), the out-of-work father; Maria (Caterina Sylos Labini), the mother helping to support her family by working as a singer in a small café; Bruno (Federico Rizzo), their young son who contributes to the family's welfare by working at a local gas station; and Paolo (Mattio Auguardi), the toddler with a talent for playing with knives, electrical outlets, and other hazardous objects.

Antonio objects to Maria's work, how she neglects her duties at home, and how the family always eats such wretched food. As the two quarrel at the dinner table, a soap commercial featuring a slinky model soaking in a luxurious bubble bath breaks into the dramatic scene. Nichetti is outraged at the interruption as he watches from a monitor at the TV station, while the film critic prepares another ponderous introduction to another classic film, and the suburban family ignores the broadcast except for Father, who amorously eyes the slinky model. The program segues from a candy bar commercial back to the film, where the scene has shifted to an evening mass in a local church. Don Italo (Renato Scarpa) presides over the ceremony with Bruno serving as altar boy. After the ceremony, Don Italo asks Bruno if there is trouble at home. Bruno confesses that his mother wants his father to become involved with the black market in order to help the family survive—a confession that is not exactly true, but one that prompts the priest to find a job for Antonio in the nearby glass factory. The family rejoices over the prospect of finally having enough money to live adequately. Maria tells Antonio about her frivolous desire to one day have enough money to buy a beautiful chandelier, one with elaborate glass "icicles" hanging from it. As the two stare lovingly into each other's eyes, they suddenly turn to the camera as if to acknowledge the jarring commercial interruption that breaks into their world. Again, Nichetti is outraged over the interruption. Again, the suburban family is oblivious to the show's content, the boy chewing a candy bar as he watches a commercial advertising the candy he is eating. When the commercial ends and the film begins again, Bruno stares into the camera at the suburban boy eating the candy bar. Suddenly he announces that he wants a candy bar and begins singing the jingle from the candy bar commercial.

The next day, Antonio bikes to the glass factory and learns how to manipulate the hot glass for molding into various objects, one of the objects being beautiful glass chandeliers. As he stares at the chandeliers, he remembers Maria's wish to own one. At the end of the day, he steals one of the chandeliers in the factory. Meanwhile, Maria has quit her singing job and has returned home, where she cleans the small apartment and prepares an elaborate dinner. Another commercial break interrupts the drama, this time featuring a gorgeous, scantily clad model preparing to dive into a swimming pool. In mid-dive, there is a power failure and the television studio and surrounding areas are plunged into darkness. When the power is restored and the film's action continues, Antonio is pedaling home while balancing the chandelier on his bike's handle bars. His ride home is interrupted by frantic cries for help coming from the nearby canal. When he stops to investigate, he is stunned by the sight of the beautiful, scantily clad model in glorious color drowning in the murky gray water. In the film's most technically dazzling scene, Antonio saves the model, who shimmers in color while surrounded by the gritty black-and-white film world. Antonio leans over the woman and, as he dries her off with his coat, her body slowly loses its color until she has merged with her black and white surroundings.

When Antonio arrives home with his stunning, nearly naked companion, Maria screams in outrage, thinking her husband is having an affair. Heidi, the model (Heidi Komarek), speaks only English and therefore cannot clear up the misunderstanding. To prove that he is innocent of any betrayal, Antonio takes Maria to the canal to show her where he rescued Heidi and where he dropped Maria's chandelier. While Antonio frantically searches for the chandelier, a despondent Maria decides to kill herself and walks into the canal. When a commercial for laundry detergent interrupts the action, however, Maria suddenly appears in the ad and skips happily away, thankful for being rescued from her dreary, depressing world.

Meanwhile, Nichetti is horrified over what is happening to his film. Determined to straighten out its plot, he runs out of the television studio, takes a train to the town where the film's story is set, merges with the black-and-white world, and begins to search for the characters. He eventually finds Antonio's apartment, where he learns from Bruno that Antonio has been arrested for the murder of Maria. Heidi appears with a birthday cake for Bruno and announces that she prefers this world to the flashy, sterile world she came from. Nichetti bemoans the turn of events his film has taken, telling Bruno that Antonio was supposed to have been hit by a truck after stealing the chandelier, forcing Maria into prostitution to support the family, and that the kids are sent to an orphanage. Bruno, not wanting Nichetti to restore the film to its original depressing conclusion, runs to Don Italo and tells him that it was Nichetti, not Antonio, who murdered Maria. After Antonio is freed from prison, Nichetti is arrested but escapes and begins to chase Bruno through the streets of the city. The two run into the television world where they participate in various commercials before Nichetti runs into Maria dancing with some other women in a floor-wax ad. Nichetti tries to force Maria to return to the film world but she refuses,

saying she prefers the colorful fantasy world of commercials to her depressing cinematic world. Meanwhile, Antonio returns to his dreary apartment accompanied by
Don Italo. When they are greeted at the door by Heidi, Don Italo runs away, convinced that Antonio actually did kill Maria. As Antonio ponders his fate, clutching
baby Paolo and contemplating suicide, Maria, Bruno, and Nichetti suddenly arrive at
the apartment pushing shopping carts filled with trinkets, gadgets, and food from
the commercial world.

The suburban Mother, who has finally stopped talking on the phone, views the
chaotic ending of the film with sentimental tears in her eyes, then commands the rest
of her family, who are all asleep, to get ready for bed. Nichetti, realizing that he is
trapped in his now completely uncontrollable film world, tries to escape by yelling at
the suburban Mother for help as she cleans the living room. He yells and pounds on
the television screen to no avail; the woman finishes tidying up the living room,
turns, and switches off the television.

The structure of *The Icicle Thief*, with its blending of four views of the effects that
television can have on life and art, is a delight to watch. Nichetti first presents each
world separately, then gradually begins to interweave the neorealistic film world
with the commercial television world, the blasé viewing public point of view, and the
exasperated view of Nichetti's director persona. The way Nichetti juxtaposes each
world with the other—cutting from the gray, demeaning neorealistic world to the
sleek, flashy commercials—emphasizes the total incompatibility of the images and
how damaging such interruptions are to the dramatic flow of the film. It also dramatically illustrates how such absurd juxtapositions can result in anesthetizing the viewing audience. The result is an amusing farce filled with sight gags, technical wiz-
ardry, and satire.

Nichetti's underlying message is a serious one: how television butchers and dis-
torts the content and meaning of great cinematic art and how the viewing public has
adapted to television's warped reality by developing a nearly nonexistent attention
span. The outrage over television's treatment of films, its endless commercial interruptions and shameless editing practices, is not a new topic. Countless filmmakers
have voiced their anger over the presentation of their televised motion pictures since
the beginning of the television era. Because the concern is not a new one, the message of *The Icicle Thief*, although presented with great technical bravado, ultimately
fails to have a lasting impact. In fact, the clever structure of the film, which is its
strongest asset, is also the film's greatest detriment; the film becomes merely a
clever trick with no emotional core. The characters, although charming, are carica-
tures who represent various points of view but who are never given any real life of
their own. What little identities they do have are negated by the film's rigid structure
and by badly staged sight gags. For example, when Nichetti enters his black-and-
white film world and searches for the principal characters, he encounters Don Italo,
who gives him information on the whereabouts of the other characters but then
insists that Nichetti mop the floor of the church before he leaves. This illogical
request is used only so that Nichetti can cleverly segue into a commercial for floor

wax. Later, an even cheaper joke is made as Antonio talks to baby Paolo about committing suicide if Maria and Bruno cannot be found, then nonchalantly tosses the baby on its head into one of the shopping carts to embrace Maria when the two suddenly arrive. Other attempts by Nichetti to create clever sight gags achieve the same effect: They encourage the audience to perceive the characters as lifeless props to be manipulated at the director's whim. The film becomes a visually exciting yet emotionally uninvolving joke.

Nichetti has been compared to Woody Allen, not only because he bears a slight resemblance to Allen but also because of his humorous blending of slapstick with intellectually stimulating subjects. Indeed, *The Icicle Thief*, with its playful interaction between cinematic characters and "real" world characters, is reminiscent of Allen's *The Purple Rose of Cairo* (1985). Both directors have in turn acknowledged their indebtedness to Buster Keaton, specifically his film *Sherlock, Jr.* (1924), which also deals with real-world characters invading the world of film. What both Allen and most specifically Nichetti fail to achieve in their films dealing with multiple realities, however, Keaton perfected so many years ago in his film: the masterful blending of technical brilliance and clever sight gags that enhance rather than undermine the integrity of the characters.

One cannot fault Nichetti's intention to take a facsimile of de Sica's *The Bicycle Thief*, one of the most genuinely moving films of all time, and show how the integrity and compassion of a cinematic work of art can be corrupted when subjected to the confines of television. By subjecting his own film to a new set of technical confinements at the expense of character development, however, Nichetti is guilty of the same crime of which he accuses television: sacrificing content for format.

Jim Kline

Reviews

Boxoffice. October, 1990, p. R79.
Chicago Tribune. September 7, 1990, VII, p. 33.
The Christian Science Monitor. August 16, 1990, p. 12.
Film Quarterly. XLIII, Spring, 1990, p. 34.
The Hollywood Reporter. CCCXI, February 27, 1990, p. 4.
Los Angeles Times. September 7, 1990, p. F12.
Los Angeles Times. October 5, 1990, p. F12.
Maclean's. May 14, 1990, p. 69.
The New Republic. CCIII, October 1, 1990, p. 26.
The New York Times. August 24, 1990, p. C8.
Playboy. May, 1990, p. 22.
The Times-Picayune. January 4, 1991, p. LAG17.
Variety. CCCXXXVIII, February 7, 1990, p. 22.
The Washington Post. September 7, 1990, p. B7.

INTERNAL AFFAIRS

Production: Frank Mancuso, Jr., in association with Pierre David; released by
  Paramount Pictures
Direction: Mike Figgis
Screenplay: Henry Bean
Cinematography: John A. Alonzo
Editing: Robert Estrin
Production design: Waldemar Kalinowski
Art direction: Nicholas T. Preovolos
Set decoration: Florence Fellman
Sound: Gary Gerlich
Costume design: Rudy Dillon
Music: Mike Figgis, Anthony Marinelli, and Brian Banks
MPAA rating: R
Running time: 116 minutes

> *Principal characters:*
> Dennis Peck .... Richard Gere
> Sergeant Raymond Avila .... Andy Garcia
> Kathleen Avila .... Nancy Travis
> Amy Wallace .... Laurie Metcalf
> Lieutenant Sergeant Grieb .... Richard Bradford
> Van Stretch .... William Baldwin
> Dorian .... Michael Beach
> Penny .... Faye Grant

Sergeant Raymond Avila (Andy Garcia) has been assigned to the division of internal affairs in the Los Angeles Police Department. Although he receives the standard
lecture from his superior officer about how the police officers respect the division for
its staunch efforts to rid the department of corruption, it is soon made clear to Avila
by his partner, Sergeant Amy Wallace (Laurie Metcalf), that most officers hate internal affairs. Any police officer in that division is immediately suspect as an ambitious
desk type who will use the failings of officers to advance his or her career. Yet neither Avila nor Wallace fit this stereotype; on the contrary, they seem to be loners—
not particularly impressed with authority but attracted to the work of the division
precisely because it appeals to their hard-won sense of integrity. Wallace is a lesbian
who has nothing but contempt for the peer pressure exerted by male policemen upon
one another; Avila is a Hispanic who has married an Anglo art dealer and apparently
has assimilated middle-class values of the majority culture.

During an investigation of a policeman he knew during his training at the police
academy, Avila becomes intensely curious about the policeman's partner, Dennis
Peck (Richard Gere). Although Peck has been cited as an outstanding officer, Avila

notices that Peck has extraordinary influence over his fellow officers. Peck and his partner are suspect because they drive expensive cars and live a luxurious life-style, a fact that no one in the department wants to question. There is something disturbing in the way Peck controls people, however, and, when he tries to manipulate Avila's investigation, Avila decides to go after Peck, sensing that he is at the root of widespread corruption.

From this point on, the film becomes a struggle between two equally ruthless men. Peck is all polish and deviousness, knowing how to lead Avila on while seeming to be a good policeman. Gere plays Peck with a seasoned nonchalance—the air of a man who has seduced many women and corrupted many men. He does not perceive Avila as a serious threat, because Avila is so easy to read. All Peck has to do is contrive a meeting with Avila's wife to make Avila think that Peck has made her another of his lovers. In a rage, Avila almost ruins not only his case against Peck but also his marriage.

At first, Avila's sudden madness over his wife's suspected adultery seems contrived. He has, after all, shown enormous cool and self-possession, qualities that must have earned for him his promotion to internal affairs. That he should now exhibit such jealousy and not even suspect that Peck has set him up seems improbable and cannot be explained by resort to the stereotype that he is a hotheaded Hispanic. On the other hand, Avila has been portrayed as a man who will not discuss his cases with his wife, a man who pursues Peck without authorization from his division, a man, in short, who is somewhat alienated from reality—an obsessive policeman who is not comfortable among his fellow police officers or among his wife's art crowd. It is no accident, then, that Avila feels comfortable with a lesbian, who in her own way is as alienated from the department and society as he is. Film critic Pauline Kael interprets the film as "a dirty sexy twist on the Iago-Othello relationship." Gere is the Iago who "torments the stiff-backed Othello (Garcia)." Avila's jealousy, in other words, and Peck's smooth distortions of reality work hand in hand to destroy Avila's reason.

All the major performances in this film are outstanding. Gere, with his graying hair, looks the part of the veteran policeman, still handsome, still doing his job, but now tinged with a fatal contempt for anyone who is not his wife, lover, or family. In one extraordinary scene, he has arranged to have his partner, Van Stretch (William Baldwin), shot and then finds (after he has killed the hit man) that Van Stretch is still alive murmuring for help. Peck cradles Van Stretch's head in his arms in what at first seems like a reassuring, soothing gesture and then slowly chokes the remaining life out of him, at the same time stifling his own humanity by shouting at Van Stretch in a suppressed, constricted voice to remain quiet. Although Peck is thoroughly evil, he loves women and children and can be good to them. The power of Gere's performance inheres in his knowledge that this monster is still a human being: "People are part-angel and part-devil. Some of us are predominantly one or the other; or both of them at the same time—which I think is the case with Dennis Peck," Gere concludes.

With an entirely different kind of performance, Garcia portrays the opposite side of Peck. Compared to Gere, Garcia is immobile and dominates the screen, as one reviewer suggests, by "sheer presence." Pauline Kael in a dissenting opinion criticizes the actor's "one-note, glaring-eyed performance," but the seemingly stolid, impassive aspect of Avila's character demands a certain stiffness from Garcia, for Avila is trying to maintain control over the fierce forces inside him that Peck knows how to exploit. Like Peck, Avila breaks some of the rules, but unlike Peck he cannot tolerate the immorality and violence of his actions. Whereas Peck feeds on and stimulates corruption by appealing to peer pressure, Avila is aloof from everyone and unwilling to accept that he is as susceptible to temptation as the next policeman.

Even the minor roles in this film shine because of fine performances and succinct writing. Metcalf makes the most of sharply drawn scenes involving Sergeant Amy Wallace, a character given relatively few lines, by staring levelly at her male superiors and colleagues with the same no-nonsense and perceptive vision as Avila. Perhaps it is too obvious to make Wallace a lesbian, yet Metcalf's matter-of-fact and incisive performance makes her character striking and credible.

The police milieu of the film is convincing, a product of the screenwriter's research into police department corruption and Gere's and Garcia's rides with the Los Angeles Police Department during night operations. Both actors also had the technical advice of Richard Whitaker, an eighteen-year veteran of the police force. As a result, the film shows not only the predictable action sequences of a police film but also the culture of being a police officer, of those moments when officers gather to exchange the day's intelligence, to gauge the tenor of events.

In two respects, *Internal Affairs* diverges from most conventional police or crime and punishment films. Wallace is shot as she and Avila close in on Peck. It is a serious wound, and, after leaving her at the hospital where the doctor assures Avila that Wallace has a chance if she is a fighter, he rushes home to the expected confrontation with Peck, who has gone to Avila's house to take possession of his wife. In the film's concluding scene, Avila kills Peck, and it becomes clear that Avila has wanted to kill Peck and that Peck does not want to survive after his corruption has been exposed. At that moment, Avila is not a policeman, he is a husband in his wife's bedroom killing the man who has invaded it. The film never makes clear what happens to Wallace, and the frightening emotions aroused in Avila suggest that on the level of both plot and theme the film acknowledges a depth of feeling that is uncontrollable. The film is, indeed, about internal affairs, about massive personal passions that go far beyond the typical range of feelings in a crime drama.

Carl Rollyson

Reviews

Chicago Tribune. January 12, 1990, VII, p. 30.
Films in Review. XLI, May 9, 1990, p. 303.

Los Angeles Times. January 12, 1990, p. F12.
New Statesman and Society. III, May 18, 1990, p. 47.
New York Magazine. January 29, 1990, p. 57.
The New York Times. January 12, 1990, p. C10.
The New Yorker. LXV, February 5, 1990, p. 111.
Time. CXXXV, February 5, 1990, p. 73.
Variety. CCXXVIII, January 10, 1990, p. 2.
Village Voice. January 23, 1990, p. 82.
The Wall Street Journal. January 18, 1990, p. A12.
The Washington Post. January 12, 1990, p. D1.

JACOB'S LADDER

Production: Alan Marshall for Carolco Pictures; released by Tri-Star Pictures
Direction: Adrian Lyne
Screenplay: Bruce Joel Rubin
Cinematography: Jeffrey L. Kimball
Editing: Tom Rolf
Production design: Brian Morris
Art direction: Jeremy Conway and Wray Steven Graham
Set decoration: Kathleen Dolan
Special effects: Conrad Brink
Costume design: Ellen Mirojnick
Music: Maurice Jarre
MPAA rating: R
Running time: 115 minutes

Principal characters:
Jacob	Tim Robbins
Jezzie	Elizabeth Peña
Louis	Danny Aiello
Michael	Matt Craven
Paul	Pruitt Taylor Vince
Geary	Jason Alexander
Sarah	Patricia Kalember
Gabe	Macaulay Culkin

With *Jacob's Ladder,* versatile director Adrian Lyne demonstrates again his keen interest in disturbing subjects. This grim, haunting picture combines a psychological text about war atrocities with a methodology most often associated with effective horror films. What results is a film which generates deep fear, a nagging sense of chronic fright that threatens to stay. Its emotional repercussions seem strong enough to overcome even happy digressions.

In *Nine and a Half Weeks* (1986), Lyne explored the way in which erotic urgency can grow into profound danger when the oppositions of pleasure and pain merge, blurred further by neurosis in one or both sex partners. The extraordinarily popular *Fatal Attraction* (1987) showed Lyne taking this danger to an extreme, featuring a transformation of adventurous lust into angry, psychotic violence. *Jacob's Ladder* is a more serious project, one that manipulates its viewers through uncertainty, mystifying them with alternate flashes of truth and terror.

Bruce Joel Rubin's screenplay is not only punctuated with fright but also contains such complexities as dreams-within-dreams and biblical allusions, most of which lead nowhere. It starts with the harshest (and ultimately clearest) reality in the film: an assault on a squad of American infantrymen during hostilities in the Mekong Delta in the fall of 1971. Among the casualties is a tall, likeable recent Ph.D. named

Jacob Singer (Tim Robbins). The scene in which he is bayoneted in the abdomen is shown at several, irregular intervals, indicating that writer Rubin wants his audience to hold onto that brutal image. More important to director Lyne's overall purpose, however, is a set of shots immediately preceding the attack on Jacob. One minute his fellow soldiers are passing the time eating snacks and smoking marijuana; the next minute some of them are writhing in some strange delirium or thrashing in violent convulsions, their heads bobbing, mouths foaming and bleeding. A heavyset private sits trembling and staring out, his mouth open but soundless.

Jacob wakes in a different uniform, that of a U.S. postal employee. He has apparently fallen asleep on his way home from working an overtime shift. The subway car in which he sits is strewn with litter, and a homeless man sleeps under newspapers. Jacob thinks that he sees the tail of a reptilian creature slithering beneath the man's cover. In one of the film's most subtly frightening sequences, Jacob finds himself locked inside his subway station which, like the passenger car, is dimly lighted and filthy with debris. He tries to reach an open door on the other side of the tracks and is nearly run down by a train which appears to be occupied by phantoms who grin and wave evilly at him.

Gradually, the structure of *Jacob's Ladder* becomes discernible. The former GI lives in the present time with a fellow employee named Jezebel (Elizabeth Peña), who is not so evil as her name might imply. Interspersed with scenes from the present are chapters from his actual civilian past and the hallucinatory nightmares with which he is currently beset. In both present and past, there are numerous waking-up scenes, some of them on hospital tables. Certain facts can be pieced together from his fleeting glimpses of the distant, or pre-Vietnam, past. While a doctoral student at a university somewhere in New York City, Jacob held a job at the post office to pay the bills for his family—his three sons and wife Sarah (Patricia Kalember). One day, his son Gabriel (Macaulay Culkin) was riding the bicycle that his father had recently bought for him when the boy was struck by a car and killed. Jacob sank into guilt-ridden depression. Up to that time, his marriage had been a strong one of mutual trust, even to the point that Jacob shared with Sarah a nighttime dream in which he was living with his coworker Jezebel. They joke about the matter.

In the present time, Jacob's dilemma grows. Even his philosophical chiropractor Louis (Danny Aiello) worries about him, about his broken marriage and his insistence on staying at the post office despite his advanced education. One morning, Jacob is almost run down by a carload of demonic figures, who wave and grin at him just like the ones on the phantom subway. Shortly thereafter, he rushes to the veterans' hospital, where he apparently had once been a patient. They have no record of him, and the doctor that he alleges to have seen was killed in a car accident. Before running out of the hospital in panic, he sees a monstrous growth on the head of the receptionist. Jacob begins to suspect a massive conspiracy. He attends a party with Jezebel, where he is told by a palm reader that he is already dead. A few minutes later, the partygoers begin to turn into demons and Jacob shrieks in fear. Jezebel angrily takes him home, but soon he is burning up in fever. After Jacob has responded positively to being iced down, his doctor says that only a miracle had saved him.

By coincidence, he meets another survivor from his military outfit who has also been suffering from hallucinations. What appears to be a turning point in Jacob's condition becomes yet another element of terror, however, when the old acquaintance is blown up by a car bomb. Jacob feels more alone than ever, as he has thoroughly alienated Jezebel, who cannot understand what he is going through. After the funeral for the dead veteran, he meets a few others who had been in the combat outfit. Most of them suffer from one symptom or another, and they realize they may have been given something in their food or drink which has caused their current condition. Collectively, they secure the services of a lawyer (Jason Alexander) who decides in favor of a class-action suit against the government. As their meeting ends, however, a car from the federal motor pool is shown observing them from a distance. Later, when Jacob calls, the lawyer explains that he is backing down because the others want no part of the suit. The angry counselor adds that he and his friends were discharged after war games in Thailand, and that none had ever set foot in Vietnam.

Despite what appears to be a depressingly final disclosure, complications continue to develop for Jacob. Government agents abduct him, but after a wild ride he escapes, only to be temporarily paralyzed because of his chronic back injury. While he is prone and nearly immobile on the pavement, a streetcorner Santa Claus steals his wallet. The sequence which follows is the most surreal in *Jacob's Ladder*, as the apparently delirious man is wheeled through a hospital that looks increasingly like an abandoned wreck, then a madhouse, and finally a grotesque place of slaughter, where severed limbs lie rotting on the floor and walls are smeared with blood in swirls in hideous graffiti. In the middle of Jacob's hospital stay, Louis the chiropractor rushes to the rescue, spiriting him away to a manipulation table, where after several strategic shoves and pulls, Jacob is able to walk. His walk is even somewhat reassured, perhaps owing to Louis' advice, "If you've made your peace, the devils you've been seeing will become angels, who will free you from the earth."

The final messenger Jacob encounters is a nervous former drug dealer named Michael Newman (Matt Craven), who tells him about a secret drug. Years before, Newman had been coerced by government agents into developing a chemical which would increase aggression among draftees in combat who otherwise might not be able to kill sufficiently. It was a mixture called BZ, commonly referred to as "the ladder," small doses of which had turned the combat unit into uncontrollable beasts who tore each other apart. In other words, Jacob and the others had been attacked by fellow Americans. The Vietcong had not been involved at all.

Jacob takes a taxi to his old residence, where the doorman greets him as "Dr. Singer." Upstairs, no one is there, but his old drawing instruments look as if they had only recently been put down. Before long, he feels the misty presence of Gabriel, his dead son, who takes him up a ladder of a very different sort. As they climb upward, the screen fades to bright white, then abruptly transfers to a mobile hospital in 1971. The field surgeon pronounces Private Jacob Singer dead.

Director Lyne takes some interesting liberties in order to objectify a long, vivid dream which contains bliss as well as horror. *Jacob's Ladder* is more than a modern, flashy version of the old boxing films, however, in which the battered hero, looking up from the canvas, would see his whole life instantly replayed between the counts of four and ten. In this film, the dreamer's suffering inside the dream is just as significant as those deepest recesses of the past that yield a bit of meaning here, a dash of possibility there. Most of this could have happened, and because much of it was dreamed does not diminish its hold on the eyes and in the mind.

Although a disclaimer before the end credits states that the federal government has denied ever using a drug such as BZ for any reason, the dramatic, visual point made by Rubin and Lyne is too powerful to discard as mere make-believe. The look of frantic pain on Jacob's face, as his unknown comrade—glassy-eyed and motivated by fake savagery—leads the ensuing torture, is an unforgettable image. Bloodied and in shock, the young man whom the others had called "professor" crawls through the green jungle toward rescue and death.

Yet Jacob's is not the only death that functions importantly. There is the accidental killing of Gabe, the ironic, angelic child who eventually liberates his father from the prison of dreams, but whose own death may have had something to do with the changing of Jacob's induction status. A father of two, no less than a holder of a doctorate, is certainly not the foxhole prototype, except to allow Rubin and Lyne the means to articulate a greater death. This is the death of the young and healthy on behalf of the old and convenienced. The eternally young smile and laugh at each other and reach, in their moment of death, for beauty—just as in the final, deathly image of Lewis Milestone's *All Quiet on the Western Front* (1930).

Robbins plays the key role very effectively, following the necessarily drastic mood shifts of a man out of control. His grin is more boyish and appreciative than is ordinarily found in motion pictures designed to jolt and scare. Most convincing among the supporting cast is Aiello as the chiropractic guardian angel, who only ventures into moral territory in his last lines.

Andrew Jefchak

Reviews

American Film: Magazine of the Film and Television Arts. XV, November, 1990, p. 63.
Chicago Tribune. November 2, 1990, VII, p. 31.
Films in Review. XLII, January, 1991, p. 48.
The Hollywood Reporter. CCCXIV, October 31, 1990, p. 5.
Los Angeles Times. October 30, 1990, p. F1.
The New York Times. November 2, 1990, p. B6.
Newsweek. November 12, 1990, p. 77.
Variety. CCCXLI, October 30, 1990, p. 2.
The Washington Post. November 2, 1990, p. C1.

JOE VERSUS THE VOLCANO

Production: Teri Schwartz for Amblin Entertainment; released by Warner Bros.
Direction: John Patrick Shanley
Screenplay: John Patrick Shanley
Cinematography: Stephen Goldblatt
Editing: Richard Halsey
Production design: Bo Welch
Art direction: Tom Duffield
Set decoration: Cheryl Carasik
Special visual effects: David L. Carson
Sound: Keith A. Wester
Costume design: Colleen Atwood
Music: Georges Delerue
MPAA rating: PG
Running time: 102 minutes

Principal characters:
Joe	Tom Hanks
DeDe/Angelica/Patricia	Meg Ryan
Graynamore	Lloyd Bridges
Dr. Ellison	Robert Stack
Waponi chief	Abe Vigoda
Waturi	Dan Hedaya
Marshall	Ossie Davis
Luggage salesman	Barry McGovern

Joe Versus the Volcano contains its share of maxims about how to live. It is a parable for all times in the tradition of Aesop, Grimm, or, even, the Carpenter from Nazareth; at one point it is reminiscent of the Book of Job. Because the fantasy comes from the whimsical and romantic mind of John Patrick Shanley and is graced with the charming performances of Tom Hanks and Meg Ryan, the lesson is more than palatable—in fact, it adds up to a delightfully humorous entertainment that leaves the viewer with food for thought and a pleasant aftertaste.

Shanley keeps reminding the viewer that this is a fable and not a realistic depiction. His choice to film primarily on Hollywood sound stages rather than on location makes sense considering his stylistic approach. He begins with the words "Once upon a time" and shoots pictures that look as if they were out of a splendid children's storybook. A shot of the New York skyline from a boat at night is spectacular, with windows glowing in many different colors of light. Another stunning shot shows a leviathan of a moon rising gloriously out of the Pacific Ocean.

The story has a highly unlikely premise and along the way raises a number of questions in reasonably literal minds. Improbabilities, however, become acceptable within the framework of the fable, where the storyteller is concerned with bigger-than-usual questions, sometimes of a supernatural nature, about a person's relationship to the cosmos or, at the very least, about what one should do with this gift of life; Shanley is not concerned with trivial questions of logic or probability. Another effect of putting the story clearly in the realm of make-believe is that the viewer, while delighting in the victories of the protagonist, can remain comfortably distanced from his suffering.

When the tale begins, Joe Banks (Tom Hanks) is an employee of a medical supply firm, American Panascope, located in an industrial complex that is, among other things, the home of the rectal probe: There are grim reminders of that fact on signs that greet workers along the grisly way as they arrive each morning. Everything about the working environment is depressing except the presence of DeDe (Meg Ryan), who sits at a desk near Joe. She is a bit simple-minded but looks good and is certainly of a gentle nature. Before getting to see DeDe, however, Joe must approach the complex through a field of muddy holes; inside there are no windows, the place is poorly lit, with fluorescent bulbs constantly flickering, and Joe's boss, Waturi (Dan Hedaya), is either gratingly justifying his own mistakes in incessant telephone conversations or picking on Joe. It is no wonder that Joe is a hypochondriac and spends too large a percentage of his measly earnings on doctors.

Early in the story, Doctor Ellison (Robert Stack) tells Joe that he has a rare disease and no more than six months to live. The news is, indeed, overwhelming and sobering, and causes him to reflect on his unsatisfactory life-style. When he gets back to the office, he quits his job and—in one of his less imaginative forays against life's negative energy—effects some minor wreckage in the workplace. For the first time, he has the courage to ask DeDe out, and she accepts. On their date, Joe, not for the last time, exhibits bad timing: He makes the mistake of telling an admiring and attracted woman, who is ready to give herself to him, that he has only six months to live, news almost certain to douse her ignited passion.

Eventually, he departs on a far-ranging adventure from the east to west coast of the United States and across the Pacific Ocean: Along the way he meets two intriguing women, both also played by Meg Ryan, and is given ample opportunity to display his newfound courage. Vivid moments in his odyssey include several days at sea on a raft made of four tied-together steamer trunks, with Joe getting baked and blistered by the sun because he valiantly uses the one umbrella to protect the woman who accompanies him; they are rescued by cheerful natives, who wear necklaces of crushed soda pop cans—orange soda being the favorite drink on the island. The film's climax takes Joe to the portal of death itself in the likeness of the mouth of a fire-spitting volcano. This fateful odyssey allows him, and the viewer (without much distress), to reflect upon life's meaning. One of the author's intentions, similar to that of Thornton Wilder in his play, *Our Town* (1938), is to nourish an appreciation for even the everyday occurrences in life.

The film is never subtle but perhaps that is part of its appeal. Shanley—or editor Richard Halsey—occasionally miscalculates in terms of rhythm: For example, to suggest his discarding of former restraints, Joe's uninhibited but clumsy dance need not go on as long as it does. Yet, for the most part, Shanley's first directing job for the cinema is skillfully executed. In the opening segment, the hordes of employees at the beginning of the workday moving toward their eight hours of tedium and misery are reminiscent of Fritz Lang's subterranean, robotlike workers in *Metropolis* (1927). An overhead crane shot shows them wending their way along a zigzag path that looks, from a bird's-eye view, very much like a trap. Images of Joe at the Hotel Pierre—sitting alone at a table in the formal dining room or in an elegant wood-carved bed with white, fluffy bed linens all around him—convey his sad isolation in the midst of luxurious trappings. Shanley finds very direct, striking images to convey information.

Shanley is helped by the collaboration of two outstanding leading players. Meg Ryan demonstrates that her major-league status is well-deserved with three quirky but distinct characterizations, all of which are different from her critically praised performance in *When Harry Met Sally* (1989). She is winsome whether playing the simple coworker or Angelica, a rich man's neurotic daughter, or her half-sister Patricia, who has the potential to pull herself out of a mire of self-doubt. Besides it being a tour de force for Ryan, having the same actress play the three roles has thematic justification: Each woman reflects a stage in Joe's psychological journey.

Tom Hanks projects the kind of ingenuousness that, while it could not salvage a repetitive, one-joke film like *The Money Pit* (1986), often makes potentially cloying moments in this film enjoyable. The delicate balance that *Joe Versus the Volcano* maintains to keep its didacticism from becoming simplistically offensive, or its essentially optimistic perspective from seeming overly cheerful or inane, is the result in large part of his unpretentious, appealing performance. His casual stroll to the roaring-red volcano near the film's climax could well represent everyone's fantasy of how to face a clearly life-threatening situation with aplomb.

Shanley has sprinkled the film with cameos featuring some of his favorite actors: The result is a supporting cast of distinguished names. The most impressive of these portrayals is that of Marshall (Ossie Davis). Davis has created quite an opposite character from the one he played in *Do the Right Thing* (1989), his other recent notable performance. Marshall is a classy chauffeur, who knows exactly where to take Joe for the best in clothing, luggage, and accommodations. His characterization of a man with impeccable taste is elegant and amusing.

From the writing of the script to the casting of supporting roles to guiding the performances of his leading players, Shanley has evidently undertaken his job with enthusiasm. He has found the way to translate his personal experience into salutary and witty entertainment. He toys with the idea that, in order to live, one must be liberated from the necessity of living. Joe Banks's death sentence opens up possibilities he otherwise would never have experienced. For the viewer, it is a most painless way to face fundamental, often troublesome, questions.

Cono Robert Marcazzo

Reviews

American Film: Magazine of the Film and Television Arts. XV, April, 1990, p. 20.
Chicago Tribune. March 9, 1990, VII, p. 33.
The Hollywood Reporter. CCCXI, March 9, 1990, p. 4.
Los Angeles Times. March 9, 1990, p. F1.
New York Magazine. XXIII, March 26, 1990, p. 77.
The New York Times. March 9, 1990, p. C16.
The New Yorker. LXVI, March 26, 1990, p. 81.
Premiere. II, May, 1990, p. 82.
Variety. CCCXXXVIII, March 7, 1990, p. 34.
Video. XIV, October, 1990, p. 69.
The Washington Post. March 9, 1990, p. D1.

KINDERGARTEN COP

Production: Ivan Reitman and Brian Grazer for Imagine Entertainment; released by Universal Pictures
Direction: Ivan Reitman
Screenplay: Murray Salem, Herschel Weingrod, and Timothy Harris; based on a story by Salem
Cinematography: Michael Chapman
Editing: Sheldon Kahn and Wendy Greene Bricmont
Production design: Bruno Rubeo
Art direction: Richard Mays
Set design: Joseph B. Pacelli, Jr., Beverli Eagan, and Larry Hubbs
Set decoration: Anne D. McCulley
Sound: Gene S. Cantamessa
Costume design: Gloria Gresham
Music: Randy Edelman
MPAA rating: PG-13
Running time: 110 minutes

Principal characters:
Kimble	Arnold Schwarzenegger
Joyce	Penelope Ann Miller
Phoebe	Pamela Reed
Miss Schlowski	Linda Hunt
Crisp	Richard Tyson
Eleanor Crisp	Carroll Baker
Dominic	Joseph Cousins
	Christian Cousins

Although *Kindergarten Cop* may not be great drama, it is an example of professional Hollywood craftsmanship at its best. Making Arnold Schwarzenegger funny was enough of a challenge in itself; however, the authors achieved this effect in a manner similar to that employed in *Twins* (1988), a highly successful film that was created by the same producer/director and some of the same writers. In *Twins*, the contrast between the gigantic Schwarzenegger and the five-foot-tall professional comedian Danny DeVito provided an ongoing source of comedy which reflected favorably on the muscular hero. In *Kindergarten Cop*, a similar effect is achieved by surrounding Schwarzenegger with tiny children, making him look like Gulliver among the Lilliputians. Showing big, strong men as hopelessly incompetent at handling small children is a perennial source of film comedy, as proven by the popular *Three Men and a Baby* (1987). Having a whole army of children in *Kindergarten Cop* also puts the film squarely in the category of "family entertainment" and attracts the segment of the population that was responsible for the phenomenal success of films such as *E.T.: The Extra-Terrestrial* (1982) and *Home Alone* (1990; reviewed in this volume).

As John Kimble, Schwarzenegger plays a tough Los Angeles police officer who has been trying for years to obtain a conviction on Cullen Crisp (Richard Tyson), a drug dealer who demonstrates that he is also a psychopath and a vicious killer. Crisp has an Achilles heel: His former wife ran away with their little boy, and Crisp and his equally vicious mother, Eleanor (Carroll Baker), want the child. Crisp learns from an informant that his former wife is living under an assumed name in Astoria, Oregon, where their son is attending kindergarten. Crisp kills his informant to keep him from telling anyone else what he knows. When he finds out that the informant's girlfriend overheard the conversation and told the police, he has her killed also in order to prevent her from testifying against him. Kimble's only chance to obtain a conviction is to find Crisp's former wife and persuade her to tell everything that she knows on the witness stand.

Astoria is a picturesque town of about ten thousand people that is situated on the lush green hills near the mouth of the Columbia River. It is fully exploited for its photographic potential in the same way that the town of Nelson, British Columbia, was used in the Steve Martin comedy *Roxanne* (1987). When Kimble arrives in Astoria, he is forced to assume the undercover role of kindergarten teacher because his female partner is confined to bed with food poisoning. Pamela Reed, as his partner Phoebe, provides comedy with her spunky wisecracking in a manner resembling Tyne Daly, who costarred with Clint Eastwood in his third Dirty Harry film, *The Enforcer* (1976). Kimble and Phoebe know that Crisp's son will be in the class, but they do not know what the boy looks like or what name he may be using.

The only person at the school who is aware of Kimble's true identity is the principal, Miss Schlowski, played by Linda Hunt, who received a Best Supporting Actress Oscar for her role in *The Year of Living Dangerously* (1982). The casting of such a charismatic actress in a relatively minor role is an example of how the filmmakers have buttressed the towering Schwarzenegger with supportive talent. Another example is their casting of Carroll Baker, who has a long acting career going back to *Baby Doll* (1956), in which she costarred with Karl Malden and received an Academy Award nomination for Best Actress. Miss Schlowski has grave doubts about turning the inexperienced Kimble over to a group of kindergartners. The enormous policeman who knows how to handle thugs and killers is soon reduced almost to tears by the boundless energies and mischievous minds of his tiny charges.

Kimble turns to a fellow teacher for help. Penelope Ann Miller, as a third-grade teacher named Joyce, shows him how to cope with children and quickly develops a personal interest in the big, handsome stranger. Miller is another gifted actress, and her warmth and sensitivity cast a flattering light on the impassive Schwarzenegger. After they have fallen in love, Kimble begins to suspect that Joyce herself was Crisp's wife and that her son—and his kindergarten pupil—Dominic (played by the twins Joseph and Christian Cousins) is the boy whom Crisp and his wicked mother are planning to abduct.

The authors of the film have set up a central comic situation that is entirely plausible and produces all the laughter that they had expected. They have also displayed admirable craftsmanship in constructing a plot that is full of potentially dramatic circumstances. Kimble does not know which of his pupils is Crisp's son or which of their mothers is Crisp's former wife. The teachers, the pupils, and the parents do not know that Kimble is an undercover police officer. Crisp does not know that Kimble is working as his son's kindergarten teacher. Joyce does not know that the man with whom she is falling in love represents a grave threat to her security. The complications continue to thicken, foreshadowing a violently emotional finale.

With Joyce's help, Kimble begins to learn about children. He sees that each of his pupils has his or her own unique personality and that many of them are carrying heavy burdens on their young shoulders. Some have fathers who refuse to work, others have no fathers at all, and some are neglected. One is so badly abused that Kimble reports the parents to the authorities. This aspect of the story is reminiscent of François Truffaut's *Argent de Poche* (1976; *Small Change*). Director Ivan Reitman and his assistants have done a fine job of handling the thirty children that were involved in the production.

Kimble begins to understand that the hoodlums that he deals with as a police officer were all children themselves and that one way to solve the crime problem is to help children before they are too badly warped by their environments. The change that takes place in the viewpoint character is another example of highly professional screenwriting. Schwarzenegger becomes a far more sympathetic character than he was in his one-dimensional roles in such films as *The Terminator* (1984), *Commando* (1985), *Raw Deal* (1986), and *Predator* (1987). Eventually, Kimble makes a radical career decision and gives up police work to become a real schoolteacher. There is an implicit message that is contained in this plot development—that it would be a good thing if more men went into teaching elementary-school children, providing wholesome male role models that are missing in so many contemporary American homes.

When Crisp and his mother arrive in Astoria, the sadistic killer immediately recognizes his son, who is, in fact, also Joyce's son. Tyson is an excellent actor but is handicapped by the role of a villain whose behavior is illogical. Instead of waiting for an appropriate opportunity to abduct little Dominic, Crisp grabs him in a hallway after setting the school on fire and causing a mass evacuation. This leads to a predictable confrontation in which both Kimble and his partner Phoebe are wounded and Crisp and his mother are sent to prison on stretchers. Kimble tells Joyce that he wants her and her son to be his family and that he intends to remain in Astoria for the rest of his life.

In *Kindergarten Cop*, Schwarzenegger is so attractively packaged that this formidable giant is made to appear not only a funnier comedian than he actually is but a better actor as well. To do this, the filmmakers have placed him in an intrinsically amusing situation, given him a comical sidekick, surrounded him with charming children and highly skilled supporting actors, provided a credible love story, set that story in a cinematically attractive locale, and made sure that their offering has social significance, with the themes of divorce, neglect, and abuse. It is a textbook example of how an offbeat idea can be developed by solid craftsmanship. As a result of all this professional input, *Kindergarten Cop* became one of the most successful films that was released in 1990.

Bill Delaney

Reviews

Chicago Tribune. December 21, 1990, VII, p. 22.
The Hollywood Reporter. CCCXV, December 17, 1990, p. 10.
Los Angeles Times. December 21, 1990, p. F1.
The New York Times. December 21, 1990, p. B7.
Newsweek. December 24, 1990, p. 62.
Premiere. IV, December, 1990, p. 22.
The Saturday Evening Post. CCLXIII, January, 1991, p. 58.
USA Today. December 21, 1990, p. D5.
Variety. December 17, 1990, p. 3.
The Wall Street Journal. January 10, 1991, p. A12.
The Washington Post. December 21, 1990, p. D1.

THE KRAYS

Origin: Great Britain
Released: 1990
Released in U.S.: 1990
Production: Dominic Anciano and Ray Burdis for Parkfield Entertainment and Fugitive Features; released by Miramax Films
Direction: Peter Medak
Screenplay: Philip Ridley
Cinematography: Alex Thomson
Editing: Martin Walsh
Production design: Michael Pickwoad
Sound: Godfrey Kirby
Makeup: Jenny Boost
Costume design: Lindy Hemming
Stunt coordination: Stuart St. Paul
Music: Michael Kamen
MPAA rating: R
Running time: 119 minutes

Principal characters:
Violet Kray	Billie Whitelaw
Ronald Kray	Gary Kemp
Reginald Kray	Martin Kemp
Rose	Susan Fleetwood
May	Charlotte Cornwell
Cannonball Lee	Jimmy Jewel
Helen	Avis Bunnage
Frances	Kate Hardie
Jack "The Hat" McVitie	Tom Bell
Charlie Kray, Sr.	Alfred Lynch
Steve	Gary Love
George Cornell	Steven Berkoff

Among the most colorful figures in London during the 1960's—a decade notable for its original and outlandish characters—were Ronald and Reginald Kray. Twin brothers, the Krays instigated a violent campaign that placed them at the forefront of the East End's criminal underworld. At the same time, their glamorous reputation as Saville Row-suited nightclub owners made them favorites of London's café society, where they mingled with wealthy customers and show business celebrities. By the time of their downfall and arrest in 1968, the Krays had acquired a mystique that continues to generate public interest despite their subsequent years of imprisonment and hospitalization.

Director Peter Medak and writer Philip Ridley's cinematic portrait of the brothers is a stylish and intriguing, if ultimately unsatisfying, look at the pair's life. Born in 1934, the Krays were the sons of Violet and Charlie Kray, and Medak's film opens with their birth and christening. From the beginning, Violet Kray (Billie Whitelaw) is a force to be reckoned with in her sons' lives. Strong, outspoken, and fiercely attached to her boys, Violet instills in them an isolating "us against them" mentality that will bind them to her and to each other with disturbing intensity. When young Ronnie (Gary Kemp) falls ill with diphtheria, Violet removes him from the hospital, knowing that only the presence of his brother, Reggie (Martin Kemp), will pull him through the disease.

The Krays spend their childhood surrounded by strong women, including a doting aunt (Charlotte Cornwell) and a grandmother (Susan Fleetwood) who is emphatic on the subject of the innately childlike behavior of grown men. Throughout their early years, the twins seem to possess an almost psychic bond, as well as a growing penchant for violence and trouble. Thrown into military prison for their refusal to obey orders, the pair are advised by a fellow prisoner to make their living collecting money from those people who are willing to pay in order to avoid being hurt. The Krays take his message to heart and are soon establishing a name for themselves by forcing their way into other gangsters' territories.

The two open an ornate nightclub, which is soon attracting the elite of show business society, and they ricochet between flaunting the trappings of their wealth and notoriety and extending their influence with horrifying attacks on anyone who crosses them. Using bayonets and tommy guns as their weapons of choice, the brothers establish themselves as East End crime lords. They remain devoted to their mother, however, holding their gang meetings in her house as Violet serves tea and cakes. One of their henchmen, Jack "The Hat" McVitie (Tom Bell), receives a warning after attempting to cheat the brothers. His refusal to recognize the full measure of the Krays' capacity for violence will eventually prove fatal.

Ronnie Kray, who is homosexual, begins an affair with a young man named Steve (Gary Love) but is increasingly jealous of Reggie's relationship with Frances (Kate Hardie), the young woman that he eventually marries. Frances is unprepared for life with the pathologically possessive Reggie, however, and she gradually turns to pills as she suffers a breakdown that leads to her suicide. Reggie is thrown into a period of unshakable despair by his wife's death, and only Ronnie is able to reach him, reminding him that his marriage led to a breach in their own closeness. Ronnie's plan for his brother's recovery involves the bloody elimination of their taunting rival, Cornell (Steven Berkoff), and the murder of Jack, whom Reggie stabs repeatedly in an uncontrollable fury. The film's final scene takes place in 1982 at Violet Kray's graveside where Ronnie and Reggie, in handcuffs and with a police escort, are watching her burial. A postscript notes that Reginald Kray is serving a thirty-year prison term, while Ronald remains a patient in a maximum-security psychiatric hospital.

Since the time of their criminal reign in the 1960's, the Krays have remained something of a national obsession in Great Britain. Books and articles on the pair have appeared periodically throughout their incarceration, and a number of well-known show business figures are said to have visited them in jail. The source of the Krays' appeal has been the cause of much speculation. It seems likely that their popularity is the result of factors as varied as their East End background, their donations to charitable causes, and their much-publicized devotion to their mother. Yet the public fascination with the brothers remains largely unexplored in the film, as do their friendships with numerous celebrities, a particularly unfortunate omission for audiences outside of Great Britain who may be unaware of the cultural phenomenon that the Krays became at the peak of their power. The glamour that sometimes attaches itself to violence and crime is itself an intriguing subject, and the Kray twins would seem to offer an ideal framework for its exploration.

What the film does do with considerable success is paint a picture of the brothers' lives that captures the style, the perverse emotional bond, and the violence that marked their behavior. *The Krays* is a technically well-made film, occasionally even stylized in its use of imagery and staging, and director Medak, best known for the savagely satirical *The Ruling Class* (1972), succeeds in conveying visually the difference between the cramped, economically straitened circumstances of the twins' childhood and the life-style that they later acquire. Perhaps the most vivid—and amusing—contrast occurs in a scene in which expensive cars line the narrow street outside Violet Kray's small home, where the brothers and their gang are holding a meeting while Violet serves them tea and cakes.

That scene, along with many others in the film, also points up the ironic contrast between the Krays' surface nods to notions of gentility and the brutal reality of their lives. Preparing to attend the opening of their nightclub, which the pair have acquired through violence and intimidation, Ronnie and Reggie show off their new Saville Row-tailored suits to their family, winning praise as "proper little gentlemen." It is a contrast that is felt throughout the film, as the twins' veneer of wealth and style slips repeatedly and with chilling suddenness to reveal their true natures. The reasons for the development of those natures and the Krays' early and ongoing proclivity for violence remain obscure, although the film points its finger at Violet Kray and also seems to suggest a link to the social climate in Great Britain that was created by the events of World War II. The second connection is a tenuous one. Although the film makes repeated references to the war years and, at one point, intercuts a series of violent actions by the brothers with shots of Violet weeping as she watches a television documentary on the war, a sense of any real link between the two is never convincingly established.

Violet Kray, whatever the true extent of her role in shaping her sons' behavior, quickly emerges as a fascinating character. Strong and direct, she adores her boys and fosters in them a powerful sense of family loyalty. As Ronnie and Reggie begin their life of crime, Violet turns a blind eye to their activities, focusing instead on the physical trappings of their new life. Billie Whitelaw, a noted stage actress who has appeared in such films as *The Omen* (1976) and Alfred Hitchcock's *Frenzy* (1972), gives a striking performance as Violet, never allowing the character to slip into caricature despite Violet's excesses of motherly love. The film makes it clear, however, that the twins' violent behavior began when they were children, and nothing in Violet's adoring manner seems reason enough for their shockingly brutal actions as adults or Ronnie Kray's subsequent confinement in Broadmoor, a maximum-security psychiatric hospital. One aspect of the Krays' life that the film ignores is Ronnie's hospitalization for schizophrenia in the mid-1950's—a seemingly important piece of information in any examination of the twins' lives.

The film achieves a casting coup, however, with the performances of brothers Martin and Gary Kemp as Reggie and Ronnie Kray. Founding members of the British rock group Spandau Ballet, the Kemps bring the film an eerie verisimilitude that is crucial to its success in establishing the strange bond between the Krays. The Kemps did not come to the film as amateurs—they had studied acting throughout their teens—and their performances reflect a degree of polish not generally evident in rock stars-turned-actors. The film is well-served by both their prior experience and the aura of glamour that they bring to their roles.

Arresting performances and stylish filmmaking are an inadequate substitute for depth and real character analysis, but *The Krays* succeeds well enough on the level of pure entertainment to compensate for some of its omissions. Although it fails to fully explore many aspects of the Kray brothers' mystique and motivations, the film remains an interesting and well-made account of their lives.

Janet Lorenz

Reviews

Boxoffice. September, 1990, p. R68.
Chicago Sun-Times. November 9, 1990, p. 46.
Chicago Tribune. November 9, 1990, VII, p. 38.
The Christian Science Monitor. November 30, 1990, p. 12.
Film Comment. XXVI, September, 1990, p. 47.
The Hollywood Reporter. May 17, 1990, p. 10.
Interview. November, 1990, p. 50.
Los Angeles. November, 1990, p. 220.
Los Angeles Times. November 9, 1990, p. F4.
New Statesman and Society. III, May 4, 1990, p. 41.
The New York Times. November 9, 1990, p. B9.
Newsweek. CXVI, November 26, 1990, p. 78.
The Spectator. CCLXIV, May 12, 1990, p. 48.
Vanity Fair. October, 1990, p. 220.
Variety. March 1, 1990, p. 2.
The Washington Post. November 9, 1990, p. C1.

LANDSCAPE IN THE MIST
(TOPIO STIN OMICHLI)

Origin: Greece
Released: 1988
Released in U.S.: 1990
Production: Theo Angelopoulos for Paradis Films, Greek Film Centre, Television ET-1, and Basicinematografica; released by New Yorker Films
Direction: Theo Angelopoulos
Screenplay: Theo Angelopoulos, Tonino Guerra, and Thanassis Valtinos
Cinematography: Giorgos Arvanitis
Editing: Yannis Tsitsopoulos
Art direction: Mikes Karapiperis
Sound: Marinos Athanassopoulos
Music: Eleni Karaindrou
MPAA rating: no listing
Running time: 126 minutes

> *Principal characters:*
> Alexander . . . . Michalis Zeke
> Voula . . . . Tania Palaiologou
> Orestes . . . . Stratos Tzortzoglou

Acclaimed Greek director Theo Angelopoulos has added the third entry to his trilogy of classicized "road" films. The recent release of Angelopoulos' *Landscape in the Mist* completes the circle of this oeuvre, which includes the two previous road adventures *Voyage to Cythera* (1984) and *The Beekeeper* (1986).

Characteristic of Angelopoulos' signature style, *Landscape in the Mist* has a daringly sparse plotline. Two children, eleven-year-old Voula (Tania Palaiologou) and her five-year-old brother Alexander (Michalis Zeke) embark upon a journey to seek their mythical father, who they have been led to believe lives in Germany. Voula and Alexander ride a train leading to the Greek/German "border" (in actuality Greece and Germany do not share such a border). As they traverse their homeland, they experience the pain inflicted upon them by an indifferent and often brutal adult world. The penniless children are taken off of trains; they are disavowed by an uncle, who reveals the futility of their search (Voula and Alexander are illegitimate and their mother does not know the whereabouts of their father); Alexander is traumatized when he witnesses the last throes of a dying horse; and Voula is raped by a lecherous lorry driver.

There is a brief interlude of tenderness in the film when the two are befriended by the youth Orestes (Stratos Tzortzoglou). Orestes is one of the members of a theater troupe. (This troupe reappears from Angelopoulos' 1975 film *The Travelling Players.*) The players are themselves on a journey transecting Greece in search of an

auditorium at which to perform their sad play. Orestes resonates a breath of optimism into the plot, as he assumes the role of sympathetic protector. This breath of
hopefulness, however, is cut short when Voula, who has developed a schoolgirl infatuation for Orestes, comes to discover that her would-be boyfriend is homosexual.
Dismayed and ravaged, Voula can hardly summon the strength to continue forth, but
the children do continue as Alexander buoys Voula's spirits by reminding her that the
end is near and that they shall soon be united with their father.

The children reach their destination as Voula and Alexander paddle a boat across
a river into Germany. As sister and brother disembark, a mysterious mist lifts away
and a lone tree standing tall is revealed. This landscape in the mist is at best an
ambiguous and debatable triumph for the children, but seen through the eyes of
Voula and Alexander it represents a mystical experience of untranscribable proportions.

Angelopoulos' landscape is certainly more surreal than realistic; this is a story
told elegiacally rather than narratively. The piercing bleakness of the isolated beaches,
the deserted railway stations, the empty roads, the seemingly vacant villages, and the
oppressive turgid sky forever swelling forth with sheets of rain visually express the
societal, political, and cultural desolation of modern-day Greece: a country which
has repudiated its past and has been undermined by the inexorable abrading of traditional values. This is the central theme of Angelopoulos' trilogy of his motherland.
The children's odyssey is a journey of enlightenment, in the sense that it is a progressive loss of innocence and illusion in the same manner in which postwar Greece
has lost its national idealism.

Destitute, homeless, rootless—this is the condition of the children as they reach
their destination. They have endured so much that their existence is fragile. They
stand at the precarious edge of an uncertain future, hoping at least to move out of the
mist. Voula and Alexander thus serve as Angelopoulos' allegory of Greece, a nation
he sees as poised on the precipice of destruction.

Angelopoulos reveals his subtlety and complexity as a filmmaker not only in this
contextual manner but also in the visual stylization of imagery. Angelopoulos is a
master of the composed long take, slow crane shot, and the unstopping pan. The use
of these cinematic devices clearly shows the influence of the famed Japanese director
Kenji Mizoguchi. Like Mizoguchi, Angelopoulos utilizes the long take, the tracking,
crane shots, and the 360-degree pan to create the illusion of real time and real
movement and to force the viewer to savor the moment, even if the savoring brings
with it an element of pain. Especially memorable is the protracted scene of the dying
horse which comes at midpoint in the film. As Alexander sobs in the foreground
over the flailing animal, in the background a bride briefly escapes a wedding party to
come outside in the snow and weep. The bride is quickly rejoined to the party and
merriment continues as the celebrators sing and dance offscreen. During this pro-
cessional, Alexander has continued to cry, unconsolable. The interminable close-up
of the little boy is nearly unbearable. The impact is such that the viewer is made to
feel Alexander's agony.

Another breathtaking moment in the film comes near the end when Voula, Alexander, and Orestes stand amazed on the windswept shore and watch as a helicopter winches from the sea a colossal stone hand. The camera moves with the dangling ancient stone fragment as, helicopter-borne, it disappears over Salonica. This disquieting scene is strangely beautiful. Angelopoulos' debt to Federico Fellini is obvious, as seen in surreal images such as this which transform simple narrative objects into visual poetry.

Finally, a discussion of this film would not be complete without praising the cinematographer Giorgos Arvanitis for his inimitable camerawork and flawless lighting, and lauding the musical score of Eleni Karaindrou, which stirs, rouses, and soars in perfect harmony with the film.

Jo Lauria

Reviews
Boston Globe. September 28, 1990, p. 47.
Chicago Tribune. November 19, 1990, V, p. 3.
Film Comment. XXVI, November, 1990, p. 38.
The Hollywood Reporter. April 27, 1990, p. 63.
Los Angeles Times. October 31, 1990, p. F3.
The Miami Herald. February 7, 1990, p. D1.
The New York Times. September 14, 1990, p. C10.
Punch. CCXCVI, June 23, 1989, p. 44.
San Francisco Chronicle. September 21, 1990, p. E4.
Variety. September 6, 1988, p. 16.
The Village Voice. XXXV, September 18, 1990, p. 57.
The Washington Post. February 1, 1991, p. C7.

LAST EXIT TO BROOKLYN

Production: Bernd Eichinger; released by Cinecom Entertainment Group
Direction: Uli Edel
Screenplay: Desmond Nakano; based on the novel by Hubert Selby, Jr.
Cinematography: Stefan Czapsky
Editing: Peter Przygodda
Production design: David Chapman
Art direction: Mark Haack
Set decoration: Leslie Ann Pope
Costume design: Carol Oditz
Music: Mark Knopfler
MPAA rating: R
Running time: 103 minutes

Principal characters:
Harry Black	Stephen Lang
Tralala	Jennifer Jason Leigh
Big Joe	Burt Young
Vinnie	Peter Dobson
Boyce	Jerry Orbach
Donna	Ricki Lake
Georgette	Alexis Arquette
Regina	Zette
Georgette's mother	Rutanya Alda
Spook	Cameron Johann

Hubert Selby, Jr.'s *Last Exit to Brooklyn* stirred murky controversy when it first was published in the United States in 1964. Composed of six interrelated stories, the book examined the underbelly of an era, the 1950's, once popularly labeled "fabulous." Attacked as vile obscenity in both the United States and England, it was nevertheless praised as honest and compassionate by such literary figures as Allen Tate and Stanley Kunitz. German director Uli Edel's film adaptation shows fascinated affection for the original, even as it acknowledges the often sordid nature of Selby's stories, visually stressing the persistent nightmares that have dominated urban reality for decades. The book withstood legal assaults well into the 1960's, ultimately serving as a test case that helped overthrow the 1959 Obscene Publications Act. Shortly afterward, it was purchased as a potential film property by three young graduates of the Munich Film and Television Academy: Edel himself, and producers Bernd Eichinger and Herman Weigel. Nearly two decades of false starts and changed plans later, along came a screenplay by Desmond Nakano which wove together Selby's loose connections into something unified.

Edel and his associates chose the Nakano script because it invited strong images and connected the characters in one narrative stream. Edel himself explained to press interviewers, "we always wanted to do the whole book as a kind of neighborhood." The area they chose, the Red Hook section of Brooklyn, seemed to them to carry forward enough of the necessary 1950's atmosphere and lend itself well to the grim, sometimes dreamlike expressions of fear, desire, and brutal anger which characterize the film's residents. *Last Exit to Brooklyn* looks at times foreign, a displaced memory or delusion. Some scenes recall passages in Orson Welles's adaptation of Franz Kafka's *The Trial* (1963). It also retains some of the stock imprints of *film noir.* Emptiness and uncertainty dominate strangely vacated streets at times. Shifting to a wide-angle lens, cinematographer Stefan Czapsky can turn the wet, paper-strewn pavement into a momentary stage for dangerous assignations.

This certainly is not a film for everyone, for it can offend in the same ways that coarse reality can. Still, readers who appreciated the book's uncompromising studies of trapped people will find Edel's cinematic transfer interesting. Producer Eichinger, expressing his hope in the power of Selby's story, stated in a press release, "I wanted to throw a rock at the audience with this film. They can either throw the rock back in my face or take it and run."

Giving shape to Selby's several stories, scriptwriter Nakano focuses on a long-lasting strike in a Brooklyn metal plant, circa 1952. Neither Dwight Eisenhower nor the Dodgers are mentioned prominently here, and there is enough familiar evidence of poverty, garbage, and crime that, with minimal costume and automobile changes, viewers might be inclined to mistake the setting for 1990. Because the factory employs so many neighborhood men, the work stoppage directly affects everyone's lives, including those of the brazen hooker Tralala (Jennifer Jason Leigh) and the idealistic adolescent Spook (Cameron Johann), whose naïve longing for her is surpassed only by his dream of a motorcycle on which he will rescue her from life's hardships. With crass nonchalance, she tolerates the youth. Less gracious is her pimp, a recently released convict named Vinnie (Peter Dobson), who stirs his local goons to beat savagely a Korea-bound soldier from a nearby base, ostensibly because the latter has cast aspersions on Tralala's purity. When police arrive, no one tells the truth about the fight, not even a witness, Harry Black (Stephen Lang), who figures to profit more in reputation and self-importance by validating Vinnie's lies.

Black is the most complex of a bevy of pathetic characters. While publicly strutting and exhibiting self-assurance, he privately smolders with fear and doubt. When approached by the local transvestite, a flirtatious young man who calls himself Georgette (Alexis Arquette), Black feels strangely aroused, but he knows that to give in to his urge will mean ridicule from his peers, thus spoiling his self-image as a macho labor leader. Confused, he retreats to his dingy apartment. His child sleeps uneasily next to a bed where his wife virtually begs him for sex. After trying to fake sleep, he grabs her quickly and enters her with violence and hatred. In addition to further characterizing Black, the crude sex scene foreshadows several other moments in the film. That is, whenever the potential for affection or gentleness develops, it is annihilated by some variant of the opposite emotional force. Pleasure soon gives way to pain, every time.

Spook's father, called Big Joe (Burt Young), is another turbulent sort who may just as easily throw things at his wife as embrace her. Angry about being out of work for so long, he discovers that his fat, unmarried daughter Donna (Ricki Lake) is pregnant. The frightened Spook guesses that a fun-loving lad named Tommy might be the father. Big Joe goes into a rage. Later, as union groceries are being distributed and the organizer, named Boyce (Jerry Orbach), exhorts his men to stay together, Joe sees Tommy and tries to strangle him. Tommy cracks the older man over the head with a chair, but he still promises to marry Donna.

In the middle portion of *Last Exit to Brooklyn*, director Edel alternates scenes from the essentially comic Tommy/Donna story with scattered scenes of gruesome or anonymous violence. He also weaves in two quasi-romantic developments. One focuses on Tralala and an impressionable, Korea-bound army officer named Steve, whom she picks up in a Manhattan bar after an earlier client passes out. The other story follows Harry Black to a drug party, where he meets and falls in love with a gay young man named Regina (Zette), who, like Tralala, is less interested in sex than in financial rewards. Soldier Steve quickly falls in love with the streetwalker. He speaks politely of her rare beauty, buys clothes for her, and acts as if their lovemaking is the rhapsodic zenith of his life. He does not even get upset when he catches her trying to steal his wallet. Before long, the foulmouthed prostitute begins speaking with more care and, encouraged by the compliments that Steve pays her, stays with him, confident that he will leave her a bundle of cash. When he ships out, however, he leaves her only an envelope containing a love letter.

Harry is also smitten, so much so that he stays with Regina until late the next morning. Completely forgetting his responsibilities at the plant gate, he jokes with his lover while a convoy of nonunion trucks breaks through the picket line for loading inside. That same evening, police arrive to help the trucks take their cargo out of the city. A bloody riot ensues, with casualties on both sides, but the trucks get through. Later, Boyce, angry over Harry's negligence and for mindless spending on Regina and elsewhere, fires him from the strike leadership post. Without access to union cash, Harry no longer interests Regina. Later, he is caught trying to sodomize a frightened young neighborhood boy. As Harry shrieks for mercy, the local crowd brutally beats him and ties him up, spread-eagled, behind a billboard.

During the neighborhood violence, Big Joe has become a grandfather. He decides on a double celebration: the christening of the grandson and the wedding of Donna and Tommy. Just when it seems that the new young family will serve as beacons of love for the community, Tommy and his father-in-law get into another fierce argument and fight, even jeopardizing the safety of the cradled infant. Then Boyce appears with good news: The strike has been settled. Wrestling holds turn into handshakes and embraces, and the party reverts to celebration.

Tralala, however, is elsewhere, in a dark, profane place called Willie's Bar, lamenting the soldier's love letter and drinking herself into a stupor. With little encouragement, she starts to undress and pledges to give herself to every man in sight. With glazed eyes and sick grins, the unreal men charge her. In an abandoned car across the road, they gang-rape her. Young Spook, who has managed to start an old motorcycle and wants to give her a ride, finds her with her last assailant. She looks nearly dead, but when the boy weeps uncontrollably, she manages to take him in her arms and comfort him. The next morning, in the final scene of the film, Big Joe and the other men happily return to work. The epilogue is the only scene of pleasantry which does not disintegrate into chaos or brutality of some kind.

Last Exit to Brooklyn is clearly meant to be acknowledged or perhaps studied, but not enjoyed. That there is so little joy springing from the docks and channels of Selby's and Edel's Brooklyn is the very point of the film—or at least one of its points. "These are real people," Selby told an interviewer for *The New York Times* before the release of the film that his book had inspired. "How can anybody look inside themselves and be surprised at the hatred and violence in the world?" In recent decades, literary analysts and film scholars have generally found this kind of literary naturalism irrelevant, or at least aesthetically unfashionable. To the general viewing public, such recognition of relentless woe as that herein represented may seem too far from entertainment. Films such as *Last Exit to Brooklyn* may also imply that, for every individual tale of financial success and hedonistic fulfillment (in any era), there are potential volumes about whole communities, filled with ugly failure and miserable disillusionment.

Best in the talented cast is Lang, who did an absorbing job of character-creation as Happy Loman in Volker Schlondorff's Broadway and television productions of Arthur Miller's *Death of a Salesman*. Here he delivers a paradox in personality, a frantic man capable of passion yet also an opportunist given to self-revulsion. Lang seems to be used by his director to manifest and almost surrealistically dramatize the pervasive fear and panic in the community. The rest of the characters are attached more fully to stark reality, particularly Leigh as Tralala, who swaggers and swears through life blissfully ignorant of her own beauty until her self-imposed barriers are shattered by the silly words of a sentimental hick who goes off to fight in a distant war.

Andrew Jefchak

Reviews
Boxoffice. July, 1990, p. R49.
Chicago Tribune. May 11, 1990, VII, p. 39.
Films in Review. XLI, August, 1990, p. 425.
The Hollywood Reporter. CCCXII, May 1, 1990, p. 4.
Los Angeles Times. May 4, 1990, p. F8.
The Nation. CCL, May 28, 1990, p. 755.
The New Republic. CCII, June 4, 1990, p. 24.
The New York Times. May 2, 1990, p. B1.
Variety. CCCXXXVII, November 8, 1989, p. 32.
The Washington Post. May 11, 1990, p. D7.

LISTEN UP
The Lives of Quincy Jones

Production: Courtney Sale Ross; released by Warner Bros.
Direction: Ellen Weissbrod
Cinematography: Stephen Kazmierski
Editing: Milton Moses Ginsberg, Pierre Kahn, Andrew Morreale, Laure Sullivan,
    and Paul Zehrer
Production management: Melissa Powell
Music: Quincy Jones
MPAA rating: PG-13
Running time: 114 minutes

> *Principal personages:*
> Quincy Jones, Jolie Jones, Billy Eckstine, Clark Terry, Clarence Avant, George Benson, Richard Brooks, Tevin Campbell, Ray Charles, Miles Davis, Sheila E., Ella Fitzgerald, Dizzy Gillespie, Lionel Hampton, Herbie Hancock, Ice-T, James Ingram, Jesse Jackson, Sydney Lumet, Bobby McFerrin, Frank Sinatra, Steven Spielberg, Barbra Streisand, Sarah Vaughan, Oprah Winfrey, and Michael Jackson, among others.

While the music of Quincy Jones has become legendary and his achievements almost innumerable, the man himself remains something of an enigma. Because Jones's life has been varied and unusual, a different approach is taken by the filmmakers of *Listen Up: The Lives of Quincy Jones.* Instead of following traditional lines, this documentary weaves together a collection of interviews and old film footage, as well as excerpts from Jones's chosen profession—music making.

From the outset, it is quite clear that the journalistic approach of interviewing is to be left far behind. In fact, the style is so innovative that at times the structure becomes more important than the subject. Indeed, the approach to the subject takes a very immediate, visceral, and often frenzied look at the world of the famous composer, arranger, and musician. This style is almost entirely attributable to the vision of the producer, Courtney Sale Ross. Her idea of continually collapsing time, by bringing the past into the present, is an attempt to show that the past influences the present. Whether this approach to film documentary is a valid one still remains to be seen, as Ross's approach is unique. In order to achieve her goal, Ross has at least three different threads running through the documentary. The first is, understandably, Jones himself being interviewed. The second and by far the most impressive thread is the assembly of writers, musicians, actors, and actresses that are brought together to give their impressions of the leading man. Among them are Frank Sinatra, Steven Spielberg, Dizzy Gillespie, Alex Haley, Jesse Jackson, Sidney Lumet, Ray Charles, and Michael Jackson, as well as Jones's family and friends. The third thread which intertwines with the rest is the montage of film clips which seem to have the purpose of uniting the film. Because this last part is the most manipulative, there is often an interpretation given to Jones's life which is not apparent when he is interviewed.

This unusual approach can be seen in particular in a segment which deals with racism in the 1960's. Starting with scenes from the Watts riots in Los Angeles, in which blacks are shown being beaten by the police, the film depicts, with short segments, different kinds of racism and segregation. There is the Ku Klux Klan, the black townships of South Africa, signs which show that blacks are not welcome, and then more blacks rioting in the streets of America's inner cities. Throughout all this, prominent black personalities are asked their feelings about what went on during those times. Despite the obvious pressure, most diplomatically sidestep the issue and describe them merely as unsettling times. The message which is perceived is one of the "white world" against the "black world." Because the music of Jones was little influenced by the black-white question, there seems to be little justification for examining such an inflammatory subject. Had Jones himself shown that much of his music was influenced by the difficulties that blacks experienced during those times, then a good social comment would have been made. The truth is that Jones wrote what he felt, which had nothing to do with segregation and white supremacy.

From racism to the world of jazz, the documentary signals a shift of focus and the possibility of learning what really motivates Jones to write and arrange such memorable pieces. There can be no question that the black musical community, with its distinctive African-American rhythms and vocalization, embodies jazz wholeheartedly. Again, the filmmakers give only the briefest of moments to portray the great jazz musicians; Nat King Cole appears for only a second on the screen. Interestingly, Jones speaks of Count Basie as more than just a mentor. This relationship sounds interesting, but nothing more comes of this line of questioning. In fact, this is perhaps the film's trademark: Interesting ideas are brought into the arena but there is no time to stop and explore a little deeper. It is as if there is an overburdening need to move along into the next interview, the next film clip, the next piece of information that might just unlock the secret as to what really makes up "the lives of Quincy Jones."

Jazz allows the expression of something that is very dear to the black musician but which was not appreciated by the average white American. In fact, it was through his many tours and appearances in Europe that Jones, in his own estimate, received the most immediate understanding of the kind of music that he wrote and played. Despite this seeming appreciation of his music, his one major tour in Europe almost broke Jones, financially as well as emotionally. By his own admission, he was no businessman, and this lack of know-how caused an enormous strain on his band, which he had taken to Europe in the summer of 1957. Taking care of a large group of musicians, who were constantly on the road, was too much of a task for Jones. In fact, if it had not been for a number of benefactors who sent money to him in Europe, the whole tour might have been an even worse disaster than it already had become.

Jones returned feeling so low that he even contemplated suicide. As is so often the case in show business, a great fall is often followed by some equally astounding rise, and Jones was not immune to this law. Mercury Records offered him a job and as a result, he soon rose in the company to become vice president. The extremely handsome Jones became tied to a routine that required him to wear tailored Italian suits and to become a part of the establishment, which everyone except Jones thought was a good idea. While his talents as a composer and arranger were acknowledged, the free-loading Jones was not happy, as he had focused his attention on Hollywood and hoped to compose for motion pictures.

To date, Jones has written scores for more than forty major motion pictures. Success apparently comes easy for Jones as, if success could be measured by the number of Grammies and singles sold, his career ranks with the all-time greats. It is at this point that Jones shows his insecurity, and the fact that he is sought after by the music industry does not convince him of his great contribution to that industry. Soon the old story would emerge, that Jones was writing to formula and that films no longer inspired him. Around about this time a young singer named Michael Jackson teamed up with Jones. When Jackson's management approached Jones, the idea, even in the beginning, was to make Jackson a "megastar." The result of the Jones/Jackson collaboration was the solo album "Off the Wall," which launched Jackson as an international superstar and Jones as one of the major record producers in America.

Commercial success again put Jones on a new emotional high, but his third divorce brought him crashing back to earth again. While Jones may have wanted to remain on the crest of the wave, his family life caused him to look deeper. During one of his interviews, Jones confesses to being a workaholic and claims that he did not see the breakup coming. The situation caused him to work even harder, and the continual stress and long hours caused him to have two brain aneurysms. Recovering from surgery, Jones realized that this may be a sign from God that he needs to slow down. Through such traumatic events, Jones finally realized that his work had been all-consuming. He had put his family life on permanent hold and now more than ever he needed that emotional security which, up until then, had been provided solely by his music. It is on this note that the documentary ends. What better ending than observing, at very close quarters, a man who recognizes the need for his family over and above that of his career.

Quincy Jones won six Grammys for his eclectic album *Back on the Block*. Those Grammys were: Album of the Year, Best Rap Performance by a Duo or Group, Best Jazz Fusion Performance (Vocal or Instrumental), Best Arrangement on an Instrumental, Best Engineered Recording—Non-Classical, and the most prestigious award of Producer of the Year—Non-Classical.

Music was Jones's life, and, as such, it might not be unreasonable to expect that some of the focus would be on the physical side of music composition, but this never happens. This omission constitutes one of the more obvious weaknesses of *Listen Up: The Lives of Quincy Jones*. All of the famous people who were interviewed spoke in glowing colors of Jones except for his daughter from his first marriage,

Jolie. She speaks candidly and from the heart, and she saw sooner than anyone else what was happening to her father. The viewer is left with the impression that, had he taken her advice, Quincy Jones might not have had to experience the many peaks and troughs of his career.

Richard G. Cormack

Reviews

Boxoffice. November, 1990, p. R83.
Chicago Tribune. October 5, 1990, VII, p. 22.
The Christian Science Monitor. November 2, 1990, p. 13.
Down Beat. LVII, December, 1990, p. 12.
The Hollywood Reporter. August 27, 1990, p. 6.
Los Angeles Times. October 5, 1990, p. F8.
The New York Times. October 3, 1990, p. B5.
Premiere. IV, September, 1990, p. 22.
Rolling Stone. October 18, 1990, p. 49.
Variety. CCXXVIII, August 23, 1990, p. 2.
The Village Voice. XXXV, October 9, 1990, p. 67.
The Washington Post. October 5, 1990, p. D1.

THE LONG WALK HOME

Production: Howard W. Koch, Jr., and Dave Bell for New Visions Pictures; released
  by Miramax Films
Direction: Richard Pearce
Screenplay: John Cork
Cinematography: Roger Deakins
Editing: Bill Yahraus
Production design: Blake Russell
Costume design: Shay Cunliffe
Music: George Fenton
MPAA rating: PG
Running time: 97 minutes

Principal characters:
Miriam Thompson	Sissy Spacek
Odessa Cotter	Whoopi Goldberg
Norman Thompson	Dwight Schultz
Herbert Cotter	Ving Rhames
Tunker Thompson	Dylan Baker
Selma Cotter	Erika Alexander
Mary Catherine Thompson	Lexi Faith Randall
Theodore Cotter	Richard Habersham
Franklin Cotter	Jason Weaver
Narrator	Mary Steenburgen

Set against the backdrop of the rising racial tensions threatening to destroy segregated Southern life in Montgomery, Alabama, in the 1950's, *The Long Walk Home* unfolds the intimate drama of two women who become unwitting heroines in the battle against racism. The film focuses on the relationship between Miriam Thompson (Sissy Spacek), an affluent white suburban housewife, and her black maid, Odessa Cotter (Whoopi Goldberg). The story is narrated in the present from the perspective of the now mature Mary Catherine (voice of Mary Steenburgen), Miriam's youngest daughter, and it swiftly zeroes in on the segregationist attitudes that were all-pervasive in Southern society.

Miriam is the middle-class prim and proper housewife who takes great pride in managing domestic affairs as well as maintaining her family's position on the social roster. Junior League meetings, bridge and tennis dates, community involvement, and cocktail parties require so much of Miriam's attention that she finds herself relying heavily on the efficiency of Odessa, her dedicated maid of nine years, to keep her household running smoothly and to do the "mothering" of Mary Catherine (Lexi Faith Randall). Odessa performs her duties pleasantly and without complaint; she is unobtrusive and silently accepts the injustices and little indignities that go with the territory. Odessa has a family of her own, a husband and three children, and it is clear that she sacrifices her pride and endures the daily hard work and degradation in order to help provide for them.

The domestic routine of the Thompson house is disturbed, however, when the Reverend Martin Luther King, Jr., urges a black boycott of the city's transit system in response to the arrest of Rosa Parks, a black woman who had refused to vacate her seat for a white passenger. What the bus boycott means for Odessa, who supports the protest movement, is that she must now walk the nine miles to and from Miriam's house if she is to keep her job. What this means for Miriam is that she is now inconvenienced by Odessa's late arrival in the mornings and by her maid's utter physical exhaustion, which limits her performance. Therefore, it is practicality that motivates Miriam to sidestep the boycott issue and drive Odessa to work twice a week, an act that she keeps secret from her overbearing husband Norman (Dwight Schultz).

The protest escalates and tensions mount in urban Alabama. Norman learns of his wife's chauffeuring activities and demands that she stop interfering. An ambitious real-estate developer, Norman does not want anyone in his family to be identified as a Negro sympathizer. This is Miriam's time of awakening. She realizes that her prejudiced husband is forcing her to take a stand and that, up to now, she has "done all the right things for all the wrong reasons." In a poignant living room scene when Miriam attempts to communicate with Odessa on a human level, it is Odessa who highlights for Miriam the contradiction in her life: Odessa flatly asks Miriam, "What's scaring you, Mrs. Thompson? Who you are, or who Mr. Thompson wants you to be?" Miriam chooses sides. Barely able to comprehend her own motivations, the white suburban housewife begins driving for the black-run carpool system. By so doing, Miriam stands opposed to the overwhelming majority of white Montgomery citizens who live by their bigotry, including Miriam's husband, who has shown his anger toward her by moving out of their bedroom.

The film races to the climax. Determined to break the back of the boycott resistance, racist whites brandishing baseball bats storm the carpool lot. Among the offenders are Norman and his hard-line segregationist brother, Tunker (Dylan Baker). Standing on the lot awaiting a carpool assignment is Miriam; nearby hover Odessa and Mary Catherine, as well as several black women waiting on a ride. This is baptism by fire. Tunker verbally and physically abuses Miriam, but threatened as she is, Miriam proves her commitment by standing her ground. Odessa, sensing imminent violence, starts singing a hymn. Almost immediately, Odessa is joined by her sisters in song. With hands linked, the women, including Miriam, form a human chain across the carpool lot. Odessa's singular show of bravery silences the surging mob and passive resistance triumphs. Two women, one white and one black, clasping hands and singing a spiritual, face the future with hope for a better, more equitable world. The film ends on Mary Catherine's narration: "It would be years before I understood what standing in that line meant to my mother—and as I grew older, to me."

The Long Walk Home deftly portrays an incendiary incident that sparked widespread black involvement in the Civil Rights movement by holding the focus on two central characters whose lives are forever altered by the choices that they make. While this domestic perspective is a narrow one, the film succeeds because of the tightness of the script, which never allows the viewer's attention to stray, and the command performances by Spacek and Goldberg. In the beginning, Spacek is completely convincing as the well-to-do suburbanite who is happily self-absorbed and naïve in worldly affairs. As the story progresses, her evolution to a sympathetic character who condescends neither to her husband nor to blatant bigotry is equally believable because Spacek plays the part with great insight and depth. Her performance is matched scene for scene by Goldberg's. Goldberg, who actually says very little throughout the film, renders her character supremely credible by acting downtrodden with masterful control and restraint. The dynamics between the two actresses make for compelling drama.

If this film is to be faulted, the fault lies in its sentimental tone. Particularly glaring are the portrayals of Odessa's family members, who are depicted as veritable models of virtue. Additionally, all the existent hardships that the blacks suffer in a racist society are romanticized for the sake of keeping the film rising on an upbeat arc. Yet, *The Long Walk Home* is a commercial endeavor and does not pretend to be a documentary, although the writer and producers do claim absolute historical accuracy. In the final analysis, *The Long Walk Home* deserves to be viewed as a small but significant period piece, made most notable by the superb performances of its two lead actresses.

Jo Lauria

Reviews
The Christian Science Monitor. January 11, 1991, p. 12.
The Hollywood Reporter. September 14, 1990, p. 10.
L.A. Life. December 21, 1990, p. 20.
Los Angeles Times. December 20, 1990, p. F1.
New Woman. XXI, January, 1991, p. 28.
The New York Times. December 21, 1990, p. B6.
Newsweek. CXVII, January 14, 1991, p. 54.
Premiere. IV, January, 1991, p. 12.
Time. CXXXVI, December 17, 1990, p. 92.
Variety. September 13, 1990, p. 2.
The Village Voice. XXXV, December 25, 1990, p. 84.

LONGTIME COMPANION

Production: Stan Wlodkowski for Companion Productions and American Playhouse
Theatrical Films; released by Samuel Goldwyn Company
Direction: Norman René
Screenplay: Craig Lucas
Cinematography: Tony Jannelli
Editing: Katherine Wenning
Production design: Andrew Jackness
Art direction: Ruth Ammon
Set decoration: Kate Conklin
Sound: Paul Cote
Makeup: Nina Port
Costume design: Walter Hicklin
Music: Greg DeBelles
MPAA rating: R
Running time: 96 minutes

Principal characters:
David	Bruce Davison
Willy	Campbell Scott
Fuzzy	Stephen Caffrey
Sean	Mark Lamos
Howard	Patrick Cassidy
Lisa	Mary-Louise Parker
Paul	John Dossett
Bob	Brian Cousins
John	Dermot Mulroney
Alec	Brad O'Hare
Michael	Michael Schoeffling

It is a reflection on history, rather than on the film itself, that *Longtime Companion* is a simple film. The plot consists of nothing more than excerpts of the daily lives of a group of gay men between 1981 and 1989. By the film's end, however, daily life includes an omnipresent death threat in the form of the AIDS epidemic. Everyday life, and, horrifyingly, everyday death.

The action begins on July 3, 1981, a beautiful day on Fire Island, where wealthy David (Bruce Davison) and his lover, Sean (Mark Lamos), a soap-opera writer, are enjoying their beach house and a little boy-watching. Meanwhile, in Manhattan, lovers Howard (Patrick Cassidy) and Paul (John Dossett), an actor and lawyer, respectively, start their busy day. Next door to Howard and Paul, Lisa (Mary-Louise Parker) calls her best friend, Fuzzy (Stephen Caffrey), an entertainment lawyer who happens to be spending the weekend on Fire Island. In a series of cuts that begin with

Lisa reading to Fuzzy, the characters are shown reading *The New York Times* story covering a new disease afflicting gay men. Someone quips that it is "like the CIA trying to scare us from having sex." Unconcerned, the Islanders go out for an evening of dancing. Willy (Campbell Scott) and his best friend, John (Dermot Mulroney), who are visiting David and Sean, notice Fuzzy. Despite John's jokes about Fuzzy's beard, Willy is attracted to him. The day ends happily on both Fire Island and Manhattan, with Willy and Fuzzy in a romantic embrace on the beach, and Howard and Paul beginning a night of lovemaking.

By April 30, 1982, the situation is slightly less joyful. The group from Fire Island meet at the hospital, where John lies dying from pneumonia. The friends are unsure whether it is AIDS-induced, but the attending physician implies that it is, although everyone is reluctant to name the disease. Waiting in the lounge, the friends talk despairingly of the fact that John has never participated in those aspects of the "gay life" currently being blamed for AIDS: casual bath-house sex or drugs. Willy goes home to Fuzzy, now his live-in lover, devastated at the thought of losing his best friend.

On June 17, 1983, David, Sean, Fuzzy, and Willy and assorted friends, including Lisa, are back on Fire Island. They reminisce with love about John, but their AIDS consciousness is not yet raised, and they sneer when a neighbor, covered with Kaposi's sarcoma and ostracized on the Island, stares longingly over the back fence. Later, they watch an episode of Sean's soap opera, while Sean explains how hard it is for him to be accepted as a writer, defined by his skill, rather than labeled a "gay writer."

A bit more than a year later, September 7, 1984, the disease once again closes in on the group. This time, it is Sean who is in the hospital, although he seems healthy. In a shocking scene, Willy slips into the bathroom after unavoidably getting a greeting kiss from Sean. He washes his cheek, his mouth, his hands and arms, using paper towels to touch anything that Sean might have touched. After he emerges and chats falsely for a few minutes he flees, his face strained with equal parts of guilt and fear.

By March 22, 1985, AIDS has become the overwhelming factor in everyone's life. Sean continues to deteriorate, losing as much mental acuity as physical strength. David struggles with an exasperation at once poignant and comic as he takes care of Sean. In one scene, David futilely tries to feed lines to Sean on the extension while Sean, parroting hopelessly inappropriate responses, talks to his unwitting producer on the telephone. In another, David takes Sean to the park. As he leans back against the bench with a look of fatigued relief, he follows the horrified eyes of a mother and child and sees Sean happily urinating on the grass. Meanwhile, Paul has been diagnosed with AIDS, leaving Howard frantic enough to consider stopping work. In the political climate of the times, it is a question that might become one of necessity rather than choice: Fuzzy's sole work, lately, seems to consist of trying to defend clients who are in danger of being dropped from projects as the result of rumors of homosexuality or AIDS.

On January 4, 1986, Sean lies nearly unidentifiable in a sick room at home. Going to Sean's bed, David looks at the gray-skinned, spastic skeleton that used to be his vibrant companion. In the film's most riveting scene, he strokes Sean's face, and as the dying man chokes for breath, David soothes him and tells him to let go, easing him calmly into death. Later, he sits numbly as the body is removed, while Fuzzy, Willy, and Lisa call the AIDS hotline to find a morgue that will handle AIDS victims.

David's funeral is held on May 16, 1987. Willy eulogizes him with humor, covering his financial stinginess and spiritual generosity. Afterward, at an upbeat wake, old friends regale Lisa's new husband with stories about David. In one, David takes advantage of his parents' empty house, on the day before his sister's wedding, to try on her wedding dress. He trips down the stairs, destroying the dress; the family returns to find him unconscious, in drag.

September 10, 1988, sees Willy and Fuzzy deeply committed to the battle against AIDS. Both volunteer with Gay Men's Health Crisis, and Willy does housework for housebound AIDS patients, including a straight Hispanic man. Howard has also become an activist, following Paul's death. As a well-known actor, openly gay and diagnosed with AIDS, he heads benefits and serves as a role model for People with AIDS.

The film ends on July 19, 1989, as Willy, Fuzzy, and Lisa walk along the beach at Fire Island. In marked contrast to the beautiful day that opened the film eight years before, the day is overcast, the beach deserted. The three try to remember what life was like before AIDS, finding the joy and freedom of those times nearly inconceivable. All of a sudden there is a shout, and John comes running down to the beach, and embraces Willy. Soon the friends are surrounded by all the old inhabitants of Fire Island, including, among all their friends dead of AIDS, a serene David and Sean. The collective fantasy fades, however, leaving Fuzzy, Willy, and Lisa alone again on the cold sand. "What do you think it'll be like when they find a cure?" one asks. "Like the end of World War II."

Longtime Companion has been criticized for being less than an atomic device in this worldwide battle. Some people have found the lack of minority characters and the economically disadvantaged to be unrealistic, if not racist. As one critic noted, however, focusing on white, well-to-do characters permitted the filmmakers to study the emotional toll of AIDS itself, rather than the extenuating circumstances of AIDS in the face of racism or poverty (vital questions, of course, which merit separate films). Several lesbian critics have taken exception to the fact that, while a great number of lesbians are involved with AIDS care and AIDS protests, there is no depiction of such in the film. The most basic criticism of the film, however, is its even-tempered political discussion of AIDS. While various points are raised—from the question of AIDS as antigay conspiracy, through the morality of the baths-poppers-disco scene of the late 1970's and early 1980's, to the New Age disease-as-metaphor offered by Michael (Michael Schoeffling), a member of the group who pushes self-love and high colonics—none is seriously engaged. The film has been accused of having the depth of a "movie-of-the-week," and, since it was developed for American Play-house, this criticism is not inaccurate, only unfair in its implication. As the first major motion-picture release that focuses on AIDS and the gay male community—versus Bill Sherwood's independent release *Parting Glances* (1986), in which AIDS was a subplot—*Longtime Companion* exhibits sufficient bravery by simply standing alone in the middle of the road.

It is a nicely made, often effectively acted film. It is most notable, perhaps, for its generosity in allowing heterosexual audiences entry into what its author, Craig Lu-cas, calls "the culture of our lives." That culture is well presented in the camera's—and characters'—pleasure in the male body; in the evocation of the sexual dyna-mism of Fire Island, circa 1980; in the biting humor that sends Sean's body to be cremated in a lovely dress or that shows Fuzzy lip-synching coyly to "Dreamgirls." It is shown tenderly by the transvestite who visits her AIDS-stricken boyfriend in the bed next to Paul's.

During Howard's AIDS benefit, a chamber trio of "retro nerds" begins a ponder-ous, cello-driven piece. As one begins to sing, the song is revealed to be "YMCA" by the Village People, a near-anthem of gay culture from the late 1970's, a golden time: post-Stonewall, pre-AIDS. The audience howls in recognition, with pleasure at both the parody and the memory. It is a strong reminder that the music has slowed but will not stop.

Gabrielle J. Forman

Reviews
Boxoffice. April 9, 1990, p. R32.
Chicago Tribune. May 25, 1990, VII, p. 28.
Film Comment. XXVI, May, 1990, p. 11.
Films in Review. XLI, October, 1990, p. 483.
The Hollywood Reporter. CCCXI, January 24, 1990, p. 4.
Los Angeles Times. May 17, 1990, p. F1.
The Nation. CCL, May 28, 1990, p. 752.
The New Republic. CCII, May 28, 1990, p. 25.
The New York Times. May 11, 1990, p. B1.
The New Yorker. LXVI, May 21, 1990, p. 71.
Newsweek. CXV, May 14, 1990, p. 70.
Time. CXXXV, May 14, 1990, p. 96.
Variety. January 30, 1990, p. 12.

LOOK WHO'S TALKING TOO

Production: Jonathan D. Krane; released by Tri-Star Pictures
Direction: Amy Heckerling
Screenplay: Amy Heckerling and Neal Israel
Cinematography: Thomas Del Ruth
Editing: Debra Chiate
Production design: Reuben Freed
Set decoration: Barry W. Brolly
Art direction: Richard Wilcox
Visual effects (title sequence): Gary Platek
Sound: Ralph Parker
Costume design: Molly Maginnis
Special creature effects: Chris Walas, Inc.
Music: David Kitay
MPAA rating: PG-13
Running time: 81 minutes

Principal characters:

James	John Travolta
Mollie	Kirstie Alley
Mikey	(voice of Bruce Willis)
Julie	(voice of Roseanne Barr)
Eddie	(voice of Damon Wayans)
Rosie	Olympia Dukakis
Stuart	Elias Koteas
Rona	Twink Caplan
Joey	Gilbert Gottfried
Mr. Toilet Man	(voice of Mel Brooks)
Mikey	Lorne Sussman
Julie (1 year old)	Megan Milner
Julie (4 months old)	Georgia Keithley
Julie (newborn)	Nikki Graham
Eddie	Danny Pringle
Mr. Ross	Neal Israel
Mikey's dream friend	Mollie Israel

The formula worked spectacularly the first time, to the tune of $300 million collected (worldwide) at the box office. Therefore, as has been the case in Hollywood for seventy years, *Look Who's Talking Too*, the sequel, followed the unexpected hit *Look Who's Talking* (1989). *Look Who's Talking Too* brought everyone back for an encore, including much of the talent behind the camera, headed by director Amy Heckerling, and a cast topped by Kirstie Alley and John Travolta, as mismatched lovers who are now married. In the original, Mollie (Alley) is in love with her boss, Albert, but after an accidental pregnancy, she alone struggles to raise Mikey (the voice of Bruce Willis) properly. Seeking a husband and father, Mollie first spurns the attentions of the earnest young cab driver, James (Travolta), who drove her to the hospital during labor. What made *Look Who's Talking* so special was that baby Mikey had audible thoughts that could be heard only by the audience. With Mikey's "help" (that only the audience knows about) Mollie does marry James, setting the stage for the sequel.

In the sequel, Willis once again does the offscreen talking, but he has help from the voices of Roseanne Barr (as his no-nonsense sibling Julie) and *In Living Color*'s Damon Wayans (as his street-smart African-American infant friend Eddie). The sequel's plot twists revolve around Mikey learning to live with his kid sister, and James and Mollie struggling with their marriage. The sequel continues the offbeat style of the original from the opening sequence. For example, baby Mikey (with Willis at his wisecracking best) spies sister Julie and screeches: "She's up! She's mobile! She's movin'! She's headin' right for my toys!" Sadly, however, the sequel seems unable to find as much humor in situations of raising newborns. For example, *Look Who's Talking Too* devotes too much attention to crude potty training jokes, to the point of offering a musical number with the lyrics: "You have to fight . . . for the right . . . to potty!" Even Mel Brooks as the voice of Mr. Toilet Man, a fantasy bathroom bowl come to life, cannot rescue this simpleminded comedy.

At first glance, *Look Who's Talking Too* seems to be yet another example of the new genre of Yuppie comedies about the pratfalls of parenthood. The late 1980's produced a spate of "bringing up baby" films: *Three Men and a Baby* (1987), followed by *Baby Boom* (1987), *She's Having a Baby* (1988), and *Three Men and a Little Lady* (1990; reviewed in this volume), offer significant examples. Yet, the filmgoing public of 1990 seemed to want a new variation on that theme, and so the hits of the Christmas season were *Home Alone* and *Kindergarten Cop* (both reviewed in this volume). *Look Who's Talking Too* can also be thought of as a throwback to the screwball comedies of the 1930's. In the film's best moments, Alley and Travolta act out marital spats that seem both comical and pathetic at the same time. Their struggle to form a marriage forms the heart of the best moments of the film.

Look Who's Talking Too, however, is very different from the far more successful original. In the sequel, for example, there is a far greater use of popular songs. "Catch Us If You Can" (performed by the Dave Clark Five) is the background tune as sperm cells race to attack an egg. The two children, expectedly, frolic to Sonny and Cher's "I Got You Babe." True Hollywood insider's musical commentary comes when baby Julie is about to take her first steps. The camera angle seems to foreshadow strains of Richard Strauss's "Thus Spake Zarathustra," following the influence of *2001: A Space Odyssey* (1968). Instead, director Heckerling added the music signature of Tri-Star's leaping white horse logo (composed by Dave Grusin).

Despite moments of cinematic fun, of the eighteen New York City, Washington, D.C., and Los Angeles-based film critics that it polled, *Variety* could find none who would recommend *Look Who's Talking Too.* Most panned the film, objecting to the abundance of superfluous sequences—in particular, the trapping of terrified youngsters in an accidental fire that did little to advance the basic plot line.

Still, *Look Who's Talking Too* is far more complex than the usual Hollywood sequel. It takes a complex look at the trials and tribulations of contemporary motherhood. Indeed, *Look Who's Talking* and *Look Who's Talking Too* were written and directed by a woman, Heckerling, a rare successful female Hollywood filmmaker. After training at the American Film Institute, Heckerling made her directorial debut with *Fast Times at Ridgemont High* (1982), one of the few films to treat male and female teenagers as complex individuals. Suddenly, Heckerling stood as a filmmaker sought after by the moguls of Hollywood's major studios. She signaled that she was willing to pay her dues with *Johnny Dangerously* (1984) and *National Lampoon's European Vacation* (1985). *Look Who's Talking*, presenting a woman's point of view of the hardships of married life and of the necessary compromises of rearing a child, served as the first true Heckerling cinematic creation. Indeed, it was based on personal experience. The idea had come to her in the mid-1980's with her own experience with childbirth. It is instructive to know that Heckerling's daughter's name is Mollie.

Making a film about babies is not easy. The sequel, in particular, required delicate work with not just the on-screen images of each of the three principal newborns. There were numerous required "stand-ins" and "photo doubles." The shooting schedule was dictated by the needs of these young aspiring thespians. Their meals and naps, by strict agreement, took precedence over all other filmmaking activities. For their comfort, a full nursery, with separate sleeping rooms, cribs, a diaper service, dozens of types of food and formula, a television set, and sitters, operated next to the set. This burden may, in part, explain why the sequel failed to achieve the spontaneity and success of the original. The production history of *Look Who's Talking Too* tells of a constantly rushed Heckerling, working around the clock at the end with a team of editors in order to meet an impending Christmas release deadline. Still, Heckerling, with a new contract with the Disney studio, remains in the top echelons of Hollywood filmmakers.

Douglas Gomery

Reviews

Atlanta Constitution. December 17, 1990, p. B8.
Boston Globe. December 14, 1990, p. 55.
Chicago Tribune. December 17, 1990, V, p. 5.
Entertainment Weekly. December 21, 1990, p. 46.
Film Journal. XCIV, January, 1991, p. 47.
The Hollywood Reporter. CCCXV, December 12, 1990, p. 5.
Los Angeles Times. December 14, 1990, p. F8.

The New York Times. December 14, 1990, p. B6.
People Weekly. XXXV, January 21, 1991, p. 21.
The Philadelphia Inquirer. December 17, 1990, p. E1.
Premiere. IV, December, 1990, p. 22.
USA Today. December 14, 1990, p. 5D.
Variety. CCCXLI, December 12, 1990, p. 2.
The Washington Post. December 14, 1990, p. B7.

MARKED FOR DEATH

Production: Michael Grais, Mark Victor, and Steven Seagal for Victor & Grais
   Productions, in association with Steamroller Productions; released by Twentieth
   Century-Fox
Direction: Dwight H. Little
Screenplay: Michael Grais and Mark Victor
Cinematography: Ric Waite
Editing: O. Nicholas Brown
Production design: Robb Wilson King
Art direction: James Burkhart
Set decoration: Robert Kensinger
Set design: Gilbert Wong
Sound: John Pritchett
Costume design: Isabella van Soest Chubb
Music: James Newton Howard
MPAA rating: R
Running time: 96 minutes

   Principal characters:
   John Hatcher .... Steven Seagal
   Screwface .... Basil Wallace
   Max .... Keith David
   Charles .... Tom Wright
   Leslie .... Joanna Pacula
   Melissa .... Elizabeth Gracen
   Kate Hatcher .... Bette Ford

   Martial-arts expert Steven Seagal has emerged as one of America's hottest action/
adventure stars. He first fought his way to fame with *Above the Law* (1988), a very
dense political thriller. Newcomer Seagal wrote the script, produced it, and persuaded Warner Bros. to cast him in the lead role. He has been in the public eye ever
since. In *Above the Law*, he played a tough Chicago cop who battled drug dealers,
police corruption, and political assassins. One year later, Seagal returned in *Hard to
Kill*, starring with his wife, actress Kelly LeBrock. In this film, he played a tough
cop who was seriously wounded and lapsed into a seven-year coma. He swore bloody
revenge on the hoodlums who shot him and killed his family and achieved his goal.
Hard to Kill was very successful at the box office and reaffirmed Seagal as a rising
star.
   Seagal's third film, *Marked for Death*, follows the pattern of the first two films,
offering yet another version of the tough cop protecting his family from drug dealers. In *Marked for Death*, the hero is disillusioned and wants to retire. The crazed
drug dealers have been recast as Jamaicans. The motion picture opens with John

Hatcher (Seagal), ace troubleshooter for the Drug Enforcement Agency (DEA), involved in a shoot-out with drug runners. His longtime partner is killed and an angry Hatcher decides to resign from the agency. He seeks solace from a priest: "I have become what I most despise," he confesses. "Find the gentle soul inside you," advises the priest. On a leave of absence from the DEA, Hatcher returns to his old hometown, the Chicago suburb of Lincoln Heights, to visit his sister and niece. Things have changed in his neighborhood since he was a boy. A Jamaican "posse" has moved into town and is selling crack to anyone interested, especially to children.

Hatcher ignores the ominous signs around him and is determined to live a quiet and peaceful life. One evening, the bar that he is patronizing is destroyed in a crossfire between rival Jamaican and Colombian gangs. Hatcher steps in, ends the violence in his own efficient way, and earns the enmity of the Jamaicans, who are led by a sadistic practitioner of voodoo called Screwface (Basil Wallace). Screwface decides to eliminate Hatcher and marks him and his family for death. The Jamaicans begin their quest by shooting his sister's house with Uzi machine guns, Chicago gangland style, wounding his niece. An enraged Hatcher declares war on Screwface and his posse, and thereafter the action escalates. Hatcher seeks the help of an old childhood friend, Max (Keith David), who is the Lincoln Heights high school football coach. Soon they are stalking Screwface. Hatcher, who apparently has no time for women or romance, also gets in touch with an attractive anthropology professor (Joanna Pacula), who informs him of the rites of voodooism and Jamaican culture but does not warm his heart. "I got a lot on my mind for now," he explains.

Hatcher's quest to find Screwface brings him in constant contact with hoodlums, whom he disposes of in a cold-blooded manner. One criminal, for example, is simply thrown out of a high-rise building. Eventually, Hatcher and Max force Screwface to flee from Lincoln Heights to Jamaica and then follow him to his homeland— some quick scenic shots of Jamaica are shown to establish location. Hatcher soon discovers where Screwface resides on the island, and he and Max pay him a nighttime visit while a party is in progress. Despite the large number of guards present, Hatcher boldly enters the villain's home, hunts him down, and finally destroys him in a bitter and bloody fight. He brings Screwface's head back to Lincoln Heights because the posse will be neutralized only if Hatcher can convince the gang members that he has more power than they.

The final major sequence shows Hatcher and Max, armed only with their courage and Screwface's head, confronting the members of the posse in an abandoned building. The hoodlums are intimidated by the sight of their former leader, and Hatcher appears to have won. Suddenly, another Screwface appears and a second major confrontation begins between Hatcher and the newcomer. This man is Screwface's twin brother, and Hatcher must pit his martial-arts skill against yet another demonic killer who relies on voodoo and witchcraft. A furious battle ensues, with Hatcher once again victoriously destroying his nemesis. The film comes to a close with Hatcher and Max leaving the building in triumph.

Marked for Death is easily Seagal's worst film of the three that he has made. The actor himself has denounced the B-picture as stupid, demeaning, and unoriginal. Seagal has created the persona of a rugged lawman who is incorruptible, fearless, and skilled with his hands and feet, his wit, and his sophisticated weaponry. The latest film features a very high level of violence, which is often gratuitous, with many people killed, cars careening down pedestrian-filled sidewalks, and crashes through jewelry store windows. Furthermore, the plot makes little or no sense upon close examination. One moment Hatcher swears off violence completely and the next he is obsessed with revenge. His friend Max, who was introduced as a high school football coach, appears to have suddenly quit in mid-season to work with Hatcher. The use of two Screwfaces as a plot twist lacks effectiveness as a finale because it was telegraphed earlier. The Jamaican accents are very difficult to comprehend and could have used subtitles for clarification. There is also a moral smugness inherent in the scenario of one superior white man definitively defeating many inferior black men from a Third World country. Finally, the screen credits at the end of the film claim that not all Jamaicans are drug dealers, but that fact would be difficult to deduce from this motion picture. Despite all of the above reservations, however, the film's saving grace is Seagal's commanding presence. His performance creates an authentic action/adventure hero.

Seagal is acclaimed as a virtuoso in the discipline of aikido, a style considered one of the most difficult and spiritual of the martial arts. He is certainly one of the most interesting action/adventure stars to watch on the screen. Seagal is very tall, always dresses in black, has sloping shoulders and close-set eyes, wears a distinctive ponytail, and possesses a loping gait. The actor becomes something else again when he moves into action. Unlike his martial-art counterparts Jean-Claude Van Damme, Dolph Lundgren, and Chuck Norris, Seagal's fighting style is simple yet devastating. Using his aikido skill he turns the strength of his opponents against themselves and does not resort to kicks, blocks, or punches. He is like a force of nature when riled, which is quite often in *Marked for Death*.

Before pursuing a career in the film industry, Seagal had already accomplished many things. He is a sixth degree black-belt master of aikido and holds black belts in a wide array of other martial arts. He is an expert marksman and a master of weaponry. Seagal has been an international security operative and bodyguard to several heads-of-state. He became interested in martial arts and eventually earned black belts in numerous Japanese martial arts, including karate, judo, kendo, and aikido, while studying in Japan. Next, he focused his attention on motion pictures, but he chose to work behind the scenes rather than in front of the camera, choreographing fight scenes and coaching numerous actors, including Sean Connery and James Mason. In all three of his films, he coached and choreographed all the martial-art fighting. After fifteen years in Asia, Seagal finally returned to Los Angeles and opened a martial-arts academy where he teaches classes which stress the spiritual values that make a true martial artist. He also composed and performed the song "John Crow" with reggae star Jimmy Cliff on the soundtrack of *Marked for Death*. The highly intelligent Seagal promises to have a long and exciting screen career if he can overcome his propensity for simplistic revenge yarns, such as this film, and select suitable screen material.

Terry Theodore

Reviews

Boston Globe. October 6, 1990, p. 25.
Chicago Tribune. October 8, 1990, VII, p. 7.
The Hollywood Reporter. CCCXIV, October 8, 1990, p. 5.
Los Angeles Times. October 8, 1990, p. F4.
The New York Times. October 6, 1990, p. 12.
People Weekly. XXXIV, November 5, 1990, p. 18.
Premiere. IV, October, 1990, p. 61.
USA Today. October 8, 1990, p. D4.
Variety. CCCXLI, October 22, 1990, p. 61.
The Washington Post. October 8, 1990, p. D4.

MEMPHIS BELLE

Production: David Puttnam and Catherine Wyler for Enigma Productions; released
  by Warner Bros., in association with Fujisankei Communications Group, British
  Satellite Broadcasting, and County Natwest Ventures
Direction: Michael Caton-Jones
Screenplay: Monte Merrick
Cinematography: David Watkin
Editing: Jim Clark
Production design: Stuart Craig
Art direction: Norman Dorme
Set decoration: Ian Giladjian
Special effects direction: Richard Conway
Sound: David John
Costume design: Jane Robinson
Music: George Fenton
MPAA rating: PG-13
Running time: 106 minutes

> *Principal characters:*
> Dennis Dearborn .... Matthew Modine
> Danny Daly .... Eric Stoltz
> Luke Sinclair .... Tate Donovan
> Phil Rosenthal .... D. B. Sweeney
> Val Kozlowski .... Billy Zane
> Richard "Rascal" Moore .... Sean Astin
> Clay Busby .... Harry Connick, Jr.
> Virgil .... Reed Edward Diamond
> Eugene McVey .... Courtney Gains
> Jack Bocci .... Neil Giuntoli
> Commanding officer .... David Strathairn
> Colonel Bruce Derringer .... John Lithgow

The plot that propels *Memphis Belle* is a simple one: Will ten airmen survive their
final, frightening mission over Germany and return home to their loved ones? It is
filled with almost every cliché of plot and character ever to appear in a World War II
film. It has the heroic pilot, the singing tail gunner, the intellectual good guy, the
warring best buddies, and the faithful dog awaiting his master's return. Even the
dialogue lapses into clichés. "I know you're scared; we're all scared." What makes
Memphis Belle so effective, however, is its presentation—and the time-tested appeal
of these clichés on audiences.

In the summer of 1943, bombing raids went deep into Germany, and fewer and
fewer planes were coming back. The "Memphis Belle," a B-17 with the impressive

accomplishment of having successfully flown twenty-four missions with its original crew of ten men, is about to fly its twenty-fifth, and final, mission. If all return, as the first plane and crew in the Eighth Air Force to complete their tour of duty, they will be sent back to the United States to participate in war bond drives.

To chronicle this achievement, the Army Air Force has sent Colonel Bruce Derringer (John Lithgow) of public relations. He has no real conception of the dismaying destruction and toll being taken on these men. His upbeat attempts at publicity distress the commanding officer (David Strathairn) and seem completely out of place. At a morning's briefing, the final bombing target is divulged. There will be a daylight bombing raid on Bremen. The last time Bremen was bombed, one-quarter of the squadron was lost. It looks as if it will not be easy for the "Memphis Belle" and her crew to survive this mission.

The crew of the "Memphis Belle" consists of ten men—some no more than boys. They are pilot Dennis Dearborn (Matthew Modine), copilot Luke Sinclair (Tate Donovan), radioman Danny Daly (Eric Stoltz), tailgunner Clay Busby (Harry Connick, Jr.), bombardier Val Kozlowski (Billy Zane), navigator Phil Rosenthal (D. B. Sweeney), waistgunners Eugene McVey (Courtney Gains) and Jack Bocci (Neil Giuntoli), top-turret gunner Virgil (Reed Edward Diamond), and ball-turret gunner Richard "Rascal" Moore (Sean Astin).

As is usual for a 1940's World War II film, each crewman has a distinctive personality which is representative of a segment of America. The pilot is taciturn, seemingly humorless, and ultimately heroic. The copilot feels like a runner-up who does not get the credit or action he deserves. The radioman is the college graduate who writes poetry, and the tailgunner was a singer in a whorehouse. The bombardier is the handsome medical student and the navigator is the pessimistic soldier who is sure it is his day to die. The two waistgunners are bickering buddies who constantly test the limits of their friendship only to rally to each other in the pinch. The top-turret gunner is the virgin and the ball-turret gunner the ladies' man who constantly teases him. The interaction of these ten men, from different segments of American society, provides half of the film's story.

The other half of the story focuses on the final mission itself. It is as action-packed as any film in which John Wayne ever flew in the 1940's. Although aided by fighter planes, the B-17's had to fly first through the Luftwaffe's attack planes. When the Allied fighters retreated because of dwindling fuel, the Luftwaffe's attack continued. Near the target, antiaircraft flak attacks begin. Then, more Messerschmitts attack as the B-17's fly or limp home, depending on whether they have been hit.

The "Memphis Belle" is among the limping. Of the twenty-four planes which started the mission, less than half return. One by one, they fly back to their home base in Great Britain. Time passes, and some begin to give up hope that the "Memphis Belle" will return. With a severely wounded radioman and two of its four engines out, however, the plane has trailed the pack. Finally coming into view, it attempts a tricky landing with almost all of its fuel gone and one landing gear needing to be slowly and laboriously hand-cranked into position at the very last moment.

Memphis Belle is a romanticized bit of nostalgia which still manages to capture the horror and heroics of war. One of the film's producers, Catherine Wyler, has a very personal connection to this topic. Her father, famed director William Wyler, flew five missions on the "Memphis Belle" and filmed a documentary of the plane's final mission. (It is available on videotape.) In this newest film, much artistic license is taken with that mission. In reality, the B-17 was given a different city as its final target and came in without a scratch, but that would hardly have made a stirring film. Even the crew's names and civilian occupations have been changed. (Eight of the ten original crew members are still alive and acted as advisers for the actors in the motion picture.)

The film's other producer is David Puttnam, late of Columbia Pictures and now running his own company, Enigma Productions. The producer of such films as *Midnight Express* (1978), *Chariots of Fire* (1981), and *The Killing Fields* (1984), Puttnam has a track record for producing quality films on a grand scale. *Memphis Belle* is in keeping with his record. It is beautifully photographed, has movingly emotional music, and presents an epic story through individual efforts.

Memphis Belle is director Michael Caton-Jones' second feature film. (His first was 1989's *Scandal*.) He does a credible job of bringing both the small story of the crew's interactions and the large story of the war into focus for audiences who are at least fifty years removed from the event.

Aiding the director in bringing depth to the crew's story are ten young actors who transcend the usual "brat pack" image and performance level. Matthew Modine, as the pilot, was memorable in *Birdy* (1984) and *Full Metal Jacket* (1987) and has yet to turn in a bad performance on screen. Eric Stoltz, as the poetic radioman, won rave reviews for *Mask* (1985) and lends empathy and humanity to his characters. Billy Zane, who riveted and terrified audiences in 1989's *Dead Calm*, here provides a startling handsomeness worthy of any 1940's matinee idol. The rest of the ten-man crew is played by equally gifted, though not as well known, actors. Among them are D. B. Sweeney (*Eight Men Out*, 1988); Sean Astin, son of Patty Duke and John Astin (*The War of the Roses*, 1989); Courtney Gains (*Colors*, 1988); and singer/pianist Harry Connick, Jr., in his acting debut.

Within the film, Caton-Jones subjects his actors (and his audiences) to the constricted internal world of the B-17. This majestic behemoth rattles on land and in the air, and in the thin air and freezing temperatures of cruising altitudes has an interior to which exposed skin would stick. Yet its daring daylight bombing raids, costly in both men and planes, are credited with turning the tide of the war in Europe.

At one time, a sky filled with B-17's must have been an overwhelming and common sight. Finding bombers which are still operable today, however, was quite a chore. Only one B-17, the "Sally B," remained in Britain, where the film was shot. Two more were recruited from France, the "Lucky Lady" and the "Chateau de Verneuil." (The latter is technically a B-17G and is the only plane that has been in continuous operation through 1989—after demobilization in 1947, it was used by the Institut Géographique National for aerial surveillance work.) Two more B-17's, of the few left in the world, were flown to Britain from the United States. (The original "Memphis Belle," which still exists but does not fly, is on permanent display in Memphis, Tennessee.) Added to these B-17's were three Messerschmitts (ME-109's) and eight Mustangs. With only five original bombers (one of which unfortunately crashed during filming with no casualties) and eleven fighter planes, Caton-Jones did an amazing job of re-creating the flying sequences so essential for the integrity and tension required in this film genre.

Beverley Bare Buehrer

Reviews

Chicago Tribune. October 12, 1990, VII, p. 35.
The Christian Science Monitor. October 17, 1990, p. 10.
Cosmopolitan. December, 1990, p. 32.
Film Comment. XXVI, November, 1990, p. 64.
Films in Review. XLII, January, 1991, p. 51.
Glamour. November, 1990, p. 172.
The Guardian. September 6, 1990, p. 24.
The Hollywood Reporter. CCCXIV, October 11, 1990, p. 5.
Los Angeles Times. October 12, 1990, p. F1.
Maclean's. October 15, 1990, p. 80.
New Republic. November 12, 1990, p. 27.
The New York Times. October 12, 1990, p. B7.
Newsweek. CXVI, October 22, 1990, p. 74.
People Weekly. October 29, 1990, p. 19.
Playboy. December, 1990, p. 25.
Rolling Stone. November 1, 1990, p. 96.
Time. CXXXVI, October 15, 1990, p. 71.
Variety. September 11, 1990, p. 2.
The Wall Street Journal. October 11, 1990, p. 12.

MEN DON'T LEAVE

Production: Paul Brickman and Jon Avnet, for Geffen Company; released by
　Warner Bros.
Direction: Paul Brickman
Screenplay: Barbara Benedek
Cinematography: Bruce Surtees
Editing: Richard Chew
Production design: Barbara Ling
Art direction: John Mark Harrington
Set decoration: Karen O'Hara and Cricket Rowland
Set design: William Arnold
Special effects: Rodman Kiser
Sound: Curt Frisk
Makeup: Susan Mayer
Costume design: J. Allen Highfill
Music: Thomas Newman
MPAA rating: PG-13
Running time: 113 minutes

Principal characters:

Beth Macauley	Jessica Lange
Chris Macauley	Chris O'Donnell
Matt Macauley	Charlie Korsmo
Charles Simon	Arliss Howard
John Macauley	Tom Mason
Jody	Joan Cusack
Lisa Coleman	Kathy Bates
Winston Buckley	Corey Carrier
Mr. Buckley	Jim Haynie
Mrs. Buckley	Belita Moreno
Dale Buckley	Shannon Moffett
Nina Simon	Lora Zane
Polka dancer	Theresa Wozniak

Families dealing with major upheavals, fighting to adjust, stay together, and re-define themselves, have always been a favorite theme in literature, theater, and film, namely because such a theme mirrors the realities of life so closely. The passage of time affects all families, and each family adjusts and reacts to change differently from the next. The variety is infinite; the chance for drama is rich.

Men Don't Leave chronicles the struggle of one family attempting to adjust after the sudden death of the husband/father. John Macauley (Tom Mason), the strong, authoritative leader of his family, is shown as a caring and commanding husband to his wife, Beth (Jessica Lange), and an attentive father to his sons, teenager Chris (Chris O'Donnell) and ten-year-old Matt (Charlie Korsmo). Soon after his character is introduced, however, he meets with a fatal accident on his job as a construction foreman. Housewife Beth, devastated by the loss of her decisive husband, is suddenly thrust into the role of sole provider. Soon after the tragedy, Beth discovers that the family debt is more serious than she had realized. She concludes that drastic changes must take place if the family hopes to survive financially. When she proposes selling her husband's truck, teenager Chris protests that his father promised the truck to him. Reluctantly, he agrees to help sell the truck. When bills continue to mount, Beth announces that she intends to sell their house and move to nearby Baltimore, where job opportunities are more plentiful. The boys are at first adamantly opposed to such a radical move and protest loudly. Later, they realize that selling the house and moving to Baltimore is their only option for survival.

The family moves into an apartment near the city's noisy downtown area. Beth, a skilled cook, lands a job as assistant manager in a catering store. Her boss, Lisa (Kathy Bates), who also owns the store, is an aggressive and demanding woman, and Beth has trouble adjusting to Lisa's offensive style of management. During one of her delivery runs, Beth meets Charles Simon (Arliss Howard), an avant-garde musician, who invites her to one of his concerts. She at first declines his offer but later changes her mind and attends the concert. They end up going out after the concert, and Beth meets some of Charles's friends, including his former wife. Beth then accompanies Charles to his apartment where he talks about his previous marriage and his young son. The two come close to intimacy, but then Beth confesses that an intimate relationship is low on her list of priorities at the moment, with work and keeping her family together taking precedence over everything else.

While Beth struggles to adjust to her new life, the boys have their own unique ways of coping with their new surroundings. Chris meets Jody (Joan Cusack) in the elevator of their apartment complex. She is an eccentric X-ray technician, who lives on the floor above the Macauleys and begins an affair with Chris. Matt is befriended by a schoolmate, Winston Buckley (Corey Carrier), who turns out to be a thief specializing in stealing videocassette recorders from apartments. Matt, craving acceptance and friendship, joins his new friend's activities and quickly becomes a skilled and savvy crook. Beth's tangles with Lisa become more heated until finally Beth quits and seeks comfort with Charles. When she returns home late in the evening, Chris announces that he has decided to move in with Jody. Beth, infuriated, commands Chris to return home. Meanwhile, Matt has also left to spend the night at Winston's house and is reluctant to come home.

Determined to bring her family together, Beth organizes family outings to museums and other attractions. Her superficial attempts, however, are greeted with limp enthusiasm. Beth, feeling totally defeated, retreats to her room and falls into a deep, listless depression. She begins to sleep all day long, neglecting the boys and the upkeep of the apartment, and refusing to look for another job. Chris becomes alarmed by his mother's deepening depression and seeks the help of Charles, whom he had initially greeted with violent hostility when his mother first introduced the two. Charles's attempts at helping Beth fail. Jody then takes it upon herself to help Beth. Jody, full of methodical, almost fanatical, patience, forces Beth to eat, bathe, and dress. Jody then cleans the apartment and takes Beth on a drive in the country and later for a ride in a hot-air balloon. Beth, who at first greeted Jody's presence with as much hostility as Chris's first meetings with Charles, recognizes the strong-willed kindness of Jody's actions, and the two become affectionate friends. While Beth and Jody enjoy their outing, Matt learns that Winston has won a large sum of money from the state lottery after purchasing lottery tickets with money the two earned from selling their stolen goods. When Matt confronts his friend and demands that he split the lottery winnings, Winston refuses. Matt ultimately runs away.

Beth becomes frantic when Matt does not return home. She calls Charles, who helps notify the police. Finally, they receive word that Matt has been spotted by the new owners of the Macauley's former home. Beth and Chris drive to their old home and find Matt cowering in the backyard playhouse that his father had built for him. Matt says that he wishes he could see his father one more time. When the family returns home, they begin in earnest to remain together. Beth makes up with Lisa and enters into a business arrangement with her, supplying the store with homemade desserts. The family outings begin again and include Charles and Jody, who have become part of their extended family. The film ends with Matt's voice-over narration telling how secure he feels now that the family is once again whole.

Men Don't Leave is loosely based on the French film *La Vie continue* (1982), written and directed by Moshe Mizrahi. The two films share the basic premise of a woman thrust into the role of sole provider for her family after the sudden death of her husband. Yet the French film has a much colder, superficial tone than its American counterpart. The two boys in the French film are marginal figures, obedient, polite, supportive, and almost nonexistent, while the boys in *Men Don't Leave* play pivotal roles of near-equal importance with the mother's character. While the woman in *La Vie continue* recovers quickly from the death of her husband, even admitting that she was not even sure if she loved him, Beth's character is devastated by the loss of her husband, and the entire family is haunted by his absence. Throughout *Men Don't Leave*, there are slow-motion flashbacks of John Macauley playing with his boys, a potent reminder of the effect that he had on his family and the loss that they feel without him.

Because *La Vie continue* lacks an emotional core, it plays as a rather ordinary melodrama, merely a series of tepid, uninvolving events. *Men Don't Leave* could have easily followed in its French predecessor's footsteps. The subject lends itself to melodrama, a built-in hazard with family dramas. What saves the film from soap opera bathos, however, is the subtle shading given to the principal characters and the overall excellent, restrained acting of the main cast. Credit must be given to screenwriter Barbara Benedek for emphasizing subtlety and three-dimensional shading over melodramatic outbursts. Her most acclaimed screenwriting credit prior to *Men Don't Leave* is a shared credit for *The Big Chill* (1983), another film alive with full-dimensional characters. Most of the film's effectiveness, however, must be attributed to director Paul Brickman. As in his previous film, *Risky Business* (1983), Brickman establishes a realistic yet dreamy, almost otherworldly tone. The use of moody, slow-motion flashbacks and wispy, voice-over narration by ten-year-old Matt, gives the film a fablelike mood that enhances the film's universal theme of families coping with change. As in *Risky Business*, the acting by the principals is subtle, polished, and natural, especially Jessica Lange as Beth, Chris O'Donnell as Chris, and Charlie Korsmo as Matt.

If there is a flaw in the film, it is with the adult male characters, who are all too nice to be fully believable. The characters of Charles, John Macauley, and Winston's father are all basically the same character, too eager to please, always having ample time to frolic and play, never showing any trace of pettiness or obnoxiousness. Fortunately, the main focus is on Beth and her boys, whose stories are told in effective, crosscutting spurts, which emphasize the characters' individuality and later make for an effective climax when their stories collide and come together in the final moments of the film.

Overall, *Men Don't Leave* is a radical departure from the black-comedy ribaldry of Brickman's *Risky Business*. Both films, however, share a controlled and effective moodiness and, in their own distinct way, a keen insight into the values and attitudes of the modern family.

Jim Kline

Reviews

American Film: Magazine of the Film and Television Arts. XV, August, 1990, p. 52.
Chicago Tribune. February 23, 1990, VII, p. 37.
Films in Review. XLI, May, 1990, p. 299.
The Hollywood Reporter. CCCXI, February 1, 1990, p. 4.
Los Angeles Times. February 2, 1990, p. F1.
The New York Times. February 2, 1990, p. B10.
Newsweek. CXV, February 5, 1990, p. 72.
Rolling Stone. February 22, 1990, p. 39.
Time. CXXXV, February 5, 1990, p. 73.
Variety. CCCXXXVIII, January 31, 1990, p. 28.
The Washington Post. February 23, 1990, p. B1.

MERMAIDS

Production: Lauren Lloyd, Wallis Nicita, and Patrick Palmer; released by Orion Pictures
Direction: Richard Benjamin
Screenplay: June Roberts; based on the novel by Patty Dann
Cinematography: Howard Atherton
Editing: Jacqueline Cambas
Production design: Stuart Wurtzel
Art direction: Steve Saklad and Evelyn Sakash
Set decoration: Hilton Rosemarin
Set design: Deborah Kanter and Philip Messina
Sound: Richard Lightstone
Costume design: Marit Allen
Music: Jack Nitzsche
MPAA rating: PG-13
Running time: 111 minutes

> *Principal characters:*
> Mrs. Flax .... Cher
> Lou Landsky .... Bob Hoskins
> Charlotte Flax .... Winona Ryder
> Joe .... Michael Schoeffling
> Kate Flax .... Christina Ricci

It seems that, whenever a film depicts a teenager having sex for the first time, it is called a "coming-of-age" film. This is the case with *Mermaids*, but there is a twist. In this film, it is the teenager's mother who really learns, grows, and as they say, "comes of age."

Mrs. Flax (Cher) is a most unconventional mother. In 1963, when the ideal family was represented in sugarcoated sitcoms such as *Leave It to Beaver* and *Father Knows Best*, any single mother was unusual. A Jewish single mother of two daughters from different fathers who wears tight dresses, hands out tubes of toothpaste for Halloween treats, and refuses to cook anything except hors d'oeuvres because anything more is too much of a commitment, is exceptionally bizarre. Also out of the ordinary is the frequency with which the Flax family moves. The family motto, coined by Mrs. Flax, is "Life is change, and death is dwelling on the past or staying in one place too long." This philosophy is illustrated by the Flaxes' packing up and moving to a new city every time something unpleasant occurs. It was Mrs. Flax's failed affair with her boss that instigated their most recent move to East Port, Massachusetts.

Mrs. Flax's elder daughter, Charlotte (Winona Ryder), does not share her mother's philosophy but, as a minor, is nevertheless bound by it. Charlotte's resentment of this unstable life-style manifests itself in her search for religious enlightenment.

Charlotte views her mother, whom she refers to exclusively as "Mrs. Flax," as loud, brash, irresponsible, immoral, and altogether embarrassing. In an effort to become as different from her mother as possible, Charlotte turns to Catholicism. She dresses in as close to a nun's habit as she can without drawing unwanted attention, prays at a shrine that she creates and re-creates in every new home, and listens intently and impatiently for the word of God.

Having arrived in East Port, the family goes about the business of setting up their new household and establishing their new routines. For Charlotte, this is the worst part of each move. She hates waking up and not knowing where she is. Petrified of again being the new kid in school, Charlotte spends most of the first day hiding in a stall in the girls' washroom. There, Charlotte eavesdrops on some girls giggling about their boyfriends, and she is torn between her own budding interest in boys and her revulsion at what she considers to be impure thoughts. The one pleasing aspect of this new situation is the Flaxes' proximity to a convent. After school, Charlotte sneaks onto the convent grounds and observes the nuns as they walk, sing, and even play soccer. The observation itself is a spiritual experience for Charlotte, a refuge from her life among the sinners.

For Mrs. Flax's younger daughter, Kate (Christina Ricci), the adjustment is some-what easier; it means finding a swimming pool. Kate is the character who most literally embodies the film's title. At ten years old, Kate is an accomplished swim-mer and intends to vie for an Olympic medal one day. Until then, she is content to swim on a school team. In between schools, Kate strives to improve her holding her breath underwater by immersing her body, except for one hand which holds a stop-watch, in her mother's bathtub—a practice which provokes considerable anxiety in Mrs. Flax.

Mrs. Flax quickly finds a job as a secretary, and having done so, makes her first task that of sneaking out of work to take her children shopping for school shoes. This is how the Flaxes meet Lou Landsky (Bob Hoskins). Lou is the proprietor of Foot Friendly Shoes and an amateur painter who falls for Mrs. Flax on sight. Though taken aback by Lou's brutal honesty and inquisitiveness, Mrs. Flax encourages Lou's attentions and soon they are an item. To her horror, Charlotte also finds herself in love—or worse yet, lust—at first sight. The object of her infatuation is Joe Peretti (Michael Schoeffling), the convent's caretaker. Joe is heartbreakingly handsome and a man with a past. Rumor has it that Joe's former girlfriend had to leave town in order to avoid a scandal, and that his working part-time at the convent is a self-imposed penance for his supposed sin. Charlotte conveniently perceives meeting Joe, and the sudden infusion of hormones that accompanies that encounter, to be her long-awaited sign from God.

Up to this point in the film, the characters are all clearly and very humorously drawn. From here on, however, things become complicated. As Lou and Mrs. Flax become closer, so do Lou and Mrs. Flax's children. Charlotte and Kate have never had a father or, by any conventional definition, a family. Suddenly, they find them-selves sitting down to normal family dinners and a variety of other so-called normal family activities, and they love it. Mrs. Flax, on the other hand, does not. She is terrified that, if she allows herself to become attached to Lou and what he brings into her life, she will be hurt when she inevitably loses him as she has lost all the men that she has loved. Mrs. Flax painfully reminds Lou that this is her family, not his. At a neighborhood Halloween party, Lou proposes marriage, but Mrs. Flax makes a joke of it. Unable to go on as if everything is all right between them, Lou leaves her at the party. Mrs. Flax asks for a ride home from Joe, who has stopped by to deliver the drinks. Charlotte, who had been waiting for her to return, sees Joe helping her always flirtatious and now drunken mother out of her seat and assumes that Mrs. Flax has seduced Joe. Charlotte declares, "You want to drive Lou away— that's your business. You want Joe—that's war!"

The next time that Mrs. Flax leaves the house, Charlotte dons one of her mother's skintight dresses, teases her hair into a bouffant and applies makeup, all the while force-feeding herself wine. Kate, whom Charlotte is supposed to be watching, is entertained by what she perceives as a game of "dressup," and she joins Charlotte in drinking the wine. Charlotte suggests she and Kate take a walk, then leaves her drunken little sister in the woods outside the convent. Charlotte runs up to the bell-tower, where she knows that she will find Joe, and breathlessly throws herself at him. In the midst of the sexual act, it finally dawns on Charlotte that this is not part of the pretend persona that she adopts in order to make her life more tolerable: This is real. Also real are the screams that Charlotte hears from below. Kate has fallen into the stream that runs past the convent and is drowning. As the nuns pull Kate out of the water and rush her to a hospital, Charlotte fears that this time she has truly sinned and that Kate's death may be her punishment.

Mrs. Flax is brought to the hospital to where Kate lies unconscious in an oxygen tent. Seeing her elder daughter wearing one of her dresses, smeared makeup, and Joe standing sheepishly nearby, there is no mistaking why Kate was left alone and vulnerable to this accident. Later, Lou calls Charlotte at home to report that Kate is going to be all right. When Mrs. Flax comes home in order to pack some things that Kate will need in the hospital, she advises Charlotte to stay far away from her, as she is too angry to speak, but Charlotte insists on settling the conflict. For the first time, Charlotte openly rebels against her mother's chosen way of life and half-begs, half-demands that they stay in one place long enough for her to finish high school. Mrs. Flax confesses to Charlotte the events that led to Charlotte and Kate's births, and her fear that Charlotte and Kate might become like her: young, unwed mothers with no one to love them and help them support their families. This cathartic conversation changes the lives of Mrs. Flax, her daughters, and Lou. The Flaxes stay in East Port. Lou does not move in, but continues to spend much time with the family. Joe leaves town, and Charlotte, whose popularity has increased enormously because of the rumors of her tryst with Joe, recognizes that her fanatical pursuit of Catholicism was merely an adolescent phase and replaces it with an interest in Greek mythology.

Although love/hate relationships are natural among mothers and their teenage daughters, June Robert's screenplay relies on some disturbing incongruities to make its points. For example, Charlotte, and indeed the whole country, is devastated by the assassination of President John F. Kennedy on November 22, 1963, but by Thanksgiving, no one seems to remember that they were even depressed a few days ago. Even more disturbing is the inconsistency in Charlotte's knowledge. She genuinely fears that she may be pregnant as the result of one kiss with Joe, then seems to know exactly what she is doing when they have sex on the floor of the bell tower.

The producers of *Mermaids* hired and fired a number of directors before Richard Benjamin finally accepted the job. This is the eighth successful film directed by Benjamin, but he is probably best known for his starring role in *Goodbye Columbus* (1969). The original music budget of $150,000 was eventually tripled to $450,000, not including the music video (Cher singing "The Shoop Shoop Song: It's in His Kiss") and Jack Nitzsche's original score, making it one of the most expensive music budgets Orion Pictures has ever done.

Eleah Horwitz

Reviews
American Film: Magazine of the Film and Television Arts. XV, December, 1990, p. 48.
Chicago Tribune. December 14, 1990, VII, p. 40.
The Christian Science Monitor. January 22, 1991, p. 13.
The Hollywood Reporter. CCCXV, December 10, 1990, p. 10.
Los Angeles Times. December 14, 1990, p. F1.
The New York Times. December 14, 1990, CXL, p. B1.
Newsweek. CXVI, December 17, 1990, p. 70.
Premiere. IV, October 4, 1990, p. 74.
Time. CXXXVII, January 7, 1991, p. 75.
Variety. CCXXX, December 10, 1990, p. 2.
The Washington Post. December 14, 1990, p. B1.

METROPOLITAN

Production: Whit Stillman for Westerly Films; released by New Line Cinema
Direction: Whit Stillman
Screenplay: Whit Stillman
Cinematography: John Thomas
Editing: Chris Tellefsen
Production design: Brian Greenbaum
Sound: Antonio Arroyo
Costume design: Mary Jane Fort
Music: Mark Suozzo and Tom Judson
MPAA rating: PG-13
Running time: 98 minutes

Principal characters:
Audrey Rouget	Carolyn Farina
Tom Townsend	Edward Clements
Nick Smith	Christopher Eigeman
Charlie Black	Taylor Nichols
Jane Clarke	Allison Rutledge-Parisi
Sally Fowler	Dylan Hundley
Cynthia McClean	Isabel Gillies
Fred Neff	Bryan Leder
Rick Von Sloneker	Will Kempe
Serena Slocum	Elizabeth Thompson

The remarkably literate screenplay written by Whit Stillman, *Metropolitan*'s director, contains far more words of dialogue than is the norm: Characters sit around and talk for large segments of the film. Topics of discussion include the novels of Jane Austen, Lionel Trilling, socialism, God, and old values versus new. The talk is from the perspective of wealthy young preppy friends from Manhattan's upper East Side and one outsider from the disdained, not-quite-so-affluent West Side. Fortunately, the talk is often extremely amusing—characters sometimes display a cynical wit but more often a naïveté that shines through despite the very sophisticated milieu. Youth, in a way, is a great leveller. Whatever their degree of wealth and education, these young men and women, including the outsider, Tom (Edward Clements), often speak with audacious certainty on subjects about which they know little. Therein lies much of the film's humor.

Tom, for example, offers strong opinions about Jane Austen's novels before his partner in discussion, Audrey (Carolyn Farina), learns that his conclusions are based on his reading of literary criticism: He has never read Jane Austen. In fact, he proudly asserts that he does not read novels at all. Tom's East Side "better," Nick (Christopher Eigeman), who seems to be the catalyst for much of the discourse, spews a relentless stream of pronouncements on various subjects from parents to the symbolic importance of wearing detachable collars. At one point, he scoffs at Tom's patronizing manner by asking him if, instead of sitting around eating hors d'oeuvres, he would prefer to be at home thinking about the less fortunate.

Snobbishness provides humor and is often a springboard for discussion; Tom's reverse snobbishness serves the same purpose. He states that he does not like debutante balls, yet he has just attended one. Later, he refuses an invitation to share a taxicab with Nick and his coterie; afterward, they see Tom get on a bus to the West Side and feel smugly enlightened. Nick condescends to continue to invite Tom to their gatherings, but encourages him to get rid of his shabby raincoat. Tom, trying to save face, justifies his use of the coat by saying that it has a warm lining, but he fools no one. Eventually, he does admit that his resources are limited. A nice touch is Tom at home sniffing the same shirt he wore the previous night and then dabbing Old Spice onto it to make it tolerable.

The viewer learns about the backgrounds of these youths through their conversations. Although very little of their lives outside parties with their peers is seen on the screen, subtextual hints fill in the biographical picture and lend the characters depth and credibility. Nick, in particular, goes through a progress in the viewer's perception: first impressions are likely to be that he is cynically callous as he brazenly offers cutting comments on nearly every subject that comes up for discussion; but eventually it is apparent, in his relationship to Tom, that he is capable of deep friendship and that he is sensitive to the plight of others.

Metropolitan is relatively plotless, capturing a series of get-togethers in Chekhovian fashion (or Rohmerian, which is a cinematic equivalent); with plot movement kept to a minimum, the viewer can examine, as if under a microscope, this species of society. The technique works effectively in Anton Chekhov's full-length plays, but one can question whether the medium of cinema can bear the burden of so many words. Eric Rohmer succeeds by juxtaposing lengthy scenes of talk with scenes that are almost totally visual. For example, in *Le Rayon vert* (1986; *Summer*), Delphine (Marie Rivière) wanders the beach at Biarritz alone, lost in her thoughts as she weaves through the throngs of vacationers; eventually, after this extended sequence without dialogue, she overhears a small group of middle-aged people discussing Jules Verne's novel *Le Rayon vert* (1882). The audience is more disposed to listen receptively because of the variety offered by such juxtapositions. Also, Rohmer's talky sequences tend more to forward the internal action: Although both films consist of a series of social gatherings, Delphine is actively searching for answers as she talks and listens, while the characters in *Metropolitan* are talking because they have a certain amount of time in which to socialize.

In still another way, the abundant dialogue is a double-sided coin. It is refreshing to find characters who are this literate and enjoy expressing themselves with words; however, much of what they say comes out of a very specific social and cultural context that is not familiar to most potential filmgoers. There is also a sense that inside banter abounds: Voguish comments about the Hamptons, for example, even in

New York City, get big responses from segments of the audience, while others try to decipher the humor. It is likely that parts of *Metropolitan* will successfully address certain New Yorkers but will seem elitist to many other viewers across the country. These objections notwithstanding, Stillman's screenplay has earned for him an Academy Award nomination.

The simple plot involves a romantic quadrangle: Charlie (Taylor Nichols) loves Audrey, who loves Tom, who loves Serena (Elizabeth Thompson). Another plot thread involves Nick's antagonism for Rick Von Sloneker (Will Kempe), who, Nick says, entices, exploits, and eventually ruins women foolish enough to fall for him. One of the film's climaxes involves a confrontation between the two after a debutante ball. Nick is caught in a lie: Having previously told the others about a young woman driven to suicide because of her destructive relationship with Rick, he now must admit that the woman never existed. He tries to extricate himself by saying that his fictional creation is, however, a composite of women Rick has ruined.

The character, among all these wealthy friends, who seems the most unaffected is Audrey. It is partly a result of her infatuation with Tom that he is continually invited, despite his poorer circumstances. Her preparations for a debutante ball at the film's beginning reveal her uncertainty about herself. She becomes an object of sympathy later when, in a cruel game of candor whose rules dictate that the loser of a round answer honestly any question asked, Tom makes it clear that he loves another. Not long after, Audrey tries to escape her misery by going with Rick to his place in the Hamptons. Charlie and Tom assume she has to be rescued, because of Rick's randy reputation. They decide to rent a car and go after her but then realize that neither one knows how to drive. They solve the problem by taking a cab for a triple-digit fare, which Charlie just happens to have in his pocket. They barge into Rick's house, and Audrey, pleased by the attention, assures her two deliverers that all is well; nevertheless, she allows herself to be rescued. The film's resolution is an idyllic scene in which the three friends walk contentedly beside one of the typical high hedges surrounding a Hampton estate. They were abandoned by the cab driver but feel no alarm. One senses their deepening pleasure in one another and an underlying innocence which contradicts typical, superficial impressions of the wealthy.

Stillman, a former journalist, has stated that he wanted to provide an accurate portrait of the American upper class; such portraits have been available in fiction, particularly in the novels of Louis Auchincloss, but absent in cinema. Ironically, in order to accomplish his purpose with very limited funds (the film was shot for under one million dollars), Stillman had to bivouac outside the Plaza Hotel and other plush sites, sometimes shooting members of his cast intermingled with genuine debutantes and their escorts. Visually, the film is pleasing, particularly in its outdoor shots of Southhampton and of Manhattan at Christmastime. One is reminded of Woody Allen's stunning, poetic views of New York City in *Manhattan* (1979) and *Hannah and Her Sisters* (1986). Although *Metropolitan*'s camera focuses on many clichéd subjects, such as the Christmas tree at Rockefeller Center, one senses the filmmaker's love of these locales. Cinematographer John Thomas frames these scenes simply but vividly, allowing the viewer to enjoy their postcardlike familiarity, which is, however, altered and made particular by the presence of individuals who have been intimately revealing themselves in the indoor scenes.

The film seems to start and stop between segments, and the indoor scenes sometimes look like they are being acted for the stage, with performers carefully positioned before the cameras by their director. Sensing the machinery behind the filmmaking prohibits a total release of the viewer into this fictional world and the lives of its characters. Despite these minor flaws, *Metropolitan* is an impressive directorial debut.

Cono Robert Marcazzo

Reviews

America. CLXIII, November 3, 1990, p. 330.
American Film: Magazine of the Film and Television Arts. XV, May, 1990, p. 62.
Chicago Tribune. August 10, 1990, VII, p. 32.
The Christian Science Monitor. August 15, 1990, p. 11.
Los Angeles Times. August 10, 1990, p. F10.
The Nation. CCLI, August 13, 1990, p. 178.
New York Magazine. XXIII, August 13, 1990, p. 64.
The New York Times. March 23, 1990, p. C18.
The New York Times. August 3, 1990, p. C6.
Newsweek. CXVI, August 27, 1990, p. 61.
Variety. CCCXXXVIII, January 31, 1990, p. 32.
The Washington Post. September 14, 1990, p. C9.

MIAMI BLUES

Production: Jonathan Demme and Gary Goetzman for Tristes Tropiques; released
   by Orion Pictures
Direction: George Armitage
Screenplay: George Armitage; based on the novel by Charles Willeford
Cinematography: Tak Fujimoto
Editing: Craig McKay
Production design: Maher Ahmad
Sound: Dan Sable
Costume design: Eugenie Bafaloukos
Music: Gary Chang
MPAA rating: R
Running time: 99 minutes

   Principal characters:
   Frederick J. Frenger, Jr. . . . . Alec Baldwin
   Sergeant Hoke Moseley . . . . Fred Ward
   Susie Waggoner . . . . Jennifer Jason Leigh
   Sergeant Bill Henderson . . . . Charles Napier
   Ellita Sanchez . . . . Nora Dunn
   Blink Willie . . . . Obba Babatunde
   Pablo . . . . Jose Perez
   Sergeant Frank Lackley . . . . Paul Gleason
   Edie Wulgemuth . . . . Shirley Stoler

Frederick J. Frenger, Jr. (Alec Baldwin), known as "Junior," is a man in a hurry.
He wants his share of the American dream, and he is unwilling to wait for it to
happen. Fresh out of prison, Junior quickly resorts to making a living the only way
he knows how, by crime. He has stolen credit cards, and, as he sits in the first-class
section on an airplane, he practices forging the signature of his latest victim. Once
on the ground, Junior steals a suitcase from a sleeping woman and breaks the finger
of an annoying Hare Krishna who impedes his getaway.

When the Hare Krishna dies from shock, Sergeant Hoke Moseley (Fred Ward), a
likable but world-weary veteran homicide policeman who takes pleasure in popping
out his dentures in front of people, is soon in pursuit of Junior. Eager to make up for
lost time, Junior joins up with a naïve, slightly dim amateur prostitute named Susie
Waggoner (Jennifer Jason Leigh). Susie dreams of giving up the "life" for marriage,
a house with a white picket fence, and a Burger World franchise for security. She
finds Junior charming, and before long she and Junior are sharing their ideas about
marriage. Recognizing several benefits to having a woman in his life, Junior soon
announces to Susie that they are engaged. The two set up housekeeping, and Susie
"retires" in order to take care of her man full-time. Junior confesses his past, say-

ing, "I rob people who rob people." Hopeful, Susie suggests his similarity to Robin
Hood. Junior agrees but notes that he does not give the money to the poor.

Susie demands that Junior retire from his life of crime, and Junior promises to do
so, professing that he longs for a "regular life." Before long, however, Hoke disrupts
the couple's idyllic yet perversely normal domesticity. The policeman insinuates himself into Susie's life, accepting her generous hospitality and sharing a family dinner
with the loving couple. He then proceeds to interrogate Junior. Junior, no fool, realizes what the policeman is doing and, annoyed, later pays Hoke a visit at the seedy
hotel where he lives. Junior beats the veteran policeman senseless and steals his gun,
his badge, and even his dentures.

Before long, Junior is posing as a police officer. He halts crimes-in-progress with
the aid of Hoke's badge, but when the perpetrators escape, Junior surprises their
victims by finishing the job. While masquerading as Hoke, Junior sets up the policeman as trying to cut himself in for half of the five-hundred-dollar payoff normally
extracted from Pablo (Jose Perez) by crooked vice policeman Frank Lackley (Paul
Gleason). Returning from the hospital, Hoke is surprised to find two envelopes, each
containing anonymous payoff money. Lackley does not appreciate Hoke's apparent
attempt to move in on his territory and goes to the hotel to confront him and to get
his money back.

Humiliated by the beating he received from Junior, Hoke is determined to stop the
crime spree of this psychopath, as well as regain possession of his gun and badge.
Hoke returns to Susie's apartment, only to find it vacated. Reluctantly accepting the
aid of Officer Ellita Sanchez (Nora Dunn), Hoke succeeds in correctly identifying
Junior from fingerprints obtained from beer bottles left behind. For Junior, life becomes far more complicated than he could ever have imagined. Once having thought
those police credentials would simplify his life of crime, Junior instead begins to
suffer an identity crisis, forgetting at times which side of the law he is really on. Any
confusion he may have had, however, is suddenly resolved when Junior, armed with
a bottle of spaghetti sauce, tries to talk a convenience store robber out of his crime
and ends up instead with a battered leg and glass in his face after the criminal has
driven through the plate-glass doors of the store.

When Junior returns home, bloody and battered and asking to be sewn up with an
everyday needle and thread, Susie begins to realize that the life she was hoping for
with Junior is nothing more than a dream. Officer Sanchez learns of Susie's application for a telephone at their rented house down in Coral Gables, and Hoke arranges
an accidental meeting with Susie at the neighborhood supermarket. She tries to
maintain her composure and denies still being in touch with Junior, but she is nevertheless visibly shaken when Hoke informs her that Junior is a murderer. Susie returns home and deliberately ruins her homemade vinegar pie in an attempt to test
Junior's sincerity. He forces down the dessert, remarking, "This is one of your best,
honey."

Susie reluctantly agrees to drive Junior to the local pawnshop to cash in his stolen
coin collection. Unaware that Hoke has followed them, Susie waits in the car while

Junior, still posing as a policeman, limps his way into the shop. When he pulls a gun on the formidable owner, Edie Wulgemuth (Shirley Stoler), however, Junior discovers that the shop is not the easy target he thought it was. The woman chops off his fingers with a machete before Junior shoots her and steals one of the cocktail rings from the case—a feeble attempt to divert Susie's attentions from his latest battle wound. He is not successful this time, however, and Susie drives off, leaving Junior behind for a showdown with Hoke. Junior commandeers a car and makes his way back to Susie's house, but Hoke finds him and eventually shoots him dead. When Susie returns home and discovers Junior's lifeless body lying on the kitchen table, she calmly remarks to Hoke: "I had to give him the benefit of the doubt 'cause he had some good qualities. He always ate everything I ever made for him."

It is easy to dismiss *Miami Blues* as yet another exploitative B-film, replete with fast-action and graphic violence. It is the filmic adaptation of the first of several pulp police procedural novels written by Charles Willeford during the period of 1980-1984, immediately prior to his death. George Armitage's laconic directorial style, combined with the droll camerawork of Tak Fujimoto, captures the essence of the book and molds the film into a wry, hard-edged piece of filmmaking. Armitage's previous film, the disastrous *Vigilante Force* (1975), seemed to portend an end to a promising filmmaker who had begun as one of several protégés of the King of Exploitation, Roger Corman, in the early 1960's. After essentially disappearing from the Hollywood scene for nearly thirteen years, Armitage, with the help of his old friend, fellow director Jonathan Demme, was able to persuade Orion Pictures to allow him not only to write the screenplay but to direct the film as well.

While the film does contain several scenes depicting graphic violence, particularly the machete scene, *Miami Blues* displays a surprising wit and an unusual sense of humor. It never attempts to transcend its genre or make lame excuses for itself by interjecting self-important social commentary. The film moves steadily along, never forcing a false sense of urgency yet never lingering too long or straying from its narrative. The action is continual, pausing only for an occasional laugh or a dose of Junior's insouciant charm.

Alec Baldwin imbues the character of Junior with charm and humor, as well as an unpredictability and sense of danger befitting a criminal psychopath. Baldwin has been quietly stealing scenes in major motion pictures since his debut in *Forever, Lulu* (1987), displaying a versatility that has helped him build an impressive array of supporting roles in a relatively short period of time. Like his character in *Miami Blues*, Baldwin seems content to pull off the small caper, impressing audiences and critics alike with his subtle, never grandiose, yet stealthily captivating acting style. He appeared as the two-timing boyfriend of Melanie Griffith in Mike Nichols' *Working Girl* (1988), the hot-blooded hitman in Jonathan Demme's *Married to the Mob* (1988), Geena Davis' benign ghost-husband in *Beetlejuice* (1988), the tough radio station owner in Oliver Stone's *Talk Radio* (1988), and a young Jimmy Swaggart in Jim McBride's *Great Balls of Fire!* (1989). Most recently, Baldwin garnered critical acclaim for his costarring role as the CIA analyst opposite Sean Connery in the film adaptation of Tom Clancy's novel, *The Hunt for Red October* (1990; reviewed in this volume).

Reviews of *Miami Blues* were mixed. Most critics praised the acting of all three of the leads, but some concluded that the story line was not sufficiently compelling to warrant attention, while others argued that Moseley should have remained the central character, as he was in the novel. *Miami Blues* will most probably never be regarded as a "significant" piece of filmmaking, appearing to be merely old-fashioned disposable entertainment designed to amuse its audience; below the surface, however, lies a cynical indictment of the American dream.

Patricia Kowal

Reviews

American Film: Magazine of the Film and Television Arts. XV, May, 1990, p. 61.
Boxoffice. CXXVI, April, 1990, p. R27.
Chicago Tribune. April 20, 1990, VII, p. 37.
The Christian Science Monitor. April 20, 1990, p. 10.
Films in Review. XLI, May, 1990, p. 298.
The Hollywood Reporter. CCCXIII, April 16, 1990, p. 4.
Los Angeles Times. April 20, 1990, CIX, p. F1.
Monthly Film Bulletin. LVII, December, 1990, p. 359.
The New York Times. April 20, 1990, CXL, p. B3.
The New Yorker. LXVI, April 23, 1990, p. 90.
Premiere. III, March, 1990, p. 39.
Time. CXXXV, April 23, 1990, p. 90.
Variety. XXVII, April 18, 1990, p. 2.
Village View. April 20-26, 1990, p. 10.
The Village Voice. April 3, 1990, XXXV, p. 61.
The Wall Street Journal. May 3, 1990, A16.

MILLER'S CROSSING

Production: Ethan Coen for Circle Films and Ted and Jim Pedas/Ben Barenholtz/
  Bill Durkin Productions; released by Twentieth Century-Fox
Direction: Joel Coen
Screenplay: Joel Coen and Ethan Coen
Cinematography: Barry Sonnenfeld
Editing: Michael Miller
Production design: Dennis Gassner
Art direction: Leslie McDonald
Set design: Kathleen McKernin
Set decoration: Nancy Haigh
Sound: Allan Byer
Costume design: Richard Hornung
Music: Carter Burwell
MPAA rating: R
Running time: 114 minutes

> *Principal characters:*
> Tom Reagan . . . . Gabriel Byrne
> Leo . . . . Albert Finney
> Verna . . . . Marcia Gay Harden
> Johnny Caspar . . . . Jon Polito
> Bernie Bernbaum . . . . John Turturro
> Eddie Dane . . . . J. E. Freeman
> Mink . . . . Steve Buscemi

In a film season with more than the usual percentage of gangster epics, *Miller's Crossing* stood somewhere between the pop art approach of *Dick Tracy* (1990; reviewed in this volume) and the gritty realism of *GoodFellas* (1990; also reviewed in this volume). It is the most cartoonish in its depictions of violence. Tom Reagan (Gabriel Byrne), the major character, for example, is beaten up in every other scene, yet the only mark of this mayhem to face, head, and guts is an occasional cut lip. In similar fashion, blazing submachine guns are used as much for visual as for lethal effect. At the same time, however, the dingy lives of gangsters squabbling over petty sums are conveyed in a naturalistic manner.

The story line, highly convoluted in its detail, is a simple formula: Two men in love with the same woman dissolve a lifelong friendship. The year is 1929 and the locale is an anonymous industrial city in what appears to be the northeastern United States. Leo (Albert Finney), a classic Irish gangster type, controls the mayor and the police chief and is overboss of the city's gambling dens and speakeasies. He is tough, sometimes shrewd, but not particularly bright. His hard thinking is done by Reagan, a tight-lipped fellow who drinks incessantly but is never seen drunk. Their partnership collapses when they both become involved with Verna (Marcia Gay Harden), the sister of Bernie Bernbaum (John Turturro), a petty gambler who violates the underworld code of ethics.

The film opens with a parody of the opening sequence of *The Godfather* (1972). Johnny Caspar (Jon Polito) sits at a desk across from Leo and complains that Bernie has been cheating him. Caspar wants permission to take revenge or the assurance that Leo will redress the grievance. Leo refuses the request even though a gang war will surely result from his inaction. When Caspar has departed, Reagan is furious, saying the only reason Leo has declined to do what he should is that he has made a promise to Verna to shield her brother. In a final effort to stave off full-fledged bloodletting, Reagan is eventually forced to reveal his own involvement with Verna. This outrages Leo, who punches Reagan and expels him from mob headquarters.

The film's point of reference is always Reagan. He is the smartest of the gangsters, and he has a code of honor based on the assumption that no one ever knows anyone else. He calls Verna a whore, castigating her for sleeping with Leo only to protect her brother, yet refuses to admit that his own lust for her may have elements of love. He fashions a complex scheme to keep Leo in power, to keep Bernie alive, and possibly to keep Verna at his side. Unwilling to confide in anyone, he carries out the plan single-handedly.

Like all the film's characters, Reagan speaks in a terse manner modeled on the language of Dashiell Hammett. The result is often wooden or artificial, but occasionally, it is poetic in its simplicity. Explicit homage to Hammett was very much in the minds of Joel and Ethan Coen, the brothers who wrote, produced, and directed the film. Their major problem is that Reagan is not a Hammett-style private eye who is an outsider; Reagan is a gangster and an insider. Part of the plot revolves around Reagan's inability to pay a rather small gambling debt. He wanders around the underworld trying to sort out information about fixed horse races and boxing matches. Given his status, he should be the fixer, and he should be making odds, not taking them. When Leo offers to pay his debt, Reagan turns the money down, even though it would only be a loan. This decision lacks sense, aside from the fact that, as Leo's principal adviser, Reagan would have his own steady source of income from his own rackets. As an important insider with a wide circle of contacts, Reagan is not credible as an honorable loner fighting the system.

Many of the other characters are also poorly conceived. Johnny Caspar is shown to have a formidable gangster apparatus that is able to best Leo's momentarily, yet most of Caspar's scenes are played as Italian farce with Johnny as the buffoon. Verna's behavior is unfathomable, to say the least, and only brilliant acting by Marcia Gay Harden in her film debut invests her lines with credibility. The basic failing is that the Coens have attempted a mixed genre. They want to parody the gangster formulas and at the same time pay homage to the world of Dashiell Hammett, the source of many of those very formulas. Yet a third concern is to provide a realistic antidote to the glorification and mystification of gangsters that characterize *The Godfather* films and their many imitators. Like mixed metaphors in literary works, this mixed genre does not succeed.

Nevertheless, the film has many fine qualities. The ethnic mix of criminals—Irish, Italian, and Jewish—is rendered flawlessly. While the ethnic digs are constant, as in the real world, they do not get in the way of business. The lampooning of corrupt political figures would do credit to director Preston Sturges. Considerable effort has also gone into the look of the film. Period buildings were found in New Orleans, and the regal gambling halls, street scenes, and rooming-house interiors are exactly right. Equal consideration has been given to the choice of costumes. The only excess is that the Coens appear to have developed a fetish for the 1920's hat. Reagan's hat, in particular, is asked to do symbolic duty that is inappropriate. Ethnic and social differences are skillfully underscored by an outstanding musical score that ranges from "Decatur Street Tutti" to "Come Back to Erin" and "King Porter Stomp." Especially effective is the singing of "Danny Boy" by Frank Patterson.

An important element in the plot involves the homosexual relationship between rival gang members. Eddie Dane (J. E. Freeman), Johnny Caspar's ruthless enforcer and the only gangster with an intelligence approaching Reagan's, is homosexual. Verna's brother, Bernie, is also homosexual, as is Mink (Steve Buscemi), one of Leo's subordinates. Mink has liaisons with both Bernie and Eddie, and although only seen on screen for one scene, Mink is central to the plot's key developments. Mink is rendered stereotypically, Bernie in a slightly more complex manner, and Dane as the toughest guy around and a man who remains completely loyal to his lover.

The film's title refers to an area in the forest near the city where the mobsters conduct their executions. In the most important single sequence in the film, the Caspar mob orders Reagan to shoot Bernie and thus establish his loyalty to his new boss. Reagan and Bernie go into the woods alone, and Bernie falls to his knees, pleading that they may be gangsters but they are not killers and they do not betray their friends. Before the film is over, however, neither will be able to make that statement.

The moments at Miller's Crossing are the cinematic high points of the film, particularly the shots of interlocking treetops caught by a moving camera. Also visually strong are scenes in which Leo's house is set ablaze. Less dramatic but completely realistic is the way in which the camera reveals the ugliness of mob life. A few shots made from what would be below floor level provide artificial elongations that the Coens would have done better without. The violence quotient is high, with no fewer than five major characters slain in graphic fashion.

The Coens have built a critical and popular following with their first two films, *Blood Simple* (1985) and *Raising Arizona* (1987). *Miller's Crossing* was eagerly awaited for its anticipated blend of fine and popular art, and it was selected to open the prestigious New York Film Festival. The film, however, received only a cool reception. The critical and popular acclaim that the Coens were seeking for a gangster film went, instead, to Martin Scorsese's *GoodFellas*, which was released at approximately the same time.

Dan Georgakas

Reviews

Boxoffice. September, 1990, p. R64.
Chicago Tribune. October 5, 1990, VII, p. 22.
Film Comment. XXVI, September, 1990, p. 32.
Films in Review. XLII, January, 1991, p. 46.
The Hollywood Reporter. CCCXIII, August 20, 1990, p. 14.
Los Angeles Times. October 5, 1990, p. F10.
The New York Times. September 21, 1990, p. B1.
Newsweek. CXVI, September 17, 1990, p. 54.
Sight and Sound. LX, Winter, 1990, p. 64.
Time. CXXXVI, September 24, 1990, p. 83.
Variety. August 20, 1990, p. 2.

THE MISADVENTURES OF MR. WILT

Origin: Great Britain
Released: 1989
Released in U.S.: 1990
Production: Brian Eastman; released by Samuel Goldwyn Company
Direction: Michael Tuchner
Screenplay: Andrew Marshall and David Renwick; based on the novel *Wilt*, by Tom Sharpe
Cinematography: Norman Langley
Editing: Chris Blunden
Production design: Leo Austin
Art direction: Richard Elton and Diane Dancklefsen
Sound: Christian Wangler
Costume design: Liz Waller
Music: Anne Dudley
MPAA rating: R
Running time: 93 minutes
Also known as: Wilt

Principal characters:
Henry Wilt .... Griff Rhys Jones
Inspector Flint .... Mel Smith
Eva Wilt .... Alison Steadman
Sally .... Diana Quick
Hugh .... Jeremy Clyde
Dave .... Roger Allam
Reverend St. John Froude .... David Ryall

Mel Smith and Griff Rhys Jones are two of Great Britain's most popular comedians, perhaps best known for their television show *Alas Smith and Jones* (not to be confused with *Alias Smith and Jones*, a popular Western television show from the 1970's). The screenplay for *The Misadventures of Mr. Wilt* was adapted from the Tom Sharpe novel entitled *Wilt* (1976), which was also the title of the film when it was first released, in Great Britain. Sharpe is well known for his satirical views on education in England, and, taken all together, Sharpe, Smith, and Jones would seem an unbeatably humorous combination. Yet, the translation of Sharpe's humor to the screen, at least as played in the farcical manner of Smith and Jones, does not work.

Henry Wilt (Griff Rhys Jones) is a weak-willed college lecturer who is a failure: His shrewish and brutally insensitive wife, Eva (Alison Steadman), despises him for his spinelessness; he is physically intimidated by bullying students in his class; and he is continually denied promotion. There is, however, a secret side to Wilt: He regularly fantasizes about his wife's coming to a violent end. Ironically, the story hinges on what Wilt does when he is indeed accused of murdering his wife, while all he has ever done is to envision her death, lacking the courage to murder her in reality.

Eva is a silly woman who readily adopts fads from others and then berates Wilt for his stuffiness in not joining. Her present fancies include self-defense and herbal remedies such as colonics. She is easily swayed by her friends, and one in particular, named Sally (Diana Quick), whom Wilt particularly despises. Married to the impotent Hugh (Jeremy Clyde), Sally is a voraciously egotistical bisexual nymphomaniac who is trying to seduce Eva, though Eva does not realize it; Eva thinks that Sally is a feminist who is merely looking out for Eva's rights. Wilt, however, divines Sally's real intentions and, at a party at her house, insults Sally to her face, leading her to take revenge.

Revenge comes in the very shapely form of Angelique, an inflatable, anatomically correct sex doll. After Wilt accidentally wanders upstairs into Sally's bedroom, Sally knocks Wilt unconscious and ties him—naked—to Angelique. For the rest of the night, Wilt wanders about the English countryside trying to rid himself of his unwelcome partner. Finally, he stuffs the doll down a contractors' hole at the technical college where he teaches. Predictably, during these nocturnal adventures, Wilt is spotted by several people, who are just as predictably outraged by what they see as his licentious behavior with a beautiful, if strangely passive, woman.

The next day, while pouring concrete into the hole containing Angelique, a construction worker spots what he misconstrues as a female body. About this time, Wilt goes to the police to report that his wife is missing, as she has not returned from Sally and Hugh's party. Unfortunately, Eva's disappearance and the eyewitnesses to Wilt's strange antics the night before combine with the recent activities of the so-called Swaffam Strangler to land Wilt in serious trouble with Inspector Flint (Mel Smith), a policeman with whom he has been in trouble before. In one of the few truly comic scenes of the film, Wilt, unable to persuade Flint of his innocence, confesses to all the hideous crimes for which Flint could ask and even signs a confession— except he uses the name Sweeney Todd, "the demon barber of Fleet Street," leading to Flint's crushing humiliation.

Meanwhile, it is revealed that Eva has gone away with Sally and Hugh aboard their boat, which then breaks down. When Eva realizes the exact nature of Sally's intentions, she swims ashore in search of a telephone in order to call Wilt, but she ends up at a deserted church, ministered by a psychotic who is the real Swaffam Strangler. Wilt manages to get to the church in time to save her, but the denouement is more anticlimactic than dramatic, for by this point any sympathy for Eva has evaporated, and the audience is rooting for the strangler. Steadman plays a role that evokes as little audience sympathy as the one she played in *Shirley Valentine* (1989); Eva is a thoughtless woman whose self-involvement is so complete that she is oblivious to the fact that she could be driving her husband to murder. Ironically, it is the intervention of the murderous vicar that saves her marriage and her life.

Smith plays Inspector Flint as an obsessively ambitious bumbler. Sent out to the provinces to redeem himself, Flint has an important drug bust ruined by Wilt. When Wilt becomes a suspect in the Swaffam Strangler case, Flint sees his chance to regain his career and to exact revenge at the same time. The contest between Flint and Wilt becomes an extension of their appearances: the hulkingly brutal and physical Flint versus the slight and almost effeminately cerebral Wilt. Jones's Wilt is not much more sympathetic than Smith's Flint. For such a supposedly intelligent man, the situations in which he finds himself are too ridiculous to be watched for long without cringing. Ultimately, watching *The Misadventures of Mr. Wilt* is like watching a horrendous—and horrendously drawn-out—*Alas Smith and Jones* skit.

There are many levels on which this film could have been attempted, including bawdy sex farce and deeply black comedy. Unfortunately, the sexual tension of Sharpe's novel has been cut for sophomoric sex jokes, while the edge of black humor has been sacrificed for a silly, sitcom approach to Sharpe's characters. Wilt's inadvertent destruction of Flint's drug bust (by dropping a shopping cart on his head) is improbable. It therefore comes as no surprise that the scene was not in the book, where, more logically, Flint and Wilt meet during the course of the investigation of Eva's disappearance.

Though *Wilt* was written by Sharpe in the mid-1970's, the film version seems to catalog the woes of what is commonly called "Margaret Thatcher's Britain." The degeneration of education, the abuse inflicted on teachers by both the students and the government, the collapse of the economy, and the licentious behavior and excesses at Sally and Hugh's party are all recognizable signs of a disintegrating empire. The decades of rule by generally inept politicians have left Great Britain a crumbling edifice not too dissimilar from the broken-down technical college where Wilt teaches. Obsolete equipment and underutilized and unrewarded knowledge have contributed to the ruin of Great Britain as surely as to that of Wilt's career.

While it is not difficult to describe the worst excesses of this film, it is difficult to comprehend how it could have happened. The cast members, who include many seasoned performers, are intelligent and talented. Jones studied English at the University of Cambridge, where he was president of the famous Footlights Dramatic Society. Smith began studying experimental psychology at the University of Oxford, but left to become the assistant director of London's Royal Court Theatre and made his motion-picture directing debut in 1989 with the film *The Tall Guy*. Diana Quick also attended Oxford, where she studied English, and has been a columnist for a British women's magazine called *She*. Both the director, Michael Tuchner, and the producer, Brian Eastman, have produced respectable work in the past. One is led to suspect that, ultimately, this film's failure is the fault of a weak and unfunny script (adapted from Sharpe's novel by Andrew Marshall and David Renwick).

Jo-Ellen Lipman Boon

Reviews

Films in Review. XLI, October, 1990, p. 490.
The Hollywood Reporter. CCCXIII, June 20, 1990, p. 8.
The Houston Post. October 1, 1990, p. B1.
Insight. VI, July 16, 1990, p. 62.
Los Angeles Times. June 29, 1990, p. F4.
The New York Times. June 22, 1990, p. B10.
Newsweek. CCV, June 18, 1990, p. 62.
People Weekly. XXXIV, July 23, 1990, p. 11.
Playboy. XXXVII, August, 1990, p. 25.
The Sunday Times (London). November 5, 1989, p. C5b.
The Times (London). November 2, 1989, p. 21G.
The Village Voice. XXXV, June 26, 1990, p. 65.

MISERY

Production: Andrew Scheinman and Rob Reiner for Castle Rock Entertainment, in association with Nelson Entertainment; released by Columbia Pictures
Direction: Rob Reiner
Screenplay: William Goldman; based on the novel by Stephen King
Cinematography: Barry Sonnenfeld
Editing: Robert Leighton
Production design: Norman Garwood
Sound: Robert Eber
Costume design: Gloria Gresham
Music: Marc Shaiman
MPAA rating: R
Running time: 107 minutes

Principal characters:
Paul Sheldon .... James Caan
Annie Wilkes .... Kathy Bates (AA)
Virginia .... Frances Sternhagen
Buster .... Richard Farnsworth
Marcia Sindell .... Lauren Bacall
Libby .... Graham Jarvis
Chief Sherman Douglas .... J. T. Walsh
Pete .... Jerry Potter

Stephen King is a writer and a clever one at that, but not much of a filmmaker. His stories have fared far better when treated by experienced directors such as Brian DePalma, Stanley Kubrick, and Rob Reiner than when King himself has been immediately involved, as with *Pet Sematary* (1989), which he scripted. Reiner's first King project, *Stand by Me* (1986), was not exactly typical King material, but a coming-of-age picture based on King's short story "The Body."

Misery is closer to the Gothic world of the typical King thriller, except the horror is psychological rather than supernatural. Moreover, it has a serious allegorical dimension that suggests that King may be thinking of his own talent and craft and the purpose and audience that it has served. *Misery* is clearly a gory allegory concerning a writer who must pay the consequences of writing popular, exploitative fiction. The purpose of this confessional seems to be to put the writer at ease with himself.

Stephen King films have become commonplace, but *Misery* should not be judged by the weak *Pet Sematary*, which generally followed the novel but was hardly a cut above a typical horror-slasher epic. Not only is *Misery* a more thoughtful story, but it represents the collaboration of many talented people as well. The screenplay was written by Academy Award winner William Goldman, and the film was directed by Rob Reiner, whose *Stand by Me* is arguably the best adaptation of a King vehicle captured on film so far. Add to this a splendid ensemble cast, and the result is far better than what could be expected from the usual King film. It is interesting especially to see Goldman, who created the sadistic dentist of *Marathon Man* (1976), creating a parallel character in King's demented nurse.

The writer-hero of King's novel is Paul Sheldon (James Caan), who created a popular series of bodice-rippers involving a romantic heroine named Misery Chastain. In order to liberate himself from his creation, he has written a final Misery novel in which he describes the death of his heroine at the end. While this novel is in production, Paul goes to the Silver Creek Lodge in Colorado and writes a "serious" personal novel, in order to change his image. Paul thinks that he has escaped from his Misery, but King locks him into a bizarre set of circumstances that proves otherwise.

For an unexplained reason—perhaps in a state of giddy expectation because he believes he has recaptured his integrity—Sheldon leaves the lodge in a blizzard in order to send his manuscript to his agent. The roads are icy, however, and his 1965 Mustang slides off the road and down the mountainside. He is rescued by Annie Wilkes (Kathy Bates), a nurse who saves his life and carries him to her isolated home to care for him until his health returns. Annie claims to be Paul's "number-one fan," but there is later reason to suspect that the fact that she was following him in a blizzard might not have been a matter of coincidence. She tells him that the telephone lines are out and that there is no way to take him to a hospital.

Paul is seriously disabled with a broken arm and compound fractures to both legs. Annie is delighted to offer what nurses call "tender loving care," and, as an expression of gratitude, Paul permits her to read his unpublished manuscript. Annie soon discovers this is not a Misery novel, and forty pages into the manuscript she begins to act like his editor. She is offended by the swearing: "It has no nobility," she asserts. She launches into a tantrum, the first outward sign of her psychic disturbance. Bates portrays Annie's mood swings expertly. As Annie recovers her composure, she coos: "I love you Paul. You're mine."

Meanwhile, the local sheriff, Buster (Richard Farnsworth), has been alerted to the fact that Sheldon is missing after Paul's New York agent, Marcia Sindell (Lauren Bacall), calls to discover his whereabouts. Buster and his wife, Virginia (Frances Sternhagen), decide to investigate. In a nice exercise of camera irony, Buster stops just short of finding Paul's snow-covered Mustang, which is finally spotted from the air weeks later.

Back at Annie's, Paul is becoming more intimate with his hostess, who becomes increasingly more demanding, petulant, and possessive. Paul slowly begins to realize that he is her prisoner and that she is a demented psychopath. When the last Misery novel is published and Annie reads it, she is outraged to discover that Paul has killed her favorite heroine. Upset at the turn his career has taken, she forces him to burn his latest manuscript and to begin writing another Misery sequel that will bring the heroine back to life. She forces her own vulgar tastes in literature and music (Liberace) onto her captive. When he becomes well enough to think of escaping, she "hobbles" him by smashing his ankles with a sledgehammer. One obvious means of rescue would be the telephone, but Paul discovers that Annie's telephone is nothing more than a hollow shell; it is not functional.

Buster has been reading the eight Misery novels and is struck by one sentence: "There is a justice higher than man. I will be judged by Him." Buster is also suspicious of Annie, who was banned from the profession of nursing after a series of mysterious hospital deaths. Checking the newspapers, Buster discovers that Annie quoted that same sentence at her trial. When Buster visits Annie to investigate and hears Paul, who is locked in the basement and making noises, Annie kills him with a shotgun. She then becomes depressed and decides that a double-suicide would bring her and Paul's affair to a dramatic closure. Paul has other plans, however, and the two of them become locked in a life- and-death struggle at the film's end.

"I don't want to fictionalize myself," Paul writes at the end of King's novel. "Writing may be masturbatory, but God forbid it should be an act of autocannibalism." The novel is more bloody, grim, and disturbing than the film and has a broader self-reflexive context, but the film is sufficient. Bates is a marvel in her role. She researched the psychology of the sociopath in order to prepare herself and was surprised to learn that criminal sociopaths often appear "normal." The way in which she is able to insinuate the sinister into the "normal" is brilliant. Her performance won the Academy Award for Best Actress of 1990.

It is a little surprising that Reiner would turn to a King property after making *The Princess Bride* (1987), an inventive comic fantasy, and *When Harry Met Sally* (1989), a comedy-romance in the style of Woody Allen. In fact, in a pre-release interview done with *The New York Times*, Reiner remarked that "I don't like horror movies." His point is, however, that *Misery* is more than simply a horror film: "It's exactly what I've been through in my life," Reiner explained, "being successful at one thing and wanting to do something else and being terrified that you won't be accepted at that."

Reiner and screenplay writer Goldman took an unconventional and contrary approach to shaping the story for the screen by stripping away much of the horror and emphasizing the psychological interplay, "the opposite of what people typically do with a Stephen King adaptation; usually they strip away the character and leave the horror," which was exactly the approach that had been taken with *Pet Sematary*. Reiner seems to respect King as a writer whose "characters are very well drawn, very real, and his descriptions are powerful." Reiner worked with the preconception that Paul Sheldon was "a guy who is dying to do something other" than what he has been doing, "and yet he knows there's an audience out there and they buy the stuff that he writes and he's great at it, so he's going to keep doing it." The message rather resembles the conclusion reached by the fictional director of Preston Sturges' *Sullivan's Travels* (1941), who wants to make a serious film but cannot escape his talent for making comedies. *New York Magazine* scoffed at *Misery*, however, calling it a self-justifying parable: "If success is his prison, he has someone other than his fans to blame."

Goldman won Oscars for *Butch Cassidy and the Sundance Kid* (1969) and *All the President's Men* (1976), but his later work on *Marathon Man* and *Magic* (1978) more closely resembles this film, as Goldman knows how to touch nerves. Barry Sonnenfeld, whose camera work for Joel and Ethan Coen's *Blood Simple* (1985) and *Miller's Crossing* (1990; reviewed in this volume) was outstanding, was the cinematographer for *Misery*, and no one shoots odd angles, telling close-ups, and tense tracking shots better. It is entirely appropriate that Lauren Bacall should have a cameo in this film, as the story recalls *The Fan* (1981), adapted from Bob Randall's epistolary novel, in which she starred as a stage actress who is stalked by a psychopathic fan. *Misery* is a far better variation of that theme. Not only is *Misery* superior to the horrors portrayed by King's *Graveyard Shift* and the television production of *It*, both released in 1990, but the film is one of the year's best all-around films as well.

James M. Welsh

Reviews

Baltimore Sun. November 30, 1990, Maryland Live, p. 12.
Chicago Tribune. November 30, 1990, VII, p. 29.
The Christian Science Monitor. December 14, 1990, p. 10.
The Hollywood Reporter. CCCXV, November 26, 1990, p. 5.
Los Angeles Times. November 30, 1990, p. F1.
New York Magazine. December 10, 1990, p. 88.
The New York Times. June 17, 1990, p. 13.
The New York Times. November 30, 1990, p. B1.
New York Times Magazine. January 27, 1991, p. 25.
Premiere. IV, October, 1990, p. 74.
Time. CXXXVI, December 10, 1990, p. 87.
Variety. November 26, 1990, p. 2.
The Wall Street Journal. December 6, 1990, p. A16.
The Washington Post. November 30, 1990, p. F1.

MR. AND MRS. BRIDGE

Production: Ismail Merchant for Cineplex Odeon Films and Merchant Ivory/Robert Halmi; released by Miramax Films
Direction: James Ivory
Screenplay: Ruth Prawer Jhabvala; based on the novels *Mr. Bridge* and *Mrs. Bridge*, by Evan S. Connell
Cinematography: Tony Pierce-Roberts
Editing: Humphry Dixon
Production design: David Gropman
Set decoration: Joyce Gilstrap
Art direction: Karen Schultz
Sound: Ed Novick
Costume design: Carol Ramsey
Music: Richard Robbins
MPAA rating: PG-13
Running time: 127 minutes

> *Principal characters:*
> Walter Bridge . . . . Paul Newman
> India Bridge . . . . Joanne Woodward
> Grace Barron . . . . Blythe Danner
> Ruth Bridge . . . . Kyra Sedgwick
> Douglas Bridge . . . . Robert Sean Leonard
> Carolyn Bridge . . . . Margaret Welsh
> Harriet . . . . Saundra McClain
> Mr. Gadbury . . . . Austin Pendleton
> Julia . . . . Diane Kagan
> Dr. Alex Sauer . . . . Simon Callow
> Virgil Barron . . . . Remak Ramsey

The creative team that made *A Room with a View* (1986) has reunited to produce *Mr. and Mrs. Bridge*. Director James Ivory had wanted to make this film since the 1960's when he read Evan S. Connell's novels, *Mrs. Bridge* (1959) and *Mr. Bridge* (1969). Ivory discussed the book with screenwriter Ruth Prawer Jhabvala, but she did not share his interest. Almost twenty years later, when actress Joanne Woodward expressed her desire to one day play India Bridge, Ivory not only proposed a film combining both of Connell's novels but also implied that Jhabvala was interested in such a project. Their enthusiasm was so contagious that Woodward's husband, actor Paul Newman, offered to take the role of Walter Bridge.

Newman and Woodward have performed together few times over the years. Woodward appeared briefly in Newman's film *Harry and Son* (1984), and they costarred in *The Drowning Pool* (1975). Though best known for acting in such hit films as *Butch*

Cassidy and the Sundance Kid (1969), Newman is also a respected director. He has directed his wife in several projects, including *Rachel, Rachel* (1968), for which Newman won the Best Director Award from the New York Film Critics Society and Woodward won the Academy Award for Best Actress.

Mr. and Mrs. Bridge opens with a series of home movies, presumably shot years ago by Walter Bridge (Newman). Shown are his wife, India (Woodward), and their three children frolicking at the Mission Hills Country Club, the mecca of the upper-middle-class, in their hometown of Kansas City. The sequence is indicative of the film's style: a series of vignettes, days in the life of the Bridge family, with no discernible beginning, middle, or end.

On a hot summer day, the Bridges sun themselves in the backyard while Walter helps his daughter Ruth (Kyra Sedgwick) rehearse a scene from a play. Walter plays Romeo to Ruth's Juliet, hinting at the unnatural, almost incestuous relationship that they have. Later, watching Ruth sunbathe alone, Walter is so overcome with desire that he grabs his unsuspecting wife and throws her to the bed. His passion is not so easily satisfied when late one night, thinking he hears a prowler, Walter loads a pistol and searches the house, only to find Ruth making love to a boyfriend on the living-room floor. Days later, when they are finally able to face each other, Walter asks if Ruth intends to marry the boy. Ruth rolls her eyes at what she considers to be her father's outdated morals, but she is embarrassed when he admits that he still feels a great desire for Ruth's mother. Father and daughter awkwardly share their views on love, respect, and trust.

Ruth tells her father of her plan to go to New York and become an actress. Even in this outrageous breach of propriety and parental expectations, Walter is unable to resist his daughter and agrees to support her in her adventure. India is never consulted on any part of this decision. Hurt by this oversight, India punishes Ruth with a tool that some mothers wield expertly: guilt. In a letter calculated to make Ruth weep, India states that, while she may not always understand Ruth, she will always love her. Except for brief visits on holidays and special occasions, Ruth never returns to her family.

The Bridges' relationship with their son Douglas (Robert Sean Leonard) is no less strained. Though his Eagle Scout manual tells him that a boy's best friend is his mother, Douglas flinches every time India attempts to approach him. He is the only boy at the Eagle Scout's award ceremony who refuses to kiss his mother. India attempts to hide her hurt feelings but is, in fact, devastated. Walter's fury at his son's lack of respect is less concealed, but even Walter's tenderness is too little and too late to soothe India's feelings. Still, India wants to be a part of her son's life in any way that he will allow. When she finds a lingerie catalog in Douglas' bureau drawer, she nervously presents him with a pamphlet called "The Mysteries of Marriage." It is an excruciating moment; both mother and son are so embarrassed that they can hardly speak. Later, the three Bridge siblings will laugh about the pamphlet that they each received when their mother thought it prudent, but India will be left with only the fear that she was unable to help her children when they needed her.

The Bridges' youngest daughter, Carolyn (Margaret Welsh), promises to be their pride and joy but then proves to be yet another disappointment. She returns from college engaged to a boy whom the Bridges do not consider to be of their social sphere. Walter instructs Carolyn to call the boy and break off the engagement. Having never been defied before, Walter is astonished when the fiancé appears in his office and vows not to leave until he and Carolyn have Walter's blessing. Caught off guard, Walter is eventually won over. The wedding takes place, but the family's happiness is brief. Carolyn makes a habit of leaving her husband and coming home for days at a time, when the simple life-style she had defended proves to be as dull and dreary as her parents had predicted.

Other relationships prove to be equally disappointing and emotionally draining for the Bridges. An acquaintance from the country club, Dr. Alex Sauer (Simon Callow), accuses Walter of priggishness and flaunts his own marriage to a younger woman, finally forcing Walter to admit that, while he has known contentment, he has never in his life experienced joy. India's best friend, Grace Barron (Blythe Danner), seems to be the only one who understands and appreciates India's childlike and nurturing qualities. Tragically, the monotony of life that India hesitates to question drives Grace to madness. When Grace commits suicide, India's loss is exacerbated by what she perceives as her husband's misplaced priorities. Walter's first reaction is to be offended on behalf of Grace's husband, Virgil (Remak Ramsay), that Grace could cause him such pain. India furiously points out that she too is in pain and needs comfort, not the condemnation of her lost friend.

Most interesting are the scenes in which the Bridges can be examined as a couple. Walter is as arrogant as India is insecure. One evening at a country club dinner, the guests run for cover to the basement as a violent tornado approaches. Walter stubbornly remains in his chair, cutting his roll and complaining about the lack of butter. Terrified, India searches the abandoned tables for butter while she begs Walter to let them join the others in the basement. Walter reminds India that, in the twenty years that he has been telling her when something will or will not happen, he has been wrong on no significant occasion. As he finishes his sentence, the tornado passes. Walter's intuition again proves sound when he insists that they cut short a second honeymoon in Paris and return immediately to the United States after hearing radio reports that the Nazis have invaded Poland.

Though Walter and India Bridge may be the perfect picture of 1940's, suburban, middle-class marriage, they are emotionally mismatched. Walter is as stingy with his approval and affection as India is in need of those qualities. When India, feeling neglected, demands a divorce, Walter merely sits her on his knee and has her drink beer until she forgets what the problem was. When Walter, concerned about his failing health, tries to acquaint India with the contents of their safe-deposit box, India only wants to know if Walter loves her. He wearily replies that he would not be here if he did not.

In the film's poignant final sequence, India is trapped in her car, in the garage, during a snowstorm. Walter has stopped on his way home to buy her roses for Valentine's Day. As the home movies that opened the film are replayed, captions reveal that Walter arrived in time to rescue India but then forgot to give her the roses. The image is an accurate metaphor for their entire marriage: India is entirely dependent on Walter who, by caring for her the best way he knows, denies her the love that she most wants.

Though it would be reasonable to expect this on-screen pairing of a famous off-screen couple to be exciting, *Mr. and Mrs. Bridge* is disappointing. This is no fault of Woodward or Newman, whose performances are characteristically intense and finely tuned. Unfortunately, the adaptation from novel to screenplay has rendered Walter and India Bridge a tiresome couple. India's profound emotions—love, longing, fear, and her awkwardness with her husband, children, and friends—are portrayed beautifully but never explained. Also unexplained is Walter's apparent lack of emotion and his unsettling relationships with his family, colleagues, and employees. The Bridge family remains an enigma, reviewed but never resolved.

Eleah Horwitz

Reviews

American Film: Magazine of the Film and Television Arts. XV, December, 1990, p. 48.
Boxoffice. November, 1990, p. R83.
Commonweal. CXVIII, February 8, 1991, p. 101.
Films in Review. XLII, January, 1991, p. 42.
The Hollywood Reporter. CCCXV, November 19, 1990, p. 7.
Los Angeles Times. November 23, 1990, CC, p. F1.
The New Republic. December 24, 1990, p. 26.
The New York Times. November 23, 1990, CXL, p. B1.
The New Yorker. LXVI, December 3, 1990, p. 170.
Sight and Sound. LX, Winter, 1990, p. 63.
Time. CXXXVI, November 26, 1990, p. 86.
Variety. CCCXL, September 10, 1990, p. 2.
The Village Voice. XXXV, November 27, 1990, p. 108.
The Wall Street Journal. CXXIII, November 21, 1990, p. A10.

MO' BETTER BLUES

Production: Spike Lee for 40 Acres and A Mule Filmworks; released by Universal
    Pictures
Direction: Spike Lee
Screenplay: Spike Lee
Cinematography: Ernest Dickerson
Editing: Sam Pollard
Production design: Wynn Thomas
Set decoration: Ted Glass
Sound: Skip Lievsay
Costume design: Ruth E. Carter
Music: Bill Lee
MPAA rating: R
Running time: 127 minutes

Principal characters:
Bleek Gilliam	Denzel Washington
Giant	Spike Lee
Shadow Henderson	Wesley Snipes
Left Hand Lacey	Giancarlo Esposito
Indigo Downes	Joie Lee
Clarke Bentancourt	Cynda Williams
Butterbean Jones	Robin Harris
Bottom Hammer	Bill Nunn
Moe Flatbush	John Turturro
Big Stop Gilliam	Dick Anthony Williams
Josh Flatbush	Nicholas Turturro
Petey	Rubén Blades

Mo' Better Blues is writer-director-producer Spike Lee's fourth film, and it is as
different from the preceding three as each of those is from the others. It has become
a hallmark of Lee's brief but already controversial career that he has characteristics
but no fingerprint; he changes genres and styles more frequently than he changes
actors. Nevertheless, *Mo' Better Blues* follows up on some of Lee's earlier concerns,
while exploring much new terrain.

Mo' Better Blues looks in some ways like a traditional jazz film. It follows trum-
peter Bleek Gilliam (Denzel Washington) from a brief childhood scene through his
peak as leader of a quintet to the violent destruction of his career. The film does not,
however, move like the standard jazz biopic. It is slow and static. Most of it takes
place over a very short period of time. It focuses more on character exposition,
camera work, and music than on any kind of plot development. The film devotes its
attention to Bleek's relationship to his business manager, Giant (Spike Lee), who is

a compulsive gambler; to his sax player, Shadow Henderson (Wesley Snipes), who is his competitor; and to his lovers Indigo Downes (Joie Lee, Spike's sister) and Clarke Bentancourt (Cynda Williams).

The plot is simple. Bleek and his group are packing the house at a New York club, and they want more money. Giant ought to get it for them, but he does not seem to be able to do so, mainly because he negotiated their contract poorly. In the meantime, Giant himself needs money to cover his gambling debts. Simultaneously, Bleek's two lovers are getting tired of sharing his attention; they both dump him. Giant is severely beaten by his bookie's protectors, and in an attempt to intervene, Bleek gets his mouth split open. After a period of severe depression, Bleek tries to make a comeback, fails, and begs Indigo to take him back; she does, they marry, they have a son, and everyone lives happily ever after. (Giant is doorman at the club where Clarke and Shadow, who are now a couple, play backed by the rest of Bleek's old quintet.)

As must be obvious from this plot synopsis, the writing is weak. Although complex plot development is not a necessary ingredient for a good film, what plot there is must be important or compelling. Bleek's relationships are interesting, but Lee spends so much time showing how quirky they are that he does not get to serious explanations for them. That, too, would be fine, except that some very clichéd explanations substitute for much-needed character development. For example, Bleek has two girlfriends because he is shallow and self-centered. There is no indication either of why Bleek is self-centered or why his egotism expresses itself in that particular way. Why can he commit to Giant, a blatant liability, but not to the women? Some critics have gone so far as to suggest a kind of homoeroticism in the Bleek/Giant relationship, but the film itself does not support that notion. (It might be more enlightening to consider Bleek and Shadow along these lines.)

The much-criticized anti-Semitism of this film demands particular notice. The brothers Moe (John Turturro) and Josh Flatbush (Nicholas Turturro) who own the club where Bleek plays parade the worst stereotypes of "New York Jews." They are cheap, money-grubbing, brash, loud, and offensive. Their characterization, or, better, caricature, is beneath the dignity of further comment.

One other factor, which has always been problematic in Lee's work, remains troubling. He does not have much sympathy for, insight into, or interest in women. Both Clarke and Indigo get very few chances to speak. Neither has the room to develop a character nor to participate in striking dialogue, as the men do. Lee's women manage at their best to be uninteresting, a consequence of their poorly written roles. The writing for the men, by contrast, is often truly wonderful. The first scene in the dressing room, into which Left Hand (Giancarlo Esposito) brings his white girlfriend, crackles with barbs and bites in particularly vibrant language. The rap song (cowritten by Lee and Branford Marsalis) is sharp, brittle, and humorous—well worth the price of the sound-track recording. Perhaps the most important success of the screenplay is its ending. The syrup that was promised by the final sequence is undercut by the very last scene, the basic message of which is that life goes on. That kind of move, to refuse the traditional final closure of Hollywood storytelling, goes a long way toward making some of the film's sap palatable.

The direction is as uneven as the writing. In fact, the most serious flaw of this film may have been a direction issue: The pace is intolerably choppy. The film moves like a bucking bronco, and eventually this produces a feeling not unlike motion sickness. Lee shows real strength, however, in his camera work. The sex scenes pour sensuality into the theater; Lee has brought his audience the best screen sex from any filmmaker in some time. The beating at the film's climax was far more violent, though far less graphic, than any of the summer's violence extravaganzas, such as *Total Recall* (1990; reviewed in this volume) and *Die Hard II: Die Harder* (1990; also reviewed in this volume).

While some reviewers have called *Mo' Better Blues* self-involved and film-schoolish, it is hard to see those accusations as anything less than racist. The negative reviews seem to suggest that what is "art" from Francis Coppola or David Lynch or Martin Scorsese is poor judgment from Lee. (This criticism is not done explicitly or consciously; but what got accolades in some films gets criticism in Lee's work.) In comparison, for example, to *The Cotton Club* (1984), *Mo' Better Blues* puts obvious technique on productive display. Where *The Cotton Club* seems clumsy and self-indulgent, *Mo' Better Blues* provides its audience with a highly personal vision. There is a very fine line between self-indulgence and personal vision, but Spike Lee manages to stay on the right side of it here. With the help of some outstanding cinematography by Ernest Dickerson and Wynn Thomas' rich, warm set designs, Lee turned *Mo' Better Blues* into an essay on the beauty of brown; and in this sea of honey and cinnamon and skin, he let some very accomplished actors loose to play.

Denzel Washington's performance exhibits a tremendous degree of control and discipline. His Bleek is an egotist near the edge of megalomania, but without a single excess gesture or intonation. The moment, soon after the beating, when Bleek is shown lying on the floor of his apartment surrounded by album jackets and then pulling out yards of cassette tape proves how little, in both time and energy, it takes to be convincingly mad on screen. Like Glenn Close with her lamp switch in *Fatal Attraction* (1987), Washington needs minimal accoutrements to show just how low Bleek has sunk.

To the credit of both Lee and Wesley Snipes, Shadow Henderson not only does not collapse into villainy, but even manages to stay appealing. Shadow, along with Clarke, keeps music on the level of a job, if, admittedly, one that is extremely significant to him. Because both of them can do what Bleek cannot—separate the music from themselves—they rise quickly to a big-money gig. Even so, the film does not dismiss them as sellouts. In spite of Lee's flamboyant critiques of mass culture, he does not throw aside his characters for deciding to be popular, or for not being the protagonist. A film in which characters can disagree and compete with the "hero" and still come out okay in the end is both unusual and satisfying. Fortunately, Williams and Snipes succeed in the roles Lee wrote for them.

The film was scored by Bill Lee (Spike's father), with five songs by Branford Marsalis, trumpet work by Terence Blanchard, and some excerpts from John Coltrane. Jazz rules here: Bill Lee has the grace and taste to be able to move among jazz idioms to meet all of his scoring needs. The climactic beating tears apart both screen and audience almost exclusively because of Marsalis and Blanchard's overwhelming outpouring of sound. From the club to the streets to the bedroom, the music makes an unforgettable contribution to each piece of this film.

Anahid Kassabian

Reviews

Billboard. CII, August 11, 1990, p. 68.
Boxoffice. October, 1990, p. R76.
The Christian Science Monitor. LXXXII, August 1, 1990, p. 15.
Commonweal. CXVII, September 28, 1990, p. 546.
Films in Review. XLI, November, 1990, p. 555.
The Hollywood Reporter. CCCXIII, July 30, 1990, p. 5.
Insight. VI, August 13, 1990, p. 62.
Los Angeles Times. August 3, 1990, p. F1.
The Nation. CCLI, August 13-20, 1990, p. 179.
The New Republic. CCIII, September 3, 1990, p. 28.
The New York Times. August 3, 1990, CXXXIX, p. B1.
The New Yorker. LXVI, August 13, 1990, p. 82.
Newsweek. CXVI, August 6, 1990, p. 82.
People Weekly. XXXIV, August 13, 1990, p. 11.
Time. CXXXVI, August 20, 1990, p. 62.
Variety. July 30, 1990, p. 2.
The Village Voice. XXXV, August 7, 1990, p. 63.
The Wall Street Journal. August 9, 1990, p. A6.

MONSIEUR HIRE

Origin: France
Released: 1989
Released in U.S.: 1990
Production: Philippe Carcassonne and René Cleitman for Cinea-Hachette Première et Compagnie Europe 1 Communication and F. R. 3 Films Productions; released by Orion Classics
Direction: Patrice Leconte
Screenplay: Patrice Leconte and Patrick Dewolf; based on the novel *Les Fiançailles de Monsieur Hire*, by Georges Simenon
Cinematography: Denis Lenoir
Editing: Joëlle Hache
Art direction: Ivan Maussion
Music: Michael Nyman
MPAA rating: PG-13
Running time: 88 minutes

Principal characters:
Monsieur Hire . . . . Michel Blanc
Alice . . . . Sandrine Bonnaire
Émile . . . . Luc Thuillier
Police inspector . . . . André Wilms

It is as if René Magritte's *The Menaced Assassin* (1926) has come to life. In the painting, a woman lies murdered while the apparent murderer, his hat and coat thrown carelessly over a chair, listens to the gramophone. Two pale men in dark coats and bowlers (or are they two facets of the same man?) hide suspiciously behind the door, and the whole scene is observed by voyeurs at the window.

Monsieur Hire begins with a murder. A young girl lies dead in a field, being photographed by the police inspector (André Wilms) who must find her killer. The only apparent suspect is Monsieur Hire (Michel Blanc), a neighbor of the victim and a very strange man. Hire is always clad in a long black coat and black hat that contrast sharply with his chalky complexion. He keeps a cage full of white mice at his tailor shop and places food on the table with his tools, allowing the mice out of their cage to feed among the scissors and needles. Is he negligent of or, even more frightening, fully aware of the possibility of injury to the mice? Although Hire is seen playing some sort of game with a little girl in an early scene, he has no friends or family and is ridiculed by the neighborhood children. His only entertainment, indeed his only relationship with other humans, is that of a voyeur. Every evening this solitary gentleman stands at his window, the lights in his apartment off, the shadows and curtains hiding him, and watches the people in the other apartments, such as the one of the murdered woman. Hire also has a criminal record. He was once convicted of exposing himself in public. Thus, when witnesses report a cloaked man running from the nearby field toward the apartment complex the night of the murder, the inspector naturally suspects Monsieur Hire.

So does the audience. Monsieur Hire, whose first name is never revealed, is a mysterious and frightening character—not because he is alone or lonely, but because he seems to do everything in his power to aggravate his own isolation. He does not respond when greeted by his neighbors, he makes no effort to feign normality or even hide his perversions from the inquisitive inspector, and by applying talcum powder to his face and neck he encourages the perception of himself as ghostly or surreal.

Determined to prove Hire guilty, the inspector orders him to run between the buildings of the apartment complex in a reenactment of the scene witnessed the night of the murder. The witnesses will not testify that it was in fact Hire they saw. It could have been any man in a long coat. Undaunted, the inspector continues to follow the humiliated Hire, this time to a bowling alley. To the inspector's surprise, Hire is a star there. Though bowling alone, Hire performs for and is applauded by the establishment's patrons. When Hire offers this as evidence that he is not antisocial after all, the inspector counters with a disturbing accusation regarding Hire's sexuality, which Hire cannot bring himself to deny.

Hire returns to his apartment. As is his ritual, he plays a romantic Brahms piece on the phonograph and takes his spot at the window. The current object of his attention is Alice (Sandrine Bonnaire), the beautiful young woman whose window directly faces Hire's. Hire watches her bathe, dress, and leave her apartment. Though her apartment is empty and dark, Hire remains at the window. Alice has gone to meet her boyfriend, Émile (Luc Thuillier). Émile meets her, but only to explain that he cannot keep their date; an appointment with his friends is more important than Alice. Hurt and angry, Alice returns home, where she continues unknowingly to perform for Hire. He watches her eat, read, undress, and go to sleep. Even then Hire does not move, merely waits, hidden at his window, for Alice to rise.

It is only by accident that Alice discovers Hire's interest in her. One evening during a thunderstorm, the power goes out in Alice's apartment. Suddenly a streak of lightening crosses the courtyard between the apartments, illuminating Hire's face in the window. Alice gasps. Hire ducks behind the curtains. Alice's fear is only temporary, however: Whereas others might call for help or at least pull down the window shade, Alice is intrigued by Hire and by the idea of being watched. She begins to take an active part in Hire's voyeurism. When Émile visits, she encourages him to make love to her, all the while throwing glances to Hire. Not satisfied with this, Alice endeavors to meet Hire. She waits in the hallway for him to return from work and purposely spills a bag of tomatoes at his feet. Hire stands paralyzed with inexpressible desire while Alice crawls seductively on all fours, retrieving the tomatoes. Delighting in Hire's discomfort, Alice attempts a second meeting. This time Hire admits her to his apartment. Once inside, Alice frustrates and confuses Hire by reprimanding him for his misbehavior, then stretching out on his bed and inviting him to join her there. Unable to withstand the temptation and unable to give in to it, Hire explodes with temper, ordering Alice out of the apartment. Hire's obsession with Alice grows. He follows her everywhere. On a crowded bus, Alice conducts a cool conversation with Émile, while caressing Hire's hand under the pretense of holding the handrail for support.

Émile is running from the police. As his tension grows, his interest in Alice wanes. He asks Alice to marry him but later confesses that he asked in a moment of panic, wishing that such a thing were realistic when he must instead be concerned with saving his own life. Though he treats her badly and through association places her in danger, Alice will not leave him. She explains, "You only love me a little, but I love you enough for two." Then why, the viewer wonders, is she becoming involved with Hire?

Hire reveals to Alice that he had been watching her long before she was aware of him. He was at his window the night Émile rushed in after committing the crime for which he is being pursued. He saw them hide the evidence, a woman's pocketbook and Émile's bloodstained coat, in Alice's closet. Hire explains to Alice that by doing so she has become an accomplice. Hire tells Alice of a house he has in Switzerland where the two of them could live, alone, away from the police and from Émile and from people in general. Hire shows Alice two train tickets and begs her to meet him at the station.

On his way to the meet Alice, Hire stops at his tailor shop to pick up the cage of mice. Placing piles of seed at intervals along a train track, Hire releases the hungry mice and stands back to wait for the train. The scene is highly symbolic, for in a sense Hire is Alice's mouse, as she is his: Alice never arrives at the train station. Dejected, Hire returns home to find not only Alice but also the police inspector waiting for him. While Alice sits guiltily by the window in which she first saw Hire, the inspector shows Hire the murdered woman's pocketbook, turned in by Alice, who supposedly found it while hired to clean Hire's apartment. Hire runs, beginning the film's climactic chase through the buildings and rooftops of the apartment complex. What the conniving Alice does not know is that, while she was placing the pocketbook in his closet, he was taking the bloodied coat from hers and placing it in a locker at the train station with a note to the inspector, offering, too late, the truth.

Though *Monsieur Hire* is not the first collaboration for director Patrice Leconte and actor Michel Blanc, it is a departure from their usual comedic format. Leconte and Blanc are well known in France for such films as *Les Bronzés* (1978), *Les Bronzés font du ski* (1979), *Ma femme s'appelle reviens* (1982), and *Circulez y'a rien à voir* (1983). As a child, Leconte was a fan of Georges Simenon, the author of *Les Fiançailles de Monsieur Hire*, from which *Monsieur Hire* and the earlier screen version *Panique* (1947) were adapted.

Michael Nyman composed the haunting score, utilizing the Brahms quartet for string and piano that becomes Monsieur Hire's theme. Nyman's music can also be heard in Peter Greenaway's film *The Cook, the Thief, His Wife, and Her Lover* (1990; reviewed in this volume). Denis Lenoir's cinematography is exceptional. With the muted hues of a hand-tinted photograph, Lenoir's light and color render each shot a distinct and separate composition. The visually as well as emotionally compelling *Monsieur Hire* could be hung shot by shot in a museum, comfortable among the works of Salvador Dalí and René Magritte.

Eleah Horwitz

Reviews

Boxoffice. July, 1990, p. R54.
Chicago Tribune. June 15, 1990, VII, p. 42.
The Christian Science Monitor. April 23, 1990, p. 11.
Film Comment. XXVI, May, 1990, p. 22.
Films in Review. XLI, August, 1990, p. 433.
The Hollywood Reporter. October 25, 1989, p. 7.
Los Angeles Times. May 4, 1990, p. F6.
The New Republic. CCII, April 23, 1990, p. 26.
The New York Times. October 5, 1989, p. C22.
Newsweek. CXV, April 23, 1990, p. 73.
People Magazine. XXX, June 18, 1990, p. 13.
Rolling Stone. May 3, 1990, p. 36.
Variety. CCCXXXV, May 24, 1989, p. 26.
Village View. May 4-10, 1990, p. 10.
The Village Voice. April 24, 1990, p. 6.
The Washington Post. June 9, 1990, p. B2.

MOUNTAINS OF THE MOON

Production: Daniel Melnick; released by Tri-Star Pictures
Direction: Bob Rafelson
Screenplay: William Harrison and Bob Rafelson; based on the biographical novel
　　Burton and Speke, by Harrison, and on original journals by Richard Burton and
　　John Hanning Speke
Cinematography: Roger Deakins
Editing: Thom Noble
Production design: Norman Reynolds
Art direction: Maurice Fowler and Fred Hole
Set decoration: Harry Cordwell
Special effects: David Harris
Sound: Simon Kaye
Makeup: Christine Beveridge
Costume design: Jenny Beavan and John Bright
Choreography: Eleanor Fazan
Music: Michael Small
MPAA rating: R
Running time: 135 minutes

Principal characters:
Richard Burton	Patrick Bergin
John Hanning Speke	Iain Glen
Oliphant	Richard E. Grant
Isabel	Fiona Shaw
Lord Murchison	John Savident
Lord Oliphant	James Villiers
Edward	Adrian Rawlins
Lord Houghton	Peter Vaughan
Sidi Bombay	Paul Onsongo
Ngola	Bheki Tonto Ngema
Mabruki	Delroy Lindo

Those familiar with Irish explorer Richard Burton, and, especially, his 1850's expeditions into Africa with John Hanning Speke to search for the true source of the River Nile, have always proclaimed that the characters and their journey are the stuff of which epic cinema is made. *Mountains of the Moon*—an amazingly belated first attempt to tell this story as a theatrical feature (it did provide the basis for a 1971 television docudrama, *In Search of the Nile*)—confirms that view. The characters and events may derive from history, but they have a larger-than-life quality of a kind that at least suggests the magic of big-screen adventure in the classical era of cinema.

It is possible, though—as much as this film evokes that bigger-than-life spirit of adventure—to wish it had been made in that earlier era, when Errol Flynn might have incarnated Burton and Douglas Fairbanks, Jr., could have played Speke. The present actors are fine, just as the screenplay and direction are intelligent; yet while many details in the production are more authentic than they would have been in the 1930's, 1940's, and 1950's—and very appealingly so—and while an earlier film would probably have been more fanciful about history, the present work is afflicted with problems partly attributable to its own era. In emphasizing the darker aspects of the Burton-Speke relationship—including the subtext of an unexpressed homosexual relationship between the two men that director and cowriter Bob Rafelson might have created—and views of society's support and recognition of venturous exploration that are dispiritingly cynical, the film sadly forsakes what is implicit in both its genre and its specific historical action: a vision of the quest as a beautiful and ennobling experience.

If the film lacks true sweep and grandeur, though, at least its narrative does have density and scope. It begins in 1854, when Burton (Patrick Bergin), already on an expedition to search for the mouth of the Nile though also interested in many other aspects of African culture and geography, meets Speke (Iain Glen). While the Irish Burton is a rugged adventurer—not only an explorer but also a geologist, botanist, and collector and translator of erotica, among other things—Speke is a reserved aristocrat, interested in guns and hunting but otherwise drifting through life. So different, the two men nevertheless feel an instinctive connection and venture into central Africa together to look for the fabled "mountains of the moon," where the source of the Nile is believed to be.

This first expedition is a disaster, dismantled by a violent native attack that grievously wounds both Burton and Speke. Separated, they do both survive and find their way back to England, where Burton meets and falls in love with the free-spirited Isabel (Fiona Shaw) and eventually marries her, while Speke temporarily settles into life at the family manor. In 1857, backed by Lord Houghton (Peter Vaughan), Burton is able to mount another African expedition, and Speke once again joins him, this time with a self-interested friend, Oliphant (Richard E. Grant), determined that the Royal Geographical Society will accord at least equal recognition to the English Speke as to the Irish Burton no matter what the outcome of the quest.

This second journey is a very eventful one and shows the explorers interacting with various tribes as they traverse the landscape, guided by the resourceful Sidi Bombay (Paul Onsongo). They come to one lake but doubt it is the Nile's true source and move on. In the meantime, Speke helps to nurse Burton through a serious illness at one juncture, and on another occasion Burton saves the life of another native, Mabruki (Delroy Lindo), who becomes devoted to him and later aids him in key ways. The most harrowing ordeal endured by the Burton-Speke group finds them held captive by the brutal Ngola (Bheki Tonto Ngema). Seeing his violent ways with his own people, they fear for their lives but eventually arrive at an uneasy understanding with him after Speke gives him a small firearm. In better health than Burton, Speke is allowed to go on with a small group including Sidi Bombay, and he finds another, much larger lake, which he names Lake Victoria and which he is certain is the Nile's source. Burton, whom he rejoins afterward, never sees it, insisting that they head back to the coast.

Upon the return of the two men to England, dissension is cleverly created between them, largely through the lies and machinations of Oliphant (who seems to be overtly jealous of Speke's closeness to Burton). The Royal Geographical Society prepares to hear the two men debate their findings—Speke is adamant that Lake Victoria, which he discovered, was the object of their search, while Burton, much the more-practiced and knowledgeable explorer of the two, vigorously disputes that claim—but Speke tragically shoots himself while hunting, either accidentally or by deliberation, and dies. Sadly, the misunderstandings that breached the friendship and caused Speke to set out to discredit the reputation of his mentor are never given a chance to be mended, while, ironically, a footnote informs the viewer that later it was proven by others that Speke was right—Lake Victoria is the true source of the Nile.

Much of *Mountains of the Moon* was filmed on location, with production designer Norman Reynolds doing a superb job of erasing the traces of a century's progress and re-creating nineteenth century African life in a way that imposes its own subtle sense of immediate reality rather than a well-researched past. Taking care to preserve this illusion, director Rafelson and cinematographer Roger Deakins record the action mostly in muted, somber images, which not only discourage the viewer from experiencing the film as excessively gaudy or exotic but also create a severe emotional distance from the unfolding story. There is considerable action in the eventful narrative, but in proportion to it the film does not register as physically exciting. Perhaps as valuable as documentary detail, which does add much to an adventure film, is a bit of the unreality of legend or a talespinner's account of things. One film that comes to mind in this context is the 1950 version of *King Solomon's Mines*, which is not a great dramatic work and certainly not a subtle one but which is still, in its way, the model for the filmed-in-Africa adventure, simply because its neatly contrived romanticism, matinee-style action, and exploitation of colorful imagery are so well integrated with a location reality no less vivid and imposing than that of *Mountains of the Moon*.

Given these limitations, the film stands to gain most through a presentation of compelling characters and a complex relationship, the basis of which are undeniably there in the raw material; the same problem prevails, however, as Rafelson grimly holds both heroes within a circumscribed vision that reflects more fascination with their psychological makeup (though only in terms that would be of particular interest to a contemporary sensibility) than with any visionary attributes, heroic stature, or even—in the pure form celebrated by a classical director such as Raoul Walsh—glory-seeking. When Burton is delirious with fever, Speke kisses him on the mouth. In the context of the real story, this kiss could have actually happened and been the kiss of a heterosexual trying to warm his friend back to life. Homosexuality would not diminish either figure—as a comparison with *Lawrence of Arabia* (1962) and that film's presentation of its mysterious real-life protagonist attests—but when it is so vague and speculative as it is throughout *Mountains of the Moon*, it is simply dull and can only diminish the protagonists. By his own account, Rafelson shares many of Burton's specific interests and has the same heart of the explorer, and so it is mystifying why that particular kind of energy and spirit are made an essential part of the narrative, with some bearing on virtually every bit of character interplay, without ever really being artistically celebrated.

Somehow the real force that drives Rafelson, in both his style and sensibility, registers as a deep-rooted belief that restlessness of spirit (which other of his characters have also possessed, like the protagonist of his famous 1970 film *Five Easy Pieces*) is bound to be ultimately disappointed by experience. It is interesting to note that he could respond this way to a historical adventure so fabulous as the one treated here and one that may still be regarded as impressively courageous, mature, and purposeful. Rafelson moves through most scenes quickly and cursorily, with an editing style that consistently keeps his shots brief without imbuing them with the vitality they lack. The film is long and episodic but always curiously underdeveloped, without expansiveness but equally without an appreciation of the intimate side of its story. Possessing neither a compelling introversion to draw the viewer in, nor a *Lawrence of Arabia*-like awe of the page of history it illuminates, it finally registers as a lucid and coherent but very restricted and uninspiring adventure film. Its greatest virtue may be simply that it teaches something about the marvelous Burton-Speke journey to those who had no previous knowledge of it, with allowances being made for the inevitable coloring of the presentation of the facts.

Rafelson does not appear to be a very interesting or impressive filmmaker in the face of this material, yet this would probably be true of most of his contemporaries as well; as a group, they are perhaps too self-conscious and too attuned to modern angst to grasp properly a subject such as this one. No doubt, *Mountains of the Moon* would have fared well in the hands of a classical director such as *Lawrence of Arabia*'s David Lean or the aforementioned Raoul Walsh. Based on most of his work, Nicholas Ray would have perfectly balanced the neurotic and heroic aspects of both protagonists, while creating a richly dramatic relationship between them and also appreciating and delineating the cultural detail of the background in a near-documentary manner—as, for example, in *Wind Across the Everglades* (1958) or *The Savage Innocents* (1959). Perhaps the perfect director for this story, though, would have been Henry Hathaway, for if his appreciation of Africa in *The Last Safari* (1967) as a magnificent culture inevitably suffering a gradual erosion seems enlightened and his hero (Stewart Granger) a melancholy figure, no less moving and true are his beliefs that the landscape of adventure always remains beautiful and that the adventurer is a giver both to his own spirit and to the world.

Blake Lucas

Reviews
Chicago Tribune. March 23, 1990, VII, p. 46.

The Christian Science Monitor. February 28, 1990, p. 15.
Films in Review. XLI, August, 1990, p. 427.
Los Angeles Times. February 23, 1990, p. F1.
New York Magazine. March 5, 1990, p. 66.
The New York Times. February 23, 1990, p. C12.
The New Yorker. LXVI, March 12, 1990, p. 72.
Newsweek. CXV, February 26, 1990, p. 65.
Sight and Sound. LIX, Spring, 1990, p. 134.
Variety. CCCXXXVIII, January 31, 1990, p. 31.
The Washington Post. March 23, 1990, p. D6.

MY TWENTIETH CENTURY

Origin: Hungary
Released: 1989
Released in U.S.: 1990
Production: Gabor Hanak and Norbert Friedlander for Budapest Film-Studio/
Mafilm, Friedlander Filmproduktion/Hamburger Film Büro, and I.C.A.I.C.
Direction: Ildikó Enyedi
Screenplay: Ildikó Enyedi
Cinematography: Tibor Mathe
Editing: Maria Rigo
Production design: Zoltan Labas
Music: Laszlo Vidovszky
MPAA rating: no listing
Running time: 100 minutes

Principal characters:

Dora/Lili/Mother	Dorotha Segda
Z	Oleg Jankowski
Thomas Edison	Peter Andorai
X	Gabor Mate

My Twentieth Century marks the feature film debut of Hungarian writer/director Ildikó Enyedi, who received the 1989 Camera d'Or at the Cannes Film Festival. Set on the eve of the twentieth century, the film is a comical exploration of changes—both social and technological—that marked the world's passage from one century to the next, and the often chaotic effect they have had on human life in the modern age.

Although Enyedi's story takes the form of a jumble of set pieces and vignettes, it is held together by its central focus on the lives of twin sisters, Dora and Lili (both played by Dorotha Segda), born in Hungary in 1880. The film opens, however, in Menlo Park, New Jersey, where Thomas Edison (Peter Andorai) is staging a demonstration of the telegraph, complete with a marching band wearing lightbulb-bedecked helmets. As the father of modern technology readies his latest invention, the mother (also played by Segda) of Dora and Lili is giving birth in Budapest. The twins are soon orphaned and are next seen several years later as street urchins, selling matches on a snowy Christmas Eve. In a life-altering twist of fate, each is carried away into the night by a different man.

The story resumes on New Year's Eve, 1900, aboard the Orient Express. In another twist of fate—always a crucial part of any identical twin story—both sisters are traveling on the train, Dora in first class and Lili in third. The difference in their accommodations is symbolic of the divergent courses that their lives have taken: Dora has become a con artist and seductress, using her charms to earn her keep and maintain her luxurious life-style, while Lili is an earnest—and virginal—political revolutionary, toting carrier pigeons, pamphlets, and a bomb on board the train. Although the sisters themselves do not meet on the journey, both encounter and are wooed by a mysterious stranger, Z (Oleg Jankowski), who mistakenly believes that the two are the same woman. Puzzled by the marked contrasts in their behavior from meeting to meeting, he nevertheless pursues the pair as they, in turn, follow their own destinies. For Dora, this involves the seduction of a number of men, sometimes for pleasure but more often with an eye to financial gain. Lili's plans, on the other hand, include political assignations, suffragette meetings, and the assassination of a government minister.

Interspersed with the sisters' stories are a series of vignettes connected only by their ties to the monumental changes that will shape the new century. Edison makes periodic appearances, a chimpanzee in a zoo relates the story of his capture by the "strange animal"—man—that he mistakenly approaches, and a dog, the subject of a laboratory experiment, finally breaks free of his confinement, experiences the world outside the lab for the first time, and lies down in the path of the oncoming Orient Express. There are also a pair of astral voices who offer sympathetic commentary on the plights of the films' characters, human and otherwise.

As their story unfolds, it becomes clear that Dora and Lili have come to represent the conflicting roles of women in the twentieth century, struggling to strike a balance between body and soul, sexuality and intellect, and feminine role playing and independence. When the pair are at last reunited, in a funhouse hall of mirrors, they find reflected in their identical images the complex qualities that make up the total character of a modern woman.

My Twentieth Century is an impressive directorial debut for Enyedi. Released to wide critical acclaim, the film shows a distinct visual style that makes full use of its black and white cinematography. Enyedi's decision to film in black and white, evoking memories of silent films and early newsreel footage, provides her story with a visual link to its theme of the twentieth century as the age of invention—Edison was also the inventor of the film camera. Edison's light bulb also plays an important role in the film, illuminating some scenes brilliantly and leaving others in shadow and darkness. Behind the film's fascination with early technology, however, is Enyedi's message that it has failed to emerge as the socially transforming force that its enthusiasts once promised. Originally viewed by many as capable of bringing society both literally and metaphorically from darkness into light, technology has in many ways, according to Enyedi, plunged society still further into chaos. The same is also true of the political and social changes—women's suffrage, revolutions—that arrived alongside the new age's many scientific advances.

Women, in particular, are seen in the film as victims of the profound changes that the new century is bringing. In its portraits of Dora and Lili, the film addresses the schism that modern women face in a society that thrusts them forward as newly independent social equals while demanding the preservation of traditional feminine charms and seductive beauty. In Lili, the dedicated revolutionary, one finds the image of women taking their place in the front ranks of history, no longer relegated to a supporting role. Yet when the crucial moment arrives, Lili finds herself unable to throw her bomb at the minister: She has looked into his eyes and made a human connection that arouses the tenderness that she has tried to suppress.

Dora, too, has lost sight of her feelings in her role as a courtesan. As the embodiment of female sexuality, she has learned to trade on her charms, holding her emotions at a distance in most of her relationships with men. This estrangement, represented symbolically by the sisters' physical separation, is an outgrowth of lives forced into roles and patterns by social pressures and expectations—a familiar problem for many women and one not solved by simply replacing one set of outside expectations with another. If women are to come into their own, Enyedi argues, they must unite all aspects of their character, rejecting preset roles and allowing individual complexity to have its voice.

A onetime philosophy student who abandoned the field because she disagreed with the manner in which it was taught, Enyedi went on to study at Budapest's film academy. Her love of filmmaking and film history is apparent throughout her feature debut; observant viewers will spot references to Orson Welles and Jean Renoir, among others, throughout the film. While such filmic quotes are frequent in the work of young directors, they seem particularly appropriate here—in a film concerned with the failed dream of technology—as a tribute to those directors who took technology and transformed it into an art. Enyedi made several experimental short films before beginning *My Twentieth Century*, and her nontraditional roots show in the film's sometimes chaotic structure and its inclusion of set pieces that are unrelated to the central story. It was on this aspect of its style that the film drew its weakest reviews, with several critics arguing that the sometimes arbitrary nature of modern life does not translate well as a method of filmmaking. The same is also true for the film's whimsical humor, which struck some critics as witty and others as tiresome and self-conscious. Technically, however, the film drew almost universal praise, with its cinematography and lighting singled out for special comment.

Segda is an engaging actress, and she handles all three of her roles well. Among the supporting actors, Andorai in the role of Edison may prove something of a surprise to English-speaking audiences—this Edison speaks only in Hungarian. Some of the film's most enjoyable performances are given by its nonhuman actors: the chimpanzee, the dog, the cat that is present at the twins' birth, and the donkey that is mysteriously present at both their separation and their eventual reunion.

My Twentieth Century is an ambitious film that undertakes a vast and complicated subject. How well one thinks that it succeeds will differ from viewer to viewer, but it is clear that Enyedi is a director with an intriguing style, a strong personal voice, and an encouraging willingness to tackle complex issues.

Janet Lorenz

Reviews

Chicago Tribune. February 1, 1991, V, p. 37.
The Christian Science Monitor. November 16, 1990, p. 12.
Los Angeles Reader. October 20, 1989, p. 20.
Los Angeles Times. November 23, 1990, p. F16.
Los Angeles Weekly. November 23, 1990, p. 29.
The Nation. CCLI, December 10, 1990, p. 742.
The New Republic. CCIII, December 3, 1990, p. 26.
The New York Times. November 9, 1990, p. C10.
Variety. CCCXXXIV, February 22, 1989, p. 257.
The Village Voice. XXXV, November 13, 1990, p. 86.
The Wall Street Journal. November 15, 1990, p. A16.

NARROW MARGIN

Production: Jonathan A. Zimbert for Carolco Pictures; released by Tri-Star Pictures
Direction: Peter Hyams
Screenplay: Peter Hyams; inspired by the 1952 screenplay *The Narrow Margin*, by
 Earl Fenton, from a story by Martin Goldsmith and Jack Leonard
Cinematography: Peter Hyams
Editing: James Mitchell
Production design: Joel Schiller
Art direction: David Willson, Kim Mooney, and Eric Orbom
Set decoration: Kim MacKenzie
Special effects: Stan Park
Sound: Ralph Parker
Stunt coordination: Glenn Wilder
Music: Bruce Broughton
MPAA rating: R
Running time: 97 minutes

> *Principal characters:*
> Robert Caulfield .... Gene Hackman
> Carol Hunnicut .... Anne Archer
> Nelson .... James B. Sikking
> Michael Tarlow .... J. T. Walsh
> Sergeant Dominick Benti .... M. Emmett Walsh
> Kathryn Weller .... Susan Hogan
> Jack Wootton .... Nigel Bennett
> Martin Larner .... J. A. Preston
> Leo Watts .... Harris Yulin

Film remakes are dangerous undertakings. Unless a remake can enhance, give
substance to, or somehow avoid the blatant weaknesses of the original, there is little
point in remaking a successful film. To remake a film that is already regarded as a
classic is to risk alienating the audience already familiar with the original. Some of
the greatest films made, however, are remakes. John Huston's *The Maltese Falcon*
(1941) was the third filmed treatment of Dashiell Hammett's hard-boiled detective
novel and is considered the definitive version. Howard Hawks's *His Girl Friday*
(1940) is considered the best cinematic version of Ben Hecht and Charles Mac-
Arthur's play *The Front Page* (1928), which had been filmed once previously in 1931
and has been remade twice since (1974, and 1988 as *Switching Channels*). The reaction to certain remakes, however, can be so hostile that careers are noticeably damaged. Dino De Laurentiis' disastrous, big-budgeted remakes of *King Kong* (1976)
and *Hurricane* (1979) signalled the beginning of the end for his production company.
 One of the most common mistakes filmmakers commit when attempting a remake

is to take a modestly-budgeted B-film original and create a lavishly produced extravaganza with top-name stars and flashy technical effects which tend to distract from the original charm and effectiveness of the story. Director Peter Hyams' *Narrow Margin,* a remake of the classic 1952 B-film *film noir The Narrow Margin,* is an example of just such a film.

Carol Hunnicut (Anne Archer), on a friend's recommendation, agrees to a blind date with Michael Tarlow (J. T. Walsh). The two meet for dinner at his hotel where he is staying while on a business trip. When Michael tells Carol that he has to make an important phone call from his hotel room, she follows him and freshens up in the bathroom while he makes his call. While she is still in the bathroom, Michael receives an unexpected visitor: mob boss, Leo Watts (Harris Yulin). Unknown to Carol, Michael is an attorney for Leo, who has discovered that Michael has been stealing funds from his organization. As Carol watches from the shadows of the hallway, Leo orders his companion, a professional hit man, to shoot Michael. The two men then leave, oblivious to the fact that Carol has witnessed the killing.

The scene shifts to the local district attorney's office where assistant D.A. Robert Caulfield (Gene Hackman) and police sergeant Dominick Benti (M. Emmett Walsh) interrupt Caulfield's boss, chief deputy D.A. Martin Larner (J. A. Preston), with some breakthrough news on the mob killing case involving Michael. Caulfield tells Larner that the fingerprints found in Michael's hotel room have been identified as Carol Hunnicut's and that they have tracked her to a remote cabin in the Canadian Rockies. When Caulfield asks permission to bring Carol in for questioning as a possible eyewitness to the murder, Larner hesitates. Caulfield, outraged at Larner's unwillingness to pursue the lead, comes close to accusing him of protecting mob boss Leo. Caulfield and Sergeant Benti then storm out of Larner's office. Soon they are flying in a helicopter to Carol's mountain hideout.

Carol is stunned when the two men appear at her cabin door. When they tell her that they know she was present when Michael was murdered and want her to testify so they can indict Leo, she refuses to help them. As they attempt to persuade her to testify, suddenly another helicopter appears and fires at them. Sergeant Benti is killed, the police helicopter is destroyed, and Caulfield and Carol escape through the back window of the cabin. They elude the helicopter by driving Carol's car through the surrounding forest until they catch sight of a passenger train. They arrive at the train and board it just ahead of the mob hit men, who also climb aboard.

The rest of the film is a series of hide-and-seek encounters between Caulfield and the two hit men as Caulfield attempts to hide Carol from the killers. Carol is still adamant about refusing to testify, fearing that Caulfield and others like him are too incompetent to protect her from the mob. Caulfield believes that Carol is part of the mob organization, "the girlfriend of a mob attorney," and is startled when Carol tells him that she met Michael for the first time on the evening he was killed and that the main reason for her unwillingness to testify is her young son from a previous marriage. She is fearful that the mob will find him and kill him.

Caulfield eventually meets with the main hit man, Nelson (James B. Sikking), who tells Caulfield that the mob will pay him to "look the other way" while they kill Carol. Caulfield refuses their offer and the cat-and-mouse games continue. Caulfield is befriended by an attractive woman, Kathryn Weller (Susan Hogan), who becomes so affectionate with him that Caulfield fears the hit men have mistaken her for Carol. He forces Kathryn into the cabin of the train's security officer for protection, then decides to risk hiding Carol in the security officer's cabin as well. Having lost his gun in one of the encounters with the hit men, he borrows a realistic-looking squirt gun from a young boy and prepares for a final confrontation. Using the squirt gun, he is able to disarm one of the hit men and, during a struggle with the man, pushes him off the train. In the film's finale, Caulfield and Carol have fled to the top of the train trying to elude Nelson. Caulfield and Nelson struggle until Caulfield is able to throw Nelson off the train. Kathryn suddenly appears armed with a gun, however, and reveals herself as one of Nelson's accomplices. As she prepares to shoot the two of them, the train approaches a tunnel and Kathryn dies along with her would-be assassins. The final moments of the film take place in a courtroom as Caulfield prosecutes Leo, with Carol testifying as Leo squirms in his chair.

Narrow Margin fails to generate significant interest for various reasons. For one, the action holds far too few surprises. The most effective scene occurs early in the film when Caulfield attempts to persuade Carol to testify and they are suddenly ambushed by the hit men. The scene is shocking, completely unexpected, and exciting as the cabin is inundated by sudden violent explosions and machine-gun fire. After this promising beginning, however, the cat-and-mouse shenanigans on the train are far too predictable and the film is unable to recapture that same level of suspense or excitement. Director/screenwriter Hyams uses key plot twists from the 1952 original, most significantly the relationship that develops between Caulfield and Kathryn. This plot angle adds interest to the film because Kathryn is a genuinely sympathetic character; however, when she is unmasked as an accomplice to the hit men, the shock of this final and sudden twist is not enough to justify sacrificing the sympathy already established for her character. The scene plays as a cheap trick rather than as a startling revelation.

Another fatal flaw of the film is the handling of Carol's character. She should be central to the action of the film, but is instead a very peripheral, almost nonexistent personality. Her main function for most of the film is to hide from the hit men and to ridicule Caulfield's attempts to protect her which, given the situation she is in, seems ludicrous. Her one important scene, in which she tells Caulfield that she is not the girlfriend of a mob attorney, loses much of its drama because the audience already knows this about her.

Gene Hackman's portrayal of Caulfield is the strongest asset of the film. Because of his quirky and humorous attitude in the face of life-threatening encounters and his genuine concern for the safety of both Carol and Kathryn, he is able to breathe life into his character. One of the most effective scenes of the film occurs when he confronts one of the hit men with a squirt gun and, after fooling him and gaining control of his gun, playfully cries out, "Ha-ha! Toy gun!" and squirts the man in the face. It is an outrageous moment and works surprisingly well because of Hackman's ability to play both serious and comic roles with great conviction and expertise. Given the other problems of weak plotting and characterizations, however, Hackman alone cannot save the film from mediocrity.

The main problem with the film is one common with remakes: What was successful as a modestly budgeted B-film thriller from the 1950's does not translate well when revamped as a big-budgeted A-film with elaborately staged action sequences and big-name stars. The audience's expectations and their acceptance level for wild plot twists and acting expertise are likely to be more tolerant for B-films from the past than for the more realistic, expensive, and technically sophisticated motion pictures of today.

Director Hyams has done well in the past with suspense films set in claustrophobic environments. Both *Outland* (1981), a remake of *High Noon* (1952) set in outer space, and *2010* (1984), the sequel to *2001: A Space Odyssey* (1968), benefitted from the epic treatment and technical sophistication lavished on the suspenseful, close-cramped settings. With *Narrow Margin*, however, Hyams' attempts to recapture the excitement created by the simple and unpretentious original ultimately serve to destroy rather than enhance the success of the remake.

Jim Kline

Reviews
Boston Globe. September 21, 1990, p. 44.
Chicago Tribune. September 21, 1990, VII, p. 36.
Cosmopolitan. CCIX, October, 1990, p. 52.
The Hollywood Reporter. CCCXIV, September 19, 1990, p. 10.
Los Angeles Times. September 21, 1990, p. F8.
The New York Times. September 21, 1990, p. B4.
Premiere. IV, September, 1990, p. 22.
Rolling Stone. October 4, 1990, p. 50.
USA Today. September 21, 1990, p. D6.
Variety. September 17, 1990, p. 2.
The Washington Post. September 21, 1990, p. B7.

THE NASTY GIRL

Origin: Germany
Released: 1989
Released in U.S.: 1990
Production: Michael Verhoeven for Sentana Produktion; released by Miramax
   Films
Direction: Michael Verhoeven
Screenplay: Michael Verhoeven
Cinematography: Axel de Roche
Editing: Barbara Hennings
Production design: Hubert Popp
Special effects: Heinz Ludwig
Sound: Haymo H. Heyder
Makeup: Helga Sander and Cordula Aspoc
Costume design: Ute Truthmann
Music: Mike Herting and Elmar Schloter
MPAA rating: PG-13
Running time: 95 minutes

> *Principal characters:*
> Sonja .... Lena Stolze
> Mother .... Monika Baumgartner
> Father .... Michael Gahr
> Uncle .... Fred Stillkrauth
> Grandmother .... Elisabeth Bertram
> Martin .... Robert Giggenbach
> Professor Juckenack .... Hans-Reinhard Müller
> Fraulein Juckenack .... Barbara Gallauner

It has been said that curiosity killed the cat. It almost killed Anja Elisabeth Rosmus as well. A typical schoolgirl from the typical German town of Passau, Rosmus had hoped to win an essay contest. With complete confidence in the official version of Passau's role (or lack thereof) in the Nazi persecution of Jews before, during, and after World War II, Rosmus endeavored to interview those of her neighbors who claimed to have been resistance fighters. She found that many did not play the noble roles they had claimed, but were in fact personally responsible for turning vulnerable townspeople over to the Nazis.

Apparently writer and director Michael Verhoeven also was curious. He has made two projects based on this story: a 1990 television documentary about Rosmus entitled, *The Girl and the City: Or, What Really Happened?*, and the slightly fictionalized black comedy, *The Nasty Girl. The Nasty Girl* alternates between a documentary style and conventional scenes which are initially in black and white to depict the past, with color gradually added to indicate the passing of time.

In a characterization that Rosmus herself calls "fairly accurate," Verhoeven introduces Sonja Rosenberger-Wegmus (Lena Stolze). She appears in front of a wall bearing graffiti that is the film's thesis: "Where were you from 1939-1945? Where are you now?" Sonja holds a microphone and speaks to the camera, proudly admitting that though she was known as a troublemaker even while in her mother's womb, no one could have expected the difficulty she would eventually bring to herself and her family.

Sonja's parents (Monika Baumgartner and Michael Gahr) were teachers in the religious school system of their town, Pfilzig. While pregnant, Sonja's mother is barred from teaching for fear that her presence will make the children ask improper questions. Even so, the school remained a large part of the Rosenbergers' lives. Sonja's uncle (Fred Stillkrauth), a respected priest living on seminary grounds, took the family in when they were unable to find housing. While Frau Rosenberger tends Sonja and eventually a son and another daughter in their garden beneath the windows of her husband's classroom, the seminary students struggle to catch a glimpse of the teacher's wife in her morning robe which she can never manage to keep buttoned.

While the students' corruption is amusing and forgivable, that of the adults is less so. The teaching nuns routinely alter grades and offer the answers to final exam questions for those students whose parents contribute to the church. Though Sonja's parents cannot afford to give generously, the sisters include Sonja out of respect for her uncle. The fact that Sonja is intelligent and can answer the questions even without help only makes her more endearing to them. One teacher in particular, Fraulein Juckenack (Barbara Gallauner), likes Sonja very much.

One day, Fraulein Juckenack rushes excitedly into the Rosenberger home with good news. She has entered Sonja in an essay contest. The topic is to be "Freedom in Europe," one that Fraulein Juckenack considers "very commendable." Sonja wins the contest and prepares for the trip to Paris that is her reward. She is bid a reluctant farewell by the new student teacher from Munich, Martin Wegmus (Robert Giggenbach). Martin had been attracted to Sonja from the first day he taught her giggling teenage class. Though Sonja is the soul of propriety in school and at home, she has feelings for Martin too. Visiting the Tree of Mercy, once a gallows and now a wishing well for the children of Pfilzig, Sonja places a photograph of Martin in the tree and prays for him to love her. On the day before her departure, he finds her there, sees the picture, and passionately kisses her. After Sonja awakes from her faint, Martin informs her that they are now engaged.

During her tour of Paris, Sonja meets the other winners of the contest, students from other countries in Europe. Her difficulty in explaining the political status of her homeland, the differences between democratic West Germany and the German Democratic Republic, is overwhelming. She is more interested in sightseeing, flirting with the male students, and shopping for a wedding dress. When she and Martin meet again, it is he who faints from the passion and surprise of her kiss.

Upon her return, Sonja's success is noted in the local newspaper. In a formal ceremony, she is presented with a medal. Her doctor tells her that had he known how famous she would be, he would have preserved her appendix in alcohol. Sonja thanks Fraulein Juckenack, to whom she feels she owes her success. When the Fraulein presents her with another essay contest, Sonja leaps at the opportunity. This time her topic will be, "My Hometown in the Third Reich," and this time she will not be so celebrated for her efforts.

Sonja will spend the next ten years trying to complete the research for that essay. Despite her valiant struggle to prove the citizens of Pfilzig heroic, and her own initial disbelief in the guilt of her neighbors, Sonja discovers information indicting residents of Pfilzig. A newspaper article from 1934 reports a scandal in which two clergymen denounced a Jewish businessman, supposedly for cheating the church in the sale of a large order of underwear. The names of the businessman and of the two priests are not mentioned in the article. Sonja inquires of neighbors who lived in Pfilzig at the time, but no one can seem to remember, and they express anger at Sonja for digging up the past. Professor Juckenack (Hans-Reinhard Müller), the brother of Sonja's beloved teacher, is also the editor-in-chief of the local newspaper and controls access to the newspaper's records. As he becomes more secretive, Sonja becomes more intrigued. The townspeople become enraged, and even Fraulein Juckenack tries to silence Sonja. She tells Sonja that study is "very commendable" as long as one does not "poke around in the wrong things."

The contest deadline comes and goes. Sonja marries Martin and bears two children. Still, she cannot suppress her need to know the truth about Pfilzig. Against Martin's wishes, Sonja enrolls in the university and continues to investigate Pfilzig. The higher Sonja searches for information, the more vehemently she is denied access. Sonja repeatedly outwits the city officials who withhold the needed records, and eventually she sues the city for access. When Sonja enlists the aid of local television news crews to intimidate those who would shut her out, she is again brought to the attention of the town, including the surviving relatives of those suspected of committing war crimes and the neo-Nazis that still honor those criminals.

Sonja begins to receive anonymous threats. Sonja and her family listen to one call after another on the answering machine, picking up the phone only when they recognize the voice of Fraulein Juckenack, who identifies herself only as a concerned friend and urges the family to pack their things and disappear. She is shocked to hear her former student respond with a sarcastic echo of her own catchphrase, "very commendable."

While Pfilzig tries to punish and silence Sonja, her books are being published all over Europe. Universities in Vienna, Sweden, and France bestow her with honorary degrees. Finally, the local university invites Sonja to lecture. Those who have made things difficult and frightening for Sonja, including Professor Juckenack, sit in the front row to remind Sonja of their promise to destroy her if she continues her exposé. Challenged to reveal the names of the clergymen she has denounced, Sonja names Professor Juckenack and, regrettably, Father Brummel, who had played the organ at her wedding. Sonja is attacked in what would have become a riot if not for an old man who speaks up to confirm Sonja's accusation.

Shocked that someone with the required knowledge is on her side, Sonja meets with the old man at his shack. He explains that he was put in a concentration camp for being a Communist and is himself trying to bring local offenders to justice. Despite an attack on the two as they confer, the man agrees to testify at a trial brought against Sonja by Professor Juckenack for defamation of character. Almost magically, and certainly illogically, the trial is dismissed because the judge has fallen from a tree while picking pears. Suddenly, Sonja is once more a celebrity. In this second celebration of her work, Sonja is presented with a bust of herself that is to be placed in the town hall. It occurs to her, however, that she is not being honored but further suppressed. Accusing the town's officials of trying to force her into a position of gratitude because they are afraid she will find more discrediting information, Sonja begins to scream and becomes violent. Grabbing her youngest child, she runs from the hall and hides in the Mercy Tree that she visited and prayed to as a child.

The viewer is left to wonder how and when Sonja will ever come down from that tree. Perhaps this is Michael Verhoeven's device to necessitate a sequel. At best it inspires a small taste of the curiosity that drove Sonja, and Anja, to find their answers.

Eleah Horwitz

Reviews

American Film: Magazine of the Film and Television Arts. XV, December, 1990, p. 48.
The Christian Science Monitor. October 25, 1990, p. 14.
The Hollywood Reporter. CCCXIV, August 29, 1990, p. 5.
Los Angeles Times. November 11, 1990, p. F11.
The New Republic. CCIII, November 26, 1990, p. 28.
The New York Times. October 7, 1990, CXL, p. 23.
Time. CXXXVI, October 29, 1990, p. 115.
Variety. CCCXXXVIII, March 7, 1990, p. 24.
*Variety..*CCIX, November 2, 1990, p. 2.
Village View. November 2-8, 1990, V, p. 11.
The Wall Street Journal. November 15, 1990, p. A16.
The Washington Post. December 7, 1990, p. D1.

PACIFIC HEIGHTS

Production: Scott Rudin and William Sackheim for Morgan Creek; released by
    Twentieth Century-Fox
Direction: John Schlesinger
Screenplay: Daniel Pyne
Cinematography: Amir Mokri
Editing: Mark Warner
Production design: Neil Spisak
Art direction: Gershon Ginsburg and Sharon Seymour
Set decoration: Clay A. Griffith and Debra Shutt
Costume design: Ann Roth and Bridget Kelly
Music: Hans Zimmer
MPAA rating: R
Running time: 102 minutes

Principal characters:
Patty Palmer	Melanie Griffith
Drake Goodman	Matthew Modine
Carter Hayes	Michael Keaton
Toshio Watanabe	Mako
Mira Watanabe	Nobu McCarthy
Stephanie MacDonald	Laurie Metcalf
Lou Baker	Carl Lumbly
Dennis Reed	Dorian Harewood
Greg	Luca Bercovici
Florence Peters	Tippi Hedren
Liz Hamilton	Sheila McCarthy

Not since *The Grapes of Wrath* (1940) has eviction been a central issue in a motion picture. John Schlesinger's *Pacific Heights* tells the story of a couple trying to evict a nonpaying tenant, but in this film audience sympathy is for the landlords, not the tenant. Loosely based on screenwriter Daniel Pyne's legal battle to evict a bad tenant, *Pacific Heights* takes the experience to the edge of believability.

Michael Keaton's portrayal of sociopathic Carter Hayes, the "tenant from hell," provides a menacing contrast to the naïve sincerity of Patty Palmer (Melanie Griffith) and Drake Goodman (Matthew Modine). The relatively innocent couple have combined all their savings to renovate and rent downstairs apartments in a Victorian house in Pacific Heights. By creating this tense encounter between a con artist and an upwardly mobile middle-class couple, Schlesinger explores psychological, social, and ethical issues. He effectively uses sets, props, colors, lighting, and casting to weave a symbolic web of the characters' entrapment in an evil game. While the villain ultimately loses, the film's closure suggests that the protagonists have also lost something—their naïve belief in society's ability to protect the innocent.

With the opening shots of windmills in the dry, white mountains of Southern California, Hans Zimmer's brooding musical score establishes a mood of foreboding. The scene shifts to a condominium, with the camera tracking into the dark interior of a room where Hayes and a woman (Beverly D'Angelo, who is not listed in the credits) lie under white sheets, playing with ice cubes and each other. Two men burst into the room and beat Hayes, who says after their departure, "The worst part's over now," indicating that this character is accustomed to playing rough.

The action moves to sunny San Francisco, where Patty and Drake are buying a house in which they will live while renting the two downstairs apartments. Although the unmarried pair are sweet and likable, they talk about "fudging the numbers— everybody does it," a hint that they may be subject to corruption. They renovate the house, painting everything white, and the appearance of prospective tenants in colors from black to white to yellow establishes color symbolism that runs throughout the rest of the film. One very white middle-class couple brings with them their child, who runs his toy car along the walls, leaving broad black skid marks. Two young men, clad all in black, complain that the place is too "chalky"; they want to repaint in black. When an Asian couple, Toshio and Mira Watanabe (Mako and Nobu McCarthy) arrive, Patty gladly accepts them as reliable tenants with a proven credit record.

African American Lou Baker (Carl Lumbly) arrives to look at the other apartment and bristles at Patty's request for his credit record. As he leaves, however, he apologizes for suspecting her of giving him the "runaround" because of his color. In a twist of irony, it is the Asian couple who inadvertently misplace the yellow credit form Baker later leaves in the mail drop. Whether Schlesinger intended all of this color symbolism or he simply wanted to create an evenhanded ethnic mix, the film plays with and occasionally reverses traditional associations. White does not always indicate innocence, nor does black portend evil, but yellow does seem to operate as a transitional color, one that represents the exigencies of survival, from the crucial yellow credit application to the sunny yellow jeep that Drake drives to his job as the manager of Asian seamstresses making colorful kites.

Just as an underlying racial tension fuels the plot, so gender plays a role in the unfolding of events. While Patty intuitively trusts the black man and suspects Carter Hayes for lying about having talked to her, Drake is dazzled by Hayes's black Porsche and glib references to wealthy clients. As in countless suspense and horror genre films, the hero ignores the sage advice of the heroine. Drake insists on justifying his decision to give the key to Hayes, claiming that he can handle the situation himself, a phrase to be echoed and disproved throughout the remainder of the film.

When Hayes moves in without permission, Drake's masculine pride first prevents him from admitting his mistake and then drives him to commit more serious errors. He finally begins to suspect that Hayes is not all that he appears to be when a polite but firm Asian bank cashier insists that Hayes, "for his own reasons," did not have rent money transferred as he had promised. Hayes wakes the other tenants by hammering at two o'clock in the morning, and Drake discovers that he has also changed the locks. Drake then tries to outwit Hayes by turning off the heat and the electricity.

Drake soon discovers that the law in California is on the tenant's side, regardless of whether the rent is paid. When the police officer delivers this news, Drake rages in colorful epithets, insulting the police officer and reinforcing the case Hayes is carefully constructing against his landlord. Patty tries to calm Drake, but to no avail. In talking to her equestrian class, Patty makes a statement that foreshadows her relationship to both hero and villain: "Why are we the boss? Because we're smarter." For as long as Drake insists on "being the boss," the young couple loses, because Drake, for all his boyish charm, is unbelievably obtuse.

As in other works by John Schlesinger, such as *Midnight Cowboy* (1969), *Sunday, Bloody Sunday* (1971), *Marathon Man* (1976), and *The Falcon and the Snowman* (1985), *Pacific Heights* focuses on the effects of extreme pressure on a relationship. When Patty tells Drake she is pregnant he tries to act pleased, but the strains of impending bankruptcy and legal battles override his attempts to put on a happy face. The couple go to court to try to evict Hayes, but their lawyer Stephanie MacDonald, played with the right touch of martyred resignation by Laurie Metcalf, knuckles under when the judge scolds Drake for cutting off Hayes's utilities. In one of the few obtrusive shots of the film, Amir Mokri's camera circles dizzyingly around Patty in the elegant rotunda of the Los Angeles City Hall, as she realizes the hopelessness of their situation.

When Hayes unleashes his cockroach farm on the Asian couple next door, the film achieves some of its more clever touches. Unable to control the avalanche of insects with his vacuum cleaner and spray, an Orkin exterminator suggests that they get "little tiny leashes and pretend they're pets." Indulging in this kind of humor lessens the tension of the film, however, and it caused Orkin to sue for unfavorable presentation of the product that they had paid to have in the film. When Drake crawls under the floor grate, witnesses Hayes saying that "screwing people over is just a job," and quietly endures dozens of cockroaches falling on his face, the audience groans with revulsion. The notion of Hayes having a cockroach farm is, in itself, a risky choice; what the film gains in its ability to horrify the audience is offset by the humor of an insect-breeding villain.

The turning point in the film occurs when Patty miscarries and then receives flowers from Hayes, a move calculated to drive Drake over the edge. Drake knocks Hayes down the stairs and through the glass front door in time for the arrival of the police, who take Drake away, screaming, to jail. Hayes's next move is to file an injunction against Drake, forbidding him from entering his own property. Drake obligingly returns and is shot by Hayes, putting Drake in the hospital and Patty in charge of revenge. In one of the least believable scenes of the film, Patty confronts Hayes's old girlfriend and discovers that he is at a hotel in Southern California. She persuades the maid to let her into his room, where she discovers that he has stolen and falsified Drake's credit cards. After she charges lavish room service and champagne to his account, the hotel runs another credit check and discovers that the real Drake has cancelled the cards. As the manager stops Hayes in the lobby, the camera repeats its dizzying circle, only this time it is around Hayes, who has been outsmarted. Before he parts ways with Patty, Hayes returns to her house and tries to kill her; instead, he falls and impales himself on the wreckage that he had left behind.

In this penultimate scene, Hayes claims that Patty has "crossed the line," that she herself has been tainted, and the close of the film implies that this may be true. Patty has kept some of Hayes's money, and with it she and Drake re-renovate the house in order to sell it. When the buyers ask if they had not put their hearts into the building, Patty replies, "No, it was just an investment." Perhaps the couple did put their hearts into the large white edifice, and, like the building, they have been bludgeoned, blackened, and scarred underneath their smooth refinished exterior. Despite the apparently happy ending, after miscarriage, theft, and killing, Patty Palmer may have taken a bit of the villain into her own heart.

Rebecca Bell-Metereau

Reviews

Boxoffice. November, 1990, p. R82.
Chicago Tribune. September 28, 1990, VII, p. 25.
The Christian Science Monitor. October 12, 1990, p. 14.
Films in Review. XLII, January, 1991, p. 53.
The Hollywood Reporter. CCCXIV, September 21, 1990, p. 6.
Los Angeles Times. September 28, 1990, p. F4.
The New York Times. September 28, 1990, p. B3.
The New Yorker. LXVI, October 22, 1990, p. 104.
Newsweek. CXVI, October 1, 1990, p. 70.
People Weekly. October 8, 1990, p. 12.
Rolling Stone. October 18, 1990, p. 49.
Variety. September 21, 1990, p. 2.
Vogue. September, 1990, p. 398.
The Washington Post. September 28, 1990, p. C7.

POSTCARDS FROM THE EDGE

Production: Mike Nichols and John Calley; released by Columbia Pictures
Direction: Mike Nichols
Screenplay: Carrie Fisher; based on her novel
Cinematography: Michael Ballhaus
Editing: Sam O'Steen
Production design: Patrizia Von Brandenstein
Art direction: Kandy Stern
Set decoration: Chris A. Butler
Sound: Stan Bochner
Costume design: Ann Roth
Music: Carly Simon
Song: Shel Silverstein (writer), Meryl Streep and Blue Rodeo (performers), "I'm Checkin' Out"
MPAA rating: R
Running time: 101 minutes

> *Principal characters:*
> Suzanne Vale .... Meryl Streep
> Doris Mann .... Shirley MacLaine
> Jack Falkner .... Dennis Quaid
> Lowell .... Gene Hackman
> Doctor Frankenthal .... Richard Dreyfuss
> Joe Pierce .... Rob Reiner
> Grandma .... Mary Wickes
> Grandpa .... Conrad Bain
> Evelyn Ames .... Annette Bening
> Aretha .... Robin Bartlett

Struggling to regain control over her life after a serious substance-abuse problem, a young actress must also finally confront her feelings of deep resentment toward her mother. *Postcards from the Edge* is an entertaining comedy of satiric wit and wry humor.

Suzanne Vale (Meryl Streep) is a cocaine-snorting, pill-popping actress with a show-stopping motion-picture star mother (Shirley MacLaine). Having spent her entire life as Doris Mann's daughter, Suzanne seems bent on self-destruction: Her quip, "Instant gratification takes too long," is typical of her driven personality. After a near-fatal overdose, Suzanne finds herself in a drug detoxification center. While Suzanne struggles through rehabilitation, Doris attempts to be supportive, which is clearly not her strong point; she is far too self-centered and needy herself to be able to give to her daughter. When she arrives late for group therapy and an ecstatic fan tells her that since he was a child he has wanted to be her, Doris pulls out the charm the way the old studios taught her. Under her breath, however, Doris mutters to Suzanne, "Sorry, but you know how much the queens love me."

As Suzanne attempts to rebuild her career, the actress learns she must move back home and live with her "responsible" mother for the duration of the shooting schedule of her film in order to be insured. Ironically, Suzanne's mother has a drinking problem, but she is still in denial and quick to point out that she only drinks "like an Irish person." Despite their mutual love and respect, mother and daughter cannot stop competing with each other. When Doris throws a welcome-home party for Suzanne following her stint in rehabilitation, Doris pressures Suzanne to sing. Suzanne hesitates, but she performs pleasantly. Then, with little cajoling and obvious forethought, Doris takes to the stage and belts out an over-the-top rendition of Stephen Sondheim's "I'm Still Here." The crowd erupts in applause, and once again Doris has succeeded in upstaging her daughter. When Doris complains that Suzanne is wasting her talent by not singing, it is not hard to understand her daughter's reluctance.

On her first day back at work, after being subjected to a drug screen, Suzanne, armed with a continuous supply of junk food, overhears the director and the costumer commenting about her overweight thighs, receives advice about the comedic delivery of lines, and is told by the producer's son that her performance thus far has displayed "low enjoyment levels." Suzanne spots a bottle of pills, but she resists the temptation to use them. Leaving the set, she runs into Jack Falkner (Dennis Quaid), the man who left her at the hospital when she attempted to overdose in his bed. At first Suzanne does not recognize him, but Jack confesses and manages to persuade Suzanne to go on a date. Before long she succumbs to his charming seduction. "I think I love you," he tells her. "When will you know for sure?" the wisecracking Suzanne quips. When she learns from a fellow actress that Jack's sincerity is questionable, Suzanne returns to confront him. Feeling precariously vulnerable, Suzanne later tells her mother: "Thank God I got sober so I could be hyperconscious for this series of humiliations."

As the tensions between the two build, Suzanne bitterly confronts her mother with the fact that Doris gave her sleeping pills when she was only nine years old. Doris defends her actions, pointing out that they were only of the over-the-counter variety and not at all harmful. Distraught, Suzanne leaves to complete some work on the last film she shot before her overdose and receives support and a much-needed shot of self-esteem from the film's director, Lowell (Gene Hackman). Later, when Doris lands in the hospital emergency room and is arrested for drunk driving, mother and daughter forge a tentative truce.

Actress Carrie Fisher's first novel, *Postcards from the Edge*, published in 1987, was a compelling account of the pain and pathos stemming from drug rehabilitation. For the film adaptation, however, Fisher and director Mike Nichols have chosen to jettison most of that material and concentrate instead on the relationship between mother and daughter. It is interesting to note that while the story's protagonist complains of being overshadowed by her egocentric mother, the screenwriter has inadvertently done the same thing to her main character. About two-thirds of the way through the film, the focus seems to shift to Doris, and once again she overshadows her daughter. This time, however, the fault is the writer's.

This film is light on plot, which may explain that empty, down feeling with which the viewer is left after the end credits roll and the euphoria of wry witticisms dissipates. (Interestingly, that feeling parallels the feelings drug users experience when the high wears off.) The film is very amusing, and it does contain some of the best performances from some top-flight actors. For those, however, who want motion pictures to tell a story, who long for a sense of closure, of resolution, *Postcards from the Edge* may be a disappointment. It starts out with clever, incisive characters and dialogue, then sputters to a virtual standstill as Suzanne calls a tentative truce with her mother. Yet because nothing has been resolved between the two characters (although they have perhaps a bit more insight into each other's pain, and Suzanne gets a much-needed ego-boost), one is hard-pressed to believe that they will not fall back into their same old modi operandi once the cameras stop rolling. What the viewer is left with, then, are character sketches and not a story (which is yet another argument against making films out of novels). As good as *Postcards from the Edge* is, it should have been better. It is filled with razor-sharp quips and amusing behind-the-scenes looks at the Hollywood film industry, past and present, but the film flounders for direction and suffers from tonal problems. Moreover, the moment the film enters the realm of melodrama, it loses all of its life, vitality, and energy and becomes another *Terms of Endearment* (1983), hospital scenes and all.

Meryl Streep hits all the right notes in her portrayal of the wise-cracking yet insecure Suzanne. She even delivers a surprisingly affecting vocal performance as she belts out a country and western tune during the film's finale. The actress has a natural talent for comedy, one that was exploited in Susan Seidelman's failed *She-Devil* (1989). It seems as though there is nothing Streep cannot do. This film may silence the critics who have complained of the actress' penchant for characters with foreign accents. Streep won her first Academy Award for Best Supporting Actress opposite Dustin Hoffman in *Kramer vs. Kramer* (1979) and another for Best Actress for her portrayal of the tormented Polish concentration camp survivor in *Sophie's Choice* (1982). For her work in *Postcards from the Edge*, she was nominated for, but did not win, an Academy Award for Best Actress.

Although thinly written, all three of the main male parts are superbly acted. Gene Hackman imbues the director, Lowell, with a complexity that combines warmth and sensitivity with the toughness it takes to survive in the film business. The sheer power of Hackman's own captivating presence leaves the viewer longing for his return throughout the story, but his is basically a cameo role with only two brief scenes. Hackman's acting style is in direct contrast to that of Dennis Quaid, who gets the opportunity once again to give a dynamic performance as the smooth-talking, womanizing film producer, although here he is a bit more restrained than in *Great Balls of Fire!* (1989). This kind of flamboyant acting suits the type of character he is portraying, who is the most vile and unscrupulous denizen of the Hollywood jungle.

It is not surprising, then, that his character, Jack Falkner, should be awarded one of the best comic lines in the film when he attempts to seduce Suzanne: "You're the realest person I've ever met in the abstract."

Postcards from the Edge is a superb title. It is also an inadvertently revealing, insightful one that summarizes the film quickly and efficiently. Postcards are moments frozen in time and space, designed to capture the feeling of a specific setting or a fleeting emotion. Seldom, if ever, do they allow the author to tell an entire story; space will not permit it. So it is with this film: Many pretty pictures leave the viewer longing for more.

Patricia Kowal

Reviews
Chicago Tribune. September 12, 1990, V, p. 1.
Commonweal. CXVII, November 9, 1990, p. 652.
Films in Review. XLII, January, 1991, p. 47.
The Hollywood Reporter. CCCIV, September 10, 1990, p. 5.
Los Angeles Magazine. Vol. 35, October 22, 1990, p. 232.
Los Angeles Times. September 12, 1990, p. F1.
The New York Times. September 12, 1990, p. B1.
The New Yorker. LXVI, October 22, 1990, p. 104.
Newsweek. CXVI, September 24, 1990, p. 70.
Rolling Stone. DLXXXVIII, October 4, 1990, p. 50.
San Francisco Examiner. September 14, 1990, CXXVI, p. C3.
Time. CXXXVI, September 17, 1990, p. 70.
Variety. CCCXL, September 10, 1990, p. 2.

PRESUMED INNOCENT

Production: Sydney Pollack and Mark Rosenberg for Mirage; released by Warner
  Bros.
Direction: Alan J. Pakula
Screenplay: Frank Pierson and Alan J. Pakula; based on the novel by Scott Turow
Cinematography: Gordon Willis
Editing: Evan Lottman
Production design: George Jenkins
Art direction: Bob Guerra
Set decoration: Carol Joffe
Sound: James Sabat
Costume design: John Boxer
Music: John Williams
MPAA rating: R
Running time: 127 minutes

> *Principal characters:*
> Rusty Sabich .... Harrison Ford
> Raymond Horgan .... Brian Dennehy
> Sandy Stern .... Raul Julia
> Barbara Sabich .... Bonnie Bedelia
> Judge Larren Lyttle .... Paul Winfield
> Carolyn Polhemus .... Greta Scacchi
> Detective Lipranzer .... John Spencer
> Tommy Molto .... Joe Grifasi
> Nico Della Guardia .... Tom Mardirosian
> "Painless" Kumagai .... Sab Shimono

  A tautly told tale based on a best-selling novel, *Presumed Innocent* was one of the
most popular summer films of 1990. Interwoven with a suspenseful mystery pro-
pelled by passionate feelings and relationships, it presents a contemporary, at times
very cynical, view of justice—felt to be credible because the author of the novel on
which it was based, Scott Turow, is an attorney. While the film is reasonably absorbing throughout, however, the double-leveled narrative, which subjects both modern
marriage and the legal system to cold-eyed scrutiny, does not make it the resonant
achievement it might be. Director Alan J. Pakula seems to enjoy the twists and turns
of the plot—some of them very contrived—and works hard with production designer George Jenkins and cinematographer Gordon Willis to give the film a drab,
forbidding texture. Beyond irony and a certain ruefulness, though, plot revelations
seem to exist here more for the sake of surprise than to create an ambivalent empathy and so to allow intimations of genuine complexity. Still, even an intriguing surface is not negligible and may be considered an artistic quality in an era of over-

blown yet empty productions.

A somber tone is established at once as the voice of the protagonist, Rusty Sabich (Harrison Ford), introduces the story in voice-over narration while the camera glides over an empty courtroom. Sabich's words are straightforward, but his tone is grim and fatalistic: The audience learns immediately that he is a prosecutor and senses that he has had a deeper, more personal experience of the workings of the law than even his profession has allowed. The past-tense story that makes up the body of the film confirms this. It begins as Rusty's boss, Raymond Horgan (Brian Dennehy), the district attorney of a large metropolitan city (Detroit locations were used, though it has been suggested that Cook County in Illinois was Turow's model), is on the verge of political defeat at the hands of Nico Della Guardia (Tom Mardirosian), an adversary who, like the more loyal Rusty, comes from the ranks of Horgan's own prosecutors. The final negative development in Horgan's hopeless campaign for reelection comes when still another of his prosecutors, Carolyn Polhemus (Greta Scacchi), is found murdered. Rusty is assigned to head the investigation, and he enlists the help of his loyal friend Detective Lipranzer (John Spencer) of the police force, but following further developments both men are dismissed. It develops that Carolyn, an attractive and ambitious young woman, had many affairs while advancing her career, one of them with the married Rusty (and another, afterward, with the recently divorced Raymond Horgan). Through strong physical evidence, Rusty becomes the prime suspect at about the time that Horgan loses the election. Della Guardia and his right-hand man Tommy Molto (Joe Grifasi), who seems to harbor unreasoning envy and resentment toward Rusty, take over the case with a view toward vigorously prosecuting it. In the meantime, Rusty's problems are compounded by the fact that he is still obsessed by Carolyn, much to the chagrin of his unhappy but still loyal wife, Barbara (Bonnie Bedelia).

Rusty hires a top defense attorney, brilliant and silkily smooth Sandy Stern (Raul Julia), and the case comes before Judge Larren Lyttle (Paul Winfield), a tough but fair jurist. Surprisingly, while there is physical evidence against Rusty—Carolyn had apparently been raped and his blood type matches—there is no direct evidence that can be presented of his earlier affair with her. Stern makes much of a missing file of a bribery case on which she had been working at the time of the murder and of a glass found at the scene of the crime with Rusty's fingerprints which also turns out to be missing. Stern dismantles the testimony of Horgan, who has turned on Rusty in the wake of his defeat, and, more vitally, the testimony of the coroner "Painless" Kumagai (Sab Shimono), who has apparently bungled the autopsy, suggesting the prosecution's willful manipulation of evidence. There are finally enough inconsistencies to warrant dismissal of the case by Judge Lyttle.

Rusty, who has proclaimed his innocence from the beginning, is relieved and ready to move on with his life but quickly learns a truth difficult for a principled man to accept. His friend Lipranzer had stolen the incriminating glass to protect him—it is clear that the detective had suspected Rusty was guilty but felt in some way that Carolyn had deserved it. This is only a prefiguration, though, of a far more challenging revelation. Rusty's wife Barbara was the actual killer—somehow she meant for Rusty to see the truth, presuming he would be leading the investigation, even while planting the evidence against him. Transfixed by Rusty's betrayal to the point of extreme psychological disturbance, she remains hopelessly bound to the husband she still loves, and who, alone with her, knows the truth. Rusty and Barbara have a young child, and as the film closes with the returning image of the still courtroom, Rusty says in his narration that this is one reason why he would not turn her in. He is plainly horrified and emotionally destroyed by the reality of her guilt, partly because of his deep belief in the law and justice, mocked by his wife's crime, but more perhaps, because his own moral lapse with Carolyn pushed Barbara to the act.

The extent to which law-and-order representatives Sabich, Horgan, Stern, Lipranzer, Della Guardia, Molto, Lyttle, and Polhemus all treat the law immorally at some point is mildly interesting to the extent that each of these individuals seems to have principles—not many, in some cases, but quite significant ones, in others. Even in the case of Rusty, though, it is mostly the possibility of his innocence—encouraged by the casting of Ford, though the audience knows this might be deliberately deceptive—which gives a feeling of ambiguity to his more expeditious decisions at the beginning and his rueful gratitude later for Lipranzer's suppression of evidence. The revelation of the latter act provides the film with one of its best moments, not because it is startling or even because it suggests Rusty is guilty after all (though he does not deny it, his reaction only seems to affirm his steady posture of innocence), but because of the nuances in the Lipranzer character: As played by John Spencer, the detective at once displays pride in his handiwork, warm friendship for Rusty that he is glad to have had the opportunity to prove, an edge of misogynistic distaste for Carolyn, and an undertone of shame and even moral disgrace that he has so unambiguously subverted his job.

On the other hand, the film is never able to penetrate any character's psyche with any depth. Symptomatic is Carolyn Polhemus: even the motives behind her affairs, which she cold-bloodedly breaks off when they are no longer useful, are obscure. Given her treatment of Rusty, it seems that she uses men to advance in her career, which makes sense. Yet the filmmakers are not content with this; they appear to believe that they must make her personally lustful as well, perhaps to exploit Scacchi's blatant appeal as a sexual fantasy figure, so the audience is treated to an overheated, artistically meaningless first sexual encounter with Rusty, in the same register as those which have dominated contemporary Hollywood thrillers since the success of *Fatal Attraction* (1987). As for Carolyn's penchant for prosecuting cases of rape, child abuse, and similarly unpleasant crimes, it is never remotely explained or connected with her own highly active and dangerous sex life. Even so, *Presumed Innocent* is not a film callous about women, as shown by the character of Barbara Sabich, to which it at least attempts to impart some depth. To the credit of Turow and the screenwriters, she is the most logical person dramatically to be Carolyn's murderer, well-motivated and with a clear idea of what she hoped to gain—the restoration of her home and marriage. The film has subtly suggested the two strands of her present relationship with her husband—psychological dependence and emotional wariness—and in the climactic confession, a single-take, medium close-up of her describing her actions and feelings runs for some time before Rusty's response is given a chance to register. Strangely, though, the account of the murder finds her suddenly becoming completely demented, a development that is perhaps plausible but one which leaves her, finally, only a figure of pathos.

Thinness of characterization where there was some chance of density makes this film anemic and insubstantial. This is unfortunate because the dark side of relationships and the consequences of infidelity are at least perceived as serious subjects here, even if *Presumed Innocent* shares some of the faults of a less thoughtful film such as *Fatal Attraction*. The themes, and those relating to the perversion of justice, too, are not at all new in cinema—a *film noir* such as *Pitfall* (1948), directed by Andre de Toth, arguably treats similar material more powerfully and subtly—but each era returns to familiar themes and moral perceptions with its own inflections. A work that engages the contemporary mood in addressing provocative issues could be profound, cathartic, and starkly forceful. *Presumed Innocent* is not it; it is a film more likely to be enjoyed and then forgotten quickly. It does not encourage analysis of its imagery, mostly gloomy, or other aspects of the direction, mostly straightforward if at least intelligent. The actors are all excellent in spite of the limitations of the roles, with Spencer a clear standout, creating more of a character than the screenplay has really suggested. It is the elegant Julia as defense attorney Stern, though, who provides the film's single most memorable moment—the lengthy pause in his courtroom interrogation of Horgan, after he has exposed the shabbiness of the other's easily undone loyalty to Rusty, when he stares at Horgan with magisterial contempt and then continues in the same gentlemanly tone with an extra edge to the words "All right."

Blake Lucas

Reviews

ABA Journal. LXXVI, August, 1990, p. 42.
Chicago Tribune. July 27, 1990, VII, p. 27.
Films in Review. XLI, November, 1990, p. 552.
The Hollywood Reporter. CCCXIII, July 23, 1990, p. 5.
Los Angeles Times. July 27, 1990, p. F1.
The New York Times. July 27, 1990, p. B1.
The New Yorker. LXVI, August 13, 1990, p. 82.
Newsweek. July 30, 1990, p. 56.
Sight and Sound. LIX, Autumn, 1990, p. 279.
Time. CXXXVI, July 30, 1990, p. 57.
Variety. July 23, 1990, p. 2.

PRETTY WOMAN

Production: Arnon Milchan and Steven Reuther for Touchstone Pictures, in
 association with Silver Screen Partners IV; released by Buena Vista
Direction: Garry Marshall
Screenplay: J. F. Lawton
Cinematography: Charles Minsky
Editing: Priscilla Nedd
Production design: Albert Brenner
Art direction: David Haber
Set decoration: Garrett Lewis
Set design: Antoinette J. Gordon
Special effects: Gary Zink
Sound: Jim Webb
Makeup: Bob Mills
Costume design: Marilyn Vance-Straker
Music: James Newton Howard
MPAA rating: R
Running time: 117 minutes

> *Principal characters:*
> Edward Lewis .... Richard Gere
> Vivian Ward .... Julia Roberts
> James Morse .... Ralph Bellamy
> Philip Stuckey .... Jason Alexander
> Kit De Luca .... Laura San Giacomo
> David Morse .... Alex Hyde-White
> Elizabeth Stuckey .... Amy Yasbeck
> Hotel manager .... Hector Elizondo
> Bridget .... Elinor Donahue

Pretty Woman is a film about voyeurism. It gambles on how much viewers will submit to falling in love with images that mirror back a grand need for wish-fulfillment:
that is, it banks on how much people on the screen substitute for the lives in the
audience. In this way the film takes as its subject the love of looking that marks any
film experience. Yet it also conflates the idea of the "look." What is seen here are
images of characters, of actors, who also seem to adore the very act of being looked
at. *Pretty Woman* is a creature of its time: It is a film that tells people that images
may be more important than what lies behind them and that looking is perhaps the
most fulfilling activity anyone can have.

In loving to look at the actors in *Pretty Woman*, by necessity viewers must understand their separateness from the audience—a fundamental operation of filmic voyeurism. Pleasure comes not only from looking at actors but also from unconsciously
accepting them as objects of desire who can never be touched. The characters' lives,

therefore, take on the quality of fairy tale. *Pretty Woman* has the romance of 1930's screwball comedies, yet the substantial characters from those films are gone; what is left is the act of looking.

In this fantasy, where nothing really goes wrong and everything turns out right, Edward Lewis (Richard Gere) is a corporate mogul who buys and sells businesses and seems to treat people as stepping-stones to more and more success. He is a divorced man nearing middle-age, and his live-in mistress has just told him she is moving out of their New York apartment. While at a party in Beverly Hills, Lewis takes the Lotus automobile of his good friend and lawyer, Philip Stuckey (Jason Alexander), and goes for a ride through the city. He passes through Hollywood and, while on the boulevard, meets Vivian Ward (Julia Roberts, who earned an Oscar nomination for her role), a prostitute who seems none-too-wise for a woman working the streets. Lewis asks her for directions, and she responds by getting into the car, a machine that she seems to know better than he does. After they arrive at the Beverly Hills Hotel, where he is staying, Lewis asks Vivian up to his room. He does not so much want her as a prostitute as much as he is intrigued by her childlike curiosity and seeming vitality for life. A jaded woman-of-the-streets she definitely is not. Rather, she embodies a quality of innocence, a kind of naïveté that attracts Lewis. He is interested in her for obvious reasons: Vivian's emotional vitality serves to accentuate the vapidness into which his emotional life has plummeted. Lewis has long since given up on expecting anything from life; instead, he does business through a psychological vacuum. He surrounds himself with expensive hotel suites, business meetings, and multimillion-dollar telephone deals. Yet through it all, he walks as if in a daydream. Nothing that he accomplishes has the feel of emotional fulfillment.

So it is that Lewis is taken with Vivian's verve for living, her found excitement in everything she encounters. After the two spend the night together, Lewis asks Vivian to stay with him for a week; he tells her that he needs a female companion to accompany him to his business and social engagements, and he will pay her for her time and company. This is strictly a business deal for both of them, yet the audience knows what will develop; it is a predictable love story in the making. This proposal also establishes the possibility of foibles to come. Vivian becomes a resident of the Beverly Hills Hotel, making herself a visual embodiment of contradiction. She dresses like a prostitute, and, as she walks in and out of the hotel lobby, she wreaks havoc on hotel employees and guests alike. Yet underneath, because she is a nymph, and because she is played by Julia Roberts, she seems a transformation waiting to happen. Lewis gives Vivian a thousand dollars with which to buy herself some new clothes befitting the job of companion she has incurred. This ploy sets off some visual sight plots that beg for the audience's voyeurism. Few people in this audience, so director Garry Marshall has presumed, could help but wish for the adventure that awaits them through watching Vivian. She roams the streets of Beverly Hills with money to burn in her pocket. She is Cinderella on the verge of having all her dreams come true: She can buy anything she wants, and she has a handsome prince awaiting her at home. In fact, though, Vivian is playing house, and her audience can jump into the fantasy along with her.

Some clinkers in this fantasy await Vivian. Because she looks like a prostitute, a store owner will not wait on her when she walks into the shop of a particular clothing store on Rodeo Drive. Vivian simply cannot get anyone to take her seriously, and so she becomes brokenhearted and returns to the hotel, humiliated and depressed. She attracts the attention of the hotel manager (Hector Elizondo), who calls a friend (a friend who happens to run another clothing store), and Vivian at last is outfitted to the hilt. Parading into the hotel after she is transformed by the simplest of things, a wardrobe, Vivian commands the respect of hotel guests and film audience alike. She has successfully climbed to the side of such a respectability that the film's narrative now takes her as seriously as the audience does. Joining Lewis for business lunches and casual parties, she becomes a desirable object for all eyes. Previously desirable only as a prostitute, she is now desirable as a woman. She thus reinforces director Marshall's strongest condemnation of her—that she is a female whose body alone delineates her availability and her self-worth in the viewer's eyes.

Now that Vivian is restored to the viewer's serious contemplation of her, she begins to teach Lewis about relationships. Because she has gained respectability, she is suddenly capable of filling the gaping emotional void in his life. Yet this is no easy task. Vivian goes along with Lewis, pretending she is with him as part of a paid venture, yet all along the two are falling in love with each other and not admitting it. It will be up to Vivian, however, because she is the female, to show Lewis how much he needs her in life after their business arrangement has ended. While much of the pleasure of looking has been focused on Vivian, Lewis also commands attention in the film. Richard Gere is a fine choice to portray a character who is a tortured soul, a man gone dry at the core. Gere can get away with looking sullen and not talking any more than necessary. In this way he is also a figure of visual pleasure for his audience. He exudes a willful confidence, and he can get the camera to love him while doing so. He is, in short, a perfect match for the visual attention commanded by Julia Roberts. He speaks with his body, through imploded insolence and demeanor, rather than with his words. *Pretty Woman* is a film where bodies are the ultimate means of expression.

As Vivian carries the weight and responsibility of emotionality in the film, it is she who must realize the growing affection between Lewis and herself. It is she who must make him realize that he cannot fully experience life except through her. So she is set up by the camera to perform visual sight gags that will allure both Lewis and the film's spectator. She commits small acts of impropriety that are intended to be endearing. She must learn not only how to dress the part of an expensive companion but also how to eat in expensive restaurants and conduct herself at social functions of the very wealthy. All this she accomplishes, and, as the plot would have it, the more she learns, the more Lewis views her through a different set of expectations.

Vivian successfully makes her transformation: Toward the film's conclusion she becomes a desirable object, not simply a female body but a female whom Lewis takes seriously. He is, however, stuck in his emotional absence, although growing out of it all the time. He realizes his emotional attachment to Vivian yet is holding fast to his bad habit: He cannot convince himself that a new relationship—a long-lasting one—would work. Vivian has certainly transformed herself; she has been the good student as it were. Yet this is not enough for Lewis, or so it would seem.

Working on the premise that the relationship between Lewis and Vivian will fail, director Marshall keeps his audience in suspense until the final minutes of *Pretty Woman*. Vivian has offered herself to Lewis as his lifelong partner, yet all Lewis can cope with is the idea of her as a mistress. When she refuses his offer, the couple separates: Lewis will fly back to New York, and Vivian will go back to her apartment in Hollywood to pack her bags, leave town, and abandon the life of prostitution in order to find a way to live that is, to her, more honest. It seems that being with Lewis has helped her to realize her potential for happiness; she believes now that she has something worthwhile to offer the world: herself. The audience cannot help but know that this type of plot device will lead only to a fairy-tale ending, and thus it does. After Lewis leaves his hotel room, he experiences a change of heart. Realizing that he loves Vivian and does not want to lose her, he finds his way to her apartment and, in spite of his fear of heights, ascends the fire escape. The two fall into each other's arms and into each other's lives.

Thus *Pretty Woman* fulfills its promise as a modern-day Cinderella fairy tale. The two characters here have been romancing each other throughout the entire scenario of the film as if operating within a self-consciously configured design that spells out the desire all spectators share: a life transformed through a series of nonthreatening, often amusing, plot devices. In this film, people are pretty, food is delicious, and room service is unbeatable. This is the stuff of filmic voyeurism. It is also the stuff of fantasy. *Pretty Woman* made a grand sweep of the box office, and this fact indicates that many people's hearts and minds lie centered in wish fulfillment. The lives of filmic characters who denote a society's communal leap into fantasy are the real stuff of voyeuristic fiction.

Marilyn Ann Moss

Reviews

Boxoffice. CXXVI, June, 1990, p. R43.
Chicago Tribune. March 23, 1990, VII, p. 43.
Films in Review. XLI, June, 1990, p. 359.
The Hollywood Reporter. CCCXI, March 19, 1990, p. 5.
Los Angeles Times. March 23, 1990, VI, p. 1.
The New York Times. March 29, 1990, p. A12.
Newsweek. CXV, March 26, 1990, p. 52.
Time. CXXXV, April 2, 1990, p. 70.
Variety. CCXXVII, March 19, 1990, p. 2.
The Wall Street Journal. March 15, 1990, p. B9.
The Washington Post. March 23, 1990, p. D1.

PUMP UP THE VOLUME

Origin: USA and Canada
Released: 1990
Released in U.S.: 1990
Production: Rupert Harvey and Sandy Stern for New Line Cinema, in association
   with SC Entertainment International; released by New Line Cinema
Direction: Allan Moyle
Screenplay: Allan Moyle
Cinematography: Walt Lloyd
Editing: Janice Hampton and Larry Bock
Production design: Robb Wilson King
Set decoration: Kathy Curtis Cahill
Set design: Bruce Bolander
Sound: Russell C. Fager
Costume design: Michael Abbott
Music: Cliff Martinez
MPAA rating: R
Running time: 100 minutes

Principal characters:

Mark Hunter	Christian Slater
Nora Diniro	Samantha Mathis
Jan Emerson	Ellen Greene
Brian Hunter	Scott Paulin
Paige	Cheryl Pollak
Murdock	Andy Romano
Marta Hunter	Mimi Kennedy
Mrs. Creswood	Annie Ross
Janie	Lala Sloatman
Mazz Mazzilli	Billy Morrissette
Malcolm	Anthony Lucero
Jamie	Ahmet Zappa

Pump Up the Volume was a surprising motion picture for the summer of 1990 and a deceptive one as well. It is a good coming-of-age film in the tradition of *Rebel Without a Cause* (1956) that, according to David Ansen of *Newsweek*, managed to transcend its "teen-pic trappings and sometimes clunky plotting" to make several convincing points about teenage rebellion, frustration, and anxiety. It has the harsh colors and high sheen of a low-budget film, but it is driven by a very high level of manic energy (provided by its star, Christian Slater) and by an intelligent script (provided by writer-director Allan Moyle) that convincingly conveys a sense of teenage alienation. *Pump Up the Volume* is arguably the best film about teenagers since *The Breakfast Club* (1985).

Christian Slater plays Mark Hunter, a shy, introverted student at Hubert Humphrey High School in Paradise Hills, Arizona. Mark's father, Brian (Scott Paulin), has moved the family to Arizona from New York to become the high school commissioner. Mark's family is liberal; Arizona is conservative. Mark's high school is ruled by a tyrant, Mrs. Creswood (Annie Ross, formerly a member of the vocal jazz trio Lambert, Hendricks and Ross), who maintains a high S.A.T. average at her school by expelling her weakest students. Mark knows that the high school's image is false, but his father is impressed by the school's academic record. It is a little odd that Mark's father refuses to listen to what his son tells him about the school.

Mark is bright, verbal, and inventive, consciously designed as a combination of Holden Caulfield and Lenny Bruce, according to Moyle. Out of sheer frustration, Mark creates a pirate radio station in his family's basement and uses it to speak his mind to his fellow students. His radio persona, Hard Harry, is Mark's flamboyant and outspoken alter ego. At first Harry uses vulgar language to gain the attention of his classmates, but later he becomes an adviser and spokesman for his peers, articulating their common complaints and concerns. "Sex is out," Harry tells his listeners. "Drugs are out. Politics are out. Spiritualism is out. Everything's on hold. We definitely need something new." Hard Harry speaks his mind on values, morality, drugs, suicide, sexual identity, and the corrupt school system in which he is trapped. "I keep waiting for some new voice to come out of somewhere. Someone who says, 'Hey, wait a minute, look around.' Someone to say, 'What's wrong with this picture?'"

Mark's classmates are fascinated by this anonymous voice that "can go somewhere· uninvited and just hang out." Hard Harry develops a following that includes all types and all classes, from the punk rocker Mazz Mazzilli (Billy Morrissette) to the all-American cheerleader Paige (Cheryl Pollak), who destroys her costume jewelry in the microwave after listening to Hard Harry, a strange reflective moment of rebellion against middle-class materialism. Hard Harry has a responsive audience and quickly becomes a local outlaw celebrity. Eventually, Mark rents a post-office box so that his fans can write to him and enclose their telephone numbers. Every night at ten o'clock, Mark goes on the air and calls his fans. A suicidal misfit named Malcolm (Anthony Lucero) tells Hard Harry that he is going to kill himself, but Mark does not consider the death threat to be serious. When the student commits suicide, the community holds Hard Harry responsible.

Meanwhile, Mrs. Creswood, the principal, is determined to stop Hard Harry's radio transmissions, as Mark has threatened to expose her and her ruthless policies. The Federal Communications Commission (FCC) finally comes to investigate, and a net begins to close around Mark. The student body is so agitated, however, that Mrs. Creswood has created more trouble than she realizes.

What is amazing about this film is the way it is able to generate excitement by filming a single actor talking into a microphone. Radio is portrayed as the natural medium for teenagers, while only adults seem to be addicted to television. Slater's performance as Mark is nicely complemented by that of Samantha Mathis as Nora, the one student who discovers Hard Harry's true identity and helps him with his final battle with the establishment and the FCC. Mark is clearly disturbed by Malcolm's suicide and intends to discontinue his show. Nora does not agree, however, and urges him to continue what he has started, presumably as an act of symbolic protest. To evade escape, Mark rigs his transmitter to a moving Jeep. He drives toward a field where his fans have gathered, but he finally is apprehended by the authorities. Mark advises his listeners to carry on what he has started, to "steal the air," to "talk hard," and to "find their voices."

This idealistic conclusion only works on an emotional level, nevertheless it is nicely dramatized. The idea for the screenplay came from writer-director Moyle's own high school experience, as well as the experience of his sister, who taught at a high school that expelled students with low test scores. Moyle describes the story of *Pump Up the Volume* as being "about one angry young man's attempt to convert his confusion and pain into something cool. Of course, it gets out of hand and our hero unwittingly ends up as a voice of hope and affirmation."

Pump Up the Volume works as a typical teenage film, as it generally presents adults as buffoons or villains. Brian Hunter, Mark's father, is an essentially decent but burned-out 1960's liberal who has lost touch with his ideals and is now consumed by his work. He does not seem to have much time for his son. Annie Ross plays Mrs. Creswood, the high school principal, as a one-dimensional tyrant. The only sympathetic adult character is Jan Emerson (Ellen Greene), Mark's English teacher and an idealist who is willing to put her career on the line in order to defend her students. The cast also includes Ahmet Zappa, who has already made his recording debut. He is the son of Frank Zappa, whose rock group, The Mothers of Invention, became an anti-establishment icon during the 1960's.

The stand-out performance in *Pump Up the Volume*, however, is provided by Christian Slater, who appeared in two other 1990 films—*Young Guns II* and *Tales from the Darkside: The Movie*. Slater also won acclaim for his roles in *The Name of the Rose* (1986), Francis Ford Coppola's *Tucker: The Man and His Dream* (1988), and *Heathers* (1989), another cult film about teenagers. Slater excels in what amounts to a double role in *Pump Up the Volume*, and he makes Mark's transformation into Hard Harry believable. His voice control is perfect, and his energy reminds the viewer of a young Jack Nicholson. Slater's talent explains the surprising success of *Pump Up the Volume*, a low-budget motion picture that became one of the top films of the summer market and may become a teenage cult classic. This success also can be attributed to an outstanding progressive rock soundtrack, and the motion picture's sound mix is particularly effective.

Mark defines his classmates as belonging to the "Why Bother Generation." He understands their fears and their vulnerability. He wants to offer them a message of hope. His understanding of teenage angst may be more typical than profound, but it is certainly universal.

James M. Welsh

Reviews

American Film: Magazine of the Film and Television Arts. XV, September, 1990, p. 56.

Boxoffice. September, 1990, p. R68.

Chicago Tribune. August 22, 1990, V, p. 5.

The Christian Science Monitor. September 12, 1990, p. 11.

The Hollywood Reporter. CCCXIII, August 22, 1990, p. 7.

Los Angeles Times. August 22, 1990, p. F5.

Los Angeles Times. September 19, 1990, p. F4.

The New York Times. August 22, 1990, p. B4.

Newsweek. CXVI, September 10, 1990, p. 58.

Time. September 3, 1990, p. 72.

Variety. CCCXXXIX, May 23, 1990, p. 26.

The Wall Street Journal. August 23, 1990, p. A12.

The Washington Post. August 22, 1990, p. B1.

Q&A

Production: Arnon Milchan and Burtt Harris for Regency International Pictures/
  Odyssey Distributors; released by Tri-Star Pictures
Direction: Sidney Lumet
Screenplay: Sidney Lumet; based on the novel by Edwin Torres
Cinematography: Andrzej Bartkowiak
Editing: Richard Cirincione
Production design: Philip Rosenberg
Art direction: Beth Kuhn
Set decoration: Gary Brink
Costume design: Ann Roth and Neil Spisak
Music: Rubén Blades
MPAA rating: R
Running time: 132 minutes

Principal characters:

Mike Brennan	Nick Nolte
Al Reilly	Timothy Hutton
Bobby Texador	Armand Assante
Kevin Quinn	Patrick O'Neal
Leo Bloomenfeld	Lee Richardson
Luis Valentin	Luis Guzman
Sam Chapman	Charles Dutton
Nancy Bosch	Jenny Lumet
Roger Montalvo	Paul Calderon
Jose Malpica	International Chrysis
Larry Pesch	Dominick Chianese
Nick Petrone	Leonard Cimino
Preston Pearlstein	Fyvush Finkel
Alfonse Segal	Gustavo Brens
Armand Segal	Martin E. Brens
Lubin	Tommy A. Ford
Hank Mastroangelo	John Capodice
District Attorney	Frederick Rolf
Altshul	Hal Lehrman

Lieutenant Mike Brennan (Nick Nolte) is a legend in the New York City police force. When Brennan shoots a small-time Latino drug dealer outside an after-hours club, Al Reilly (Timothy Hutton), a new assistant district attorney, is called in to investigate his first case. Reilly's boss, Kevin Quinn (Patrick O'Neal), tells him that it is an open-and-shut case. All Reilly has to do is interview the people involved, collect the facts, and present them to the grand jury. To Quinn, it is a clear case of justifiable homicide. During the question-and-answer (Q&A) interviews (the official transcripts of the investigation), however, Reilly begins to suspect that the murder may not be justifiable, that perhaps Brennan had a motive for the killing and that a cover-up is involved.

A key clue comes from Bobby Texador (Armand Assante), a major drug dealer who was a friend of the murdered man. According to Texador, the victim carried only a .32 gun in his boot. He was found with a .45, a gun which Brennan had placed near the body. Soon, even one of Brennan's fellow police officers, Luis Valentin (Luis Guzman), begins to think that there is something strange about the homicide. For Reilly, however, Texador's testimony is complicated by the fact that Texador's live-in girlfriend, Nancy Bosch (Jenny Lumet, the daughter of director Sidney Lumet and granddaughter of Lena Horne), was Reilly's fiancée six years before. What had separated them was Reilly's initial and automatic refusal to accept the fact that Nancy's father was black. Even the film's hero could not hide the ingrained racism implied in a character from an Irish, Catholic, New York City background whose father was also a cop.

Reilly is suspicious of Texador's statements. After a meeting with Quinn in which the young assistant district attorney sees his boss plotting for political power (he plans on running for attorney general), however, Reilly begins to wonder if perhaps he was chosen specifically because of his inexperience. Quinn was hoping Reilly would miss the cold-bloodedness of the murder, and he certainly never expected Reilly to discover the deeper conspiracy taking place.

Reilly, along with Valentin and Sam Chapman (Charles Dutton), Hispanic and black officers who have been on the force with Brennan for a while, begin to dig into Brennan's story. It takes them into the worlds of drug lords, street gangs, transsexuals, and homosexuals. As the film progresses, it peels away layer after layer of corruption, constantly elevating the level of threat to Reilly and keeping audiences uncertain as to whom Reilly can trust and worried for his safety. Evil lurks in every corner of Lumet's film, not only in the political and police corruption that drive the story but also in the rampant racism, which is even more insidious because of the way it underlies the entire system and society. Racist jokes are bandied about the police station, each ethnic group relies on its own version of the "old boy network" to advance its goals, and oftentimes loyalty to race takes precedence over truth.

Once again, director Lumet has brought to the screen a chilling and taut police thriller. Like his earlier *Serpico* (1973) and *Prince of the City* (1981), *Q&A* exposes the rotting influences of corruption among those whom society desperately needs to have above reproach: the police and the politicians. Like *Serpico*, *Q&A* is based on a previously published work. In this instance, the story is from an original novel written by Edwin Torres, one of the first Hispanic judges in the New York judicial system. Lumet has characteristically written his film's screenplay. The last time he did so (for *Prince of the City*), he won an Academy Award nomination with his cowriter Jay Presson Allen. (Lumet also won a New York Film Critics Circle Award for Best Director for that film.) Award nominations are nothing new to Lumet's films. They have accrued more than forty, including those for *Twelve Angry Men* (1957), *The Pawnbroker* (1965), *Dog Day Afternoon* (1975), *Network* (1976), *The Verdict* (1982), *The Morning After* (1986), and *Running on Empty* (1988).

Many of the crew who worked with Lumet on *Q&A* have worked with him before. Director of photography Andrzej Bartkowiak worked with Lumet on nine films, production designer Philip Rosenberg on ten, and producer and first assistant director Burtt Harris on nearly twenty.

Q&A is a bleak film, with a visual point of view that enhances the action and gives the film a resonant atmosphere. Lumet has made the police officers' world flat and gray, lit by fluorescent lighting and devoid of any tangible attractiveness. Outside, however, Lumet presents everything from drug lords' homes to gay bars as filled with color, life, and freedom. By contrasting the officers' world with that occupied by those whom they must patrol, Lumet underscores Brennan's words: "Everyone's raking it in, but if we [the police] take one hamburger it's goodbye badge, goodbye pension, but meanwhile it's *our* widows and *our* orphans. . . ." This world is compellingly rendered onscreen by Lumet and his fine cast of actors. Before filming began, several of them, including Hutton, Nolte, and Guzman, spent several weeks with the police officers of Manhattan's 34th Precinct—the same precinct in which many of the film's scenes occur. The actors went out on calls with the officers and saw everything from domestic disputes to homicides.

While a few characters may be simplistically drawn (O'Neal's politically ambitious Quinn oozes evil even from his first appearance), the acting in *Q&A* is top-rate, proving once again that Lumet is an actor's director. Nick Nolte brings bravado, crudeness, and malevolence to his portrayal of the veteran Irish cop Brennan. Initially he takes in the impressionable Reilly with his legendary status on the force, but eventually he unleashes his pathological brutality as Reilly discovers more of the truth and his innocence is stripped away. Armand Assante's Bobby Texador manages to be both sinister and eventually, improbably, likable—possibly because many other characters in the film are so unlikable. It is Hutton's steady and underplayed Reilly, however, that propels the plot. It is common for Lumet to make his main character sensitive and suffering. His heroes have lofty liberal ideals that inevitably clash with the reality of corrupt organizations and people who find it more convenient or lucrative to look the other way. The audience wants Lumet's heroes to be victorious over the evil they encounter, but as in life, that does not often happen. *Q&A* is no different.

Despite the fine acting and the strong story line, *Q&A* is a rough and discouraging film. It is violent and uses foul language liberally. Its virtually nihilistic ending leaves the viewer with a feeling of helplessness and hopelessness that remains long after this engrossing, unsettling, and chilling film is over.

Beverley Bare Buehrer

Reviews

America. CLXII, June 2, 1990, p. 553.
Boxoffice. June, 1990, p. R42.
Chicago Tribune. April 27, 1990, VII, p. C7.
The Christian Science Monitor. April 27, 1990, p. 10.
Commonweal. CXVII, June 15, 1990, p. 387.
Cosmopolitan. July, 1990, p. 18.
The Hollywood Reporter. CCCXII, April 20, 1990, p. 14.
Los Angeles Magazine. June, 1990, p. 206.
Los Angeles Times. April 27, 1990, p. F1.
Maclean's. April 30, 1990, p. 63.
The Nation. CCL, May 7, 1990, p. 647.
The New Republic. May 21, 1990, p. 26.
New York Magazine. April 23, 1990, p. 92.
The New York Times. April 27, 1990, p. C20.
Newsweek. CXV, May 7, 1990, p. 65.
People Weekly. May 7, 1990, p. 17.
Rolling Stone. May 17, 1990, p. 27.
Variety. CCCXXXIX, April 25, 1990, p. 28.
Video. XIV, December, 1990, p. 70.
The Wall Street Journal. April 26, 1990, p. 12.

THE RESCUERS DOWN UNDER

Production: Thomas Schumacher for Walt Disney Pictures, in association with
  Silver Screen Partners IV; released by Buena Vista
Direction: Hendel Butoy and Mike Gabriel
Screenplay: Jim Cox, Karey Kirkpatrick, Byron Simpson, and Joe Ranft; based on
  characters created by Margery Sharp
Cinematography: John Aardal, Chris Beck, Mary E. Lescher, Gary W. Smith, and
  Chuck Warren
Editing: Michael Kelly
Animation supervision: Glen Keane, Mark Henn, Russ Edmonds, David Cutler,
  Ruben A. Aquino, Nik Ranieri, Ed Gombert, Anthony De Rosa, Kathy Zielinski,
  and Duncan Marjoribanks
Computer animation: Tina Price and Andrew Schmidt
Character leads supervision: Bill Berg, Brian Clift, Renee Holt, Emily Jiuliano,
  Marty Korth, and Vera Lanpher
Art direction: Maurice Hunt
Story supervision: Joe Ranft
Effects supervision: Randy Fullmer
Background supervision: Lisa Keene
Layout supervision: Dan Hansen
Sound: Louis L. Edemann and Paul Timothy Carden
Music: Bruce Broughton
MPAA rating: G
Running time: 74 minutes

Voices of principal characters:

Bernard	Bob Newhart
Miss Bianca	Eva Gabor
Wilbur	John Candy
Jake	Tristan Rogers
Cody	Adam Ryen
McLeach	George C. Scott
Frank	Wayne Robson
Krebbs	Douglas Seale
Joanna	Frank Welker
François	Ed Gilbert

Setting their story in Australia gave the Disney artists an opportunity to depict a
relatively unfamiliar assortment of animals, such as kookaburras, wombats, platy-
puses, and flying squirrels. They have wisely resisted any temptation to overwork
two Australian stereotypes: bouncing kangaroos and cuddly koalas. The only kangaroo in the film does not jump at all because it is being held captive in a dungeon,

and the only koala, another captive, is old and cynical, like baggy-eyed Friend Owl in Disney's *Bambi* (1942). In fact, many of the characters will remind older viewers of the classic animated features of the era when Walt Disney was a highly intelligent and creative human being and not a multi-billion-dollar corporation.

An eight-year-old boy named Cody (the voice of Adam Ryen) who lives in the Outback of Australia spends his time rescuing animals from the traps of the treacherous and sadistic McLeach (the voice of George C. Scott). Cody himself falls into one of McLeach's traps and is spirited away like a character that he so closely resembles: the little stringless puppet-hero of Disney's *Pinocchio* (1940). Echoing the Pleasure Island sequence in *Pinocchio*, Cody finds himself in a cage in McLeach's dungeon, along with an assortment of animals who are due to be shipped off to zoos or skinned and made into belts and wallets. McLeach, who is always looming in doorways like Stromboli, the traveling impresario in *Pinocchio*, wants to force Cody to tell him how to find Marahute, an enormous eagle who is worth a fortune if the poacher can capture her and sell her to a zoo. The fact that Marahute belongs to a nearly extinct species adds the theme of humanity's ecological depredations to the familiar Disney theme of humanity's cruelty to animals and gives *The Rescuers Down Under* educational significance.

As is always the case with Disney's full-length animated features, there are scenes that may terrify the smaller members of the audience and give them a few nightmares. Most of these involve McLeach clenching his hairy fists and threatening little Cody in the raspy voice that Scott used to intimidate whole armies as the fiery World War II tank commander in *Patton* (1970). Older viewers may wonder why an Australian poacher happens to have an American accent; however, authenticity has never been a matter of great concern in Disney films. Australia is treated with the same poetic license that characterized Disney's portrayal of South America in *Saludos Amigos* (1943). Although *The Rescuers Down Under* contains no bouncing kangaroos or cuddly koalas, Australians will probably feel that their enormous country has once again been "Hollywoodized" by an American film, as it was in *Quigley Down Under* (1990), for example, which was an American Western incongruously superimposed on an Australian setting. The Disney story contains a few Australian animals, but otherwise it could have been set in North America, Africa, or Asia.

To Cody's rescue come the two top mouse agents from the International Rescue Aid Society, Bernard (the voice of Bob Newhart) and Miss Bianca (the voice of Eva Gabor), who starred in Disney's highly successful *The Rescuers* (1977). One of the most amusing sequences in the sequel involves their bumpy flight to Australia in a sardine can that is strapped to the back of a reckless and incompetent albatross named Wilbur (the voice of John Candy). Many minutes of the film's running time are taken up with simulated high-altitude views of the landscape from the perspectives of Cody flying on the back of the eagle and Bernard and Miss Bianca on the back of the albatross. The scenes require little animation but consist mainly of a gliding bird silhouetted against panning shots of painted backdrops. This effective cost-cutting device is symptomatic of the economic dilemma that has been haunting

Disney for years. Production expenses, particularly the cost of the highly skilled human labor that is needed to produce the thousands of individual illustrations that go into a full-length animated film, have skyrocketed since Disney's first animated feature, *Snow White and the Seven Dwarfs* (1937). Inflationary pressures have forced the introduction of limited animation devices which, however skillfully employed, make it impossible for a contemporary Walt Disney feature to compare with one of the classics of his golden era.

Bernard and Miss Bianca team up with a kangaroo mouse named Jake (the voice of Tristan Rogers), who immediately falls in love with Miss Bianca and makes poor Bernard desperately jealous. Like Penny (the voice of Michelle Stacy) in *The Rescuers*, Cody is a bland and rather passive character who is intended to serve as a counterpoint to the zany animal characters that surround him. In the meantime, McLeach has released Cody from his dungeon, telling the boy that he has killed his friend Marahute and that her unborn eaglets will die inside their unprotected eggs. The crafty McLeach knows that Cody will try to save the eggs and will lead him straight to Marahute. The scheme nearly succeeds, but Bernard, Miss Bianca, and Jake, after many mishaps, arrive just in time to help Cody save the eagle from Mc-Leach, who falls into the river and has to swim for his life to escape from crocodiles. The scene is reminiscent of the ones involving Captain Hook and the ticking crocodile in *Peter Pan* (1953).

The older viewer has the feeling that there is a new generation of artists at Disney who are trying to introduce innovative ideas, but that they are fighting an uphill battle against conservative elements who cling to the tried and true characters and situations that have proved so lucrative in the past. A few of the animals who provide background are somewhat expressionistic, reflecting the trickle-down influence of artists like Pablo Picasso and Paul Klee. The principals, however, are typically romanticized Disney animals with soft, cuddly bodies and big, glistening eyes like those of Bambi and his rabbit friend, Thumper. Of all the Disney animated features, *The Rescuers Down Under* most closely resembles *Bambi*. It presents a strong message on the theme of humanity's cruelty to fellow creatures. It goes beyond *Bambi* in teaching that humankind is in danger of destroying the environment through greed. Like another memorable Disney animated feature, *The Jungle Book* (1967), it emphasizes humanity's kinship with other animals, which is a priceless heritage.

This film is a sequel to the Disney production of 1977 which was based on a sincerely written children's book by Margery Sharp. Like many sequels, *The Rescuers Down Under* lacks the unique charm of the original. Much of the comedy consists of "visual gags." If there is anything to bump into or fall over, one of the characters will do it. If silence is of the essence, then one of them is sure to create a horrible clatter. The plot itself is banal. Bernard and Miss Bianca come to Australia to rescue Cody, but the boy himself is never in serious danger—except the danger to which he exposes himself by clambering around on high places. McLeach has no intention of skinning the little boy or selling him to a zoo, and eventually he releases him unharmed. The mice are trying to save Cody, Cody is trying to save the eagle's eggs (thinking Marahute herself is dead), and McLeach is trying to capture the eagle. This confusion over characters' motivations and goals creates confusion in the story: The viewer is never quite sure who is going where and for what purpose. For example, it is not clear what Cody intends to do with the three large eagle's eggs when he reaches them, as he can hardly sit on them himself. The Disney people still know how to captivate young children, however, and *The Rescuers Down Under* proved by its box-office receipts that it will be a profitable addition to the Disney treasure chest of full-length animated features.

Bill Delaney

Reviews

Boston Globe. November 16, 1990, p. 77.
Chicago Tribune. November 16, 1990, VII, p. 42.
The Christian Science Monitor. November 23, 1990, p. 12.
The Hollywood Reporter. September 16, 1990, p. 8.
Los Angeles Times. November 16, 1990, p. F15.
The New York Times. November 16, 1990, p. B7.
Newsweek. CXVI, December 3, 1990, p. 67.
Time. CXXXVI, November 19, 1990, p. 112.
USA Today. November 16, 1990, p. D4.
Variety. November 14, 1990, p. 2.
The Washington Post. November 17, 1990, p. D9.

REVERSAL OF FORTUNE

Production: Edward R. Pressman and Oliver Stone, in association with Shochiku
  Fuji and Sovereign Pictures; released by Warner Bros.
Direction: Barbet Schroeder
Screenplay: Nicholas Kazan; based on the book by Alan Dershowitz
Cinematography: Luciano Tovoli
Editing: Lee Percy
Production design: Mel Bourne
Art direction: Dan Davis
Set decoration: Beth Kushnick
Sound: Tom Nelson
Costume design: Judianna Makovsky
Music: Mark Isham
MPAA rating: R
Running time: 110 minutes

> *Principal characters:*
> Sunny von Bülow .... Glenn Close
> Claus von Bülow .... Jeremy Irons (AA)
> Alan Dershowitz .... Ron Silver
> Carol .... Annabella Sciorra
> Maria .... Uta Hagen
> David Marriott .... Fisher Stevens
> Andrea Reynolds .... Christine Baranski

Reversal of Fortune documents one of the most sensational criminal cases of modern times—the conviction and ultimate acquittal of Claus von Bülow, accused of murdering his millionairess wife, Sunny. Blending facts and speculation with fantasy narration from the comatose Sunny (Glenn Close), the film examines the case from various points of view including von Bülow's (Jeremy Irons), his attorney Alan Dershowitz (Ron Silver), and Dershowitz' youthful investigative team.

The film opens with beautiful aerial shots of luxurious, castlelike mansions along the Eastern coast near Newport, Rhode Island, where the von Bülows reside. The scene shifts to a depressing hospital corridor and glides into the room of Sunny von Bülow, comatose for a decade, who, in a voice-over narration, explains the events that led to her vegetablelike existence. Sunny quickly sums up the story from the point of view of the prosecution's case against her husband, how the evidence pointed to Claus von Bülow having attempted to cold-bloodedly kill Sunny by injecting her with lethal doses of insulin on two separate occasions. Von Bülow was convicted in two separate sensational trials.

Sunny's narration stops here and the emphasis of the film shifts to the point of view of Harvard law professor and attorney Alan Dershowitz, who is first glimpsed playing an intense, solitary game of basketball at his modest home in Cambridge,

Massachusetts. His game is interrupted by a phone call from von Bülow, who wants Dershowitz to defend him in his state supreme court appeal. Dershowitz, an emotionally passionate civil libertarian lawyer and human rights activist, first balks at the thought of defending the rich and publicly despised von Bülow. He agrees to meet, however, and talk over the case.

Dershowitz meets with von Bülow at von Bülow's elegant Newport mansion. Thinking von Bülow guilty, he tells the cold, priggish millionaire—whose bail is set at one million dollars—not to relate his side of the story because it will make the case less defensible if von Bülow's "facts" turn out to be lies. He tells von Bülow that he will take the case and that the one thing in von Bülow's favor is that "Everybody hates you." Dershowitz then begins to gather his research and investigative team, made up primarily of his Harvard law students. Some object to the idea of defending such a despicable character as von Bülow, who appears to be an unfeeling monster. Dershowitz points out to his youthful team, however, that what is important is that von Bülow, like any person accused of a crime, must receive a fair trial regardless of the charges against him or his social position.

Dershowitz, still believing von Bülow guilty, hopes to win an acquittal by finding technical flaws in the trials that convicted him. As his team researches the previous trials and uncovers conflicting and questionable evidence, however, Dershowitz realizes that the best approach is to prove von Bülow innocent of the charges. In a series of meetings with von Bülow at the Newport mansion in the presence of von Bülow's mistress, and at Dershowitz' home with his team present, Dershowitz finally asks von Bülow to relate his side of the story. Von Bülow shocks the team members with his emotionless, sterile demeanor and the perverse delight he takes in relating jokes he has heard about himself as the infamous insulin murderer. His story, however, is convincing in its detached straightforwardness. He tells them that Sunny was addicted to various drugs and was continually ingesting them in massive quantities. He tells of her overdose on aspirin, her inability to handle alcohol, her sugar binges, and her bouts with depression. He believes that Sunny's two comas were the result of suicide attempts caused by von Bülow's intentions to divorce her. He also states that there was no insulin in the mansion at any time and that he believes his stepchildren might have planted the insulin after Sunny's second coma to implicate him in attempted murder and to cover up their mother's addictive and depressive habits.

After a more extensive investigation, much of von Bülow's story is substantiated. Yet Dershowitz is worried about being able to present new evidence at an appeals trial. After one of his student investigators discovers such a precedent—a Rhode Island law case in which new evidence was allowed when the theory on which the original case was based was found to be faulty—Dershowitz feels confident that he will be able to present his new evidence and win the case. When the day of the trial finally arrives, von Bülow and his mistress watch comfortably from his Newport mansion as the televised proceedings unfold. Ultimately, von Bülow is found innocent. Afterward, Dershowitz and his staff present varying scenarios which attempt to explain what really happened. In the end, Sunny, from her hospital bed, poses more questions and the film ends in a shroud of doubt over von Bülow's guilt or innocence.

The major problem with *Reversal of Fortune* is a common one with films dealing with recent factual and controversial events which involve people who are still alive and able to sue the filmmakers for libel or defamation of character. The filmmakers have to be very careful not to incriminate or defame the people involved, which results in major compromises in the film's depiction of the events. The subject of the film is a fascinating one and perfect for dramatization: A devious, amoral man methodically and remorselessly attempts to kill his rich, defenseless wife in order to inherit her fortune and live with his mistress, and, after a series of sensational trials, is found innocent. Because of the controversy surrounding the scandal and the fear of a lawsuit, however, the filmmakers cannot dramatize the full story.

The most obvious and dramatically damaging compromise that the filmmakers made in approaching the film involves the depiction of von Bülow's stepchildren. The stepchildren, who initially filed the murder charges against their stepfather, are depicted as passive and almost nonexistent. They are glimpsed eating at the dinner table and playing card games in the mansion, but they never appear outraged or upset over von Bülow's behavior toward their mother. In contrast to their portrayal, Dershowitz' own son is depicted as a fiery, passionate youth full of questions and doubts about the case, mirroring Dershowitz' own emotional and vibrant character. Because the film is based, for the most part, on Dershowitz' book of the same name and was co-produced by his son Elon, the filmmakers had little to worry about lawsuits from Dershowitz and his family and had more freedom to add substance to these characters and more fully dramatize their points of view.

The most outrageous and intriguing dramatic touch of the film, the comatose Sunny's narration of certain events from her hospital bed, proves to be the most dramatically unsatisfying aspect of the film. Because it is impossible to present Sunny's side of the story, her comments serve only as a means for the filmmakers to tell certain expository facts about the case in a less conventional manner and ultimately add nothing to understanding the questions raised about von Bülow's guilt or innocence. Sunny, the one person who knows the truth, sounds even more confused than the other characters, posing such questions as "Is he (von Bülow) the devil? If so, can the devil get justice?" In an attempt to add dimensions to Sunny and von Bülow's characters and to explain how two such loveless and decadent people could have ever been attracted to each other, Sunny narrates a flashback showing how they met. Again, the feeling of dramatic compromise affects the scene, as Sunny and von Bülow timidly engage in a brief clandestine meeting and later stare affectionately at each other at an outdoor luncheon as a tiger cub suddenly appears and begins to eat Sunny's food. Although Sunny's unconventional "narration from the grave" is similar to William Holden's outrageous voice-over comments in Billy Wilder's *Sunset Boulevard* (1950), the effect is spoiled by the filmmakers' inability to tell Sunny's side of the story without resorting to total fantasy.

The major strength of the film is the superb acting by Ron Silver as Alan Dershowitz and especially Jeremy Irons who won the 1990 Academy Award for Best Actor for his portrayal of the enigmatic Claus von Bülow. Silver, playing the intense, noble lawyer and author of the book on which the film is based, not surprisingly has all the best lines, which are full of passionate pleas for truth and justice. Silver delivers his lines with conviction and gives his character human quirks, such as a feverish love for basketball and a brooding concern about his client's innocence. Irons, his hair grayed and thinned, speaking in a priggishly proper English/Dutch accent, also brings human dimensions to a character regarded by most as an emotionless fiend. Irons portrays von Bülow as an objectively honest man who guards his emotions yet is capable of showing affection and concern, and who finally rebels against the demands of his highly neurotic and unstable wife. The two characters make for an interesting contrast, Silver embodying the squat, scruffy Dershowitz with energy and fire, Irons playing the towering, elegant von Bülow with a haughty yet slyly humorous aloofness, both characters sharing a fervent concern with uncovering the truth of the events.

Unfortunately, Glenn Close's portrayal of Sunny von Bülow is hampered by the fact that her character is usually shown either drunk, in a druglike stupor, or comatose. Her voice-over narration serves only to advance the plot and offers no opportunity to understand the woman who holds the truth to the tragic events.

Producer Oliver Stone's *Born on the Fourth of July* (1989) is an example of a motion picture based on the life of a still-living legend—antiwar activist Ron Kovac—that shows no evidence of dramatic compromise even when depicting less-than-flattering factual events. Such films are rare, most becoming timid television movie-of-the-week dramatizations of facts already well known by the public. *Reversal of Fortune*, although filled with strong performances and revealing an expensive lavishness, unfortunately cannot rise above its timidity to capture effectively the sensationalistic aura that surrounded one of the most intriguing and infamous court cases of the twentieth century.

Jim Kline

Reviews

America. CLXIII, December 15, 1990, p. 486.
Chicago Tribune. October 17, 1990, V, p. 2.
Glamour. October, 1990, p. 191.
The Hollywood Reporter. CCCXIV, October 18, 1990, p. 10.
Los Angeles Times. October 17, 1990, p. F1.
The New York Times. October 17, 1990, p. B1.
Newsweek. CXVI, November 5, 1990, p. 79.
Rolling Stone. November 15, 1990, p. 159.
Time. CXXXVI, October 22, 1990, p. 63.
Variety. September 13, 1990, p. 2.
The Wall Street Journal. October 18, 1990, p. A14.
The Washington Post. November 9, 1990, p. C1.

ROBOCOP II

Production: Jon Davison; released by Orion Pictures
Direction: Irvin Kershner
Screenplay: Frank Miller and Walon Green
Cinematography: Mark Irwin
Editing: William Anderson, Deborah Zeitman, Lee Smith, and Armen Minasian
Animation: Phil Tippett
Production design: Peter Jamison
Art direction: Pam Marcotte
Set decoration: Ronald R. Reiss
Set design: Colin Irwin
Special effects: Robert K. Worthington and Jim Rollins
Costume design: Rob Bottin and Rosanna Norton
Stunt coordination: Conrad E. Palmisano
Music: Leonard Rosenman
MPAA rating: R
Running time: 117 minutes

Principal characters:
Robocop	Peter Weller
Anne Lewis	Nancy Allen
Cain	Tom Noonan
The Old Man	Daniel O'Herlihy
Donald Johnson	Felton Perry
Sergeant Reed	Robert Do'Qui
Hob	Gabriel Damon
Dr. Juliette Faxx	Belinda Bauer
Jess Perkins	Leeza Gibbons
Mayor Kuzak	Willard Pugh
Angie	Galyn Gorg
Duffy	Stephen Lee

Robocop II continues in the visual tradition of *Robocop* (1987), but without the original's biting parody. The dystopian satire remains, but the coherent political worldview of Director Paul Verhoeven has been traded in for the kinder, gentler sequels that have become a trademark of Director Irvin Kershner. These include *The Empire Strikes Back* (1980) and *Never Say Never Again* (1983).

Robocop II aims at a middle-of-the-road satire that pokes fun at conservatives and liberals alike, but it does so more out of a sense of accommodation than conviction. The shift in perspective is most evident in the use of news briefs and commercials. In the original film, these full-screen video asides stopped the narrative cold, providing a parodic counterpoint to the genre, the news media, and popular culture. In *Robocop II*, however, the news briefs provide exposition that propels the narrative. In fact, Hollywood reporter Leeza Gibbons is no longer cast as an inside joke about the news media. Instead, she becomes the voice of objectivity.

Similarly, the first film's nuclear satire is emptied of its meaning and context and made into an empty metaphor for the crack epidemic. In general, *Robocop II* retreats into symbolic displacement of the social ills that director Verhoeven confronted in the original film. For example, white children are presented here as the new drug dealers in what is shown to be a black-controlled city, and the drug epidemic is explained as a cult phenomenon and not a socioeconomic one. The depiction of Mayor Kuzak (Willard Pugh) as a modern-day Stepin' Fetchit, in fact, is one of the few that does not mask its racism. The mayor is depicted as childlike himself, and, when in physical danger, he rolls his eyes and makes an unseemly exit. Surprisingly, there was no comment on his portrayal, or on the coincidental similarities to the arrest and trial of real-life Mayor Marion Barry of Washington, D.C.

In *Robocop II*, Robocop (Peter Weller) again confronts a ruthless drug dealer, Cain (Tom Noonan), who manufactures a new designer drug called Nuke. Nuke bears striking similarities to crack, although its small container includes a needle for quick injection into the neck. Cain is modeled on Charles Manson and imbues his operation with a messianic rhetoric, if not objective. The film opens with a commercial and news brief that provides exposition on the current state of Detroit. In one news item, the surgeon general is assassinated during a press conference on the effects of Nuke. In another, the Detroit police are shown on strike after Omni Consumer Products (OCP), which contracted to run the department in *Robocop*, cuts salaries by 40 percent and cancels pensions. After the television sequence, *Robocop II* cuts to the streets of Detroit, where addicts, unencumbered by the police, rob stores and mug pedestrians. Robocop, however, is still on the job, and he arrives in time to foil a robbery in progress. The bloodied criminals tell him where the Nuke is manufactured. Meanwhile, Robocop's previous partner, Anne Lewis (Nancy Allen), is also on the job, arriving at the factory just after Robocop.

In the factory, Latina women manufacture Nuke in a kitchenlike environment complete with children and salsa music (listed as "Robo Salsa" in the credits). While young male Latinos have been stereotyped as drug dealers and gang members in the past, recent action films have expanded that stereotype to implicate the entire Latino family. Often it is "Latin" music that provides the bridge between street violence and domestic scenes, between old stereotypes about men and new stereotypes about women and children. The children trigger Robocop's memories about his human past, and when a twelve-year-old boy, Hob (Gabriel Damon), takes a shot at him, Robocop temporarily short-circuits, and the criminals escape. Later, OCP executives upbraid Robocop, because he has been parking across the street from the house of his widow and son. In fact, his wife has filed suit against the police department, so that Robocop must be persuaded to deny his humanity and leave her alone. When his wife is allowed to see him in his cage, Robocop proclaims himself a machine. Actor Peter Weller conveys Robocop's identity crisis without ever tipping the scales: Robocop remains mechanical, and what little humanity he has left manifests itself as obstinacy.

Meanwhile, OCP continues its stranglehold on Detroit, which is about to default on its police contract. The Old Man (Daniel O'Herlihy) and his new second-in-command, Donald Johnson (Felton Perry), inform Mayor Kuzak that OCP plans to foreclose on city assets and "take Detroit private." As part of its plan to control Detroit, OCP is developing a second-generation Robocop. The new cyborgs, however, all self-destruct, since the police officers used were unable to cope without the strong sense of duty that the original subject, Officer Alex Murphy (Peter Weller), possessed. Dr. Juliette Faxx (Belinda Bauer), a motivational psychologist, sees her chance for advancement and offers to screen potential candidates. To the dismay of the Robocop technicians, however, she recommends that a psychotic killer be used, since he would welcome the power. In order to circumvent the objections of Johnson and the technicians, Dr. Faxx becomes the Old Man's lover.

While Dr. Faxx proceeds with her plan, Robocop and Lewis track down the Cain gang, which includes Hob and Cain's girlfriend, Angie (Galyn Gorg). Officer Duffy (Stephen Lee) is discovered to be an informant for Hob, receiving both cash and Nuke. Robocop tortures Duffy until he reveals Cain's whereabouts: the River Rouge sludge plant, where Murphy had been brutally shot in *Robocop*. Cain and Hob, however, are prepared for Robocop. In a ritual reenactment of Murphy's execution in the first film, Hob shoots off one arm. Robocop is chained to the ground and dismantled with a jackhammer, buzzsaw, and other tools. The Cain gang then drops off the remains in front of the striking police.

OCP is slow to repair Robocop, although he is still alive. When the police insist, Dr. Faxx decides to update Robocop's computer program so that he will not pose a threat to the Robocop II project. She convenes a liberal community focus group, which provides hundreds of suggestions, including one that Robocop speak out on environmental issues. These are then written into Robocop's program as directives. When he returns to the streets, Robocop lectures juvenile delinquents on nutrition, reads Miranda rights to a corpse, and refuses to set a bad example by speeding. His liberal directives make him at once more human in appearance and completely ineffectual as a police officer. In order to free himself from the directives, Robocop electrocutes himself. When he revives, he has no directives, not even the original three directives that expressed law enforcement ideals. Robocop rallies the striking officers and leads them in an assault on Cain's base of operations. Hob and Angie escape in a truck filled with cash. Cain, however, is chased by Robocop and fatally wounded.

While Hob takes over the operation, Dr. Faxx has Cain's brain removed and placed inside Robocop II, a gigantic cyborg. Because Cain was himself a Nuke addict, Dr. Faxx promises to supply Robocop II after he kills the mayor, who has found a secret source of money to bail out the city. If OCP cannot foreclose, confidence in OCP stock will plummet, since it has transferred most of its corporate resources to "urban pacification." The mayor's secret benefactor is Hob, who offers the city $50 million in exchange for the right to sell drugs. The mayor accepts, but Robocop II breaks into the warehouse, shooting at everyone. Robocop II stops briefly when he recognizes Angie, who reciprocates his sexual advances until he realizes its futility and kills her. The mayor escapes, but Hob is fatally shot. Before he dies, Hob tells Robocop that the machine that attacked them was Cain.

The denouement comes when the Old Man, safe in the knowledge that the city will default on its contract, presents his plans for Detroit to the press in a large auditorium. Rather than participate in democratic elections, people who can afford to will be able to buy OCP stock and vote on corporate decisions. The city and its neighborhoods will be razed and replaced with high-rises. A large model of the future Detroit rises from beneath the platform, with Robocop II in its midst. In order to make a point, the Old Man holds up a cylinder filled with Nuke, which excites the addicted cyborg. Robocop II arms himself and goes on a rampage. When Robocop comes to the rescue, the special effects take over, and a drawn-out fight ensues. Robocop II is finally destroyed when Robocop is able to jump on top of him, pull out Cain's brain, and smash it against the pavement. In the end, as in *Robocop*, the Old Man remains in power, after Dr. Faxx is set up as the scapegoat. The "loose cannon" theory, which allows the Old Man to claim "plausible deniability," is even more strongly identified as a red herring in the sequel.

Once again, the film ends with Robocop affirming his humanity, although this time he no longer needs to play by the rules of law enforcement directives. Whereas in *Robocop* the parody was often violent, in *Robocop II* the violence becomes merely humorous entertainment. Beneath the humor, and the celebration of the individual *cum* machine, is a struggle over who will be the absolute and arbitrary authority: OCP or the Detroit police. In either case, the ends justify violent means. In a sense, films such as *Robocop II* create an entertaining rationale for philosopher Thomas Hobbes's "social contract," wherein fear of violent death leads people to submit to an absolute authority.

Chon A. Noriega

Reviews

Baltimore Sun. June 22, 1990, "Maryland Live," p. 12.
Boxoffice. August, 1990, p. R57.
Chicago Tribune. June 22, 1990, VII, p. 37.
The Hollywood Reporter. CCCXIII, June 22, 1990, p. 6.
Los Angeles Times. June 22, 1990, p. F1.
The New York Times. June 22, 1990, p. B10.
Newsweek. CXVI, July 2, 1990, p. 54.
Time. CXXXVI, July 2, 1990, p. 64.
Variety. June 22, 1990, p. 2.
Video. XIV, December, 1990, p. 70.
The Wall Street Journal. June 28, 1990, p. A12.
The Washington Post. June 22, 1990, p. C1.

ROCKY V

Production: Robert Chartoff and Irwin Winkler for United Artists; released by
  Metro-Goldwyn-Mayer/United Artists
Direction: John G. Avildsen
Screenplay: Sylvester Stallone
Cinematography: Steven Poster
Editing: John G. Avildsen and Michael N. Knue
Production design: William J. Cassidy
Art direction: William Durrell, Jr.
Set decoration: John Dwyer
Sound: Barry Thomas
Special makeup effects: Michael Westmore
Music: Bill Conti
MPAA rating: PG-13
Running time: 104 minutes

Principal characters:

Rocky	Sylvester Stallone
Adrian	Talia Shire
Paulie	Burt Young
Mickey	Burgess Meredith
Rocky, Jr.	Sage Stallone
Tommy	Tommy Morrison
George W. Duke	Richard Gant
Tony	Tony Burton
Jimmy	James Gambina
Karen	Delia Sheppard
Merlin Sheets	Michael Sheehan
Union Cane	Michael Williams

The predominance of sequels in recent film history seems to evidence a bankruptcy of creative imagination. The generic type of sequel, spawned by horror and action series such as *Death Wish* (1974), *Jaws* (1975), and *Friday the 13th* (1980), packages a known commodity for a given audience in an attempt to maximize profits without requiring the filmmaker or the audience to invest too much effort. So often sequels are delivered with merely external or situational conflict or are sustained by the one-line gag. It is unnecessary to give close attention to intricate plot structure or to compelling character development in a film such as *Lethal Weapon II* (1989). The big box-office returns of the sequel overshadow Shane Black's more thoughtfully written *Lethal Weapon* (1987), a film which centered on a police officer's tormented personal conflict.

In 1990, there have been further installments of even those works that have been awarded lofty critical placement. Jack Nicholson has forced a doomed, redundant offering in *The Two Jakes* (1990; reviewed in this volume), set several years after the brilliantly communicated *Chinatown* (1974), while in *Texasville* (1990; also reviewed in this volume), Peter Bogdanovich ineffectually revisited the characters from the small Texas locale with which he made such an indelible impression in his own *The Last Picture Show* (1971). These confused, self-indulgent attempts have failed even to exhibit the drawing power that the formula sequels possess.

In contrast, *Rocky V* is an unusual creation. The fifth installment of the legend that America has taken to heart, it must be discussed in relation to the original 1976 film and the three others that followed. The admittedly numerous *Rocky* films capitalize on the cultural phenomenon of "the Boxer" as a figure whose career invariably passes through different phases. This built-in context draws from the audience's collective familiarity with such real-life icons as Joe Lewis and Muhammad Ali. Thus, the first three films might have stood as a trilogy covering the distinct, dynamic phases of an achievement of championship stature, culminating in *Rocky III* (1982). Yet *Rocky IV* (1985), tipping the scales with repulsive and insulting chauvinism, rendered that impossible. The characterization seemed to be tainted by Sylvester Stallone's own egocentricity and resulted in general cynicism toward the release of another *Rocky* film. *Rocky V* actually atones for these failures, somewhat, by focusing with sincerity on some new obstacles. In its exploration of the time of life at which longstanding options are no longer feasible, this film addresses that period of adjustment after the hero's "big shot" has come and gone, while the consequences remain.

If not altogether realistic, the plot unfolds with minimal gaps and is paced in order to avoid lingering. After being bludgeoned in the Soviet Union by Ivan Drago (Dolph Lundgren), the indefatigable Rocky Balboa (Stallone) has suffered brain damage, which precludes any professional return to the ring. Upon their return, Rocky and his wife Adrian Balboa (Talia Shire) find their finances destroyed because of the mismanagement of his brother-in-law Paulie (Burt Young) and unscrupulous accountants who played the real-estate market. With the quick reminder of Rocky's inability to effectively commercialize his image, they are all forced back to Rocky's mentor's gym in Philadelphia. This exaggerated fall eerily mirrors much economic uneasiness that Americans began to experience at the end of the 1980's. The American underdog of the post-Watergate Era has worked hard and still lost the trappings of success through circumstances frustratingly beyond his control. Rocky has been knocked off balance so quickly as to override the previous episode's pomposity. Vulturelike sportswriters and exploitative promotor George W. Duke (Richard Gant) badger Rocky back toward the ring, but Adrian and his doctors prevail. Cast back to his gritty roots, Rocky must eke out a living for his family. The relentless depiction of the nature of his injuries serves to make him more tragic and lovable than ever before.

Rocky attempts to fill the mentor role that the beloved Mickey (Burgess Meredith) once played for him by training the talented young fighter Tommy Gunn (Tommy

Morrison). After much time and heart is invested, however, Tommy betrays Rocky for a chance at the title. Disillusioned, Rocky must try to repair his strained personal relationships and regain some degree of integrity. *Rocky V* is the story of a man who has already outlived his time at the top of the mountain. It adequately covers Rocky's loss, his relegation to a position on the sidelines, and his still huge heart setting itself up to be broken.

The logical finale, pitting pupil against teacher, follows through in the last reel, though in a bare-knuckled street brawl rather than in a heavyweight title event. Predictably upheld is the legacy of editing extravagance for the climactic last fight sequence. In addition to slow-motion freeze-frame techniques, there are bizarre subjective images from the brain damaged fighter's perspective that are informed by the reflexive artiness of music videos. These stylized visuals seem overdone, as do earlier flashbacks resurrecting Mickey's character. Such high production value is the most noticeable disjunction with the 1976 original.

The film succeeds in exploiting the locations themselves to counterpoint scenes which border on melodrama. Moreover, such neighborhood characters as the priest who blesses Rocky's daily run are set up to imbue a sense of humanity to the mythic overtones. It may be no accident that, for a film about Rocky's dissatisfying attempt to fill the mentor role, Stallone humbly concedes the direction of the film once again to the capable John G. Avildsen. If the villains are overly distilled and the character changes abrupt, it is for the sake of delivering narrative, rather than subverting it. The worst offense of *Rocky V* is the handling of Adrian who, as Rocky's protective wife, is overburdened with mostly propagandistic dialogue. Rocky, Jr. (Sage Stallone), however, works well as the foil to his father. This film does not contain deep subtext in the dialogue or sophisticated narrative style. It displays as much subtlety as a left hook, but it is so sincerely consistent to its own terms of overstatement as to be watchable. Reviews were divided, but a substantial portion acknowledge that *Rocky V* recaptures a great deal of the charm of the original.

The last scene depicts Rocky and his son together completing the now famous ascent to the Philadelphia Art Museum. Puffing a bit, Rocky muses that these steps keep growing taller every year. It is this wink of acknowledgement that nearly absolves the filmmakers. This latest installment comes as close to putting an old friend to rest with dignity as middle-class sentiment will allow. Hopefully, Stallone and Hollywood will quit while they are so miraculously ahead.

Mary E. Belles

Reviews
Boston Globe. November 16, 1990, CCXXXVIII, p. 78.
Chicago Tribune. November 16, 1990, VII, p. 43.
The Hollywood Reporter. CCCXV, November 13, 1990, p. 10.
Los Angeles. XXXVI, January, 1991, p. 119.

Los Angeles Times. November 16, 1990, p. F1.

The New York Times. November 16, 1990, CXL, p. B1.

Philadelphia. LXXXI, November, 1990, p. 118.

Premiere. IV, October, 1990, p. 77.

San Francisco Chronicle. November 16, 1990, CXXVI, p. E1.

San Francisco Examiner. November 16, 1990, CXXVI, p. C3.

Screen International. November 24, 1990, p. 34.

USA Today. November 16-18, 1990, p. 4D.

Variety. November 13, 1990, p. 2.

Variety. November 19, 1990, p. 79.

The Washington Post. November 16, 1990, CXIII, p. D1.

THE RUSSIA HOUSE

Production: Paul Maslansky and Fred Schepisi for Pathe Entertainment; released by
    Metro-Goldwyn-Mayer/United Artists
Direction: Fred Schepisi
Screenplay: Tom Stoppard; based on the novel by John le Carré
Cinematography: Ian Baker
Editing: Peter Honess
Production design: Richard MacDonald
Art direction: Roger Cain
Set decoration: Simon Wakefield
Sound: Chris Munro
Costume design: Ruth Myers
Music: Jerry Goldsmith and Branford Marsalis
MPAA rating: R
Running time: 123 minutes

> *Principal characters:*
> Barley .... Sean Connery
> Katya .... Michelle Pfeiffer
> Russell .... Roy Scheider
> Ned .... James Fox
> Brady .... John Mahoney
> Clive .... Michael Kitchen
> Walter .... Ken Russell
> Dante .... Klaus Maria Brandauer

The Russia House, a romantic spy thriller with political overtones, marks a new
direction in the oeuvre of talented Australian-born filmmaker Fred Schepisi, whose
previous critically acclaimed works include *The Chant of Jimmie Blacksmith* (1980),
Plenty (1985), *Roxanne* (1987), and *A Cry in the Dark* (1988).

Based on the superlative bestseller by John le Carré, with a script by award-
winning playwright Tom Stoppard (*Empire of the Sun*, 1987) and boasting a star-
studded international cast featuring Sean Connery, Michelle Pfeiffer, Roy Scheider,
and Klaus Maria Brandauer, *The Russia House* presents an attractive package for a
timely cinematic foray into the politics of spying in the era of *glasnost*. It is also the
first major Hollywood film to be made in the Soviet Union without Soviet coproduc-
tion. As such, it is a pioneering film, treating issues never before filmed in that country, as noted by producer Paul Maslansky, a veteran of Soviet coventures. Doubtless, its development was keenly observed by the Soviet bureaucracy as a model for
future foreign projects.

Unfortunately, the burden of motion-picture making under these heady distinc-
tions seems to have taken its toll. The script by Stoppard appears rushed, marked by

a discursive structure that defeats suspense and obscures the narrative, dialogue so elliptical that, at times, it verges on hermetic, and thin character development. While the principal actors deliver credible, if studied, performances (with the exception of Scheider), the romantic chemistry between Connery and Pfeiffer, the emotional core of the film, is tepid at best. The major failing, however, belongs to Schepisi, whose fawning views of Russian landmarks as backdrops—the Red Square, St. Basil's Cathedral, a gratuitous panoramic view from atop a Zagorsk bell tower, to name a few—seem pretentious and intrusive. The sheer majesty of the Soviet Union appears to have thwarted his judgment. Throughout, he sacrifices scene integrity for visual impact. Like a pre-*glasnost* tourist taking snapshots of forbidden subjects to smuggle out of Russia, he has indulged in "historical" filmmaking at the expense of his story.

The story, as told by le Carré, is a rather good one, to which Stoppard's screenplay generally adheres, in letter if not in spirit. It is about a dilettantish, loquacious, middle-aged British publisher, a bachelor named Barley Blair (Connery), who is distinguished by his saxophone playing, womanizing, drinking, and instinct for publishing unsuccessful books. Like many failures, he has devoted himself to a prolonged and bitter last hurrah. Yet, something continues to draw him to the Soviet Union and its *glasnost* bookfairs, where he peddles his titles and buys the works of obscure Soviet writers to debut in the West, usually at a loss. A cynic, he cites the Soviets' unabashed corruption and refreshing authenticity in playing catch-up with the West as the reasons for his attraction. One suspects him, however, of vaguely idealistic motives that are attached to the promise of the Soviet people. Perhaps his cynicism conceals a disillusioned romantic waiting to be rekindled with faith.

The catalyst comes in the shape of a beautiful Soviet book editor and divorced mother of two named Katya (Pfeiffer), who smuggles a manuscript by a former lover, code-named "Dante" (Brandauer), to Barley for publication. The manuscript, intercepted by the division of British Intelligence that is devoted to Soviet watching—known as the Russia House—appears to expose the Soviet's strategic missile capability as a fiasco. If true, then the West's plans to construct a "Star Wars" defense system is a monumental waste.

Once Barley is cleared of suspicion of acting as a Soviet spy, British Intelligence attempts to enlist him to meet with Dante and ascertain his reliability. Photographs of the beautiful Katya help Barley to overcome his habitual apathy and cynicism. British spymaster Ned (James Fox) is dubious of his "Joe"—craftspeak for agent—but decides to take a chance on him. Back in Moscow, Barley mixes romance with intrigue, as he tries to reassure Katya of his intentions to publish the unlikely manuscripts while soliciting information about Dante. Wearing a wire, he meets with Dante in Leningrad and makes it known that the British are interested in an ongoing relationship. The tapes reveal that Dante is a highly placed Soviet scientist working on strategic defense. This confirmation raises the ante, and the U.S. Central Intelligence Agency (CIA) is brought in.

Barley undergoes further "vetting," or interrogation, in the United States by the

CIA. Reluctantly, Russell (Scheider), Ned's skeptical American counterpart, commits CIA resources. Barley must return to the Soviet Union and attempt to "turn" Dante. An elaborate publishing scam is designed to account for his new American "partners," the CIA. Privately, Barley acknowledges that Katya is his only motivation. Meanwhile, Ned regrets losing control of his "Joe." Amid this intrigue and danger, Katya and Barley's romance progresses soberly. Her children take to him as well, and he marvels at her ability to sacrifice all, even her children, for a cause— the future of her country.

Katya receives a suspicious letter from Dante, writing from a hospital where he claims to be recuperating from hepatitis. He requests a meeting in Moscow, at which time Barley is to bring a definitive shopping list of questions about Soviet defense systems from the CIA and British Intelligence. It will be their last meeting. Back at the Russia House, informed of the letter, Russell celebrates the meeting as a coup, while Ned demurs, sensing something ominous in Dante's forwardness and in the shopping list, which, in design, might reveal as much about the West as they hope to discover about the Soviets. Barley, fearing that Dante has been caught by the KGB, tells Katya of his cooperation with British Intelligence. That night, after they make love for the first time, he resolves to protect her from herself and to save both her and the children.

Dante's scheduled telephone call to Katya reveals, through code, that he has indeed been taken by the KGB. Barley, an astonishingly quick study in spycraft, launches his own campaign of subterfuge. After convincing the Americans that the meeting with Dante is on, he arranges a deal with the Soviets to turn over the shopping list in exchange for Katya and her children. His own safety is of secondary concern. As progress reports filter back to the Russia House of Barley's supposed meeting with Dante, who is already dead, Ned realizes in an intuitive flash that his "Joe" has gone over to the other side. For Barley, however, this apparent treason is a redeeming act of courage and sacrifice. Surprisingly, the Soviets keep their end of the bargain, eventually releasing Katya and the children to Barley in Lisbon.

Unlike numerous films based on bestsellers that disappoint by diverging from the original, Schepisi's *The Russia House* suffers by not taking more liberties. Discursive and repetitive, recapitulating many of the story's plot twists in the course of Barley's interrogations and in his parting letter to Ned, it virtually deflates suspense. It is a film that begs to be refashioned into a more linear narrative. A very different story might have resulted, one less dependent on literary device, a trademark of le Carré's. *The Russia House*, the novel, is principally a character study of Barley Blair as told by Ned, his British spymaster, whose account is lent piquancy by Barley's betrayal. The book's tension is generated by Ned's attempt to understand a man like Barley, his "Joe," in light of his crossover to the Soviets. Interior and reflexive, its adaptability to the screen is problematic. Stoppard's screenplay, by downplaying Ned's point of view and relegating his valuable observations to a series of melodramatic confrontations with Russell over Barley's integrity, eviscerates the narrative of depth and reduces Barley to one dimension.

In the film, insight into Barley is limited to his comments to Katya, which, in the absence of Ned's subtext, ring pretentiously. Stoppard adds to their woodenness by couching them in "big scenes," denuded of amenities. The result is a series of hollow profundities, delivered by Barley to Katya—"I've never felt so alone," "All my failures were preparations for meeting you," "Now, you are my country"—which, in the absence of more overt action, are intended as turning points. Unfortunately, they do not resonate enough to be convincing. Not even Connery, stretching admirably, can give them life.

Elsewhere, Stoppard's bare-bones narrative and elliptical dialogue render Barley sketchily, as with other characters. Thus, Barley's alcoholism is only vaguely indicated by his modest request for a few fingers of scotch during his first vetting by the British, and later, in the United States, when the CIA allocates him a bottle. His womanizing is reduced to an ambiguous scene in Lisbon showing his wrecked apartment, destroyed apparently by his neglected mistress. As for Barley's alcohol-fueled wit, it is also given short shrift by Stoppard's stingy dialogue, which is almost entirely devoid of humor. With such scant character development, it is difficult to identify with Barley or feel much sympathy for his plight. Even his singular redeeming act, trading himself and the shopping list for Katya, happens offscreen, robbing the audience of a critical moment of identification.

Pfeiffer's Katya, admirably restrained and understated, is a triumphant characterization, given the dearth of material that Stoppard allots her. With her perfectly modulated Russian accent and repressed gestures, as though squelched by centuries of totalitarianism, she convincingly captures the essential Soviet citizen. Her portrayal is reminiscent of Meryl Streep's mastery of foreign cultural nuance in her films. It is a highwater mark for Pfeiffer. Unfortunately, Pfeiffer's luminous screen persona suffers in the bargain, and little heat is given off in her scenes with Connery, whose Barley smolders but never quite burns. Stoppard's minimalist scripting sustains the sober courtship that is described by le Carré, and they are given little chance to spark in their stolen moments together. These scenes are occasionally enlivened by clever double entendre, as Barley mixes spycraft with romance. Katya's reliance on the catchall phrase "it's not convenient," which also means "it's not proper" in Russian, is mildly titillating when Barley learns its alternative meaning, but overall their scenes together remain uninspired. The only unmitigated joke in the film is a faux pas by the Soviet cultural minister, who promises to get some good work out of his Gulag writers if it "kills them."

Brandauer's Dante presents an apt cameo of the passionate, idealistic Soviet scientist, naïve in his expectations for his manuscripts, easily seduced by Barley's bluff pontifications on freedom, and too willing to risk his life and Katya's for *glasnost*. James Fox's Ned finds the proper combination of British reserve and concern. Ken Russell's Walter, the flamboyant Russia House agent, is a delightful bit of eccentricity, though his role has been edited into obscurity. Roy Scheider's Russell, on the other hand, borders on caricature. At times, even he seems not to believe his own posturing.

A lack of establishing shots, with jump cuts from one interior to another, is befuddling at times, as are Schepisi's superfluous travelogue sweeps of the Soviet Union. At other times, his camera work is misleading. One telling scene takes place at Kolomenskoye, an old country estate of the Czars. Ominously dollying through the arches of a wooden courtyard at a low angle, Schepisi opens onto an idyllic picnic scene with an innocuous, if commanding, view of the Moscow River. Nothing more significant was intended. Cinematographer Ian Baker, a longtime Schepisi collaborator, must shoulder some of the blame for the film's ambiguous camera work.

Not even Academy Award-winning composer Jerry Goldsmith (*The Omen*, 1976), with an impressive list of credits that span twenty-five years, could inject more suspense into the soundtrack than the script calls for, try as he might. Saxophonist Branford Marsalis, the equally talented brother of Wynton and veteran of Art Blakey's Jazz Messengers, was the featured artist on the soundtrack.

In the final analysis, *The Russia House*, despite a formidable array of talent in front of and behind the camera, will be remembered as a well-intentioned film that is flawed by injudicious scripting, self-conscious camera work, and a tepid East/West love story. Unfortunately, le Carré's ironical commentary on the self-perpetuating machinery of the Cold War, grinding on because of and despite *glasnost*, was lost in the translation.

Eugene H. Davis

Reviews
The Christian Science Monitor. December 21, 1990, p. 12.
The Hollywood Reporter. CCCXV, December 11, 1990, p. 10.
Los Angeles Times. December 19, 1990, p. F1.
The New York Times. December 19, 1990, p. B4.
The New Yorker. LXVI, December 31, 1990, p. 84.
Newsweek. CXVI, December 24, 1990, p. 63.
Premiere. IV, December, 1990, p. 22.
Time. CXXXVI, December 17, 1990, p. 91.
Variety. December 12, 1990, p. 2.
The Washington Post. December 21, 1990, p. D1.

THE SHELTERING SKY

Production: Jeremy Thomas; released by Warner Bros.
Direction: Bernardo Bertolucci
Screenplay: Mark Peploe and Bernardo Bertolucci; based on the book by Paul
  Bowles
Cinematography: Vittorio Storaro
Editing: Gabriella Cristiani
Production design: Gianni Silvestri
Art direction: Andrew Sanders
Set decoration: Cynthia Sleiter
Sound: Ivan Sharrock
Costume design: James Acheson
Music: Ryuichi Sakamoto
Original North African music: Richard Horowitz
MPAA rating: R
Running time: 137 minutes

Principal characters:
>Port Moresby .... John Malkovich
>Kit Moresby .... Debra Winger
>George Tunner .... Campbell Scott
>Mrs. Lyle .... Jill Bennett
>Eric Lyle .... Timothy Spall
>Belquassim .... Eric Vu-An
>The Narrator .... Paul Bowles

Paul Bowles, a composer and author, and his wife, Jane, a writer of short fiction, moved to North Africa in the 1940's. They lived there for many years and produced some of the finest literature ever created by Americans. Perhaps because they both lived as expatriates in Tangier and set most of their fiction in foreign lands neither Jane nor Paul became household names in their home country. In 1949, Paul published the autobiographical novel *The Sheltering Sky* which became, if not a hugely successful bestseller, a critically acclaimed favorite of the slowly emerging beatnik generation. Almost immediately after publication, the film rights to the enigmatic story of three American travelers in the Sahara were snatched up by Hollywood and the project sat in a holding pattern for four decades. In 1986, director Bernardo Bertolucci was offered the rights and, after *The Last Emperor* (1987) won nine Academy Awards, Bertolucci acquired the clout to bring the noncommercial project to the screen. Unfortunately, what has emerged from Bowles's fascinating journey into the elusive minds of alienated wanderers is a film that is as languid and confused as its leading characters.

The film begins with snippets of post-World War II newsreels that capture the emerging optimism of American urban centers in the United States. Tacked onto these glimpses of productivity at home is the arrival of three spiritless Americans in Tangier: Port Moresby (John Malkovich), his wife, Kit (Debra Winger), and socialite George Tunner (Campbell Scott). Port, disillusioned with the modern age, has plans to travel to the most uncivilized parts of North Africa in search of some sense of connection to the world. Port seems to believe that, once stripped of any kind of cultural linkage, he will discover this illusory connection and will find new meaning in his life. Kit, desperate to rejuvenate her failing marriage, follows her husband without question, and Tunner, sexually attracted to Kit and detecting the rift between her and Port, brings up the rear.

One night early in their journey, Port visits a prostitute, whose attempted robbery of his wallet leads to an all-night escapade. With her husband noticeably away, Kit allows herself to be charmed by Tunner. When Port decides to move on to a less-civilized, less-cultured area of North Africa, he accepts a ride with priggish Mrs. Lyle (Jill Bennett) and her pimply, overbearing son, Eric (Timothy Spall), while Kit and Tunner must take a local train. Kit, terrified by trains, is soothed by champagne that is supplied by Tunner and later is seduced by her young suitor.

Feeling guilty, Kit goes bicycling with Port and, at the edge of the desert, they desperately attempt to make love. Port, however, is unable to perform; he has too many questions swirling in his mind, and he declares that they are too out of syn-chronization to meld together as lovers. All Kit can secure is a confession from Port that he loves her deeply and a small suggestion that their marriage may be salvage-able once they finish their journey. Later, Port conspires to continue on without Tunner, and Kit, feeling a new bond with her husband, complies. Eric, who has constantly harangued Port for money, steals his passport, and Port, annoyed at the loss, pushes on with Kit to an obscure town further into the desert. Riding on a crowded, fly-infested bus, Kit and Port travel farther away from modern civilization.

When they arrive at their destination, Port is struck with typhoid fever and Kit, frantic, is unable to find help. Kit is able to load Port onto a truck and drive him to a Foreign Legion fort, where she attempts to nurse him back to health. Kit, becoming more and more desperate, searches for medical help while Port suffers. Despite some last-minute assistance from the authorities, Port dies after claiming that he is sorry that he selfishly ignored the vital connection he could have had with Kit.

After Port dies, a dazed Kit, apparently taking up where Port left off, walks into the desert and wanders into a caravan of Bedouin nomads that is led by the virile Belquassim (Eric Vu-An). Kit begins to travel with the group and slowly becomes Belquassim's silent lover. When the group arrives at their settlement, Belquassim se-questers a passive Kit in his quarters, visiting her for periods of intense lovemaking. When Belquassim is away, the suspicious women of the commune taunt her, and later, when visiting the village, Kit's inability to communicate with the natives causes them to turn violently on her. Battle-scarred, she is sent to a sanitarium in Tangier where Tunner, who has been searching for her, waits. Before she can be reunited with her earnest suitor, Kit, seeking the anonymity of her life as a love slave and the lack of personal involvement that she had with the people of the Bedouin community, wanders off into the streets of the North African city.

The Sheltering Sky is filled with the luscious images that are typical of a Bertolucci film: He captures the sensuous vibrancy of the North African cities in much the same way that he re-created the opulent wonder of China's Forbidden City in *The Last Emperor.* Long-time collaborator Vittorio Storaro provides stunning cinematography that includes a harrowing sequence in which the camera appears to shrink around Kit as her husband suffers in the tight confines of the desert fort. Composer Ryuichi Sakamoto, with his moving, operatic score, is able to add force to narrative sequences when all else is unsuccessful. Together with James Acheson's costumes and Gianni Silvestri's production design, Richard Horowitz' original North African music lends a sophisticated air of authenticity to the film. Unfortunately, all these above-average accoutrements cannot save a production whose half-baked script, with dialogue made up of glaring non sequiturs, meanders hopelessly around the thematic map.

Obviously, part of Bertolucci's problem in his adaptation is built from the source material. Bowles's book, heavy on observation and insight, is light on dialogue and action. Although Port and Kit Moresby travel throughout North Africa, their journey is an internal one that takes them from self-examination to self-obliteration. More corrosive, however, is Bertolucci's tendency to douse everything that he presents with large doses of alluring sensuality, which leads to an oversimplified cinematic interpretation that substitutes sexual liberation for psychological disintegration. What once was a tale of a widow's sexual slavery and tragic loss of identity has, in Bertolucci's sensuous hands, become a tale of a newfound sexuality that is brought on by the demise of a frigid spouse. The director and his screenwriter, Mark Peploe, have turned Bowles's grim story into an erotic adventure.

Film and literature are two separate and unique mediums. Therefore, comparing a book and a film that tackle the same material is suspect. A comparison between a successful novel and its fledgling film counterpart, however, is useful in determining what happened along the adaptation's way. Even though Bertolucci mixes in a significant amount of his trademark eroticism, he and Peploe are much too faithful to Bowles's narrative. They try too hard to externalize the internal activities of the characte —in the film, Kit and Port say, often quite senselessly, what they merely think in the book. In an attempt to translate Bowles's own musings on the human condition, Bertolucci and Peploe have created an additional character called "The Narrator," played by Bowles himself, who sits in a cafe and provides commentary in voice-overs. At the film's conclusion, Bowles gives a speech that is supposed to provide a tidy moral to the narrative but instead, with its warning to never take for granted any day of life, merely trivializes what has come before it.

Bertolucci's greatest sin, however, is his ignorance of pace and focus. There are several long periods in *The Sheltering Sky* where Bertolucci devotes the film to lengthy travelogue shots that, initially breathtaking, quickly become stale. The natives beat their drums, the camels toddle, the sand glistens, but the actors, like the audience, simply watch listlessly. Malkovich, whose loony theatrical style is a perfect match for the histrionic personality of Port, and Winger, too durable an actress to play the helpless Kit, play second fiddle to the dusty environment. The ideas and themes that are contained in *The Sheltering Sky* slide in and out of the narrative like lost thoughts; not one is ever developed completely through character action or dialogue. It seems as if Bertolucci thought a languid pace, which some critics have called seductive, would emphasize Kit and Port's spiritlessness. Instead, it made his film, which ended up poison at the box office, as apathetic as his characters.

Greg Changnon

Reviews

Chicago Tribune. January 11, 1991, VII, p. 15.
Entertainment Weekly. December 14, 1990, p. 44.
The Hollywood Reporter. CCCXV, November 26, 1990, p. 5.
Los Angeles Times. December 12, 1990, p. F1.
New York Magazine. XXIII, December 17, 1990, p. 52.
The New York Times. December 12, 1990, p. B1.
The New Yorker. LXVI, December 17, 1990, p. 118.
Newsweek. CXVI, December 17, 1990, p. 68.
Sight and Sound. LX, Winter, 1990, p. 66.
The Times Literary Supplement. November 30, 1990, p. 1292.
Variety. CCCXLI, November 26, 1990, p. 2.
The Washington Post. January 11, 1991, p. D6.

SIBLING RIVALRY

Production: David Lester, Don Miller, and Liz Glotzer for Castle Rock
    Entertainment, in association with Nelson Entertainment; released by Columbia
    Pictures
Direction: Carl Reiner
Screenplay: Martha Goldhirsh
Cinematography: Reynaldo Villalobos
Editing: Bud Molin
Production design: Jeannine Oppewall
Set decoration: Lisa Fischer
Sound: Richard Goodman
Costume design: Durinda Wood
Music: Jack Elliott
MPAA rating: PG-13
Running time: 88 minutes

    Principal characters:
        Marjorie Turner .... Kirstie Alley
        Nick Meany .... Bill Pullman
        Iris Turner-Hunter .... Carrie Fisher
        Jeanine .... Jami Gertz
        Harry Turner .... Scott Bakula
        Charles Turner, Jr. .... Sam Elliott
        Wilbur Meany .... Ed O'Neill
        Rose Turner .... Frances Sternhagen
        Charles Turner, Sr. .... John Randolph
        Pat .... Bill Macy
        Casey Hunter .... Matthew Laurance
        Plotner .... Paul Benedict

Sibling Rivalry was widely praised as the return-to-form of Carl Reiner, the acclaimed genius behind the classic 1960's television series *The Dick Van Dyke Show* and the cult 1970 film *Where's Poppa?* In the early 1980's, he directed several interesting, if not always commercially successful films starring comedian Steve Martin, including *Dead Men Don't Wear Plaid* (1982) and *All of Me* (1984). Since then, however, Reiner has been overshadowed by his son, Rob Reiner, and has directed light, forgettable comedies. On closer examination, the successful *Sibling Rivalry* also belongs in that category.

In *Sibling Rivalry*, Marjorie Turner (Kirstie Alley) had planned on being a writer—"like Sylvia Plath, only happy"—but instead married a young doctor who, over the years, has turned into a workaholic. Marjorie's life consists of running errands in her late-model car and waiting on her husband, Harry (Scott Bakula), and her in-laws, all physicians as well and all prone to arriving at her home unannounced. In addition, she must constantly worry about her unconventional younger sister Jeanine (Jami Gertz), who, although on her own, has been Marjorie's responsibility since the girls were orphaned as youngsters. Across town, another pair of siblings is having difficulty. Wilbur (Ed O'Neill) is a policeman who hopes to be promoted to chief of police but is worried that his younger brother may tarnish his reputation. Young Nick (Bill Pullman) is deeply in debt to his older brother, and he is about to be fired from yet another job, this time as a salesman of vertical blinds. Desperate, Nick tells his boss Pat (Bill Macy) that he knows he can arrange a contract for blinds at a major luxury hotel.

Marjorie visits Jeanine at her job at the tropical fish store, a less-than-upwardly-mobile "career" that satisfies Jeanine and annoys Marjorie. When Marjorie chides Jeanine for her lack of stability and history of short-lived relationships, Jeanine retaliates by noting Marjorie's unhappiness with Harry and her abandoned writing career. Taunting Marjorie loudly—to the delight of the store customers—about her premarital virginity and subsequent naïveté, Jeanine suggests that Marjorie alleviate her depression by having an affair. Stung and angry, Marjorie continues on her round of domestic errands by going to the grocery store. She must prepare a feast in honor of the homecoming of yet another doctor in the Turner family: Harry's older brother Charles, the Nobel-nominated "golden boy" who has been overseas for fifteen years.

At the market, Marjorie attracts the attention of a handsome stranger (Sam Elliott), who gently flirts with her, drawing her into his selection of a fruit gift-basket. He tells Marjorie that he is due at a party, but that now he would rather not go, and solicits her help in writing the gift card. Her suggestion—"Start without me"—sends them from the store to a long, romantic lunch. Over wine, Marjorie tells the stranger how unfulfilled she feels and how much it has been incumbent upon her to be "good" her entire life. The man asks her to think of what would happen if she forgot her inhibitions, and although she is initially afraid, the two go to a hotel, where Marjorie has the first satisfying sexual experience of her inexperienced life. Afterward, cooing, Marjorie cuddles up to the man, who lies with his eyes closed, to thank him and ask him his name. When she receives no reply, she shakes him, checks his breathing, and realizes with horror that he is dead.

Meanwhile, Nick has failed to persuade the desk clerk to let him into a room to install vertical blinds. Nick attempts to pick the lock of a room when he sees Marjorie scramble from hers in a panic, stumble over the blinds, and drop her wallet. Nick tries to catch her as the elevator closes, but, having failed, he enters her open room, oblivious to the body that lies beneath a drawn sheet, and proceeds to hang the blinds. Back at home, Marjorie calls 911 and leaves an anonymous tip about the corpse in the room. When hotel security checks the room, they are stopped at the door by a nervous Nick. Once alone again, Nick proceeds with his covert installation, but loses control of a blind, which bashes the corpse in the temple. Discovering the body in the bed, Nick assumes that he is responsible for the man's death.

In the Turner kitchen, Jeanine is helping Marjorie prepare for Charles's homecoming dinner. Nick, having found Marjorie's wallet and believing her to be the wife of the man he "killed," calls and asks her to come to the hotel. On the edge of hysteria, she tells her irritable in-laws that she must leave for a moment, just as a familiar fruit basket and note—"Start without me"—arrive. Gasping, she races to the hotel. Once Marjorie and Nick are alone in the hotel room, *Sibling Rivalry* loses its manic pace and the credible sense of danger which is crucial to black comedy. Marjorie and Nick's various confessions and blackmail threats generate neither action nor emotion, coming across instead as unnecessary exposition. After several leaden minutes, Nick and Marjorie agree to work together and make Charles's death appear to be a suicide. Nick pushes the medicinal contents of Marjorie's purse down the corpse's throat with a pencil, while Marjorie composes a poetic, ambiguous suicide note.

Meanwhile, Wilbur has been sent to Marjorie's house in order to investigate the seemingly false 911 report. When Wilbur arrives, however, he finds Jeanine alone, Harry and his family having departed angrily at Charles's absence and Jeanine's cooking. Although Jeanine can offer no information, she and Wilbur are attracted to one another and spend a long time drinking tea and talking. The next day, Marjorie and Jeanine go out for lunch. While Jeanine dreams aloud about Wilbur, Marjorie sobs across the table from her, then runs to the bathroom. Jeanine follows her, and is both shocked and pleased when Marjorie confesses her infidelity and its subsequent disaster.

At the hospital, Harry and his sister Iris (Carrie Fisher) join the pathologist, Dr. Plotner (Paul Benedict), for the final autopsy results on Charles, who has finally been found and identified. Dr. Plotner, pulling undissolved laxatives, menstrual cramp remedies, and the pencil eraser from Charles's throat, concludes that Charles's suicide had been faked, and that the real cause of death was a heart attack following sexual activity. As the various clues begin to implicate Marjorie, Jeanine goes to Wilbur's house for dinner and tries to dissuade him from further investigation into Marjorie's 911 call. They spend a happy night together, but the next morning Nick calls to say that he has turned himself in for accidental murder.

Harry calls the family together and tells them that Nick has confessed to Charles's murder. Jeanine rushes over to Marjorie and silently pleads with her to confess. Her nerves frayed, Marjorie tries to speak to Harry alone in order to tell him the truth, but his family insists that she speak in front of them. Completely desperate, Marjorie quickly relates the real story. Harry's family feels vindicated in their dislike of Marjorie and try to persuade Harry to side with them, but Harry's fury is beyond their pettiness. He orders his family from his home, then runs upstairs, packs, and leaves Marjorie.

In the last minutes, *Sibling Rivalry* regains a perfunctory pace as Marjorie narrates a montage sequence that covers several months and resolves the loose ends of the story. Marjorie's confession frees Nick, who returns to the hotel to remove his blinds. The hotel manager catches him, loves the blinds, and gives him the huge sale he needs to secure his job. Wilbur receives his promotion, and he and Jeanine continue their relationship. In her solitude, Marjorie turns to writing and chronicles her fiasco with Charles, which is published. When Harry reads her book, he calls Marjorie, telling her that he has left his family's practice and opened his own. He asks if he might drop in some time and appears a few minutes later, having called from his car phone. He tells Marjorie that he recognized himself in her story and apologizes for taking her for granted; the film ends with their embrace.

Sibling Rivalry skirts the edges of competence. The film is static and suffers from several awkward cuts and overall flat lighting. Although Reiner has likened it to the black humor of *Where's Poppa?*, it has none of the former film's inspired madness. The scene in which Marjorie and Nick fake Charles's suicide, for example, with its leaden dialogue and action, crosses the border from the daring to the tasteless.

Yet *Sibling Rivalry* did well at the box office, the result of Kirstie Alley's enormous box-office appeal and the scarcity of quality adult comedies. While several performances offer bright spots, Scott Bakula, who is the brilliantly emotive wizard in the television series *Quantum Leap*, languishes in an underwritten role. Ed O'Neill, however, from Fox Broadcasting's subversive series *Married . . . With Children*, reveals surprising range, portraying a tender, attractive character quite unlike his brutish television persona. Especially amusing is the Turner family *en masse*, with a standout performance from Carrie Fisher. Indeed, Reiner's handling of the quintessential 1980's family is deft. Ironically, *Sibling Rivalry* fails to focus on the subtleties of family life that its title promises.

Gabrielle J. Forman

Reviews

Chicago Tribune. October 26, 1990, VII, p. 20.
The Hollywood Reporter. CCCXIV, October 22, 1990, p. 5.
Los Angeles. XXXV, November, 1990, p. 223.
Los Angeles Times. October 26, 1990, p. F10.
The New Republic. CCIII, November 26, 1990, p. 28.
The New York Times. October 26, 1990, p. B6.
People Weekly. XXXIV, November 26, 1990, p. 16.
Rolling Stone. November 15, 1990, p. 162.
Variety. CCCXLI, October 22, 1990, p. 2.
The Washington Post. October 26, 1990, p. C2.

STANLEY AND IRIS

Production: Arlene Sellers and Alex Winitsky for Metro-Goldwyn-Mayer; released
  by Metro-Goldwyn-Mayer/United Artists
Direction: Martin Ritt
Screenplay: Harriet Frank, Jr., and Irving Ravetch; based on the novel *Union Street,*
  by Pat Barker
Cinematography: Donald McAlpine
Editing: Sidney Levin
Production design: Joel Schiller
Art direction: Alicia Keywan
Set decoration: Steve Shewchuk
Sound: Richard Lightstone
Makeup: Suzanne Benoit
Costume design: Theoni Aldredge
Music: John Williams
MPAA rating: PG-13
Running time: 104 minutes

Principal characters:
Iris King	Jane Fonda
Stanley Cox	Robert De Niro
Sharon	Swoosie Kurtz
Kelly	Martha Plimpton
Richard	Harley Cross
Leonides Cox	Feodor Chaliapin
Elaine	Zhora Lampert
Joe	Jamey Sheridan

Some critics of American film have charged that Hollywood has never been comfortable with showing work. As a consequence, they say, even Hollywood films about the working class can be expected to avoid depicting the everyday grind of actual labor. Instead, American films comfort audiences with wish-fulfilling stories in which a protagonist rises in Horatio Alger-like fashion from rags to riches.

Nevertheless, there have been eras in which the working class and the problems of work have become an important cinematic subject. In particular, the nationwide trauma of the Great Depression in the 1930's spurred an increase in Hollywood's so-called social-consciousness films such as *The Grapes of Wrath* (1940), which detailed the plight of the newly poor or the already downtrodden. In the 1980's, in spite of the increase in the numbers of Americans who were dropping into poverty, struggling with illiteracy, or coping with being homeless, a similar cinematic commitment to revealing the problems of the nation's working class was not forthcoming. *Stanley and Iris* is one of the first commercial films of the 1990's to focus attention on the contemporary problems of the working class. More specifically, the film attempts to address the growing national crisis of illiteracy, a problem affecting some 27 million adults in the United States.

Stanley and Iris begins with a panoramic view of a dying New England town, where the economic security of one era has been transformed into the economic woes of another. In a town once thriving because of its factories, factories are now closed. Industry is gone, and the economic base for skilled and semi-skilled labor that once permitted one hardworking generation to catapult another into a better life has disappeared. At the Nevins and Davis bakery, work continues, but it is generally unskilled work, boring and backbreaking. After a day of mixing dough, packaging bread, or icing cakes, the workers leave for home. Among them is Iris (Jane Fonda), who boards the bus. On the way, she becomes the victim of a purse snatching. She pursues the thief onto the street. After a struggle, he escapes. Stanley Cox (Robert De Niro), a cook in the bakery's cafeteria, has followed her to help but catches up to her too late. She is unhurt, but he warns her that trying to stop the robber was reckless. She protests that she lost everything: her paycheck, her rosary, her family pictures.

Stanley escorts Iris to her house, a modest wooden bungalow with peeling white paint and a kitchen full of dirty dishes. Her sister Sharon (Swoosie Kurtz) and brother-in-law Joe (Jamey Sheridan) are both unemployed. They are living with Iris and her two children, but strained finances make the situation tense. Since her husband died eight months earlier, Iris has barely managed to make ends meet. Her job on the line at the bakery and looking after her two children take all of her time. She is not interested in a romantic relationship, but by chance she runs into Stanley again, at the shoe repair shop. He has no ticket for his shoes. The repairman insists that he sign for them. Stanley refuses, jumping over the counter to retrieve his shoes. Iris is mystified by his behavior since he seems to be such a quiet and kind man. One day at work, she misses her bus and accepts Stanley's offer of a ride home on his bicycle. As they ride over the dirty, deserted streets, he tells her of his aged father (Feodor Chaliapin), with whom he lives, and of his desire to move to the country.

Stanley and Iris happen to meet at work, then again at a laundry. As they wait for their clothes to dry, they share an eggroll and their lives. In the following days, she sees him cleaning up in the factory cafeteria. She asks him for an aspirin. He proceeds to bring out, one by one, an array of products—all meant for some other ailment. She is perplexed. Suddenly, she overhears his manager berate him for a shortage in supplies. Attempting to defend him, she blurts out her sudden realization: Stanley cannot read or write. Her outburst leads the manager to fire Stanley, because he fears the company could be sued if Stanley confused foodstuff packages with dangerous pesticides or cleaning agents. Stanley takes a janitor's job, digs ditches, and joins the ranks of those standing in line for manual labor, but he does not make enough to pay the rent. Reduced to living in a garage, he is forced to send his father to the state home for the aged, where he soon dies. This traumatic loss prompts Stanley to go to the bakery to beg Iris to teach him how to read. She is reluctant: She has her own problems. Iris is coping with the unexpected pregnancy of her teenage daughter, Kelly (Martha Plimpton). Despite her family troubles, she agrees to teach Stanley.

Quickly, it becomes evident that Stanley has a romantic interest in Iris. She, however, is still grieving for her husband. Their lessons continue, but Stanley fails his first practical test at reading and quits. Days later, she finds him to tell him that she was inadequate as a teacher. He refuses to let her take responsibility for his failure. He shows her his amazing mechanical inventions. He also tells her that this talent has gained for him job offers that he has had to refuse. He wants to break out of the prison of failure and isolation created by his illiteracy. He appears at her house ready to learn again.

Iris' own frustrations intensify. Her daughter quits school after the birth of her baby and takes a job at the bakery. Iris and Stanley's romantic attraction grows, but Iris finds it impossible to start a sexual relationship. Stanley quits their tutorials. Months go by, then he reappears. By this time, both Stanley and Iris have made strides. Iris tells him that she is ready to stop obsessively visiting her husband's grave. Stanley has progressed in his learning. In a short time, with her help, he is able to read anything. He goes to Detroit to interview for a job, his talent no longer stymied by his inability to read. He gets the job. In spite of Iris' fears that he will never return, he faithfully continues to write to her. One night as Iris is walking across the street with an armful of groceries, Stanley appears in a new car. He is a complete success in his new job, has picked out a house to buy for his new family, and asks her to marry him; she agrees. They affirm that anything is possible.

Stanley and Iris is a film graced by the talents of numerous award-winning actors and filmmakers, including Tony award-winning actress, Swoosie Kurtz, and the Oscar-nominated screenwriting team of Irving Ravetch and Harriet Frank, Jr. With two Academy Awards each, Robert De Niro and Jane Fonda, in the title roles, would appear to be unmatchable as box-office and performance assets, especially to a serious-minded film that actually does manage to convey a glimpse of what work is like for women on the line in a food industry. No doubt, the star power of the two leading players explains even the marginal box-office return that *Stanley and Iris* managed to achieve upon its release.

Unfortunately, such well-known, high-power Hollywood talent also brings certain drawbacks to a story of working-class people. While De Niro has frequently been associated with inarticulate or troubled working-class protagonists, such as Michael in *The Deer Hunter* (1978), Jake La Motta in *Raging Bull* (1980), and the young Vito Corleone in *The Godfather, Part II* (1974), Jane Fonda seems radically miscast in her role as Iris. Her clipped, self-assured manner of speaking gives away her patrician upbringing as a member of one of Hollywood's most famous acting families. As a personality, she has come to personify the possibility of ultra-fit, middle-aged glamour. Hence, *Newsweek* remarked on the unbelievability of the moment in the film when Iris feels too fat to step on a scale. More importantly, Fonda's trim, tan body and relentlessly bouncy walk belie the representation of Iris as a woman who has weathered not only decades of menial work but also illness (colitis) resulting from unmanageable worry.

Some critics also registered a measure of incredulity at the final twist in the film's plot. Stanley's remarkable talent for invention provides a happy ending that rang false to many reviewers who thought that a modestly hopeful ending would have been considerably more realistic. Also frequently mentioned was the film's emphasis on the romantic involvement between the pupil and his reading tutor. Some reviewers thought that the love story interfered with the social theme of illiteracy and gave a distorted impression of the close but nevertheless professional relationship formed by the thousands of participants in the many volunteer reading programs run throughout the United States.

Consequently, in spite of its valiant attempt to bring an important national issue to the screen, *Stanley and Iris* falls into familiar Hollywood traps. Rather than deal directly with illiteracy and its widely destructive influence, especially on disproportionate numbers of ethnic and racial minorities, the film indulges in easy answers and sentimental wish fulfillment, perhaps in response to a perceived need to make the audience feel good. By sugarcoating its message and glamorizing its protagonists, *Stanley and Iris* leaves it to some future film to provide a more honest revelation of working-class hardship and heartache in late twentieth century America.

Gaylyn Studlar

Reviews
American Film: Magazine of the Film and Television Arts. XV, October, 1990, p. 60.
Boxoffice. April, 1990, p. R29.
Chicago Tribune. February 9, 1990, VII, p. 39.
Films in Review. XLI, June, 1990, p. 364.
The Hollywood Reporter. CCCXIII, January 22, 1990, p. 4.
Los Angeles Times. February 9, 1990, p. F1.
The New Republic. CCII, February 26, 1990, p. 26.
The New York Times. February 9, 1990, C12.
Newsweek. CXV, February 19, 1990, p. 66.
Variety. CCXXVIII, January 22, 1990, p. 2.
The Washington Post. February 9, 1990, p. D7.

STELLA

Production: Samuel Goldwyn, Jr., for the Samuel Goldwyn Company and
   Touchstone Pictures; released by Buena Vista
Direction: John Erman
Screenplay: Robert Getchell; based on the novel *Stella Dallas*, by Olive Higgins
   Prouty
Cinematography: Billy Williams
Editing: Jerrold L. Ludwig
Production design: James Hulsey
Art direction: Jeffrey Ginn
Set decoration: Steve Shewchuk
Special effects: Doug Graham and Martin Malivoire
Sound: Bruce Carwardine
Makeup: Bob Mills, Suzanne Benoit, and Richard Blair
Costume design: Theadora Van Runkle
Choreography: Pat Birch
Music: John Morris
MPAA rating: PG-13
Running time: 114 minutes

Principal characters:

Stella Claire	Bette Midler
Ed Munn	John Goodman
Jenny Claire	Trini Alvarado
Stephen Dallas	Stephen Collins
Janice Morrison	Marsha Mason
Mrs. Wilkerson	Eileen Brennan
Debbie Whitman	Linda Hart
Jim Uptegrove	Ben Stiller
Pat Robbins	William McNamara
Bob Morrison	John Bell

Stella illustrates the power of motion pictures to change the meaning of any story, even a simple one of mother-daughter love. Olive Higgins Prouty's popular novel *Stella Dallas* was first brought to the screen in 1925, with Belle Bennett as Stella Dallas. In 1937, the novel was again brought to the screen with veteran director King Vidor at the helm. Barbara Stanwyck assumed the role of Stella Dallas, while Anne Shirley essayed the role of her beloved daughter, Laurel. The film was a phenomenal success, in spite of the fact that some critics thought the story material too old-fashioned, too overwrought for a "modern" audience.

Central to the problem of the latest updating of *Stella Dallas* is the depiction of class difference. Set in 1969, *Stella* begins with Stella Claire (Bette Midler) working as a bartender in a blue-collar bar. With her mother dead of alcoholism and her father a victim of a fatal construction accident, she has no one except Ed Munn (John Goodman), a rowdy friend who harbors an unrequited love for her. For reasons unexplained by the script, Stephen Dallas (Stephen Collins), a doctor at a local hospital, frequents the working-class bar. One night he sees Stella doing a mock striptease. He returns to ask her for a date, but Stella flatly refuses, telling him that "oil and water" do not mix, in other words, that their class differences make any relationship an impossibility. She says he is "just a little too fancy" for her, but the barriers of class difference appear to dissolve as she relents to his request and Stephen joins in her more raucous, "lower-class" ways that include disrupting a lieder recital.

One morning, he announces that he will be leaving to complete his medical residency in New York City, but Stella has her own announcement: She is pregnant. She does not know exactly how she wants to deal with this problem because, as she says, she does not know what she wants. Stephen proposes marriage, but Stella refuses his offer as one prompted by a feeling of duty rather than love. Unlike Stanwyck's Stella, this Stella has no apparent ambitions to escape her class origins even though she remarks on the unhappy fate of her parents. Stephen leaves, and she is left alone, with only Ed to help her through her pregnancy.

As in the 1937 version, Stella is more interested in a good time than in motherhood until she realizes the pleasures of parenting. Almost immediately, her life begins to revolve around her child, Jenny (Trini Alvarado), to the exclusion of all other relationships. Jenny is approximately three years old before Stephen comes to visit. In the 1937 version, Stella accepts money from her husband so that she and her daughter can lead an acceptably comfortable middle-class existence. In *Stella*, mother and daughter live in poverty, because Stella steadfastly refuses to accept money from her former lover, even though that money might give her daughter the things she needs and wants. Although this may establish Stella as a product of the liberal side of the 1960's, it also makes the audience wonder exactly how much Stella considers the welfare of her child in such a decision.

When Stephen visits for the first time since his daughter's birth, he criticizes the spontaneous party that has erupted among Stella's friends. Although Jenny has never seen him, she immediately accepts him as her "daddy." A deep bond is formed between them. The film shows, over the course of many years, their dinners together in expensive New York City restaurants, as the daughter grows into adolescence. This change from the earlier film versions of the story creates one of the central dramatic problems with *Stella*. In trying to prevent Stephen Dallas from being the cardboard villain of the piece, *Stella* delays and downplays the special bonding between mother and daughter that formed the heart-tugging emotional core to the Stanwyck/Shirley version. Instead, the mother/daughter relationship appears characterized as much by conflict as by loving commitment. The conflict increases as Jenny reaches college age. In the presence of her father, Jenny is polite, content, and happy. With her mother, she is sullen and judgmental, particularly in regard to Stella's friendship with Ed Munn.

For reasons that can only be attributable to the film's representation of the lower class, Stella sees Jenny slipping away from her longstanding ambition to be an architect and from the hope of a better life. Jenny takes up with an abusive, cocaine-sniffing boyfriend, Jim Uptegrove (Ben Stiller), who literally throws her out of his car when she refuses to have sex with him. When she returns home from this incident, she argues violently with her mother.

In this respect, the film seems to be the inadvertent ideological product of the Reaganite 1980's and its much-discussed emphasis on material acquisition. Through its comparative treatment of the rich and the poor, *Stella* could very well be seen as promoting the notion that being poor is a crime, even as being rich is the reward for being a superior (and appropriately ambitious) person. Sympathetic portraits of Stephen and his love interest, Janice Morrison (Marsha Mason), rescue the upper class from the old stereotype of the rich as self-interested and greedy. In contrast, Ed Munn's drunken, sexualized play around Jenny, Jenny's boyfriend's abusive conduct, and the disgusting sexual advances made by Ed's drinking buddy toward Stella serve to confirm a vision of the working class as virtually devoid of any positive attributes. This stands in marked contrast to the 1937 version, which established Ed as a much more benign and likable sort, even as Stella's energy and enthusiasm served as wordless critical commentary on the "undertaker" attitude of Stephen Dallas.

When Jenny goes to her father for her regular visit, he introduces her to Janice, a widow and mother who works as a Random House editor. Ironically, she married rich and raised herself out of rural poverty into wealth and happiness. Janice nurtures Jenny's "finer" social aspirations. At a dance, Jenny meets Pat Robbins (William McNamara), a student at Brown University who has rejected his parents' monetary ambitions for him: He wants to teach elementary school. Jenny and Pat become romantically attracted to each other. When Jenny returns home, Stella realizes that Janice and Stephen are rivals with her for her daughter's affection. Stella obtains a credit card to take Jenny to the resort in Florida where Pat and his parents are vacationing. Jenny and Pat have a wonderful time until Stella emerges from her room and makes a sexual spectacle of herself by donning an outrageous dress and drunkenly attempting to dance with a bartender.

In Vidor's *Stella Dallas*, a similar though much more restrained scene becomes the impetus for an emotionally wrenching climax: As they ride back on the train, Stella overhears some of Laurel's friends ridicule her appearance at the resort. Until this moment Stella never knew she was a barrier to her daughter's social advancement. Laurel also overhears them; she crawls down to her mother's sleeping berth. Stella acts as if she has been asleep. Neither one admits to hearing the cruel comments. Instead, Laurel wordlessly holds Stella in her arms. Because Vidor does not allow the characters to cry for themselves and because Stella's only sin is one of style, the viewer willingly assumes the burden of crying for the characters' plight.

In *Stella*, the daughter's sympathy for her mother at this critical moment in the narrative is totally blunted by her own self-involvement. When they return home from Florida, Jenny despairs that she will never hear from Pat. She resumes her relationship with Uptegrove and temporarily ends up in jail when she is picked up in a drug raid. Consequently, in *Stella*, social norms and upper-class judgments based on superficial standards do not assume the role of villain, but the dangers of poverty work to separate a loving mother and her daughter. As a result, the film gives credence to the view that Stella is, inadvertently, a bad mother since she stubbornly refuses to take Stephen's money and protect her daughter from the bad influences that are constructed by the film as the inevitable norm for their social class.

The only answer is for Stella to give Jenny to Stephen. Stella tricks Jenny into thinking that she no longer cares about or wants her. Jenny goes to live with her father and Janice, his new wife. Months later, Jenny and Pat are married as Stella, thought to be married to Ed Munn and thousands of miles away, looks upon her daughter's high society marriage as an anonymous outsider, left standing on the street to peer through a rain-streaked window and her own tears.

In reference to *Stella Dallas* (1937), Barbara Stanwyck once remarked that there is a difference between honest sentiment and the sentimental. It is that difference that the makers of *Stella* have seemingly forgotten. Not surprisingly, critical and box-office response to the film was lackluster. Although the film draws upon the talents of Academy Award-nominated screenwriter Robert Getchell, veteran television director John Erman, and Academy Award-winning cinematographer, Billy Williams, the film's considerable technical polish cannot hide its desperate attempt to break the viewer's heart. While the acting, in particular, frequently relies on shamelessly sentimental maneuvers to elicit viewer emotion, Stella unwittingly undermines our sympathy for Stella's plight. She is made the victim of her own stubborn independence; her relationship to Jenny is undercut by the film's idealization of the realm of the rich. In this order, parents can afford to tell their children, as Janice does, that on the level of personal style, "less is always more." In the case of *Stella's* revision of a classic story of maternal love, the filmmakers should have taken that succinct bit of advice to heart.

Gaylyn Studlar

Reviews
Boxoffice. April, 1990, p. R29.
Chicago Tribune. February 2, 1990, VII, p. 37.
The Christian Science Monitor. March 9, 1990, p. 10.
Entertainment Weekly. February 12, 1990, p. 24.
The Hollywood Reporter. CCCXI, January 31, 1990, p. 4.
Los Angeles Times. February 2, 1990, p. F1.
The New Republic. CCII, March 5, 1990, p. 26.
New Statesman and Society. III, September 14, 1990, p. 27.
The New York Times. February 2, 1990, p. B1.
Newsweek. CXV, February 19, 1990, p. 66.
Variety. CCXXVIII, February 1, 1990, p. 2.
The Washington Post. February 2, 1990, p. C1.

SWEETIE

Origin: Australia
Released: 1989
Released in U.S.: 1990
Production: John Maynard and William MacKinnon for Arena Film; released by Avenue Pictures
Direction: Jane Campion
Screenplay: Jane Campion and Gerard Lee
Cinematography: Sally Bongers
Editing: Veronika Haussler
Art direction: Peter Harris
Costume design: Amanda Lovejoy
Music: Martin Armiger
MPAA rating: R
Running time: 100 minutes

Principal characters:

Kay	Karen Colston
Louis	Tom Lycos
Sweetie	Genevieve Lemon
Gordon	Jon Darling
Flo	Dorothy Barry
Bob	Michael Lake
Clayton	Andre Pataczek

One of the advantages that a director who works outside the production and distribution that controls most standard American films has is the freedom to develop a narrative and stylistic structure that does not follow the conventions of presentation that audiences are conditioned to accept. This can lead to an eccentricity that lapses into incoherence, or it can provide the opportunity to fashion a particular form that is uniquely suited to the subject of the film. Wayne Wang's *Chan Is Missing* (1982) and Jim Jarmusch's *Stranger than Paradise* (1984) are notable examples of films that demonstrated how a distinctly imaginative approach can produce a strikingly singular work. Australian director Jane Campion's *Sweetie* is a similarly personal and effective film that utilizes an unusual and original visual style that has been designed to express the psychological sensibilities of its characters. Set in a relatively nondescript semi-urban landscape in New South Wales, it examines an aspect of Australian life that is far removed from the wild outback of *Walkabout* (1971) or the soaring Sydney skyline that is emblematic of a vital nation. Instead, it concentrates on a small group of people whose lives are profoundly affected by the demands of the title character, a young woman named Dawn (Genevieve Lemon) who is called Sweetie by her family and whose enormously self-centered manner of living ranges from amusing peculiarity to lethal self-absorption.

Although Sweetie is the agent of much of the action, she is not its primary focus, a decision Campion wisely made to locate the film's central point of view in a more accessible and more sympathetic person, Sweetie's sister, Kay (Karen Colston). The cinematic strategy that Campion has developed to present Kay depends, to a significant extent, on Colston's ability to capture and project the character's elusive charm—her shyness, her sensitivity, her uncertainty, and her flashes of intense, passionate seriousness. It succeeds, however, because Campion and her cinematographer, Sally Bongers, have been able to depict the rhythms of Kay's life through the composition and editing of the scenes in which she initially appears. The sequence that opens the film establishes this method immediately. The first shot shows a figure in a landscape, the body at an odd angle amidst a gorgeous floral pattern with Kay's voice describing a tree that was a special place for Sweetie during their childhood. The almost surreal quality of Sweetie's presence is suggested, and the following sequence in which Kay muses about the symbolic power of trees and her fears of the mysterious forces of the universe further expresses her inward, reflective nature. When she visits a spiritualist and hears a prophecy that she will meet an important man with a question mark on his face, the gravity of her response, projected in an interior monologue, reveals her faith in omens and portents and prepares her sudden assertion to a friend's fiancé, "I'm destined to be with you . . . it's in the spirits!"

During these introductory passages, Bongers and Campion photograph Kay in a series of discrete, angular shots, the duration of each shot not directly connected to what she is doing or saying. Partial views of her body at the edge of the frame serve to arouse curiosity, while separate segments of her anatomy in close-up instill a feeling of disconnection. Stanley Kaufmann in *The New Republic* complained that the camera work was designed to show off and call attention to its own cleverness, but the rhythms of the editing frequently correspond to the jagged pace of Kay's thoughts, the sudden shifts and non sequiturs of her flow of consciousness, while the impersonal observations of the camera reflect the director's nonjudgmental acceptance of an idiosyncratic person living at angles to the more conventional flow of society around her. Frequent blackouts between short sequences further underscore this disjunction.

Kay's own apartness stands in appealing contrast to the babbling gaggle of her coworkers in a small factory, and her dependence on a kind of New Age amalgam of meditation, casual spiritualism, and intuition is balanced by an inherent decency and an essential practicality. Her obvious affection for her new boyfriend, Louis (Tom Lycos), and her interest in his welfare anchors her character in a fundamental friendliness that is one of the values that Campion approves of and that is also a key to Lou's engaging affability. A passage of thirteen months occurs offcamera after their relationship begins, and when the narrative resumes, Lou has dug up a clothesline (Kay worries about drying the wash) in order to plant an alder tree amid a barren patch of concrete as a celebration of their first anniversary. Although this act is in accordance with Kay's general outlook, her faith and fear in portents is so strong that she digs it up at night so that it will not adversely affect their lives if it dies. At the same time, she moves into a spare room, rationalizing that they have shifted to a "non-sex phase" that is "more spiritual," but both of her acts are impulsive responses to uncertainties in their relationship that she wishes to avoid confronting. Consequently, Lou and Kay continue to drift, the dissonances in their lives causing some pain and confusion, but far short of fracture, both of them adjusting to and accommodating conditions that they do not know how to influence, victims of a modern malaise that is disquieting if not really dangerous.

The casual drift of their lives is violently wrenched in an unpleasant direction when Kay and Lou return one night to discover that Sweetie has moved in with them, accompanied by a man named Bob (Michael Lake) who is euphemistically referred to as her "producer." He is a useless layabout whose inertial, sponging existence is more pathetic than parasitical, but he complements Sweetie's worst tendencies. She is a master of manipulation who has been spoiled since childhood, pampered by her father who has indulged her proclivities for performing, and now she is a demon of self-enclosed touchiness, her manner of living derailed by spasms of mental instability that verge on psychosis. Working from a shrewd sense of others' feelings of responsibility, while playing on her own diminishing appeal as a free-spirited, beguiling overgrown child, Sweetie increasingly lapses into vulgar tantrums and has begun to career into frightening displays of anger and obscene self-gratification. She has become a monstrous obstacle to ordinary living, and the relatively placid flow of Lou and Kay's life, including the pensive, private moments that are crucial for their existence, has been obliterated by her arrival.

Kay is thus caught in a complex situation, both angry at and feeling sorry for Sweetie—a recapitulation of their entire mutual life—and Campion presents the early incidents of conflict in comic terms, making Bob's mumbling and Sweetie's seductive overtures toward Lou little more than minor irritations. These scenes are underscored by Kay's good-natured exasperation, but the film shifts toward a mood of ominous uncertainty as the sisters' father, Gordon (Jon Darling), arrives. He and his wife are at the start of a trial separation that has left him distraught (he inadvertently thaws all the frozen meals that she has prepared for him), and his distress compounds the calamitous nature of the events so that the entire family is sent spinning gradually out of control. A sense of futility and meaninglessness pervades everyone's life, and a kind of near-despair begins to take hold when the family's failures to handle Sweetie's constant demands and refusals to cooperate remove the slightly whimsical mood that previously made most setbacks seem minor and temporary.

The film shifts tone again, however, because one of Campion's concerns is the resilience that most people can call on in trying times. Resorting to deception, Kay, Lou, and Gordon trick Sweetie into staying behind as they travel to a Jackaroo camp where Kay's mother, Flo (Dorothy Barry), is cooking and entertaining the men. As the men dance together and listen to Flo's surprisingly stylish singing, a feeling of serenity gradually envelops everyone, leading Kay's parents to rejoin in a confirmation of Kay's (and her mother's) recognition that everyone needs some space and variety to regain equilibrium. Minor depression gives way to a curious therapeutic combination of meditation, retreat, and odd personal gestures of companionship. Campion's contention that late twentieth century life is marked by uncertainty that results from the failure of conventional arrangements leads to the words of straight wisdom that Kay hears when she consults another spiritualist: "Love equals courage plus sex," the woman tells her, and this admonition echoes Campion's comment that the film has something to do with "a quest for love," and that it is also a "look at the underbelly and the way people see things and their behavior."

The dramatic conclusion is a logical advance from the initial thrust of Sweetie's arrival. There have been several indications of how dangerous Sweetie's anger can be when she is met with continued resistance, but the tone of most of these scenes is muted by everyone's feelings of resignation. When the rest of her family returns, Sweetie, in a rage of frustration and confusion, attempts to reassert her control and regain her position at the center of the family's attention by climbing into a tree house with a boy from the neighborhood. She refuses to descend, and the family's responses are initially ludicrous and ineffectual, like a television sitcom with Dad stumbling about below, alternately pleading and insisting, and Mom threatening to call the rescue squad. Sweetie enjoys orchestrating this little charade, resorting to progressively vulgar gestures to register her amusement and disdain, but a slapstick struggle on the ladder becomes tragic when the entire structure collapses. The boy falls unhurt, but Sweetie is mortally wounded. The undercurrent of real damage that has been implicit throughout surges into the open in a scene in which Kay cradles the broken body of her sister, its heretofore overblown burlesque dimensions horribly transformed into an image of blood, bewilderment, and pain. Sweetie's physical presence has been destroyed in the wreckage, her death inevitable now that her ruined body cannot compensate for the weakness of her mind. The full impact of Lemon's extraordinary unselfconscious performance is evident, another indication of the strength of Campion's direction of the actors, which matches her inventive use of cinema in the service of her declaration that "We believed the order of the day was taking risks."

The vividness of this sequence does not substantially exceed the most intense moments of the film, but its somber tone is jarring in the context of what has previously taken place. Yet, even the extreme nature of its emotional pressure is consistent with Campion's exploration of psychic survival. In a world in which uncertainty is a given, the only possibility—as Kay realizes—is to give love without reservation. Even if this does not always work, however, there is no other viable choice.

Leon Lewis

Reviews
American Film: Magazine of the Film and Television Arts. XV, January, 1990, p. 59.

Boston Globe. September 21, 1989, p. 60.
Boxoffice. May, 1990, p. R40.
Chicago Tribune. March 23, 1990, VII, p. 42.
Harper's Bazaar. CXXIII, February, 1990, p. 63.
Los Angeles Times. February 14, 1990, p. F2.
The Nation. CCL, February 19, 1990, p. 252.
New Leader. LXXIII, January 8, 1990, p. 23.
The New Republic. CCII, February 26, 1990, p. 27.
The New York Times. October 6, 1989, p. C3.
The New York Times. February 4, 1990, p. B17.
Newsweek. CXV, January 22, 1990, p. 60.
Variety. CCCXXXV, May 10, 1989, p. 18.
The Wall Street Journal. January 25, 1990, p. A12.
The Washington Post. March 2, 1990, p. D1.

TEENAGE MUTANT NINJA TURTLES

Production: Kim Dawson, Simon Fields, and David Chan for Limelight; a
   presentation of Golden Harvest, released by New Line Cinema
Direction: Steve Barron
Screenplay: Todd W. Langen and Bobby Herbeck; based on an original story by
   Herbeck and on cartoon characters created by Kevin Eastman and Peter Laird
Cinematography: John Fenner
Animation: David Greenaway, Mark Wilson, David Rudman, Martin P. Robinson,
   Ricky Boyd, and Robert Tygner
Production design: Roy Forge Smith
Art direction: Gary Wissner
Set decoration: Brendan Smith and Barbara Kahn
Set design: Jerry Hall
Special effects: Joey Di Gaetano
Sound: Lee Orloff, Steve Maslow, Michael Herbick, and Gregg Landaker
Makeup: Jeff Goodwin
Costume design: John M. Hay
Choreography: Pat Johnson
Music: John Du Prez
MPAA rating: PG
Running time: 87 minutes

> *Principal characters:*
> April O'Neil .... Judith Hoag
> Casey Jones .... Elias Koteas
> Raphael .... Josh Pais
> Michaelangelo .... Michelan Sisti
>   (voice of Robbie Rist)
> Donatello .... Leif Tilden
>   (voice of Corey Feldman)
> Leonardo .... David Forman
>   (voice of Brian Tochi)
> Danny Pennington .... Michael Turney
> Splinter .... (voice of Kevin Clash)
> Charles Pennington .... Jay Patterson
> The Shredder .... James Saito
> Chief Sterns .... Raymond Serra

On Monday, April 3, 1990, after the weekend film grosses had been counted,
Teenage Mutant Ninja Turtles emerged as the biggest surprise since *Batman* (1989).
Never before had an independent film earned $25 million in its opening weekend. In
fact, *Teenage Mutant Ninja Turtles* had the third-biggest opening weekend ever and

broke all records for a nonsummer, nonholiday release. Added to these accomplish-ments, the film also became the first independent release to gross more than $100 million. What makes these numbers even more amazing is the fact that an estimated 50 percent of the audience was under twelve years of age and therefore paid one half as much as adolescent and adult filmgoers.

Teenage Mutant Ninja Turtles is a live-action screen version of the popular televi-sion cartoon and comic book "heroes on a half shell." Peter Laird and Kevin East-man created the turtles in 1983 as a send-up of traditional comic book superheroes, publishing a black-and-white comic book on their own until 1986. Since then, licens-ing agent Mark Freedman has transformed the turtles into a marketing phenomenon aimed at children. Archie Comics distributes 500,000 copies of the comic book every six weeks, while Playmate Toys underwrites a weekly syndicated cartoon show that implicitly promotes its line of turtle figures. In 1989, the total revenue from the more than one hundred companies that license turtle merchandise had doubled to $350 million and is expected to double again in 1990.

In a pretitle sequence, *Teenage Mutant Ninja Turtles* depicts New York City, where crime has been on the rise. Television reporter April O'Neil (Judith Hoag) stumbles upon a group of adolescent males loading a truck with stolen goods. She is about to become their next victim, when the lights go out and a fight ensues. When the lights are back on, the criminals are tied up, and April discovers a scythe that one of the vigilantes dropped. Beneath the city, in the sewer system, the Teenage Mutant Ninja Turtles—Raphael (Josh Pais), Michaelangelo (Michelan Sisti), Donatello (Leif Til-den), and Leonardo (David Forman)—celebrate their triumph over evil. The human-size turtles return to their ninja master, Splinter (voice of Kevin Clash), a wizened, four-foot-tall rat. Splinter admonishes the turtles. Despite their Renaissance names and ninja skills, they have teenage minds, as evident in their surfer lingo and ap-petite for pizza.

Despite Splinter's warnings to remain invisible, Raphael dons a trench coat and fedora, and heads for Central Park. Unlike the other turtles, he alone suffers from teenage angst. Raphael encounters Casey Jones (Elias Koteas), a vigilante armed with sports equipment, and the two engage in a playful fight that Raphael loses. Meanwhile, April uncovers the source of the recent crime wave, the Foot Clan, a Japanese-run organization that trains adolescents as ninjas. Blue-suited ninjas are about to attack April, when Raphael rescues her. Raphael carries April to the turtle's sewer den, where Splinter explains their genesis. Splinter, once the pet of a ninja master, fled to New York after his master's murder. In the sewers, he came upon four abandoned baby pet turtles who were mired in radioactive waste. The radioactivity caused Splinter and the turtles to grow in size and intellect and to acquire speech. The turtles also acquired an insatiable appetite for pizza.

Despite her fear of rodents, April befriends the superheroes, and the turtles escort her to her apartment. Returning to their den, the turtles discover that Splinter has been kidnapped by the Foot Clan. The turtles return to April's apartment in despair, whereupon hordes of Foot Clan ninjas descend upon the building. Raphael is seriously injured, but the other turtles hold the ninjas at bay while flinging flip remarks. Casey arrives and helps the turtles and April escape the now-burning building.

The Foot Clan is run by the Shredder (James Saito), an evil ninja master dressed like Darth Vader of George Lucas' *Star Wars* trilogy (1977, 1980, 1983). The Shredder runs his operation beneath an urban bar, where he recruits disaffected adolescents. "I am your father," he implores, and refers to the clan as the teenagers' family. Danny Pennington (Michael Turney), whose father, Charles Pennington (Jay Patterson), is also April's boss, has fallen in with the Foot Clan. When Danny is arrested, Police Chief Sterns (Raymond Serra) blackmails his father into firing April in order to stop her accusatory investigation. Now on their own, April, Casey, and the turtles retreat to April's rural childhood home. In a lengthy sequence, the turtles are shown to be despondent over Splinter's capture. One night, however, the turtles realize Splinter's dictum that the true ninja is not of the body, but of the mind, and conjure up Splinter's holographic image through meditation. Splinter congratulates the turtles and expresses his love for them. In the meantime, April and Casey overcome their differences and begin a tentative romance.

The group returns to the turtles' den, where they find Danny, who has begun to question the clan after a talk with Splinter. While the others sleep, Danny sneaks back to the clan's bar, with Casey on his trail. Danny again questions Splinter, who tells him that the Shredder appears to be the same person who killed his former master and his wife. The Shredder and his ninjas have left for the turtles' den. When the second in command confronts Danny and Splinter, Casey knocks him out with a golf club. The adolescents, now without a leader, disband, and Casey helps Splinter walk back to the den.

The turtles have managed to defeat the Foot Clan ninjas. Now atop a building, they take turns attacking the Shredder, but are no match for him in a one-on-one fight. Shredder is about to kill one of the turtles, when Splinter appears and challenges the Shredder. He tells the Shredder that he is the small rat who attacked the Shredder after he had killed Splinter's master. The Shredder removes his mask to reveal a scarred face and charges at Splinter, who then flips the Shredder over the top of the building. The police arrive, and a repentant Danny is reunited with his father, who rehires April on the spot. True to their code, Splinter and the turtles retreat to the sewers, unseen by the authorities.

Teenage Mutant Ninja Turtles draws upon the most popular science-fiction films of two generations: the *Godzilla* cycle of the late 1950's and 1960's, and the *Star Wars* trilogy of the late 1970's and 1980's. Like the Japanese monsters Godzilla, a giant dinosaur, and Gammera, a giant space turtle, Splinter and the turtles are radioactive mutants who battle various social ills. The Shredder's dress and Oedipal challenge—"I am your father"—are direct references to *Star Wars* (1977), while Splinter evokes the charismatic Jedi master Yoda in the film's two sequels. A central theme in both of these genres is the battle between good and evil for control of the male adolescent. Interestingly, good is depicted as nonhuman, with the exception of reporters in *Godzilla* films and mercenaries in the *Star Wars* films. In *Teenage Mu-*

tant Ninja Turtles, these two roles are fulfilled by April and Casey, respectively.

For all its commercial success, *Teenage Mutant Ninja Turtles* displays poor production values. The pace of the film is erratic when the turtles are not involved in a fight scene; and the photography is so dimly lit that it raises questions about the efficacy of the turtle and Splinter puppets, designed by Jim Henson's Creature Shop in London. Furthermore, lighting the set in order to accommodate the dark green turtles and light-skinned actors results in a monochromatic image that flattens out the differences between the turtles.

More troublesome, however, are the merchandise tie-ins that drive the narrative. Food, toys, and clothing items are strategically placed within the mise-en-scène. *Teenage Mutant Ninja Turtles* also participates in the Japan-bashing of recent Hollywood films, most notably Ridley Scott's *Black Rain* (1989). The message in both films is that Japan's economic power stems from criminal sources.

Since the box-office success of Richard Donner's *Superman* (1978) and its sequels, Hollywood has turned to other comic book heroes, such as *Batman* and *Dick Tracy* (1990; reviewed in this volume). While these films held significant appeal for adult audiences, *Teenage Mutant Ninja Turtles* guarantees sequels and none-too-subtle imitators designed to exploit what has become the children's market. In fact, Eclipse comics plans a comic book and television cartoon show called *Adolescent Radioactive Black Belt Hamsters*. Ten years ago, before the deregulation of the Federal Communications Commission (FCC), such product tie-ins were illegal in children's television shows. In all the excitement about how *Teenage Mutant Ninja Turtles* shellshocked the film industry, however, journalists failed to ask what the merchandising of entertainment has done to children.

Chon A. Noriega

Reviews
Chicago Tribune. March 30, 1990, VII, p. 37.
The Christian Century. CVII, May 2, 1990, p. 468.
Los Angeles Times. March 30, 1990, p. F4.
New Statesman and Society. III, November 30, 1990, p. 33.
The New York Times. March 30, 1990, p. C8.
Premiere. IV, February, 1991, p. 84.
Time. CXXXV, April 2, 1990, p. 59.
USA Today. March 30, 1990, p. D1.
Variety. CCCXXXVIII, March 28, 1990, p. 23.
The Village Voice. April 3, 1990, p. 68.
The Wall Street Journal. April 12, 1990, p. A12.
The Washington Post. March 30, 1990, p. B1.

TEXASVILLE

Production: Barry Spikings and Peter Bogdanovich for Nelson Entertainment and
   Cine-Source; released by Columbia Pictures
Direction: Peter Bogdanovich
Screenplay: Peter Bogdanovich; based on the novel by Larry McMurtry
Cinematography: Nicholas von Sternberg
Editing: Richard Fields
Production design: Phedon Papamichael
Set decoration: Daniel Boxer
Sound: Kirk Francis and Michael Haines
Costume design: Rita Riggs
Music: Karyn Rachtman
MPAA rating: R
Running time: 123 minutes

Principal characters:
Duane Jackson	Jeff Bridges
Jacy Farrow	Cybill Shepherd
Karla Jackson	Annie Potts
Sonny Crawford	Timothy Bottoms
Ruth Popper	Cloris Leachman
Lester Marlow	Randy Quaid
Genevieve	Eileen Brennan
Dickie Jackson	William McNamara
Marylou Marlow	Angie Bolling
Suzie Nolan	Su Hyatt
Junior Nolan	Earl Poole Ball

In this long-awaited sequel to the critically acclaimed *The Last Picture Show*
(1971), Peter Bogdanovich fails to move beyond an antiquated directing style that
attempts to imbue every frame of film with intense meaning. Little of *Texasville* is
compelling, and the film resonates with lingering moments of nothingness in the
midst of low farce. The result is merely a meandering slice of life in a small Texas
town, with the most significant moments happening offscreen and not dramatized
within the framework of the filmic text. This leaves the audience, as well as the
film's main protagonist, squinting beyond the frame, wondering what is happening.
   Immersed in his midlife crisis, as well as in his hot tub, Duane Jackson (Jeff
Bridges) fires random shots at his best friend's multilevel doghouse. After making
millions in the oil business, Duane, like so many other Texan barons, is in serious
trouble: He is $12 million in debt. His sharp-tongued wife, Karla (Annie Potts)—an
angry woman with a fondness for dressing in clothes that, as Duane says, "you have

to read"—is a woman full of subtext. The problem is that the film never reveals what it is masking.

Texasville begins thirty years after the events of *The Last Picture Show*, and Bogdanovich has reassembled most of the original cast. Sonny Crawford (Timothy Bottoms) is now the mayor and chief entrepreneur of Anarene, no longer involved with his high school coach's wife, Ruth Popper (Cloris Leachman), but still frequenting the Picture Show. The only difference now is that the theater is an empty shell and the films that Sonny sees are figments of his own imagination. As at the end of the previous film, Sonny seems to be near rock bottom, leading one to wonder how he ever was voted mayor. His is a thankless role in *Texasville*, a sleepwalker who watches others flounder in their frantic moments of forced joviality as he sinks deeper into some undisclosed mental illness. It is amusing to note that Bottoms had serious reservations about returning to work with the same cast and director, revealing that he feared a rerun of the romantic dramas, apparently centering on Cybill Shepherd, that unfurled offscreen during the filming of *The Last Picture Show*. Bottoms was only twenty years old at the time and admittedly felt overwhelmed by the emotional intensity that resulted from the young actress's flirtatious entanglements.

As for Ruth, somehow she has become Duane's devoted secretary. It is sad that her character appears for little more than cheap exposition in the early part of the film, then cheap sentiment at the melodramatic end. Furthermore, it is disappointing that two characters who have so much history together, Ruth and Sonny, should have so few scenes together. Even when Ruth offers to take Sonny into her home—the actual reconciliation happens offscreen—there is a sense that this is one of the first times the two have spoken. This continual distancing from the characters is one of the most infuriating flaws of *Texasville*. Something is happening somewhere but, like the film's protagonist, the viewer always misses the action and only learns of it secondhand.

There is a sense that Duane is mad at Sonny at the film's end, but that implication is never explained. A vein of underlying resentment or hostility between any of the characters would have been helpful. Instead, forced melodrama is employed as a smoke screen to divert the viewer's attention from the fact that there is no story to drive this film. The significant amount of unresolved tensions between the characters needs more than a cursory examination. The relationship between Duane and Sonny is one of the few moments of interest, a glimmer of hope that something was to be dramatized, not merely whitewashed over. Yet nothing happens. Instead the characters all decide to go to breakfast, where their most active moments undoubtedly will be deciding what to order.

Bogdanovich launched former cover-girl Shepherd's acting career with *The Last Picture Show* and became somewhat obsessed with his leading lady, losing sight of her limited acting range. He made her the focus of several films, a move that nearly ended his own directing career with such unsuccessful films as *Daisy Miller* (1974) and *At Long Last Love* (1975). When he met and later became romantically involved with Playboy centerfold Dorothy Stratten, Bogdanovich again tried to shape his lover's acting career by starring her in *They All Laughed* (1981), a work that was long on style and short on substance. Stratten was murdered by her husband two weeks after filming was completed and Bogdanovich was slow to recover from the tragedy. His obsession with Stratten culminated with his recent marriage to her younger sister. He finally returned to the screen with *Mask* (1985).

One expects more from Bogdanovich in terms of filmmaking, particularly since he was a film critic, having written several books on films and directors. He seems to be most comfortable in the past, either working on projects that are set in the past, such as *Paper Moon* (1973), or attempting to revive a motion-picture form whose time has come and gone, such as the screwball comedy *What's Up, Doc?* (1972).

Jeff Bridges once again rises far above his material, imbuing the disillusioned and floundering Duane with a smoldering sensuality and vulnerability that do not appear to stem from the characterization drawn by the screenplay. Bridges has consistently given beautifully restrained and refined performances in recent years, particularly as the frustrated piano lounge player opposite his real-life brother, Beau, in the overlooked *The Fabulous Baker Boys* (1989), as well as the lead in Francis Ford Coppola's *Tucker: The Man and His Dream* (1988).

Shepherd, however, offers one of the most stilted performances in recent memory. Perhaps part of the problem is that her character, Jacy, has supposedly undergone massive changes which have occurred in the interim, giving the viewer no access, except for superficial references made through the dialogue, to her internal workings. When the audience last glimpsed Jacy in *The Last Picture Show*, she was a self-involved beauty queen who knew no pain. Thirty years later, after a floundering third-rate acting career in Italy, Jacy returns to her hometown, still recovering from the death of her only son. She strikes up an immediate friendship with Karla and proceeds to rob Duane of his family and even his dog. Showing little depth and understanding of her character's emotions, Shepherd plays Jacy with a frostiness that never does thaw.

Reviews of the film were surprisingly forgiving, despite an acknowledgment of the absence of a discernible story. It is amusing to note that critics who disapproved of the lack of movement in Martin Scorsese's *GoodFellas* (1990; reviewed in this volume), released within a month of *Texasville*, accepted the presence of the latter's likable quirky characters as sufficient to overshadow the need for dramatic tension. If a director of lesser renown had made *Texasville*, he probably would never be granted another directing assignment. Perhaps it is beneficial to be in the throes of one's own midlife crisis to appreciate this film's meandering quality.

Texasville is the first major undertaking of cinematographer Nicholas von Sternberg, son of director Joseph von Sternberg, who is regarded by many as one of Hollywood's greatest visual stylists, creating such classic films as Marlene Dietrich's *The Blue Angel* (1930) and *Blonde Venus* (1932). Von Sternberg has chosen to film in washed-out arid colors, rather than in the rich black and white used for *The Last Picture Show*.

Bogdanovich has created a telling metaphor: The Picture Show is now an empty shell of a building in the same way that *Texasville* is merely an empty shell of *The Last Picture Show*. Perhaps it would have been more appropriate to name this film *The Last Dairy Queen*: a place to go while waiting for something to happen.

Patricia Kowal

Reviews

American Film: Magazine of the Film and Television Arts. XV, October, 1990, p. 27.
Boxoffice. CXXVI, November, 1990, p. R85.
Chicago Tribune. September 28, 1990, VII, p. 24.
The Christian Science Monitor. September 28, 1990, p. 14.
Daily Variety. LVII, 1990 Anniversary Issue, p. 310.
Film Journal. XCIII, September, 1990, p. 15.
Film Review. January, 1991, p. 42.
The Hollywood Reporter. CCCXV, September 28, 1990, p. 6.
The Houston Post. September 28, 1990, p. E1.
Los Angeles Times. September 28, 1990, CX, p. F1.
The New York Times. September 29, 1990, CXL, p. B1.
Newsweek. CXVI, October 1, 1990, p. 70.
Rolling Stone. RS 589, October 18, 1990, p. 45.
Variety. September 19, 1990, p. 2.
The Wall Street Journal. October 11, 1990, p. A12.
The Washington Post. September 28, 1990, p. C7.

THREE MEN AND A LITTLE LADY

Production: Ted Field and Robert W. Cort for Touchstone Pictures and Jean
   Francois Lepetit/Interscope Communications; released by Buena Vista
Direction: Emile Ardolino
Screenplay: Charlie Peters; based on a story by Sara Parriott and Josann McGibbon
   and on the film *Trois hommes et un couffin*, by Coline Serreau
Cinematography: Adam Greenberg
Editing: Michael A. Stevenson
Production design: Stuart Wurtzel
Art direction: David M. Haber
Set design: Mark Poll and Sig Tinglof
Set decoration: Ethel Richards
Sound: C. Darin Knight
Costume design: Louise Frogley
Music: James Newton Howard
MPAA rating: PG
Running time: 100 minutes

   Principal characters:
   Peter .... Tom Selleck
   Michael .... Steve Guttenberg
   Jack .... Ted Danson
   Sylvia .... Nancy Travis
   Mary .... Robin Weisman
   Edward .... Christopher Cazenove
   Vera .... Sheila Hancock
   Miss Lomax .... Fiona Shaw
   Barrow .... John Boswall
   Vicar Hewitt .... Jonathan Lynn

   When a film is as successful as the box-office hit, *Three Men and a Baby* (1987),
a sequel is inevitable. Yet, rarely is a sequel as ambitious, clever, and amusing as
this one.
   Three Men and a Little Lady begins five years after its predecessor ended. Baby
Mary is now a bright, pretty, and completely normal five-year-old girl living in a
most abnormal home. Mary (Robin Weisman) has one mother, Sylvia (Nancy Travis),
and three fathers, Peter (Tom Selleck), Michael (Steve Guttenberg), and Jack (Ted
Danson). Though Jack is Mary's biological father, the three men share parenting
duties, each one bringing his own special talents to the relationship. Michael, an
artist, decorates Mary's room with murals depicting her life in this unique family.
Jack, a largely unsuccessful actor, helps Mary find her shoes, and Mary helps Jack
choose the correct tie to wear for an audition. Peter, who is an architect and was the

first of the men to accept the responsibility of rearing Mary, is the one who seems most concerned with Mary's long-term welfare.

Sylvia, who left Mary at the bachelors' doorstep when she could no longer cope with childcare while trying to pursue an acting career, is now the toast of Broadway. Between performances, she makes feeble and often comic attempts at domesticity, but the fathers are able to save themselves and Mary from Sylvia's culinary horrors. The men are the ones who are closest to Mary. Because Mary is about to enter kindergarten, however, this arrangement begins to be problematic. When the four parents decide on a school that they feel is suitable for Mary, they must then convince its administration that Mary is suitable for the school. Naturally in question is the matter of how four single people of two different sexes behave in front of one impressionable child. The parents hasten to assure the school board that, while they are a loving and affectionate family, everybody sleeps in his or her own bedroom and, though the adults have healthy social lives, dates are never brought into the home. The meeting goes well and Mary is accepted into the school.

Meanwhile, Mary has been playing with the other kindergartners. When asked about her family, Mary confidently explains that she has one Mommy, one biological Daddy, and two honorary Daddies. Another child tells Mary that it is against the law to have more than one father at a time. Mary's first day of kindergarten apparently is her first exposure to other children and thus to the knowledge that her family is different. Mary's parents tell her that it is okay to be different, but they see that a trite maxim is small comfort to a little girl with no friends. As Mary begins to question her family's arrangement, so does Sylvia.

Sylvia's mother, Vera (Sheila Hancock), comes to visit. Disdainful of her daughter's and granddaughter's situation, Vera encourages Sylvia to pursue a different kind of relationship. Vera guesses that Sylvia has feelings for Peter, but tells her that Peter seems unable to communicate his feelings to anyone but Mary and that Sylvia would be wasting her time with him. Sylvia is also involved with the director of her play, Edward (Christopher Cazenove). Edward has asked Sylvia to marry him and return with him to England. Peter, Michael, and Jack are horrified at the thought of their family breaking up, but Sylvia insists that it would be better for all of them to return to a normal way of life. She knows that she wants to marry and have more children and is sure that the men would like wives and children of their own. Furthermore, Sylvia is anxious for Mary to experience normal family life. Jack gallantly offers to marry Sylvia and is greatly relieved when she declines. The men try to persuade Sylvia not to break up their family, but Sylvia responds that someone has to be the grown-up and think of Mary's welfare. Peter, who is in love with Sylvia, remains silent.

Later, while looking for Jack, who was supposed to help her rehearse a scene for her acting class, Sylvia finds Peter. Frustrated and unable to express his feelings, Peter instead offers to rehearse with Sylvia. When the script calls for a kiss, Peter and Sylvia are moved, but Peter still cannot tell Sylvia how he feels. When he visits Sylvia in her dressing room at the theater, she hopes it is to confess his feelings.

Peter only wishes to say, however, that he will support Sylvia in whatever decision she makes. It is difficult for him to live up to that promise when Sylvia announces her decision to accept Edward's proposal. Though Peter is the one who is most hurt, he is the first to help Mary adjust to the imminent change. After meeting Edward, however, who is an obsequious flatterer and clearly not interested in children, Peter challenges Sylvia's decision. Sylvia accuses Peter of thinking only of himself. He sarcastically asks Sylvia if that is not what she was doing when she abandoned Mary at their door five years ago. Sylvia slaps Peter and runs from the room. The men bid Sylvia and Mary a tearful goodbye. They have no plans to attend Sylvia's wedding because no one can bear to face the end of their family. One of them suggests throwing a party, just like the wild parties they used to have before Mary arrived. The party is a disaster, however, when the guests become bored looking at photos of Mary and the stereo plays Big Bird singing "Rubber Duckie."

Edward's family home in the English countryside is beautiful, but Mary is unhappy there because Peter, Jack, and Michael are in New York without her. There is no one to dispose of Sylvia's cooking and Edward criticizes the manners that Mary has learned from her roommates. In her letters, Mary writes that she is happy, but the men sense that something is wrong and decide to go to England for Sylvia's wedding after all. There they find that Edward has enrolled Mary in a boarding school without Sylvia's knowledge. In the film's comic final scenes, the men try to stall the wedding until they can produce proof of Edward's villainous conduct. Michael kidnaps Vicar Hewitt (Jonathan Lynn) and Jack dons an elaborate disguise as a replacement vicar, deciding that, if a ceremony must take place, he can at least ensure that it is not a legal one. Peter enlists the aid of the hilarious headmistress of Pileforth Academy, Miss Lomax (Fiona Shaw), in proving that Edward has arranged to send Mary to live there.

As Sylvia and Edward walk back up the aisle, believing themselves to be married, Peter rushes in with Mary's enrollment forms. Unable to defend himself, Edward reveals his contempt for Mary, as well as her extended family. Peter asks Sylvia to marry him, for Mary's sake, but she refuses. Peter amends his request, asking Sylvia to marry him for his own sake, because he loves her. Jack reveals himself as the fraudulent vicar, the real vicar arrives to marry Peter and Sylvia, and Edward is punched in the face. Mary is now part of a normal family, and Michael and Jack can remain in Mary's life. This ending seems so neatly wrapped that there should be nothing more to say, but that was also the way it seemed at the end of *Three Men and a Baby*. Given the success of this sequel, if a third film appeared to show what this group of characters was doing five years after the wedding, it would be no surprise.

The actors, writers, producers, and the director of *Three Men and a Little Lady* all possess impressive lists of credits. Leading men Selleck, Danson, and Guttenberg are favorites of American film and television audiences. Brooklyn-born Nancy Travis has had a busy career since her film debut as Sylvia in *Three Men and a Baby*. The English actors—Christopher Cazenove, Fiona Shaw, Sheila Hancock, and Jonathan Lynn—are well known and much respected for their work on stage and screen in

Great Britain. Award winner Emile Ardolino made his film directing debut in the surprise success *Dirty Dancing* (1987).

Eleah Horwitz

Reviews

Chicago Tribune. November 21, 1990, V, p. 1.
The Christian Science Monitor. December 7, 1990, p. 12.
The Hollywood Reporter. CCCXV, November 20, 1990, p. 10.
Los Angeles. XXXVI, January, 1991, p. 119.
Los Angeles Times. November 21, 1990, CC, p. F3.
The New York Times. November 21, 1990, CXL, p. B3.
Newsweek. CXVI, December 3, 1990, p. 67.
Premiere. IV, October 4, 1990, p. 78.
Variety. CCXXIX, November 20, 1990, p. 2.
The Washington Post. November 21, 1990, p. D1.

TIE ME UP! TIE ME DOWN!
(ATAME)

Origin: Spain
Released: 1990
Released in U.S.: 1990
Production: Agustín Almodóvar for El Deseo; released by Miramax Films
Direction: Pedro Almodóvar
Screenplay: Pedro Almodóvar
Cinematography: José Luis Alcaine
Editing: José Salcedo
Production direction: Esther García
Set decoration: Ferran Sanchez
Special effects: Reyes Abades
Sound: Goldstein & Steinberg
Makeup: Juan Pedro Hernandez
Costume design: José María de Cossio
Music: Ennio Morricone
MPAA rating: no listing
Running time: 105 minutes

> *Principal characters:*
> Marina .... Victoria Abril
> Ricky .... Antonio Banderas
> Lola .... Loles Leon
> Maximo Espejo .... Francisco Rabal
> Alma .... Julieta Serrano
> Berta .... María Barranco
> Girl with moped .... Rossi De Palma

Somewhere in the heart of *Tie Me Up! Tie Me Down!* there beat the psychological rhythms of famed surrealist and filmic visionary Luis Buñuel. Director Pedro Almodóvar makes it obvious that Buñuel is indeed his cinematic mentor, and this film proves him right. *Tie Me Up! Tie Me Down!*, more than Almodóvar's previous *Women on the Verge of a Nervous Breakdown* (1988), displays many of the same comic turns that characterized Buñuelian cinema. For one thing, there is the sharp social criticism that marked many of Buñuel's stronger films, such as *Le Charme discret de la bourgeoisie* (1972; *The Discreet Charm of the Bourgeoisie*, 1972), where his middle-class victims could never sit down and complete a meal, much to their repeated frustrations in attempting to do so. Then, again, there was, in *Cet obscur objet du désir* (1977; *That Obscure Object of Desire*, 1977), the brutally humorous string of visual jokes played on Buñuel's frustrated lover, Mathieu, who could never make love to the woman he desired, simply because, in Buñuel's sharp vision, Mathieu was too narcissistic to see beyond his own self's desire. While Almodóvar's jokes on society and individuals are never quite as biting as were the master's, nevertheless, the same sharp social criticism is prominent. Almodóvar never overlooks the minutiae of the social mores he satirizes, and, much like Buñuel, he uses comedy as a weapon for enlightenment. He strikes most often at the funniest if not the most obvious site of relationships within modern society: the sexual conduct (or misconduct) between men and women. Almodóvar is comfortable not only in poking fun at sexual mores but also in being a brilliant prankster when he focuses on the hypocrisy and irony that dwell within these mores. Overall, what ties him to Buñuel is his knack for treating, with seeming irreverence, delicate subjects about sexuality between men and women.

Almodóvar's subject in *Tie Me Up! Tie Me Down!* is, most obviously, the sexual abuse of women by men who appear to be in a more powerful position than the victims they choose. For most of the film, it is almost painful to see these women put into such a subservient position. By the time the film concludes, however, the audience has come to understand that deeper subjects are being explored within the narrative. Women take on a stronger role in their own society, and men are reduced to the level of simple human beings who no longer appear to control their environment, let alone their own psychologies. Sexual games collapse into metaphors for the pain and confusion of living in the modern world. What is more, men and women are not so much separate as they are equal players in this world.

Sexual and emotional violence appear to take precedence in *Tie Me Up! Tie Me Down!*, or so it would first seem. A young man named Ricky (Antonio Banderas), who is a mental patient at an institution, is released after serving a long sentence. His one goal, upon gaining his freedom, is to find a young woman with whom he had slept during one of his previous escapes from the institution. This woman, Marina (Victoria Abril), is a minor pornography star and former drug addict whom Ricky has no trouble locating. He steals into her dressing room and, disguising himself as a woman (using her wig), he then proceeds to the film set where Marina is currently involved in shooting a film. She is surrounded by her own group of crazies on the set, including the film's director, the partially paralyzed yet nevertheless lecherous Maximo Espejo (Francisco Rabal, who, himself, starred in several of Luis Buñuel's films more than twenty years ago). Also on hand and running in and out of the narrative is Marina's sister, Lola (Loles Leon), who will figure more prominently in the story as Ricky drags Marina into his scheme.

It seems that Ricky has some very definite plans about his future, plans that result from some very real obsession. He wants only to settle down, get married, and start a family. He wants, that is, to have a normal life after having spent most of his years in the institution. He has chosen Marina as the object of his desire, the woman with whom he wants to begin this normal life. Yet his means of procuring his dream is unconventional to say the least—or is it? Finding that Marina has no recollection of who Ricky is and remembers nothing about their previous time together, Ricky simply kidnaps her. Even his mode of kidnapping is rather bizarre. He forces his way into Marina's apartment one night and holds her hostage in her own home. More than holding her hostage, he makes her his psychological prisoner—certain that in time she will fall in love with him and help him fulfill his fantasy of family and children. What follows is a strange mix of sexual violence and comedy, as well as some very misdirected affection between Ricky and Marina. Ultimately, however, the two are brought together by their shared experiences. This film is, above all else, a love story, yet its means of signaling the love that develops is unconventional at the very least.

Ricky has chosen a badly timed hour to hold Marina hostage: She has just become afflicted with a terrible toothache. Thus, in addition to having to endure the terror of this strange man in her apartment, who will not let her get away from him, she must endure the pain of an infected tooth. The juxtaposition of these two kinds of pain is intended by director Almodóvar to become a means of making the spectator of this drama feel as uncomfortable as possible. More so, the absurdity of a female hostage with a toothache is played for laughs. Almodóvar thereby directs this double dose of satire at an audience that is assumed to be part of the society he wishes to disturb. Clearly, Marina is the victim of some sexual violence that Almodóvar perceives to be inherent in today's society. The violence that women must endure as sexual objects is not always easy to tag; rather, it lies buried in modern culture's collective unconscious. To witness this kind of sexual abuse on the screen is to become disturbed, yet the viewers realize soon enough that they are disturbed by something in which they all participate, perhaps without being aware of it.

The dichotomy here is that Ricky wants to love Marina (and have her love him) no less than he wants to control her. He simply does not see that he is doing anything immoral. In this way, Ricky becomes a metaphor for all controlling men in modern society, just as Marina becomes a metaphor for all women who are emotionally as well as sexually abused by a society that conceives of them as sexual objects or as second-class citizens. Almodóvar is so adept at establishing this scenario that, before the audience recognizes the satire, there is a moment in which one must first flinch and wonder if this director might not be a misogynist of the first order. Ricky perpetrates all kinds of violence that is strangely comingled with care and affection: He ties up Marina in her own bed if he has to leave her apartment for any period of time, yet he also labors over the rope that he uses to ensure that she is as comfortable as possible. He allows her to seek relief from her toothache by visiting a doctor who lives nearby, but only if he goes with her to make sure that she does not escape. When the doctor writes Marina a prescription for a painkiller and the two "lovers" travel to the local pharmacy, only to find that no medicine is available there, Ricky offers to go out on the street and find the medicine for Marina (the medicine is the same drug that can be purchased from dope dealers in dark alleys). Before Ricky leaves on this venture, however, he must tie Marina up yet again.

Once out on the street, Ricky runs into trouble with some members of a gang and is beaten quite badly. When Ricky returns to Marina's apartment, Marina cares for him and tends his wounds. (In Ricky's absence, and unbeknown to him, Marina had untied herself, yet she does not reveal this to Ricky.) Marina has developed some affection for Ricky, and after she washes his wounds, the two of them make passionate love. After this turn of events, Marina seems to be in love with Ricky, and the audience may rightly wonder about Almodóvar's intentions. Is he trying to commit the ultimate crime against women by saying that a woman will fall in love with a man if she is mistreated by him? Is this director also saying that women will allow men to mistreat them yet fall in love at the drop of a passionate physical encounter? At this point, the film seems to be heading in the direction of a huge sexist ploy.

Yet Almodóvar wants his audience to be disturbed so he can turn the tables. Up until this point in the film, Marina has been the victim. Hereafter, it is Ricky's turn to become an object: not an object of sexual abuse but instead an object of emotional healing. It is at this point that *Tie Me Up! Tie Me Down!* is transformed from a tale of biting satire into a tale of shared human emotion. The issue of sexuality collapses into issues of love, and this has nothing whatsoever to do with gender control. Marina has fallen in love with Ricky, and Ricky has become educated in a fundamental way simply by Marina's act of loving him. He is reduced from a man who needed to control Marina to a man who now needs her. Her generosity of affection has won him over, and it is clear that ultimately she is the stronger of the two. With this, the film ends on a note of pure glee. While Ricky is out of the apartment, Marina's sister comes to rescue her. The two women go to find Ricky, and the three of them travel back in a car, singing along to a song on the radio. What began as an act of violence ends in high comedy. Yet even with this ironic turn of events, it is clear that Almodóvar has not bailed out of a sticky situation. Rather, he has chosen to teach his audience a lesson about themselves. In a society brimming with covert sexuality, no less than with complex sexual politics, a potent means of exposing these elements is to play an enormous joke on every serious subject available. This is the Buñuelian method, and in *Tie Me Up! Tie Me Down!* Almodóvar has been successful in keeping alive Buñuel's great social criticism and comic genius.

Marilyn Ann Moss

Reviews
Boxoffice. May, 1990, p. R39.
Chicago Tribune. May 25, 1990, VII, p. 30.
The Hollywood Reporter. CCCXII, May 3, 1990, p. 4.
The Hudson Review. XLIII, Winter, 1991, p. 645.
Los Angeles Times. May 4, 1990, p. F12.
The Nation. CCL, May 28, 1990, p. 752.
The New York Times. May 4, 1990, p. B1.
The New Yorker. LXVI, May 7, 1990, p. 88.
Newsweek. CXV, May 7, 1990, p. 65.
Variety. January 4, 1990, p. 2.
The Washington Post. May 25, 1990, p. D1.

TIME OF THE GYPSIES

Origin: Yugoslavia
Released: 1989
Released in U.S.: 1990
Production: Mirza Pasic for Sarajevo; released by Columbia Pictures
Direction: Emir Kusturica
Screenplay: Gordan Mihic and Emir Kusturica
Cinematography: Vilko Filac
Editing: Andrija Zafranovic
Production design: Jelena Silajdzic
Art direction: Miljen Kljakovic
Special effects: Jiry Simunek
Sound: Ivan Zakic and Srdan Popovic
Makeup: Halid Redzebasic
Costume design: Mirjana Ostojic
Music: Goran Bregovic
MPAA rating: R
Running time: 136 minutes

Principal characters:

Perhan	Davor Dujmovic
Danira	Elvira Sali
Ahmed	Bora Todorovic
Perhan's grandmother	Ljubica Adzovic
Azra	Sinolicka Trpkova
Uncle Merdzan	Husnija Hasimovic

Shot on location in Yugoslavia and Italy, *Time of the Gypsies* is a vivid exploration of European gypsy life, revealing its peculiarities and treating universal themes and values such as the importance of family relationships, respect for loyalty and honesty, and the corrupting influences in the world that contend with those high values.

The film follows chiefly the exploits of Perhan (Davor Dujmovic), who early in the narrative is an unaffected youth, lovingly tender in caring for his handicapped sister Danira (Elvira Sali). She is afflicted with a stunted leg, and he accompanies her to a distant hospital reported to have a procedure for lengthening bones. Medical costs presumably are to be paid by Ahmed Djida (Bora Todorovic), also known as the Sheik, a man whose status in the gypsy domain is equivalent to that of Michael Corleone (Al Pacino) in *The Godfather, Part III* (1990; reviewed in this volume). He is ostensibly doing this favor because he is grateful to Perhan's grandmother (Ljubica Adzovic); with her healing powers she saved the life of his son. The two youngsters unwittingly go with Ahmed on their hopeful journey, unaware that he is in the business of buying and stealing children, whom he adds to his entourage so that they can be beggars, thieves, and prostitutes. After leaving Danira at the hospital, Fagin-like, he persuades Perhan to steal for him, supposedly so they will have enough money to pay for Danira's costly medical treatment; meanwhile, she is not being treated but has been removed from the hospital and is begging for coins with another branch of Ahmed's criminal network. Perhan eventually discovers this and seeks revenge in the film's spectacular climax.

Between his innocent initiation into the world of corruption and the grim resolution of his story, Perhan goes through an amazing progress, one that is extreme in the range of its passions, yet forceful in its authenticity. Beginning as an awkward adolescent obedient to his worshipping grandmother, he develops into a love-stirred young man courting the woman he loves. Soon after departing with Ahmed and his sister, he becomes an abused and exploited victim; necessity, however, makes him a successful thief, so much so that Ahmed, after suffering a stroke, selects him over his own brothers to head the criminal operation. Perhan, arrogant with power, is brought low by warring members within the gypsy band. Interspersed with the above events are Perhan's return to his home village, his discovery that the woman he loves is pregnant with—he believes—another man's child, his marriage to her, the birth of the child, and Perhan's eventual conviction that the boy is his. This story is replete with dramatic incidents.

Throughout the film, audiences are predisposed to believe even the most extreme occurrences, because gypsy life implies an exotic and impetuous existence. Indeed, one of the film's strongest attractions is that it provides a safe but intimate view of an alien culture—dangerous, colorful, and strange. Such instances as when a lovelorn Perhan hangs himself by the neck with the cord from a church bell and then rings the bell wildly in his desperate, bobbing efforts to keep from choking, or when, enraged upon learning that his beloved is pregnant, he bites a piece out of a drinking glass, or when Perhan's Uncle Merdzan (Husnija Hasimovic), resentful that his mother will not help him pay gambling debts, ties their house to a truck's tow line and pulls it up off its foundation are both intriguing and convincing because of their extremity. Even the magic powers possessed by both Perhan and his grandmother seem credible in this unusual milieu. (Perhan has telekinetic powers that can move objects at some distance, a skill that serves him well in one of the story's critical moments.)

Many incidents are unpleasant, both in substance and in their graphic depiction. For example, Ahmed's stroke leaves his face partially paralyzed and deformed, his lower lip turned out in a manner that is utterly real. Also, when Perhan arrives with the gypsies at a trailer camp after leaving his sister at the hospital, he senses an aberrance in the surroundings. His foreboding is caught by a camera placed behind him with its wide-angle lens, slightly out of focus, capturing his back in the center of the frame and what he sees to the right and left, as if through a distorting haze. His feeling is soon proven to have a basis when an unwilling young woman is forced to prostitute herself for the gypsies' profit. Her screams as she is being brutally used cause Perhan considerable disquiet as he lies on his cot wondering what the future holds.

Many of the film's principal roles are played by actual gypsies, a fact that might be distracting to some, particularly early in the footage, because the performers are somewhat self-conscious. As the drama unfolds, however, and the emotional situations become more intense, the performers are up to the challenge; self-consciousness falls away as they abandon themselves to the passionate lives of their respective characters. This is certainly true of Ljubica Adzovic, a gypsy who was found by director Emir Kusturica's associates in Sutomor. As Perhan's grandmother, she is the matriarchal rock who gives fullness of meaning to family rituals and feels most intensely the empathetic connection when members of the clan suffer.

Particularly admirable in the central role is Davor Dujmovic, who is a professional, having appeared in Kusturica's *When Father Was Away on Business* (1985). Kusturica has aptly called Dujmovic ugly but beautiful; he does, indeed, bring to the demanding role a chameleonlike quality that enables him to portray the radical transformations of Perhan, who is at first so unpretentious as to go unnoticed but is then, in turn, spiritually aglow, sexually aroused, smug, paternally caring, and hell-bent on revenge. His emotional palette has an astonishing number of colors, and Kusturica knows how to use them.

It is perplexing that Janet Maslin, in her review in *The New York Times*, wrote that one of the most amazing things about the film is Emir Kusturica's winning of the Best Director Award at Cannes in 1989. The award seems well deserved. Except for the cliché of juxtaposing panning shots of brother and sister as they run toward each other to be reunited after long separation, his choices seem unerring. Although the film is long, often unpleasant, and will not appeal to merely escapist filmgoers, it has a potentially appreciative, perhaps ardent, audience that should have the opportunity to see it on the large screen. Kusturica has found some stunning visual metaphors for powerful human emotions. The rich images are sometimes mesmerizing. Particularly striking is the vision of Perhan's bride, Azra (Sinolicka Trpkova), in labor, her body raised above the grassy ground by his telekinetic powers, her white bridal gown bloodied from the waist down; also striking is one of Perhan's dream sequences, shot through a warm-colored filter, showing himself and his glowing bride in formal wedding attire partially immersed in the sun-lit river, with guests frolicking in the water nearby and Grandma on the bank shedding tears of joy. This and the many surreal dream sequences are Dali-esque in their fantastic but suggestive imagery. A bridal veil blowing in the wind, Grandma playing the accordion outside the Duomo in Milan, Perhan's sister dancing on two good legs, the house that was home, aflame and floating upward toward the sky—these and numerous other images, both in and outside Perhan's dreams, linger in the viewer's memory long afterward.

Images of boxes recur throughout the film. Cardboard boxes serve as hiding places for playing children, a cratelike outhouse proves to be one gunned-down victim's deathtrap, a coffin is another character's final box, and, in the film's closing image, a large corrugated carton is the means of getaway for Perhan's son after he steals two coins. The images are often playful, but they metaphorically reinforce the idea that these characters, despite the zest with which they attack life, are nevertheless trapped. Uncle Merdzan has a nightmare during which he screams that he wants to go back to Germany; his wailful cries are the most explicit statement of frustration of a people ensnared in socioeconomic and psychological conditions from which there seems to be no escape. Nevertheless, Kusturica has made a positive statement about an exuberant, passionate people, whose lives are fuller than many. *Time of the Gypsies* is the best kind of unconventional filmmaking.

Cono Robert Marcazzo

Reviews
Boxoffice. April, 1990, p. R32.
Chicago Tribune. February 21, 1990, V, p. 7.
The Christian Science Monitor. March 5, 1990, p. 10.
Films in Review. XLI, May, 1990, p. 304.
Los Angeles Times. February 9, 1990, p. F6.
The Nation. CCL, March 5, 1990, p. 322.
The New York Times. February 9, 1990, p. C16.
Newsweek. CXV, March 5, 1990, p. 63.
Time. CXXXV, February 19, 1990, p. 82.
Variety. CCCXXXV, May 17, 1989, p. 8.
The Washington Post. February 21, 1990, p. D4.

TO SLEEP WITH ANGER

Production: Caldecot Chubb, Thomas S. Byrnes, and Darin Scott for Edward R.
  Pressman Film Corp., in association with SVS Films; released by Samuel
  Goldwyn Company
Direction: Charles Burnett
Screenplay: Charles Burnett
Cinematography: Walt Lloyd
Editing: Nancy Richardson
Production design: Penny Barrett
Art direction: Troy Myers
Sound: Veda Campbell
Costume design: Gaye Shannon-Burnett
Music: Stephen James Taylor
MPAA rating: PG
Running time: 95 minutes

> *Principal characters:*
> Harry Mention .... Danny Glover
> Babe Brother .... Richard Brooks
> Gideon .... Paul Butler
> Suzie .... Mary Alice
> Junior .... Carl Lumbly
> Linda .... Sheryl Lee Ralph
> Pat .... Vonetta McGee
> Preacher .... Wonderful Smith
> Hattie .... Ethel Ayler
> Sonny .... Devaughn Walter Nixon
> Okra Tate .... Davis Roberts
> Marsh .... Sy Richardson

To Sleep with Anger opens with a stunning sequence: an older man in a pearl-gray
suit sits next to a table upon which burns a bowl of pears. The flames lick slowly at
the fruit, then move onto an apple half of which lies beside the bowl. As the man
twiddles his thumbs, oblivious, the flames crawl down the table leg and engulf his
shoes. He drops to sleep while the fire climbs up his legs. In a dissolve, the man
awakes barefooted, sitting on a stump in his backyard and holding the Bible.

It is the poetic fusion of these biblical and vernacular images of black culture that
have made Charles Burnett one of the more critically acclaimed directors in the
United States, despite the mere handful of low-budget, narrowly distributed films
that he has written and directed since the 1970's. In 1988, Burnett received the Mac-
Arthur Foundation Fellowship, or "genius grant." In 1990, the National Film Regis-
try declared his film *Killer of Sheep* (1977) a "national treasure," ensuring its preser-

vation. *To Sleep with Anger*, distributed by the Samuel Goldwyn Company, represents Burnett's first chance at a much needed national audience. Despite their critical acclaim, Burnett's previous films remain (as of 1990) unavailable, either on videotape or through the revival-house circuit.

Gideon (Paul Butler) awakes in his miniature homestead of a backyard in south central Los Angeles. Comfortably retired far from the South, he nevertheless clings to the old ways that he learned as the grandchild of slaves and later as a sharecropper. Gideon's wife, Suzie (Mary Alice), is a traditional midwife; because of a reappreciation for the art, she teaches a birthing class at home. After his disturbing dream, Gideon ambles into the house, where he finds Suzie caring for their grandson, Sonny (Devaughn Walter Nixon). Sonny is the child of the couple's younger son, Babe Brother (Richard Brooks). Because Babe Brother and his wife, Linda (Sheryl Lee Ralph), are busy with their professional careers, they are disrespectful of Gideon and Suzie's generation and lack the time to rear Sonny. Gideon, sensitive to both slights, complains to Suzie, especially because Babe Brother has forgotten her birthday. Gideon also notes with sadness that he has lost his toby jug, an African good luck charm.

The familial tensions are further revealed when Junior (Carl Lumbly), a carbon copy of Gideon's sober stability, joins his father in berating Babe Brother. Later, as Gideon amuses Sonny with some mildly irreligious jokes, Suzie drops a fruit bowl, that earlier symbol of Gideon's anger and temptation. As Sonny begins to sweep up the glass, the door bell rings, announcing the arrival of Harry Mention (Danny Glover), a friend from the South whom Gideon and Suzie have not seen since they left thirty years before. Harry is on his way to Oakland, but he receives an open invitation to stay. Junior and his wife Pat (Vonetta McGee), pregnant with their second child, arrive. In a second omen, Pat's baby kicks to the point of pain each time Pat tries to extend her hand to Harry. When this extended family leaves for church, Harry proceeds to go through their drawers, read their mail, and examine their other possessions. The film crosscuts between these transgressions and scenes of the family at church. When Babe Brother and Linda interrupt Harry, he engages in the first of several trickster tales. To Linda's disgust, Harry cleans his fingernails with a huge knife as he relates a tall tale about a knife fight on New Orleans' Beale Street. The story intrigues Babe Brother, who snaps at Linda when she interrupts. In an ironic counterpoint, Babe Brother's seduction is crosscut with shots of a baptism at the church.

Next, Harry provides Pat and Junior with the sinister, because somewhat true, motivation for their extensive charity work: It distances them from direct involvement and at the same time fulfills their attraction to pain and suffering. Harry also confronts an old Southern friend, Hattie (Ethel Ayler), who used to run a house of ill repute but has found religion in her later years. More of a match for Harry, Hattie responds to his insults with old country platitudes. As a last assault on Hattie, Harry suggests that Gideon and Suzie host a fish fry for all their old Southern friends. With the arrival of corn liquor, Harry gathers the men together in the kitchen, including

Babe Brother. As the men recall the old days, one accuses Harry of hanging his cousin and—in a move that endangered the entire community—giving it the appearance of a lynching. Outside, Gideon and Babe Brother, both drunk, scream at each other until Suzie forces the men to shake hands.

The next day, Harry takes the out-of-shape Gideon on a midday hike through the train yards. That night, Gideon has a stroke that leaves him an invalid. While Suzie nurses Gideon, Harry consolidates his hold on the house by inviting his resurrected friends and further tempting Babe Brother with the promise of how to make money at cards. As Babe Brother becomes more violent, Linda is forced to take refuge with Sonny in Junior and Pat's home. For Suzie, the final straw comes when Okra Tate (Davis Roberts), one of Harry's old friends, proposes to Suzie in order to be first in line if Gideon dies. When Suzie orders Harry to leave, however, he reminds her that she invited him, suggesting the myth of the vampire or devil which is empowered by his victim's consent. Nevertheless, he agrees to leave and returns to Babe Brother's kitchen and to his gang, who make vague plans for a life on the run. In order to enlist Babe Brother, Harry gives him his knife. Putting the knife in his sock, Babe Brother returns to his parents' home for his suitcase.

Babe Brother tells Suzie he is going "home" with Harry. Junior, Pat, and Linda arrive to help Suzie move Gideon's sickbed from under a leak in the ceiling. In an imitation of Harry, Babe Brother sits in the kitchen cleaning his nails with his new knife. Junior, who likewise "sleeps with anger" beneath his upright appearance, confronts and overpowers Babe Brother. He is about to stab Babe Brother when the women intervene, and Suzie grasps the knife's blade, cutting her hand. This near fratricide and Suzie's sacrifice reunite the family. In the hospital waiting room, Junior and Babe Brother share first concern over the long wait and then laughter when a nurse blames it all on the full moon.

Returning home the next morning, the family ignores Harry. Babe Brother is about to confront him, but Linda sends Babe Brother upstairs. Just as the broken fruit bowl announced Harry's arrival, a bowl of scattered marbles signals his exit. Alone downstairs, Harry trips on the marbles and, as he falls, suffers a heart attack and dies. As Harry lays dead on the kitchen floor, the family gathers around the dinner table, and Gideon staggers downstairs to rejoin them. Because of a city mix-up or possible bureaucratic racism, the paramedics refuse to remove the body, and the family is forced into an impromptu wake. Harry's friends, then Suzie's minister, arrive. Meanwhile, Babe Brother apologizes to Linda, explaining that his time with Harry was like what the old country people describe as hell. Linda rewards him with his given name, which is Sam.

This humorous scene with Harry's corpse, reminiscent of Alfred Hitchcock's *The Trouble with Harry* (1955), ends with a more biblical allusion: an earthquake, although a mild one. Afterward, a neighbor invites the family to an impromptu picnic, and everyone leaves the house. A neighbor child, whose atonal trumpet squawks have sounded throughout the film, suddenly bursts into a clear, fluent melody. As with the trumpet—invoking not only the biblical Gideon, but a gentle antistereotype

Magill's Cinema Annual 1991

to the "musical" African American—many symbols and leitmotifs run through *To Sleep with Anger*. Writer and director Burnett renders a delicate visual and narrative counterpoint. The devillike Harry is underscored by red light, while the apple, that devil-red forbidden fruit, is a recurring image. Besides biblical allegory, Burnett invokes rich images of the South: Harry's superstitions, the river gambler's suit of Gideon's dream, and Harry's hypnosis of a chicken. Nevertheless, the film is not purely symbolic. It raises questions about the politics of nostalgia, about the dangers as well as the pleasures of the past. In an early exchange, Suzie notes Harry's good Southern manners but adds with some bitterness that he learned them at a time and in a place where "we knew our place." Both Harry and Gideon are, in fact, crippled by their allegiance to the past: Gideon having become too soft, Harry too hard. Burnett, however, is no polemicist.

In addition to the story, writing, and fine production values, the acting is exceptional. These are naturalistic performances infused with the bit of mysticism that these characters' histories encompass. In fact, the only unfortunate thing about *To Sleep with Anger* is how few people may have enjoyed it in a theater. The Samuel Goldwyn Company relied on the dubious notion of a "built-in" audience for films by and about African-Americans, failing to implement the grassroots campaign that most specialty films require. When traditional promotion and exceptional reviews failed to generate sufficient interest, the company then turned to grassroots efforts, but too late. The film may, however, be successful with videotape rentals. Because it is an intimate and thoughtful film, its power should not be diminished in a small format.

Gabrielle J. Forman

Reviews
Afro-American. October 13, 1990, p. B6.
Chicago Tribune. October 26, 1990, VII, p. 26.
The Hollywood Reporter. January 29, 1990, p. 8.
Los Angeles Times. October 24, 1990, p. F1.
The Nation. CCLI, November 5, 1990, p. 537.
The New York Times. October 5, 1990, p. B3.
The New Yorker. LXVI, November 5, 1990, p. 138.
Newsweek. CXVI, October 22, 1990, p. 74.
Time. CXXXVI, October 22, 1990, p. 63.
Variety. January 26, 1990, p. 2.
The Washington Post. October 26, 1990, p. C7.

TOO BEAUTIFUL FOR YOU
(TROP BELLE POUR TOI)

Origin: France
Released: 1989
Released in U.S.: 1990
Production: Cine Valse, D.D. Productions, Orly Films, S.E.D.I.F., T.F.1, and Films
 Productions; released by Orion Classics
Direction: Bertrand Blier
Screenplay: Bertrand Blier
Cinematography: Philippe Rousselot
Editing: Claudine Merlin
Set decoration: Théobald Meurisse
Sound: Louis Gimel and Paul Bertault
Makeup: Joel Lavau
Costume design: Michele Marmande-Cerf
Music: Franz Schubert and Francis Lai
MPAA rating: no listing
Running time: 91 minutes

> *Principal characters:*
> Bernard Barthelemy .... Gérard Depardieu
> Colette Chevassu .... Josiane Balasko
> Florence Barthelemy .... Carole Bouquet
> Marcello .... Roland Blanche
> Pascal Chevassu .... François Cluzet
> Léonce .... Didier Bernureau
> Tanguy .... Philippe Loffredo
> Marie-Cathérine .... Sylvie Orcier
> Geneviève .... Myriam Boyer

The premise of Bertrand Blier's eleventh film is a clever twist on the often-examined phenomenon of male middle-age crisis. Bernard (Gérard Depardieu) is a successful businessman married to an elegant woman whom French society regards as the epitome of beauty and sophistication. The father of two bright and well-adjusted children, Bernard is the central figure in a group of individuals who have done well financially and maintain an active social life. He appears to have no problems with his wife, Florence (Carole Bouquet), but his emotions are turned upside-down when he looks into the eyes of Colette Chevassu (Josiane Balasko), a temporary secretary sent to work in an adjoining office separated from his by glass rather than walls. The plot twist is that Colette is not nearly as beautiful as Florence and offers Bernard no social advantages, not even the thrill of a mysterious and alluring mistress. In a conventionally cast film, Colette would have been the plain wife who was dumped for Florence, "the other woman."

The romantic attraction between Bernard and Colette is registered in their very first encounter, which is the film's first fully realized scene. Colette boldly signals her interest, and, after the briefest of hesitations, Bernard responds to her availability. The existential and expressionistic style of this initial scene is maintained for most of the film. Characters will speak their thoughts into the camera or in voice-overs, and they will imagine a scene that may or may not materialize. When the lovers converse, they seem to be talking at each other rather than with each other. Reality and fantasy merge without any hint from the director as to when the viewers are in actual time and space and when they are in the imagination of one or another character. Individuals enter scenes in which they could not be present in a gentle but surreal manner. The film's quality is enhanced by the playing of twelve brooding selections from Franz Schubert as background music.

As Bernard and Colette become more involved, their hand-holding and other affectionate gestures make their relationship obvious to some of Bernard's friends. He begins to consider the option of leaving his glamorous wife for the ordinary but surprisingly compelling Colette. His children's propriety and accomplishments become irritating. His male friends are amazed at the strength of his new sexual attachment. They can empathize with a man having an affair and even offer their rooms when needed, but they are appalled to think the affair would ever disrupt Bernard's marriage. Most of them have secretly coveted Florence and cannot imagine anyone abandoning her. At age forty, Depardieu should be ideal for the role of Bernard, but in his fifth time working with Blier, he is not able to realize his character. Bernard never seems interesting enough to warrant the attention of the two women, each strong in her own manner, who vie for him. Rather than being a complex man of conflicting desires, he seems a vacuous personality who is a stranger to genuine feelings.

Carole Bouquet does what she can with the role of Florence, but her dialogue is so contrived and ambiguous that she, too, never becomes wholly credible. Florence proves to be other than the sophisticate her admirers believe her to be. Her self-image is bound up with being Bernard's wife, the mother of perfect children, the entrancing hostess. Her goal in life appears to be no more than being the female part of a couple that perfectly meets the social expectations of a certain slice of the French upper-middle class. Part of those expectations apparently require that she address her dinner partners in a somewhat regal, even pompous manner. Her lines have a quasi-erotic edge that makes her love for the thoroughly pedestrian Bernard difficult to comprehend. The same lines make her sound neurotic and explain why Bernard might respond so positively to the clarity of Colette's character. Florence's problem with Bernard does not seem to be that she is "too beautiful" but that Blier's conception has not gone beyond surface values.

Colette, in contrast, is not as unattractive as the film's characters insist. She has a full figure that can be as enticing as the svelte shape of her rival. Her features, if not remarkable, are pleasant; her candor and enthusiasm, refreshing. From the onset, she has a good grasp of what the affair is and what it is not. She is certain that

Bernard eventually will leave her to return to Florence and the social milieu exemplified by his Yves St. Laurent wardrobe. Her single wish is that their affair last as long as possible. Underscoring her strength is her ability to remain steadfast to her vision of herself and never attempt a transformation into what Bernard might want or imagine he wants. She insists that he bend to her reality even though she knows that can never happen.

Working against the development of sexual chemistry between the film's lovers is the abstract and distancing style Blier uses to tell his tale. As often as Bernard and Colette claim that they love as they have never loved before, that kind of passion is never captured on the screen. Viewers who are not simply bored by all the talk about love and by uninspired sex scenes will still find it hard to believe that Bernard is risking the whole shape of his life for an emotion he demonstrates so poorly. Pascal (François Cluzet), Colette's previous lover, adds no heat to the emotional temperature. He is a fledgling writer more interested in shaping good prose than in reclaiming lost love. His chats with Bernard, his expressed desire for Colette's return, and his talk about writing are tepid.

Blier is uncertain of where his film should go and what it should be exploring. For most of *Too Beautiful for You*, Bernard is said to be thoroughly beguiled by Colette. Although he is not ashamed to be in public with her—she is as attractive and appropriately dressed as anyone else—he is very distressed when seen with her in a restaurant by old friends. One consequence of his embarrassment is that the couple go to the south of France to be alone. While in the country, Bernard seems unduly upset by the rustic character of the life offered him, an ambiance that could just as easily be considered charming or romantic. A major schism occurs when Colette insists on riding her bike to the greengrocer and baker rather than being driven in Bernard's car. Judging this decision insufferable, Bernard momentarily ends the relationship by driving away. When Bernard utilizes this trivial dispute to sever the relationship, the writer-director, rather than the character, seems to be straining to find credible motivation. That Bernard returns to continue the involvement does not mask the episode's weaknesses.

The film's general characterizations and pacing are largely unsatisfying. Florence is on screen too briefly to be a credible contender in the love triangle, while Bernard is on far too long for the little that the audience comes to know of his inner life. Minor characters, such as Marcello (Roland Blanche), one of Bernard's nicer cohorts, are not sufficiently developed to register as individuals. Marcello is given the statement that Italians have invented the sun and the opera. Whether such utterances are thought to be urbane or are meant to be sarcastic or farcical is unclear.

A whirlwind conclusion to what has been a light comedy gives the film some unanticipated somber aspects. After having spent nearly the entire film on a romance of about a month's duration, Blier moves to the final breakup and its four-year emotional fallout in one jump cut. Colette has a husband and two children. She continues to regard Bernard as the love of her life and recalls their time together fondly. Florence, for reasons never explicated, has changed dramatically. Bernard's return has not reestablished the old order. In an angry final encounter, she tells him that she has been faking emotions and orgasms for four years. Now she is going to leave him. Bernard is devastated. He has lost the plain girl who made him feel so wanted and he has lost the woman society had cultivated for him. He shouts at the camera angrily and in a moment typical of the film berates the Schubert music that has been trailing him throughout the film.

Colette, although unhappy, emerges as the most positive character. She understands that plain is not ugly, and she is totally at ease with her features, shape, and life-style. She understands that her problems with Bernard had to do with class, not aesthetics. Precisely because she has such a clear view of life's circumstances, she often seems prettier than the nominally lovelier Florence. This suggests some irony in the title about just who is too beautiful for whom.

Too Beautiful for You may be one of those films that plays better for a domestic audience that can recognize certain nuances of language, cleverness of sites, and aspects of national character that are not easily exported. Regardless of whether this is the case, *Too Beautiful for You* has not been well received in the United States. This is in decided contrast to the reception of Blier's earlier *Préparez vos mouchoirs* (1977; *Get Out Your Handkerchiefs*, 1978), which also starred Depardieu and won the Oscar for Best Foreign Language Film (1978) and was rated as Best Foreign Film of the Year (1978) by the National Society of Film Critics. An even earlier Blier-Depardieu film, *Les Valseuses*, (1973; *Going Places*), had considerable box-office success in the United States, and Blier's *Beau-Père* (1981) had premiered in the United States at the prestigious New York Film Festival. Both *Going Places* and *Beau-Père* were adapted by Blier for the screen from his own novels respectively entitled *Les Valseuses* and *Beau-Père*.

Dan Georgakas

Reviews

Boxoffice. June, 1990, p. 47.
Chicago Tribune. April 20, 1990, VII, p. 36.
The Christian Science Monitor. March 14, 1990, p. 11.
Commonweal. CXVII, May 4, 1990, p. 296.
Films in Review. XLI, August, 1990, p. 434.
Los Angeles Times. April 13, 1990, p. F1.
The Nation. CCL, April 2, 1990, p. 466.
The New Leader. LXXIII, January 8, 1990, p. 22.
The New York Times. September 22, 1989, p. C22.
Variety. May 15, 1989, p. 10.
The Washington Post. April 11, 1990, p. D2.

TOTAL RECALL

Production: Buzz Feitshans and Ronald Shusett for Carolco Pictures; released by
Tri-Star Pictures
Direction: Paul Verhoeven
Screenplay: Ronald Shusett, Dan O'Bannon, and Gary Goldman; based on a story
by Shusett, O'Bannon, and Jon Povill, and inspired by the short story "We Can
Remember It for You Wholesale," by Philip K. Dick
Cinematography: Jost Vacano
Editing: Frank J. Urioste
Production design: William Sandell
Art direction: James Tocci and José Rodriguez Granada
Set decoration: Robert Gould
Set design: Marco Trentini, Miguel Chang, and Carlos Echeverria
Special effects: Scott Fisher, William Gregory Curtis, Dale Martin, and James
Rollins
Visual effects: Eric Brevig (AA), Alex Funke (AA), and Tim McGovern (AA)
Sound: Nelson Stoll, Michael J. Kohout, Carlos Delarios, and Aaron Rochin
Special sound effects: John Pospisil and Alan Howarth
Special makeup effects: Rob Bottin (AA)
Costume design: Erica Edell Phillips
Stunt coordination: Vic Armstrong and Joel Kramer
Music: Jerry Goldsmith
MPAA rating: R
Running time: 109 minutes

Principal characters:
Quaid/Hauser	Arnold Schwarzenegger
Melina	Rachel Ticotin
Lori	Sharon Stone
Cohaagen	Ronny Cox
Richter	Michael Ironside
Kuato	Marshall Bell
Benny	Mel Johnson, Jr.
Helm	Michael Champion
Dr. Edgemar	Roy Brocksmith

Seldom have science-fiction films achieved the fantastic, challenging thoughtful-
ness that is the hallmark of speculative literature. *Total Recall*, an epic, financially
ambitious, and narratively complex film, comes surprisingly close to succeeding.
The film opens with a space-suited couple, who, while gazing at a pyramid-like
mound, slip and tumble down a rust-red hill. The film suddenly cuts to Doug Quaid
(Arnold Schwarzenegger), who sits bolt upright in bed. What the audience has seen
is his recurring dream. For the first of many times, the viewer, and he, will be unable

to distinguish between genuine experiences and mental fantasies.

Total Recall does a compact job of establishing its initial narrative premises and futuristic setting. Quaid is a construction worker; the year is 2084. Both in his dream and in his waking moments, Quaid finds himself oddly drawn to the thought of a Martian vacation. Mars has become a frontier mining colony, operated by a steely-jawed entrepreneur named Cohaagen (Ronny Cox). Since his salary could hardly cover such a space voyage, Quaid decides to visit Rekall, a company which can, at a relatively reasonable price, implant in his mind false memories of a Martian vacation. Quaid helps plot out his own dream: He will be a secret agent, be involved in violent mayhem, have an affair with a brunette, athletic woman, and "save the entire planet." During the dream implantation, however, Quaid suffers a "paranoid embolism." He explodes violently from Rekall's facility and immediately finds himself pursued by murderous, mysterious operatives. What follows is perhaps the most intense and energetic portion of the film: Cars crash, bystanders are killed (including one used as a human shield), and hide-and-seek shoot-outs occur in rapid succession, all reinforced by Frank J. Urioste's nimble, ferocious editing and Jost Vacano's inky, low-angled cinematography. Even Quaid's wife, Lori (Sharon Stone), tries to shoot him—she, too, turns out to be an operative.

Quaid seeks refuge in a cheap hotel room; there Quaid is contacted by a mysterious caller, who tells him where to pick up a briefcase. Having found it, Quaid opens the case to find several odd gadgets and a video screen: A videotaped image of a slightly different-looking and differently acting Quaid (who calls himself Hauser) tells him that Quaid is in reality a former operative working for Cohaagen, that he then became an ally of Martian freedom fighters, that Cohaagen had Hauser's memories erased and replaced with those of Quaid, and that the Rekall process has now inadvertently resurrected images of his former life.

Total Recall's second act begins with Quaid's arrival on Mars, a place of antiseptic decor, sordid bars, and mutant, telepathic workers (Cohaagen has built substandard protective domes over the work area; incoming ultraviolet radiation has wreaked genetic mayhem). After evading guards at Mars immigration (he disguises himself as a large woman), Quaid checks into a hotel and contacts someone who is supposed to help him: Melina (Rachel Ticotin), a doe-eyed prostitute who has allied herself with the rebels and who resembles the woman whom the audience saw in the opening, space-suit sequence, as well as the "choice" Quaid made before going to Rekall. Is this all happening, one wonders, or is Quaid in a Rekall-induced hallucination? He himself begins to wonder when a prissy Dr. Edgemar (Roy Brocksmith), an official from Rekall whom the audience has seen before in a Rekall television ad, arrives with Lori by his side. They tell him that he is in the throes of an uncontrolled nightmare and that they have come to save him. A heavy drop of sweat from Edgemar's forehead, however, betrays his quite real fear: Quaid kills him, soldiers burst in, and Lori and Melina launch into a fight of their own. Once again, Quaid and Melina manage to escape.

The film's chase/violence mix reheats as Quaid bores toward his ultimate goal: to reach Kuato (Marshall Bell), a mutant rebel leader who, in an oddly moving bit of grotesquerie, turns out to be a creature implanted as a sort of telepathic Siamese twin on the stomach of another man. Cohaagen's soldiers burst in and kill Kuato. Unwittingly, Quaid has led them to their prey, and Cohaagen announces to Quaid that his Hauser alter-ego never really did defect to the rebel side. It has all been a plot to deceive the revolutionaries—Hauser volunteered to have his personality and memories erased so that the mind-reading mutants would fail to identify Quaid as an enemy. To prove it, Cohaagen plays a tape in which Hauser himself admits to the ploy.

This second plot reversal sets Quaid's—and the audience's—perceptions on end. It also unleashes the film's somewhat weaker third act, which turns on Cohaagen's genuine goal to prevent the alien technology that was discovered in the pyramid-like mound (seen in the opening dream sequence) from being activated. This machine was apparently created by unknown creatures to generate a breathable atmosphere on Mars. A functioning machine, however, would deprive Cohaagen of his stranglehold on the settlers' air supply. (Cohaagen claims that the machine will in fact destroy the planet.) First, however, Cohaagen needs his old ally, Hauser, back. He orders Quaid strapped into the device that will transform him back into Hauser. Yet Quaid once again breaks free. He and Melina enter the gargantuan device, outduel various thugs (including Cohaagen), and switch on the device, which, after considerable pyrotechnics, restores the atmosphere of Mars.

Total Recall's intricate plot and special effects certainly merit praise. To appreciate the film's effectiveness fully, however, one must trace back the film's origins. Its primary source is Philip K. Dick's short story "We Can Remember It for You Wholesale." Screenwriters Ronald Shusett, Dan O'Bannon, and Gary Goldman have taken many narrative liberties. For example, the short story's central character—as in most of Dick's work—is a hapless misogynist whose life has degenerated into clammy paranoia. The film's Quaid is hardly such a man. The screenwriters also offset Dick's own anger toward relationships (he had several failed marriages) by counterbalancing Quaid's cool, deceitful wife, Lori, with the feisty, high-purposed character of Melina.

O'Bannon and Shusett wrote the original script a full twelve years before the film's release. A reported fifty rewrites ensued, the latter ones reflecting Schwarzenegger's own concerns (including a modest collection of the one-liners that have become the actor's trademark). The many rewrites have also led to several dangling plot threads. Why did Quaid's disguise machinery go awry at immigration? What is the audience to make of the resemblance of Kuato's four-fingered hand to the one imprinted on the alien reactor's start-up device? Why was this machine never used by its alien creators? These and other questions are left unanswered. Yet considering the numerous changes, *Total Recall*'s narrative lapses seem acceptably few. Moreover, much remains of O'Bannon and Shusett's own early ideas. The authors of *Alien* (1979) and *Blue Thunder* (1983) have always been drawn to tales of paranoia and slippery reality. Kuato may even be an echo of *Alien*'s gut-exploding creature; the pyramid mound comes directly from an early draft of *Alien*; the writers' fondness for old science-fiction classics leads to a cavernous alien machine that recalls that of *Forbidden Planet* (1956) and the massive earth-boring machines of *Things to Come* (1936).

It also is certain that director Paul Verhoeven layered *Total Recall* with his own obsessions. Verhoeven makes much of the fact that, as a child, he witnessed Nazi atrocities in his native Holland. The film's Grand Guignol violence, its traitorous characters (even Quaid's mind betrays him), and its Gestapo-like, trenchcoated villains point to Verhoeven's anxieties.

Two themes, however—seemingly the product of all artists involved—especially enrich *Total Recall*'s subtext. The first and most obvious is the question of what, indeed, is real. Are we watching the dream of an escapist construction worker, a reformed villain who is haunted by a doppelgänger, or an unrepentant villain who, unintentionally, has come to prefer his new identity? The film yields a cascade of clues that point, conflictingly, to each of these options. Also, is this ambiguity deliberate and clever, or is it a failure of foreshadowing and plot, made fragile by the rewrites? That reality and fantasy are difficult to separate from any of these perspectives makes *Total Recall*'s central conceit—whether deliberate or semiaccidental—a compelling one. More elegant, subtle, and coherent is the film's second leitmotif: that what is within is often at odds with what is at the surface. A helpful taxi driver and a commonsense coworker turn out to be betrayers; a wife is a spy; deformed mutants hold winsome motives; Quaid uses a holographic alter ego to confuse his pursuers; Kuato lives within an otherwise normal person; and the central character himself may be a villain turned inside out. Even Mars is not what it seems: The alien reactor melts subsurface ice to transform a hostile planet into a felicitous paradise. This second theme thus joins the first to generate the film's controlling question: Whether a person can ever know who he or she is.

Marc Mancini

Reviews

Boxoffice. August, 1990, p. R58.
Chicago Tribune. June 1, 1990, VII, p. 21.
Film Comment. XXVI, July, 1990, p. 24.
Films in Review. XLI, October, 1990, p. 483.
The Hollywood Reporter. CCCXII, June 1, 1990, p. 9.
Los Angeles Times. June 1, 1990, p. F1.
The New York Times. June 1, 1990, p. B1.
The New Yorker. LXVI, June 18, 1990, p. 91.
Newsweek. CXV, June 11, 1990, p. 62.
Premiere. III, June, 1990, p. 70.
Time. CXXXV, June 11, 1990, p. 85.
Variety. June 1, 1990, p. 3.
Video. XIV, December, 1990, p. 70.

THE TWO JAKES

Production: Robert Evans and Harold Schneider; released by Paramount Pictures
Direction: Jack Nicholson
Screenplay: Robert Towne
Cinematography: Vilmos Zsigmond
Editing: Anne Goursaud
Production design: Jeremy Railton and Richard Sawyer
Art direction: Richard Schreiber
Set decoration: Jerry Wunderlich
Sound: Julia Evershade
Costume design: Wayne Finkelman
Music: Van Dyke Parks
MPAA rating: R
Running time: 137 minutes

> *Principal characters:*
> Jake Gittes .... Jack Nicholson
> Jake Berman .... Harvey Keitel
> Kitty Berman .... Meg Tilly
> Lillian Bodine .... Madeleine Stowe
> Cotton Weinberger .... Eli Wallach
> Mickey Nice .... Rubén Blades
> Chuck Newty .... Frederic Forrest
> Loach, Jr. .... David Keith
> Earl Rawley .... Richard Farnsworth
> Tyrone Otley .... Tracey Walter
> Lawrence Walsh .... Joe Mantell
> Kahn .... James Hong
> Captain Lou Escobar .... Perry Lopez
> Ralph Tilton .... Jeff Morris

When a screenwriter sits down to write a film script, she or he is bound by certain expectations inherent to the craft. The writer has an obligation to structure a story that has a beginning, a middle, and an end, a story that by its very nature is self-contained within the limitations of the medium. That is not to suggest that the characters have no history or future, but that those aspects of their lives must be dramatized within the framework of the story. Simply put, a writer must have a reason to write, he must have a story to tell, and that story must have an end. Yet Hollywood, in its never-ending search for commercial box-office success, insists on bringing back, via the sequel, characters whose stories have already been told. Some have been perfectly presented, some slightly more flawed, but more often than not, these stories have served their purpose. They have said whatever the writer set out to say and thus, the sequel simply rehashes the same old material without shedding any new light on the lives of the characters. There is a cliché: let sleeping dogs lie. One could say the same about private detective J. J. Gittes. His story was already told in *Chinatown* (1974).

In *The Two Jakes*, the successful and prosperous Jake Gittes (Jack Nicholson) agrees to help another Jake, a real-estate developer named Berman (Harvey Keitel), gather proof of his wife's adultery. Unbeknown to Gittes, Berman acquires a gun and, in a presumed moment of passion, kills Bodine, the lover of Kitty (Meg Tilly), during a tryst at a local motel. Complications begin when Gittes discovers that the dead man is also Berman's business partner. Bodine's widow, Lillian (Madeleine Stowe), accuses the Bermans of framing her husband in order to gain control over the entire development plan and all its profits. When Gittes hears Katherine Mulwray's name mentioned on a wire recording from the motel room, he is once again drawn back into the past as he attempts to unravel the mystery.

There are things to like about *The Two Jakes* if the viewer has an eye for detail and can divorce himself from making comparisons to *Chinatown*. Director Jack Nicholson gives the film very American sensibilities that echo post-World War II sentiments and captures the textural fabric of life in Los Angeles in 1948 in the smallest of details. There are references to anti-Semitism, while the recurring earthquake tremors underscore the instability of life and remind viewers that one is never on solid ground. It is these small touches that give the film a fully developed richness. The problems lay in the story itself, a mystery that is no mystery (to anyone but Gittes, that is), and a cast of characters who operate with little motivation. One glance at Kitty Berman and anyone who has seen *Chinatown* immediately knows Kitty's true identity merely from her attire and her nervous smoking gestures. This lack of suspense is further exacerbated by the film's length, unnecessarily long and encumbered by a forced, poetic voice-over narration, laden with metaphor, that was written in postproduction by Nicholson in an attempt to clarify certain story elements for those viewers unfamiliar with *Chinatown*.

When screenwriter Robert Towne wrote the nouveau *film noir* classic *Chinatown*, he succeeded in telling a story in which the underlying message was that one can never escape the past. It resurfaces at the most inopportune times and without warning. That message came through poignantly and powerfully. The story was so finished, so complete that by the time the end credits rolled, *Chinatown* became a paradigm of storytelling. By the film's end, there simply was nowhere left to go. The audience knew everything it needed to know about the characters, and *Chinatown* had the good sense to let its backstory, its history, be the driving force of the film. Perhaps it was the reputed conflict between director Roman Polanski and screenwriter Robert Towne over the altered ending of *Chinatown* that motivated Towne to revive Jake Gittes. Towne accused Polanski of imposing a more cynical, fatalistic tone than the writer had originally conceived. (Towne had envisioned that Evelyn Mulwray would escape with her sister/daughter, Katherine.) Without Polanski's more cynical sense of irony, pervasive evil, and personal tragedy, however, the life and times of Mr. Gittes become boring and trite. In *The Two Jakes*, Towne has his character relive the same old story but without the eloquent fashion of the original. Instead of insight, the audience is left with myriad unanswered questions about what happened during those ten years that followed the events of *Chinatown* that could have turned J. J. Gittes into the man he is in *The Two Jakes*.

In some screenwriting circles it is expected that there should be a modicum of character movement within the course of a story. That is, by the end of the film, the main character must have learned something, must have undergone some degree of change. Unfortunately, it has become the accepted modus operandi in Hollywood filmmaking to deliver sequels in which all the character change occurs in the earlier film, if at all. Some films, such as *Robocop II* (1990; reviewed in this volume), attempt to disguise this lack of evolution by having the main character merely repeat the same internal conflict he faced previously. Other films, such as *The Two Jakes* and *Lethal Weapon II* (1989), forget about character change altogether and simply send their men to do battle with only external forces, unencumbered by any internal self-exploration.

Jack Nicholson is an actor best known for subtle, controlled performances that masked an unpredictability behind his rakishly seductive smile. Nicholson had displayed a depth of character that few other actors could match, even in supporting roles such as his portrayal of Eugene O'Neill in Warren Beatty's *Reds* (1981). Yet his more recent performances, particularly the Joker in *Batman* (1989), show no restraint or finesse of technique and seem to be little more than a parody of his own offscreen persona. The actor has become bigger than the sum of his parts.

One of the characteristics of *film noir*, those darkly pessimistic films that emerged in the 1940's, was the presence of the femme fatale, the sexually appealing and conniving female who would lure the male into danger. She was a wantonly wicked woman whose *raison d'être* was like that of the black widow spider: seduce and kill. Men seemed threatened by the new woman that emerged during the war years, and when American GIs prepared to return to the workplace, women were encouraged to surrender their new-found sense of independence and return to the role of homemaker. It was a turning point—or so it seemed at the time—and in retrospect, one can excuse this cinematic treatment of women as transitional. One cannot accept the misogynistic depiction of women that is present in *The Two Jakes* as merely being a convention of *film noir*; the filmmakers had an obligation to move their film beyond the previous constructs of the genre. The French did when New Wave filmmakers, such as Jean-Luc Godard with his brilliant *À bout de souffle* (1960; *Breathless*, 1961), took *film noir* in a new and exciting direction. *Chinatown* also succeeded in adding another layer of texture and complexity to the genre. *The Two Jakes*, however, seems content to rely on old form without exploring new content.

In an interview, Nicholson said that he believed the message conveyed by *Chinatown* was such a powerful one that it needed to be said again. As a filmmaker, he had an obligation to find either new characters or a new story through which to say it. Reviews for the film were decidedly mixed with most negative criticism citing

Nicholson's labored and unfocused direction and uninteresting performance as major faults.

Patricia Kowal

Reviews

Boxoffice. CXXVI, October, 1990, p. R75.
Chicago Tribune. August 10, 1990, VII, p. 27.
The Christian Science Monitor. LXXXII, August 10, 1990, p. 10.
Commonweal. CXVI, October 12, 1990, p. 579.
Drama-Logue. August 30-September 5, 1990, p. 23.
Entertainment Weekly. I, March 1, 1991, p. 62.
Films in Review. XLII, January, 1991, p. 43.
The Hollywood Reporter. CCCXIII, August 8, 1990, p. 5.
L.A. Weekly. XII, August 17-August 23, 1990, p. 40.
Los Angeles. XXXV, September, 1990, p. 170.
Los Angeles Times. August 10, 1990, p. F1.
The New York Times. August 10, 1990, p. B1.
The New York Times Magazine. September 10, 1990, p. S28.
Newsweek. CXVI, August 20, 1990, p. 60.
Rolling Stone. September 20, 1990, p. 47.
San Francisco Chronicle. August 10, 1990, p. E1.
San Francisco Examiner. CXXVI, August 10, 1990, p. C1.
Time. CXXXVI, August 20, 1990, p. 62.
Variety. CCCXL, August 8, 1990, p. 2.
Video. XIV, March, 1991, p. 50.

VINCENT AND THEO

Origin: Great Britain and France
Released: 1990
Released in U.S.: 1990
Production: Ludi Boeken for Belbo Films; released by Hemdale Film Corp.
Direction: Robert Altman
Screenplay: Julian Mitchell
Cinematography: Jean Lepine
Editing: Françoise Coispeau and Geraldine Peroni
Production design: Stephen Altman
Art direction: Dominique Douret, Ben Van Os, and Jan Roelfs
Art coordination: Karin Van De Werff
Set decoration: Pierre Sicre
Sketch and reproduction art: Robin Thiodet
Sound: Alain Curvelier
Costume design: Scott Bushnell
Music: Gabriel Yared
MPAA rating: PG-13
Running time: 138 minutes

Principal characters:

Vincent van Gogh	Tim Roth
Theo van Gogh	Paul Rhys
Sien Hoornik	Jip Wijngaarden
Jo Bonger	Johanna Ter Steege
Paul Gauguin	Wladimir Yordanoff
Dr. Paul Gachet	Jean-Pierre Cassel
Marguerite Gachet	Bernadette Giraud
Uncle Cent	Andrian Brine
Léon Bouscod	Jean-François Perrier
René Valadon	Vincent Vallier
Andries Bonger	Hans Kesting
Marie	Anne Canovas

Late in Robert Altman's boldly cerebral *Vincent and Theo*, Theo van Gogh (Paul Rhys) arrives in Arles to look after his brother Vincent (Tim Roth), who has just been hospitalized for slicing off a piece of his ear. Theo visits Vincent's small living quarters and examines some graffiti the troubled artist has painted on the wall. Beneath the writing is Vincent's smudged handprint, and as Theo looks closer at it, he presses his own hand over it. This short scene, more than any other in the film, comes closest to capturing Altman's motive for his reinvention of the van Gogh myth. This moment—Theo's hand fitting perfectly over Vincent's—illuminates the spiritual bond between the two siblings, an interconnection that allowed them to survive in an increasingly difficult world and, ironically, led ultimately to their mutual disintegration.

Vincente Minnelli provided his version of the life of Vincent van Gogh in a gorgeous Hollywood version that was as romantic as it was beautiful. *Lust for Life* (1956) was the textbook version of the van Gogh story, a primer for those who were unfamiliar with the legend. Altman, however, is less concerned with the melodramatic details of the Postimpressionist's life than the dynamics of the most important and influential relationship in his tragic existence. Altman scrubs off Minnelli's romanticism and replaces it with an even-tempered intensity that allows a viewer to enter not only the lives of Vincent and Theo but their minds as well. In Minnelli's version, which won a Supporting Actor Oscar for Anthony Quinn despite his nine minutes of screen time as Paul Gauguin, every character is secondary to Kirk Douglas' flamboyant portrayal of Vincent van Gogh. Even Theo, played in *Lust for Life* by little-known actor James Donald, was delegated to the background. Altman, who has made a career of breaking the boundaries of a variety of genres, avoids the conventions of the biographical film and pulls the figure of Theo into the foreground, making him another protagonist.

Altman knows that his audience has a rudimentary knowledge of van Gogh's career; it is not important for this wildly original filmmaker to reinterpret facts. In Altman's biographical film, the artist's life is not as important as the psychology of the artist. What Altman and his screenwriter, Julian Mitchell, mean to do is investigate the emotional connection between the artist and his art-dealer brother and, more broadly, the tenuous connection between art and business. Taking the pages and pages of letters between the two brothers as their inspiration, screenwriter Mitchell and director Altman have made a film that is a dual story of fraternal interdependency. Throughout *Vincent and Theo*, the filmmakers parallel Vincent's struggle for intellectual success as a painter with Theo's struggle to achieve public success for his brother. In order for Vincent to survive, Theo must provide financial rewards, and in order for Theo to thrive as an independent art dealer, Vincent must provide him with artistic wonders. It is an endless circle—one that, like the brothers' mutual fight for public and critical acceptance, will be a fruitless endeavor that drags both men through intense frustration and into insanity.

Altman presents the brothers as so dependent on each other that they emerge as two dysfunctional parts of one complete and successful being. Theo is the social entity; he is able to connect with others, holds down a permanent job in a Paris gallery, provides the financial support for his brother, and starts a family with a wife (Johanna Ter Steege) and child. Vincent is the internal being who is intensely single-minded in his pursuit of artistic success, avoiding most of the people around him and living in various states of near-poverty. Instead of the lengthy courtships that Theo undergoes in order to secure lovers, Vincent merely lives with the prostitute (Jip Wijngaarden) he uses as a model. Even the performers, two virtually unknown British actors, supply portrayals that are essentially two sides of a full performance.

Rhys's Theo is full of nervous external tricks; he stumbles over his feet, his lips quiver and twist, and his eyes bulge out of his head. His acting is almost entirely on the surface while Roth makes Vincent a brooding, stifled ogre by providing an intensely internal performance. With his face covered by a blanket of dirty orange fuzz and his body splattered with paint, Roth is not so much performing as being. One senses a fever under this character's skin, a bubbling of emotion that only occasionally bursts out in volcanic explosions.

Unfortunately, neither brother is successful at the task to which they have been assigned. Theo offends his customers with his intolerance of popular art and disappoints his employers with his obsessive campaign to herald Vincent's work. He suffers from syphilis, a social disease, and his marriage becomes a sorry second to his relationship with his brother. Theo's meager salary continues to go to Vincent rather than to a sick baby and a tired wife. Meanwhile, Vincent wages an obsessive war with technique. His dissatisfaction with his inability to capture nature tears at his soul and disrupts his productivity. Because he has always been allowed to depend on others, he finds himself unable to be self-sufficient; Vincent is in constant need of all kinds of support. When he invites his friend Gauguin (Wladimir Yordanoff) to Arles, he is deeply distressed by the artist's independence. Vincent is shocked by Gauguin's ability to cook an attractive meal with things lying around the kitchen and his willingness to use the crude paints that are available in the local area. Vincent's disappointment in Gauguin's failure to be a sympathizer leads to a verbal battle that ends with Vincent's attempt to kill himself by self-mutilation.

By film's end, Theo and Vincent's failures are too much for either to bear. Vincent's artistic strength fails when he is sent to live with a doctor (Jean-Pierre Cassel) who is also an art patron and a van Gogh supporter. When an attraction between Vincent and the doctor's daughter (Bernadette Giraud) is squashed by the doctor's claims that both Vincent's art and his sanity are hopeless, Vincent finds his already-suffering confidence shattered. Finally unable to paint, Vincent shoots himself. Consequently, Theo, who failed to keep Vincent working, surrenders his own social battles. He walks out of Vincent's public funeral and, once back in Paris, throws his wife and child out of the apartment that he had once shared with his dead brother. In the end, he is seen naked in a mental institution, crying out for Vincent.

Altman is especially adroit at depicting the overpowering perfection of nature, a menacing brilliance that stirs up extreme frustration in a painter who fails to capture it on canvas. Together with cinematographer Jean Lepine, an Altman veteran, and production designer Stephen Altman, the director's son, Altman creates several sequences that contain both the ravishing beauty of van Gogh's art and the overwhelming sublimity that threatens an artist trying to do it justice. In the middle of the film, a lengthy scene involves Vincent trying to paint a field of sunflowers. The image of the field, stretching endlessly to all edges of the frame, is vibrantly beautiful; the only sign of imperfection is the sole figure of Vincent struggling with his easel. As the scene progresses, the sunflowers appear to be closing in around him. The sound-track begins to buzz discordantly, the camera weaves from one flower to the next, and Vincent struggles to remain lucid. The scene, the most viscerally powerful in an otherwise subdued film, ends with Vincent frantically folding up his canvas, tearing a few stalks out of the ground, and retreating to his studio. At film's end, Vincent is once again in the midst of nature. This time, all he can manage is a single line before he walks into the wheat field that he has tried to paint and shoots himself.

The conflict between art and business, a major theme that runs through *Vincent and Theo*, is a fight which Altman knows well. Creating such films as *M*A*S*H* (1970), *McCabe and Mrs. Miller* (1971), *The Long Goodbye* (1973), and *Nashville* (1975), Altman enjoyed a fruitful relationship with the Hollywood studio system during the 1970's, but the union cooled soon after *Popeye* (1980) met with marginal box-office success. Several flops later, the studios began to consider the eccentric director to be an unsound investment. Altman was forced to search for other sources to support his daring, unconventional work. Altman stayed away from the profit-conscious Hollywood studios, staging an opera, *The Rake's Progress*, in Michigan (1983) and France (1987), directing the brilliant one-man Richard Nixon drama *Secret Honor* (1986) for an independent film company, and creating the innovative television program *Tanner '88* with Gary Trudeau. *Vincent and Theo* allowed Altman to work with characters who fought these same artistic battles, and consequently, it became his most personal film to date.

Greg Changnon

Reviews

American Film: Magazine of the Film and Television Arts. XV, November, 1990, p. 62.
Boxoffice. November, 1990, p. R86.
Chicago Tribune. November 16, 1990, VII, p. 48.
Entertainment Weekly. November 2, 1990, p. 45.
The Hollywood Reporter. CCCXIV, October 22, 1990, p. 5.
Los Angeles Times. November 16, 1990, p. F8.
The Nation. CCLI, December 10, 1990, p. 742.
The New York Times. November 2, 1990, p. B6.
The New Yorker. LXVI, November 19, 1990, p. 127.
Newsweek. CXVI, November 26, 1990, p. 77.
Variety. April 27, 1990, p. 2.
The Washington Post. November 16, 1990, p. D1.

WHITE HUNTER, BLACK HEART

Production: Clint Eastwood for Malpaso/Rastar; released by Warner Bros.
Direction: Clint Eastwood
Screenplay: Peter Viertel, James Bridges, and Burt Kennedy; based on the novel by Viertel
Cinematography: Jack N. Green
Editing: Joel Cox
Production design: John Graysmark
Art direction: Tony Reading
Set decoration: Peter Howitt
Sound: Peter Handford, Les Fresholtz, Vern Poore, and Michael Jiron
Costume design: John Mollo
Music: Lennie Niehaus
MPAA rating: PG
Running time: 110 minutes

Principal characters:
John Wilson	Clint Eastwood
Pete Verrill	Jeff Fahey
Paul Landers	George Dzundza
Ralph Lockhart	Alun Armstrong
Kay Gibson	Marisa Berenson
Hodkins	Timothy Spall
Mrs. MacGregor	Mel Martin
Phil Duncan	Richard Vanstone
Mrs. Duncan	Jamie Koss
Irene Saunders	Catherine Neilson
Basil Fields	Richard Warwick
Kivu	Boy Mathias Chuma
Alec Laing	Geoffrey Hutchings
Tom Harrison	Christopher Fairbank
George	Norman Lumsden
Miss Wilding	Charlotte Cornwell

White Hunter, Black Heart is director/star Clint Eastwood's salute to mavericks, people obsessed with a vision, an idea, or a project who wear out the patience of friends and associates as they attempt to fulfill their mad desires. By bringing to the screen Peter Viertel's *roman à clef* about his experiences with legendary director John Huston during the making of *The African Queen* (1951), Eastwood not only pays tribute to Huston's cantankerous yet charismatic spirit, but also to Eastwood's own fiercely independent, risk-taking career.

Writer Peter Verrill (Jeff Fahey) is summoned to England by his friend, American film director John Wilson (Eastwood). Wilson has been assigned to direct a film set in Africa and wants Verrill to help him with the screenplay. Wilson is a brash, outspoken, and reckless Hollywood legend, known for his single-minded stubbornness and his undeniable genius as a filmmaker. Wilson admits to Verrill that his main reason for wanting to direct this particular motion picture is so that they can travel to Africa and indulge in big-game hunting. Wilson is persuasive, and soon the two are meeting with the film's producer Paul Landers (George Dzundza) and the principal British financial backers. Wilson and Verrill then begin working on rewriting the script and immediately clash over the direction the film should take.

The two travel to Africa to scout locations with assistant producer Ralph Lockhart (Alun Armstrong) and to finish polishing the script. Wilson tells Verrill to spend less time with "sub-plots" and to hurry and finish the script so they can arrange a safari. Wilson is especially interested in elephant hunting and has come laden down with safari equipment, elephant rifles, and an assortment of hunting outfits which he wears while he and Verrill work on the script.

During their stay at the luxurious hotel located near Victoria Falls, they meet British vacationers and residents, most of them blatantly prejudiced toward the native Africans and the non-British aristocrats. In one of the most effective scenes of the film, Wilson and Verrill have dinner with Mrs. MacGregor (Mel Martin), a young and attractive upper-class Englishwoman with a hatred of Jews. When Verrill objects to her slanderous anti-Semitic remarks, telling her that he is Jewish, she playfully ignores him and continues her diatribe. Wilson then very eloquently and powerfully tells her a mesmerizing story about an encounter he had with another woman who, very much like her, also had a severe hatred for Jews. Wilson tells his story calmly and sincerely and, by his story's end, has reduced his attractive and refined dinner companion to "the goddamnedest ugliest bitch of them all." After his encounter with Mrs. MacGregor, Wilson starts a fight with the hotel's head waiter, who has been abusing his black subordinates. Wilson, dressed in a tuxedo, is beaten severely by the burly waiter as the elegantly dressed hotel guests look on. News of Wilson's recklessness reaches Landers in England, and he sends telegrams to Wilson warning him to stay out of trouble and concentrate on his preproduction duties. Wilson ignores the telegrams and instead prepares for his big-game hunting expedition.

To scout film locations and to find hunting sites, Wilson and Verrill charter a plane and fly over the Congo, finally landing at a remote hunting lodge where they set up temporary residence. Wilson hires a professional guide as well as a local native guide, Kivu (Boy Mathias Chuma), and embarks on an elephant hunt. The hunting party soon encounters a huge herd of elephants, but the professional guide warns Wilson that it is too dangerous to risk shooting the bull of the herd because of the possibility of causing a stampede. Wilson, bitterly disappointed, returns to the hunting lodge where he dismisses the professional guide and vows to return to the bush to shoot his "big tusker." Verrill, becoming more and more disgusted with Wilson's obsession with big-game hunting and the shameful neglect of his directorial duties, flies back to the main hotel, meets with the rest of the film crew, and tells Landers of the problems with Wilson. Everyone then joins Wilson at the lodge.

Wilson has transformed the lodge's interior into a luxurious setting complete with a fleet of attendants. Over a lavish dinner, Wilson and Landers trade playful but vicious insults while a pet monkey scatters the film's shooting script all over the lodge. The following day, the crew moves to Kivu's village and prepares to begin shooting. Rain interrupts the filming, however, and while the crew languishes around the lodge, Wilson, Kivu, and another professional hunter return to the bush in search of an elephant. The rain finally stops and, with the crew prepared to film, Wilson again ventures into the African wilds, this time accompanied by Verrill.

The safari soon encounters a huge herd of elephants. Wilson prepares to shoot the huge bull elephant but then hesitates and lowers his rifle. The bull charges anyway, and Kivu pushes Wilson aside and is trampled by the wild animal. Wilson, stunned and ashamed of his obsession, returns to the village, where news of Kivu's death brings shrieks of outrage and sorrow from the rest of the villagers. Soon, drumbeats send a message to the surrounding villages. When Wilson asks what message the villagers are sending, he is told, "White hunter, black heart." Wilson then slumps in his director's chair and gives the command to begin filming.

The most fascinating aspect about *White Hunter, Black Heart* is Eastwood's portrayal of John Wilson, who is a thinly disguised John Huston. Because Huston is such a well-known figure, both as an actor and as a maverick writer/director, it is impossible to separate the real Huston from Eastwood's interpretation of the legendary figure. Eastwood attempts to embody Huston's personality by mimicking his physical mannerisms and slow, dramatic voice inflections. At first, the characterization is unsettling because of the audience's association with Eastwood's own long-established film persona.

The success of Eastwood's characterization is aided considerably by the excellent script by Viertel, Burt Kennedy, and James Bridges, which is full of colorful, vivid dialogue and which captures Huston's own outrageous and charismatic style of speech. The confrontations between Eastwood's Wilson and Fahey's Verrill, specifically when they are arguing over the film's script, are especially well executed, both characters fighting in their own way for their individual point of view. The differences in their characters are sharply dramatized in these confrontations, Verrill emerging as a down-to-earth, outspoken-yet-idealistic, and passionate writer, not afraid to challenge the grandiose and destructively cynical Wilson. Even though their styles of expression are nearly opposite, their characters complement one another because both are filled with passion and conviction.

Throughout the film, Eastwood continually plays against his own well-established screen persona. The elaborate and dramatic stories he tells, the scene in which he is soundly beaten by the bully head waiter, the fact that he is humiliated at the end of the film—all refute his tough image and establish his portrayal as a new and different Eastwood, one willing to take a chance on screen. In the past, Eastwood has taken risks behind the camera, specifically with his film *Bird* (1988), about the life of jazz saxophonist Charlie Parker. Here, Eastwood takes risks both behind and in front of the camera, exploring new terrain as an actor and as a director. The most effective scenes are the ones relying on the excellent dramatic dialogue, as opposed to the action scenes involving hunting and fighting, which is surprising from a director known for his expertise with action films. An especially well written and acted scene occurs late in the film, when Verrill vents his rage against Wilson for indulging in his obsessive passion for elephant hunting. Verrill views hunting as a crime against nature, and Wilson, after a dramatic pause, corrects him by saying that it is not a crime but a sin, and that Wilson believes he must commit a sin against nature before he can do anything else. The scene offers a key insight into the character of Wilson, and Eastwood captures Wilson's self-destructive tendencies with a moody intensity.

The fact that this film is built around the creation of the classic film *The African Queen* contributes to its interest and success. The brief scenes with Marisa Berenson, as Kay Gibson/Katharine Hepburn, and Richard Vanstone, as Phil Duncan/ Humphrey Bogart, are effectively underplayed and add to the legendary aura of the story. Other scenes involving Wilson and Verrill arguing over dialogue from *The African Queen* and the wild, impromptu ride the two take down a river on the old boat used in the classic film lend excitement and believability to the filmmaking process in which their characters are involved.

The major fault of the film is its poorly staged climax. In the book, Wilson does in fact shoot the bull elephant, triggering a stampede in which Kivu is trampled. This would have been a difficult scene to film but it would have made for a much more powerful and effective climax. The actual scene, with Wilson ultimately deciding not to shoot the elephant and then Kivu saving Wilson from the animal, dilutes Wilson's established character as a man obsessed with killing a huge, savage beast for his own egotistic gratification. That in the end Wilson is humiliated and ashamed is not convincing because Kivu's death lacks the drama required to shock Wilson out of his egotistic and self-destructive passions. Wilson has been portrayed as a man living in a grandiose world of his own making, one similar to the action films he has directed. Kivu's brutal death is too theatrical, too much like Wilson's own distorted view of the world, when it should be bloody, disgusting, and brutally real, a shocking reminder to Wilson of the dangers of mixing personal fantasies with harsh realities.

Aside from the weak climax, *White Hunter, Black Heart* succeeds in capturing the wild and flamboyant spirit of a legendary filmmaker and, in doing so, reaffirms the independent and daring reputation of Eastwood, another one of Hollywood's most endearing artists.

Jim Kline

Reviews
American Spectator. July, 1990, p. 33.

Chicago Tribune. September 14, 1990, VII, p. 33.
Commonweal. CXVII, December 21, 1990, p. 757.
Films in Review. XLI, November, 1990, p. 552.
The Hollywood Reporter. CCCXII, May 14, 1990, p. 4.
Los Angeles Times. September 14, 1990, p. F1.
The New York Times. September 14, 1990, p. B1.
Premiere. September, 1990, p. 22.
Rolling Stone. October 18, 1990, p. 45.
Sight and Sound. LIX, Autumn, 1990, p. 278.
Time. CXXXVI, September 24, 1990, p. 84.
Variety. May 11, 1990, p. 3.
The Washington Post. September 21, 1990, p. B1.

WHITE PALACE

Production: Mark Rosenberg, Amy Robinson, and Griffin Dunne for Mirage/
  Double Play; released by Universal Pictures
Direction: Luis Mandoki
Screenplay: Ted Tally and Alvin Sargent; based on the novel by Glenn Savan
Cinematography: Lajos Koltai
Editing: Carol Littleton
Production design: Jeannine C. Oppewall
Art direction: John Wright Stevens
Set decoration: Lisa Fischer
Sound: Stephan von Hase
Costume design: Lisa Jenson
Music: George Fenton
MPAA rating: R
Running time: 104 minutes

> *Principal characters:*
> Nora Baker .... Susan Sarandon
> Max Baron .... James Spader
> Neil .... Jason Alexander
> Rosemary .... Kathy Bates
> Judy .... Eileen Brennan
> George .... Spiros Focas
> Stephanie .... Gina Gershon
> Sol Horowitz .... Steven Hill
> Rachel .... Rachel Levin
> Larry Klugman .... Corey Parker
> Edith Baron .... Renée Taylor

White Palace is director Luis Mandoki's second film to deal with the subject of unconventional love affairs. In his previous film, *Gaby—A True Story* (1987), Mandoki dramatized the life of Gabriela Brimmer, a woman born with cerebral palsy who overcomes her physical limitations to enjoy a rich and dynamic life, which includes a love affair with a young man with similar physical handicaps and a lifelong loving relationship with her Mexican nanny. With *White Palace*, Mandoki examines a less unique but still atypical relationship, one between a financially successful and fastidious young Jewish man and a sloppy, middle-aged, former Catholic waitress from the poor side of town.

Max Baron (James Spader) is a successful account executive for a large advertising firm with a beautiful apartment located in upscale St. Louis. He is young, handsome, and has many friends who are continually trying to arrange dates for him with young, attractive women. Max is still suffering from the loss of his beautiful young wife, Janey, however, who died in a car crash two years earlier.

After preparing for a bachelor party given for his best friend, Neil (Jason Alexander), Max—wearing an elegant tuxedo—picks up a large supply of hamburgers at a fast-food restaurant, the White Palace. When he arrives at the party, he discovers that he has been cheated out of some of the burgers that he ordered. Feeling demeaned and wanting revenge against the waitress who cheated him out of his forty-nine-cent burgers, Max returns to the restaurant and creates a scene in front of the crowd of hungry customers. The haggard and overworked waitress, sweaty, unkempt, and irritated over Max's loud demands for a refund, still possesses enough sense of humor to give Max a slow, piercing glare and refer to him as "Mr. Astaire," because of his elegant outfit, before giving him his refund.

On his way home from the party, Max impulsively stops at a sleazy bar and orders a drink. Sitting across the bar is the waitress from the White Palace, who recognizes Max. She stumbles over to him, introducing herself as Nora Baker (Susan Sarandon) and offering to buy him a drink. Max wants nothing to do with the cheaply dressed, brazenly forward older woman and, after two strong drinks and some polite conversation, he prepares to leave. When Nora asks about his wife and he answers that she died, Nora suddenly bursts into a fit of raucous laughter, then calms down and mutters that the same thing happened to her with her twelve-year-old son, whom she says died of leukemia several years earlier. Max mumbles that he is sorry for her, then stumbles out to his car. Nora follows and asks for a ride home, to which Max reluctantly agrees.

Arriving at Nora's house, a chain of events concludes with the two making love. In the morning, Max briefly examines Nora's home which, amid the dirt and clutter, is adorned with posters and cheap statuettes of Marilyn Monroe, Nora's idol. When Nora asks him if she will ever see him again, he says no and walks out of the house. Later, when he is visiting Janey's grave with his mother (Renée Taylor), however, Max recalls the passion and excitement he felt when making love with Nora. He returns to her house with a new mailbox, offering to replace the one he damaged. Before he has time to install the mailbox, he and Nora are in each other's arms, rolling on her messy floor. Max then begins spending most of his spare time with Nora, neglecting his job and his friends.

Max cannot decide if he should invite Nora to Neil's upcoming wedding and ends up attending the event alone. Afterward, he visits Nora and finds her sitting in darkness, her electricity shut off because of her inability to pay her bills. When Max tries to comfort her, she rejects his concern and accuses him of lying about his whereabouts for the evening. He admits that he had not told her the truth, and she replies that she cannot tolerate deception in a relationship. The two realize that their attraction for each other has progressed beyond frenzied lust and they are drawn even closer together. The next morning, Max is awakened by the unexpected arrival of Nora's sister, Judy (Eileen Brennan), a borderline gypsy with psychic abilities. When she attempts to give Max a psychic reading, he scoffs at first but soon becomes frightened by her uncanny ability to read his troubled soul. Before she leaves, Judy tells Max the truth about Nora's son Charlie, that he died of drug and alcohol abuse, not leukemia. When Max visits Nora again, it is with more tenderness and compassion than ever before.

While Max and Nora shop for groceries one evening, Max encounters Neil's new wife, Rachel (Rachel Levin), who invites him to their Thanksgiving dinner. Initially hesitant, he finally agrees to take Nora with him to the Thanksgiving dinner and introduce her to his friends. When they arrive at the dinner, Nora is put off by the upscale sophistication of Max's friends. Nora insults one of the female guests and later berates Neil's father when he tries to call himself a member of the working class. She storms out of the house, and she and Max argue.

After several days, Max tries to contact Nora, only to find that she has quit her job and moved from her house, leaving no forwarding address. He drives to New York, where Nora's sister lives. Judy tells Max where to find Nora, and he discovers her at her new job as a waitress at an upscale restaurant. Nora is first outraged that Max has followed her. She tells him that she has just begun to feel better about herself and that their relationship is over, ruined by their differences and Max's inability to accept her for who she is. Max confesses that he is not ashamed of her, that he is ashamed of himself. He tells her that he has quit his job and moved from his apartment, and that he wants to return to his former profession as a teacher. Nora realizes his sincerity, and the two playfully hug each other while lying on top of one of the restaurant tables, to the delight of the other patrons.

White Palace is a standard boy-meets-girl story with a couple of quirky variations. Director Mandoki wants to present Max and Nora as almost completely opposite in their beliefs and backgrounds. Max is young, Jewish, successful, and neat. Nora is crass, middle-aged, poor, and sloppy. Mandoki and screenwriters Ted Tally and Alvin Sargent nearly overdo the differences between Max and Nora. They also overemphasize the key likeness of the two characters, the fact that they are both traumatically scarred by the loss of the greatest love of their individual lives. The filmmakers come dangerously close to trivializing the lives of their characters, making the film a simplistic love story based on the "opposites attract" cliché. What saves the film from buckling under its story line, however, is the tough, sincere dialogue, the emphasis in the directing on intimate and honest confrontations between the principals, and the superb acting by James Spader and, most especially, Susan Sarandon.

Mandoki's handling of a more traditional love story is more successful than his previous film. With *White Palace*, the story seems tame while the relationship between the two principals is filled with blunt, raw honesty. Filmed with numerous close-ups in intimate interior settings and lit with warm, earthy browns and muted reds, the confrontations between Nora and Max become much more intense and direct. Sarandon delivers her lines with a flat and basic honesty, her observations and insights into Spader's character ringing true every time. Even though the two characters are opposites, it is easy to see why Max is attracted to Nora—she is honest, something he is not used to in his sterile, upscale world of appearances.

Spader has a more difficult time with his lines, which are full of apologies and theatrical flourishes that seem jarring when compared with Sarandon's less showy delivery. Spader is much better communicating with body language and facial expressions, especially in the scene where he confronts Nora in the bar; he is able to show dread, revulsion, bewilderment, and ultimately compassion without saying a word.

Sarandon dazzles as the crass, aging, fleshy Nora. When she is first glimpsed behind the counter at the White Palace, she is almost unrecognizable, her face smeared with sweat, her hair and her cheap waitress uniform spattered with grease, and her voice laced with an irritating Southern twang. She is hardly the sexy temptress that she has played in such films as *Atlantic City* (1981), *The Witches of Eastwick* (1987), and *Bull Durham* (1988). Nevertheless, because of the intense honesty she brings to her character, to the explicit sex scenes and to the scenes in which she insists that Max quit deceiving her about his reluctance to accept her for who she really is, Sarandon's Nora is the sexiest and most attractive character that she has portrayed to date.

White Palace could have easily become a bland and uninspired Yuppie-boy-meets-lower-class-girl love story. The success of the film must be attributed primarily to the filmmakers' belief in the film's message—that love can transcend impossible obstacles—as well as the skill of the actors in communicating that message to the viewer with honesty and conviction.

Jim Kline

Reviews

America. CLXIII, November 24, 1990, p. 407.
Chicago Tribune. October 19, 1990, VII, p. 47.
The Hollywood Reporter. CCCXIV, October 17, 1990, p. 5.
Los Angeles Times. October 19, 1990, p. F1.
The New York Times. October 19, 1990, p. B4.
Newsweek. CXVI, October 22, 1990, p. 72.
Rolling Stone. November 15, 1990, p. 162.
Time. CXXXVI, November 12, 1990, p. 103.
Variety. October 17, 1990, p. 2.
The Wall Street Journal. October 18, 1990, p. A14.
The Washington Post. October 19, 1990, p. D1.

WILD AT HEART

Production: Monty Montgomery, Steve Golin, and Sigurjon Sighvatsson for
    Polygram/Propaganda Films; released by Samuel Goldwyn
Direction: David Lynch
Screenplay: David Lynch; based on the novel *Wild at Heart: The Story of Sailor and
    Lula,* by Barry Gifford
Cinematography: Frederick Elmes
Editing: Duwayne Dunham
Production design: Patricia Norris
Special pyrotechnic effects: David Domeyer
Sound: John Wentworth, John Power, and Randy Thom
Special makeup effects: David B. Miller and Louis Lazzara
Costume design: Patricia Norris
Music: Angelo Badalamenti
MPAA rating: R
Running time: 127 minutes

> *Principal characters:*
> Sailor Ripley .... Nicolas Cage
> Lula Pace Fortune .... Laura Dern
> Marietta Pace .... Diane Ladd
> Bobby Peru .... Willem Dafoe
> Perdita Durango .... Isabella Rossellini
> Johnnie Farragut .... Harry Dean Stanton
> Dell .... Crispin Glover
> Juana .... Grace Zabriskie
> Marcello Santos .... J. E. Freeman
> Mr. Reindeer .... W. Morgan Sheppard
> Good Witch .... Sheryl Lee
> Bob Ray Lemon .... Gregg Danddridge

For David Lynch, 1990 was a banner year. First he produced a successful television series, then his film *Wild at Heart* won the prestigious Palme d'Or (Golden
Palm) Award at the Cannes Film Festival. When David Lynch and Mark Frost designed *Twin Peaks* for ABC television in 1990, media critics wondered if the series
would be too weird for prime time. In a way it was, but it developed a cult following
and was continued into the following season. As *Wild at Heart* clearly demonstrates,
Lynch reserves his high-definition weirdness for the motion-picture screen. *Twin
Peaks* was certainly daring for the timid medium of television, but no episode has
offered anything approaching the outrageous and mystifying violence and weirdness
of *Wild at Heart,* an episodic road picture that is also an extended homage to *The
Wizard of Oz* (1939).

The screenplay was adapted by Lynch from Barry Gifford's novel *Wild at Heart: The Story of Sailor and Lula*, which was not published until after the film had won the Golden Palm at the Cannes festival. Sailor Ripley (Nicolas Cage) is a drifter who has worked as a driver for a local crime lord. He is in love with Lula Pace Fortune (Laura Dern), whose wealthy mother, Marietta Pace (Diane Ladd, who is Laura Dern's mother in real life), is determined to separate them. Lynch's film presents the mother as a woman scorned. She makes a drunken pass at Sailor in a public toilet and is rejected by him. Soon thereafter (and apparently at her instigation), Sailor is attacked by a black hit man, Bob Ray Lemon (Gregg Danddridge), armed with a knife and apparently intent on castrating Sailor. The film, anchored in sex and violence, thus begins in a violent spasm as Sailor literally beats his attacker's brains out.

Sailor then serves time for manslaughter at the Pee Dee Correctional Prison. Upon his release, Sailor decides to break parole and leave Cape Fear ("somewhere on the border between North Carolina and South Carolina") with Lula, driving to California in her Cadillac convertible. The mother is furious, partly because she hates Sailor but mainly because he has taken her daughter. Marietta is a cracker gothic variant of the bad mother stereotype; flashbacks indicate that she has betrayed her husband and was involved in a conspiracy to have him murdered in a burning building. Sailor worked for her gangster coconspirator and tells Lula that he was at the scene of the crime when her father died.

Sailor and Lula first drive to New Orleans, then head farther west through Texas. Marietta sends her lover, private investigator Johnnie Farragut (Harry Dean Stanton), after them. Then, to protect her bets, she goes to crime boss Marcello Santos (J. E. Freeman) to put a contract on Sailor's life. Farragut misses Sailor and Lula in New Orleans, but the gangster's hit man, Bobby Peru (Willem Dafoe), catches up with Sailor in Big Tuna, Texas. Sailor has stopped by Big Tuna to ask a friend, Perdita Durango (Isabella Rossellini), if a contract is out on him, but he does not get a straight answer from her, since she is in cahoots with Bobby Peru.

Bobby seduces Sailor, who is running short of money, into committing armed robbery, and in the course of the robbery, plans to murder him. The victims are armed, however; the attempted robbery turns into a fiasco, and Bobby, not Sailor, is killed. Sailor is in trouble with the law again. In a surreal ending that first has Sailor rejecting Lula because he thinks it would be best for her, then later changing his mind after he is beaten and then visited by Sheryl Lee as the Good Witch (another borrowing from *The Wizard of Oz*), the lovers are finally reunited, and the film ends with Sailor singing "Love Me Tender" to Lula, ready to accept the responsibility of family and fatherhood.

David Lynch is the strangest and most distinctive talent now working in American film and television. No one creates atmosphere the way Lynch does, suggesting evil and menace, perversion and corruption in *Blue Velvet* (1986) and *Twin Peaks*, for example. The atmosphere of *Wild at Heart*, his most violent film to date, is also corrupt and perverse, but oddly, more gentle in this peculiar allegory of innocence and experience on the Yellow Brick Road. It seems to be a psychic fairy tale that equates Lula with Dorothy from *The Wizard of Oz* and ends with a positive message: Love conquers all.

The world of *Wild at Heart* is still creepy, however—violent, random, and insane. Weird people are constantly encountered. As in *Twin Peaks* and *Blue Velvet*, Lynch merely springs these creatures on the unsuspecting audience without bothering to establish context. All of a sudden, there they are, cavorting and babbling insanely. Some of them are kinky, like the mysterious and sinister Mr. Reindeer (W. Morgan Sheppard); some are dangerous, like Bobby Peru; others are merely crazy. All of them, however, are strange. At one point, Lula's witch mother paints her whole face red with lipstick, providing an astonishing spectacle that makes no sense whatsoever. Lula's Uncle Dell (Crispin Glover) puts cockroaches in his underwear. Small wonder, then, that Lula concludes: "The whole world is wild at heart and weird on top."

Lula is innocent but oversexed and constantly carnal. Sailor has had underworld connections and has killed a man with his bare hands, but he is otherwise sweet and gentle. While Lula is defined by the iconography of *The Wizard of Oz* (she even wears red slippers and clicks her heels three times), Sailor, oddly dressed in a snakeskin coat, is set up as an Elvis Presley type, a jailhouse rock-hard nutcase drifter. He sings Elvis' songs twice in the picture, first creating some sexual excitement in a bar and later singing "Love Me Tender" to Lula as the film concludes. These scenes are oddly touching and arguably fascinating, even if they are nothing more than an indulgent, demented dream fantasy.

Lynch ornaments Gifford's realistic novel with pop-culture allusions: Sailor as Elvis, Lula as Marilyn Monroe, and the perverse allusions to the Land of Oz (although this is not the first time Lynch has borrowed from L. Frank Baum). James Lindroth, writing in *Literature/Film Quarterly*, has drawn parallels between *Blue Velvet* and *The Wizard of Oz*, contending that, as did Victor Fleming in *The Wizard of Oz*, David Lynch punctuated "his grotesquerie with humor" that had "a distinctly dark, Freudian twist." Lindroth points out that the Isabella Rossellini character in *Blue Velvet*, "like Judy Garland's innocent, is named Dorothy." When *Blue Velvet* was released, Lynch told *The Village Voice* that "Dennis Hopper was the perfect Frank because he's from Kansas." Lindroth's thesis—that Lynch has taken "everybody's favorite, sun-drenched fairytale" and turned it into a nightmare—at first seems outrageous, but the Oz connection in *Wild at Heart* would seem to confirm his speculation about *Blue Velvet*. Offended by the more obvious parallels in *Wild at Heart*, *Time* magazine critic Richard Corliss wrote that *Wild at Heart* has "precisely nothing in common with *Oz*."

Some critics found *Wild at Heart* indulgent and disappointing, and American reviews were mixed. Peter Travers of *Rolling Stone* picked *Wild at Heart* as the best picture of the summer and Laura Dern as the best actress. David Denby of *New York Magazine* described the film as "almost a malignant work—an instant fetish object, an appalling, self-destroying voodoo doll." David Ansen of *Newsweek* speculated that Lynch had lost "his true muse" and was dredging his "pool of images" from "surprisingly shallow waters." *Time* critic Richard Corliss found a "sense of mystery" lacking in Lynch's "first flat-out comedy" and described the director as a "master of movie style on his way to becoming a mannerist." Terrence Rafferty in *The New Yorker* found the weirdness "inexpressive and trivial, even silly." American reviews tended to be favorable in Los Angeles and Chicago and unfavorable in New York and Washington, D.C.

C. Kenneth Pellow, writing on *Blue Velvet* in *Literature/Film Quarterly*, described a tendency in Lynch that weakens *Wild at Heart* as well as *Blue Velvet*. As a filmmaker, Lynch tends to think in scenes rather than in terms of character development. Pellow criticizes Lynch for the way he establishes a narrative frame and then casually departs from it when "something thematically clever appeals to him." Critics trained in literature who tend to "read" films disliked *Blue Velvet* intensely, but those who "view" films, Pellow asserts, found it more satisfactory. American film critics and reviewers seduced by the visual were hypnotized by the inventive grotesquerie of *Blue Velvet*, but they had apparently grown more demanding by the time *Wild at Heart* was released. The French were apparently less discerning in this regard: They embraced the film at the Cannes Film Festival. American critics were even more surprised when Diane Ladd was nominated by the Motion Picture Academy for Best Supporting Actress, and no doubt relieved when the Oscar went to Whoopi Goldberg for *Ghost* (1990; reviewed in this volume).

James M. Welsh

Reviews

Boxoffice. October, 1990, p. R72.
Chicago Tribune. August 17, 1990, VII, p. 27.
Films in Review. XLI, Nov./Dec. 1990, p. 554.
The Hollywood Reporter. August 17, 1990, p. 9.
Los Angeles Times. August 17, 1990, p. F4.
New York Magazine. August 27, 1990, p. 60.
The New York Times. August 17, 1990, p. B1.
The New Yorker. LXVI, August 27, 1990, p. 90.
Newsweek. August 27, 1990, p. 61.
Rolling Stone. September 6, 1990, p. 35.
Sight and Sound. LIX, Autumn, 1990, p. 277.
Time. CXXXV, June 4, 1990, p. 79.
Time. CXXXV, August 20, 1990, p. 63.
Variety. May 21, 1990, p. 3.
Video. XIV, March, 1991, p. 47.
The Washington Post. August 17, 1990, p. C-1.
The Washington Post Weekend. August 17, 1990, p. 45.

THE WITCHES

Origin: Norway and Great Britain
Released: 1990
Released in U.S.: 1990
Production: Mark Shivas for Jim Henson Productions and Lorimar Film
  Entertainment; released by Warner Bros.
Direction: Nicolas Roeg
Screenplay: Allan Scott; based on the novel by Roald Dahl
Cinematography: Harvey Harrison
Editing: Tony Lawson
Production design: Andrew Sanders
Special makeup effects: Creature Shop
Costume design: Marit Allen
Creature design: Creature Shop
Music: Stanley Myers
MPAA rating: PG
Running time: 92 minutes

> *Principal characters:*
> Miss Ernst/Grand High Witch . . . . Anjelica Huston
> Helga . . . . Mai Zetterling
> Luke . . . . Jasen Fisher
> Mr. Stringer . . . . Rowan Atkinson
> Mr. Jenkins . . . . Bill Paterson
> Mrs. Jenkins . . . . Brenda Blethyn
> Miss Ernst's assistant . . . . Jane Horrocks
> Bruno Jenkins . . . . Charlie Potter

The Witches is an interesting motion picture, in part because of the international talent that combined to make it and in part because of the diversity of that talent. It is a children's picture, ornamented with special effects created by executive producer and Muppet creator Jim Henson in what proved to be his final film, but it was directed by Nicolas Roeg, whose films are generally intended for adult audiences. Roeg, a gifted but offbeat British cinematographer, turned to directing in 1970 with *Performance*, a challenging film starring Mick Jagger, and later followed with equally mystifying films such as *The Man Who Fell to Earth* (1976), starring David Bowie as a visitor from outer space, and *Bad Timing* (1980), starring Art Garfunkel. Roeg's *Walkabout* (1971) took an adolescent novel about two British children lost and stranded in the Australian Outback and turned it into an adult vehicle that argued for the need to respect and emulate "primitive" culture. In *Don't Look Now* (1973), Roeg made a provocative film that revolved around the central character's psychic powers. Roeg has a talent for fantasy and the supernatural and was an excellent choice to direct

Roald Dahl's cautionary story about witchcraft.

Dahl, who wrote the novel, was born in Wales in 1916 of Norwegian parents, and in this respect resembles the boy Luke in *The Witches*, adapted for the screen by Allan Scott. Dahl has specialized in writing children's stories, some of which were later reworked for adult markets as well. Dahl's children's stories are sometimes designed to frighten children in order to gain and keep their attention, a very different approach to entertaining children from that of Jim Henson, who created Kermit the Frog and a whole community of Muppets for television's *Sesame Street* and *The Muppet Show*. Henson, who started his illustrious television career in 1954, died unexpectedly on May 15, 1990, before the theatrical release of *The Witches*.

No one writes children's fantasy quite like Dahl, who knows how to mesmerize children with his bizarre and witty stories. In *The Enormous Crocodile* (1978), for example, the crocodile is a ravenous beast who loves to eat children. In *The Witches*, which won the prestigious Whitbread Prize for fiction in Great Britain, the Grand High Witch hates children in general and little boys in particular and conspires to change all the children in England into mice. Remarkably, Dahl does not write down to children, nor does he refrain from using his full power to frighten. He scares little children because, like Stephen King, he knows that children enjoy being frightened.

A witch in this fairy tale is a vile hag who hates children, as defined by Helga, the Norwegian grandmother. She is played by Mai Zetterling, an icon on Swedish cinema, acting in her first role since she turned to film directing fifteen years ago. "Real witches look very much like ordinary women," Helga tells her grandson Luke (Jasen Fisher), but they hate children, and witches' eyes glow purple with rage at the sight of them. Witches often scratch their heads because they are bald and have to wear uncomfortable wigs. They wear sensible shoes because they lack toes and their feet are squared off. They are not very comfortable with themselves. "Witches are witches because they are extremely unhappy, viciously ugly, and hate everybody," explained Anjelica Huston, who played the Grand High Witch, in a publicity statement.

Luke's grandmother is a natural storyteller; he is enthralled by her story about a childhood friend who disappeared after an encounter with a witch. The friend was later trapped as a reappearing figure that aged, as the years passed, in a landscape painting on the wall of her family's home. After being frightened by this story, Luke meets a woman who might be a witch, but he is able to escape her designs. The grandmother has lost a finger in an earlier encounter with the Grand High Witch, whom she describes as "the most evil woman in all creation." Zetterling is entirely convincing as the grandmother who believes so fervently in witches that her strongly held conviction lends credibility to a fairy tale that might otherwise seem impossibly far-fetched. "You can never be sure if it's a witch you're looking at or a kind lady," she advises, matter-of-factly. "Witches spend their time waiting to hurt children."

Luke's parents die in an automobile accident, but the film does not dwell on this misfortune. His grandmother intends to take him home to the United States, but she has a diabetic stroke in England. Her doctor prescribes rest by the sea, so they stay at the Excelsior Hotel and are there for a convention of the Society to Prevent Cruelty to Children, which is, perversely, a front for the witches who want to eradicate children from the planet. Miss Ernst, the leader of the convention, is in fact the Grand High Witch. The film builds to a ghastly spectacle when Luke is trapped in the room where the witches' society is meeting. Hiding behind a screen, he watches Miss Ernst remove her mask to reveal her true self, a hateful, monstrous hag with a deformed face and clawlike hands. All the witches in the room undergo a similar transformation, but none so awful as that of the Grand High Witch. When this coven of witches sniffs out Luke and captures him, the film becomes effectively creepy.

The Grand High Witch has concocted a potion that will transform children (and grown-ups as well, it turns out) into mice. When Luke and his fat friend Bruno (Charlie Potter) are caught by the witches, they are so transformed but are still able to think and talk like little boys. They escape, and, as mice, work with Luke's grandmother to stop the witches' conspiracy against the children of Great Britain. As a tough old woman who has dealt with the Grand High Witch before and who believes in sorcery, Helga takes Luke's transformation in stride, searching pragmatically for a reversing charm. Bruno's parents, especially his father, are less imaginative and become hysterical when introduced to their mouse-son.

The late Jim Henson, the creator of the Muppets who had presented fantastic worlds in his films *The Dark Crystal* (1982, codirected with Frank Oz) and *Labyrinth* (1986), helped to realize *The Witches* project as executive producer. His Creature Shop provided animatronic and special makeup effects that enabled Roeg to turn the stately Angelica Huston into a horrible crone. Roeg was delighted to work with "such a wonderful actress" as Huston, the daughter of the late director John Huston, who can be "very glamorous, intelligent and, at the same time, very dark and mysterious." For her part, Huston relished the challenge of playing two roles, Miss Ernst and the Grand High Witch. Huston plays the Grand High Witch with wicked abandon, claiming that she found the discomfort of her prosthetic makeup useful in finding the anger and hostility she needed to project. Jasen Fisher was only seven years old at the time the film was made but gives an effective, well-focused performance. Mai Zetterling's cigar-smoking Norwegian grandmother gives the film its heart and charm, however, and she is the outstanding performer.

Some reviewers were daunted by the film, which has its grim moments and is effectively grotesque. In her review in *The New York Times*, Caryn James added a cautionary note: "Its ideas—witches everywhere and parents who die—are probably scarier than the images, though the witches at their ugliest are horrific sights. This is not a film for very small children." Perhaps these concerns are justified; however, one could suppose that Roald Dahl knows his audience better than that. Beyond its fairytale framework, the story dramatizes a battle between Good and Evil, and it is a shame to warn off the potential audience for what Rita Kempley of *The Washington Post* called a "wickedly funny" film. After all, Luke does survive his nasty encounter with the witches and is finally changed back into a little boy. Pointing out that Luke loses both of his parents in an automobile accident, Roeg stressed that the film is "about facing up to things," making the most of a bad situation, and triumphing over adversity.

Nicolas Roeg has specialized in the cinema of the dark, the sinister, the kinky, and the supernatural. By contrast, *The Witches* seems fairly tame, but Roeg gives the film an edge while preserving much of Dahl's distinctive humor. The film is flawed only in the way in which it moves too quickly toward the end in order to free Luke and Bruno from their existential mousetrap. Otherwise, it is fine entertainment for both adults and children who like to be scared. Anjelica Huston believes that children love to be terrified, within reason, and applauds the film for respecting Dahl's perspective and attitude. "Children are a lot brighter than most filmmakers give them credit for," she noted.

James M. Welsh

Reviews

Chicago Tribune. August 28, 1990, V, p. 4.
The Christian Science Monitor. August 24, 1990, p. 14.
Films in Review. XLI, November-December, 1990, p. 557.
The Hollywood Reporter. CCCXIII, August 24, 1990, p. 6.
Los Angeles Times. August 24, 1990, p. F6.
The New York Times. August 24, 1990, p. B3.
Newsweek. CXVI, September 24, 1990, p. 70.
Variety. March 15, 1990, p. 2.
Video. XIV, March, 1991, p. 48.
The Washington Post. August 24, 1990, p. C7.

MORE FILMS OF 1990

Abbreviations: *Pro.* = Production *Dir.* = Direction *Scr.* = Screenplay *Cine.* = Cinematography *Ed.* = Editing *P.d.* = Production design *A.d.* = Art direction *S.d.* = Set decoration *Mu.* = Music *MPAA* = MPAA rating *R.t.* = Running time

THE ADVENTURES OF FORD FAIRLANE

Pro. Joel Silver and Steve Perry for Silver Pictures; Twentieth Century-Fox *Dir.* Renny Harlin *Scr.* Daniel Waters, James Cappe, and David Arnott; based on a story by Cappe and Arnott and on characters created by Rex Weiner *Cine.* Oliver Wood *Ed.* Michael Tronick *P.d.* John Vallone *A.d.* Christiaan Wagener *S.d.* Linda Spheeris *Mu.* Yello *MPAA* R *R.t.* 104 min. *Cast:* Andrew Dice Clay, Wayne Newton, Priscilla Presley, Morris Day, Lauren Holly, Maddie Corman, Gilbert Gottfried, David Patrick Kelly, Brandon Call, Robert Englund, Ed O'Neill, Vince Neil, Sheila E.

The Adventures of Ford Fairlane is an action/adventure film focusing on the exploits of a Hollywood "rock and roll detective." As the title character, comedian Andrew Dice Clay brings his controversial stage persona to the screen in a story about the search for a rock music groupie who holds the key to a series of recording industry murders.

AIR AMERICA

Pro. Daniel Melnick for Carolco Pictures and Daniel Melnick/Indieprod; Tri-Star Pictures *Dir.* Roger Spottiswoode *Scr.* John Eskow and Richard Rush; based on the novel by Christopher Robbins *Cine.* Roger Deakins *Ed.* John Bloom and Lois Freeman-Fox *P.d.* Allan Cameron *A.d.* Steve Spence, Tony Reading, and Cate Bangs *S.d.* Fred Carter and Cricket Rowland *Mu.* Charles Gross *MPAA* R *R.t.* 112 min. *Cast:* Mel Gibson, Robert Downey, Jr., Nancy Travis, Ken Jenkins, David Marshall Grant, Lane Smith, Art La Fleur, Ned Eisenberg, Marshall Bell, David Bowe, Burt Kwouk, Tim Thomerson.

Naïve Los Angeles pilot Billy Covington (Robert Downey, Jr.) is recruited by a secretive CIA agent to fly for Air America airline in Laos. Billy teams with gonzo pilot Gene Ryack (Mel Gibson), and together they engage in many hairbreadth flying escapades involving political corruption, drug trafficking, gun smuggling, and rescuing refugees.

ALLIGATOR EYES

Pro. John Feldman and Ken Schwenker for Laughing Man Partnership; Castle Hill Productions *Dir.* John Feldman *Scr.* John Feldman *Cine.* Todd Crockett *Ed.* John Feldman, Cynthia Rogers, and Mike Frisino *A.d.* Jeff Tandy *Mu.* Sheila Silver *MPAA* R *R.t.* 95 min. *Cast:* Annabelle Larsen, Roger Kabler, Mary McLain, Allen McCullough, John MacKay.

Three reunited college friends making a car trip from New York City to Virginia pick up a mysterious blind hitchhiker, Pauline (Annabelle Larsen), who persuades them to make a detour to a music festival in North Carolina.

ALMOST AN ANGEL

Pro. John Cornell for Ironbark Films; Paramount Pictures *Dir.* John Cornell *Scr.* Paul Hogan *Cine.* Russell Boyd *Ed.* David Stiven *P.d.* Henry Bumstead *A.d.* Bernie Cutler *S.d.* Richard Goddard *Mu.* Maurice Jarre *MPAA* PG *R.t.* 95 min. *Cast:* Paul Hogan, Elias Koteas, Linda Kozlowski, Charlton Heston, Doreen Lang, Joe Dallesandro, Robert Sutton, Sammy Lee Allen.

Paul Hogan stars as Terry Dean, a crook convinced that he has become an angel after being involved in a car accident. This "born-again" Robin Hood then sets out to perform acts of "kindness," befriending a paraplegic (Elias Koteas) and falling in love with his sister (Linda Kozlowski).

ANGEL TOWN

Pro. Ash Shah and Eric Karson for Imperial Entertainment; Taurus Entertainment *Dir.* Eric Karson *Scr.* S. Warren *Cine.* John LeBlanc *Ed.* Duane Hartzell *A.d.* Brian Densmore *S.d.* John Kaye *Mu.* Gil Karson *MPAA* R *R.t.* 106 min. *Cast:* Olivier Gruner, Theresa Saldana, Frank Aragon, Tony Valentino, Peter Kwong, Mike Moroff.

When Jacques (Olivier Gruner), a French foreign exchange student, moves to Southern California and becomes part of the university community, he finds that local gangs led by Angel (Tony Valentino) are terrorizing his neighbors and especially the family in whose home he takes a room. Fortunately, Jacques is a former kick-boxing champion and ultimately vanquishes the gang members in this low-budget action picture.

ANY MAN'S DEATH

Pro. John Karie and S. D. Nethersole for Goldenberg Films and International Entertainment Corporation, in association with Independent Networks Inc.; INI Entertainment Group *Dir.* Tom Clegg *Scr.* Iain Roy and Chris Kelly *Cine.* Vincent G. Cox *Ed.* Max Lemon *P.d.* Robert van de Coolwijk *Mu.* Jeremy Lubbock *MPAA* R *R.t.* 110 min. *Cast:* John Savage, William Hickey, Mia Sara, Ernest Borgnine, Michael Lerner, James Ryan.

Burnt-out reporter Leon Abrams (John Savage) is sent to Africa to investigate a mysterious photograph. This leads him into a series of adventures that results in the discovery of a notorious former Nazi, Eric Schiller (William Hickey), attempting to redeem himself by experimenting with snakes in the search for an anticancer venom. Ultimately, Abrams must face the moral dilemma of what to do with his knowledge.

ARIEL (Finland, 1990)

Pro. Aki Kaurismaki for Villealfa Filmproductions; Kino International *Dir.* Aki Kaurismaki *Scr.* Aki Kaurismaki *Cine.* Timo Salminen *Ed.* Raija Talvio *S.d.* Risto Karhula *R.t.* 74 min. *Cast:* Turo Pajala, Susanna Haavisto, Matti Pellonpaa, Eetu Hilkamo, Erkki Pajala, Matti Jaaranen, Hannu Viholainen.

An inept, hapless man, Taisto Kasurinen (Turo Pajala), is the subject of this Finnish film. After having lost his job at the mines, he receives a car from a fellow miner who subsequently commits suicide. Taisto then undertakes a road trip and is attacked and robbed, becomes a criminal, is imprisoned, and finds a steady girlfriend with a son, with whom he will travel on a boat, the Ariel, to a new life somewhere over the rainbow.

BAD INFLUENCE

Pro. Steve Tisch for Epic Productions; Triumph *Dir.* Curtis Hanson *Scr.* David Koepp *Cine.* Robert Elswit *Ed.* Bonnie Koehler *P.d.* Ron Foreman *A.d.* William S. Combs *S.d.* Leslie Morales *Mu.* Trevor Jones *MPAA* R *R.t.* 99 min. *Cast:* Rob Lowe, James Spader, Lisa Zane, Christian Clemenson, Kathleen Wilhoite, Tony Maggio, Marcia Cross.

In this highly stylized mood piece, Michael Boll (James Spader) is, unknowingly, a man on the brink of psychic disintegration. In meeting his alter ego, Alex (Rob Lowe), Michael's worst nightmares come to pass, setting up a horrifying maze of intrigue and murder from which he will never be able to recover.

BAIL JUMPER

Pro. Josephine Wallace; Angelika Films *Dir.* Christian Faber *Scr.* Christian Faber and Josephine Wallace *Cine.* Tomasz Magierski *Ed.* James Bruce *P.d.* Lynn Ruth Appel *Mu.* Richard Robbins *R.t.* 96 min. *Cast:* Eszter Balint, B. J. Spalding, Tony Askin, Bo Brinkman, Alexandra Auder, Joie Lee, Ishmael Houston-Jones, Brad Warner, Christine Vlasak.

In this combination road film and offbeat comedy, two petty thieves fall in love and jump bail to drive to New York. On the way, they are plagued by a tornado, a flood, locusts, a meteorite, and other natural disasters—reflections of their tempestuous relationship.

BASHU, THE LITTLE STRANGER (Iran, 1990)

Pro. Ali Reza Zarrin for The Institute for the Intellectual Development of Children and Young Adults; International Home Cinema, Inc. *Dir.* Bahram Beizai *Scr.* Bahram Beizai *Cine.* Firooz Malekzadeh *Ed.* Bahram Beizai *R.t.* 120 min. *Cast:* Susan Taslimi, Adnan Afravian, Parvis Pourhosseini.

When Bashu (Adnan Afravian), an Iranian boy, abruptly finds himself orphaned as a result of war, he travels from his village in the South to the North of the country. There, amid scorn and prejudice, he ultimately finds a home as a result of the compassion of one earthy peasant woman, Nai (Susan Taslimi).

BASKET CASE II

Pro. Edgar Ievins for Ievins/Henenlotter; Shapiro Glickenhaus Entertainment *Dir.* Frank Henenlotter *Scr.* Frank Henenlotter *Cine.* Robert M. Baldwin *Ed.* Kevin Tent *P.d.* Michael Moran *Mu.* Joe Renzetti *MPAA* R *R.t.* 89 min. *Cast:* Kevin Van Hentenryck, Annie Ross, Kathryn Meisle, Heather Rattray, Jason Evers, Ted Sorel.

Separated Siamese twins Duane (Kevin Van Hentenryck)—the normal half—and Belial— the deformed half, carried in a basket by his brother—are given refuge by Granny Ruth (Annie Ross), a crusader for the rights of "unique individuals" (or, as they are more commonly called, freaks). Granny Ruth proves to be as demented as Belial, complicating Duane's attempt to live a quiet life and ultimately provoking to violence those she protects.

BERKELEY IN THE SIXTIES

Pro. Mark Kitchell; Kitchell Films/P.O.V. *Dir.* Mark Kitchell *Cine.* Stephen Lighthill *Ed.* Veronica Selver *R.t.* 117 min.

This historical documentary, covering the major events of the radical student activity in the 1960's, uses a combination of historical newsreel footage and present-day interviews to re-examine the actions and motivations of the Civil Rights and antiwar protesters of that era.

BETSY'S WEDDING

Pro. Martin Bregman and Louis A. Stroller; Touchstone Pictures *Dir.* Alan Alda *Scr.* Alan Alda *Cine.* Kevin Pike *Ed.* Michael Polakow *P.d.* John Jay Moore *S.d.* Barbara Kahn *Mu.* Bruce Broughton *MPAA* R *R.t.* 99 min. *Cast:* Alan Alda, Madeline Kahn, Molly Ringwald, Ally Sheedy, Anthony LaPaglia, Joe Pesci, Joey Bishop, Nicolas Coster, Bibi Besch, Dylan Walsh, Catherine O'Hara, Burt Young, Julie Bovasso.

Writer-director Alan Alda's latest film is not the story of the eponymous Betsy (Molly Ringwald), but rather that of her father Eddie Hopper (Alan Alda) and his attempts to bring both his mob-financed housing development and his daughter's increasingly lavish wedding to fruition.

THE BIG BANG

Pro. Joseph H. Kanter; Triton Pictures *Dir.* James Toback *Cine.* Barry Markowitz *Ed.* Stephanie Kempf *MPAA* R *R.t.* 81 min. *Cast:* Emma Astner, Missy Body, Max Brookman, Darryl Dawkins, Eugene Fodor, Polly Frost, Veronica Geng, Julius Hemphill, Fred H. Jess, Elaine Kaufman, Anne Marie Keyes, Don Simpson, Tony Sirico, Jose Torres, Barbara Traub.

A philosopher/nun (Anne Marie Keyes), an Auschwitz survivor (Barbara Traub), a filmmaker (Don Simpson), a boxer (Jose Torres), a jazz saxophonist (Julius Hemphill), a gangster (Tony Sirico), and others are assembled as guests. They sit together and discuss their experiences, aspirations, and beliefs on love, madness, family, creativity, and death.

BLIND FURY

Pro. Daniel Grodnik and Tim Matheson for Tri-Star and Interscope Communications; Tri-Star Pictures *Dir.* Phillip Noyce *Scr.* Charles Robert Carner; based on a screenplay by Ryozo Kasahara *Cine.* Don Burgess *Ed.* David Simmons *P.d.* Peter Murton *Mu.* J. Peter Robinson *MPAA* R *R.t.* 85 min. *Cast:* Rutger Hauer, Brandon Call, Terrance O'Quinn, Lisa Blount, Noble Willingham, Meg Foster, Nick Cassavetes, Rick Overton, Randall ("Tex") Cobb, Charles Cooper, Sho Kusugi.

The protagonist of this action film, Nick Parker (Rutger Hauer), a blind Vietnam veteran who bests a host of villains while reuniting a father (Terrance O'Quinn) and son (Brandon Call), is based on the famed cinematic character Zatoichi, the blind samurai, played by Shintaru Katsu in a number of Japanese films of the 1960's and 1970's.

THE BLOOD OF HEROES

Pro. Charles Raven; New Line Cinema *Dir.* David Peoples *Scr.* David Peoples *Cine.* David Eggby *Ed.* Richard Francis-Bruce *P.d.* John Stoddart *Mu.* Todd Boekelheide *MPAA* R *R.t.* 90 min. *Cast:* Rutger Hauer, Joan Chen, Vincent D'Onofrio, Anna Katarina, Delroy Lindo, Gandhi MacIntyre, Justin Monjo.

In a futuristic, post-apocalyptic landscape, a team of five people who engage in the unusual, brutal sport of Jugger travels to the Red City to engage in a major competition. Headed by Sallow (Rutger Hauer), who seeks to re-establish himself after an old scandal, the team thrives with the help of its newest member, Kidda (Joan Chen), with whom Sallow reluctantly falls in love.

BLOOD SALVAGE

Pro. Martin J. Fischer and Ken C. Sanders for High Five Productions; Paragon Arts International *Dir.* Tucker Johnston *Scr.* Tucker Johnston and Ken C. Sanders *Cine.* Michael Karp *Ed.* Jacquie Freeman Ross *P.d.* Robert Sissman *A.d.* Robert Sissman *S.d.* Sarah Quinn and James Bradley Smith *Mu.* Tim Temple *MPAA* R *R.t.* 98 min. *Cast:* Danny Nelson, Lori Birdsong, John Saxon, Ray Walston, Christian Hesler, Ralph Pruitt Vaughn, Laura Whyte, Andy Greenway, Evander Holyfield.

Junkyard man Jake Pruitt (Danny Nelson) and his sons (Christian Hesler and Ralph Pruitt Vaughn) force vehicles into accidents, then salvage both car and human body parts. The plot develops when Jake falls in love with a beautiful teenager, who is confined to a wheelchair (Lori Birdsong), and he and his sons trap her and her family in their recreation vehicle. The film is grotesque, tasteless, and gory, but it is also at times funny and inventive.

BLUE STEEL

Pro. Edward R. Pressman and Oliver Stone for Mack-Taylor Productions; Metro-Goldwyn-Mayer/United Artists *Dir.* Kathryn Bigelow *Scr.* Kathryn Bigelow and Eric Red *Cine.* Amir Mokri *Ed.* Lee Percy *P.d.* Toby Corbett *S.d.* Susan Kaufman *Mu.* Brad Fiedel *MPAA* R *R.t.* 102 min. *Cast:* Jamie Lee Curtis, Ron Silver, Clancy Brown, Elizabeth Peña, Louise Fletcher, Philip Bosco, Kevin Dunn, Richard Jenkins.

Megan Turner (Jamie Lee Curtis), a rookie policewoman in New York City, begins dating Eugene Hunt (Ron Silver), a wealthy commodities broker. When Megan learns that the disturbed Eugene is responsible for a series of killings, the two become engaged in a violent cat-and-mouse game in which Megan struggles to prove her capabilities to both her family and fellow officers.

BODY CHEMISTRY

Pro. Alida Camp; Concorde *Dir.* Kristine Peterson *Scr.* Jackson Barr *Cine.* Phedon Papamichael *Ed.* Nina Gilberti *P.d.* Gary Randall *A.d.* Ella St. John Blakey *S.d.* Michele Munoz *Mu.* Terry Plumeri *MPAA* R *R.t.* 87 min. *Cast:* Marc Singer, Lisa Pescia, Mary Crosby, David Kagen, H. Bradley Barneson, Doreen Alderman, Lauren Tuerk, Joseph Campanella, Rhonda Aldrich.

Married laboratory director Tom Redding (Marc Singer) works in a sexual behavior research laboratory. Redding is seduced by outside researcher Claire Archer (Lisa Pescia), who controls a lucrative contract needed by his laboratory. By the time Redding's wife, Marlee (Mary Crosby), confronts Claire at a party the situation is out of control and violence ensues.

BRAIN DEAD

Pro. Julie Corman; Concorde Pictures *Dir.* Adam Simon *Scr.* Charles Beaumont and Adam Simon; based on an original story by Beaumont *Cine.* Ronn Schmidt *Ed.* Carol Oblath *P.d.* Catherine Hardwicke *A.d.* Gilbert Mercier *S.d.* Gene Serdena *Mu.* Peter Francis Rotter *MPAA* R *R.t.* 85 min. *Cast:* Bill Pullman, Bill Paxton, Bud Cort, Nicholas Pryor, Patricia Charbonneau, George Kennedy.

When neurologist Rex Martin (Bill Pullman) attempts to unlock the secrets in the brain of a demented mathematician, Jack Halsey (Bud Cort), he gets caught in the dreams and delusions of the other man. The line between fantasy and reality becomes increasingly blurred as the narrative by former *Twilight Zone* writer Charles Beaumont unravels.

BYE BYE BLUES (Canada, 1989)

Pro. Arvi Liimatainen and Anne Wheeler for Allarcom-True Blue Films; Circle Releasing *Dir.* Anne Wheeler *Scr.* Anne Wheeler *Cine.* Vic Sarin *Ed.* Christopher Tate *P.d.* John Blackie *A.d.* Scott Dobbie *S.d.* Barry Kemp *Mu.* George Blondheim *MPAA* PG *R.t.* 110 min. *Cast:* Rebecca Jenkins, Michael Ontkean, Luke Reilly, Robyn Stevan, Kate Reid, Leslie Yeo, Stuart Margolin, Vincent Gale, Wayne Robson, Sheila Moore, Aline Levasseur, Chad Krowchuck, Kirk Duffee.

Daisy Cooper (Rebecca Jenkins) tries to support herself and her two children as a singer-pianist in a local swing band after her husband is reported missing in action during World War II. A trombonist named Max (Luke Reilly) sees potential in the marginally talented singer and eventually falls in love with her.

CADILLAC MAN

Pro. Charles Roven and Roger Donaldson for Donaldson/Roven-Cavallo; Orion Pictures *Dir.* Roger Donaldson *Scr.* Ken Friedman *Cine.* David Gribble *Ed.* Richard Francis-Bruce *P.d.* Gene Rudolf *A.d.* Patricia Woodbridge *S.d.* Justin Scoppa, Jr. *Mu.* J. Peter Robinson *MPAA* R *R.t.* 95 min. *Cast:* Robin Williams, Tim Robbins, Pamela Reed, Fran Drescher, Zack Norman, Annabella Sciorra, Lori Petty, Paul Guilfoyle, Bill Nelson, Eddie Jones, Mimi Cecchini, Tristine Skyler, Judith Hoag, Lauren Tom, Anthony Powers, Elaine Stritch, Paul Herman, Paul J. Q. Lee, Jim Bulleit, Erik King, Richard Panebianco.

Joey O'Brien (Robin Williams) is a divorced car salesman whose job is on the line. He is a ladies' man whose sales have fallen off. When Larry (Tim Robbins) discovers that his wife (Annabella Sciorra), the secretary at the car dealership, is cheating on him, he rides his motorcycle into the showroom and takes everyone, including Joey, hostage until he discovers who her boyfriend is.

THE CAMP AT THIAROYE (Senegal, 1990)

Pro. Senegal-Argelia-Tunisia; New Yorker Films *Dir.* Ousmane Sembène and Thierno Faty Sow *Scr.* Ousmane Sembène and Thierno Faty Sow *Cine.* Ismail Lakhdar Hamina *Ed.* Kahena Attia Riveil *Mu.* Ismaila Lo *R.t.* 157 min. *Cast:* Ibrahima Sane, Sijiri Bakaba, Mohamed Camara, Ismaila Cisse, Ababacar Sy Cissè, Moussa Cissoko, Eloi Coly, Ismaila Lo, Jean-Daniel Simon.

In this film about African identity and racial prejudice, black soldiers returning triumphantly from the battlefields of World War II find that only injustice and insults await them at the French army camp in Dakar where they are temporarily interned. When they discover they are to be paid half what the white soldiers earned for their war service, rebellion breaks out.

CHATTAHOOCHEE

Pro. Faye Schwab for Hemdale Film Corp.; Hemdale Film Corp. *Dir.* Mick Jackson *Scr.* James Hicks *Cine.* Andrew Dunn *Ed.* Don Fairservice *P.d.* Joseph T. Garrity *A.d.* Patrick Tagliaferro *Mu.* John Keane *R.t.* 103 min. *Cast:* Gary Oldman, Dennis Hopper, Frances McDormand, Pamela Reed, Ned Beatty, M. Emmet Walsh.

Emmett Foley (Gary Oldman), a Deep South war hero returning from Korea, has emotional scars which cause him to go on a shooting spree in his hometown while attempting suicide. He is sent to a maximum-security hospital for the criminally insane, where he discovers and campaigns against barbaric conditions before ultimately obtaining his release.

CHICAGO JOE AND THE SHOWGIRL (Great Britain, 1990)

Pro. Tim Bevan for Polygram/Working Title and BSB; New Line Cinema *Dir.* Bernard Rose *Scr.* David Yallop *Cine.* Mike Southon *Ed.* Dan Rae *P.d.* Gemma Jackson *A.d.* Peter Russell and Richard Holland *Mu.* Hans Zimmer and Shirley Walker *MPAA* R *R.t.* 103 min. *Cast:* Emily Lloyd, Kiefer Sutherland, Patsy Kensit, Keith Allen, Liz Fraser, Alexandra Pigg, Ralph Nossek, Colin Bruce, Roger Ashton-Griffiths, Harry Fowler, John Junkin.

An American soldier (Kiefer Sutherland), a deserter during World War II, is attracted to an English stripteaser (Emily Lloyd). Together, they go on a rampage of robbery and mayhem in London, fulfilling her fantasy to be a gangster's moll. They are caught and tried. David Yallop's screenplay is based on a true story.

CHILD'S PLAY II

Pro. David Kirschner; Universal Pictures *Dir.* John Lafia *Scr.* Don Mancini; based on characters created by Mancini *Cine.* Stefan Czapsky *Ed.* Edward Warschilka *P.d.* Ivo Cristante *A.d.* Donald Maskovich *S.d.* Debra Combs *Mu.* Graeme Revell *MPAA* R *R.t.* 85 min. *Cast:* Alex Vincent, Jenny Agutter, Gerrit Graham, Christine Elise, Brad Dourif (voice), Grace Zabriskie, Peter Haskell, Beth Grant.

Chucky's back, the evil, swearing, possessed doll bent on taking over little boy Andy's body, to wreak further havoc and horror.

CHINA CRY

Pro. Don LeRoy Parker for Parakletos Productions and Trinity Broadcasting Network (TBN) Films; Penland Incorporated *Dir.* James F. Collier *Scr.* James F. Collier; based on the book *China Cry,* by Nora Lam and Irene Burke *Cine.* David Worth *Ed.* Duane Hartzell *P.d.* Norman Baron *S.d.* Linda Allen *Mu.* Al Kasha and Joel Hirschhorn *MPAA* PG-13 *R.t.* 103 min. *Cast:* Julia Nickson-Soul, Russell Wong, James Shigeta, France Nuyen, Philip Tan, Elizabeth Sung.

Based on the life of evangelist Nora Lam, *China Cry* is the story of a spirited young woman, Sung Neng Yee (Julia Nickson-Soul), who, after enduring years of persecution in revolutionary China for her beliefs in Christianity and the rights of the individual, ultimately gained freedom for herself and her family.

A CHINESE GHOST STORY II (Hong Kong, 1990)

Dir. Chen Siu-Tung *Scr.* Leung Yu-Ming. *Cast:* Leslie Cheung, Jacky Cheung, Wang Tsu-Hsin, Michelle Ries, Lau Su-Ming.

Set in the late Ming Dynasty and featuring action and swordplay, this Hong Kong period adventure features a naïve tax collector (Leslie Cheung) who befriends a sorcerous Taoist monk (Jacky Cheung) in an abandoned mansion, where they meet two sisters posing as ghosts and an evil other-worldly creature.

CIRCUITRY MAN

Pro. Steven Reich and John Schouweiler for I.R.S. Media Inc.; Skouras Pictures *Dir.* Steven Lovy *Scr.* Steven Lovy and Robert Lovy *Cine.* Jamie Thompson *Ed.* Jonas Thaler *P.d.* Robert Lovy *Mu.* Deborah Holland *MPAA* R *R.t.* 87 min. *Cast:* Jim Metzler, Dana Wheeler-Nicholson, Lu Leonard, Vernon Wells, Barbara Alyn Woods, Paul Willson.

In a polluted future, where Los Angeles and New York City inhabitants must live underground, and cross-country travel involves a maze of underground tunnels or carrying one's own oxygen supply, bodyguard Lori (Dana Wheeler-Nicholson) undertakes the trip with android Danner (Jim Metzler), pursued by bad guys, to deliver a load of narcotic microchips and achieve her freedom from her cruel boss (Lu Leonard).

CLASS OF 1999

Pro. Mark L. Lester; Taurus Entertainment *Dir.* Mark L. Lester *Scr.* C. Courtney Joyner *Cine.* Mark Irwin *Ed.* Scott Conrad *P.d.* Steven Legler *Mu.* Michael Hoenig *MPAA* R *R.t.* 98 min. *Cast:* Bradley Gregg, Traci Lind, Malcolm McDowell, Stacy Keach, Patrick Kilpatrick, Pam Grier, John P. Ryan, Darren E. Burrows, Joshua Miller, Sharon Wyatt, Jimmy Medina Taggert, Jason Oliver, Jill Gatsby, Sean Haggerty, Sean Gregory Sullivan.

In the year 1999, gangs of heavily armed students roam Free Fire Areas around a Seattle high school dealing drugs and killing all who oppose them. New principal Dr. Miles Langford (Malcolm McDowell) enlists robotics entrepreneur Dr. Bob Forrest (Stacy Keach), who brings in three android teachers, Ms. Connors (Pam Grier), Mr. Hardin (John P. Ryan), and Mr. Bryles (Patrick Kilpatrick). The teachers are programmed to maintain classroom order at any price.

COUPE DE VILLE

Pro. Larry Brezner and Paul Schiff for Morgan Creek; Universal Pictures *Dir.* Joe Roth *Scr.* Mike Binder *Cine.* Reynaldo Villalobos *Ed.* Paul Hirsch *P.d.* Angelo Graham *A.d.* Jim Murakami *S.d.* Don Ivey *Mu.* James Newton Howard *MPAA* PG-13 *R.t.* 99 min. *Cast:* Patrick Dempsey, Arye Gross, Daniel Stern, Annabeth Gish, Rita Taggart, Joseph Bologna, Alan Arkin.

While delivering a vintage Coupe de Ville to their mother in Florida from their father (Alan Arkin) in Detroit, three brothers, Bobby (Patrick Dempsey), Buddy (Arye Gross), and Marvin (Daniel Stern), grow much closer.

COURAGE MOUNTAIN

Pro. Stephen Ujlaki for Epic Productions Inc., a Stone Group Ltd.-France production; Triumph Releasing Corp. *Dir.* Christopher Leitch *Scr.* Weaver Webb; based on a story by Fred and Mark Brogger *Cine.* Jacques Steyn *Ed.* Martin Walsh *P.d.* Robb Wilson King *Mu.* Sylvester Levay *MPAA* PG *R.t.* 98 min. *Cast:* Juliette Caton, Joanna Clarke, Nicola Stapleton, Charlie Sheen, Jan Rubes, Leslie Caron, Yorgo Voyagis, Laura Betti.

The famous fictional character of Heidi (here portrayed by Juliette Caton), the Swiss girl who lived with her grandfather in the Alps, is updated in a story set at the outbreak of World War I. When Heidi goes away to school in Italy, circumstances turn her into a virtual slave at an orphanage, but she and her friends eventually effect a heroic escape, aided by her childhood friend Peter (Charlie Sheen).

CRAZY PEOPLE

Pro. Tom Barad; Paramount Pictures *Dir.* Tony Bill *Scr.* Mitch Markowitz *Cine.* Victor J. Kemper *Ed.* Mia Goldman *P.d.* John J. Lloyd *Mu.* Cliff Eidelman *MPAA* R *R.t.* 90 min. *Cast:* Dudley Moore, Daryl Hannah, Paul Reiser, Mercedes Ruehl, J. T. Walsh, Ben Hammer,

Dick Cusack, Alan North, David Paymer, Danton Stone, Doug Yasuda, Bill Smitrovich, Paul Bates, Floyd Vivino, John Terlesky.

A burned-out copywriter (Dudley Moore) becomes obsessed with telling the truth in advertising and ends up in a mental hospital, where he falls in love with a beautiful woman (Daryl Hannah). With the help of a group of eccentric patients, he turns the advertising business upside down.

CRY-BABY

Pro. Rachel Talalay for Imagine Entertainment; Universal Pictures *Dir.* John Waters *Scr.* John Waters *Cine.* David Insley *Ed.* Janice Hampton *P.d.* Vincent Peranio *A.d.* Delores Deluxe *S.d.* Chester Overlock III and Virginia Nichols *Mu.* Patrick Williams *MPAA* PG-13 *R.t.* 89 min. *Cast:* Johnny Depp, Amy Locane, Susan Tyrrell, Polly Bergen, Iggy Pop, Ricki Lake, Traci Lords, Kim McGuire, Darren E. Burrows, Stephen Mailer, Kim Webb, Troy Donahue, Mink Stole, Joe Dallesandro, Joey Heatherton, David Nelson, Patricia Hearst, Willem Dafoe.

This satire of the 1950's teen genre nevertheless celebrates, if not romanticizes, the music and styles of the period. Essentially a musical, the film depicts the romance between Cry-Baby (Johnny Depp), a "drape" or juvenile delinquent, and Allison (Amy Locane), a "square" from the upper-middle class.

A CRY IN THE WILD

Pro. Julie Corman; Concorde-New Horizons Corp. *Dir.* Mark Griffiths *Scr.* Gary Paulsen and Catherine Cryan; based on the novel *Hatchet*, by Paulsen *Cine.* Gregg Heschong *Ed.* Carol Oblath *P.d.* Michael Clausen *Mu.* Arthur Kempel *MPAA* PG *R.t.* 81 min. *Cast:* Jared Rushton, Pamela Sue Martin, Stephen Meadows, Ned Beatty.

In this family film, 13-year-old Brian (Jared Rushton), living with his mother (Pamela Sue Martin) and very angry over his parents' recent divorce, is sent by plane to visit his father (Stephen Meadows) in Canada. When the pilot (Ned Beatty) of the small plane suffers a fatal heart attack in mid-flight, Brian is forced to crash land alone in the wilderness, where his bitterness and self-pity will have to cede to his need to survive.

CURRENT EVENTS

Pro. Ralph Aryck *Dir.* Ralph Aryck *Scr.* Ralph Aryck *Cine.* Ralph Aryck.

In this documentary film, filmmaker and activist Ralph Aryck has taken on several tasks: to communicate to Americans the hardship and suffering in other areas of the world, to discuss what it means to be a caring person, and to try to find a balance between activism and responsibilities to family and self.

DADDY'S DYIN': WHO'S GOT THE WILL?

Pro. Sigurjon Sighvatsson, Steve Golin, and Monty Montgomery for Propaganda Films; Metro-Goldwyn-Mayer/United Artists *Dir.* Jack Fisk *Scr.* Del Shores; based on his stage play *Cine.* Paul Elliott *Ed.* Edward A Warschilka, Jr. *P.d.* Michelle Minch *S.d.* Susan Eschelbach *Mu.* David McHugh *MPAA* PG-13 *R.t.* 95 min. *Cast:* Beau Bridges, Beverly D'Angelo, Tess Harper, Judge Reinhold, Amy Wright, Patrika Darbo, Molly McClure, Bert Remsen, Keith Carradine.

Four adult siblings, their grandmother, and their spouses embark on a search for their father's lost will. They race against time (Daddy cannot help if he is dead) and one another and learn almost too late that the family is more precious than the money.

DARKMAN

Pro. Robert Tapert for Darkman Prods.; Universal Pictures *Dir.* Sam Raimi *Scr.* Chuck Pfarrer, Sam Raimi, Ivan Raimi, Daniel Goldin, and Joshua Goldin; based on the story by

Sam Raimi *Cine.* Bill Pope *Ed.* David Stiven, Bud Smith, and Scott Smith *P.d.* Randy Ser *A.d.* Phil Dagort *S.d.* Julie Kaye Fanton *Mu.* Danny Elfman *MPAA* R *R.t.* 95 min. *Cast:* Liam Neeson, Frances McDormand, Colin Friels, Larry Drake, Nelson Mashita, Jessie Lawrence Ferguson, Rafael H. Robledo, Danny Hicks, Theodore Raimi.

This action/adventure with the look and feel of a graphic comic book deals with the hideous disfigurement of Peyton Westlake (Liam Neeson) and his transformation from a gifted scientist into a vengeance-seeking madman. With references to other legendary human monsters such as the Phantom of the Opera, the Hunchback of Notre Dame, and the Mummy, the film follows Peyton as he systematically tracks down and destroys the people responsible for his disfigurement, resulting in estrangement from his girlfriend, Julie Hastings (Frances McDormand), and ultimately society itself.

DEATH WARRANT

Pro. Mark DiSalle; Metro-Goldwyn-Mayer/United Artists *Dir.* Deran Sarafian *Scr.* David S. Goyer *Cine.* Russell Carpenter *Ed.* G. Gregg McLaughlin and John A. Barton *P.d.* Curtis Schnell *A.d.* Robert E. Lee *S.d.* Richard Hummel *Mu.* Gary Chang *MPAA* R *R.t.* 88 min. *Cast:* Jean-Claude Van Damme, Robert Guillaume, Cynthia Gibb, George Dickerson, Art La Fleur, Patrick Kilpatrick, Joshua Miller, Hank Woessner, George Jenesky, Jack Bannon, Abdul Salaam El Razzac.

Jean-Claude Van Damme returns to the screen in yet another martial-arts film as Louis Burke, a Los Angeles police officer sent undercover to investigate a series of mysterious deaths inside a prison. The plot winds to its inevitable, violent conclusion, with lots of action along the way.

DEF BY TEMPTATION

Pro. James Bond III for Lloyd Kaufman-Michael Herz and Bonded Filmworks Prods.; Troma Team *Dir.* James Bond III *Scr.* James Bond III *Cine.* Ernest Dickerson *Ed.* Li-Shin Yu *P.d.* David Carrington *A.d.* Marc Henry Johnson *Mu.* Paul Laurence *R.t.* 95 min. *Cast:* James Bond III, Kadeem Hardison, Bill Nunn, Cynthia Bond, Minnie Gentry.

When Joel (James Bond III), a Southern divinity student, comes to New York City to stay with a friend, fast-talking and slick K (Kadeem Hardison), he begins to get a tempting taste of a more sophisticated life-style. The dark side of city life, however, catches up with him when a temptress (Cynthia Bond), actually a succubus, sets her sights on him in a potentially deadly situation.

DELTA FORCE II: OPERATION STRANGLEHOLD

Pro. Yoram Globus and Christopher Pearce for Cannon Entertainment; Metro-Goldwyn-Mayer/United Artists *Dir.* Aaron Norris *Scr.* Lee Reynolds; based on characters created by James Bruner and Menahem Golan *Cine.* Joao Fernandes *Ed.* Michael J. Duthie *P.d.* Ladislav Wilheim *A.d.* Rodell Cruz *S.d.* Pia Fernandez *Mu.* Frederic Talgorn *MPAA* R *R.t.* 105 min. *Cast:* Chuck Norris, Billy Drago, John P. Ryan, Richard Jaeckel, Begonia Plaza, Paul Perri, Hector Mercado, Mark Margolis, Mateo Gomez, Ruth de Sosa.

Two members of the Delta Force commando group (Chuck Norris and John P. Ryan) pursue a Latin American drug lord (Billy Drago) in order to rescue several captured Drug Enforcement Administration agents, as well as to exact revenge for the villain's murder of one commando and his family.

DESPERATE HOURS

Pro. Dino De Laurentiis and Michael Cimino for Dino De Laurentiis Communications; Metro-Goldwyn-Mayer/United Artists *Dir.* Michael Cimino *Scr.* Lawrence Konner, Mark Rosenthal, and Joseph Hayes; based on the novel and play by Hayes *Cine.* Doug Milsome *Ed.* Peter

Hunt *P.d.* Victoria Paul *A.d.* Patricia Klawonn *S.d.* Tom Lindblom and Crispian Sallis *Mu.* David Mansfield *MPAA* R *R.t.* 105 min. *Cast:* Mickey Rourke, Anthony Hopkins, Mimi Rogers, Lindsay Crouse, Kelly Lynch, Elias Koteas, David Morse, Shawnee Smith, Danny Gerard, Gerry Bamman, Matt McGrath.

In this remake of the 1955 classic film, a suburban family is held hostage and terrorized by a psychotic prison escapee (Mickey Rourke) and his two accomplices. Loosely based on a factual incident, this story served as star vehicle for Paul Newman on the stage and Humphrey Bogart on film.

DIAMOND'S EDGE (Great Britain, 1990)
Pro. Linda James for Red Rooster Films, in association with Coverstop Film Finances Ltd., The Children's Film and Television Foundation, and British Screen; Castle Hill *Dir.* Stephen Bayly *Scr.* Anthony Horowitz; based on the book *The Falcon's Malteser,* by Horowitz *Cine.* Billy Williams *Ed.* Scott Thomas *P.d.* Peter Murton *Mu.* Trevor Jones *MPAA* PG *R.t.* 83 min. *Cast:* Colin Dale, Dursley McLinden, Rene Ruiz, Susannah York, Patricia Hodge, Michael Robbins.

In this British satire of the *film noir* detective genre, two teenage brothers, Nick (Colin Dale) and Tim Diamond (Dursley McLinden), run a detective business struggling to find clients, when a dwarf with a package shows up. The brothers are to guard the package for the large sum of two hundred pounds, a job made difficult by the number of people who come looking for it, and meet many interesting characters, including a worldly saloon singer Lauren Bacardi (Susannah York) and the Fat Man (Michael Robbins).

DISTURBED
Pro. Brad Wyman; Live Entertainment/Odyssey Distributors *Dir.* Charles Winkler *Scr.* Emerson Bixby and Charles Winkler *Cine.* Bernd Heinl *Ed.* David Handman *P.d.* Marek Dobrowolski *A.d.* Anna Ritti Raineri *Mu.* Steven Scott Smalley *MPAA* R *R.t.* 96 min. *Cast:* Malcolm McDowell, Geoffrey Lewis, Priscilla Pointer, Pamela Gidley, Irwin Keyes, Clint Howard, Peter Murnik, Carrie Lynn.

In this grim thriller, Malcolm McDowell stars as Dr. Derek Russell, chief psychiatrist at an insane asylum, who has a penchant for drugging, then raping his female patients.

DIVING IN
Pro. Martin Wiley; Skouras Pictures *Dir.* Strathford Hamilton *Scr.* Eric Edson *Cine.* Hanania Baer *Ed.* Marcy Hamilton *A.d.* Marty Bercaw *Mu.* Paul Buckmaster and Guy Moon *MPAA* PG-13 *R.t.* 92 min. *Cast:* Matt Adler, Burt Young, Yolande Gilot, Kristy Swanson, Matt Lattanzi.

A high school senior, Wayne Hopkins (Matt Adler), who has ambitions to become an Olympic diver, faces two major obstacles: an uninterested coach and a fear of heights. Although its outcome is predictable, the film does probe such topics as peer pressure and the competitive spirit.

DON'T TELL HER IT'S ME (also known as *The Boyfriend School*)
Pro. George G. Braunstein and Ron Hamady; Hemdale *Dir.* Malcolm Mowbray *Scr.* Sarah Bird; based on her novel *The Boyfriend School Cine.* Reed Smoot *Ed.* Marshall Harvey *P.d.* Linda Pearl *S.d.* Debra Schutt *Mu.* Michael Gore *MPAA* PG-13 *R.t.* 101 min. *Cast:* Steve Guttenberg, Jami Gertz, Shelley Long, Kyle MacLachlan, Kevin Scannell, Mädchen Amick, Beth Grant, Caroline Lund, Sally Lund.

Romance novelist Lizzie (Shelley Long) transforms her shy, introverted brother, Gus (Steve Guttenberg), into a motorcycle-riding hunk in order to win favor with a pretty reporter (Jami Gertz).

DOWNTOWN
Pro. Charles H. Maguire for Gale Anne Hurd; Twentieth Century-Fox *Dir.* Richard Benjamin *Scr.* Nat Mauldin *Cine.* Richard H. Kline *Ed.* Jacqueline Cambas and Brian Chambers *P.d.* Charles Rosen *A.d.* Gregory Pickrell *S.d.* Don Remacle *Mu.* Alan Silvestri *MPAA* R *R.t.* 96 min. *Cast:* Anthony Edwards, Forest Whitaker, Penelope Ann Miller, Joe Pantoliano, David Clennon, Art Evans, Rick Aiello, Roger Aaron Brown, Ron Canada, Wanda De Jesus, Frank McCarthy, Kimberly Scott.

When Alex Kearney (Anthony Edwards), an inexperienced young white policeman, is transferred to the Diamond Street section of Philadelphia from a crime-free suburb, he matures in a hurry, aided by a reluctant partner, streetwise black detective Dennis Curren (Forest Whitaker). Curren is reluctant to befriend Kearney after earlier losing a partner in the line of duty, but, despite cultural differences, they do come to care about each other while breaking up a ring of drug-dealing criminals.

DUCKTALES, THE MOVIE: TREASURE OF THE LOST LAMP
Pro. Bob Hathcock for Disney Movietoons and Walt Disney Animation; Buena Vista *Dir.* Bob Hathcock *Scr.* Alan Burnett *P.d.* Skip Morgan *Mu.* David Newman *MPAA* G *R.t.* 73 min. *Voices:* Alan Young, Russi Taylor, Rip Taylor, Christopher Lloyd, Richard Libertini, June Foray, Joan Gerber, Chuck McCann, Terence McGovern.

Miser Scrooge McDuck (voice of Alan Young) and his nephews foil the attempts of the evil shape-changing magician Merlock (voice of Christopher Lloyd) and his cringing kleptomaniac sidekick Dijon (voice of Richard Libertini) to rob them of the magic lamp they discover when they unearth the lost ancient treasure of Collie Baba. Their success frees the lamp's genie (voice of Rip Taylor), who is granted his wish to become a real, all-American boy.

EATING
Pro. Judith Wolinsky; International Rainbow Pictures *Dir.* Henry Jaglom *Scr.* Henry Jaglom *Cine.* Hanania Baer *Ed.* Henry Jaglom *R.t.* 110 min. *Cast:* Lisa Richards, Mary Crosby, Gwen Welles, Nelly Alard, Frances Bergen, Elizabeth Kemp, Marlena Giovi, Daphna Kastner, Marina Gregory.

Three women celebrating birthdays gather with their women friends for a party, during which they discover that they are all obsessed by food and how it affects their appearance.

ELLIOT FAUMAN, PH.D.
Pro. Ric Klass for Ventcap Film Partners; Taurus Entertainment *Dir.* Ric Klass *Scr.* Ric Klass *Cine.* Erich Roland *Ed.* Judith Herbert *P.d.* Henry Shaffer *A.d.* Tony Cisek *Mu.* Roger Trefousse *MPAA* PG-13 *R.t.* 86 min. *Cast:* Randy Dreyfuss, Jean Kasem, Tamara Williams, Shelley Berman, Bryan Michael McGuire, John Canada Terrell, Michael Willis.

Elliot Fauman, Ph.D. (Randy Dreyfuss), a psychology professor, is researching what he hopes will be a breakthrough paper on prostitutes. Attempting to gain firsthand information, he first approaches the streetwalker Stella (Tamara Williams) but alienates her when he refuses her sexual solicitations. Immediately afterward, though, his defenses crumble when he falls in love with Meredith (Jean Kasem), an actress who is posing as a prostitute to get his attention, and comic complications ensue.

THE END OF INNOCENCE
Pro. Thom Tyson and Vince Cannon for O.P.V. Productions; Skouras Pictures *Dir.* Dyan Cannon *Scr.* Dyan Cannon *Cine.* Alexander Nepomniaschy *Ed.* Bruce Cannon *P.d.* Paul Eads *A.d.* Mindy Roffman *Mu.* Michael Convertino *MPAA* R *R.t.* 102 min. *Cast:* Dyan Cannon, John Heard, George Coe, Lola Mason, Steve Meadows, Rebecca Schaeffer.

A woman (Dyan Cannon) struggles against a drug addiction and poor self-esteem on the way to self-discovery. The film also was written and directed by Cannon.

ERNEST GOES TO JAIL

Pro. Stacy Williams for Emshell Producers Group for Touchstone Pictures, in association with Silver Screen Partners IV; Buena Vista *Dir.* John Cherry *Scr.* Charlie Cohen *Cine.* Peter Stein *Ed.* Sharyn L. Ross and Farrel Levy *P.d.* Chris August *A.d.* Mark Ragland *S.d.* Connie Gray *Mu.* Bruce Arntson and Kirby Shelstad *MPAA* PG *R.t.* 82 min. *Cast:* Jim Varney, Gailard Sartain, Bill Byrge, Barbara Bush, Barry Scott, Randall ("Tex") Cobb, Dan Leegant, Charles Napier, Jim Conrad, Jackie Welch.

Ernest P. Worrell (Jim Varney), a bank employee serving on a jury, looks exactly like Nash (also played by Jim Varney), a ruthless criminal serving time in prison. Through the machinations of another convict, Rubin Bartlett (Barry Scott), a switch is pulled which finds the innocent Ernest trying to survive prison life while Nash impersonates him on the outside. After further comic complications, right triumphs.

L'ETAT SAUVAGE (France, 1978)

Pro. Louis Wimpf for Films 66-Gaumont S.A.; Interama *Dir.* Francis Girod *Scr.* Georges Conchon and Francis Girod; based on the novel by Conchon *Cine.* Pierre Lhomme *Ed.* Genevieve Winding *A.d.* Guy-Claude François *Mu.* Pierre Jansen *R.t.* 111 min. *Cast:* Jacques Dutronc, Marie-Christine Barrault, Doura Mane, Michel Piccoli, Claude Brasseur, Rudiger Vogler.

In a relatively new West African nation, Doumbe (Doura Mane), a black cabinet minister, lives with a white woman, Laurence (Marie-Christine Barrault). The interracial love affair stirs the animosity of everyone in the couple's sphere, including other cabinet members and Laurence's former husband, Avit (Jacques Dutronc), a Frenchman. Events become increasingly dramatic as the personal story unfolds against a complex political background.

EVERYBODY WINS

Pro. Jeremy Thomas for Karel Reisz Film; Orion Pictures *Dir.* Karel Reisz *Scr.* Arthur Miller *Cine.* Ian Blake *Ed.* John Bloom *P.d.* Peter Larkin *A.d.* Charley Beal *S.d.* Hilton Rosemarin *Mu.* Mark Isham *MPAA* R *R.t.* 97 min. *Cast:* Debra Winger, Nick Nolte, Will Patton, Judith Ivey, Kathleen Wilhoite, Jack Warden, Frank Converse, Frank Military, Steven Skybell, Mary Louise Wilson.

Everybody Wins is a detective story. Set in a rural Connecticut town, it follows Tom O'Toole (Nick Nolte), a private detective, as he unravels a complex mystery involving false conviction, strange cults, drug addiction, corruption, and a very attractive, but slightly crazy, young woman (Debra Winger).

THE EXORCIST III

Pro. Carter DeHaven for Morgan Creek Prods.; Twentieth Century-Fox *Dir.* William Peter Blatty *Scr.* William Peter Blatty; based on his novel *Legion* *Cine.* Gerry Fisher *Ed.* Todd Ramsay and Peter Lee-Thompson *P.d.* Leslie Dilley *A.d.* Robert Goldstein and Henry Shaffer *S.d.* Hugh Sciafe *Mu.* Barry Devorzon *MPAA* R *R.t.* 110 min. *Cast:* George C. Scott, Ed Flanders, Brad Dourif, Jason Miller, Nicol Williamson, Scott Wilson, Nancy Fish, George DiCenzo, Viveca Lindfors, Mary Jackson.

William Peter Blatty picks up his own story seventeen years after the release of his controversial script for *The Exorcist* (1973). A fiendish serial killer terrorizes Washington, D.C. A detective named Kinderman (George C. Scott) traces the gruesome crimes to a large hospital, only to learn that they were committed by more than one person.

FAR OUT MAN

Pro. Lisa M. Hansen; New Line Pictures *Dir.* Tommy Chong *Scr.* Tommy Chong *Cine.* Greg

Gardiner and Eric Woster *Ed.* Stephen Myer and Gilberto Costa Nunes *A.d.* David B. Miller *Mu.* Jay Chattaway *MPAA* R *R.t.* 91 min. *Cast:* Tommy Chong, Shelby Chong, Paris Chong, C. Thomas Howell, Martin Mull, Rae Dawn Chong, Bobby Taylor, Reynaldo Taylor, Peggy F. Sands, Al Mancini, Judd Nelson, Paul Bartel, Cheech Marin.

In his first film without former partner Cheech Marin, brilliant but erratically inspired writer/director/star/comedian Tommy Chong plays a burned-out former hippie living in the present as if it were still the 1960's. Members of Chong's family, including wife Shelby Chong and daughter Rae Dawn Chong, play other characters in the loosely constructed story which finds the eponymous aging free spirit going out on the road as work therapy.

THE FEUD

Pro. Bill D'Elia and Carole Kivett; Castle Hill *Dir.* Bill D'Elia *Scr.* Bill D'Elia and Robert Uricola; based on the novel by Thomas Berger *Cine.* John Beymer *Ed.* Bill Johnson *P.d.* Charles Lagola *Mu.* Brian Eddolls *R.t.* 96 min. *Cast:* Rene Auberjonois, Ron McLarty, Joe Grifasi, Scott Allegrucci, Gale Mayron, David Strathairn, Stanley Tucci, Lynn Killmeyer.

A feud between two neighboring families, the Beelers and the Bullards, escalates into a comic frenzy after Reverton Bullard (Rene Auberjonois), a demented railroad detective, pulls a gun on Dolf Beeler (Ron McLarty) when the latter refuses to toss out an unlighted cigar while in the store of Bud Bullard (Joe Grifasi). Set in the 1950's, this adaptation of a Thomas Berger novel is a satirical, mordant observation of Americana.

FIRE BIRDS

Pro. William Badalato for Nova International Films; Touchstone Pictures *Dir.* David Green *Scr.* Nick Thiel and Paul F. Edwards; based on a story by Step Tyner, John K. Swensson, and Dale Dye *Cine.* Tony Imi *Ed.* Jon Poll, Norman Buckley, and Dennis O'Connor *P.d.* Joseph T. Garrity *S.d.* Jerie Kelter *Mu.* David Newman *MPAA* PG-13 *R.t.* 85 min. *Cast:* Nicolas Cage, Tommy Lee Jones, Sean Young, Bryan Kestner, Dale Dye, Mary Ellen Trainor, J. A. Preston.

Fire Birds is a military adventure involving high-tech helicopters and the men and women who fly them, battling the war against drugs in South America. Jake Preston (Nicolas Cage), a would-be hotshot pilot, must first earn his wings before being assigned to his mission against the drug cartel in an unnamed South American country. Of course the mission is successful.

THE FIRST POWER

Pro. David Madden for Interscope Communications and Nelson Entertainment; Orion Pictures *Dir.* Robert Resnikoff *Scr.* Robert Resnikoff *Cine.* Theo Van de Sande *Ed.* Michael Bloecher *MPAA* R *R.t.* 98 min. *Cast:* Lou Diamond Phillips, Tracy Griffith, Jeff Kober, Mykel T. Williamson, Elizabeth Arlen, Dennis Lipscomb, Carmen Argenziano, Julianna McCarthy, Nada Despotovich, Sue Giosa.

Detective Russell Logan (Lou Diamond Phillips), an expert in tracking down serial killers, gets much more than he can handle from the spirit of an executed murderer (Jeff Kober). The satanically inspired fiend resumes his string of crimes while temporarily occupying the bodies of random victims. His main target is the man who tracked him down, Logan. The latter's task is essentially impossible, but he is nevertheless helped by Tess Seaton (Tracy Griffith), a sympathetic psychic.

FLASHBACK

Pro. Marvin Worth; Paramount Pictures *Dir.* Franco Amurri *Scr.* David Loughery *Cine.* Stefan Czapsky *Ed.* C. Timothy O'Meara *P.d.* Vincent Cresciman *A.d.* James Terry Welden *S.d.* Cecilia Rodarte *Mu.* Barry Goldberg *MPAA* R *R.t.* 108 min. *Cast:* Dennis Hopper, Kiefer Sutherland, Carol Kane, Cliff De Young, Paul Dooley, Richard Masur, Michael Mc-Kean, Kathleen York.

This action-comedy plays with the value differences between the eras of the 1960's and the 1980's by throwing together a legendary radical-prankster from the 1960's and a young, contemporary FBI agent. The agent, John Buckner (Kiefer Sutherland), escorts his prisoner, hippie radical Huey Walker (Dennis Hopper), from San Francisco to Spokane, Washington. Along the way, the two end up switching identities and reassessing their values, while eluding the maniacal pursuit of a corrupt police sheriff.

FOOLS OF FORTUNE (Great Britain, 1990)

Pro. Sarah Radclyffe for Polygram and Working Title Films, in association with Film Four International; New Line Cinema *Dir.* Pat O'Connor *Scr.* Michael Hirst; based on the novel by William Trevor *Cine.* Jerzy Zielinski *Ed.* Michael Bradsell *P.d.* Jamie Leonard *Mu.* Hans Zimmer *MPAA* PG-13 *R.t.* 109 min. *Cast:* Iain Glen, Julie Christie, Mary Elizabeth Mastrantonio, Michael Kitchen, Sean T. McClory, Tom Hickey, Niamii Cusack, Neil Dudgeon, Frankie McCafferty, Catherine McFadden, Ronnie Masterson.

Post-World War I Ireland during the Irish War of Independence is the backdrop for this historical family saga. The plot revolves around Willie (Iain Glen): the devastation of his comfortable life, his revenge and exile, and his redemption through love.

THE FORBIDDEN DANCE

Pro. Marc S. Fischer and Richard L. Albert for 21st Century Corp. and Menahem Golan; Columbia Pictures *Dir.* Greydon Clark *Scr.* Roy Langsdon and John Platt; based on a story by Joseph Goldman *Cine.* R. Michael Stringer *Ed.* Robert Edwards and Earl Watson *P.d.* Don Day *A.d.* Frank Bertolino *S.d.* Shirley Starks *Mu.* Vladimir Horunzhy *MPAA* PG-13 *R.t.* 94 min. *Cast:* Laura Herring, Jeff James, Barbra Brighton, Miranda Garrison, Sid Haig, Angela Moya, Richard Lynch, Shannon Farnon, Linden Chiles.

Nisa (Laura Herring), a princess from the Amazon rain forests, goes to Los Angeles to try to help her cause—saving the rain forests and her tribe, its native inhabitants. Befriended by Jason (Jeff James), a rich young man, she enters a television dance contest with him and they do the lambada—the "forbidden dance" of the title coming into popularity at the time of the film's release.

THE FOURTH WAR

Pro. Wolf Schmidt for Kodiak Films; New Age Releasing (Cannon/Pathe) *Dir.* John Frankenheimer *Scr.* Stephen Peters and Kenneth Ross; based on *The Fourth War*, by Peters *Cine.* Gerry Fisher *Ed.* Robert F. Shugrue *P.d.* Alan Manzer *Mu.* Bill Conti *MPAA* R *R.t.* 91 min. *Cast:* Roy Scheider, Jürgen Prochnow, Tim Reid, Lara Harris, Harry Dean Stanton, Dale Dye, Bill MacDonald.

On the Czechoslovakia-West Germany border, the shooting of a would-be defector provokes outrages in hard-line U.S. Colonel Jack Knowles (Roy Scheider), who throws a snowball at Soviet Colonel Valachev (Jürgen Prochnow). Conflict between the two men escalates as they continually retaliate against and try to outdo each other in a darkly comic charade of Cold War attitudes.

FRANKENHOOKER

Pro. Edgar Ievins for Ievins/Henenlotter; Shapiro Glickenhaus Entertainment *Dir.* Frank Henenlotter *Scr.* Robert Martin and Frank Henenlotter *Cine.* Robert M. Baldwin *Ed.* Kevin Tent *Mu.* Joe Renzetti *R.t.* 90 min. *Cast:* James Lorinz, Patty Mullen, Charlotte Helmkamp, Shirley Stoler, Louise Lasser, Joseph Gonzalez, Lia Chang, Jennifer Delora, Vicki Darnell, Kimberly Taylor, Heather Hunter, Sandy Colisimo, Stephanie Ryan, Paul Felix Montez.

Comedy dominates a gory contemporary version of the Frankenstein story, as demented scientist Jeffrey Franken (James Lorinz) tries to give new life to his fiancée, Elizabeth (Patty

Mullen), after she is cut into pieces by a runaway lawn mower. Jeffrey accomplishes his task by murdering a group of prostitutes and using parts of their bodies together with Elizabeth's head to create the eponymous creature, whose legs carry her back to 42nd Street for further misadventures.

FUNNY ABOUT LOVE

Pro. Jon Avnet and Jordan Kerner; Paramount Pictures *Dir.* Leonard Nimoy *Scr.* Norman Steinberg and David Frankel; based on the article "Convention of the Love Goddesses," by Bob Greene *Cine.* Fred Murphy *Ed.* Peter E. Berger *P.d.* Stephen Storer *A.d.* Nathan Haas and Robert Guerra *Mu.* Miles Goodman *MPAA* PG-13 *R.t.* 101 min. *Cast:* Gene Wilder, Christine Lahti, Mary Stuart Masterson, Robert Prosky, Stephen Tobolowsky, Anne Jackson, Susan Ruttan, Jean De Baer, David Margulies, Tara Shannon.

Cartoonist Duffy Bergman (Gene Wilder), seeking the ever-elusive family life, woos and weds his caterer (Christine Lahti) and tries to start a family. But infertility and his affair with a young girl (Mary Stuart Masterson) pose a threat to their happiness.

GENUINE RISK

Pro. Larry J. Rattner, Guy J. Louthan, and William Ewart; I.R.S. Media, Inc. *Dir.* Kurt Voss *Scr.* Kurt Voss; based on a story by Larry J. Rattner and Voss *Cine.* Dean Lent *Ed.* Christopher Koefoed *P.d.* Elisabeth A. Scott *A.d.* Christopher Neely *Mu.* Deborah Holland *MPAA* R *R.t.* 89 min. *Cast:* Terence Stamp, Peter Berg, Michelle Johnson, M. K. Harris, Max Perlich, Teddy Wilson, Sid Haig.

A gambler (Peter Berg) down on his luck takes the job of debt-collecting for a racketeer (Terence Stamp), at the advice of an old buddy (M. K. Harris). When he has an affair with the racketeer's mistress (Michelle Johnson), he finds himself in even more debt than before.

GHOST DAD

Pro. Terry Nelson for SAH Enterprises; Universal Pictures *Dir.* Sidney Poitier *Scr.* Chris Reese, Brent Maddock, and S. S. Wilson; based on a story by Maddock and Wilson *Cine.* Andrew Laszlo *Ed.* Pembroke Herring *P.d.* Henry Bumstead *A.d.* Bernie Cutler *S.d.* Richard Goddard *Mu.* Henry Mancini *MPAA* PG *R.t.* 88 min. *Cast:* Bill Cosby, Kimberly Russell, Denise Nicholas, Ian Bannen, Barry Corbin, Salim Grant, Brooke Fontaine, Dana Ashbrook, Omar Gooding, Christine Ebersole.

Busy corporate climber and befuddled widower-father Elliot Hopper (Bill Cosby) sets off to work one morning and, unfortunately, meets up with a crazed cab driver who plunges the two of them into a river. Upon recovering, Hopper realizes that he is now a partial ghost. The laughs are abundant as Hopper sets out to keep his family and their future intact while finding his way back to normality.

GHOSTS CAN'T DO IT

Pro. Bo Derek for Epic Productions; Triumph *Dir.* John Derek *Scr.* John Derek *Cine.* John Derek *Mu.* Junior Homrich and Randy Tico *MPAA* R *R.t.* 95 min. *Cast:* Bo Derek, Anthony Quinn, Don Murray, Leo Damian, Julie Newmar, Donald Trump.

When Scott (Anthony Quinn) dies, his beautiful young wife, Kate (Bo Derek), feels that she will not be satisfied with a less virile man, and she and Scott's ghost devise a plan to put his spirit into the body of a young man, Fausto (Leo Damian), just as he himself dies. Kate is a not very willing murderess, but fortunately for her, nothing goes exactly as planned.

THE GODS MUST BE CRAZY II

Pro. Boet Troskie for Weintraub Entertainment Group; Columbia Pictures (United States) and Twentieth Century-Fox (international) *Dir.* Jamie Uys *Scr.* Jamie Uys *Cine.* Buster Reynolds *Ed.* Renee Engelbrecht and Ivan Hall *S.d.* Joy Design *Mu.* Charles Fox *MPAA* PG *R.t.*

97 min. *Cast:* N!xau, Lena Farugia, Hans Strydom, Eiros, Nadies, Erick Bowen, Treasure Tshabalala, Lourens Swanepoel, Pierre Van Pletzen.

A New York corporate lawyer (Lena Farugia), Kalahari desert zoologist (Hans Strydom), Bushman (N!xau) and his two children (Nadies and Eiros), two elephant tusk poachers (Lourens Swanepoel and Pierre Van Pletzen), and two soldiers (Erick Bowen and Treasure Tshabalala) spend an hour and a half converging on one spot in the Kalahari in order to resolve a plot full of implausible complications and sight gags in this highly amusing sequel.

GRAFFITI BRIDGE
Pro. Arnold Stiefel and Randy Phillips for Paisley Park; Warner Bros. *Dir.* Prince *Scr.* Prince *Cine.* Bill Butler *Ed.* Rebecca Ross *P.d.* Vance Lorenzini *Mu.* Prince *MPAA* PG-13 *R.t.* 95 min. *Cast:* Prince, Ingrid Chavez, Morris Day, Jerome Benton, Mavis Staples, George Clinton, Tevin Campbell, Robin Power.

Prince returns to the screen in this film about a beleaguered rock singer, deserted by friends and fans, dueling fellow artist Morris Day for control of their nightclub. To his aid comes an angel (Ingrid Chavez), in this tale of spirituality versus capitalism.

THE GREAT BARRIER REEF
Pro. George Casey for Graphic Films *Dir.* George Casey *Scr.* Bill Kurtis and Soames Summerhays *Cine.* Mal Wolfe, James Niehose, and Steve Craig *MPAA* PG *R.t.* 37 min.

A presentation in the comparatively new IMAX system (where the frame is ten times the size of a standard 35mm frame), this documentary view of Australia's Great Barrier Reef, and underwater structure said to be the earth's oldest life-sustaining natural wonder, provides insights into how the undersea life regenerates while also displaying environmental concerns.

GRIM PRAIRIE TALES
Pro. Richard Hahn for East/West Film Partners Productions; Coe Hahn *Dir.* Wayne Coe *Scr.* Wayne Coe *Cine.* Janusz Minski *Ed.* Earl Ghaffari *P.d.* Anthony Zierhut *A.d.* Angela Levy *S.d.* Shirley Starks *Mu.* Steve Dancz *MPAA* R *R.t.* 90 min. *Cast:* James Earl Jones, Brad Dourif, Will Hare, Marc McClure, Michelle Joyner, William Atherton, Lisa Eichhorn, Wendy Cooke, Scott Paulin, Bruce Fischer.

In the setting of the Old West, two travelers, one a crude bounty hunter (James Earl Jones), the other a timid merchant (Brad Dourif), pass the time and entertain each other around the campfire telling grim tales.

THE GUARDIAN
Pro. Joe Wizan; Universal Pictures *Dir.* William Friedkin *Scr.* Steven Volk, Dan Greenburg, and William Friedkin; based on the novel *The Nanny* (1987), by Greenburg *Cine.* John A. Alonzo *Ed.* Seth Flaum *P.d.* Gregg Fonseca *A.d.* Bruce Miller *S.d.* Sarah Burdick *Mu.* Jack Hues *MPAA* R *R.t.* 98 min. *Cast:* Jenny Seagrove, Dwier Brown, Carey Lowell, Brad Hall, Miguel Ferrer, Natalia Nogulich.

Kate (Carey Lowell) and Phil (Dwier Brown) hire a too-perfect nanny, Camilla (Jenny Seagrove), to care for their newborn, without thoroughly investigating her references. When they discover that she is a druid who regularly sacrifices babies to an ancient malevolent tree spirit, the Guardian, Phil and Kate must fight for their own lives as well as their baby's, eventually destroying both the nanny and the Guardian.

HAPPILY EVER AFTER
Pro. Lou Scheimer for Filmation and First National Film; Kel-Air Entertainment *Dir.* John Howley *Scr.* Robby London and Martha Moran *Cine.* Fred Ziegler *Ed.* Jeffrey C. Patch and Joe Gall *A.d.* John Grusd *Mu.* Frank W. Becker *MPAA* G *R.t.* 74 min. *Voices:* Irene Cara,

Edward Asner, Carol Channing, Dom DeLuise, Phyllis Diller, Zsa Zsa Gabor, Linda Gary, Jonathan Harris, Michael Horton, Sally Kellerman, Malcolm McDowell, Tracey Ullman, Frank Welker.

Devised as a sequel to *Snow White and the Seven Dwarfs* (though there is no relationship to the Disney film of that name in terms of production company or personnel), this animated fantasy finds Snow White (voice of Irene Cara) trying to rescue the Prince (voice of Michael Horton) from a spell cast by the late evil queen's brother, Lord Maliss (voice of Malcolm McDowell), while she is aided and given refuge by the Seven Dwarfelles, female cousins of the Dwarfs.

HAPPY TOGETHER

Pro. Jere Henshaw for Apollo Pictures; Borde Releasing Corporation *Dir.* Mel Damski *Scr.* Craig J. Nevius *Cine.* Joe Pennella *Ed.* O. Nicholas Brown *P.d.* Marcia Hinds *A.d.* Bo Johnson *S.d.* Jan K. Bergstrom *Mu.* Robert Folk *MPAA* PG-13 *R.t.* 102 min. *Cast:* Patrick Dempsey, Helen Slater, Dan Schneider, Kevin Hardesty, Marius Weyers, Barbara Babcock.

Would-be playwright Chris (Patrick Dempsey) and aspiring actress Alex (Helen Slater) wind up as freshmen roommates in a university dorm because of her unisex name. He is serious-minded and she's free-spirited. Alex's extroverted personality and whimsical ways drive Chris to desperation, yet in the three weeks it takes him to arrange a room transfer they fall in love.

HARD TO KILL

Pro. Gary Adelson, Joel Simon, and Bill Todman, Jr.; Warner Bros. *Dir.* Bruce Malmuth *Scr.* Steven McKay *Cine.* Matthew F. Leonetti *Ed.* John F. Link *P.d.* Robb Wilson King *A.d.* Louis Mann *Mu.* David Michael Frank *MPAA* R *R.t.* 95 min. *Cast:* Steven Seagal, Kelly Le Brock, Bill Sadler, Frederick Coffin, Bonnie Burroughs, Zachary Rosencrantz, Branscombe Richmond, Jerry Dunphy.

A tough policeman, Mason Storm (Steven Seagal), is gunned down by hoodlums who also kill his wife (Bonnie Burroughs) and, presumably, his son (Zachary Rosencrantz). Somehow, Storm survives, awaking from a coma seven years later to seek revenge and show appropriate romantic appreciation to his nurse Andrea (Kelly Le Brock).

HARDWARE (Great Britain and USA, 1990)

Pro. Joanne Sellar and Paul Trybits for Wicked Films; Palace Pictures and Millimeter Films, in association with British Screen and British Satellite Broadcasting *Dir.* Richard Stanley *Scr.* Richard Stanley *Cine.* Steve Chivers *Ed.* Derek Trigg *P.d.* Joseph Bennett *A.d.* Max Gottlieb *Mu.* Simon Boswell *MPAA* R *R.t.* 92 min. *Cast:* Dylan McDermott, Stacey Travis, John Lynch, Iggy Pop, William Hootkins, Mark Northover, Oscar James, Paul McKenzie, Carl McCoy, Lemmy.

In this postapocalyptic horror story about a terrible, futuristic experiment gone awry, Mo (Dylan McDermott) gives his girlfriend, Jill (Stacey Travis), a sack of robot components. Unknown to them, these parts belong to the MARK 13, a government experiment in deadly population control. The robot regenerates itself in Jill's apartment and begins to fulfill its program.

HEART CONDITION

Pro. Steve Tisch; New Line Cinema *Dir.* James D. Parriott *Scr.* James D. Parriott *Cine.* Arthur Albert *Ed.* David Finfer *P.d.* John Muto *Mu.* Patrick Leonard *MPAA* R *R.t.* 96 min. *Cast:* Bob Hoskins, Denzel Washington, Chloe Webb, Roger E. Mosley, Janet DuBois, Alan Rachins, Ray Baker, Jeffrey Meek, Frank R. Roach.

This offbeat "buddy film" stars Bob Hoskins as a bigoted police detective who receives the heart of a murdered black attorney (Denzel Washington). The attorney's ghost returns to haunt the detective, and the two become friends as they work together to solve the attorney's murder and help the call girl (Chloe Webb) they both love.

HENRY: PORTRAIT OF A SERIAL KILLER

Pro. John McNaughton, Lisa Dedmond, and Steven A. Jones; Greycat Films *Dir.* John McNaughton *Scr.* Richard Fire and John McNaughton *Cine.* Charlie Lieberman *Ed.* Elena Maganini *A.d.* Rick Paul *Mu.* Robert McNaughton, Ken Hale, and Steven A. Jones *R.t.* 83 min. *Cast:* Michael Rooker, Tom Towles, Tracy Arnold.

Henry (Michael Rooker), a psychopathic murderer, lives with Otis (Tom Towles), a friend from prison, and Otis' sister Becky (Tracy Arnold), who has just left her wife-beating husband. Henry kills at random, eventually drawing Otis into the crimes before complex emotions rupture the strange, uneasy triangle formed by the two men and Becky. Director John McNaughton treats the material very differently from a conventional genre film with violent subject matter; his emphasis is on the aftermaths of the murders more than the acts, and the film's tone resembles that of a documentary.

HIDDEN AGENDA (Great Britain, 1990)

Pro. Eric Fellner and Rebecca O'Brien; Hemdale *Dir.* Ken Loach *Scr.* Jim Allen *Cine.* Clive Tickner *Ed.* Jonathan Morris *P.d.* Martin Johnson *Mu.* Stewart Copeland *MPAA* R *R.t.* 107 min. *Cast:* Frances McDormand, Brian Cox, Brad Dourif, Mai Zetterling, Maurice Roeves, Jim Norton, Patrick Kavanagh, Brian McCann.

In this British thriller, two American human-rights activists, Ingrid Jessner (Frances McDormand) and Paul Sullivan (Brad Dourif), investigate civil rights injustices in Northern Ireland, leading to the death of Sullivan. Senior British inspector Kerrigan (Brian Cox) arrives to investigate, only to discover mass corruption in high places.

HOLLYWOOD MAVERICKS

Pro. Florence Dauman; American Film Institute and NHK Enterprises *Dir.* Don McGlynn *Scr.* Todd McCarthy and Michael Henry Wilson *Cine.* John Bailey, Steve Baum, Frederick Elmes, Marc Gerard, Mead Hunt, Todd McClelland, Peter S. Rosen, and Steve Wacks *Ed.* Stacey Foiles *R.t.* 90 min. *Cast:* Martin Scorsese, Paul Schrader, Peter Bogdanovich, King Vidor, Samuel Fuller, Dennis Hopper, Francis Coppola, Alan Rudolph, David Lynch, Robert De Niro.

Featuring Martin Scorsese, Peter Bogdanovich, and Paul Schrader, this montage of film clips and interviews examines the work of those Hollywood film directors who have earned a reputation for following their own artistic visions.

HOMER AND EDDIE

Pro. Moritz Borman and James Cady; Skouras Pictures *Dir.* Andrei Konchalovsky *Scr.* Patrick Cirillo *Cine.* Lajos Koltai *Ed.* Henry Richardson *P.d.* Michel Levesque *Mu.* Eduard Artemyev *MPAA* R *R.t.* 100 min. *Cast:* James Belushi, Whoopi Goldberg, Karen Black, Ernestine McClendon, Nancy Parsons, Anne Ramsey, Beah Richards.

Homer (James Belushi), a mentally retarded man, decides to travel from Arizona to Oregon to visit his parents. Along the way he is befriended by Eddie (Whoopi Goldberg), an escaped mental patient with an inoperable brain tumor. The odyssey of the two continues, with Eddie occasionally robbing and killing along the way before both find disillusionment in their respective homes.

HONEYMOON ACADEMY

Pro. Tony Anthony for Trans World Entertainment of a Sarlui/Diamant presentation of a Fidelity Films/Maslansky production; Triumph *Dir.* Gene Quintano *Scr.* Gene Quintano and

Jerry Lazarus; based on a story by Quintano *Cine.* John Cabrera *Ed.* Hubert C. de la Bouillerie *A.d.* Gumpsindo Andres *Mu.* Robert Folk *MPAA* PG-13 *R.t.* 94 min. *Cast:* Kim Cattrall, Robert Hays, Leigh Taylor-Young, Charles Rocket, Lance Kinsey, Christopher Lee, Jonathan Banks, Doris Roberts, Gordon Jump, Max Alexander, Jerry Lazarus.

A secret agent working for the State Department, Chris (Kim Cattrall) falls in love with Sean McDonald (Robert Hays) without telling him what she does for a living. On their honeymoon in Madrid, Chris is maneuvered back to work and into tracking down some counterfeit plates.

THE HOT SPOT

Pro. Paul Lewis; Orion Pictures *Dir.* Dennis Hopper *Scr.* Nona Tyson and Charles Williams; based on the novel *Hell Hath No Fury,* by Williams *Cine.* Ueli Steiger *Ed.* Wende Phifer Mate *P.d.* Cary White *A.d.* John Frick and Michael Sullivan *Mu.* Jack Nitzsche *MPAA* R *R.t.* 120 min. *Cast:* Don Johnson, Virginia Madsen, Jennifer Connelly, Charles Martin Smith, William Sadler, Jerry Hardin, Barry Corbin, Jack Nance.

Harry Madox (Don Johnson), a cynical drifter and small-time crook, brings danger and excitement to the lives of the citizens of a backwater Texas town in this modern *film noir* thriller. Soon after his arrival, Madox has aroused the interest of the wife (Virginia Madsen) and young accountant (Jennifer Connelly) of his new boss as well as the security guards at the local bank.

HOW TO MAKE LOVE TO A NEGRO WITHOUT GETTING TIRED (France and Canada, 1989)

Pro. Richard Sadler, Ann Burke, and Henry Lange; Angelika Films *Dir.* Jacques W. Benoit *Scr.* Dany Laferrière and Richard Sadler; based on the novel by Laferrière *Cine.* John Berrie *Ed.* Dominique Roy *P.d.* Gaudeline Sauriol *A.d.* Gaudeline Sauriol *Mu.* Manu Dibango *R.t.* 98 min. *Cast:* Isaach de Bankolé, Maka Kotto, Antoine Durand, Jacques Legras, Roberta Bizeau, Miriam Cyr, Marie-Josee Gauthier, Susan Almgren, Alexander Innes, Nathalie Coupal, Isabelle L'Ecuyer, Patricia Tulasne, Tracy Ray, Dominique James, Nathalie Talbot, Julien Poulin, Roy Dupuis, Denys Trudel, Mark Bromilow.

Man (Isaach de Bankolé), a Haitian immigrant newly arrived in Montreal, pursues young white women (exclusively and successfully) while becoming a writer, sharing ideas with his laid-back roommate Bouba (Maka Kotto) and making ruefully bemused observations about various forms of racism.

I COME IN PEACE

Pro. Jeff Young for Vision p.d.g. and Damon/Saunders; Triumph Releasing *Dir.* Craig R. Baxley *Scr.* Jonathan Tydor and Leonard Maas, Jr. *Cine.* Mark Irwin *Ed.* Mark Helfrich *P.d.* Phillip M. Leonard *A.d.* Nino Candido *S.d.* Phillip M. Leonard *Mu.* Jan Hammer *MPAA* R *R.t.* 93 min. *Cast:* Dolph Lundgren, Brian Benben, Betsy Brantley, Matthias Hues, Jay Bilas, Jim Haynie, David Ackroyd, Sherman Howard, Sam Anderson, Mark Lowenthal, Michael J. Pollard.

In this science-fiction thriller, Dolph Lundgren plays Jack Caine, a Houston policeman pursuing local drug lords. Complications arise when a large alien arrives to knock off the drug dealers, steal their heroin, and use it on humans to obtain the endorphins heroin produces in their brains.

I LOVE YOU TO DEATH

Pro. Jeffrey Lurie and Ron Moler for Chestnut Hill; Tri-Star Pictures *Dir.* Lawrence Kasdan *Scr.* John Kostmayer; based on events in the lives of Anthony Toto, Frances Toto, and Barry Giacobe *Cine.* Owen Roizman *Ed.* Anne V. Coates *P.d.* Lilly Kilvert *A.d.* Jon Hutman *S.d.*

Cricket Rowland *Mu.* James Horner *MPAA* R *R.t.* 96 min. *Cast:* Kevin Kline, Tracey Ullman, Joan Plowright, River Phoenix, William Hurt, Keanu Reeves, James Gammon, Jack Kehler.

Based on the true story of Frances Toto's five unsuccessful attempts to murder her husband Tony, this is an amusing and moving love story with a bravura performance by Kevin Kline, backed up by Tracey Ullman's unusually restrained appearance, and William Hurt's low-keyed but eccentric supporting role.

IMPULSE

Pro. Albert S. Ruddy and Andre Morgan; Warner Bros. *Dir.* Sondra Locke *Scr.* John De Marco and Leigh Chapman; based on an original story by De Marco *Cine.* Dean Semler *Ed.* John W. Wheeler *P.d.* William A. Elliott *S.d.* Tom Bugenhagen *Mu.* Michel Colombier *MPAA* R *R.t.* 108 min. *Cast:* Theresa Russell, Jeff Fahey, George Dzundza, Alan Rosenberg, Nicholas Mele, Eli Danker, Charles McCaughan, Lynne Thigpen, Shawn Elliott, Christopher Lawford.

Undercover policewoman Lottie Mason (Theresa Russell) is overworked, financially extended, and sexually harassed by her superior. Burned out and frustrated by her job, Lottie allows herself to be picked up in a bar by a stranger, who turns out to be a drug dealer. Her mistake leads to legal and ethical entanglements beyond her control.

IN THE SPIRIT

Pro. Julian Schlossberg and Beverly Irby for Running River; Castle Hill Productions *Dir.* Sandra Seacat *Scr.* Jeannie Berlin and Laurie Jones *Cine.* Dick Quinlan *Ed.* Brad Fuller *P.d.* Michael C. Smith *A.d.* Jacqueline Jacobson *Mu.* Patrick Williams *MPAA* R *R.t.* 93 min. *Cast:* Elaine May, Marlo Thomas, Peter Falk, Olympia Dukakis, Melanie Griffith, Jeannie Berlin, Chad Burton, Thurn Hoffman.

A Manhattan free spirit named Reva (Marlo Thomas) is hired by a newly arrived West Coast couple, Marianne (Elaine May) and Roger Flan (Peter Falk), to decorate their apartment, which results in the dismantling of their marriage through a series of darkly comic catastrophes. Then, after Reva's prostitute neighbor Crystal (Jeannie Berlin) is murdered, Reva and Marianne must go on the run together before exacting justice and becoming unlikely friends.

INSTANT KARMA

Pro. Dale Rosenbloom, Bruce A. Taylor, and George Edwards for Rosenbloom Entertainment and Desert Wind Films; Metro-Goldwyn-Mayer/United Artists *Dir.* Roderick Taylor *Scr.* Bruce A. Taylor and Dale Rosenbloom *Cine.* Thomas Jewett *Ed.* Frank Mazzola *P.d.* George Edwards and Michele Seffman *Mu.* Joel Goldsmith *MPAA* R *R.t.* 95 min. *Cast:* Craig Sheffer, Chelsea Noble, David Cassidy, Glenn Hirsch, James Gallery, Alan Blumenfeld, William Smith, Orson Bean, Marty Ingels.

Young, successful television writer-producer Zane Smith (Craig Sheffer) lives the Yuppie dream: He has a successful television series, a beautiful Hollywood Hills home, and a red Mercedes. Yet Zane realizes the superficiality of his "successful" life and seeks to escape.

THE INTERROGATION (*Przesluchanie.* Poland, 1982)

Pro. Tadeuz Drewno for Andrezej Wajda Film Studio and Unit X, Zespoly Filmowe; Circle Releasing Corporation *Dir.* Richard Bugajski *Scr.* Richard Bugajski, in association with Janusz Dymek *Cine.* Jacek Petrycki *Ed.* Katarzyna Maciejko *P.d.* Janusz Sosnowksi *R.t.* 122 min. *Cast:* Krystyna Janda, Janusz Gajos, Adam Ferency, Agnieszka Holland, Anna Romantowska, Olgierd Lukaszewicz.

A cabaret singer (Krystyna Janda) is unjustly arrested and held prisoner for five years in this grim prison drama set in Poland in the 1950's. The film pits the state's aggressive inhumanity against the woman's indomitable spirit of resistance as police try to force her to give them information about other, politically important people.

JETSONS: THE MOVIE

Pro. William Hanna and Joseph Barbera for Hanna-Barbera Studios, Wang Film Productions, and Cuckoos Nest Studios; Universal Pictures *Dir.* William Hanna and Joseph Barbera *Scr.* Dennis Marks, with additional dialogue by Carl Sautter; based on the television series *The Jetsons* *Ed.* Pat Foley, Terry W. Moore, and Larry C. Cowan *P.d.* Al Gmuer *Mu.* John Debney *MPAA* G *R.t.* 82 min. *Voices:* George O'Hanlon, Mel Blanc, Penny Singleton, Tiffany, Patric Zimmerman, Don Messick, Jean VanderPyl, Ronnie Schell, Patti Deutsch, Dana Hill, Russi Taylor, Paul Kreppel, Rick Dees.

The combined efforts of the Jetson family produce a happy solution when it is discovered that the Spacely Sprocket Company's new automated Outer Space plant is destroying the environment of thousands of furry little creatures.

JOURNEY OF LOVE (*Viaggio d'amore.* Italy, 1990)

Pro. Ottavio Fabbri; Centaur Releasing *Dir.* Ottavio Fabbri *Scr.* Tonino Guerra *Cine.* Mauro Marchetti *Ed.* Mauro Bonanni *P.d.* Tommaso Bordone *Mu.* Andrea Guerra *R.t.* 98 min. *Cast:* Omar Sharif, Lea Massari, Ciccio Ingrassia, Florence Guerin, Stephane Bonnet.

Omar Sharif and Lea Massari star in this Italian drama as an elderly couple who travel on foot from their small mountain village to the Adriatic Sea, a voyage they have been meaning to make for the last forty years. As they reminisce on their past, they meet various people along the way, foremost a young woman who loses her fiancé to another woman.

THE KILL-OFF

Pro. Lydia Dean Pilcher for Cabriolet; Filmworld International Productions *Dir.* Maggie Greenwald *Scr.* Maggie Greenwald; based on the novel by Jim Thompson *Cine.* Declan Quinn *Ed.* James Y. Kwei *P.d.* Pamela Woodbridge *Mu.* Evan Lurie *MPAA* R *R.t.* 100 min. *Cast:* Loretta Gross, Steve Monroe, Cathy Haase, Andrew Lee Barrett, Jorjan Fox, Jackson Sims.

Seedy, underworld characters populate this pessimistic film, at the center of which resides a malicious old woman who knows all the local gossip and thus sets herself up as a prime murder victim.

KING OF NEW YORK (Italy and USA, 1990)

Pro. Mary Kane for Reteitalia and Scena International; Seven Arts through New Line Cinema *Dir.* Abel Ferrara *Scr.* Nicholas St. John *Cine.* Bojan Bazelli *Ed.* Anthony Redman *P.d.* Alex Tavoularis *A.d.* Stephanie Ziemer *S.d.* Sonja Roth *Mu.* Joe Delia *MPAA* R *R.t.* 103 min. *Cast:* Christopher Walken, David Caruso, Larry Fishburne, Victor Argo, Wesley Snipes, Janet Julian.

Violence and nihilism permeate this chilling film about gangster Frank White (Christopher Walken) who, having been released from prison, returns to take over New York's illegal drug industry. With his demented efforts to take from the rich and give to the poor, White is portrayed as a paradox of good and evil, as the film itself seeks to blur the distinction between the good guys and the bad guys, the cops and the criminals.

LABYRINTH OF PASSION (Spain, 1982)

Pro. Alphaville Production; Cinevista *Dir.* Pedro Almodóvar *Scr.* Pedro Almodóvar *Cine.* Angel L. Fernández *Ed.* José Salcedo *P.d.* Pedro Almodóvar *R.t.* 100 min. *Cast:* Cecilia Roth, Imanol Arias, Helga Line, Marta Fernández-Muro, Angel Alcazar, Antonio Banderas, Agustín Almodóvar, Pedro Almodóvar.

Approximately fifty characters figure in this Madrid-set story, contemporary to the time the film was made (1982), which focuses on the different sexual problems, humorously treated, of these characters, most of whom are wildly promiscuous in a permissive time.

LAMBADA

Pro. Peter Shepherd for Cannon Pictures, in association with Film and Television Company; Warner Bros. *Dir.* Joel Silberg *Scr.* Joel Silberg and Sheldon Renan; based on a story by Silberg *Cine.* Roberto D'Ettorre Piazzoli *Ed.* Marcus Manton *P.d.* Bill Cornford *A.d.* Jack Cloud *Mu.* Greg DeBelles *MPAA* PG *R.t.* 98 min. *Cast:* J. Eddie Peck, Melora Hardin, Shabba-Doo, Ricky Paull Goldin, Basil Hoffman, Dennis Burkley, Keene Curtis.

Kevin (J. Eddie Peck), a Beverly Hills schoolteacher who moonlights as a superb lambada dancer named "Blade," uses his dancing to win the admiration of East Los Angeles Hispanic dropouts so that he can encourage them to pursue their education. One of his students, Sandy (Melora Hardin), finds out about his double life and attempts to provoke trouble, but Kevin is ultimately vindicated by his crusading motives.

THE LASERMAN

Pro. Peter Wang; Original Cinema *Dir.* Peter Wang *Scr.* Peter Wang *Cine.* Ernest Dickerson *Ed.* Grahame Weinbren *P.d.* Lester Cohen *MPAA* R *R.t.* 93 min. *Cast:* Marc Hayashi, Tony Leung, Peter Wang, Joan Copeland, Maryann Urbano, David Shoichi Chan.

Arthur Weiss (Marc Hayashi), a Chinese-American laser scientist, falls into the hands of criminals who attempt to use his lethal technology for their own ends. At the same time, he must contend with his Jewish mother, Ruth (Joan Copeland), who is convinced she has a Chinese soul, and a girlfriend, Janet (Maryann Urbano), who is immersed in New Age mysticism at the expense of a normal relationship. Producer-director-writer Peter Wang attempts comically but ambitiously to treat cross-cultural complexity within the fanciful narrative.

THE LAST OF THE FINEST

Pro. John A. Davis for Davis Entertainment; Orion Pictures *Dir.* John Mackenzie *Scr.* Jere Cunningham, Thomas Lee Wright, and George Armitage; based on a story by Cunningham *Cine.* Juan Ruiz-Anchia *Ed.* Graham Walker *P.d.* Lawrence G. Paull *S.d.* John Thomas Walker *Mu.* Jack Nitzsche and Michael Hoenig *MPAA* R *R.t.* 106 min. *Cast:* Brian Dennehy, Joe Pantoliano, Jeff Fahey, Bill Paxton, Deborra-Lee Furness, Guy Boyd, Henry Darrow, Lisa Jane Persky, Michael C. Gwynne, Henry Stolow, John Finnegan, J. Kenneth Campbell.

In the fight against drugs, Los Angeles police detective Frank Daly (Brian Dennehy) leads a small band of uncorrupted cohorts—Wayne (Joe Pantoliano), Ricky (Jeff Fahey), and Hojo (Bill Paxton). The group, suspended by higher-ups in league with the drug dealers, continues to pursue its investigation, finding that bureaucrats in the police department and federal government are allowing a trade of drugs for arms to supply Central American guerrillas (in a situation vaguely similar to the Iran-Contra affair).

LEATHERFACE: TEXAS CHAINSAW MASSACRE III

Pro. Robert Engelman; New Line Cinema *Dir.* Jeff Burr *Scr.* David J. Schow; based on characters created by Kim Henkel and Tobe Hooper *Cine.* James L. Carter *Ed.* Brent A. Schoenfeld *P.d.* Mick Strawn *Mu.* Jim Manzie and Pat Regan *MPAA* R *R.t.* 81 min. *Cast:* Viggo Mortensen, Kate Hodge, William Butler, Ken Foree, Joe Unger, Tom Everett, Toni Hudson, Miriam Byrd-Nethery, R. A. Mihailoff.

A young couple, Michelle (Kate Hodge) and Ryan (William Butler), en route across the country, are entrapped by a family of cannibals in a remote area of Texas. The plot which develops is virtually a remake of the famous 1974 film *The Texas Chainsaw Massacre*, unlike the first sequel in 1986 by original director Tobe Hooper.

THE LEMON SISTERS

Pro. Joe Kelly for Lightyear Entertainment; Miramax Films *Dir.* Joyce Chopra *Scr.* Jeremy Pikser *Cine.* Bobby Byrne *Ed.* Joseph Weintraub and Michael R. Miller *P.d.* Patrizia Von Brandenstein *Mu.* Dick Hyman *MPAA* PG-13 *R.t.* 93 min. *Cast:* Diane Keaton, Carol Kane, Kathryn Grody, Elliott Gould, Rubén Blades, Aidan Quinn, Estelle Parsons.

Diane Keaton, Carol Kane, and Kathryn Grody star in this serio-comic look at friendship. Set in Atlantic City, *The Lemon Sisters* puts the long-term friendship of three amateur singers to the test when a series of challenges disrupts their lives.

LIFE IS A LONG QUIET RIVER (*La Vie est un long fleuve tranquille.* France, 1988)

Pro. Charles Gassot; MK2 Productions *Dir.* Etienne Chatiliez *Scr.* Florence Quentin and Etienne Chatiliez *Cine.* Pascal Lebègue *Ed.* Chantal Delattre *P.d.* Geoffroy Larcher *Mu.* Gerard Kawczynski *R.t.* 95 min. *Cast:* Benoit Magimel, Hélène Vincent, André Wilms, Christine Pignet, Maurice Mons, Catherine Hiegel, Catherine Jacob, Daniel Gélin, Claire Prévost, Patrick Bouchitey.

In a fit of pique, the mistress, Josette (Catherine Hiegel), of a married man, Doctor Mavial (Daniel Gélin), switches two babies he has delivered. Twelve years later—when the action of the film is set—she becomes angry again and confesses, beginning a series of ruptures and comic reversals of fortune involving two very different families: the comfortable, bourgeois Le Quesnoys and the larcenous, amoral Groseilles.

LISA

Pro. Frank Yablans for United Artists; Metro-Goldwyn-Mayer/United Artists *Dir.* Gary Sherman *Scr.* Gary Sherman and Karen Clark *Cine.* Alex Nepomniaschy and Stanley Lazan *Ed.* Ross Albert *P.d.* Patricia Van Ryker *S.d.* Stewart Kane McGuire *Mu.* Joe Renzetti *MPAA* PG-13 *R.t.* 95 min. *Cast:* Cheryl Ladd, D. W. Moffett, Staci Keanan, Tanya Fenmore, Jeffrey Tambor, Edan Gross, Julie Cobb.

Lisa (Staci Keanan), a fourteen-year-old girl at odds with her divorced mother, Katherine (Cheryl Ladd), over sexual issues and her relative lack of freedom, makes provocative phone calls to a man she does not know named Richard (D. W. Moffett). Richard turns out to be a pathological killer, and when he searches out Lisa, she and her mother both wind up in jeopardy.

LITTLE VEGAS

Pro. Peter Macgregor-Scott for Maclang; I.R.S. Releasing *Dir.* Perry Lang *Scr.* Perry Lang *Cine.* King Baggot *Ed.* John Tintori *P.d.* Michael Hartog *A.d.* Daniel Brewer *Mu.* Mason Daring *MPAA* R *R.t.* 92 min. *Cast:* Anthony John Denison, Catherine O'Hara, Anne Francis, Michael Nouri, Perry Lang, P. J. Ochlan, John Sayles, Bruce McGill, Jay Thomas, Sam McMurray, Michael Talbot, Jerry Stiller.

In this character-study film consisting mainly of intertwining subplots, former gangster Carmine (Anthony John Denison), attempting to escape his past in a Nevada trailer park, is sought out by his gangster brother (Michael Nouri) to help him on a job back east. Carmine is counseled through flashbacks by his now-deceased lover Martha (Anne Francis), and begins to fall in love with her daughter Lexie (Catherine O'Hara). Lexie's brother schemes to buy the trailer park and turn it into a gambling haven called Little Vegas.

LOOSE CANNONS

Pro. Aaron Spelling and Alan Greisman; Tri-Star Pictures *Dir.* Bob Clark *Scr.* Richard Christian Matheson, Richard Matheson, and Bob Clark *Cine.* Reginald H. Morris *Ed.* Stan Cole *P.d.* Harry Pottle *A.d.* William J. Durrell, Jr. *S.d.* Denise Exshaw *Mu.* Paul Zaza *MPAA* R *R.t.* 94 min. *Cast:* Gene Hackman, Dan Aykroyd, Dom DeLuise, Ronny Cox, Nancy Travis,

Robert Prosky, Paul Koslo, Dick O'Neill.

Mac (Gene Hackman), a straightforward, old-fashioned cop, is chagrined to be partnered with Ellis (Dan Aykroyd), who has bouts of brilliance but also suffers episodes of delusion and multiple personalities. Somehow the two partners survive a number of chases and solve a murder case involving a pornographic film of Hitler.

LORD OF THE FLIES

Pro. Ross Milloy for Castle Rock Entertainment, in association with Nelson Entertainment; Columbia Pictures *Dir.* Harry Hook *Scr.* Sara Schiff; based on the novel by Sir William Golding *Cine.* Martin Fuhrer *Ed.* Tom Priestley and Harry Hook *P.d.* Jamie Leonard *Mu.* Philippe Sarde *MPAA* R *R.t.* 90 min. *Cast:* Balthazar Getty, Chris Furrh, Danuel Pipoly.

A group of boys between the ages of eight and thirteen are marooned on a tropical island without adult supervision. Their struggle for survival eventually divides them into two factions, one led by the thoughtful, decent Ralph (Balthazar Getty) and the other by the impulsive, selfish Jack (Chris Furrh). Before an adult presence returns, they regress to a point of bestiality that questions the ultimate nature of humanity.

LOVE AT LARGE

Pro. David Blocker; Orion Pictures *Dir.* Alan Rudolph *Scr.* Alan Rudolph *Cine.* Elliot Davis *Ed.* Lisa Churgin *P.d.* Steven Legler *Mu.* Mark Isham *MPAA* R *R.t.* 97 min. *Cast:* Tom Berenger, Elizabeth Perkins, Anne Archer, Ted Levine, Annette O'Toole, Kate Capshaw, Ann Magnuson, Barry Miller, Kevin J. O'Connor, Neil Young.

In a contemporary urban landscape, private detective Harry Dobbs (Tom Berenger) is hired by elegant Miss Dolan (Anne Archer) to trail her allegedly errant lover, but Harry somehow follows the wrong man, while he is followed by Stella (Elizabeth Perkins), a novice detective hired by his jealous girlfriend Doris (Ann Magnuson). Harry and Stella wind up falling in love, while the wrongly identified suspect (Ted Levine) turns out to be a bigamist with an intriguingly splintered personality.

MACK THE KNIFE

Pro. Stanley Chase; 21st Century Film *Dir.* Menahem Golan *Scr.* Menahem Golan; based on the musical *Die Dreigroschenoper (The Threepenny Opera)* by Bertolt Brecht and Kurt Weill *Cine.* Elemer Ragalyi *Ed.* Alain Jakubowicz *P.d.* Tivadar Bertalan *Mu.* Dov Seltzer *MPAA* PG-13 *R.t.* 120 min. *Cast:* Raul Julia, Richard Harris, Julia Migenes, Roger Daltrey, Rachel Robertson, Clive Revill, Bill Nighy, Erin Donovan, Julie T. Wallace.

The lowlife characters of the famous Brecht-Weill musical *The Threepenny Opera* sing and emote once again in this new cinematic adaptation of the play.

MADHOUSE

Pro. Leslie Dixon for Boy of the Year Productions; Orion Pictures *Dir.* Tom Ropelewski *Scr.* Tom Ropelewski *Cine.* Denis Lewiston *Ed.* Michael Jablow *P.d.* Dan Leigh *A.d.* C. J. Simpson *S.d.* Leslie Rollins *Mu.* David Newman *MPAA* PG-13 *R.t.* 90 min. *Cast:* John Larroquette, Kirstie Alley, Alison LaPlaca, John Diehl, Jessica Lundy, Bradley Gregg, Dennis Miller, Robert Ginty.

An affluent young married couple, Mark (John Larroquette) and Jessie (Kirstie Alley), are abruptly besieged by a horde of unwanted houseguests, including relatives, neighbors, and children. Comic complications, of the broad and often scatological variety, accumulate as the intruders fail to leave.

THE MAHABHARATA (USA and France, 1989)

Pro. Michel Propper for Channel Four Television Company, Les Productions du Troisieme

Etage, and Reiner Moritz Associates; MK2 Productions *Dir.* Peter Brook *Scr.* Jean-Claude Carrière, Marie-Helene Estienne, and Peter Brook; based on the Sanskrit epic poem *Cine.* William Lubtchansky *Ed.* Nicolas Gaster *P.d.* Chloe Obolensky *A.d.* Emmanuel de Chauvigny and Raul Gomez *Mu.* Toshi Tsuchitori, Djamchid Chemirani, Kudsi Erguner, Kim Menzer, and Mahmoud Tabrizi-Zadeh *R.t.* 171 min. *Cast:* Robert Langdon-Lloyd, Antonin Stahly-Vishwanadan, Bruce Myers, Vittorio Mezzogiorno, Andrzej Seweryn, Mamadou Dioume, Jean-Paul Denizon, Mahmoud Tabrizi-Zadeh, Mallika Sarabhai, Miriam Goldschmidt, Erika Alexander, Georges Corraface, Ryszard Cieslak, Helene Patarot, Urs Bihler, Jeffrey Kissoon, Yoshi Oida, Sotigui Kouyate, Tuncel Kurtiz, Tapa Sudana.

Director Peter Brook and writer Jean-Claude Carrière's adaptation of the epic Sanskrit poem offers an absorbing, arrestingly staged distillation of one of the world's great religious and philosophical works. The film's story centers on two families and the rivalry between them that finally erupts into war.

MAMA, THERE'S A MAN IN YOUR BED (*Romuald et Juliette*. France, 1989)
Pro. Jean-Louis Piel and Philippe Carcassonne; Miramax Films *Dir.* Coline Serreau *Scr.* Coline Serreau *Cine.* Jean-Noel Ferragut *Ed.* Catherine Renault *S.d.* Jean-Marc Stehle *R.t.* 110 min. *Cast:* Daniel Auteuil, Firmine Richard, Pierre Vernier, Maxime Leroux, Gilles Privat, Muriel Combeau, Catherine Salviat.

When the cleaning lady Juliette (Firmine Richard) helps the corporate president Romuald (Daniel Auteuil) uncover insider trading and industrial sabotage within his yogurt company, he falls in love with her. She rejects him, telling him how he has taken advantage of her. Eventually, they reach an understanding.

A MAN CALLED SARGE
Pro. Gene Corman; Cannon Pictures *Dir.* Stuart Gillard *Scr.* Stuart Gillard *Cine.* David Gurfinkel *Mu.* Chuck Cirino *MPAA* PG-13 *R.t.* 88 min. *Cast:* Gary Kroeger, Marc Singer, Jennifer Runyon, Gretchen German, Michael Mears, Andy Greenhalgh, Bobby Di Cicco, Travis McKenna, Andrew Bumatai.

During World War II, a company of American soldiers led by Sarge (Gary Kroeger) faces hordes of German soldiers led by Von Kraut (Marc Singer) in North Africa, though the action of the story is played for laughs.

THE MAN INSIDE
Pro. Philippe Diaz; New Line Cinema *Dir.* Bobby Roth *Scr.* Bobby Roth; based on the selected writings of Günter Wallraff *Cine.* Ricardo Aronovitch *Ed.* Luce Grunewaldt *A.d.* Didier Naert *Mu.* Tangerine Dream *MPAA* PG *R.t.* 93 min. *Cast:* Jürgen Prochnow, Peter Coyote, Nathalie Baye, Dieter Laser, Monique Van de Ven, Philip Anglim, Henry G. Sanders, James Laurenson, Sylvie Granotier.

Based on the real-life exploits of West German journalist Günter Wallraff, this political thriller features Jürgen Prochnow as the master of disguise who goes undercover as a reporter for the most powerful newspaper in Europe in order to expose its yellow journalism and propaganda. Wallraff must now write bogus stories conforming with the *Standard*'s policies to maintain his cover, as well as endure the state security's harassment of his family, all in pursuit of justice.

MARTIANS GO HOME
Pro. Michael D. Pariser for Edward R. Pressman Productions; Taurus Entertainment *Dir.* David Odell *Scr.* Charlie Haas; based on the novel by Frederic Brown *Cine.* Peter Deming *Ed.* M. Kathryn Campbell *P.d.* Catherine Hardwicke and Don Day *A.d.* Tom Cortese *S.d.* Gene Serdena *Mu.* Alan Zavod *MPAA* PG-13 *R.t.* 85 min. *Cast:* Randy Quaid, Margaret

Colin, Anita Morris, John Philbin, Gerrit Graham, Barry Sobel, Vic Dunlop.

Just coming into his own as a composer of motion-picture and television themes, Mark (Randy Quaid) creates a theme song for a science-fiction film that his girlfriend Sara (Margaret Colin) inadvertently plays on the radio. Martians are attracted by it and soon invade Earth, peacefully but obnoxiously. Earth's inhabitants come to appreciate how much happier existence was before this happened, while Mark finally finds a way to persuade the green men to leave.

MAY FOOLS (France, 1989)

Pro. Vincent Malle for Nouvelles Editions de Films, TF1 Films, and Ellepi Films; Orion Classics *Dir.* Louis Malle *Scr.* Louis Malle and Jean-Claude Carrière *Cine.* Renato Berta *Ed.* Emmanuelle Castro *Mu.* Stephane Grappelli *MPAA* R *R.t.* 105 min. *Cast:* Michel Piccoli, Miou-Miou, Michel Duchaussoy, Dominique Blanc, Harriet Walter, Bruno Carette, Francois Berleand, Martine Gautier, Paulette Dubost, Hubert Saint-Macary, Rozenn Le Tallec, Renaud Danner, Jeanne Herry-LeClerc, Marcel Bories.

At the time of the student demonstrations of May, 1968, in France, Madame Vieuzac (Paulette Dubost) dies. Her son, Milou (Michel Piccoli), gathers the family together to pay their respects, but the relatives find themselves too obsessed with their own greed, anger, and fear to take much notice of the late family matriarch.

MEN AT WORK

Pro. Cassian Elwes for Epic/Elwes/Euphoria and Epic Prods.; Triumph Releasing *Dir.* Emilio Estevez *Scr.* Emilio Estevez *Cine.* Tim Suhrstedt *Ed.* Craig Bassett *P.d.* Dins Danielsen *A.d.* Patty Klawonn *S.d.* Kathy Curtis Cahill *Mu.* Stewart Copeland *MPAA* PG-13 *R.t.* 99 min. *Cast:* Charlie Sheen, Emilio Estevez, Leslie Hope, Keith David, Dean Cameron, John Getz, Hawk Wolinski, John Lavachielli, Darrell Larson.

Two garbage men (played by real-life brothers Emilio Estevez and Charlie Sheen) stumble upon the body of a murdered politician who was involved in a toxic waste dumping scheme led by a corrupt businessman. Reluctant to go to the police, the two men soon find themselves embroiled in Laurel-and-Hardy-type shenanigans as they try to foil the cover-up.

MR. DESTINY

Pro. James Orr and Jim Cruickshank for Touchstone Pictures in association with Silver Screen Partners IV; Buena Vista *Dir.* James Orr *Scr.* James Orr and Jim Cruickshank *Cine.* Alex Thomson *Ed.* Michael R. Miller *P.d.* Michael Seymour *A.d.* Catherine Hardwicke *S.d.* Naomi Shohan and Kathleen McKernin *Mu.* David Newman *MPAA* PG-13 *R.t.* 112 min. *Cast:* James Belushi, Linda Hamilton, Michael Caine, Jon Lovitz, Hart Bochner, Bill McCutcheon, Rene Russo, Jay O. Sanders, Maury Chaykin, Pat Corley, Douglas Seale, Courteney Cox.

When Larry Burrows (James Belushi) decides that the first thirty-five years of his life have been unfulfilling, a mysterious stranger (Michael Caine) gives him the chance to see what his life would have been like had he hit a home run in a high school championship game instead of striking out.

MR. FROST (Great Britain and France, 1990)

Pro. Xavier Gélin for SVS, Inc., and AAA/Hugo Film; Triumph Films *Dir.* Philippe Setbon *Scr.* Philippe Setbon and Brad Lynch *Cine.* Dominique Brenguier *Ed.* Ray Lovejoy *P.d.* Max Berto *Mu.* Steven Levine *MPAA* R *R.t.* 92 min. *Cast:* Jeff Goldblum, Alan Bates, Kathy Baker, Roland Giraud, Jean-Pierre Cassel, Daniel Gélin, François Negret, Maxime Leroux, Catherine Allegret.

English gentleman Mr. Frost (Jeff Goldblum), an institutionalized mass murderer, wages a mind war on psychiatrist Sarah Day (Kathy Baker), trying to convince her that he is the devil incarnate.

MY BLUE HEAVEN

Pro. Herbert Ross and Anthea Sylbert for Hawn/Sylbert; Warner Bros. *Dir.* Herbert Ross *Scr.* Nora Ephron *Cine.* John Bailey *Ed.* Stephen A. Rotter *P.d.* Charles Rosen *A.d.* Richard Berger *S.d.* Jim Bayliss, Robert Maddy, Nick Navarro, and Don Remacle *Mu.* Ira Newborn *MPAA* PG-13 *R.t.* 95 min. *Cast:* Steve Martin, Rick Moranis, Joan Cusack, Melanie Mayron, Carol Kane, Bill Irwin, William Hickey, Deborah Rush.

This broad comedy deals with the problems that arise when Vinnie Antonelli (Steve Martin), a small-time gangster and participant in the government's Witness Protection Program, tries to adjust to the life-style of a small San Diego suburb. While waiting to testify at two mob trials, he becomes involved in several illegal activities that exasperate local assistant district attorney Hannah Stubbs (Joan Cusack) and the FBI agent, Barney Coopersmith (Rick Moranis), assigned to protect him.

MY UNCLE'S LEGACY (Yugoslavia, 1989)

Pro. Ben Stassen; International Film Exchange Ltd. *Dir.* Krsto Papic *Scr.* Ivan Aralica and Krsto Papic; based on the novel *Framework of Hatred*, by Aralica *Cine.* Boris Turkovic *Ed.* Robert Lisjak *A.d.* Tihomir Piletic *Mu.* Branislav Zivkovic *R.t.* 105 min. *Cast:* Davor Janjic, Alma Prica, Anica Dobra, Miodrag Krivokapic, Fabijan Sovagovic, Filip Sovagovic, Branislav Lecic, Ivo Gregurevic, Radko Polic.

In present-day Yugoslavia, an old man (Miodrag Krivokapic) seeks the forgiveness of his nephew Martin (Davor Janjic), whom he has not seen in thirty-six years. The relationship is explained in an extended flashback when the young Martin, then a student, fell in love with Martha (Alma Prica), a romance that ended tragically. The flashback events take place in the wake of Tito's break with Stalin in 1951, giving a political coloration to a personal story.

NAVY SEALS

Pro. Brenda Feigen and Bernard Williams; Orion Pictures *Dir.* Lewis Teague *Scr.* Chuck Pfarrer and Gary Goldman *Cine.* John A. Alonzo *Ed.* Don Zimmerman *P.d.* Guy J. Comtois and Veronica Hadfield *S.d.* Malcolm Stone and Debra Schutt *MPAA* R *R.t.* 113 min. *Cast:* Charlie Sheen, Michael Biehn, Joanne Whalley-Kilmer, Rick Rossovich, Cyril O'Reilly, Bill Paxton, Dennis Haysbert, Paul Sanchez, Nicholas Kadi, Ron Joseph.

When the elite unit of the Navy SEALs, led by Lieutenant James Curran (Michael Biehn) and sparked by Lieutenant Dale Hawkins (Charlie Sheen), springs into action to save the helicopter crew taken hostage by Mideast terrorists, they discover a cache of Stinger missiles as well as an "Egyptian prisoner" (Nicholas Kadi), who proves to be an important terrorist leader and whom they naïvely release. After several frustrating attempts to track down both, with the aid of Lebanese-American reporter Claire Varens (Joanne Whalley-Kilmer), the SEALs reach a final explosive confrontation with the leading terrorists.

NIGHT OF THE LIVING DEAD

Pro. John A. Russo and Russ Streiner for 21st Century Film, George A. Romero, and Menahem Golan; Columbia Pictures *Dir.* Tom Savini *Scr.* George A. Romero; based on the original screenplay by John A. Russo and Romero *Cine.* Frank Prinzi *Ed.* Tom Dubensky *P.d.* Cletus R. Anderson *A.d.* James Feng *S.d.* Brian J. Stonestreet *Mu.* Paul McCollough *MPAA* R *R.t.* 96 min. *Cast:* Tony Todd, Patricia Tallman, Tom Towles, McKee Anderson, William Butler, Katie Finneran, Bill Mosley, Heather Mazur.

In this color remake of the 1968 cult classic, seven people again are trapped in a farmhouse besieged by an army of flesh-eating zombies and must battle for survival.

NIGHTBREED

Pro. Gabriella Martinelli for Morgan Creek; Twentieth Century-Fox *Dir.* Clive Barker *Scr.* Clive Barker; based on his novel *Cabal* *Cine.* Robin Vidgeon *Ed.* Richard Marden and Mark Goldblatt *P.d.* Steve Hardie *A.d.* Ricky Eyres *Mu.* Danny Elfman *MPAA* R *R.t.* 100 min. *Cast:* Craig Sheffer, Anne Bobby, David Cronenberg, Charles Haid, Hugh Quarshie, Hugh Ross, Doug Bradley, Catherine Chevalier.

In an elaborate horror film, the hero, Boone (Craig Sheffer), plagued by nightmares, travels to the underground city of Midian, where all kinds of monsters which evoke ancient times and tales still exist. He is followed by his girlfriend, Lori (Anne Bobby), and the evil psychiatrist Dr. Decker (David Cronenberg), who has set out to frame him for a series of murders; but in a bizarre way, justice triumphs as Boone becomes a leader of the maligned inhabitants of Midian.

NOBODY'S PERFECT

Pro. Benni Korzen for Panorama Film International, in association with Steve Ader Productions; Moviestore Entertainment *Dir.* Robert Kaylor *Scr.* Annie Korzen and Joel Block *Cine.* Claus Loof *Ed.* Robert Gordon *Mu.* Robert Randles *MPAA* PG-13 *R.t.* 89 min. *Cast:* Chad Lowe, Gail O'Grady, Patrick Breen, Kim Flowers, Todd Schaefer, Robert Vaughn.

In order to get close to his school classmate Shelly (Gail O'Grady), college freshman Steve (Chad Lowe) puts on a wig and make-up and passes for Stephanie. Shelly accepts Steve/Stephanie as her roommate, primarily to get rid of another suitor, Brad (Todd Schaefer). Steve/Stephanie and Shelly become friends and eventually fall in love.

NUNS ON THE RUN (Great Britain, 1990)

Pro. Michael White for HandMade Films; Twentieth Century-Fox *Dir.* Jonathan Lynn *Scr.* Jonathan Lynn *Cine.* Michael Garfath *Ed.* David Martin *P.d.* Simon Holland *A.d.* Clinton Cavers *S.d.* Michael Seirton *Mu.* Yello and Hidden Faces *MPAA* PG-13 *R.t.* 92 min. *Cast:* Eric Idle, Robbie Coltrane, Camille Coduri, Janet Suzman, Doris Hare, Lila Kaye, Robert Patterson, Robert Morgan.

Charlie McManus (Robbie Coltrane) and Brian Hope (Eric Idle) are two bank robbers who double-cross their boss, "Case" Casey (Robert Patterson), once they realize he plans to kill them. Unable to escape, the two men must pose as nuns in a nearby nunnery that has problems of its own.

THE NUTCRACKER PRINCE (Canada, 1990)

Pro. Kevin Gillis for Lacewood Prods.; Warner Bros. *Dir.* Paul Schibli *Scr.* Patricia Watson; based on the book *The Nutcracker and the Mouseking*, by E. T. A. Hoffmann *Ed.* Sue Robertson *A.d.* Peter Moehrle *Mu.* Victor Davies, Kevin Gillis, Jack Lenz, and Peter Ilyich Tchaikovsky *MPAA* G *R.t.* 75 min. *Voices:* Megan Follows, Kiefer Sutherland, Peter Boretski, Mike MacDonald, Phyllis Diller, Peter O'Toole.

In this animated version of the classic E. T. A. Hoffmann story, young Clara (voice of Megan Follows) receives the enchanted Nutcracker from Uncle Drosselmeier (voice of Peter Boretski) at a Christmas party. That night, alone, she witnesses her Nutcracker (voice of Kiefer Sutherland) come to life to battle the Mouseking (voice of Mike MacDonald), after which he escorts her through the magical kingdom of the dolls. He proposes to her, but she refuses and returns to real life where she finds her prince to be Drosselmeier's nephew.

OPPORTUNITY KNOCKS

Pro. Mark R. Gordon and Christopher Meledandri for Brad Grey/Meledandri-Gordon Co. for Imagine Entertainment; Universal *Dir.* Donald Petrie *Scr.* Mitchel Katlin and Nat Bernstein *Cine.* Steven Poster *Ed.* Marion Rothman *P.d.* David Chapman *A.d.* Leslie A. Pope *S.d.*

Derek Hill *Mu.* Miles Goodman *MPAA* PG-13 *R.t.* 105 min. *Cast:* Dana Carvey, Robert Loggia, Todd Graff, Julia Campbell, Milo O'Shea, James Tolkan, Doris Belack, Sally Gracie, Mike Bacarella, John M. Watson, Sr., Beatrice Fredman.

Eddie (Dana Carvey) and Milt (Todd Graff), two young, small-time Chicago con artists, take up residence in a plush suburban home, with Eddie passing himself off as the son of the house's owner (Doris Belack). Complications ensue as Eddie falls in love with Annie (Julia Campbell), the sister of his supposed friend and daughter of a successful business executive, Milt (Robert Loggia). While Eddie feels the pangs of conscience, comedian Carvey (of *Saturday Night Live*) gets to show off his talent for impersonation in a number of different guises.

OVEREXPOSED

Pro. Roger Corman; Concorde Pictures *Dir.* Larry Brand *Scr.* Larry Brand and Rebecca Reynolds *Cine.* David Sperling *Ed.* Patrick Rand *P.d.* Robert Franklin *A.d.* Ella Blakey *S.d.* Tom Margules *Mu.* Mark Governor *MPAA* R *R.t.* 80 min. *Cast:* Catherine Oxenberg, David Naughton, Jennifer Edwards, William Bumiller, John Patrick Reger, Larry Brand, Karen Black.

Television soap opera star Kristen (Catherine Oxenberg) believes she is being stalked by a homicidal fan. While Kristen is harassed verbally by an overzealous viewer, Mrs. Trowbridge (Karen Black), her two co-stars suffer more permanent damage when they use doctored cold cream that proves lethal.

PATHFINDER (Norway, 1988)

Pro. John M. Jacobsen for Filmkameratene and Norsk Film; International Film Exchange *Dir.* Nils Gaup *Scr.* Nils Gaup; based on a Lapp legend *Cine.* Erling Thurmann-Andersen *Ed.* Niels Pagh Andersen *P.d.* Harald Egede-Nissen *Mu.* Nils-Aslak Valkeapaa, Marius Muller, and Kjetil Bjerkestrand *R.t.* 88 min. *Cast:* Mikkel Gaup, Nils Utsi, Svein Scharffenberg, Helgi Skulason, Sara Marit Gaup.

An adaptation of a thousand-year-old Norwegian legend, the film tells the story of a young Lapp teenager (Mikkel Gaup) whose family is murdered and who is forced to guide the killers across the Arctic terrain to another Lapp settlement. The young boy must realize that good will not necessarily triumph over evil and take forceful steps to combat the marauding outlaws.

THE PLOT AGAINST HARRY

Pro. Michael Roemer and Robert M. Young for King Screen Productions; New Yorker Films *Dir.* Michael Roemer *Scr.* Michael Roemer *Cine.* Robert M. Young *Ed.* Terry Lewis and Georges Klotz *A.d.* Howard Mandel *Mu.* Frank Lewin *R.t.* 81 min. *Cast:* Martin Priest, Henry Nemo, Ben Lang, Maxine Woods, Ellen Herbert, Julius Harris.

Harry Plotnik (Martin Priest), a numbers racketeer just out of prison, is torn between seeking revenge against the mobsters who wronged him and going straight—which would involve going into the catering business with his brother-in-law Leo (Ben Lang) as well as reuniting with his wife Kay (Maxine Woods) and children. Ultimately, he finds himself at cross-purposes with the contrasting aspects of his life, which is disastrously but comically collapsing.

PREDATOR II

Pro. Lawrence Gordon, Joel Silver, and John Davis; Twentieth Century-Fox *Dir.* Stephen Hopkins *Scr.* Jim Thomas and John Thomas; based on characters created by Thomas and Thomas *Cine.* Peter Levy *Ed.* Mark Goldblatt *P.d.* Lawrence G. Paull *A.d.* Geoff Hubbard *S.d.* Rick Simpson *Mu.* Alan Silvestri *MPAA* R *R.t.* 102 min. *Cast:* Danny Glover, Gary Busey, Rubén Blades, Maria Conchita Alonso, Bill Paxton, Kevin Peter Hall, Robert Davi, Adam

Baldwin, Kent McCord, Morton Downey, Jr., Calvin Lockhart.

In Los Angeles, 1997, policeman Mike Harrigan (Danny Glover) heads a group of outnumbered law-enforcement officers battling drug dealers, who become confused when the drug dealers are mysteriously and massively killed off, only to find out the cause is an oversized and ferocious alien.

PROBLEM CHILD

Pro. Robert Simonds for Imagine Entertainment; Universal Pictures *Dir.* Denis Dugan *Scr.* Scott Alexander and Larry Karaszewski *Cine.* Peter Lyons Collister *Ed.* Daniel Hanley and Michael Hill *P.d.* George Costello *A.d.* Michael Bingham *S.d.* Denise Pizzini *Mu.* Miles Goodman *MPAA* PG *R.t.* 81 min. *Cast:* John Ritter, Jack Warden, Michael Oliver, Gilbert Gottfried, Amy Yasbeck, Michael Richards, Peter Jurasik, Charlotte Akin.

When Ben (John Ritter) and Flo (Amy Yasbeck) decide to adopt a child, the boy they choose, seven-year-old Junior (Michael Oliver), turns out to be an antisocial misfit who becomes pen pals with a serial killer, Martin Beck (Michael Richards). It takes all the new parents' patience and nurturing skills to bring about a happy ending following numerous comic misadventures.

QUICK CHANGE

Pro. Robert Greenhut and Bill Murray for Devoted; Warner Bros. *Dir.* Howard Franklin and Bill Murray *Scr.* Howard Franklin; based on the novel by Jay Cronley *Cine.* Michael Chapman *Ed.* Alan Heim *P.d.* David Gropman *A.d.* Speed Hopkins *S.d.* Susan Bode *Mu.* Randy Edelman *MPAA* R *R.t.* 88 min. *Cast:* Bill Murray, Geena Davis, Randy Quaid, Jason Robards, Bob Elliott, Dale Grand Esq., Kurtwood Smith, Susannah Bianchi, Tony Shalhoub, Philip Bosco.

Dressed as a clown, Grimm (Bill Murray), a disillusioned city planner, robs a bank successfully and escapes with two accomplices (Geena Davis and Randy Quaid), pursued by Police Chief Rotzinger (Jason Robards). Grimm is frustrated in his attempt to get out of New York City to Kennedy Airport after the trio's automobile is stolen and they get lost in lower Manhattan.

QUIGLEY DOWN UNDER

Pro. Stanley O'Toole and Alexandra Rose for Pathe Entertainment; Metro-Goldwyn-Mayer/United Artists *Dir.* Simon Wincer *Scr.* John Hill *Cine.* David Eggby *Ed.* Adrian Carr and Peter Burgess *P.d.* Ross Major *A.d.* Ian Gracie *Mu.* Basil Poledouris *MPAA* PG-13 *R.t.* 119 min. *Cast:* Tom Selleck, Laura San Giacomo, Alan Rickman, Chris Haywood, Ron Haddrick, Tony Bonner.

In this Western set in Australia, Tom Selleck plays Matthew Quigley, a cowboy from Wyoming hired as a sharpshooter by an Australian rancher, Elliott Marston (Alan Rickman). Conflict ensues when Quigley finds that he is expected to shoot Aborigines, not dingoes as he was led to believe. Beaten up by Marston's men, Quigley is left to die in the desert with a crazy woman (Laura San Giacomo), and the two must struggle back to civilization, fending off the attacks of Marston's henchmen.

THE RAIN KILLER

Pro. Rodman Flender for Califilm; Concord *Dir.* Ken Stein *Scr.* Ray Cunneff *Cine.* Janusz Kaminski *Ed.* Patrick Rand *A.d.* Johan LeTenoux *Mu.* Terry Plumeri *MPAA* R *R.t.* 93 min. *Cast:* Ray Sharkey, David Beecroft, Tania Coleridge, Michael Chiklis, Bill LaVallee, Woody Brown.

In this mediocre thriller, a Los Angeles policeman (Ray Sharkey) hunts down a serial killer whose victims are women from the same support group for recovering substance abusers.

RED SURF

Pro. Richard C. Weinman for Arrowhead Entertainment; Academy Entertainment *Dir.* H. Gordon Boos *Scr.* Vincent Robert; based on a story by Brian Gamble, Jason Hoffs, and Robert *Cine.* John Schwartzman *Ed.* Dennis Dolan *P.d.* Lynda Burbank *Mu.* Sasha Matson *MPAA* R *R.t.* 104 min. *Cast:* George Clooney, Doug Savant, Dedee Pfeiffer, Philip McKeon, Rick Najera, Gene Simmons, Vincent Klyn, Eddie Frias.

Aging surfers Ramar (George Clooney) and Attila (Doug Savant) make a living peddling drugs but finally decide to become law-abiding when Ramar's girlfriend (Dedee Pfeiffer) becomes pregnant. Inevitably, the last big deal designed to free them from their errant way of life puts them in conflict with an East Los Angeles street gang, leading to violence.

REPOSSESSED

Pro. Steve Wizan; Seven Arts through New Line Cinema *Dir.* Bob Logan *Scr.* Bob Logan *Cine.* Michael D. Margulies *Ed.* Jeff Freeman *P.d.* Shay Austin *A.d.* Gae Buckley *S.d.* Lee Cunningham *Mu.* Charles Fox *MPAA* PG-13 *R.t.* 84 min. *Cast:* Linda Blair, Ned Beatty, Leslie Nielsen, Anthony Starke, Lana Schwab, Thom J. Sharp, Melissa Moore.

In this silly spoof of *The Exorcist* (1973), Linda Blair plays housewife Nancy Aglet. Satan flies out of the television and takes possession of her, and the Church agrees to an exorcism only if it can be televised on a popular evangelist show. Thus, possessed Nancy and a retired priest (Leslie Nielsen) battle each other in professional wrestling fashion, with running color commentary, providing the premise for endless sight gags and outlandish jokes.

THE RETURN OF SUPERFLY

Pro. Sig Shore and Anthony Wisdom for Crash Pictures; Triton Pictures *Dir.* Sig Shore *Scr.* Anthony Wisdom *Cine.* Anghel Decca *Ed.* John Muller *P.d.* Jeremie Frank *A.d.* Charlotte Snyder *S.d.* Robert Covelman *Mu.* Curtis Mayfield *MPAA* R *R.t.* 95 min. *Cast:* Nathan Purdee, Margaret Avery, Leonard Thomas, Christopher Curry, Carlos Carrasco, Sam Jackson, David Groh, Tico Wells.

In this third in the *Superfly* series, following *Superfly* (1972) and *Superfly T.N.T.* (1973), Harlem cocaine-peddler Priest (Nathan Purdee) returns to New York City after about ten years abroad in exile and stumbles into a war between the police and a cocaine ring.

REVENGE

Pro. Hunt Lowry and Stanley Rubin for Rastar, in association with New World Entertainment; Columbia Pictures *Dir.* Tony Scott *Scr.* Jim Harrison and Jeffrey Fiskin; based on the novella by Harrison *Cine.* Jeffrey Kimball *Ed.* Chris Lebenzon *P.d.* Michael Seymour and Benjamin Fernandez *A.d.* Tom Sanders and Jorge Sainz *S.d.* Crispian Sallis and Fernando Solorio *Mu.* Jack Nitzsche *MPAA* R *R.t.* 124 min. *Cast:* Kevin Costner, Anthony Quinn, Madeleine Stowe, Tomás Milián, Joaquin Martinez, James Gammon, Jesse Corti, Sally Kirkland.

This adaptation of Jim Harrison's novella details the illicit affair between a retired pilot (Kevin Costner) and a married woman (Madeleine Stowe). Once the woman's husband (Anthony Quinn) discovers the betrayal, he enacts a hideous revenge on the lovers. The wounded former pilot is then forced to seek his own revenge and find his imprisoned lover in a film that attempts to explore the nature of revenge.

ROBOT JOX

Pro. Albert Band for Empire Pictures and Charles Band Prod.; Triumph Films *Dir.* Stuart Gordon *Scr.* Joe Haldeman and Stuart Gordon *Cine.* Mac Ahlberg *Ed.* Ted Nicolaou and Lori Scott Ball *Mu.* Frederic Talgorn *MPAA* PG *R.t.* 84 min. *Cast:* Gary Graham, Anne-Marie Johnson, Paul Koslo, Robert Sampson, Danny Kamekona, Hilary Mason, Michael Alldredge.

In this world of the future, war has been replaced by symbolic combat, where robots, piloted by humans, do battle to settle disputes.

ROGER CORMAN'S FRANKENSTEIN UNBOUND (also known as *Frankenstein Unbound*)

Pro. Roger Corman, Thom Mount, and Kobi Jaeger for Mount Co.; Twentieth Century-Fox *Dir.* Roger Corman *Scr.* Roger Corman, F. X. Feeney, and Ed Neumeier; based on the novel *Frankenstein Unbound*, by Brian W. Aldiss *Cine.* Armando Nannuzzi and Michael Scott *Ed.* Jay Cassidy and Mary Bauer *P.d.* Enrico Tovaglieri *S.d.* Ennio Michettoni *Mu.* Carl Davis Warren, Jr. *MPAA* R *R.t.* 85 min. *Cast:* John Hurt, Raul Julia, Bridget Fonda, Nick Brimble, Catherine Rabett, Jason Patric, Michael Hutchence, Catherine Corman, Mickey Knox, Terri Treas.

In this take-off on the original story, scientist-of-the-future Dr. Joe Buchanan (John Hurt), working to perfect a new kind of weaponry, is accidentally transported to nineteenth century Switzerland. There he meets the legendary Dr. Frankenstein (Raul Julia) and his monster (Nick Brimble), not to mention the author, Mary Godwin (Bridget Fonda), as well as Percy Shelley (Michael Hutchence) and Lord Byron (Jason Patric).

THE ROOKIE

Pro. Howard Kazanjian, Steven Siebert, and David Valdes for Malpaso; Warner Bros. *Dir.* Clint Eastwood *Scr.* Boaz Yakin and Scott Spiegel *Cine.* Jack N. Green *Ed.* Joel Cox *P.d.* Judy Cammer *A.d.* Ed Verreaux *S.d.* Dan May *Mu.* Lennie Niehaus *MPAA* R *R.t.* 121 min. *Cast:* Clint Eastwood, Charlie Sheen, Raul Julia, Sonia Braga, Tom Skerritt, Lara Flynn Boyle.

Nick Pulovski (Clint Eastwood) is a former race-car driver who now works as a grand-theft-auto police sergeant in this high-speed action-adventure. Pulovski is a man of few words, but he vows revenge when his partner is viciously murdered by a ring of automobile-theft criminals. Saddled with an inexperienced young partner, David Ackerman (Charlie Sheen), Pulovski tracks down the operation's nefarious leaders (Raul Julia and Sonia Braga) while teaching Ackerman the true meaning of being a police officer.

ROSALIE GOES SHOPPING (West Germany, 1990)

Pro. Percy Adlon and Eleonor Adlon; Four Seasons Entertainment *Dir.* Percy Adlon *Scr.* Percy Adlon, Eleonor Adlon, and Christopher Doherty *Cine.* Bernd Heinl *Ed.* Jean-Claude Piroue *P.d.* Stephen Lineweaver *Mu.* Bob Telson *MPAA* PG *R.t.* 94 min. *Cast:* Marianne Sagebrecht, Brad Davis, Judge Reinhold, Erika Blumberger, Willy Harlander, Alex Winter, Patricia Zehentmayr, John Hawkes.

This satirical comedy deals with the eccentric behavior of German-born Rosalie Greenspace (Marianne Sagebrecht), her Arkansas husband, Ray (Brad Davis), and their seven children. While Ray supports the family with his job as a crop duster in rural Arkansas, Rosalie indulges in extravagant shopping sprees, manipulating funds from forged and fictitious bank accounts, all with the mostly enthusiastic support of her family and to the dismay of the local priest, who is privy to her illegal endeavors via her daily confessions.

A RUSTLING OF LEAVES (Canada, 1990)

Pro. Nettie Wild, a Kalasikas Production; Empowerment Project *Dir.* Nettie Wild *Scr.* Nettie Wild *Cine.* Kirk Tougas *Ed.* Peter Wintonick *R.t.* 112 min.

Canadian filmmaker Wild attempts an evenhanded documentary about the contemporary problems of the Philippines, where many factions of different political persuasions attempt to assert leadership—including current president Corazon Aquino, who is subtly undermined by the film—and the role of the United States, long a dominant presence there, is beginning to change. Wide-ranging location shooting and a thorough look at different viewpoints, individuals, and aspects of Philippine life mark the film as an ambitious effort.

SANTA SANGRE (also known as *Holy Blood*. Chile, 1990)
Pro. Claudio Argento *Dir.* Alejandro Jodorowsky *Scr.* Roberto Léoni, Alejandro Jodorowsky, and Claudio Argento *Cine.* Daniele Nannunzi *Ed.* Mauro Bonanni *P.d.* Alejandro Luna *Mu.* Simon Boswell *MPAA* R *R.t.* 115 min. *Cast:* Axel Jodorowsky, Blanca Guerra, Guy Stockwell, Thelma Tixou, Sabrina Dennison, Adán Jodorowsky, Faviola Elenka Tapia.

A mass murderer, Fenix (Axel Jodorowsky), who is hospitalized in a Mexico City insane asylum, relives his childhood traumas in a circus milieu. In a fit of jealousy, Fenix's father, El Gran Orgo (Guy Stockwell), hacks off the arms of his trapeze artist wife, Concha (Blanca Guerra). Then, Concha puts together a circus act in which she mimes with her son's hands, the beginning of their partnership in murder.

SHADOW OF THE RAVEN (Iceland, 1990)
Dir. Hrafn Gunnlaugsson *Scr.* Hrafn Gunnlaugsson *Cine.* Esa Vuorinen *Mu.* Hans Erik-Philip *R.t.* 108 min. *Cast:* Renir Brynolfsson, Tinna Gunnlaugsdottir, Egil Olafsson, Sune Mangs.

In a retelling of the Tristan and Isolde legend, two men and one remarkable woman wage a private battle touching on archetypal themes against the backdrop of a Medieval Icelandic village and the competition among its inhabitants to lay claim to an immense dead whale.

A SHOCK TO THE SYSTEM
Pro. Patrick McCormick; Corsair Pictures *Dir.* Jan Egleson *Scr.* Andrew Klavan; based on the novel by Simon Brett *Cine.* Paul Goldsmith *Ed.* Peter C. Frank and William A. Anderson *P.d.* Howard Cummings *A.d.* Robert K. Shaw, Jr. *S.d.* Robert J. Franco *Mu.* Gary Chang *MPAA* R *R.t.* 91 min. *Cast:* Michael Caine, Elizabeth McGovern, Peter Riegert, Swoosie Kurtz, John McMartin, Will Patton, Jenny Wright.

This adaptation of the novel of the same name by Simon Brett deals with the murderous pursuits of Graham Marshall (Michael Caine), who begins killing people who he believes are obstructions to his professional ambitions. The film is a black comedy, taking the corporate philosophy of "get ahead at any cost" to its ultimate, inhumane limits.

SHORT TIME
Pro. Todd Black for Gladden Entertainment Corporation; Twentieth Century-Fox *Dir.* Gregg Champion *Scr.* John Blumenthal and Michael Berry *Cine.* John Connor *Ed.* Frank Morriss *P.d.* Michael Bolton *A.d.* Eric Fraser *S.d.* Peter Hinton *Mu.* Ira Newborn *MPAA* PG-13 *R.t.* 97 min. *Cast:* Dabney Coleman, Matt Frewer, Teri Garr, Barry Corbin, Joe Pantoliano, Xander Berkeley, Rob Roy, Kaj-Erik Eriksen, Deejay Jackson, Shawn Clements.

Policeman Burt Simpson (Dabney Coleman) is misdiagnosed as terminally ill just days before he is due to retire. He is determined to get killed in the line of duty so his estranged wife Carolyn (Teri Garr) and their son Dougie (Kaj-Erik Eriksen) can cash in on his life-insurance policy. His desire for a speedy death turns him into an unwilling hero.

A SHOW OF FORCE
Pro. John Strong, in association with Golden Harvest; Paramount Pictures *Dir.* Bruno Barreto *Scr.* Evan Jones and John Strong; based on the book *Murder Under Two Flags* by Anne Nelson *Cine.* James Glennon *Ed.* Henry Richardson and Sonya Polansky *P.d.* William J. Cassidy and Sonya Polansky *A.d.* William J. Durrell, Jr. *S.d.* Rob McGraw *Mu.* Georges Delerue *MPAA* R *R.t.* 93 min. *Cast:* Amy Irving, Andy Garcia, Lou Diamond Phillips, Robert Duvall, Kevin Spacey, Erik Estrada.

Television newswoman Kate Melendez (Amy Irving), covering the death of two alleged terrorists seeking Puerto Rican independence from the United States, discovers an official whitewash by the government. In fact, the men were murdered by police provocateur Jesus

Fuentes (Lou Diamond Phillips), who framed the pair in a conspiracy masterminded by FBI agent Frank Curtin (Kevin Spacey).

THE SHRIMP ON THE BARBIE

Pro. R. Ben Efraim; Unity Pictures *Dir.* Alan Smithee *Scr.* Grant Morris, Ron House, and Alan Shearman *Ed.* Fred Chulack *MPAA* PG-13 R.t. 86 min. *Cast:* Cheech Marin, Emma Samms, Vernon Wells, Terence Cooper, Jeannette Cronin, Carole Davis, Bruce Spence.

When Carlos Munoz (Cheech Marin), a Mexican-American from Los Angeles, relocates to Sidney, Australia, he finds that the restaurant where he is working is in extreme financial trouble. That situation leads him into posing as the fiancé of an heiress, Alexandra Hobart (Emma Samms), in a bizarre scheme which finally results in the two actually falling in love.

SIDE OUT

Pro. Gary Foster for Jay Weston, in association with Aurora Prods., Inc. and Then Prods.; Tri-Star Pictures *Dir.* Peter Israelson *Scr.* David Thoreau *Cine.* Ron Garcia *Ed.* Conrad Buff *P.d.* Dan Lomino *A.d.* Bruce Crone *S.d.* Cloudia *Mu.* Jeff Lorber *MPAA* PG-13 *R.t.* 100 min. *Cast:* C. Thomas Howell, Peter Horton, Courtney Thorne-Smith, Harley Jane Kozak, Christopher Rydell, Terry Kiser, Randy Stoklos, Kathy Ireland.

Attempting to make his way in the business world, college graduate Monroe (C. Thomas Howell) finds he is happier playing volleyball on the beaches of Southern California. He and his friend Zack (Peter Horton)—who is trying to overcome a gambling addiction—find romance before winning the big tournament.

SKI PATROL

Pro. Philip B. Goldfine and Donald L. West for Epic Productions, Inc.; Triumph *Dir.* Richard Correll *Scr.* Steven Long Mitchell and Craig W. Van Sickle; based on an original story by Mitchell, Van Sickle, and Wink Roberts *Cine.* John Stephens *Ed.* Scott Wallace *P.d.* Fred Weiler *A.d.* Sven L. Nielsen *S.d.* Steven A. Lee *Mu.* Bruce Miller *MPAA* PG *R.t.* 91 min. *Cast:* Roger Rose, Yvette Nipar, Corby Timbrook, T. K. Carter, Leslie Jordan, Martin Mull, Ray Walston, George Lopez, Sean Gregory Sullivan, Paul Feig, Tess.

When an unscrupulous developer, Maris (Martin Mull), tries to sabotage the business of a Utah ski resort owner, Pops Sandrich (Ray Walston), the members of Pops's ski patrol help to set matters right. The story is a frame for comedy and romance in the style of the *Police Academy* series, also overseen by executive producer Paul Maslansky.

SONNY BOY

Pro. Ovidio G. Assonitis for Trans World Entertainment; Triumph Films *Dir.* Robert Martin Carroll *Scr.* Graeme Whifler *Cine.* Roberto D'Ettorre Piazzoli *Ed.* Claudio Cutry *P.d.* Mario Molli *Mu.* Carlo Mario Cordio *MPAA* R *R.t.* 98 min. *Cast:* David Carradine, Paul L. Smith, Brad Dourif, Conrad Janis, Sydney Lassick, Savina Gersak, Alexandra Powers, Steve Carlisle, Michael Griffin.

Sonny Boy (Michael Griffin) has had a fairly gruesome existence to date: He was accidentally kidnaped as a baby when the car he was in was stolen, and his captors, sadistic Slue (Paul L. Smith) and his transvestite wife Pearl (David Carradine), decide to keep him, torture him, and use him as a killing machine. No wonder, then, at age seventeen, he rebels, with the help of the beautiful Rose (Alexandra Powers).

SPACED INVADERS

Pro. Luigi Cingolani for Touchstone Pictures, in association with Silver Screen Partners IV for Smart Egg Pictures-Luigi Cingolani; Buena Vista *Dir.* Patrick Read Johnson *Scr.* Patrick Read Johnson and Scott Lawrence Alexander *Cine.* James L. Carter *Ed.* Seth Gaven and Daniel Gross *P.d.* Tony Tremblay *A.d.* Scott Lawrence Alexander *S.d.* Chava Danielson *Mu.*

David Russo _MPAA_ PG _R.t._ 100 min. _Cast:_ Douglas Barr, Royal Dano, Ariana Richards, J. J. Anderson, Gregg Berger, Wayne Alexander, Kevin Thompson.

A group of Martians, distracted by a Halloween rebroadcast of Orson Welles's famous "War of the Worlds" radio production while passing near Earth, presumes they should be joining the apparent invasion and lands. Kathy (Ariana Richards), a little girl, helps to set them straight and head back to outer space, with the help of a morose old farmer (Royal Dano).

SPEAKING PARTS (Canada, 1990)

Pro. Don Ranvaud for Cinephile _Dir._ Atom Egoyan _Scr._ Atom Egoyan _Cine._ Paul Sarossy _Ed._ Bruce McDonald _A.d._ Linda Del Rosario _Mu._ Mychael Danna _R.t._ 92 min. _Cast:_ Michael McManus, Arsinee Khanjian, Gabrielle Rose, David Hemblen.

Lance (Michael McManus), an unsuccessful actor who works as a hotel gigolo, becomes involved with two women, Clara (Gabrielle Rose), a screenwriter, and Lisa (Arsinee Khanjian), a chambermaid. Betrayals and jealousy account for further narrative turns as Toronto filmmaker Egoyan uses the story as a springboard for mixed media experimentation.

STATE OF GRACE

Pro. Ned Dowd, Randy Ostrow, and Ron Rotholz for Cinehaus; Orion Pictures _Dir._ Phil Joanou _Scr._ Dennis McIntyre _Cine._ Jordan Cronenweth _Ed._ Claire Simpson _P.d._ Patrizia von Brandenstein and Doug Kraner _A.d._ Shawn Hausman and Timothy Galvin _S.d._ George DeTitta _Mu._ Ennio Morricone _MPAA_ R _R.t._ 134 min. _Cast:_ Sean Penn, Ed Harris, Gary Oldman, Robin Wright, John Turturro, John C. Reilly, R. D. Call, Joe Viterelli, Burgess Meredith, Deidre O'Connell, Marco St. John.

State of Grace examines the violent gangsters (known as Westies) of a predominantly Irish, West Side Manhattan neighborhood in the late 1970's. Terry Noonan (Sean Penn) returns to this neighborhood, after a twelve-year absence, as an undercover policeman. He is torn between old loyalties, represented by his manic friend Jackie (Gary Oldman) and complicated by the rekindling of a passionate romance with Jackie's sister, Kathleen (Robin Wright), and his repulsion to the Westies' deranged violence.

STEPHEN KING'S GRAVEYARD SHIFT (also known as _Graveyard Shift_)

Pro. William J. Dunn and Ralph S. Singleton for Larry Sugar; Paramount Pictures _Dir._ Ralph S. Singleton _Scr._ John Esposito; based on the short story by Stephen King _Cine._ Peter Stein _Ed._ Jim Gross and Randy Jon Morgan _P.d._ Gary Wissner _Mu._ Anthony Marinelli and Brian Banks _MPAA_ R _R.t._ 87 min. _Cast:_ David Andrews, Kelly Wolf, Stephen Macht, Brad Dourif, Andrew Divoff, Vic Polizos, Ilona Margolis, Jimmy Woodard, Robert Alan Beuth, Jonathan Emerson.

This latest, rather poor, adaptation of a Stephen King story centers on a small-town textile mill run by fearsome boss Warwick (Stephen Macht) who is continually hiring new workers to replace the ones who mysteriously disappear while cleaning out the mill's rat-infested basement. This B horror film flaunts gruesome special effects, great sets, and a terrific performance by Brad Dourif as an exterminator who loves his work, but overall will prove a disappointment to King fans.

STRAIGHT FOR THE HEART (_A corps perdu._ Canada and Switzerland, 1990)

Pro. Denise Robert, Robin Spry, and Ruth Waldburger for Les Films Telescene and Xanadu Films; L. W. Blair Films _Dir._ Lea Pool _Scr._ Lea Pool and Marcel Beaulieu; based on the novel _Kurwenal_, by Yves Navarre _Cine._ Pierre Mignot _Ed._ Michel Arcand _A.d._ Vianney Gauthier _Mu._ Osvaldo Montes and Antonio Vivaldi _R.t._ 92 min. _Cast:_ Matthias Habich, Johanne-Marie Tremblay, Michel Voita, Jean-François Pichette.

Pierre (Matthias Habich), a photographer just returned from assignment, despairs when he finds his two roommates and lovers, Sarah (Johanne-Marie Tremblay) and David (Michel Voita), have moved out. A relationship with a young deaf mute, Quentin (Jean-François Pichette), may provide the means to bringing Pierre out of his depression.

STRAPLESS (Great Britain, 1989)

Pro. Rick McCallum for Granada Film; Miramax Films *Dir.* David Hare *Scr.* David Hare *Cine.* Andrew Dunn *Ed.* Edward Marnier *P.d.* Roger Hall *A.d.* Martin Hitchcock and Len Huntingford *S.d.* Marianne Ford *Mu.* Nick Bicat *MPAA* R *R.t.* 102 min. *Cast:* Blair Brown, Bruno Ganz, Bridget Fonda, Alan Howard, Michael Gough, Hugh Laurie, Suzanne Burden, Rohan McCullough, Joe Hare.

Dr. Lillian Hempel (Blair Brown), an American expatriate living and working as a physician in London, reluctantly falls in love with a mysterious man, Raymond Forbes (Bruno Ganz), while on vacation in Lisbon. She eventually marries him in secret and is ultimately disillusioned while maturing along with her younger sister Amy (Bridget Fonda), who gives birth to an illegitimate child while becoming a fashion designer.

STREETS

Pro. Andy Ruben; Concorde Pictures *Dir.* Katt Shea Ruben *Scr.* Katt Shea Ruben and Andy Ruben *Cine.* Phedon Papamichael *Ed.* Stephen Mark *P.d.* Virginia Lee *A.d.* Johan Le Tenoux *S.d.* Michelle Munoz *Mu.* Aaron Davis *MPAA* R *R.t.* 83 min. *Cast:* Christina Applegate, David Mendenhall, Eb Lottimer, Starr Andreef, Patrick Richwood, Alan Stock, Kay Lenz.

Dawn (Christina Applegate), a teenage runaway, lives a squalid existence in contemporary Los Angeles as a drug addict and sometime prostitute. Her existence goes from bleak to horrifying when she becomes the special target of a psychotic policeman, Lumley (Eb Lottimer), who preys on street kids.

STRIKE IT RICH (Great Britain and USA, 1990)

Pro. Christine Oestreicher and Graham Easton for Flamingo Pictures; Millimeter Films in association with Ideal Communications Films, British Screen, and the British Broadcasting Company *Dir.* James Scott *Scr.* James Scott; based on the novel *Loser Takes All*, by Graham Greene *Cine.* Robert Paynter *Ed.* Thomas Schwalm *P.d.* Christopher Hobbs *A.d.* Mike Buchanan *Mu.* Shirley Walker and Cliff Eidelman *MPAA* PG *R.t.* 84 min. *Cast:* Robert Lindsay, Molly Ringwald, Sir John Gielgud, Max Wall, Simon de la Brosse, Margi Clarke, Vladek Sheybal, Michel Blanc, Frances De La Tour, Narius Goring.

In the 1950's in London, Ian Bertram (Robert Lindsay), a straitlaced accountant, meets Cary Porter (Molly Ringwald), a vivacious young Briton reared in America. Thanks to some clever work by Ian at his job, the two are invited to Monte Carlo by a business executive, Dreuther (Sir John Gielgud), but, when he fails to meet them there, their troubles begin as Ian is overtaken by a gambling obsession. After many complications, the couple's love for each other motivates Ian to forsake convoluted schemes of wealth and revenge and win back Cary.

SURVIVAL QUEST

Pro. Roberto Quezada for Starway International; Metro-Goldwyn-Mayer/United Artists *Dir.* Don Coscarelli *Scr.* Don Coscarelli *Cine.* Daryn Okada *Ed.* Don Coscarelli *P.d.* Andrew Siegel *Mu.* Fred Myrow and Christopher L. Stone *MPAA* R *R.t.* 96 min. *Cast:* Lance Henriksen, Mark Rolston, Steve Antin, Michael Allen Ryder, Paul Provenza, Ben Hammer, Dominic Hoffman, Traci Lin, Dermot Mulroney, Catherine Keener, Ken Daly, Reggie Bannister.

Two rival wilderness survival groups, the good guys led by Hank (Lance Henriksen), who emphasize a peaceful coexistence with nature, and the bad guys, led by Jake (Mark Rolston), who specialize in machismo and psychosis, clash on an outing when bad-guy survivalist Raider (Steve Antin) shoots Hank and knifes Jake, then proceeds to hunt down the rest of Hank's group to eliminate them as witnesses.

TAKING CARE OF BUSINESS

Pro. Geoffrey Taylor for Hollywood Pictures; Buena Vista *Dir.* Arthur Hiller *Scr.* Jill Mazursky and Jeffrey Abrams *Cine.* David M. Walsh *Ed.* William Reynolds *P.d.* Jon Hutman *S.d.* Donald Krafft and Linda Spheeris *Mu.* Stewart Copeland *MPAA* R *R.t.* 103 min. *Cast:* James Belushi, Charles Grodin, Anne DeSalvo, Loryn Locklin, Stephen Elliott, Hector Elizondo, Veronica Hamel, Mako, Gates McFadden, John de Lancie, Thom Sharp.

Convict and car thief Jimmy Dworski (James Belushi) escapes prison in hopes of seeing the Chicago Cubs win the World Series. He finds the lost filofax of businessman Spencer Barnes (Charles Grodin) and uses it to assume Barnes's identity, leaving Barnes without his home, his job, and possibly his marriage.

TALES FROM THE DARKSIDE: THE MOVIE

Pro. Richard P. Rubinstein and Mitchell Galin; Paramount Pictures *Dir.* John Harrison *Scr.* Anthology film with many authors: "Lot 249," by Michael McDowell, based on a story by Sir Arthur Conan Doyle; "Cat from Hell," by George A. Romero, based on a story by Stephen King; "Lover's Vow," by Michael McDowell; "The Wraparound Story," by Michael McDowell *Cine.* Robert Draper *Ed.* Harry B. Miller III *P.d.* Ruth Ammon *Mu.* Jim Manzie, Pat Regan, Chaz Jankel, John Harrison, and Donald A. Rubinstein *MPAA* R *R.t.* 93 min. *Cast:* Deborah Harry, Christian Slater, David Johansen, William Hickey, James Remar, Rae Dawn Chong, Robert Klein, Steve Buscemi, Matthew Lawrence, Robert Sedgwick, Julianne Moore, Michael Deak.

A youth (Matthew Lawrence), about to be roasted alive by a housewife (Deborah Harry), stalls his fate by recounting horror tales about a mummy, a diabolical cat, and a gargoyle. In the end he tricks the housewife and roasts her instead.

THE TALL GUY (Great Britain, 1989)

Pro. Paul Webster for LWT and Virgin Vision, in association with Working Title Production; Miramax Films *Dir.* Mel Smith *Scr.* Richard Curtis *Cine.* Adrian Biddle *Ed.* Dan Rae *P.d.* Grant Hicks *A.d.* Andrew Rothschild *Mu.* Peter Brewis *R.t.* 92 min. *Cast:* Jeff Goldblum, Emma Thompson, Rowan Atkinson, Emil Wolk, Geraldine James, Kim Thomson, Susan Field, Hugh Thomas.

In this quirky romantic comedy, Jeff Goldblum stars as Dexter King, a struggling American actor in London, who finds love and a job, and ultimately, a happy ending.

THINK BIG

Pro. Brad Krevoy and Steven Stabler for Motion Picture Corporation of America; Concorde Pictures *Dir.* Jon Turtletaub *Scr.* Edward Kovach, David Tausik, and Jon Turtletaub; based on a story by R. J. Robertson and Jim Wynorski *Cine.* Mark Morris *Ed.* Jeff Reiner *P.d.* Robert Schullenberg *Mu.* Michael Sembello and Hilary Bercovici *MPAA* PG-13 *R.t.* 86 min. *Cast:* Ari Meyers, Peter Paul, David Paul, Martin Mull, David Carradine, Claudia Christian, Richard Kiel, Richard Moll, Michael Winslow.

Twin brothers Rafe and Vic (Peter Paul and David Paul, real-life bodybuilding twins known as the Barbarian Brothers) are truck drivers helping a beautiful and brilliant sixteen-year-old runaway, Holly (Ari Meyers), while trying to elude a host of villains and a repo man, John Sweeney (David Carradine).

THROUGH THE WIRE

Pro. Nina Rosenblum for Amnesty International; Original Cinema *Dir.* Nina Rosenblum

Scr. Nina Rosenblum and Carlos Norman *Mu.* Nona Hendryx *Documentary narration:* Susan Sarandon.

This documentary focuses on three radical political activists, Susan Rosenberg, Alejandrina Torres, and Sylvia Baraldini. These women, all given severe prison sentences, were incarcerated for two years in a high-security "control unit" in Lexington, Kentucky. There they suffered extreme sensory-deprivation, isolation, and twenty-four-hour video camp surveillance until political and human-rights groups intervened.

TO PROTECT MOTHER EARTH: BROKEN TREATY II

Pro. Joel L. Freedman; AFI, Warner Bros. *Dir.* Joel L. Freedman *Cine.* Robert Fiore, Mark Peterson, and Sandi Sissel *Ed.* Sarah Stein *R.t.* 60 min. *Narration:* Robert Redford.

The losing battle of the Western Shoshone Indians to retain their claim to some 24 million acres in Nevada is the subject of this documentary narrated by Robert Redford. Throughout, the natural beauty of the land and the Shoshone's simple life-style within its borders are contrasted with the U.S. government's present use of the area as a nuclear test site.

TORN APART

Pro. Danny Fisher and Jerry Menkin; Castle Hill Productions *Dir.* Jack Fisher *Scr.* Marc Kristal; based on the novel *Forbidden Love*, by Chayym Zeldis *Cine.* Barry Markowitz *Ed.* Michael Garvey *A.d.* Yoram Shaier *Mu.* Peter Arnow *MPAA* R *R.t.* 85 min. *Cast:* Adrian Pasdar, Cecilia Peck, Machram Huri, Arnon Zadok, Margit Polak, Michael Morim, Amos Lavi, Hanna Azulai, Barry Primus.

Ben (Adrian Pasdar), an Israeli, and Laila (Cecilia Peck), an Arab, form a bond in their youthful years and fall in love when they meet again as young adults. Despite the opposition of both families and the mistrust within their respective cultures, they attempt to go forward with their relationship. As in classical modes, though, the romance ends tragically.

TORRENTS OF SPRING (Italy and France, 1990)

Pro. Angelo Rizzoli, in association with Curzon Films Distributors, Ltd.; Millimeter Films *Dir.* Jerzy Skolimowski *Scr.* Jerzy Skolimowski and Arcangelo Bonaccorso; based on the novel by Ivan Turgenev *Cine.* Dante Spinotti and Witold Sobocinski *Ed.* Cesare D'Amico *P.d.* Francesco Bronzi *Mu.* Stanley Myers *R.t.* 98 min. *Cast:* Timothy Hutton, Nastassja Kinski, Valeria Golino, William Forsythe, Urbano Barberini, Francesca De Sapio.

A nineteenth century Russian nobleman, Dmitri Sanin (Timothy Hutton), passing through Mainz, Germany, falls in love with and proposes to the innocent Gemma Rosselli (Valeria Golino). While selling off a parcel of his land in order to take care of Gemma and her family, Sanin meets and is seduced by prospective buyer Maria Polozova (Natassja Kinski). Ultimately, Sanin loses both women as a result of his indiscretion with Maria.

TOUCH OF A STRANGER

Pro. Hakon Gundersen and Andrea Stone Guttfreund; Raven-Star Pictures *Dir.* Brad M. Gilbert *Scr.* Joslyn Barnes and Brad M. Gilbert *Cine.* Michael Negrin *Ed.* William Goldenberg *P.d.* Richard Sherman *Mu.* Jack Alan Goga *MPAA* R *R.t.* 87 min. *Cast:* Shelley Winters, Anthony Nocerino, Danny Capri, Haley Taylor-Block, Leslie Sachs.

A wounded criminal (Anthony Nocerino) holds an elderly recluse hostage (Shelley Winters) in her home (she is actually happy to have some company), and the two develop a strange mother/son relationship.

THE TRAVELING PLAYERS (*O Thiassos.* Greece, 1974)

Pro. Giorgios Samiotis for Giorgios Papalios; Kino International *Dir.* Theo Angelopoulos *Scr.* Theo Angelopoulos *Cine.* Giorgos Arvanitis *Ed.* Takis Davropoulos and Giorgios Triandfillou *A.d.* Mikes Karapiperis *S.d.* Mikes Karapiperis *Mu.* Loulianos Kilaidonis *R.t.*

230 min. *Cast:* Stratos Pachis, Eva Kotamanidou, Petros Zarkadis, Aliki Georgouli, Vangelis Kazan.

Against the backdrop of civil unrest in Greece from 1939 to 1952, the film charts the lives of a group of itinerant actors who travel from town to town playing a nineteenth century melodrama. These performers, mostly the members of a single family, play out the betrayals, vengeance, and death of the classical tragedy of the House of Atreus in modern times.

TREMORS

Pro. S. S. Wilson and Brent Maddock for No Frills/Wilson-Maddock; Universal *Dir.* Ron Underwood *Scr.* S. S. Wilson and Brent Maddock; based on a story by Wilson, Maddock, and Ron Underwood *Cine.* Alexander Gruszynski *Ed.* O. Nicholas Brown *P.d.* Ivo Cristante *A.d.* Don Maskovich *S.d.* Paul Ford *Mu.* Ernest Troost *MPAA* PG-13 *R.t.* 96 min. *Cast:* Kevin Bacon, Fred Ward, Finn Carter, Michael Gross, Reba McEntire, Bobby Jacoby, Victor Wong, Charlotte Stewart.

This parody of 1950's science-fiction films is set in Perfection, Nevada, a desert town of fourteen people faced with an unexpected crisis and no plan for action. Two local handymen (Kevin Bacon and Fred Ward) discover that recent seismographic irregularities charted by a visiting geologist (Finn Carter) are caused by giant carnivorous worms. The monstrously tentacled worms begin to rise from their subterranean haunt and attempt to devour everyone in the isolated valley.

TUNE IN TOMORROW . . .

Pro. John Fiedler and Mark Tarlov for Polar Entertainment; Cinecom Entertainment *Dir.* Jon Amiel *Scr.* William Boyd; based on the novel *Aunt Julia and the Scriptwriter,* by Mario Vargas Llosa *Cine.* Robert Stevens *Ed.* Peter Boyle *P.d.* Jim Clay *A.d.* Chris Seagers *S.d.* Jeanette Scott *Mu.* Wynton Marsalis *MPAA* PG-13 *R.t.* 105 min. *Cast:* Barbara Hershey, Peter Falk, Keanu Reeves, Bill McCutcheon, Patricia Clarkson, Jerome Dempsey, Peter Gallagher, Dan Hedaya, Buck Henry, Hope Lange, John Larroquette, Elizabeth McGovern, Robert Sedgwick, Henry Gibson, Richard Portnow.

Radio scriptwriter Pedro Carmichael (Peter Falk) plays cupid to Martin (Keanu Reeves), an aspiring writer, and his worldly Aunt Julia (Barbara Hershey), then eavesdrops on them and uses their dialogues in his soap opera skits.

TWILIGHT OF THE COCKROACHES (Japan, 1990)

Pro. Hiroaki Yoshida and Hidenori Taga for TYO/Kitty Entertainment Group and Gaga Communications; Streamline Pictures *Dir.* Hiroaki Yoshida *Scr.* Hiroaki Yoshida *A.d.* Kiichi Ichida *Mu.* Morgan Fisher *R.t.* 105 min. *Cast:* Kaoru Kobayashi, Setsuko Karamsumaru.

Combining animation and live-action, this fable anthropomorphizes cockroaches in telling a story of young love threatened by humans— principally the girlfriend (Setsuko Karamsumaru) of a young man (Kaoru Kobayashi) at whose home the cockroaches live. Many of the cockroaches do die before the hero and heroine and some others prevail in this sentimental allegorical fantasy.

TWISTED JUSTICE

Pro. David Heavener for Hero Films Inc.; Seymour Borde and Associates *Dir.* David Heavener *Scr.* David Heavener *Cine.* David Hue *Ed.* Gregory Schorer *A.d.* Dian Skinner *MPAA* R *R.t.* 90 min. *Cast:* David Heavener, Erik Estrada, Karen Black, Shannon Tweed, Jim Brown, James Van Patten Luther, Don Stroud.

In the year 2020 in Los Angeles, guns have been outlawed even to the police, but James Tucker (David Heavener), a renegade police officer with society's best interests at heart, still carries a real gun (rather than the tranquilizing weapons in general use). His foresight proves to be fortuitous when a crazed but brilliant criminal overcomes the prevailing crime-fighting methods and it is up to Tucker to stop him in a traditional manner.

TWISTED OBSESSION (Spain, 1990)

Pro. Andrés Vincente Gómez; IVE *Dir.* Fernando Trueba *Scr.* Fernando Trueba and Manolo Matji *Cine.* José Luis Alcaine *Ed.* Carmen Frías *A.d.* Pierre-Louis Thevenet *Mu.* Antoine Duhamel *MPAA* R *R.t.* 107 min. *Cast:* Jeff Goldblum, Miranda Richardson, Anemone, Dexter Fletcher, Daniel Ceccaldi, Liza Walker, Jerome Natali, Arielle Dombasle, Asuncion Blaguer.

Dan Gillis (Jeff Goldblum), a screenwriter, becomes involved in an art film against the advice of his crippled agent, Marilyn (Miranda Richardson). Dan is drawn into the project because of his fascination with the younger sister, Jenny (Liza Walker), of the director, Malcolm (Dexter Fletcher)—a fascination that becomes an obsession and complicates an already dramatically tangled web of relationships and conflicting motives.

TWISTER

Pro. Wieland Schulz-Keil; Vestron *Dir.* Michael Almereyda *Scr.* Michael Almereyda; based on the novel "Oh!" by Mary Robison *Cine.* Renato Berta *Ed.* Roberto Silvi *P.d.* David Wasco *A.d.* Don Bishop *S.d.* Dianna Freas *Mu.* Hans Zimmer *MPAA* PG-13 *R.t.* 94 min. *Cast:* Harry Dean Stanton, Suzy Amis, Crispin Glover, Dylan McDermott, Jenny Wright, Charlaine Woodard, Lois Chiles, William Burroughs.

In this quirky, somewhat surreal, and intelligent comedy, several members of a rich, bored Kansas family—including a soda-pop magnate (Harry Dean Stanton), his Byronesque "artist" son (Crispin Glover), and an unwed-mother daughter (Suzy Amis)—live through a tornado, which does little to dispel their continuing ennui.

THE UNBELIEVABLE TRUTH

Pro. Bruce Weiss and Hal Hartley; Action Features *Dir.* Hal Hartley *Scr.* Hal Hartley *Cine.* Michael Spiller *Ed.* Hal Hartley *P.d.* Carla Gerona *S.d.* Sarah Stoleman *Mu.* Jim Coleman *R.t.* 98 min. *Cast:* Adrienne Shelly, Robert Burke, Christopher Cooke, Julia McNeal, Gary Sauer, Mark Bailey, Katherine Mayfield.

Producer-director-writer Hal Hartley's first feature confidently uses experimental devices in telling a slim story of a very independent girl, Audry (Adrienne Shelly), and a taciturn mechanic, John (Robert Burke). Along with the conscious stylization, the film brings humor to its account of offbeat relationships.

THE VANISHING (The Netherlands, 1988)

Pro. Anne London and George Sluizer for Egg Films; Tara Distribution *Dir.* George Sluizer *Scr.* Tim Krabbe *Cine.* Toni Kuhn *Ed.* George Sluizer *S.d.* Santiago Tsidro Pin *Mu.* Henry Vrienten *R.t.* 107 min. *Cast:* Gene Bervoets, Johanna Ter Steege, Bernard-Pierre Donnadieu, Gwen Exkhaus.

Two young lovers (Gene Bervoets and Johanna Ter Steege) encounter unexpected peril on their French vacation during the Tour de France bicycle race. At a roadside rest stop, the girl's sudden disappearance sparks a three-year search by her boyfriend which culminates in a Hitchcockian revelation of the evil that men do.

VITAL SIGNS

Pro. Laurie Perlman and Cathleen Summers for Perlman Productions; Twentieth Century-Fox *Dir.* Marisa Silver *Scr.* Larry Ketron and Jeb Stuart; based on a story by Ketron *Cine.* John Lindley *Ed.* Robert Brown and Danford B. Greene *P.d.* Todd Hallowell *S.d.* Dan May *Mu.* Miles Goodman *MPAA* R *R.t.* 98 min. *Cast:* Adrian Pasdar, Diane Lane, Jimmy Smits, Norma Aleandro, William Devane, Jack Gwaltney, Laura San Giacomo, Jane Adams,

Tim Ransom, Bradley Whitford.

Third-year medical students, out of the classroom and working in a hospital, include charming and privileged Michael Chatham (Adrian Pasdar), intense underdog Kenny Rose (Jack Gwaltney), charismatic Gina Wyler (Diane Lane), and the more low-key Suzanne Maloney (Jane Adams). While enduring pressure and competition, the members of the group find themselves in challenging romantic situations and learn important lessons about life.

WAIT FOR ME IN HEAVEN (*Esperame en el cielo.* Spain, 1990)
Pro. Jose Calleja, in association with Televisión Española; MD Wax/Courier Films *Dir.* Antonio Mercero *Scr.* Horacio Valcarcel, Roman Gubern, and Antonio Mercero *Cine.* Manuel Rojas *Ed.* Rosa G. Salgado *Mu.* Carmelo A. Bernaola *R.t.* 111 min. *Cast:* Jose Soriano, Chus Lampreave, Jose Sazatornil.

Madrid shopkeeper Alonso Paulino (Jose Soriano) is kidnapped and trained by government agents to serve as Spanish dictator Francisco Franco's double.

WAIT UNTIL SPRING, BANDINI
Pro. Orion Classics *Dir.* Dominique Deruddere *Scr.* Dominique Deruddere *Cine.* Jean-Francois Robin *Ed.* Ludo Troch *Mu.* Angelo Badalamenti *MPAA* PG *R.t.* 100 min. *Cast:* Joe Mantegna, Faye Dunaway, Ornella Muti, Michael Bacall, Burt Young, Daniel Wilson, Alex Vincent.

In financial difficulties and dissatisfied with his life, Svevo Bandini (Joe Mantegna) deserts his wife, Maria (Ornella Muti), and children in the winter of 1928 and lives with a woman, Mrs. Hildegarde (Faye Dunaway), who has employed him as a bricklayer. Sometime afterward, though, he decides to return home and attempt to affect a reconciliation.

WAITING FOR THE LIGHT
Pro. Caldecot Chubb and Ron Bozman for Epic Productions and Sarlui/Diamant; Triumph Films *Dir.* Christopher Monger *Scr.* Christopher Monger *Cine.* Gabriel Beristain *Ed.* Eva Gardos *P.d.* Phil Peters *Mu.* Michael Storey *MPAA* PG *R.t.* 94 min. *Cast:* Teri Garr, Shirley MacLaine, Clancy Brown, Vincent Schiavelli, Hillary Wolf, Colin Baumgartner, John Bedford Lloyd, Jeff McCracken, Robin Ginsburg.

Trying to start a new life, single mother Kay (Teri Garr) moves from big-city Chicago to a small town with her two kids and wacky Aunt Zena (Shirley MacLaine). When Zena and the kids play a prank on their old neighbor, he thinks he's seen an angel and the town enters on a fervent religious conversion as pilgrims flock there to be close to the miracle.

WELCOME HOME, ROXY CARMICHAEL
Pro. Penney Finkelman Cox for ITC Entertainment Group; Paramount Pictures *Dir.* Jim Abrahams *Scr.* Karen Leigh Hopkins *Cine.* Paul Elliott *Ed.* Bruce Green *P.d.* Dena Roth *A.d.* John Myhre, Rosemary Brandenburg, and Nina Ruscio *S.d.* Tom Talbert and Maria Nay *Mu.* Thomas Newman *MPAA* PG-13 *R.t.* 98 min. *Cast:* Winona Ryder, Jeff Daniels, Laila Robins, Thomas Wilson Brown, Joan McMurtrey, Graham Beckel, Frances Fisher, Robby Kiger, Dinah Manoff, Sachi Parker, Stephen Tobolowsky.

Fifteen-year-old Dinky Bossetti (Winona Ryder), who was adopted at birth, decides that her biological mother must be Roxy Carmichael, the small-town celebrity who is returning from Hollywood for the first time in fifteen years. As the teenaged misfit makes plans for her potentially glamorous future, Roxy's former lovers face their own less-than-glamorous pasts and nostalgic passions.

WHERE THE HEART IS
Pro. John Boorman for Touchstone Pictures, in association with Silver Screen Partners IV; Buena Vista *Dir.* John Boorman *Scr.* John Boorman and Telsche Boorman *Cine.* Peter Su-

schitzky *Ed.* Ian Crafford *P.d.* Carol Spier *Mu.* Peter Martin *MPAA* R *R.t.* 94 min. *Cast:* Dabney Coleman, Uma Thurman, Joanna Cassidy, Crispin Glover, Suzy Amis, Christopher Plummer, David Hewlitt, Maury Chaykin.

In contemporary Manhattan, a demolition tycoon, Stewart McBain (Dabney Coleman), becomes tired of the indolent ways of his grown-up children, Daphne (Uma Thurman), Chloe (Suzy Amis), and Jimmy (David Hewlett), so he sends them out to a sleazy residence in Brooklyn where they must try to make it on their own. Artistic types, they do forge a fairly good life for themselves, and ultimately, they are joined in the less affluent environment by their father, who has suffered business reverses. Further fanciful developments set everything right.

THE WHITE GIRL

Pro. James Cannady for Tony Brown Productions; Tony Brown Productions *Dir.* Tony Brown *Scr.* Tony Brown *Cine.* Joseph M. Wilcots *Ed.* Tony Vigna *S.d.* Bill Webb *Mu.* George Porter Martin and Jimmy Lee Brown *MPAA* PG-13 *R.t.* 88 min. *Cast:* Troy Beyer, Taimak, Teresa Yvon Farley, O. L. Duke, DiAnne B. Shaw, Petronia Paley, Don Hannah, Donald Craig.

When Kim Barnes (Troy Beyer), a college student, becomes hooked on cocaine, it appears that she will recover with the support of fellow black students Bob (Taimak) and Debbie (DiAnne B. Shaw). Her roommate Vanessa (Teresa Yvon Farley), however, in the grip of the drug herself and obsessed with her ambitions for a television career, causes Kim greater problems than ever until a happy ending finds Kim overcoming the machinations of a host of mainly white villains.

WHY ME?

Pro. Marjorie Israel for Carolina Productions and Epic Pictures; Triumph *Dir.* Gene Quintano *Scr.* Donald E. Westlake and Leonard Maas, Jr.; based on the novel by Westlake *Cine.* Peter Deming *Ed.* Alan Balsam *P.d.* Woody Crocker *Mu.* Basil Poledouris *MPAA* R *R.t.* 88 min. *Cast:* Christophe Lambert, Christopher Lloyd, Kim Greist, J. T. Walsh, Michael J. Pollard, Tony Plana, John Hancock, Wendel Meldrum, Rene Assam, Gregory Millar, Lawrence Tierney, Jill Terashita, Thomas Callaway.

Gus Cardinal (Christophe Lambert), an amiable safecracker, steals a valuable ruby—aided by his friend Bruno (Christopher Lloyd) and girlfriend, June (Kim Greist). Afterward, various groups on both sides of the law pursue him, trying to gain possession of the stone.

WILD ORCHID

Pro. Mark Damon and Tony Anthony for Vision International; Triumph *Dir.* Zalman King *Scr.* Patricia Louisianna Knop and Zalman King *Cine.* Gale Tattersall *Ed.* Marc Grossman and Glenn A. Morgan *P.d.* Carlos Conti *Mu.* Geoff MacCormack and Simon Goldenberg *MPAA* R *R.t.* 103 min. *Cast:* Mickey Rourke, Jacqueline Bisset, Carre Otis, Assumpta Serna, Bruce Greenwood, Oleg Vidov, Milton Goncalves.

In this story, where pornography becomes the style and the substance, a young woman named Emily (Carre Otis) travels to Brazil to work as an attorney and oversee a large real-estate sale. There she meets an international playboy, Wheeler (Mickey Rourke), who leads her to understand the true nature of her own sexuality.

WITHOUT YOU I'M NOTHING

Pro. Jonathan D. Krane; Management Company Entertainment Group *Dir.* John Boskovich *Scr.* Sandra Bernhard and John Boskovich *Cine.* Joseph Yacoe *Ed.* Pamela Malouf-Cundy *P.d.* Kevin Rupnik *A.d.* Kevin Adams *S.d.* Douglas A. Mowat *Mu.* Patrice Rushen *MPAA* R *R.t.* 94 min. *Cast:* Sandra Bernhard, John Doe, Steve Antin, Lu Leonard, Ken Foree, Cynthia Bailey, Denise Vlasis.

A companion piece to Sandra Bernhard's one-woman stage show, the film contains Bernhard's comic musings on her life as a media favorite. Through stand-up comedy, musical numbers, and dramatic scenes, director John Boskovich and Bernhard provide their view on popular culture in the 1960's, 1970's, and 1980's.

YAABA (France; Switzerland; and Burkina Faso, West Africa; 1989)

Pro. Freddy Denaës, Michel David, Pierre-Alain Meier, and Idrissa Ouédraogo for Arcadia Films, Les Films de L'Avenir, and Thelma Film AG; New Yorker Films *Dir.* Idrissa Ouédraogo *Scr.* Idrissa Ouédraogo *Cine.* Matthias Kälin *Ed.* Loredana Cristelli *Mu.* Francis Bebey *R.t.* 90 min. *Cast:* Fatimata Sanga, Noufou Ouédraogo, Roukietou Barry, Adama Ouédraogo, Amadé Toure, Sibidou Ouédraogo, Adama Sidibe, Rasmané Ouédraogo.

When two twelve-year-old children, Bila (Noufou Ouédraogo) and Nopoko (Roukietou Barry), befriend an old woman (Fatimata Sanga), they learn that she is considered a witch by the other villagers, who discourage them from a relationship with her. Undeterred, they call her Yaaba ("grandmother") and prove her goodness when she finds a way to save Nopoko from a serious illness. The story unfolds against a background of simple village life in Burkina Faso in West Africa.

THE YEN FAMILY (Japan, 1990)

Dir. Yojiro Takita *Scr.* Nobuyuki Isshiki; based on a story by Tashihiko Tani. *Cast:* Takeshi Kaga, Kaori Momoi, Hiromi Iwasaki, Mitsunori Isaki, Akira Emoto, Midori Kiuchi, Akiko Kazami.

In this Japanese satire, a family of four, the Kimuras, is so obsessed with making money that, besides the father's office job, they also peddle box lunches, newspapers, and an erotic wake-up service, and each family member carries a personalized money bag. The weak link in their capitalism is their ten-year-old son, Taro, who returns the fee he charged to his visiting relatives, an action that threatens the Kimura family's established way of life.

YOUNG GUNS II

Pro. Paul Schiff and Irby Smith for James G. Robinson and Morgan Creek; Twentieth Century-Fox *Dir.* Geoff Murphy *Scr.* John Fusco *Cine.* Dean Semler *Ed.* Bruce Green *P.d.* Gene Rudolf *A.d.* Christa Munro *S.d.* Andy Bernard *Mu.* Alan Silvestri *MPAA* PG-13 *R.t.* 105 min. *Cast:* Emilio Estevez, Kiefer Sutherland, Lou Diamond Phillips, Christian Slater, William Petersen, Alan Ruck, Jenny Wright, James Coburn, Scott Wilson, Balthazar Getty, Jack Kehoe.

A sequel to *Young Guns* (1988), *Young Guns II* details the career of William Bonney, alias Billy the Kid, and his attempt to escape the pursuit of Pat Garrett across the wilds of the New Mexico Territory.

OBITUARIES

Jeff Alexander (1911-December 23, 1990). Alexander was a composer who wrote music for more than forty films in a career that spanned five decades. He was a founder of Screen Composers of America. His film credits include *Shall We Dance* (1937), *Singin' in the Rain* (1952), *Kismet* (1955), *Jailhouse Rock* (1957), and *Gigi* (1958).

Elizabeth Allan (April 9, 1908-July 27, 1990). Allan was a British actress who moved to Hollywood in the 1930's, where she made *David Copperfield* (1935) and *Camille* (1936), among others. A contract dispute with MGM ended her American film career in 1937, and she returned to England, where she acted on stage as well as in film and television. Her additional film credits include *Alibi* (1931), *A Tale of Two Cities* (1935), and *The Heart of the Matter* (1953).

Dorothy Appleby (1906-August 9, 1990). Appleby was an actress who is best known for her roles in Columbia Pictures' two-reel comedies opposite the Three Stooges, Andy Clyde, Harry Langdon, and Buster Keaton. She also appeared in such films as *Stagecoach* (1939), *The Doctor Takes a Wife* (1940), and *High Sierra* (1941).

Eve Arden (April 30, 1912-November 12, 1990). Born Eunice Quedens, Arden was a comic actress who appeared in more than fifty films, as well as on the long-running television hit *Our Miss Brooks*. She specialized in playing sarcastic characters and was nominated for an Academy Award as Best Supporting Actress for her work in *Mildred Pierce* (1945). Her additional screen credits include *At the Circus* (1939), *That Uncertain Feeling* (1941), *Our Miss Brooks* (1956), *Anatomy of a Murder* (1959), and *Grease* (1978).

Charles Arnt (August 20, 1908-August 6, 1990). Arnt was an actor who played character roles in a film career that spanned three decades. He specialized in playing meek, officious types in films such as *Ladies Should Listen* (1934), *Ball of Fire* (1941), *My Favorite Brunette* (1947), *The Boy with Green Hair* (1948), *Wild in the Country* (1961), and *Sweet Bird of Youth* (1962).

Pearl Bailey (March 29, 1918-August 17, 1990). Bailey was an exuberant black jazz singer who also acted occasionally on Broadway, in film, and in television. Her film credits include *Variety Girl* (1947), *Carmen Jones* (1955), *Porgy and Bess* (1959), and *The Landlord* (1970).

Ina Balin (November 12, 1937-June 20, 1990). Born Ina Rosenberg, Balin was an actress who was hailed as a potential star in the 1960's, appearing in such films as *The Black Orchid* (1959), *From the Terrace* (1960), and *The Comancheros* (1961). She became a political activist, and her efforts in assisting Vietnamese orphans were the subject of a made-for-television film, *The Children of An Lac* (1980). Her additional film credits include *The Young Doctors* (1961), *The Greatest Story Ever Told* (1965), and *Charro!* (1969).

Eric L. Barker (1911-June 1, 1990). Barker was a British actor and screenwriter who specialized in comic roles. He won a British Film Academy award for his work in a supporting role in *Brothers in Law* (1957). His additional screen credits include *Blue Murder at St. Trinian's* (1958), *Carry on Sergeant* (1959), *Those Magnificent Men in Their Flying Machines* (1965), and *There's a Girl in My Soup* (1970).

Madge Bellamy (June 30, 1900-January 24, 1990). Born Margaret Philpott, Bellamy was an actress who starred in numerous films in a career that spanned the silent and sound eras. Her best-remembered silent films are *Lorna Doone* (1922) and John Ford's *The Iron Horse* (1924). Bellamy's first talking picture was *Mother Knows Best* (1928), and she appeared opposite Bela Lugosi in the thriller *White Zombie* (1932). Her additional film credits include *The*

Call of the North (1921), *The Hottentot* (1922), *Lightnin'* (1925), and *Charlie Chan in London* (1934).

Joan Bennett (February 27, 1910-December 7, 1990). Bennett was a popular star in the *film noir* genre in the 1940's. She was born into a family of actors. Her father, Richard Bennett, was a stage actor who also appeared in many films from the silent era until his death in the early 1940's; and her older sisters Barbara and Constance Bennett were also actresses. Bennett broke into films as a teenager and quickly emerged as a star with roles in *Bulldog Drummond* (1929), opposite Ronald Coleman, and in *Disraeli* (1929) that same year. During the 1930's, she made dozens of films, including *Me and My Gal* (1932) and *Little Women* (1933). In 1938, she dyed her blonde hair brunette, the color it was to remain for the rest of her career. In 1940, Bennett married producer Walter Wanger, who guided her career to new heights. Working with director Fritz Lang, she made *Woman in the Window* (1944) and *Scarlet Street* (1945), among other *noir* classics. She also showed a flair for comedy, starring opposite Spencer Tracy in *Father of the Bride* (1950). Scandal struck Bennett in 1954, when her husband shot and wounded her agent, Jennings Lang, with whom he suspected the actress was having an affair. Her career never really recovered, although she appeared sporadically on television and in films over the next decade. She did enjoy a brief resurgence in popularity in the late 1960's on television's gothic soap opera *Dark Shadows*. Bennett's additional film credits include *Moby Dick* (1930), *The Trial of Vivienne Ware* (1932), *Mississippi* (1935), *Woman on the Beach* (1947), *Secret Beyond the Door* (1948), and *We're No Angels* (1955).

Leonard Bernstein (August 25, 1918-October 14, 1990). Bernstein was a renowned composer and conductor of the New York Philharmonic. He composed scores for three films: *On the Town* (1949), *On the Waterfront* (1954), which was nominated for an Academy Award, and *West Side Story* (1961). Bernstein also appeared in two films: *Satchmo the Great* (1958) and *A Journey to Jerusalem* (1969).

Juliet Berto (1947-January 10, 1990). Berto was a French actress and director who made her screen debut in Jean-Luc Godard's *Two or Three Things I Know About Her* (1967). She also directed three films, including two as codirector with Jean-Henri Roger: *Neige* (1980) and *Cape Canaille* (1982). Her additional acting credits include *La Chinoise* (1967), *Weekend* (1967), *Le Sex Shop* (1972), and *Celine and Julie Go Boating* (1974). She directed *Le Havre* (1985).

Henry Brandon (1912-February 15, 1990). Born Heinrich von Kleinbach, Brandon was an actor who was born in Germany but moved to California as a child. He broke into film by playing villains in serials such as *Jungle Jim* (1937) and *Drums of Fu Manchu* (1940). He specialized in playing exotic characters and was frequently cast as an Indian chief, most notably opposite John Wayne in John Ford's *The Searchers* (1956). His additional screen credits include *Babes in Toyland* (1934), *The Paleface* (1948), *Auntie Mame* (1958), and *Two Rode Together* (1961).

Pierre Braunberger (July 29, 1905-November 16, 1990). Braunberger was a French producer who worked with major French directors from Luis Buñuel in the 1930's to Jean-Luc Godard and François Truffaut in the 1960's. His films include *Nana* (1926), *Un Chien Andalou* (1928), *L'Âge d'or* (1930), *Shoot the Piano Player* (1960), *My Life to Live* (1962), and *A Man and a Woman* (1966).

Karl Brown (1895-March 25, 1990). Brown was a photographer, screenwriter, and director whose credits as an assistant cameraman included D. W. Griffith's *The Birth of a Nation* (1915) and *Intolerance* (1916). As director of photography, he worked primarily with director James Cruze on *The Covered Wagon* (1923). As a writer and/or director, his efforts were less auspicious; these included such B-pictures as *Tarzan Escapes* (1936) and *Under the Big Top* (1938). Brown's additional screen credits include *Ruggles of Red Gap* (1923), *The Pony Express* (1925), and *One in a Million* (1934).

Tom Brown (January 6, 1913-June 3, 1990). Brown was an actor whose youthful appearance led to a series of clean-cut boy-next-door roles in films in the silent and early sound eras. Later in his career he played supporting roles in films and was a regular in several television series, including *Gunsmoke, General Hospital,* and *Days of Our Lives.* Brown's film credits include *The Hoosier Schoolmaster* (1924), *Tom Brown of Culver* (1932), *Anne of Green Gables* (1934), *Rose Bowl* (1936), *Buck Privates Come Home* (1947), and *The Quiet Gun* (1957).

Harold Buchman (1912-June 22, 1990). Buchman was a screenwriter in the 1930's and 1940's. Like his older brother, producer Sidney Buchman, Buchman was active in leftist politics; and like his brother, Buchman was blacklisted for his beliefs. His film credits include *Shall We Dance* (1937), *It Happened in Flatbush* (1942), *Dixie Dugan* (1943), and *Cynthia* (1947).

R. Dale Butts (1912-1990). Butts was a composer for film and television. He was nominated for an Academy Award for his work on the score of *Flame of the Barbary Coast* (1945). His additional film credits include *My Buddy* (1944), *Hitchhike to Happiness* (1945), *Night Train to Memphis* (1946), and *City That Never Sleeps* (1953).

Gene Callahan (1908-December 25, 1990). Callahan was a production designer who won an Academy Award for his work on *America, America* (1964). He was nominated for an Academy Award for *The Cardinal* (1963). His additional screen credits include *Butterfield 8* (1960), *Splendor in the Grass* (1961), *Funny Girl* (1968), *Julia* (1977), and *Children of a Lesser God* (1986).

Capucine (January 6, 1933-March 17, 1990). Born Germaine Lefebvre, Capucine was a French actress who specialized in glamorous roles. She was featured in several successful Hollywood films as well as in European productions. Her acting credits include *North to Alaska* (1960), *Walk on the Wild Side* (1962), *The Pink Panther* (1964), *What's New, Pussycat?* (1965), and *Fellini Satyricon* (1969).

James Carreras (1910-June 9, 1990). Carreras was a British producer who, with producer Will Hammer, made Hammer Films the most successful studio in British cinema history. The studio specialized in low-budget action and horror films starring Peter Cushing and Christopher Lee. Carreras' film credits include *The Revenge of Frankenstein* (1958), *The Brides of Dracula* (1960), and *One Million Years B.C.* (1966).

Sunset Carson (November 12, 1922-May 1, 1990). Born Michael Harrison, Carson was an actor who specialized in playing cowboy heroes in B-Westerns. He worked most often for Republic Studios, where he was frequently paired with sidekick Smiley Burnette. He adopted the name of the character he played in films such as *Firebrands of Arizona* (1944), *Oregon Trail* (1945), *The Cherokee Flash* (1945), and *Sunset Carson Rides Again* (1948).

Don Chaffey (August 5, 1917-November 13, 1990). Chaffey was a British-born director who made both children's films such as *Pete's Dragon* (1977) and more adult-oriented action films such as *One Million Years B.C.* (1966) and *C.H.O.M.P.S.* (1979). His additional film credits include *The Mysterious Poacher* (1950), *Greyfriars Bobby* (1961), *The Prince and the Pauper* (1962), and *The Magic of Lassie* (1978).

Maurice Cloche (June 17, 1907-March 20, 1990). Cloche was a French director who began his career in the documentary field before turning to feature films in 1937. He is best known for *Monsieur Vincent* (1947), which won the Grand Prix as the best French film of the year, as well as a special Academy Award as the most outstanding foreign language film released in the United States in 1948. His additional film credits include *Docteur Laënnec* (1948), *Les Filles de la nuit* (1958), and *Mais toi tu es Pierre* (1971).

Aaron Copland (November 14, 1900-December 2, 1990). Copland was a major American composer known for incorporating folk and jazz themes into his classical works. He wrote eight film scores; his work on William Wyler's *The Heiress* (1949) won an Academy Award. Copland's other film credits include *The City* (1939), *Of Mice and Men* (1939), *Our Town* (1940), *The Red Pony* (1949), and *Something Wild* (1961).

Sergio Corbucci (1926-December 2, 1990). Corbucci was an Italian screenwriter and director who occasionally used the name Stanley Corbett. He made a variety of films during his career, including pseudohistorical epics such as *Duel of the Titans* (1961) and *The Slave* (1962), starring Steve Reeves. He is best known for developing, along with Sergio Leone, the "spaghetti western" genre, though his films, unlike those of Leone, were relatively unsuccessful in the United States. Corbucci's additional screen credits include *The Last Days of Pompeii* (1959), which he also cowrote, *Minnesota Clay* (1964), *Django* (1966), *Navajo Joe* (1966), and *Super Fuzz* (1981).

Lester Cowan (1905-October 21, 1990). Cowan was a producer best known for his involvement with the W. C. Fields vehicles *You Can't Cheat an Honest Man* (1939) and *My Little Chickadee* (1940). Prior to becoming a producer, he was executive director of the Motion Picture Academy of Arts and Sciences, where he helped to establish the Academy Awards. Cowan's additional film credits include *The Story of G.I. Joe* (1945), *One Touch of Venus* (1948), and *Love Happy* (1950).

Xavier Cugat (January 1, 1900-October 27, 1990). Born in Spain and reared in Havana, Cuba, Cugat was a bandleader best known for bringing Latin American rhythms to American popular music. He appeared in numerous musicals in the 1940's, usually playing himself. He was married to actresses Abbe Lane and Charro. His film credits include *You Were Never Lovelier* (1942), *Stage Door Canteen* (1942), *Holiday in Mexico* (1946), *A Date with Judy* (1948), and *Neptune's Daughter* (1949).

Bob Cummings (June 10, 1908-December 2, 1990). Born Clarence Robert Orville Cummings, Cummings was an actor who parlayed a successful film career in the 1940's into the long-running 1950's television series *The Bob Cummings Show*. Although he is best remembered as a comic actor, he won plaudits for his dramatic work in such films as *King's Row* (1941) and *Dial M for Murder* (1954). Cummings appeared in more than sixty films, including *Hollywood Boulevard* (1936), *It Started with Eve* (1941), *The Bride Wore Boots* (1946), *The Barefoot Mailman* (1951), *My Geisha* (1962), and *Beach Party* (1963).

Sammy Davis, Jr. (December 8, 1925-May 16, 1990). Davis was a black singer, dancer, and actor who began performing in vaudeville at the age of four. He also appeared in the Vitaphone short *Rufus Jones for President* (1933) at the age of seven. He concentrated on his musical career for the next two decades and was championed by Frank Sinatra. Davis later became a member of Sinatra's inner circle, known as the Rat Pack. He began making films again in the 1950's, with *The Benny Goodman Story* (1956) and *Porgy and Bess* (1959). He teamed with Sinatra and the rest of the Rat Pack in a series of lighthearted caper films in the 1960's, including *Ocean's 11* (1960), *Sergeants 3* (1962), and *Robin and the Seven Hoods* (1964). Davis was consistently unconventional: He converted to Judaism; was married for a time to Swedish actress May Britt; and publicly embraced Richard Nixon in 1972 after having been a Kennedy Democrat. He continued to prosper, however, in a variety of show business roles, and he found the time to write three autobiographical books while making records, films, and television appearances. His additional film credits include *The Threepenny Opera*

(1963), *Salt and Pepper* (1968), *Sweet Charity* (1969), *The Cannonball Run* (1981), and *Tap* (1989).

Jacques Demy (June 5, 1931-October 27, 1990). Demy was a French director who began his career working in the fields of animation and documentaries. Known for his romanticism, Demy's most popular film was *The Umbrellas of Cherbourg* (1964), in which the dialogue was sung to a score by Michel Legrand. The film won the Golden Palm at Cannes in 1964. Demy later made films in the United States and England, but his later work met with neither the commercial nor the critical success that his earlier films had received. Demy's additional screen credits include *Lola* (1961), *The Young Girls of Rochefort* (1967), *The Model Shop* (1969), *Donkey Skin* (1971), *The Pied Piper* (1972), and *Une Chambre en ville* (1982).

Michel Drach (October 18, 1930-February 15, 1990). Drach was a French director known for his humanism. His best-known film, *Les Violons du bal* (1973), was an autobiographical account of the filmmaker's Jewish childhood during the Nazi occupation. This film starred Drach's wife, Marie-Jose Nat, who was featured in several of the director's films. Drach's additional screen credits include *Amélie ou le temps d'aimer* (1961), *Elise ou la vraie vie* (1970), *Replay* (1977), and *Sauve-toi Lola* (1985).

Howard Duff (November 24, 1917-July 8, 1990). Duff was an actor who first gained fame for portraying the detective Sam Spade on radio. He played supporting roles in such memorable *films noirs* as *The Naked City* (1948) and was often cast as a tough-guy hero in B-action films such as *Johnny Stool Pigeon* (1949) and *Spy Hunt* (1950). He was married to actress Ida Lupino, with whom he starred in *Woman in Hiding* (1950) as well as in the television series *Mr. Adams and Eve*. Duff's additional film credits include *Illegal Entry* (1949), *Tanganyika* (1954), *Boys' Night Out* (1962), *Kramer vs. Kramer* (1979), and *Oh God! Book II* (1980).

Irene Dunne (December 20, 1898-September 4, 1990). Dunne was an actress who was one of Hollywood's leading ladies in the 1930's and 1940's. She originally aspired to be an opera singer; when those ambitions fell through, she turned to musical comedy and from the stage to films. Her first major film role was in *Cimarron* (1931), a Western that earned for her an Academy Award nomination as Best Actress. She was nominated for four additional Academy Awards, for *Theodora Goes Wild* (1936), *The Awful Truth* (1937), *Love Affair* (1939), and *I Remember Mama* (1948). She played a variety of roles, from musicals to comedy to melodrama, but projected an aura of dignity and distinction throughout all of them. She sang "Lovely to Look At" and "Smoke Gets in Your Eyes" in *Roberta* (1935) and also appeared in the second film version of *Show Boat* (1936). She appeared opposite Cary Grant in *My Favorite Wife* (1940) and *Penny Serenade* (1941). Abandoning her acting career in the 1950's, she then became active in politics, serving as an alternate delegate to the United Nations General Assembly during the Eisenhower Administration, and she was a close friend of Ronald and Nancy Reagan. Her additional film credits include *Back Street* (1932), *Magnificent Obsession* (1935), *A Guy Named Joe* (1943), *The White Cliffs of Dover* (1944), *Anna and the King of Siam* (1946), *Life with Father* (1947), and *Never a Dull Moment* (1950).

Arnaud d'Usseau (1916-January 29, 1990). D'Usseau was a playwright and a screenwriter who grew up in Hollywood as the son of producer-director Leon d'Usseau and actress Ottala Nesmith d'Usseau. He became involved in a variety of leftist causes in the 1930's and 1940's and was blacklisted by the studios in 1952. Subsequently, he worked pseudonymously on films such as *Studs Lonigan* (1960) and *Horror Express* (1973). D'Usseau's screenwriting credits also include *One Crowded Night* (1940), *Lady Scarface* (1941), *The Man Who Wouldn't Die* (1942), and *Just Off Broadway* (1942).

Helen Jerome Eddy (1897-January 27, 1990). Eddy was an actress who was featured in numerous films during the silent era, usually portraying upper-class women. Her first film was *The Red Virgin* (1915); by the advent of sound films, her career was on the wane, although she continued in smaller roles through *Strike Up the Band* (1940). Her additional screen credits include *Rebecca of Sunnybrook Farm* (1917), *The First Born* (1921), *The Flirt* (1922), *Camille* (1927), and *Mr. Smith Goes to Washington* (1939).

Rene Enriquez (1931-March 23, 1990). Enriquez was a character actor who played Hispanic roles in films as well as in a variety of television series, most prominently in *Hill Street Blues*. His film credits include *Bananas* (1971), *Serpico* (1973), and *Harry and Tonto* (1974).

Jill Esmond (January 26, 1908-July 28, 1990). Born Jill Esmond-Moore, Esmond was a British stage and film actress. Her film roles were mostly character parts. She was married to Laurence Olivier from 1930 to 1940. Her film credits include *The Skin Game* (1931), *Thirteen Women* (1932), *Random Harvest* (1942), *The White Cliffs of Dover* (1944), *The Bandit of Sherwood Forest* (1946), and *A Man Called Peter* (1955).

Aldo Fabrizi (November 1, 1905-April 2, 1990). Fabrizi was an Italian actor best known for his portrayal of the martyred priest in Roberto Rossellini's *Rome, Open City* (1945). In Italy, Fabrizi was known primarily for his comic roles; he also wrote and directed a number of films, often appearing opposite fellow comedian Toto. His screen credits include *Emigrantes* (1949), *La Famiglia Passaguai* (1951), *I Vitelloni* (1953), and *Il Maestro* (1958).

Charles Farrell (August 9, 1901-May 6, 1990). Farrell was an actor who was a popular leading man during the transition between silent and sound films. He starred opposite Janet Gaynor in a series of romantic vehicles including *Seventh Heaven* (1927), *Sunny Side Up* (1929), and *Delicious* (1931). He owned a resort hotel in Palm Springs, where he also served as mayor from 1948 to 1953. His additional film credits include *The Freshman* (1925), *Street Angel* (1928), *High Society Blues* (1930), and *Body and Soul* (1931).

Greta Garbo (September 18, 1905-April 15, 1990). Born Greta Louisa Gustafsson in Sweden, Garbo was an actress known for fiercely protecting her privacy. The sense of mystery surrounding her personal life served to enhance her popularity on the screen, and she became an international star during the transition between silent and sound films. Garbo began her film career under the wing of Swedish director Mauritz Stiller, who discovered her in drama school and gave her a prominent role in his *The Story of Gösta Berling* (1924). A similar role in G. W. Pabst's *The Street of Sorrow* (1925) followed, as did a contract from MGM's Louis B. Mayer. Garbo's first American film, *The Torrent* (1926), made her famous. MGM offered her its best scripts and directors, as well as extensive publicity. For her first sound film, *Anna Christie* (1930), they coined the advertising slogan "Garbo Talks"; for her first comedy, *Ninotchka* (1939), it was "Garbo Laughs!" Audiences were drawn to her cool sensuality, and she starred in such films as *Mata Hari* (1931), *Queen Christina* (1933), *Anna Karenina* (1935), and *Camille* (1936). Although she was nominated four times as Best Actress—for *Anna Christie, Romance* (1930), *Camille*, and *Ninotchka*—Garbo never won a competitive Academy Award. She was, however, given an honorary award in 1954 "for her unforgettable screen performances." Quite suddenly, after the release of the relatively unsuccessful *Two-Faced Woman* (1941), Garbo announced her retirement. She never offered an explanation for her decision. Public interest in Garbo continued unabated, however, and she was plagued throughout the rest of her life by reporters and photographers seeking unsuccessfully to penetrate her reserve. Her additional film credits include *Flesh and the Devil* (1927), *Love* (1927), *The Kiss* (1929), *Grand Hotel* (1932), *The Painted Veil* (1934), and *Conquest* (1937).

Ava Gardner (January 24, 1922-January 25, 1990). Gardner was an actress who was known for her beauty and her stormy love life as much as for her acting abilities. She was the daughter of a poor North Carolina tobacco farmer, and her dark, sensual good looks earned for her a starlet's contract with MGM, where she met Mickey Rooney. After a brief courtship, the two were married, but the union lasted only a year. She had similarly abbreviated marriages with bandleader Artie Shaw (1945-1947) and Frank Sinatra (1951-1957; the couple separated in 1954). As painful as these relationships undoubtedly were, the publicity they brought helped Gardner's career. She starred opposite Burt Lancaster (in his screen debut) in an adaptation of Ernest Hemingway's *The Killers* (1946) that pleased not only audiences and critics but even Hemingway himself. Her career continued in a mixture of undistinguished potboilers and significantly better films. Highlights included her portrayal of a statue brought to life in *One Touch of Venus* (1948) and the alcoholic mulatto Julie Laverne in the musical *Show Boat* (1951), though her singing was dubbed. Her role in John Ford's *Mogambo* (1953) earned for her an Academy Award nomination. By the late 1950's, she was seeking out less glamorous roles, including those in such films as *On the Beach* (1959) and *The Night of the Iguana* (1964). By then she had left Hollywood to live abroad, first in Spain and, after 1968, in London. She continued to appear in films into the 1980's, often in cameo roles. Her additional screen credits include *The Hucksters* (1947), *The Snows of Kilimanjaro* (1952), *The Barefoot Contessa* (1954), *Bhowani Junction* (1956), *The Naked Maja* (1959), *Seven Days in May* (1964), *Mayerling* (1968), and *The Life and Times of Judge Roy Bean* (1972).

Jack Gilford (July 25, 1907-June 2, 1990). Born Jacob Gellman, Gilford was a character actor who specialized in comic roles. He worked in television and on stage; he re-created his Broadway role in the film version of *A Funny Thing Happened on the Way to the Forum* (1966). He earned an Academy Award nomination as Best Supporting Actor for his work opposite Jack Lemmon in *Save the Tiger* (1973). Gilford's additional film credits include *Hey Rookie* (1944), *Main Street to Broadway* (1953), *Enter Laughing* (1969), and *Catch-22* (1970).

Paulette Goddard (June 3, 1911-April 23, 1990). Born Marion Levy, Goddard was one of Paramount's top stars in the 1940's. She began her film career with bit parts as a Goldwyn Girl and as a member of comedy producer Hal Roach's stock company in the early 1930's. She met Charlie Chaplin in 1932, and the two were married (there is controversy as to precisely when the wedding took place, with speculation ranging from 1933 to 1936). Goddard starred opposite Chaplin in two major films: *Modern Times* (1936) and *The Great Dictator* (1940). She was by no means dependent on Chaplin for her success, however. She was a leading contender for the role of Scarlett O'Hara in *Gone with the Wind* (1939); though she lost the part to Vivien Leigh, she became a popular leading lady nevertheless, in films such as *The Women* (1939) and *North West Mounted Police* (1940). She was featured opposite Bob Hope in *The Ghost Breakers* (1940) and *Nothing but the Truth* (1941), both comedies; and she demonstrated her dramatic abilities in *So Proudly We Hail* (1943) and *Kitty* (1946). Goddard's career waned rather abruptly at the end of the 1940's, and she appeared in few films after 1950. She and Chaplin were divorced in 1942, and she was married to actor Burgess Meredith from 1944 to 1950. Her additional screen credits include *The Young in Heart* (1938), *The Cat and the Canary* (1939), *Hold Back the Dawn* (1941), *Suddenly It's Spring* (1947), *Anna Lucasta* (1949), and *Sins of Jezebel* (1953).

Dexter Gordon (February 27, 1923-April 25, 1990). Gordon was a prominent jazz saxophonist who had a brief but important film career. He had a minor role as a musician in *Unchained* (1955). Three decades later, he was chosen by director Bertrand Tavernier for the lead role in *'Round Midnight* (1986); his convincing performance as an alcoholic jazz musician earned for him an Academy Award nomination as Best Actor.

Alan Hale, Jr. (1918-January 2, 1990). Born Rufus Alan McKahan, Hale was an actor who made scores of films before winning widespread popularity as the Skipper in the television series *Gilligan's Island*. He appeared in character roles over five decades in films such as *I Wanted Wings* (1941), *It Happens Every Spring* (1949), *Destry* (1954), *Hang 'Em High* (1968), and *The Fifth Musketeer* (1979).

Rex Harrison (March 5, 1908-June 2, 1990). Born Reginald Carey Harrison, Harrison was a British actor whose career on both stage and screen spanned some sixty-five years. A dapper, elegant man, he is best remembered for his performance as Professor Henry Higgins in both the Broadway and film versions of the Lerner and Loewe musical *My Fair Lady* (1964). His film performance earned for him the Academy Award as Best Actor. Harrison specialized in light comedy, making his stage debut at the age of sixteen and breaking into film six years later in *The Great Game* (1930). By 1936, he had won starring roles, appearing in *Men Are Not Gods* (1936) and *School for Husbands* (1937). After serving in the Royal Air Force during World War II, he made *Blithe Spirit* (1946) and his first Hollywood feature, *Anna and the King of Siam* (1946). During the 1950's, Harrison concentrated primarily on stage work, including two years on Broadway in *My Fair Lady* from 1956 to 1958. Back in film, he was nominated for an Academy Award for his role as Caesar in *Cleopatra* (1963). His subsequent notable roles included appearances in *The Agony and the Ecstasy* (1965), *Doctor Dolittle* (1967), and *The Fifth Musketeer* (1979). Harrison was married six times; his wives included actresses Lilli Palmer, Kay Kendall, and Rachel Roberts. His son, Noel Harrison, is an actor and singer. Harrison's additional screen credits include *The Citadel* (1938), *A Yank in London* (1945), *The Ghost and Mrs. Muir* (1947), *Unfaithfully Yours* (1948), *The Four Poster* (1952), *The Yellow Rolls-Royce* (1964), and *The Prince and the Pauper* (1977).

Jim Henson (September 24, 1936-May 16, 1990). Henson was the creator of the puppet figures the Muppets, including such characters as Kermit the Frog and Miss Piggy. Though originally aimed at children via such television shows as *Sesame Street* and *The Muppet Show*, the Muppets' gentle humor proved equally popular with adults. The Muppets first made it onto the screen in *The Muppet Movie* (1979), followed by *The Great Muppet Caper* (1981), which Henson directed, and by *The Muppets Take Manhattan* (1984), directed by Henson's associate Frank Oz. Henson's non-Muppet projects included *The Dark Crystal* (1982) and *Labyrinth* (1986). His London-based Creature Workshop also provided the costumes for the hugely successful *Teenage Mutant Ninja Turtles* (1990; reviewed in this volume).

Clair Huffaker (1926-April 2, 1990). Huffaker was a novelist and screenwriter who specialized in Westerns, often writing scripts from his own novels. These included three John Wayne vehicles: *The Comancheros* (1961), *The War Wagon* (1967), and *Hellfighters* (1969). His other film credits include *Flaming Star* (1960), *Rio Conchos* (1964), and *100 Rifles* (1969).

Raymond Huntley (April 23, 1904-1990). Huntley was a British actor who specialized in playing stuffy characters in a career that spanned five decades and more than seventy-five films. He was perhaps best known for his role in the television series *Upstairs, Downstairs*. His film credits include *Rembrandt* (1936), *Pimpernel Smith* (1941), *I See a Dark Stranger* (1947), *Passport to Pimlico* (1949), *Geordie* (1955), *I'm All Right, Jack* (1960), *The Pure Hell of St. Trinian's* (1960), and *Young Winston* (1972).

Jill Ireland (1936-May 18, 1990). Ireland was a British actress best known for her work in action films with her husband, Charles Bronson. She began her career in the British film industry, where her first significant role was in the comedy *Three Men in a Boat* (1956). She married actor David McCallum in 1957, and after moving to the United States in 1962, Ireland worked primarily in television for several years. She and McCallum were divorced in 1967; a year later, she married Bronson. Ireland and Bronson made fifteen films together, including

The Mechanic (1972), *Hard Times* (1975), *From Noon Till Three* (1976), and *Death Wish II* (1982). Her additional film credits include *Robbery Under Arms* (1957), *So Evil So Young* (1961), *Cold Sweat* (1970), *The Valachi Papers* (1972), and *Breakheart Pass* (1976). Ireland had suffered from breast cancer since 1984 and published a book about her mastectomy and its aftermath.

Gordon Jackson (December 19, 1923-January 15, 1990). Jackson was a Scottish character actor who was best known for his role as Hudson the butler in the television series *Upstairs, Downstairs*. He appeared in more than sixty films, including *Whisky Galore* (1949), *Tunes of Glory* (1960), *Mutiny on the Bounty* (1962), *The Great Escape* (1963), *The Ipcress File* (1965), and *The Prime of Miss Jean Brodie* (1969).

Gabriel Katzka (1931-February 19, 1990). Katzka was a producer who worked in film, stage, and television. His film production credits include *Soldier Blue* (1970), *Sleuth* (1972), *The Parallax View* (1974), *The Taking of Pelham One Two Three* (1974), *A Bridge Too Far* (1977), and *The Lords of Discipline* (1983).

Philip Leacock (1917-July 14, 1990). Leacock was a British director who began his career in the documentary field, producing such films as *Island People* (1940) and *The Story of Wool* (1940). By 1950, he had begun making feature films, working both in England and in the United States. He specialized in working with youthful actors during the 1950's in films such as *The Kidnappers* (1953) and *The Spanish Gardener* (1956). Later in his career, he turned to action films. His filmmaking credits include *The Brave Don't Cry* (1952), *Let No Man Write My Epitaph* (1960), and *The War Lover* (1962).

Alexander Lockwood (1901-January 25, 1990). Born Aleksander Wyrwicz in Czechoslovakia, Lockwood was a character actor who moved to the United States as a child. He appeared in numerous films over a career that spanned four decades. His screen credits include *Four's a Crowd* (1938), *King Creole* (1958), *North by Northwest* (1959), *Patton* (1970), *The Sting* (1973), and *Close Encounters of the Third Kind* (1977).

Margaret Lockwood (September 15, 1916-July 15, 1990). Born Margaret Day to British parents in Pakistan, Lockwood was an actress who became England's biggest box-office draw during the 1940's. She specialized in playing glamorous, often wicked women. Her appearance in Alfred Hitchcock's *The Lady Vanishes* (1938) brought her to the attention of Hollywood, where she made two films in 1939. She soon returned to England, however, where she spent the rest of her career. Lockwood's additional screen credits include *Lorna Doone* (1935), *Night Train to Munich* (1940), *The Wicked Lady* (1945), *Jassy* (1947), and *Trent's Last Case* (1953).

Joel McCrea (November 5, 1905-October 20, 1990). McCrea was an actor who appeared in a wide variety of roles in his career, though later in his career he specialized in the Westerns for which he is best known. Tall and handsome, McCrea grew up in Hollywood and began working in films while in his teens, appearing as a stuntman and stand-in. He had minor roles in several silent films, but his first major part was in *The Silver Horde* (1930). He was cinema's first Dr. Kildare in *Interns Can't Take Money* (1937). McCrea's early Westerns included *Wells Fargo* (1937) and Cecil B. De Mille's *Union Pacific* (1939). He made three comedies with Preston Sturges, including *Sullivan's Travels* (1941) and *The Palm Beach Story* (1942), and he starred in Alfred Hitchcock's *Foreign Correspondent* (1940). By the mid-1940's, however, he had begun to concentrate exclusively on Westerns, a genre to which he felt his talents as a rancher and outdoorsman best suited him. Highlights of his career as a screen cowboy include *Buffalo Bill* (1944), *The Virginian* (1946), *Ramrod* (1947), and *Wichita* (1955). He continued making Westerns into the early 1960's, after which he retired from acting, a wealthy man, having invested his earnings in Southern California real estate. His additional film credits include *Reaching for the Sun* (1941), *The Great Man's Lady* (1942), *The More the Merrier* (1943), *Four Faces West* (1948), *Saddle Tramp* (1950), *The Tall Stranger* (1957), and *Ride the High Country* (1962).

Dorothy Mackaill (March 4, 1905-August 12, 1990). Born in England, Mackaill was a popular actress in American films of the 1920's. A blonde Ziegfeld showgirl, she specialized in flapper roles in silent and early-sound-era films. Her screen credits include *The Streets of New York* (1922), *Just Another Blonde* (1926), *The Barker* (1928), *Bright Lights* (1930), and *Cheaters* (1934).

Mary Martin (December 1, 1913-November 4, 1990). Martin was an actress and singer best known for her stage roles in *Peter Pan, South Pacific,* and *The Sound of Music.* Her son is actor Larry Hagman. Martin made several films early in her career, including *Rhythm on the River* (1940), *Birth of the Blues* (1941), *Star Spangled Rhythm* (1942), *Night and Day* (1946), and *Main Street to Broadway* (1953).

Mike Mazurki (December 25, 1909-December 9, 1990). Born Mikhail Mazurwski in Austria, Mazurki was a burly character actor who specialized in tough-guy roles in a career that spanned four decades and more than one hundred films. He is best remembered as Moose Malloy, the dull-witted gangster in *Murder, My Sweet* (1944). His additional film credits include *Nightmare Alley* (1947), *Rope of Sand* (1949), *Night and the City* (1950), *Blood Alley* (1955), *Donovan's Reef* (1963), and *Farewell, My Lovely* (1975).

Gary Merrill (August 2, 1915-March 5, 1990). Merrill was an actor who is best remembered for his role opposite Bette Davis in *All About Eve* (1950); he and Davis were married from 1950 to 1960. Merrill made his film debut in *Winged Victory* (1944) while serving in the army. He specialized in playing determined men in dozens of films in the 1950's and 1960's. His screen credits include *Twelve O'Clock High* (1949), *Phone Call from a Stranger* (1952), *The Great Impostor* (1961), *Cast a Giant Shadow* (1966), and *Clambake* (1967).

Nathan Monaster (1911-May 19, 1990). Monaster was a screenwriter who was nominated, along with collaborator Stanley Shapiro, for an Academy Award for the script of the Cary Grant/Doris Day vehicle *That Touch of Mink* (1962). His additional film credits include *The Sad Sack* (1957), *Call Me Bwana* (1963), and *How to Save a Marriage—And Ruin Your Life* (1968).

Jackie Moran (1925-September 20, 1990). Moran was a child actor who was discovered by Mary Pickford; he played Huck Finn in *The Adventures of Tom Sawyer* (1938) and had a part in *Gone with the Wind* (1939). Moran's additional film credits include *Mad About Music* (1938), *Tomboy* (1940), *Since You Went Away* (1944), *Betty Co-Ed* (1946), and *Destination Moon* (1950).

Lois Moran (March 1, 1908-July 13, 1990). Born Lois Darlington Dowling, Moran was an actress who starred in numerous films in the silent era. She made a few films in the early days of sound but retired from film in 1931 to concentrate on a stage career. She is best remembered for her portrayal of Laurel in *Stella Dallas* (1925). Her additional screen credits include *The Road to Mandalay* (1926), *Love Hungry* (1928), *A Song of Kentucky* (1929), and *Under Suspicion* (1931).

Alberto Moravia (November 28, 1907-September 26, 1990). Born Alberto Pincherle, Moravia was a major Italian novelist known for his frankness in matters of sex as well as for his progressive social themes. His works were made into notable films, including Vittorio De Sica's *Two Women* (1960) and Bernardo Bertolucci's *The Conformist* (1970). Moravia also wrote screenplays; his film credits include *The Wayward Wife* (1952), *The Woman of Rome*

(1955), *From a Roman Balcony* (1960), and *Yesterday Today and Tomorrow* (1963).

Grim Natwick (1890-October 7, 1990). Natwick was an artist who was one of the pioneers in the field of animated cartoons. Working with Max and Dave Fleischer, he created the character Betty Boop in the animated short "Dizzy Dishes" (1930). In 1935, he joined Walt Disney and was one of the principal animators on *Snow White and the Seven Dwarfs* (1937). He also worked on Woody Woodpecker and Mr. Magoo cartoon shorts.

Edmund H. North (March 12, 1911-August 28, 1990). North was a screenwriter who wrote more than thirty films. He is best known for his collaboration with Francis Ford Coppola on the screenplay of *Patton* (1970), for which he won an Academy Award. His additional film credits include *One Night of Love* (1934), *Young Man with a Horn* (1950), *The Day the Earth Stood Still* (1951), *Cowboy* (1958), and *Sink the Bismarck!* (1960).

Jane Novak (1896-February 6, 1990). Novak was an actress who made more than one hundred films, mostly during the silent era. She was engaged for a time to Western star William S. Hart, with whom she made *The Tiger Man* (1918), *Wagon Tracks* (1919), and *Three Word Brand* (1921). She continued to appear in films after the advent of sound but never repeated her earlier successes. Her additional screen credits include *Behind the Door* (1918), *Colleen of the Pines* (1922), *Redskin* (1929), and *Hollywood Boulevard* (1936).

Susan Oliver (February 13, 1937-May 10, 1990). Born Charlotte Gercke, Oliver was an actress who worked in film and also television, where she was a regular on *Peyton Place*. Her film credits include *Up Periscope* (1959), *Butterfield 8* (1960), *Your Cheatin' Heart* (1964), and *The Disorderly Orderly* (1964).

Hermes Pan (1910-September 19, 1990). Pan was a dancer and choreographer who was best known for his work with Fred Astaire. The two were good friends and collaborated on such dance classics as *The Gay Divorcee* (1934), *Top Hat* (1935), and *Swing Time* (1936). Pan won an Academy Award for his work on *A Damsel in Distress* (1937). He also worked extensively with Betty Grable in a series of musicals that included *Springtime in the Rockies* (1942) and *Diamond Horseshoe* (1945). His film career spanned four decades and included *Flying Down to Rio* (1933), *Roberta* (1935), *Sun Valley Serenade* (1941), *Blue Skies* (1946), *Kiss Me Kate* (1953), *Pal Joey* (1957), *My Fair Lady* (1964), and *Finian's Rainbow* (1968).

Michael Powell (September 30, 1905-February 19, 1990). Powell was a British director who also produced and wrote many of his later films. He began his filmmaking career by grinding out short, low-budget films such as *Two Crowded Hours* (1931) and *The Rasp* (1931). He soon graduated to longer features, directing popular actors Leslie Banks in *Red Ensign* (1934) and Ian Hunter in *The Phantom Light* (1935). He won critical acclaim for *The Edge of the World* (1937), which brought him to the attention of producer Alexander Korda; Korda teamed Powell with writer Emeric Pressburger. Powell and Pressburger worked together from 1942 to 1958, producing films that were known for their striking, sumptuous visuals. Their major films included *One of Our Aircraft Is Missing* (1942), *The Life and Death of Colonel Blimp* (1943), and *Black Narcissus* (1947). Powell's best-known film was *The Red Shoes* (1948), which broke ground in integrating dancing into film narrative. Although Powell and Pressburger parted ways in 1958, they reunited fourteen years later for *The Boy Who Turned Yellow* (1972). Powell's films of the 1960's and 1970's were less successful than his earlier efforts, although the reputation of *Peeping Tom* (1960), a psychological thriller, has grown since its release. Powell's additional film credits include *The Thief of Bagdad* (1940; Powell codirected), *Stairway to Heaven* (1945), *The Elusive Pimpernel* (1950), *The Tales of Hoffman* (1951), and *They're a Weird Mob* (1966).

Eddie Quillan (March 31, 1907-July 19, 1990). Quillan was an actor who grew up in vaudeville and became a child actor in silent films. He later became a character actor known for his comic talents. His film credits include *A Love Sundae* (1926), *Girl Crazy* (1932), *Mutiny on the Bounty* (1935), *The Grapes of Wrath* (1940), *Song of the Sarong* (1945), *Brigadoon* (1954), and *Promises! Promises!* (1963).

David Rappaport (1951-May 2, 1990). Rappaport was an actor best known for his role on the television series *L.A. Law*. He was three feet, eleven inches tall and played a variety of dwarfs and "little people" in films such as *Mysteries* (1978), *Cuba* (1979), *Time Bandits* (1980), and *The Bride* (1985).

Anne Revere (June 25, 1903-December 18, 1990). Revere was an Academy Award-winning actress whose career was cut short when she was blacklisted by the Hollywood studios after refusing to testify before the House Committee on Un-American Activities in 1951. She won an Academy Award as Best Supporting Actress for her portrayal of Elizabeth Taylor's mother in *National Velvet* (1944). She was nominated for the award on two other occasions, for her work in *The Song of Bernadette* (1943) and *Gentleman's Agreement* (1947). Her additional film credits include *The Howards of Virginia* (1940), *The Keys of the Kingdom* (1944), *Fallen Angel* (1945), *Forever Amber* (1947), and *A Place in the Sun* (1951).

Erik Rhodes (1906-February 17, 1990). Rhodes was an actor who specialized in playing suave gigolos in a variety of films in the 1930's. He is best remembered for his work in two Fred Astaire films, *The Gay Divorcee* (1934) and *Top Hat* (1935). His additional film credits include *A Night at the Ritz* (1935), *Chatterbox* (1936), *Beg, Borrow, or Steal* (1937), *Say It in French* (1938), and *On Your Toes* (1939).

Maurice Richlin (1920-November 13, 1990). Richlin was a screenwriter who, along with director Blake Edwards, created the character of Inspector Clouseau in *The Pink Panther* (1964). Prior to this collaboration, Richlin teamed with writer Stanley Shapiro to win an Academy Award for his work in *Pillow Talk* (1959). Richlin and Shapiro received a second Academy Award nomination that same year for *Operation Petticoat* (1959). Richlin's additional film credits include *Come September* (1961), *All in a Night's Work* (1961), *What Did You Do in the War, Daddy?* (1966), and *Don't Make Waves* (1967).

Martin Ritt (March 2, 1920-December 8, 1990). Ritt was a director known for his social conscience. He began his show business career as an actor and worked extensively in the early days of television as both an actor and a director. His first feature film was *Edge of the City* (1957), which focused on race relations and political corruption on the waterfront docks. He also taught at Elia Kazan's Actors' Studio, where one of his pupils was Paul Newman. Ritt directed Newman in several of the films that helped launch the actor's career, including *The Long, Hot Summer* (1958), *Hud* (1963), and *Hombre* (1967). Ritt was nominated for an Academy Award for his work on *Hud*. Ritt's political films included *The Front* (1976), about blacklisting in Hollywood during the McCarthy era, and *Norma Rae* (1979), which starred Sally Fields in a film with a strong pro-union message. Ritt also made films about black Americans, including *The Great White Hope* (1970), *Sounder* (1972), and *Conrack* (1974). His last film was the Jane Fonda-Robert De Niro vehicle *Stanley and Iris* (1990; reviewed in this volume). Ritt's additional film credits include *The Sound and the Fury* (1959), *The Spy Who Came in from the Cold* (1965), *The Molly Maguires* (1970), *Casey's Shadow* (1978), and *Cross Creek* (1983).

Allen Rivkin (1903-February 17, 1990). Rivkin was a screenwriter who worked on more than seventy films, including Fred Astaire's first film, *Dancing Lady* (1933). In addition to his work on feature films, Rivkin worked with Frank Capra on his famous World War II "Why We Fight" series. Rivkin's additional film credits include *Picture Snatcher* (1933), *The*

Farmer's Daughter (1947), *It's a Big Country* (1951), and *Prisoner of War* (1954).

Al Roelofs (1907-July 2, 1990). Born in Holland, Roelofs was an art director who earned an Academy Award nomination for his work on Walt Disney's *The Island at the Top of the World* (1974). Prior to joining the Disney studios, he worked extensively for Paramount. His additional film credits include *Shane* (1953), *In Harm's Way* (1965), *The President's Analyst* (1967), *Escape to Witch Mountain* (1975), *The Black Hole* (1979), and *TRON* (1982).

David Rose (1910-August 23, 1990). Born in England, Rose was a composer and conductor who won honors in a variety of entertainment fields, including five Grammys during his career as a recording artist and four Emmys for his work in television. He also worked in film and was nominated for an Academy Award for the song "So in Love" in *Wonder Man* (1945). His additional film credits include *Rich, Young and Pretty* (1951), *Port Afrique* (1956), and *Please Don't Eat the Daisies* (1960).

Frank Ross (August 12, 1904-February 18, 1990). Ross was a producer who won a special Academy Award for *The House I Live In* (1945), a plea for tolerance that featured Frank Sinatra. Ross also produced *The Robe* (1953), the first film shot in CinemaScope. He was married to actress Jean Arthur from 1932 to 1949, and produced her *The Devil and Miss Jones* (1941). His additional film credits include *The Lady Takes a Chance* (1943), *Demetrius and the Gladiators* (1954), *The Rains of Ranchipur* (1955), and *Kings Go Forth* (1958).

Raymond St. Jacques (1930-August 27, 1990). Born James Arthur Johnson, St. Jacques was one of the most prominent black film and television actors of his day, with the ability to play both comic and dramatic roles. He also produced and directed *Book of Numbers* (1973). His acting credits include *The Pawnbroker* (1965), *The Comedians* (1967), *Cotton Comes to Harlem* (1970), *The Private Files of J. Edgar Hoover* (1977), and *Eyes of Laura Mars* (1978).

Luciano Salce (September 25, 1922-December 17, 1990). Salce was an Italian director best known for popular 1960's comedies that featured European stars such as Ugo Tognazzi, Monica Vitti, and Catherine Spaak. He often acted in his own films. His screen credits include *Il Federale* (1961), *Crazy Desire* (1962), *The Little Nuns* (1963), *El Greco* (1966), and *Il Provinciale* (1971).

Albert Salmi (1928-April 23, 1990). Salmi was an actor who first earned critical attention in 1955 in the role of Bo Decker in the Broadway production of *Bus Stop*. Although he turned down the same role in the film, he soon began appearing in a variety of character roles in film and television, specializing in Westerns. His screen credits include *The Brothers Karamazov* (1958), *The Unforgiven* (1960), *Hour of the Gun* (1967), *Lawman* (1971), *Brubaker* (1980), and *I'm Dancing as Fast as I Can* (1982).

Hans Schumm (1896-February 2, 1990). Schumm was a German actor who moved to the United States in the 1920's and appeared in numerous films, including Charlie Chaplin's *The Great Dictator* (1940) and *Limelight* (1952). His additional film credits include *Blonde Venus* (1932), *Algiers* (1938), and *The Sound of Music* (1965).

Delphine Seyrig (1932-October 15, 1990). Born in Lebanon of French parents, Seyrig was an actress who appeared in numerous experimental and artistic films in the 1960's and 1970's. She is best remembered for her work with director Alain Resnais, for whom she made *Last Year at Marienbad* (1961) and *Muriel* (1963); her work in the latter film earned for her the best actress award at the Venice Film Festival. Her additional screen credits include *Pull My Daisy* (1958), *Stolen Kisses* (1968), *The Discreet Charm of the Bourgeoisie* (1972), and *A Doll's House* (1973).

Stanley Shapiro (1925-July 21, 1990). Shapiro was a screenwriter and producer who specialized in light comedy in the 1950's and 1960's. He and collaborator Maurice Richlin won an

Academy Award for their work on *Pillow Talk* (1959); the pair were nominated for a second Academy Award that same year for *Operation Petticoat* (1959). Shapiro earned a final Academy Award nomination for *That Touch of Mink* (1962), written with Nathan Monaster. Shapiro's additional screenwriting credits include *The Perfect Furlough* (1958), *Come September* (1961), *Bedtime Story* (1964, which he also produced), *For Pete's Sake* (1974, which he also coproduced), and *Dirty Rotten Scoundrels* (1988).

Warren Skaaren (1946-December 28, 1990). Skaaren was a screenwriter who worked on some of the most popular films of the late 1980's. He was credited as associate producer on *Top Gun* (1986) and coauthored the screenplays of *Beverly Hills Cop II* (1987), *Beetlejuice* (1988), and *Batman* (1989).

Bella Spewack (1899-April 27, 1990). Born in Hungary, Spewack and her husband Samuel Spewack collaborated on numerous musicals and comedies from the 1930's through the 1950's. They won a Tony Award for *Kiss Me Kate* on Broadway in 1949; the musical was made into a film in 1953. The Spewacks were nominated for an Academy Award for *My Favorite Wife* (1940). Samuel Spewack died in 1971. Their additional film credits include *The Nuisance* (1933), *The Gay Bride* (1934), *The Cat and the Fiddle* (1934), *Boy Meets Girl* (1938), and *We're No Angels* (1955).

Barbara Stanwyck (July 16, 1907-January 20, 1990). Born Ruby Stevens, Stanwyck was one of the most popular film actresses of the 1940's; though she handled a variety of roles over her long career, she is best remembered for playing tough, hardbitten women. In a profession known for its temperament, Stanwyck was a favorite of directors such as Cecil B. De Mille, Frank Capra, and William Wellman, all of whom admired her solid professionalism. She broke into film in the late silent era; by the end of the 1930's, she had established herself as a major leading lady in films such as *Stella Dallas* (1937), for which she was nominated for an Academy Award as Best Actress. She was equally at home in screwball comedy, *film noir*, and conventional melodrama, as her work in *Ball of Fire* (1941), *Double Indemnity* (1944), and *Sorry, Wrong Number* (1948) attests; she won Academy Award nominations for each of these films. In the 1950's, she made *Clash by Night* (1952) and *Executive Suite* (1954), among others. By the 1960's, she had begun concentrating her energies in television, starring in the long-running Western series *The Big Valley*. She won three Emmy Awards for her television work in addition to her four Academy Award nominations. In 1982, Stanwyck received an honorary Academy Award for her career achievements. She was married to actor Robert Taylor from 1939 to 1952. Her additional film credits include *The Plough and the Stars* (1937), *Union Pacific* (1939), *Golden Boy* (1939), *The Lady Eve* (1941), *Meet John Doe* (1941), *Cattle Queen of Montana* (1954), *Walk on the Wild Side* (1962), and *Roustabout* (1964).

Jan Stussy (1922-July 31, 1990). Stussy was a documentary filmmaker who won an Academy Award for *Gravity Is My Enemy* (1978), about quadriplegic artist Mark Hicks. Stussy was a longtime art professor at the University of California at Los Angeles. His additional films include *Artanatomy: The Skeleton* (1979) and *The Mural of the Trees* (1980).

Vic Tayback (1929-May 25, 1990). Tayback was an actor who was best known for his role as Mel, first in the film *Alice Doesn't Live Here Anymore* (1975) and later in the television series *Alice*, which was based on the film. Tayback's additional screen credits include *Love with the Proper Stranger* (1963), *Bullitt* (1968), *Papillon* (1973), and *The Cheap Detective* (1978).

Terry-Thomas (July 14, 1911-January 8, 1990). Born Thomas Terry Hoar Stevens, Terry-Thomas was a British actor whose mustache and gap teeth were distinctive trademarks in a long career. He specialized in comedy, first gaining attention in *Private's Progress* (1956) and

The Green Man (1956). His additional screen credits include *Blue Murder at St. Trinian's* (1957), *I'm All Right, Jack* (1960), *Make Mine Mink* (1960), *Bachelor Flat* (1962), *Those Magnificent Men in Their Flying Machines* (1965), and *How to Murder Your Wife* (1965).

Bud Thackery (1903-July 15, 1990). Thackery was a photographer who began his career in the early days of sound films, specializing in special effects photography. He worked extensively for Republic Pictures and earned an Academy Award nomination for his work on that studio's *Women in War* (1941). His additional film credits include *Flying Tigers* (1942), *Sands of Iwo Jima* (1949), *Flame of the Islands* (1955), *Jaguar* (1956), *Stranger at My Door* (1956), and *Coogan's Bluff* (1968).

Frank Thomas (1890-November 25, 1990). Thomas was a character actor who worked extensively in television and on Broadway as well as on film. Signing with RKO, he appeared in more than seventy films in the 1930's and 1940's, including *Don't Turn 'Em Loose* (1936), *Breakfast for Two* (1937), *Bringing Up Baby* (1938), *Bachelor Mother* (1939), *Idiot's Delight* (1939), *Maryland* (1940), and *No Place for a Lady* (1943).

Ugo Tognazzi (March 23, 1922-October 27, 1990). Tognazzi was an Italian actor who specialized in comedy. He is best known to American audiences for his starring role in *La Cage aux folles* (1978). He began acting in the 1950's, and his best early role was in *Il Federale* (1961). He made a series of sex comedies with director Marco Ferreri, including *The Conjugal Bed* (1963) and *Counter-Sex* (1964). His role as a gourmand in Ferreri's international hit *La Grande Bouffe* (1973) was one of his best. A straight dramatic role in Bernardo Bertolucci's *Tragedy of a Ridiculous Man* (1981) earned for him the best actor award at the Cannes Film Festival. Tognazzi's additional film credits include *High Infidelity* (1964), *Barbarella* (1968), *Property Is No Longer Theft* (1968), and *All My Friends* (1974).

Leonid Trauberg (1901-November 14, 1990). Trauberg was a Russian filmmaker best known for the films he made with Grigori Kozintsev, with whom he collaborated for twenty years. Their Maxim Trilogy—*The Youth of Maxim* (1935), *The Return of Maxim* (1937), and *The Vyborg Side* (1939)—chronicled the events of the Russian Revolution via the fictionalized biography of a typical citizen. Trauberg's additional film credits include *The Actress* (1943), *Soldiers Were Marching* (1958), and *Dead Souls* (1960).

Bud Travilla (1921-November 2, 1990). Travilla was a costume designer who won an Academy Award for his work on the Errol Flynn swashbuckler *Adventures of Don Juan* (1948). He worked often with Marilyn Monroe, designing her famous white dress in *The Seven Year Itch* (1955). He was nominated for Academy Awards for his work in *How to Marry a Millionaire* (1953), *There's No Business Like Show Business* (1954), and *The Stripper* (1963).

Luis Trenker (October 4, 1893-April 13, 1990). Born in Italy of German parents, Trenker was an actor, screenwriter, and director who was an expert skier. As an actor, he was often featured with then-actress Leni Riefenstahl in films with a skiing motif. When he began directing his own pictures, he continued to focus on mountaineering themes. As an actor, he appeared in *Marvels of Ski* (1921), *Peak of Fate* (1924), and *The Fight for the Matterhorn* (1929), among others. As a director, his screen credits include *The Lost Son* (1934), *Condottieri* (1937), and *Monte Miracolo* (1943).

Jimmy Van Heusen (January 26, 1913-February 6, 1990). Born Edward Chester Babcock, Van Heusen was a prolific songwriter whose work was nominated for twelve Academy Awards, winning four. From 1940 to the mid-1950's, Van Heusen worked with lyricist Johnny Burke; the pair wrote songs for numerous Bing Crosby films and won an Academy Award for "Swinging on a Star" from *Going My Way* (1944). From 1955 to 1968, Van Heusen worked with Sammy Cahn and wrote songs for Frank Sinatra, including "All the Way" from *The Joker Is*

Wild (1957) and "High Hopes" from *A Hole in the Head* (1959), both of which won Academy Awards. "Call Me Irresponsible" from *Papa's Delicate Condition* (1963) won another Academy Award for Van Heusen and Cahn. Van Heusen's additional film credits include *Road to Morocco* (1942), *Young at Heart* (1954), *The Tender Trap* (1955), and *Pocketful of Miracles* (1961).

Irving Wallace (March 19, 1916-June 29, 1990). Born Irving Wallechinsky, Wallace was a best-selling novelist who was a Hollywood screenwriter in the 1950's. Several of his novels, including *The Chapman Report* (1962) and *The Man* (1972), were made into films. Wallace's screenwriting credits include *The West Point Story* (1950), *Bad for Each Other* (1953), *Bombers B-52* (1957), and *The Big Circus* (1959).

Jean Wallace (October 12, 1923-February 14, 1990). Born Jean Wallasek, Wallace was an actress known first as a leading lady during the 1940's and later for the socially conscious films she made with her husband, actor-director Cornel Wilde. Her early films included *Louisiana Purchase* (1941), *Blaze of Noon* (1947), and *Jigsaw* (1949); in the latter film, she starred opposite her first husband, Franchot Tone. She married Wilde in 1951 and appeared with him in *The Big Combo* (1955) and *Maracaibo* (1958). The couple's *Beach Red* (1967) was an anti-war film, and their *No Blade of Grass* (1970) was a futuristic environmental film. Wallace's additional screen credits include *Native Son* (1951), *The Devil's Hairpin* (1957), and *Lancelot and Guinevere* (1963).

Robert D. Webb (January 3, 1903-April 18, 1990). Webb was a director who specialized in action-oriented films. He won an Academy Award for his work as an assistant director on *In Old Chicago* (1938); his was the last such award given. Webb's additional films include *The Caribbean Mystery* (1945), *Seven Cities of Gold* (1955), *Love Me Tender* (1956), and *Pirates of Tortuga* (1961).

Lyle Wheeler (February 2, 1905-January 10, 1990). Wheeler was an art director who worked on more than four hundred films, earning twenty-nine Academy Award nominations and winning the award five times in a career that spanned four decades. His Academy Award-winning films were *Gone with the Wind* (1939), *Anna and the King of Siam* (1946), *The Robe* (1953), *The King and I* (1956), and *The Diary of Anne Frank* (1959). His additional film credits include *Laura* (1944), *All About Eve* (1950), *The Seven Year Itch* (1955), and *South Pacific* (1958).

LIST OF AWARDS

Academy Awards
Best Picture: Dances with Wolves
Direction: Kevin Costner (*Dances with Wolves*)
Actor: Jeremy Irons (*Reversal of Fortune*)
Actress: Kathy Bates (*Misery*)
Supporting Actor: Joe Pesci (*GoodFellas*)
Supporting Actress: Whoopi Goldberg (*Ghost*)
Original Screenplay: Bruce Joel Rubin (*Ghost*)
Adapted Screenplay: Michael Blake (*Dances with Wolves*)
Cinematography: Dean Semler (*Dances with Wolves*)
Editing: Neil Travis (*Dances with Wolves*)
Art Direction: Richard Sylbert and Rick Simpson (*Dick Tracy*)
Special Achievement in Visual Effects: Tim McGovern, Eric Brevig, Alex Funke, and Rob Bottin (*Total Recall*)
Sound Effects Editing: Cecelia Hall and George Watters II (*The Hunt for Red October*)
Sound: Russell Williams II, Jeffrey Perkins, Bill W. Benton, and Greg Watkins (*Dances with Wolves*)
Makeup: John Caglione, Jr., and Doug Drexler (*Dick Tracy*)
Costume Design: Franca Squarciapino (*Cyrano de Bergerac*)
Original Score: John Barry (*Dances with Wolves*)
Original Song: "Sooner or Later (I Always Get My Man)" (*Dick Tracy*: music and lyrics, Stephen Sondheim; performance, Madonna)
Foreign-Language Film: Journey of Hope (Switzerland)
Short Film, Animated: Creature Comforts (Nick Park)
Short Film, Live Action: The Lunch Date (Adam Davidson)
Documentary, Feature: American Dream (Barbara Kopple and Arthur Cohn)
Documentary, Short Subject: Days of Waiting (Steven Okazaki)
Special Oscar: Myrna Loy
Special Oscar: Sophia Loren
Irving G. Thalberg Memorial Award: Richard Zanuck and David Brown

Directors Guild of America Award
Director: Kevin Costner (*Dances with Wolves*)

Writers Guild Awards
Original Screenplay: Barry Levinson (*Avalon*)
Adapted Screenplay: Michael Blake (*Dances with Wolves*)

New York Film Critics Awards
Best Picture: GoodFellas

Direction: Martin Scorsese (*GoodFellas*)
Actor: Robert De Niro (*GoodFellas* and *Awakenings*)
Actress: Joanne Woodward (*Mr. and Mrs. Bridge*)
Supporting Actor: Bruce Davison (*Longtime Companion*)
Supporting Actress: Jennifer Jason Leigh (*Last Exit to Brooklyn* and *Miami Blues*)
Screenplay: Ruth Prawer Jhabvala (*Mr. and Mrs. Bridge*)
Cinematography: Vittorio Storaro (*The Sheltering Sky*)
Foreign-Language Film: The Nasty Girl (Germany)
New Director: Whit Stillman (*Metropolitan*)

Los Angeles Film Critics Awards
Best Picture: GoodFellas
Direction: Martin Scorsese (*GoodFellas*)
Actor: Jeremy Irons (*Reversal of Fortune*)
Actress: Anjelica Huston (*The Grifters* and *The Witches*)
Supporting Actor: Joe Pesci (*GoodFellas*)
Supporting Actress: Lorraine Bracco (*GoodFellas*)
Screenplay: Nicholas Kazan (*Reversal of Fortune*)
Cinematography: Michael Ballhaus (*GoodFellas*)
Original Score: Ryuichi Sakamoto (*The Sheltering Sky*)
Foreign-Language Film: Life and Nothing But (France)

National Society of Film Critics Awards
Best Picture: GoodFellas
Direction: Martin Scorsese (*GoodFellas*)
Actor: Jeremy Irons (*Reversal of Fortune*)
Actress: Anjelica Huston (*The Grifters* and *The Witches*)
Supporting Actor: Bruce Davison (*Longtime Companion*)
Supporting Actress: Annette Bening (*The Grifters*)
Screenplay: Charles Burnett (*To Sleep with Anger*)
Cinematography: Peter Suschitzky (*Where the Heart Is*)
Documentary: Berkeley in the Sixties (Mark Kitchell)
Foreign-Language Film: Ariel (Aki Kaurismaki, Finland)

National Board of Review Awards
Best English-Language Film: Dances with Wolves
Direction: Kevin Costner (*Dances with Wolves*)
Actor: Robin Williams (*Awakenings*) and Robert De Niro (*Awakenings*), tie
Actress: Mia Farrow (*Alice*)
Supporting Actor: Joe Pesci (*GoodFellas*)
Supporting Actress: Winona Ryder (*Mermaids*)
Foreign-Language Film: Cyrano de Bergerac (France)
The D. W. Griffith Career Achievement Award: Roy Rogers
The D. W. Griffith Career Achievement Award: Gene Autry

Golden Globe Awards
Best Picture, Drama: Dances with Wolves
Best Picture, Comedy or Musical: Green Card
Direction: Kevin Costner (*Dances with Wolves*)
Actor, Drama: Jeremy Irons (*Reversal of Fortune*)
Actress, Drama: Kathy Bates (*Misery*)
Actor, Comedy or Musical: Gérard Depardieu (*Green Card*)
Actress, Comedy or Musical: Julia Roberts (*Pretty Woman*)
Supporting Actor: Bruce Davison (*Longtime Companion*)
Supporting Actress: Whoopi Goldberg (*Ghost*)
Screenplay: Michael Blake (*Dances with Wolves*)
Original Score: Ryuichi Sakamoto, music, and Richard Horowitz, North African
    music (*The Sheltering Sky*)
Original Song: "Blaze of Glory" (*Young Guns II*: music and lyrics, Jon Bon Jovi)
Foreign-Language Film: Cyrano de Bergerac (France)

Golden Palm Awards (Forty-third Cannes International Film Festival)
Golden Palm: Wild at Heart (David Lynch)
Grand Prix: The Sting of Death (Kohei Oguri) and *Tilai* (Idrissa Ouedraogo), tie
Actor: Gérard Depardieu (*Cyrano de Bergerac*)
Actress: Krystyna Janda (*The Interrogation*)
Direction: Pavel Lounguine (*Taxi Blues*)
Jury Prize: Hidden Agenda (Ken Loach)
Artistic Contribution: Gleb Panfilov (direction, *Mother*)
Camera d'Or: Vitali Kanevski (*Don't Move, Die and Recover*)

British Academy Awards
Best Picture: GoodFellas
Direction: Martin Scorsese (*GoodFellas*)
Actor: Philippe Noiret (*Cinema Paradiso*)
Actress: Jessica Tandy (*Driving Miss Daisy*)
Supporting Actor: Salvatore Cascio (*Cinema Paradiso*)
Supporting Actress: Whoopi Goldberg (*Ghost*)
Original Screenplay: Giuseppe Tornatore (*Cinema Paradiso*)
Adapted Screenplay: Nicholas Pileggi and Martin Scorsese (*GoodFellas*)
Original Score: Ennio Morricone and Andrea Morricone (*Cinema Paradiso*)
Best Foreign-Language Film: Cinema Paradiso (Italy and France)
Fellowship Award: Louis Malle
The Michael Balcon Award: Jeremy Thomas (*The Last Emperor* and *The Sheltering
    Sky*)

MAGILL'S
CINEMA
ANNUAL

TITLE INDEX

DIRECTOR INDEX

DIRECTOR INDEX

LOVY, STEVEN
Circuitry Man 412
LUMET, SIDNEY
Q&A 303
LYNCH, DAVID
Wild at Heart 398
LYNE, ADRIAN
Jacob's Ladder 180
LYNN, JONATHAN
Nuns on the Run 433

MCGLYNN, DON
Hollywood Mavericks 423
MACKENZIE, JOHN
Last of the Finest, The 427
MCNAUGHTON, JOHN
Henry 423
MCTIERNAN, JOHN
Hunt for Red October, The 167
MALLE, LOUIS
May Fools [1989] 431
MALMUTH, BRUCE
Hard to Kill 422
MANDOKI, LUIS
White Palace 394
MARSHALL, FRANK
Arachnophobia 36
MARSHALL, GARRY
Pretty Woman 295
MARSHALL, PENNY
Awakenings 45
MEDAK, PETER
Krays, The 192
MERCERO, ANTONIO
Wait for Me in Heaven 446
MONGER, CHRISTOPHER
Waiting for the Light 446
MOWBRAY, MALCOLM
Don't Tell Her It's Me 415
MOYLE, ALLAN
Pump Up the Volume 299
MURPHY, GEOFF
Young Guns II 448
MURRAY, BILL
Quick Change 435

NICHETTI, MAURIZIO
Icicle Thief, The [1989] 171
NICHOLS, MIKE
Postcards from the Edge 287
NICHOLSON, JACK
Two Jakes, The 381
NIMOY, LEONARD
Funny About Love 420
NORRIS, AARON
Delta Force II 414
NOYCE, PHILLIP
Blind Fury 409

O'CONNOR, PAT
Fools of Fortune 419
ODELL, DAVID
Martians Go Home 430
ORR, JAMES
Mr. Destiny 431

OUEDRAOGO, IDRISSA
Yaaba [1989] 448

PAKULA, ALAN J.
Presumed Innocent 291
PAPIC, KRSTO
My Uncle's Legacy [1989] 432
PARKER, ALAN
Come See the Paradise 69
PARRIOTT, JAMES D.
Heart Condition 422
PEARCE, RICHARD
Long Walk Home, The 207
PEOPLES, DAVID
Blood of Heroes, The 409
PETERSON, KRISTINE
Body Chemistry 409
PETRIE, DONALD
Opportunity Knocks 433
POITIER, SIDNEY
Ghost Dad 420
POLLACK, SYDNEY
Havana 150
POOL, LEA
Straight for the Heart 440
POWELL, MICHAEL
Obituaries 459
PRINCE
Graffiti Bridge 421

QUINTANO, GENE
Honeymoon Academy 423
Why Me? 447

RAFELSON, BOB
Mountains of the Moon 266
RAIMI, SAM
Darkman 413
RAPPENEAU, JEAN-PAUL
Cyrano de Bergerac 78
REINER, CARL
Sibling Rivalry 332
REINER, ROB
Misery 250
REISZ, KAREL
Everybody Wins 417
REITMAN, IVAN
Kindergarten Cop 188
RENÉ, NORMAN
Longtime Companion 210
RESNIKOFF, ROBERT
First Power, The 418
RITT, MARTIN
Obituaries 460
Stanley and Iris 336
ROEG, NICOLAS
Witches, The 402
ROEMER, MICHAEL
Plot Against Harry, The 434
ROPELEWSKI, TOM
Madhouse 429
ROSE, BERNARD
Chicago Joe and the
Showgirl 411

ROSENBLUM, NINA
Through the Wire 442
ROSS, HERBERT
My Blue Heaven 432
ROTH, BOBBY
Man Inside, The 430
ROTH, JOE
Coupe de Ville 412
RUBEN, KATT SHEA
Streets 441
RUDOLPH, ALAN
Love at Large 429

SALCE, LUCIANO
Obituaries 461
SARAFIAN, DERAN
Death Warrant 414
SAVINI, TOM
Night of the Living Dead 432
SCHEPISI, FRED
Russia House, The 323
SCHIBLI, PAUL
Nutcracker Prince, The 433
SCHLESINGER, JOHN
Pacific Heights 283
SCHLONDORFF, VOLKER
Handmaid's Tale, The 146
SCHROEDER, BARBET
Reversal of Fortune 311
SCHUMACHER, JOEL
Flatliners 109
SCORSESE, MARTIN
GoodFellas 126
SCOTT, JAMES
Strike It Rich 441
SCOTT, TONY
Days of Thunder 88
Revenge 436
SEACAT, SANDRA
In the Spirit 425
SEMBÈNE, OUSMANE
Camp at Thiaroye, The 410
SERREAU, COLINE
Mama, There's a Man in Your Bed
[1989] 430
SETBON, PHILIPPE
Mr. Frost 431
SHANLEY, JOHN PATRICK
Joe Versus the Volcano 184
SHERIDAN, JIM
Field, The 105
SHERMAN, GARY
Lisa 428
SHORE, SIG
Return of Superfly, The 436
SILBERG, JOEL
Lambada 427
SILVER, MARISA
Vital Signs 445
SIMON, ADAM
Brain Dead 410
SINGLETON, RALPH S.
Stephen King's Graveyard
Shift 440

SCREENWRITER INDEX

477

SCREENWRITER INDEX

479

SCREENWRITER INDEX

SIMPSON, BYRON
  Rescuers Down Under, The 307
SKAAREN, WARREN
  Obituaries 462
SKOLIMOWSKI, JERZY
  Torrents of Spring 443
SOW, THIERNO FATY
  Camp at Thiaroye, The 410
SPEWACK, BELLA
  Obituaries 462
SPIEGEL, SCOTT
  Rookie, The 437
STALLONE, SYLVESTER
  Rocky V 319
STANLEY, RICHARD
  Hardware 422
STEINBERG, NORMAN
  Funny About Love 420
STEWART, DONALD
  Hunt for Red October, The 167
STILLMAN, WHIT
  Metropolitan 234
STOPPARD, TOM
  Russia House, The 323
STRICK, WESLEY
  Arachnophobia 36
STRONG, JOHN
  Show of Force, A 438
STUART, JEB
  Another 48 HRS. 32
  Vital Signs 445
SUMMERHAYS, SOAMES
  Great Barrier Reef, The 421

TALLY, TED
  White Palace 394
TAUSIK, DAVID
  Think Big 442
TAYLOR, BRUCE A.
  Instant Karma 425
THIEL, NICK
  Fire Birds 418
THOMAS, JIM
  Predator II 434
THOMAS, JOHN
  Predator II 434
THOMPSON, CAROLINE
  Edward Scissorhands 100

THOREAU, DAVID
  Side Out 439
TOWNE, ROBERT
  Days of Thunder 88
  Two Jakes, The 381
TRENKER, LUIS
  Obituaries 463
TRUEBA, FERNANDO
  Twisted Obsession 445
TURTLETAUB, JON
  Think Big 442
TYDOR, JONATHAN
  I Come in Peace 424
TYSON, NONA
  Hot Spot, The 424

URICOLA, ROBERT
  Feud, The 418
UYS, JAMIE
  Gods Must Be Crazy II, The 420

VALCARCEL, HORACIO
  Wait for Me in Heaven 446
VALTINOS, THANASSIS
  Landscape in the Mist
    [1988] 196
VAN SICKLE, CRAIG W.
  Ski Patrol 439
VENOSTA, LOUIS
  Bird on a Wire 53
VERHOEVEN, MICHAEL
  Nasty Girl, The [1989] 279
VICTOR, MARK
  Marked for Death 218
VIERTEL, PETER
  White Hunter, Black Heart 389
VOLK, STEVEN
  Guardian, The 421
VOSS, KURT
  Genuine Risk 420

WALLACE, IRVING
  Obituaries 464
WALLACE, JOSEPHINE
  Bail Jumper 407
WANG, PETER
  Laserman, The 427
WARREN, S.
  Angel Town 407

WATERS, DANIEL
  Adventures of Ford Fairlane,
    The 406
WATERS, JOHN
  Cry-Baby 413
WATSON, PATRICIA
  Nutcracker Prince, The 433
WEBB, WEAVER
  Courage Mountain 412
WEINGROD, HERSCHEL
  Kindergarten Cop 188
WEIR, PETER
  Green Card 130
WESTLAKE, DONALD E.
  Grifters, The 138
  Why Me? 447
WHEELER, ANNE
  Bye Bye Blues [1989] 410
WHIFLER, GRAEME
  Sonny Boy 439
WILD, NETTIE
  Rustling of Leaves, A 437
WILLIAMS, CHARLES
  Hot Spot, The 424
WILSON, MICHAEL HENRY
  Hollywood Mavericks 423
WILSON, S. S.
  Ghost Dad 420
  Tremors 444
WINKLER, CHARLES
  Disturbed 415
WISDOM, ANTHONY
  Return of Superfly, The 436
WRIGHT, THOMAS LEE
  Last of the Finest, The 427

YAKIN, BOAZ
  Rookie, The 437
YALLOP, DAVID
  Chicago Joe and the
    Showgirl 411
YOSHIDA, HIROAKI
  Twilight of the Cockroaches 444

ZAILLIAN, STEVEN
  Awakenings 45
ZEFFIRELLI, FRANCO
  Hamlet 142

481

CINEMATOGRAPHER INDEX

CINEMATOGRAPHER INDEX

CINEMATOGRAPHER INDEX

EDITOR INDEX

486

EDITOR INDEX

ART DIRECTOR INDEX

ART DIRECTOR INDEX

491

ART DIRECTOR INDEX

493

MUSIC INDEX

MUSIC INDEX

PERFORMER INDEX

PERFORMER INDEX

509

PERFORMER INDEX

513

PERFORMER INDEX

SUBJECT INDEX

The selection of subject headings combines standard Library of Congress Subject Headings and common usage in order to aid the film researcher. Cross references, listed as *See* and *See also*, are provided when appropriate. While all major themes, locales, and time periods have been indexed, some minor subjects covered in a particular film have not been included.

SUBJECT INDEX

SUBJECT INDEX